The Road to War in Serbia

The Road to War in Serbia

Trauma and Catharsis

edited by
NEBOJŠA POPOV

Central European University Press

First published in Serbian as "Srpska strana rata" by Republika,
Belgrade, 1996

English edition published in 2000 by
Central European University Press
Október 6. utca 12
H--1051 Budapest
Hungary

400 West 59th Street
New York, NY 10019
USA

English version edited by Drinka Gojković

Distributed in the United Kingdom and Western Europe by
Plymbridge Distributors Ltd., Estover Road, Plymouth, PL6 7PZ,
United Kingdom

ISBN 963-9116-55-6 Cloth
ISBN 963-9116-56-4 Paper

Library of Congress Cataloging in Publication Data
A CIP catalog record for this book is available upon request

Printed in Hungary by Akadémiai Nyomda

Contents

Introduction   1
Nebojša Popov

THE DESTRUCTION AND CREATION OF A STATE
The War for Ethnic States   9
Vesna Pešić
Yugoslavia as a Mistake   50
Olivera Milosavljević
Traumatology of the Party State   81
Nebojša Popov

ROOTS OF THE TRAUMA
The Flight from Modernization   109
Latinka Perović
An Uneasy View of the City   123
Sreten Vujović
The Unresolved Genocide   146
Srđan Bogosavljević
Who Exploited Whom?   160
Ljubomir Madžar
Kosovo in the Collective Memory   189
Olga Zirojević
The Migrations of Serbs from Kosovo during the 1970s and 1980s: Trauma and/or Catharsis   212
Marina Blagojević

IDEOLOGICAL BEARING
The Church and the "Serbian Question"   247
Radmila Radić
The Abuse of the Authority of Science   274
Olivera Milosavljević

The University in an Ideological Shell 303
Nebojša Popov
The Birth of Nationalism from the Spirit of Democracy 327
Drinka Gojković
Populist Wave Literature 351
Mirko Đordević
Football, Hooligans and War 373
Ivan Čolović

POLITICAL MOBILIZATION
The 1974 Constitution as a Factor in the Collapse of Yugo- 399
slavia or as a Sign of Decaying Totalitarianism
Vojin Dimitrijević
The Ruling Party 425
Marija Obradović
The Traumatic Circle of the Serbian Opposition 449
Dubravka Stojanović
An Alternative to War 479
Bojana Šušak
The Army's Use of Trauma 509
Miroslav Hadžić

MEDIA WAR
Politika in the Storm of Nationalism 537
Aleksandar Nenadović
Turning the Electronic Media Around 565
Rade Veljanovski
The Nation: Victim and Vengeance 587
Zoran Marković
The Nationalization of Everyday Life 608
Snježana Milivojević

CONFLICT AND COMPROMISE
The International Community and the Yugoslav Crisis 633
Vojin Dimitrijević

Bibliography 661

List of Contributors 701

Name Index 703

Introduction

NEBOJŠA POPOV

...the voice of the intellect is quiet but it does not cease until listened to.

Sigmund Freud

The spiralling violence that shook Yugoslavia in the last decade of the twentieth century has been the subject of much observation and research. There have been different interpretations, but as yet there is no widely accepted explanation regarding the war or for the motives of those who initiated it, and least of all regarding the outcome of these dramatic events. Many think that *nationalism* was the driving force and that there is still much to be investigated and clarified in this report. If we take, for instance, Isaiah Berlin's view that nationalism is the result of wounded pride and a feeling of humiliation among the more socially aware, resulting in anger and self-assertion, it is worth examining the about-turn from object-victim to subject-liberator or avenger which resulted from being offered the dangerous medicine then raging, rather than healing, throughout Central Europe and the surrounding countries before engulfing the whole world. (I. Berlin 1980).

Instead of regarding nationalism in a generalized sort of way as a product of destiny or nature which may be considered good or evil, we should rather investigate its true beginnings and how it becomes the ideology of conflict. Is it possible that there exists today, a different way of *healing*, a catharsis of the wounds associated with victim status? Why do so many turn to nationalism as an ideological practice, and is it of their own *free will?* These are the questions confronting the authors of this book and, I believe, its readers too.

Relying on a certain tradition of critical thinking and democratic tendencies in Serbia, and on the results of their own and other studies of the war, about twenty intellectuals of different professions set out to investigate one aspect of a very complex issue: the Serb side of the war. Among them were social and political scientists, scholars of language and ethnology, historians, lawyers, economists, theologians and statisticians. Aware of the intellectual impossibility of encompassing the totality of war by any kind of research, they set clear boundaries to their subject, hoping that others would do the same. The idea was that through dialogue on the results that emerged, an *understanding of all sides of the war* would gradually arise. The 'Serb side of the war' was chosen as a subject for research since this was familiar territory and affected the researchers more immediately, not only as intellectuals but as people living in Serbia. At the same time, this choice implied a repudiation of the usual tactics of imputing blame to those of other creeds, nations, countries, or in fact the whole world, for causing the war and all it entailed.

These circumstances and ideas led to the emergence of a kind of intellectual community of autonomous authors in early 1994, which was gradually to develop into a joint research project. During 1994 and 1995, at the regular bi-weekly meetings, each author explained his or her approach to the topic, and the others commented on it. The initial conceptions were published in the periodical Republika (see *Novi srpski forum* [*New Serbian Forum*] 1993: 18); each author developed his or her work independently, exposing it to criticism stage by stage, first at meetings of the research group, and then to a growing public. The meetings of the group were chaired with exemplary tolerance by Latinka Perović, and a permanent protocol was meticulously drawn up by Aleksandra Berić–Popović. (The protocols alone would provide material for an extensive and interesting book.) Conceived rather pretentiously as a movement, The New Serbian Forum turned out to be a permanent medium of communication—a rare phenomenon in this country—among autonomous researchers capable of and ready for dialogue.

Under circumstances which, to put it mildly, hardly favoured normal work, the authors were supported by the Centre for the Anti-War Campaign and the Heinrich Böll Foundation, to which they are sincerely grateful.

The essays have been grouped according to the type of underlying research, not in the order in which they were published in *The Republic*. The first part of the book contains essays concerned with the broader outlines of the theme: these are followed by essays that examine the roots of the trauma, essays that analyse the role of the cultural elite and of scientific, cultural and other institutions, and essays on the influence of the media. The book ends with a series of essays on the efforts of international organizations to end the war and to help to arrive at compromises.

However, when we consider the scale of the tragedy, and especially the atrocities carried out in and around the war zones, there is reason for fresh scepticism as to the point of trying to analyse war and what it brings in its train. We find ourselves in the same situation as those striving to hold on to their presence of mind (sanity) after the horror of World War II, who saw it as a *breakdown of civilization*, and wondered if there was any 'sense in singing' after Auschwitz (*Zivilisationbruch* anthology, Adorno et al. 1968). Igor Caruso, for instance, in his theory on *the sovereignty of the personality,* relies largely on the real and deeply contemplated experience of one of the victims of Nazism, Emmanuel Ringelblum, who, faced with the horrors of that war, left behind a message in verse (Caruso, 1962):

It is usually said that war turns people into
Animals. But we did not want war, we do not
Want it and we will not become animals.
We are people and will remain so.

We can find the same sanity today, even amongst those who have suffered most—the people of Sarajevo, for instance, who created a new oral and written (anti-)war literature. There are many others, known and unknown opponents of force and violence, in Serbia too, who show both by the written word and by deed that even when civilization—that unstable balance of contradictory elements—is in mortal danger, each single trace cannot be destroyed entirely, nor can hope for the resumption of normal life. The whole point of an expressly historical research, instead of simple narration, is to establish as precisely as possible why certain people have recourse to violence while others avoid or oppose it: in this case, why some Serbs were for war while others were not.

This present volume concentrates mainly on the period preceding the war, when the fires that fed it were being stoked, followed by the first years of conflict (1987–1993). In the foreground was the creation of a militant nationalist ideology. Its counterpoint was the destruction of institutions of learning, culture and politics. The consequences of this process are dealt with only in third place. What is lacking, however, is a knowledge of what the consequences of the war meant for culture, the economy and society. The wholesale laying waste of structures, institutions and organizations was the trademark of the war and will ultimately decide (regardless of what we may think) whether or not there is any real possibility of change.

The authors of these studies, by analysing available sources, have tried to create a solid basis for further research. Although scientific methods and techniques were employed throughout, the authors do not claim to form any 'purely scientific' final judgements.

Behind the burning lava, its source, the volcano, often goes unnoticed. Only recent research in anthropology and sociology (J. Županov 1993; Z. Golubović et al. 1995; D. Richtman-Augustin 1996) reveals the deeper layers of personality and society from which destruction springs. It is increasingly certain that nationalism serves to conceal not only complex psychological and social processes but also common 'villainy and thievery' (D. Kecmanovic 1995; 239–240). Parts of the puzzle are gradually falling into place, although the whole picture still evades us.

Trusting culture has its advantages but also its drawbacks when it comes to attitudes towards a complex and dramatic event such as the war in Yugoslavia. Advantages would include the contribution to *understanding* its sources and the paths it took, and possibly the catharsis resulting from facing up to tragic events. We should bear in mind that, as Rudi Supek wrote at the time (1986), a unique image of the world had disappeared, that there were various parallel 'worlds of life' and different cultures. The drawback would be if the importance of criticizing the ideology were to be overestimated, especially the inertia of 'the cynical mind' in the midst of the modern world (see P. Sloterdijk 1992), and the absolute orgies of cynicism in this country.[1] With due respect to culture, the question remains how to stop and place under rational control the factual machinery of war, as it is most widely understood.

If research shows that the avalanche of fear, hatred and violence was *produced* by the concrete action of individuals, groups, institutions and organizations, that it was not the result of some kind of automatism of fate or nature, there is even less possibility for alternatives to the avalanche to emerge by some kind of automatism. On the contrary, it takes a lot of effort to defend and renew culture, a great deal more than that invested in destroying it. Even this is not enough for normal life. It is necessary to *create* the appropriate values, institutions, organizations and procedures.

If one of the best authorities on human nature (especially its destructive elements), Sigmund Freud (1986: 360), placed his hopes in the ability of the human intellect to overcome its destructive urges, we present this book to the public with a similar hope and in the belief that it will be read by people who will listen to the authors and who will themselves contribute to public dialogue on a subject which is vital not only for culture: that is, on 'all aspects of the war'.

Note

1 Today, 'in the era of cynicism', says Slavoj Žižek, 'ideology can afford to reveal the secret of its actions (its central, underlying idiocy, which traditional, pre-cynical ideology had to hide) and *this doesn't influence its efficiency the least*'. See Slavoj Žižek 1996: 129.

THE DESTRUCTION AND CREATION OF A STATE

The War for Ethnic States

VESNA PEŠIĆ

For analytical purposes, the breakup of Yugoslavia and the war need to be kept separate, however much the two processes are indisputably linked. War need not have been the automatic consequence of the collapse alone, since the country could have been transformed into a confederation or could have been dissolved by peaceful means in harmony with the existing republics and borders. Dissolution or a loose association would have been basically regarded as a positive development,[1] leading to a process of integration on the basis of new, modern pre-suppositions.

The widespread view that war was an unavoidable, inherent consequence of the breakup of the state conceals the fact that their causes were not identical. In fact, by the institutionalization of quasi-sovereign states and the evident integral deficiency in the governing regime's ability,[2] the interests of the individual republics became so far removed that an association of states with new conditions of democratization could no longer be reconstructed (following the destruction of the Berlin wall). Their horizons were no longer the same. The war was not an immediate consequence of the long process of the breakup of the Yugoslav state. We attribute its cause to the creation of new national states in which the leadership of the individual republics brought them into conflict over the distribution of Yugoslav territory, borders and ethnic boundaries.

The national heterogeneity of all the republics, with the exception of Slovenia, led not only to the problem of integrating the existing states,[3] but also to the conflicts between them. To the extent to which the republics/nations narrowed the identity of the existing states (as did the leadership in Serbia and Croatia), they lost their ability to integrate, and the clashes between the nationalities of which they were composed were just as intensive as those with other republics. The narrowest identity is ethnic homogeneity, and it was exactly in that identity that the states saw their integration. The war was initiated because of boundary changes and the alteration of ethno-demographic structures (the movement of the ethnic population).

When conflicts are defined as being about border changes and the creation of ethnic homogeneity in future national states, these ends are naturally served by the leadership of individual states through unilateral decisions, *fait accompli* strategies, military force, and even genocide. A war for border changes between the republics, and the expulsion of other ethnic groups was initiated by the political leadership in Serbia as a means of creating a Serbian state. The Croatian leadership chose a similar strategy with the election of the HDZ (Croatian Democratic Union) government, as seen in the discrimination and open intolerance towards the Serbs in Croatia, and territorial pretensions towards Bosnia-Hercegovina. By agreement this republic should have been shared between Serbia and Croatia.[4]

The creation of new ethnic states which led to armed conflict, restored forgotten national questions to the centre of attention in political and theoretical discussions. In these new discussions, the question was posed as to whether, in the approaching period, new national issues along restricted ethnic lines would continuously be raised.[5] This question is critical since the case of Yugoslavia reveals that the process of creating new national states can lead to ethnic polarization which appears only 'solvable' through the use of force.

The institutional structure of multinationality

Every 'national issue' has its own special history, plans and political strategy, including current power relations. It is always a concrete, localized question which is difficult to generalize about or compare with other cases. Here, especially, there arose inadequate, popular comparisons, regardless of whose standpoint was being defended: multinational coexistence or 'restriction'. If 'restriction' is defended, one essentially tends towards the example of the population exchange between Turkey and Greece following the First World War; but if 'communal life' is defended, then the tendency is towards the example of practically all multiethnic states.

To compare Yugoslavia with the USA, since they are both multi-ethnic, would be a fruitless exercise, since the issue is about totally different conceptions of multinationalism, nations and states. The popular comparison with Switzerland is no more adequate, since that country is composed of national cantons, and not of various nations, as was Yugoslavia.[6]

For the sake of clarity, one must differentiate between multi-ethnic and multinational states. Multiethnic states differ considerably from multinational states in that the former are of one nationality regardless of the diverse ethnic, religious, linguistic or cultural origins of their citizens. In France, as in the USA and Switzerland, there exists only one nationality. The issue concerns *political* or civil nations (even if pure civil states and nations do not exist, since their cohesion and identity are lawfully created from a common tradition, memory, culture, and even ethnic origin), because a state is democratic and constitutionally founded, and as such committed to treat individual citizens equally, regardless of their actual differences in national, ethnic or religious origin.

In the case of multinational states, they are composed of *particular nations* which are institutionalized in the territorial-political sense, in order to 'guarantee the full and free development of their own culture in the best interests of their peoples. In the final analysis, they may wish to separate if they consider that their self-determination is impossible within a wider state' (W. Kymlicka 1995: 16). Such multinational states have a 'founding nation' or a significant minority, but importantly, they also differentiate themselves by the regulation of their international relations, the model of their common state (federation or some other form of association), and their understanding of membership of a nation, which may be civil, in accordance with a liberal ideal, or ethno-national, in harmony with a cultural definition of nation. Their inherent instability arises from the burden of resolving national questions when they cannot resolve these in the true sense of the word without themselves collapsing. Thus, as already underlined, each 'leap ahead' of an individual nation to resolve its national question alone in an extreme way, that is, by becoming an independent state, brings the whole multinational construct into crisis. In order to stabilize multinational states, a necessary precondition is that nationality questions are resolved on a level lower than that of the fully sovereign single nation. Only by unanimity on that question can the institutional framework and the political identity of the common state be established.

The configuration of the 'national question'

The instability of multinational states formed from the remains of former empires in Central and Eastern Europe, including Yugoslavia as the most typical example, was reflected in their never having ceased to 'resolve' the national question, always seeking new forms of 'equal rights', and a balance of power between ethno-national and political unities. However, that balance could not be achieved because of unmitigated tensions between 'people' in the ethno-cultural sense (*ethnos*), and people in the political sense (*demos*). A fragile balance was established arbitrarily by the Communist party, but without really resolving the problem, since the system, by the logic of its own function (that is, low integrated economic and political capacity), deepened the traditional and historical chasm between the civil and ethno-cultural nation models. That chasm had already drawn the Yugoslav people into ethnic war and genocide once, during the Second World War, but not even that frustration, which clearly signalled that Yugoslavia had not re-solved the relationship of state and nation, could not be overcome because these issues could not be discussed under Communist rule. Even less could those questions have been raised in the sphere of a democratic procedure to show what Yugoslavia really could be as a state, that is, in whichever scope or form a united state might take.

Yugoslavia was a state which contained all the characteristic configurations of the national question. If we accept that there exist three basic configurations, we can conclude that Yugoslavia contained all three: 1) a nation (republic) working towards the creation of independent states relying on the right of self-determination; 2) a national homeland (republic) acting with its own diaspora in mind, either in order to supervise the status of that diaspora in the country in which it arises, or in order to de-mand its unification with the mother country and a change of bor-ders; and 3) members of alienated and self-conscious minorities discriminated against, extending resistance towards the majority in order to prevent them from forming their own national state, de-manding cultural or political autonomy or secession, with the aim of uniting with their own homeland.[7] In the Yugoslav configura-tion of national questions, the most difficult of such cases arose. When two neighbouring states have large minorities on the terri-tory of a third state, that state can be attacked through the diaspora of both neighbours. Bosnia-Hercegovina is an example of this; the vulnerability of the new independent state became evident when ethnic Serbs and Croats started the process of armed separatism, in which they were both assisted by their homelands.

The first type of national question, the struggle for the independence of nations/republics, was dominant practically throughout the whole period of Yugoslavia's existence, in the form of struggles between central authority and the constituent nations or republics. However, in Yugoslavia this kind of dispute was not symmetrical. Not all nations/republics worked in the same direction, as had been the case in the imperial states in which, by rule, all strove to weaken the centre and achieve even greater autonomy and, ultimately, independence. The problem in Yugoslavia was that, historically, the ideologies raised in the resolution of individual national questions were confrontational and *asymmetric*. The politics of the largest, Serbian, nation occupied the *centre* with its own, ethno-national interest, tending towards unitarianism and centralism, since Serbia considered Yugoslavia as 'its own', territory in which all Serbs lived in one country. On the other hand, the traditional, nationalistic aim of Croatia was a struggle against centralized government, and a desire for autonomy and independence. As George Schopflin observed, the Croats, who for centuries had been subordinated to a 'distant centre', developed an extraordinary sensitivity towards the central government of Vienna and Budapest. Immediately following unification in 1918, on the creation of a centralized state through which the Serbs established their dominance, the Croats began to regard Belgrade in the same way as they had regarded Budapest, that is, the source of all their ill fortune (G. Schöpflin 1973: 125). This Yugoslav antinomy plagued the country continuously, obstructing all kinds of political stability.

This old, antagonistic division could not have been overcome in either the first, or the second Yugoslavia. Manoeuvres to resolve this question were restricted because of the still existing lack of confidence between the two peoples, and an inability to find a solution through creating a real compromise between their different nationalistic ideologies. However, the survival of Yugoslavia depended on such a compromise, since both nations had to 'achieve a security lacking to both under previous and current conditions' (ibid.: 144). Measures that would have satisfied the need for safety were not established either in the first or the second Yugoslavia. While the minimal demands of the Serbs implied the creation of an authentic federal state government, finally eliminating the problem of the survival of Yugoslavia, the maximum concession of the Croats was some form of confederation on the basis of the 'mutuality' of the southern Slavs. The unresolvable confusion revealed itself before and after the creation of Yugoslavia in 1918. It was revealed in the fact that both peoples presented themselves falsely: the Croats as federalists (but wishing to create an independent state); and the Serbs as centralists (but wishing to occupy the state government). The more the institutional organization of Yugoslavia gave independence and sovereignty to the republics and regions to the detriment of the central government (culminating in the 1974 Constitution), the more a Serbian national corpus (because of the 'surplus' of Serbian people in other republics and the view that the federal state was their own), experienced those changes to its own detriment and to the benefit of other nationalities. And vice versa. The idea of a Yugoslavia with its own political identity would seem to play into the hands of Serbian domination, and be to the detriment of Croatian (or other peoples') statehood. For the Serbs, the lack of such an identity meant the opening of the Serbian issue, the loss of a country in which all Serbs had lived together. This fundamental, historical disagreement between the Serbian and Croatian perception of Yugoslavia and the resolution of their national questions was the main lever to drive both sides to extreme positions in the critical 1990s. These positions were, as shown by events, positions of national unity (the congruity of nation and state) on the basis of ethnic purity and the redrawing of borders. When these positions were adopted politically, and when this meant the creation of independent national states, Serbia and Croatia came into conflict over the Serb minority in Croatia, who on the one hand had been frightened and discriminated against by the rise of Croatian nationalism, but who, on the other hand, had been pushed into armed conflict by Serbia in order to separate from Croatia and to enter into a future Serbian state. In the visions of independent Serbian and Croatian states, Bosnia-Hercegovina should have disappeared, that is, should have been divided between these two states.

The above configuration of the national questions emerged in extreme forms during the disintegration of Yugoslavia: separatism; unification; expulsion of minorities. Once it had been formulated in this way, and when members of the particular nations were mobilized over those goals, no one could withdraw. By the choice of extremes, the war became more or less unavoidable. Some republics chose only a separatist option, that is, the determination of an independent national state within existing republic borders (Slovenia, and then Macedonia and Bosnia-Hercegovina). Others, like Serbia and Croatia, brought their nationalistic politics into a three dimensional configuration: separatism plus unification (joining personal diaspora and so-called ethnic territory) plus discrimination against, or expulsion of, self-conscious minorities presented as an 'interfering factor' in the creation of national states. Thus, although Croatia's most important political aspiration was the creation of an independent state, it did not abandon its old, territorial pretensions towards Bosnia-Hercegovina. Serbia's policies were different from those of the other republics: in the first phase it tried to save the old Yugoslavia by force (military putsch), and in the second it introduced the unification (irredentist) politics of joining the Serbian diaspora and its 'ethnic territory' in Croatia and Bosnia-Hercegovina as a means of forming a Serbian national state.

Although during 1991 all these nations decided to form independent states (to be sure, Macedonia and Bosnia-Hercegovina made this decision because of the resulting loss of 'national balance'), which led to the collapse of Yugoslavia, the irredentist way of creating congruence between nation and state meant war. In principle, the triadic configuration of the national question which encompasses the relations between three actors—the homeland, the diaspora, and the country in which the diaspora lives—need not present the most extreme form of nationalistic conflict. It may *escalate* into irredentism,[8] which presupposes that the homeland incites its minority to enter into a separatist conflict with the state in which the minority lives, and which is in a phase of national homogenization, discriminating politically against the minority. This process can also start with the action of a minority, as is the case with the Albanian minority in Serbia, although this is not complete since the third actor—Albania, as homeland—is not fully activated. In the case of the Yugoslav crisis, four kinds of national question arose, all of which implied unification: Serbia–Serbian minority–Croatia; Croatia–Croatian minority–Bosnia-Hercegovina; Serbia–Serbian minority–Bosnia-Hercegovina; with a potential spread to the south in the same form (Albanian minority–Serbia–Albania and Macedonia–Albanian minority–Albania). All these 'triangular' combinations are practically, or potentially, war combinations, blocking, thanks to political struggles to represent the national issue, any other 'gentler' means of avoiding war. 'Gentler' means presuppose a legalistic approach to the 'national question', or a struggle for an adequate position of the minority, including non-discrimination, personal (cultural) and political-territorial autonomy, along with free cultural links with the homeland, and so on.

However, this structural description may be deceptive, suggesting that the above-mentioned actors within the respective national questions were simply given, that they presented static entities whose actions were pre-determined by 'greater' national aspirations. On the contrary, each of these actors implies a different method of action, because within each actor in the triangle the *political struggle* was led by different political powers, for the definition and representation of the national question. In view of the results of political struggles, all three actors exist within dynamic and changing relations (Brubaker 1994b). In the Yugoslav crisis, the relation between these actors in the triangle, and the 'struggle for leadership', within them can be clearly identified and followed in each case. It is enough to remember the struggle for representation of the Serbian minority in Croatia, in which each political 'set' defined its own perception of the Serbian problem in Croatia. In this way, for example, the moderate current of Opačić and Rašković, founders of the Serbian Democratic Party, was driven out by the radical, separatist, current of Milan Babić and Martić, who received support from Belgrade. The spectrum of the different positions of the Serbian minority in Croatia encompassed the Serbian National Party of Milan Đukić, which had been the closest to co-operating with the Croatian leadership; the Serbian Democratic Forum of Milorad Pupovac, seeking coexistence of Serbs and Croats by recognizing Serbian national sovereignty; through to a huge variety of local initiatives. Finally, all representatives of the Serbian minority changed their positions from moderate to radical, and vice versa. Each of these positions had a different relationship with Belgrade and Zagreb, depending on the relation of power in Serbia and Croatia.

The 'national question' or a struggle for power

The institutional organization of multinationalism shaped the *objective field* of nationalistic politics. It can be assumed that institutions form the behaviour of political antagonists and that nationalism as the politics of an ethnic collective was built into the contradictory feature of an institutionalized solution to the national problem, in which the key, indispensable element was the authoritarian rule of one party. In time, these structures enabled all spheres of public life to be crystallized into the sphere of the national (ethnic), since the dynamics of the market economy, a civil and democratic society were terminated. On one hand, they blocked the integral mechanisms of the economy, society and state, and on the other hand, they strengthened 'national statehood'. The political elite who had greatly influenced the dissolution of the country and the war, did not have to return to the past, as is usually thought. The republics had already been quasi-sovereign states. They only lacked the subjective, psychological dimension of nationalism (for a long time forbidden), but this was added by the cultural elite through selection of the collective ethnic past.

Under the previously existing Yugoslav conditions, the objective field of institutionalized structures was reinforced by deep economic, social, demographic, political and cultural differences which, in the main, coincided with ethnic-national, territorial groups. Federal units were congruent with practically all other differences. However, it was believed that these differences would eventually disappear through the work of redistributed mechanisms of the central organs of government. Those expectations were not fulfilled. In time, the differences became greater, creating new sources of conflict and argument between the republics and regions. The socialist idea of peoples' equal rights provoked more resentment (for example, the regime used the 'national key' both to reward and punish) or memories of injustice and exploitation, than it enabled the mitigation of differences and the resolution of conflicts.[9]

In numerous interpretations of the Yugoslav crisis, the noted objective fields of conflict were frequently underestimated, by reducing the whole crisis to a mere struggle for power. This popular viewpoint looks for the causes of both collapse and war in nationalism as a 'struggle for power', or in the politics of 'aggressive nationalism', introduced by the republic elite in order to renew or seize power during the collapse of the Communist regime. Aspiring to preserve its jeopardized position before emerging democratic changes, especially in Serbia (V. P. Gagnon 1994: 118) the old power structure used the 'nationalistic card'. In practically all the republics, the Communist elite faced the same challenge: reform, or the old system. In the 'power game', they found an answer in the mobilization of nationalism, by a determination to create independent national states, and to 'exit' from the old system by promising democracy and reforms, *after* consolidating the national states. The spread of nationalism was a product of the success of this 'political card' in the struggle of the republican and national elite to seize leadership and power.

Although the power struggle in the republics is an unavoidable factor in understanding the conflicts between nations in Yugoslavia (as already pointed out), the limitation of this approach is that national, long-lasting relations are treated as an epiphenomenom of momentary political struggles to keep (or take) power and privileges. It is forgotten that the very idea of multinational states, institutionalized in the form of ethno-national federalism, presupposes the constant dynamic of the 'national question'. Because of opposing national ideologies, that dynamic undermined the creation of a balance between ethno-national and civil principles, which could have prevented the danger of radical 'ethnification' of politics. Ethnicities, ('nations') were powerfully separated and defined according to the principle of citizenship, without which a 'political nation' was inconceivable both on a republican and on a federal level. In such situations, as Schöpflin states (1995: 162), a significant section of the population experiences a collective state (or republic in which they live) as an 'unnatural', 'artificial' creation which represents neither their aspirations nor their interests.[10] More precisely, Yugoslavia did not manage to reconcile the collective state identity and the narrower national identities, but those identities were conflicting.[11] Nor were the republics able to constitute this harmony. Thus, the former state can best be described as a collection of national and republican look-out towers, from which every nation unceasingly observed all the others, paying attention to any, possibly menacing, 'leaps ahead'. This institutionalized lack of confidence was the fundamental characteristic of former Yugoslavia. Above all, the suspicions of all the nations were generally connected with Serbia, not only because it was the largest republic, and the Serbian people the greatest in number, but also because of the experience of Serbian domination in the first Yugoslavia. It was believed that the Serbs had not definitely relinquished these pretensions. This apprehension was also directed towards Croatia, particularly by the Serbs, since it was suspected that Croatia would never relinquish its national separatist aspirations. There were doubts that Croatia was prepared to accept the Serbs as equal citizens.

This mutual distrust required a formula for the organization of Yugoslavia which would enable everyone to protect themselves from everyone else as much as possible. Institutionally, the changes in Yugoslavia were made in accordance with the needs of the 'new class' which wanted to keep its power, as well as with the need to ensure the security of each nation by balancing national forces and by recalling the socialist motto of 'the equal rights of peoples'. These were mechanisms of self-defence and 'non inter-vention' in internal republican (provincial) matters. Thus, in the last decade, relations in Yugoslavia were more like inter-state rela-tions built on a balance of power and coalitions,[12] than relations within a single, collective state to which loyalty was owed. This missing loyalty towards a collective state led the Yugoslav nations into a trap, the well-known mechanism described by Robert Mer-ton as 'self-fulfilling prophecy'.[13] In the end, each nation became what the others perceived, and what they were most afraid of. The more the nations/republics protected themselves from Serbian hegemony, the more certain this threat became. The more the Serbs suspected the Croats of separatist ambitions, the more real those ambitions became. The free exercise of this mechanism, without the institutional limitations of a civil state with constitu-tional rights, enabled the national elite to direct the conflict and to re-interpret the perennial national questions in accordance with their personal interests.

The turn to nation: reforms and conflicts between centre and republic

The dynamics of national conflict had already started at the begin-ning of the 1960s and lasted for the whole decade, until the pass-ing of the 1974 Constitution.[14]

At the end of the 1950s, discussions opened over the meaning of 'Yugoslav'. This concept had not been clear, being subject to inter-pretation from various political and national perspectives. At the beginning of the 1950s there was a real strengthening of 'Yugoslavism', emphasis being placed on national unity, expected as a result of introducing equal rights and decentralization

(Shoup 1968: 186). This could be traced through the Constitu-tion Law of 1953, which weakened the position of the Council of the People by not mentioning the right to self-determination and only indirectly attributing sovereignty to the republics. The same change was apparent in references to 'Yugoslav culture', based on the closeness of the Yugoslav peoples. Yugoslav cultural and scien-tific institutions were founded. In 1954 a declaration confirming that the Serbian, Croatian and Montenegrin languages were one language was issued. On that occasion it was agreed that work on a Serbo-Croatian dictionary should start. The Seventh SKJ (League of

Communists of Serbia) Congress went the furthest in expressing
these 'Yugoslav' tendencies, although nations and republics were
not brought into issue. The 1961 census introduced the category
of 'Yugoslav' as a possible declaration of nationality.

At the beginning of the 1960s there followed from Croatia and
Slovenia a 'reverse reaction' to 'Yugoslavism', which, in their estimation, exceeded the agreed scope of 'socialist patriotism'. Party
centralism and the organization of all spheres of life in society
from one centre, state unitarianism, that is, an empty form of national state, and the forcing of 'Yugoslav culture', were interpreted
in Croatia and Slovenia as a failure of Yugoslavia to be freed from
Serbian unitarianism and hegemony. For non-Serbs, the idea of
'Yugoslav' was a reminder of King Aleksandar Karadjordjević's
version of a Yugoslav nation, under whose wing was hidden Serbi-
anization (D.Rusinow 1977: 135). The question was opened publicly in sharp polemic between Dobrica Ćosić and Dušan Pirjavec
in 1961.

Although this was only an indication of future conflicts, discussions about Yugoslavism illuminated the old bipolar distinction
between centralism (the Serbian position), and particularism (the
Croatian and Slovenian position). In that context (but not exclusively), one must understand the turn in national politics, the aim
of which was the establishment of 'symmetric' inter-republic
power relations through the destruction of traditional Serbo-
Croatian rivalry.[15]

The beginning of the struggle for a new solution to the national
problem in Yugoslavia started at the Eighth SKJ Congress in 1964.
The role of nation was redefined, and it was revealed that the
'national question' had not been correctly posed. A full stop was
practically placed on discussions about the concept of 'Yugoslav':
every meaning of Yugoslav outside the context of 'socialist patriotism' was considered asymmetrical and 'hegemonistic'. The concept
of nation also changed. Most important, the Leninist concept of the
disappearance of 'nation' in a class society was rejected. 'Bourgeois
prejudice over the dying out of nations', and 'incorrect understanding' in order that 'national differences would quickly disappear after the revolution' were also rejected. These viewpoints
were held to be not only incorrect, but also bureaucratic, unitari-
anist and hegemonistic tendencies.[16] It was implied that the republics would become real bearers of sovereignty, and that this
was the right of all nations, as well as of the Yugoslavs.[17]

Discussions about Yugoslavism and the verdict of 'unscientific
ideas of the disappearance of nations', coincided with discussions

about economic reforms. From the beginning of the 1960s, talks began within the framework of the SKJ Executive concerning political and economic changes, and particular problems and deficiencies which would be confronted in the functioning of the system. This was a period of experimentation, of attempts to liberalize the economy (1961), and a return to central control. Motives for changing the method of economic decision making flowed from greater agreement in a society which would no longer bear rigid, central planning and distribution of investments. The foothold of irrationality was rightly located in the central, that is, federal, organs, but the real essence of irrationality in the system was concealed: the power of the party over the economy. Avoiding the principal problem, from 1963 to 1965 'economic and social' reforms were prepared in which the focus was on abandoning central planning (the republics could no longer agree on this), an attack on unprofitable businesses and economic inefficiency, the disturbance of price relations, inflationary tendencies, and the organization of banks. The aim of these reforms was to give companies, local authorities and the republics a greater role in this area. However, discussions about reforms and the dismantling of irrational economic centralism quickly crossed with the ethnic dimension, even though the paramount motivation appeared to be purely economic. Individual forces were against central planning, seeking a greater role for companies in investment decisions, calling for self-management and efficient operations. Others were not so much against central planning as against the *place* of planning, that is, against the federal centre for decisions making (Rusinow 1977: 124). In this confusion of different viewpoints, disagreement between the republics over economic resources, development projects,[18] and the financing of undeveloped republics and provinces, was outlined. Republican bureaucracy, being conferred as 'personal', that is, of republican interest, received local support, and it was difficult to distinguish where economic interests developed into national. The more local leadership wished to receive increased national support for their economic programmes, the more that support aroused suspicion in other republics. Economic nationalism turned into ideological and political divisions, so that in the next phase, the national question moved into the centre of the conflict (Ramet 1992: 82).

From the confusion of different viewpoints relating to economic questions, the role of the state and the party, self-management and the market, and the republics and central power, two clear currents were discernable. On one side, so-called liberal

forces were formed that supported the liberalization of the economy, the decentralization of central power ('de-etatization'), and
self-management, not bringing the party monopoly over society
into question. On the other side gathered conservative forces, who
called for socialistic values, party unity and centralism to be paramount. This division could not be expressed in terms of the *interests* of different social groups (since they only existed in outline,
not being able to have their own social and political identity in the
party state), but rather, as expected, in the inter-republican struggles and coalitions in opposition to central power which was believed to be Serbian based.

In the preparations for reform and its inception in 1965, official
Serbian politics occupied the position of defending central power,
resisting reforms and de-centralization,[19] while the leading reformist role was adopted by Croatia, behind which all the other republics were lined up, even the undeveloped, on whose support Serbia
had otherwise depended. Although the reforms ought to have
damaged these undeveloped republics the most, since they depended on the federation and its distributive function, only Montenegro joined Serbia (later moving to another 'camp'). This distortion at the creation of a coalition, that is, the neglect of economic
interests, signalled the national interests in the background: the
weakening of 'federal' power as a Serbian base was associated with
defending Yugoslavism, which also came from Belgrade.

At this time a strong Croatian offensive against the conservative
centre began (followed by other republics, especially Slovenia and
Macedonia), which skilfully sabotaged the 'economic and social
reforms'. State Security (UDBA) was blamed for the sabotage of
reforms, or rather its chief Aleksandar Ranković, as a symbol of
centralism and conservatism; in the national view of non-Serbian
people he symbolized the danger of Serbian unitarianism and hegemony. The 'liberal' coalition, led by Croatia, scored a victory in
the fall of Aleksandar Ranković (1966), which was experienced as
a 'national triumph'.[20] Ranković's fall meant the defeat of the conservatives, but in Serbia his more or less open departure was received as a Serbian national defeat. Because of this 'national humiliation' and the great purge of the predominantly Serbian cadres
of the police, the Serbian nationalistic counter-reaction was to be
expected. This was not brought into the open, since the party zeal
in Serbia following the fall of Ranković was measured by a struggle
against 'Serbian nationalism', although not openly visible. However, that reaction nevertheless existed, drawn into the 'political
underground'.[21]

Ideas about the reform of the political order were also moving outside the relation of centre to republic. These were, for example, ideas about the renewal of party pluralism, already formulated at the beginning of the 1950s by Milovan Đilas, one of the highest functionaries of the ruling party, who as a result fell from power, was arrested and convicted. Ten years later, for the same ideas, the same fate befell Mihajlo Mihajlov, an assistant at the Faculty of Philosophy in Zadar. Similar ideas would be presented by Stevan Vračar and Andrija Gams, professors at the Faculty of Law in Belgrade, during uprisings at universities, once again strongly opposed by the regime (N. Popov 1983: 155-158).

In 1968, a student movement at Yugoslav universities also threatened the party state, especially in Belgrade, not just by its criticism of the 'old left' from the position of the 'new left' which was at that time a world trend, but even more by the practice of *free* thinking, press and political activities. To this initiative the regime reacted with ideological manipulation, taking on certain ideas alongside the elimination of their protagonists (ibid.: 11-77 and 167-234).

The Yugoslav nomenclature always reacted in a united way whenever their leading supporters were threatened (ideological and political monopoly), and the more effectively they reacted, the stronger were the apparatus of the federal rule (the UDBA, for example). Also, by the movement of central power towards the republics, as shown by the research of Zagorka Golubović, the once united Yugoslav nomenclature behaved even more like the elite of different, conflicting nations, although it would remain connected by certain threads, not just to the heads of federal government, but also to the 'first country of socialism' regime (Z. Golubović 1988).

Authoritarian arbitrariness and dangerous versions of nationalism

After Ranković's fall, an extensive reconstruction of the system began, involving a radical transfer of state rule from the federation to the republics (and provinces) by a series of constitutional amendments from 1968 to 1971. This battle was led by Croatian party leaders from 1967. The aim of their offensive became the radical emptying of central power,[22] with definite intentions to settle accounts with the 'centre' as a potential danger. As long as power was not in the hands of the republics, it was considered that danger existed. The aim of the Croatian national-liberals was to 'establish a Croatian state within federal Yugoslavia, where it could secure the defence which the Croatian people had never had, but had always needed'.[23] This proposed federal reform coincided with the liberal ideas of decentralization, de-etatization, democratization, and horizontal binding through trade and self-management. However, the main force of the Croatian struggle was directed against the federation, that Gordian knot of centralism, the severing of which ought finally to have resolved the 'national question'.

Increasingly, Croatia entered into the 'national question obsession', through which all other reform questions were reflected. This was expressed most strongly when Croatia started the destruction of Belgrade's 'economic power' (foreign currency system, banks, so-called re-exporters, i.e. import-export companies, said to exploit Croatia), by non-conciliatory positions regarding 'clean accounts', about which there could not have been agreement. Complaints that Belgrade expropriated the Croatian 'surplus value' expropriated from Belgrade was 'yet another ethnic and historic metaphor' which saw in Belgrade all that was old-fashioned, centralistic and authoritarian (Rusinow 1977: 249).

Right up to the 1971 Amendment, a 'stalemate position' existed between the federation and the republic: each side was sufficiently strong to block the other. This problem was solved by amendments drafted by Edvard Kardelj in September 1970. The amendments entirely 'turned upside down the theory on which the Yugoslav federation was raised, by transferring authority to the republics as sovereign states' (Schöpflin 1973: 126). The goal of the Croatian nationalists' struggle could be seen as having been achieved,[24] since a constitutional arrangement had at last been established that secured the kind of protection that nations enjoyed in the international order.

Serbia also opposed the reforms for nationalistic reasons. Following the so-called nationalistic incident at a session of the CKSK (Central Committee of the League of Communists) of Serbia in 1968,[25] Tito appointed the liberally disposed Marko Nikezić as party leader. The 'Serbian liberals' Marko Nikezić and Latinka Perović accepted the Croatian challenge to liberalize the economy and 'de-serbianize' the centre of power. The 'liberals' considered that Serbia could only progress towards its own development and modernization if freed from these accusations and from the fears of the others. That the idea of freeing the Serbs from their role as 'protector' of Yugoslavia at any cost—even the cost of neglecting their own development and identity—was far-reaching can be seen in the endeavours of the Serbian liberals to de-polarize Yugoslavia by loosening tension in Serbian-Croatian relations. The removal of this basic Yugoslav tension could have been achieved by the principle abandonment of (real or imagined) Serbian paternalistic centralism. For this reason the liberal leadership of Serbia gave support to decentralization, a market-orientated economy (within the limits of the existing system), and horizontal relations with the other republics, removing the authority of the conservative centre of power to orientation towards the development of individual republics. The criticism by the 'liberals' of Serbian domination (also expressed in the far-reaching de-centralization of Serbia itself in the removal of the autonomous regions from Serbian Republic sovereignty) departed from the idea that Yugoslavia's being in the real interest of the Serbian and other peoples could only be preserved if Serbia turned to itself and showed all the other nations that it did not seek more for itself than they did, and did not have any special interest or part in the collective state. By such politics, the remaining but *real* strongholds of uncontrolled power—Tito and the Yugoslav People's Army (JNA)—were laid bare. The finger had been pointed at the right place, the place of the limits of reform, democratization and redefinition of Serbo-Croatian relations.

Each in its own way, the 'liberal powers' in Croatia and Serbia opened up the crisis in the system completely. There was no possibility of bringing the personal rule of Tito into question. During the 1970s it had reached grotesque proportions. In the already fairly well developed complex society, it produced a wasteland, and deep national resentment. Tito's purge first of the Croatian, and then of the Serbian leadership, with help from the JNA which from then onwards received special political power over society and the state,[26] opened up the possibility of dangerous versions of Serbian and Croatian nationalism. The Croatian nationalistic position which still had not ultimately denied the framework of Yugoslavia, had in part been satisfied by the 'dismantling' of the federation, but because of the repression the Croats felt that Croatian politics had been defeated and that this defeat had been engineered by Serbian generals.[27] The battle was completely lost with the purge of Serbian liberals. They had symbolized the possibility of modernizing Serbia, which implied that Serbian national interests were most deeply connected with the need for democracy as a test for what Serbia and Yugoslavia could be as states. But this window was firmly closed as a result of the nature of the existing political system. The battle was also lost because this group of Serbian politicians had only concentrated on criticism of Serbian nationalism, but made no attempt to focus on the Serbian national question, believing that the eradication of Serbian domination would be sufficient to solve the Serbian and Yugoslav problem or possible conflicts with other ethnic groups. From this viewpoint, the old perspective that only 'oppressed' peoples desire the creation of their own states was predominant. The closing of the democratic alternative (although it was not clearly formalized, nor even on the track of Đilas's rebellion), and the reduction of the Serbian question to anti-nationalism, led to a new national imbalance, established by the 1974 Constitution, which then facilitated the return of the Great Serbia nationalism of the mid 1980s.

From the relationship between reform, the national question and authoritative rule, emerged the famous 1974 Constitution. The complex questions of reform were simplified and selected according to two criteria: the national question and the preservation of authoritarian, personal rule. This was best shown in the transformation of the federation. The top levels of the party hierarchy supported the 'dismantling of the federation' as a way to 'depoliticize politics', that is, to save the apex of the pyramid and free it from involvement in everyday discussions which might bring it into question. By delegating the problem to lower levels in the system—the republics, provinces and local authorities—the apex was placed above the disputes as an arbiter at the 'end of the line' (Ramet 1992: 37). As a result, the reforms were reduced to the national level and given a 'form' that could be controlled by the regime. By opening the reform questions, above all in the economy, the national question appeared in its old light, as if nothing had changed, as if old Yugoslavia and the Habsburg monarchy still existed (Rusinow 1977: 273). The reforms were designed so that neither supreme power, nor the *nature of power* itself (i.e. its uncontrollability) could be brought into question; thus they filled the 'national cash registers' more than they really changed the inefficient economic system or created new integrated mechanisms. In other words, decentralization had to be introduced as *a vertical splitting of the centre of power*, the effect of which was the transformation of authoritarian, unitarian power into authoritarian, decentralized (republican) power, Tito's personal authority remaining above all as the only integrated factor. The consequences of 'splitting power' vertically (along the centre–republics axis) necessarily penetrated the federal form 'by a free fall into a confederation' (Đinđić 1988: 25). This was because federalism presumed the sharing and *control of power*, but this could not happen. The far-reaching constitutional changes confirmed the precept that authoritarian rule was incompatible with a federal arrangement: Yugoslavia could either be more than the federation (i.e. a unitarian, centralized state), or less than the federation (i.e. a kind of authoritarian confederation), as was established by the 1974 Constitution (ibid.: 32)[28]

With the 1974 Constitution, a new national and social arrangement was established. On the one hand, the authoritarian role of the party was strengthened, crowned with the metaphysics of self-management that put an end to all potential for reform, and even the previous half-way reforms.[29] On the other hand, the 1974 Constitution brought authority to the republics. The federation became a representative of agreement between the republics and the provinces, without its own, authentic power to pass resolutions and implement them. In the federal organs, resolutions were passed by consensus (each republic and province having the right of veto); all federal units had the same number of representatives (the provinces had a smaller number of representatives, although this did not influence their position); representatives in the federal parliament were 'delegations' of the republics and provinces (not even formally elected by the citizens), to whom they were accountable for their decisions, and on whose instructions they acted in these organs.[30] The republics and provinces were able to develop their overseas relations freely, and also received the right to organize the defence of republican territory (a right granted them in the first constitutional amendments in 1968).

However, the bearers of sovereignty in the republics were nations, and for each decision it was necessary for the six national states (plus two autonomous provinces) to agree. Bearing in mind that the resolution mechanisms were confederate, every question was by necessity 'nationalized', which inevitably led to daily, and open, national confrontation. Every question had to be previously decided in the republics (provinces), and having been 'nationalized', was returned to the federal level at which 'agreement' was arrived at. In terms of institutions, as there was not a single a-national body with its own source of legitimacy, there could no longer be any a-national questions.

Finally, with the 1974 Constitution, republican *symmetry* was established. However, integration within Yugoslavia, by the nature of its institutions, was brought down to the level of realistic power relations, that is, to the personal power of Josip Broz, leaning primarily on the JNA. The institutional framework of the state, as de-

termined by the Constitution, was not competent to solve problems and deal with the deep crisis which emerged at the beginning
of the 1980s. It could not do so, not only because the existing decision-making mechanisms were bad—and they were really bad—but
more significantly because the Constitution was a 'facade', behind
which stood the real relations between powers which interpreted
the Constitution in accordance with their own interests. This fundamental institutional deficiency, produced by the rule of one
party, opened the possibility for the game to be taken over by the
destructive forces of the old nomenclature and apparatus of government, which could not be restricted by any procedures when
their limits were clearly indicated by the approaching collapse of
the Communist regime.

An analysis of the institutional structures of multi-nationalism
showed the direction of the division of Yugoslavia along republican and ethnic lines. The reanimated concept of 'constitutive peoples' took on a leading role. The analysis also showed that the multinationalism thus constituted is able to survive only with the aid of
authoritarian rule. Internal struggles for ethno-national statehoods
can result either in the creation of common 'nation-states'
(political unions), able to pacify and respect ethnic identities, or in
the transformation of republics into independent states. A transitional variant–a confederation–could also have played a part in a
peaceful breakup of Yugoslavia. However, not one of these possibilities transpired. A third possibility was realized: war broke out
over internal borders and the re-allocation of Yugoslav territory,
with the ideal that areas with the greater ethnic homogeneity
should become states. The crisis in Serbia and Serbian resentful
nationalism empowered this possibility.

Nationalism and resentment

So far I have shown how fragile Yugoslavia was, as much from the
perspective of the dominant national ideologies which had shaken
it from its very creation, as from the perspective of its institutions,
within which national conflicts grew.

Tito's main strategy in maintaining national peace was seen in
the suppression of the greatest (Serbian) nation's paternalism, and
the prevention of other nations' separatism (Hassner 1993: 127).
However, after his death this peace was difficult to maintain because there was no longer a supreme 'arbiter'. No one had enough

authority to keep an eye on potential creators of conflict. Legitimate political institutions which could resolve conflicts and give support to the liberal concept of the nation in the post-communist period did not exist. These conditions were especially favourable for the growth of ethno-nationalism in multinational states.[31]

The height of the Yugoslav crisis (1990–1991), characterized by the chaotic collapse of the country and the war for the alteration of republican borders, cannot be understood without analysing the crisis that broke out in Serbia in the mid 1980s. It was expressed in a strong nationalistic movement under the leadership of the SK (the League of Communists) of Serbia. Initially, it sought the restoration of Yugoslavia based on the rule of the Communist party, but that soon grew into a movement for the creation of a Greater Serbia. That movement strengthened national conflicts from day to day, and pushed the crisis towards the swifter collapse of Yugoslavia and a war for the creation of a Serbian state. War could have been avoided if the advantages of democratization, which brought the collapse of the Communist system, had been followed, on condition that all who participated in the conflict consciously avoided ethnic clashes and pursued a *moderate* national policy.[32] That condition disappeared with the change of Serbian policy in 1987, following the victory of the conservative faction in the Serbian party, personified in Slobodan Milošević. The victory over moderate and reforming strengths in Serbia virtually signified the *rejection* of a democratic agreement about what Yugoslavia might be, that is, how it might be transformed, or how it could be dismantled in a peaceful way.

There were several elements that contributed to the igniting of the Serbian crisis, of which I shall analyse the three most significant: the constitutional position; the 'ethnic threat'; and the anti-democratic coalition.

The problematic position of Serbia: the 1974 Constitution

The Communist party could no longer be 'taken for granted' as an eternal guarantor of Yugoslavia.[33] That uncertainty was enhanced by the existing constitutional arrangement which defined Yugoslavia as an 'agreed' state of republics and provinces. Yugoslav sovereignty had been snatched up and dispersed among the republics

and provinces (Đinđić 1988: 20). The possibility of a 'Yugoslav'
solution to the Serbian national question could have been *tested*
only in the oncoming democratic process, but it was by definition
a process of uncertainty.

The creation of symmetry between the republics or provinces
and the centre, which had been divided[34] on the same principle,
left no room for the maintenance of the 'old balance' between the
Serbian 'inter-nationalist' position (which had counted on Serbian
paternalism), and the 'particularistic' position of other ethnic
groups/republics who opposed the 'centre' by strengthening republican rule.[35] The weakening of Communist authoritarian rule
directed the future Yugoslavia towards a confederation (or collapse), in accordance with the existing republican borders. As we
shall show, the Serbian cultural and political elite did not accept
such a future, calculating that (confederate) institutionalized inertia in 'the denouement years'[36] of the Yugoslav crisis, would definitely harm the fundamental Serbian national interest–life for all
Serbs in one state. Such an outcome was marked as Serbian 'loss'
which had to be corrected by the destruction of the institutionalized *status quo* and by the creation of a Serbian national state. If
that was not done, the 'Serbian question would remain unresolved'. The justification for that kind of political mobilization of
the Serbian people can be found in the wording of the Constitution by which 'peoples' and not republics had the right to self-
determination (V. Pešić 1995).[37]

The immediate source of Serbian dissatisfaction, however, lay in
the constitutional difficulties of establishing the territorial integrity and sovereignty of the Republic of Serbia. Although the 1974
institutional system prescribed 'nativization' of all nations within
their own territorial, republican limits, Serbia was frustrated. According to the 1974 Constitution, it was not a 'sovereign' negotiating party like the other republics because of the 'sovereignty' of its
provinces. In the context of the Albanian demonstrations of 1981,
this fact became an immediate *motive* for the gradual growth of an
all-Serbian movement for a national state. Anomalies in the status
of Serbia as a republic are well known, thus only the most significant are discussed here.

Under the 1974 Constitution, the republics and provinces were
made completely equal regarding their rights and responsibilities.
On a federal level, the provinces had the right of veto, equal representation in the collective Presidency of the SFRY, and the right to
present their own interests without consultation with the republic,
to which they were, in practice, most often opposed. If all the re-

publics were sovereign states, representing their complete territory, it was clear that Serbia did not possess that attribute.

Alongside its weaker position in relation to the other republics because of its violated sovereignty, 'narrower Serbia' also had a weaker position within the republic. The provinces were able to make decisions about 'narrower Serbia' in the Serbian Parliament, but Serbia could not participate in the provinces' resolutions. In the ethno-demographic sense, the position of Serbia described meant that 40 per cent of the population who were of non-Serbian nationality made decisions about 'narrower Serbia'.[38] That part of Serbia had not been constitutionally defined, or rather, Serbia had not been federalized, which would have eliminated this anomaly. The provinces seized all the attributes of statehood—legislature, judiciary, and executive—and even those which did not belong to them under the Constitution.[39] The provinces amended their constitutions independently, maintained relations with foreign countries (Kosovo most significantly with Albania), had their own territorial defence, and their laws were passed by the consensus of all three units, that is, both provinces and narrower Serbia. If proposed laws were not accepted by the provincial parliaments, they would apply only to narrower Serbia. This situation had already been established by the 1968 amendments to the Constitution.

After the passing of the 1974 Constitution, the Serbian leadership quickly demanded a change to the status of Serbia. Why had it not been changed immediately, when the anomaly was so evident? The Constitution could not be changed because unanimity of the other members of the federation could not be reached on that question.[40] In 1976, the Serbian leadership submitted a request to change the constitutional position of Serbia in a way which would integrate the provinces into the republic (but not eliminate them), by establishing defined united competence for the whole republic, without which Serbia could not function as a state. The document justifying the request for the regulation of Serbia's status, called the 'blue book', was not made public until 1990. The authors of the 'blue book' raised the question of how, in the conditions of the growing disintegration of Serbia, the status of the Serbian nation would be established in the Yugoslav federation as a whole, and whether the Serbian people could secure their historical rights according to postulates which were equal to those of other Yugoslav ethnic groups, in accordance with the right of self-determination set out in the Constitution (M. Đekić 1990: 176). The document was welcomed 'with daggers drawn' by other republics, and especially in the provinces. It was considered nationalistic, although it did not have that tone about it.[41]

The same situation continued in the 1980s, although the ethnic tension in Kosovo was growing. The Serbian leadership at the time, with Ivan Stambolić at its head, made great efforts to change the status of Serbia and the provinces, with the agreement of all members of the federation. However, the opening of discussions on that question went very slowly.[42] Since agreement to changes in the Constitution was difficult to reach on other questions too,[43] the blocking of changes to the status of Serbia began to be interpreted as 'nationalistic'—the work of the anti-Serbian coalition. In the context of demonstrations in Kosovo in 1981, emphasizing the Albanian demand that Kosovo receive the status of republic,[44] the question of Serbia's status became the pre-eminent political question–one on which politicians advanced or fell. The territorial integrity of Serbia was damaged by the fact that, from 1968, under the wing of official Albanian rule, a nationalistic movement developed in Kosovo, the roots of which reached into the recent and distant history of antagonistic Serbian-Albanian relations (L. J. Cohen 1993: 51).

Kosovo and the ethnic threat

The direct catalyst of the crisis was Albanian demonstrations in Kosovo. In the national sense, the separation of Kosovo as a *de facto* republic created the conditions for Serbia's *nationalistic defence reaction.* Kosovo represented the 'cradle' of Serbian medieval culture and was a symbol of national consciousness, statehood, history and mythology. In the first years following the Albanian demonstrations and the taking of exceptional measures in Kosovo, the Albanian rebellion and the demand for a 'Kosovo Republic' were interpreted in the official, socialistic code as a 'counter-revolution' of the Albanian separatists, by which an ethnic interpretation of the conflict was avoided. By withdrawing the army in 1983, and by leaving Kosovo to police forces, the Kosovo problem was defined as an *ethnic threat*, restoring Kosovo mythology and memories of a great medieval Serbian state.[45]

The stimulus for exploiting the historical symbolic meaning of Kosovo sprang mostly from the Serbian Orthodox Church.[46] The authorities tolerated and encouraged the Serbian ethnic reaction, at the centre of which was fear of the loss of Kosovo and opposition to the 'Albanian enemy'. The goal of the Albanian separatists—an ethnically clean Kosovo—was accomplished by the *violent* expulsion of Serbs from Kosovo,[47] by the committing of atrocities such as the rape of Serbian women, murder, robbery, desecration of Serbian graves, and various kinds of pressure for which the Albanians were not punished, since they were protected by *their own authority*. Serb departures from Kosovo were strictly defined as an exodus under the pressure of Albanian nationalism, although there were also other reasons for the Serb migration (R. Petrović and M. Blagojević 1989). Anyone who dared to mention those other reasons (economic, educational, employment-related), especially if they came from another Yugoslav republic, was ruthlessly attacked and declared a Serbian enemy (P. Tašić 1994: 71). Serb complaints were not meticulously checked,[48] since checking alone would suggest doubt about the Serbian suffering.[49] Repression of the Albanian rebels, the military occupation of Kosovo, and the presence of hundreds of Albanians in prison (I. Janković 1990: 63) did nothing to change the judgement that everything was becoming more and more difficult for the Serbian people in Kosovo, since migration continued. The leading role in defining the situation in Kosovo was played by the movement of the Kosovan Serbs who enjoyed the support of the church, and a significant part of the Serbian intelligentsia.[50] Serbs from Kosovo signed petitions and went en masse to Belgrade, bearing their petitions and threatening a collective migration if republican control was not established over the province. The petitions always aimed at constitutional changes which would establish a *united Serbia*, but which, even more importantly, would bring about a change in the *ethnic domination in Kosovo*. The main source of the 'Serbian tragedy' in Kosovo was that 'their' domination had been established, and the only cure was to halt the 'ethnic cleansing' of Serbs by restoring 'our' (Serbian) domination in Kosovo.[51] The Kosovo Serb movement no longer tolerated the socialistic, nationally neutral definition of the situation as 'counter-revolutionary', nor the symmetry of the equal 'danger of all nationalism'. *Serbs* were suffering as *Serbs*; the Serbs were victims and the Albanians were tyrants.

These interpretations of the problem distanced Serbia from diagnosing the real problem of the republic: on what basis would a political union of Serbia, with an undivided political identity and will, be formed? *Politicizing the jeopardy* of the Serbian people in Kosovo was aimed at restoring Serb domination in Kosovo, which presupposed the long-term use of force. Without exaggeration it can be stated that Yugoslavia was really destroyed in Kosovo; it did not succeed in protecting its citizens, whether Serbs or Albanians, for it did not possess instruments to neutralize or pacify the national conflicts

The politicizing of the Kosovo problem increased the number of interpretations, depending on who was pronouncing them: 'genocide' (Serbian interpretation); 'normal migration' and 'Serbian nationalism' (Slovenian); 'dispossession of Albanians' and 'terror' (Albanian). These interpretations aggravated relations between the republics, because the Serbian interpretations moved increasingly in the direction of nationalistic pressure, the justification of repression, propaganda and lies with the goal of increasing conflict with other peoples in Yugoslavia.[52] The potential for shaping ethnic relations by *invention*, which conformed with the accepted context of events and the existing animosity and fears, was discovered in Kosovo. This dramatic mechanism for directing reality, through exclusively attributing a hostile meaning to all that was done by others, became the main way to sharpen national conflicts in Yugoslavia. The idea of these interpretations was to create a feeling of *injured pride*, which brought about a 'natural' spread of sensations of danger and led to real defence preparations. The greater the emphasis on the threat to the Serbian people, the more insecure other nations felt. Their defensive reaction was used as confirmation of the threat to the Serbian people, giving Serbia justification for raising the level of its 'defence'.

On the question of Kosovo and 'injured pride', there emerged a Serbian state-creating movement, with far-reaching implications exceeding the issue of a 'united Serbia' and its place in the collective state. That movement developed into a vision of the disintegration of Yugoslavia, in which a struggle for a new division of power, security and domination on Yugoslav territory became the main cause of the future war conflicts.

Resentful nationalism

The 'national question' is usually tied to the creation of national states by a call for peoples' right to self-determination.[53] The national question in East and Central Europe, and especially in the Balkans, has continued until the present time because of the inheritance of imperial rule which had created great ethnic mixtures on this territory. In the process of creating their own states, these were not able to establish convincing congruence between nations and their political-territorial areas. Such congruence was, in fact, impossible because of the great ethnic mix. In this heritage, there is an understanding of a nation as an ethno-cultural creation; nations understanding themselves in that way could not overcome the tensions of the incongruence of nation and state by the acceptance of ethnically neutral states (the citizen principle). Rather, practically all nations on this territory stayed enslaved to belief in a state as being the possession of the ethnic majority.

If the relationship between nation and state is the central link in the forming of the 'national question', then nationalism can be defined as a political doctrine or *form of politics* which is carried out in the name of a specific nation, the aim of which is to enable this nation to create its own state. That goal governs all other interests and needs of people representing nationalistic policy.[54] When a state is created, nationalism receives its own general meaning in the framework of regular state policy.[55] The kind of nationalistic policy at stake depends on how specific national questions are defined and the kind of solution that is considered satisfactory. Thus, not all 'nationalisms' are the same, as is sometimes held. If the only satisfactory solution to the national question is the establishment of congruence between nation, in the ethnic sense, and state,[56] in circumstances of a high ethnic mix, as was the case of some nations in Yugoslavia, then the nationalistic policy will be aggressive and hostile towards peoples who 'interfere' with the establishment of congruence between the (ethnic) nation and state. That kind of nationalistic policy can grow into a policy of war, as happened in Yugoslavia.

As there is no single option for solving a specific national question, in the choice of nationalistic politics a decisive role is played by political factors and internal battles for power, and also by many other factors such as historical concepts about the state; the strength of national identity; the size of the nation; military power; historical links with other peoples; and feelings of hurt, fear and resentment. As I have already said, the understanding of nation, its readiness to be constituted as a modern society and liberal state, or as an ethno-national state demanding authoritarian rule of law, all play a decisive role (L. Greenfeld 1992: 11). 'Nationalisms', in the specific meaning of that term, therefore differ. We have attributed a special significance to nationalistic resentment[57] and its part in the outbreak of war in former Yugoslavia. What do we understand by resentful nationalism?

Resentful nationalism is popularly described as 'extreme', 'sick', 'irrational', or 'aggressive', to distinguish it from nationalism as a form of policy, the goal of which is liberation and the creation of an independent state. Resentful nationalism has nothing to do with the neutral idea of nationalism, which presumes a collection of ideas and feelings forming the conceptual framework of the national identity. In short, national resentment presumes some kind of 'neurotic' national identity, characterized by feelings of defeat because of the loss or non-creation of a state, and injured pride that the nation lags behind others, especially behind Europe. When one speaks of the 'breakdown' of national identity, one should emphasize that national identity is specific and cannot be compared with any other kind of collective identity (L. Greenfeld: 7). In the modern epoch, 'nationalism' locates the source of individual identity in the 'people', perceived as the holder of sovereignty, the central object of loyalty, and the basis of collective solidarity. That identity is believed to be fundamental, for it originates from membership in a 'people', defined as a *nation* whose organizational principle enables the stratified population of a modern society to be experienced as homogeneous, thanks to the sovereign status of the people. As the idea of nation spreads, so its meaning is changed according to what is understood by 'people', and how membership is defined. The main redefinition of nation is that, instead of ideas about individual sovereignty, a nation is understood as a 'united' people, whose being *as such* is different, and so by definition, sovereignty belongs to them. Apart from structural and cultural factors which influence the reinterpretation of the original model of nation (in which democracy was immanent), psychological factors testifying to feelings of inferiority towards an object of imitation (Western Europe) are of decisive influence. This reaction, which became an integral part of the identity of united nations, is called 'resentful' nationalism. '"Resentment" is connected to the psychological state which is created by suppressed feelings of envy and hatred (existential envy) and an inability to express them and throw them aside...'.[58] This envy, due to the negative results of comparison with Western Europe, shows itself as characteristically contradictory. On the one hand there is a borrowing from Western values, while on the other the reaction is a rejection of those values, involving the definition of pre-modern identity as contrary to the European identity. Anti-Europeanism is a basic element of resentful nationalism.

'Resentment' as an affective and psychological dimension of nationalism presents a factor of aggression, and a policy based on such an identity can be seen as psychological preparation for war (L. Greenfeld and D. Chirot 1994: 86–88). In fact, simply raising such an identity is treated as a threat of war. Bearing in mind that resentment in the Yugoslav crisis was demonstrated against people with whom life had been lived together, and that into it was brought revenge for all 'historical defeats', trauma, and the sufferings of two world wars, as was done by the Serbian elites (but not only by them), it can be contended that resentment, and the nationalism founded on it, virtually presented a mechanism for the formation of *an outward threat.* Without a convincing outward threat, war cannot break out (W. Bloom 1990: 74).

Resentment as a characteristic of national identity can be revived and chosen in a specific situation as a *possibility* which is created by protagonists, above all by the intelligentsia, producing the psychological dimension of nationalism. Due to its subjectivity and radical particularity, resentful nationalism is resistant to rational arguments and political alternatives. As we have said, it is based on the psychological dimension of nation,[59] on its subjectivity, which becomes visible by raising the issue of 'national identity' as models which the nation creates ('imagines') of itself. The national identity is susceptible to 'direction' precisely for this reason, so that it can be mobilized in one moment, then in the next demobilized, and selected as policy requires. The changing policy of the ruling party in Serbia best testifies to this.

The Serbian people, like all other ethnic groups in the Balkans, built their identity on resentment. For centuries they were subjected to imperial rule, struggling to preserve their identity (language and faith), dreaming about the restoration of their medieval empire. With this national identity, shaped by centuries of being vassals, by rebellious uprising, by the difficulties of creating a state, by lagging behind and being inferior to Europe, national resentment constituted the potential to reinterpret history as unpaid debts.

The historically formed 'injury' of the Yugoslav national identities, and their 'deeply pessimistic view of the world' (A. Đilas 1990: 25), produced *distrust* among them, and fear of domination. In Yugoslavia these came with national dreams which clashed, and wounds which had not been healed. The traumatic experience of World War II and the genocide in the Independent State of Croatia left a large scar on the Serbian national consciousness, and also on the consciousness of other peoples, especially the Muslims who were exposed to Serbian revenge (see the contribution of S. Bogosavljević, this volume). The victims of genocide during World War II, and of the massive liquidation of real and imagined conspirators or 'class enemies' (predominantly from the ranks of the three main peoples–the Serbs, Croats and Slovenes), carried out by the Communists after they came to power (see the contribution of N.

Popov, this volume), were never explained, publicly discussed, or mourned. Communist ideology prevented this, never opening space for 'national reconciliation' (as discussed above, this ideology did not accept the subjective dimension of nation). Fear and distrust were never treated or healed. Memorials were built to the victims of genocide but a veil of silence covered the fear and mutual distrust. This silence with respect to the genocide had great propaganda power in preparations for war, in which the idea of 'unpaid debts' from the 'unfinished' Second World War was exploited.[60]

Suspicion and feelings of 'national injustice' were created in the period of Communist rule. The KPJ (Yugoslav Communist Party), (or more precisely, Tito as the bearer of absolute power) defused international tensions by voluntary arbitration, applying repressive methods which have not been forgotten. A balance between national strengths and the punishment of 'disobedient' national leaders developed so that the two largest ethnic groups—Serbs and Croats—were most badly hit. This enabled them to attribute the misfortune and injustice done to them by the regime to each other at the critical moment.

From the 1980s the expression of Serb resentment started; it was reflected in an ambivalent mood, expressed in the form of offence and ill-tempered fury because of the disappearance of Yugoslavia, and disappointment in it because of 'untruthful and lying brothers'. The source of resentment was frustration because of the lost state; it was overcome by the Utopia of a great Serbian state which would realize the dream (already sacrificed for Yugoslavia) of all Serbs living together in one country. From there, contradictory thoughts about a Serbian state arose—a strong Yugoslav federation (expressed) and a Greater Serbia (implied). Such a 'combination' in itself destroyed the possibility of Yugoslavia, but this destructiveness was not noticed (like an unobserved 'black spot' on the horizon), only the reaction of others confirmed 'their hatred'. That the main drive of nationalism was resentment connected with the state, *envy* that, allegedly, 'all other peoples have a state although they never had one', is most convincingly proved in the restoration of the medieval Kosovo 'testament', which symbolizes revenge for a past defeat and for the loss of a state. Judging from the myth of Kosovo, revenge was driven by two self-perceptions: as martyrs and heroes; as victims and just conquerors. Revenge on the part of the victims represented the skeleton of selective national identity, in circumstances which demanded that something had to be done for the Serbs' 'tragic position'. Talk about 'futile sacrifices' invested in the Yugoslav state, and criticism about the inferiority of Serbian politicians (Communists) who had betrayed Serbia, were transformed into 'the moral triumph of the victim' and the present was reinterpreted as the right to revenge in 'unarmed battles, although such battles are not yet excluded', in Slobodan Milošević's speech at the 1989 anniversary of the Battle of Kosovo.

The anti-democratic coalition

The privileged strata of central and local party functionaries and agents of power (military and police) were afraid not just of local democratic currents, but also of those which had been coming from the Soviet Union, that is, from Gorbachov, *perestroika* and *glasnost*. The democratization of the 'first Socialist country' threatened the privileges that the nomenclature had enjoyed due to the *status quo*. Hesitating over the urgently needed resolution of the Kosovo and Serbian national questions, these conservative agents of power organized a putsch in the Serbian party in 1987, pushing the most conservative elements, of which Slobodan Milošević was the embodiment, into the foreground.[61] The support of military agents was not hidden.[62] Victory over the moderate wing of the Serbian party, under the charge that it had betrayed Tito's personality cult, was rightly interpreted as an accusation of the betraying of the national interest. In reality the moderate wing was indeed in strong opposition to Milošević's nationalistic policy in Kosovo. On both platforms—the defence of Tito's cult (socialism) and the resolution of the Serbian problem in Kosovo—a power struggle was going on through the 'differentiation' (purge) of cadres, the organizational strengthening of triumphant cliques, control over the most important media [63], and settlement with the opposition.[64]

By the consolidation of power along firm party lines, Serbia deviated from the rule which applied in other socialist countries. In virtually all these countries, soft Communist-reformists were in power who themselves contributed to the countries' democratization, or else old Communist sets who would later lose elections. In Serbia it was the opposite. The old power never 'fell' (see the contribution of M. Obradović, this volume). The old agents of power received new sources of energy and survival, using the inexhaustible source of Serbian national frustration. The army excelled in this, with its hidden 'appraisal of the situation', seeing the reformers as agents of the 'new world order'[65], whose goal was not to allow 'Socialism to correct its own faults and show its strength' (Kadijević 1993: 13). Europe and the West were marked as enemies of Yugoslavia, as much because of the destruction of Socialism as because of the dismantling of the Soviet Union as a state and military power on which they depended. The army was not a state but a party force and, as such, the main political factor offering decisive resistance to change (see the contribution of M. Hadžić, this volume).[66] Defending Yugoslavia from all her peoples, apart from the Serbs, and calling them 'enemies',[67] along with party factions in Serbia which brought it to power, the army and its secret agents of power pulled Serbia into an anti-modern revolution (S. Popović 1994), another name for the war which they prepared together.

Thus was formed an anti-modern, powerful and effective coalition: on one side was the extreme, nationalistic strength of the Serbian Orthodox Church and Serbian intelligentsia, whose task had been to produce nationalistic resentment; on the other side were the conservative party agents, the army and the police, who used the 'injured pride' of the nation to preserve their power. Although their motives were different, the actions of the two elements of this 'black-red' coalition were complementary, and together they launched the aggressive policy of the destruction of Yugoslavia: either Yugoslavia would be a state on Serbian terms (a 'real' federation); or Serbia, with weapons in hand ('if needed') would move along the Serbian path—the path towards the creation of Greater Serbia in which all Serbs would gather. Yugoslavia was constantly on their lips—but in the majority of cases they were thinking of some other state called by the same name.

Serbian particularism, in its integralistic, unifying form, depended on a massive popular movement (N. Popov 1993) led by a *state-creating idea* on the distribution of Yugoslav territory and the creation of a powerful Serbian state.[68] The resolution of the national question and resentful nationalism had a function in the creation of such a state. This explains why the production of national identity and emotions which attracted the intelligentsia always contained the same pictures, models, messages and historical generalizations. These models were always the same, regardless of whether they were created by the church, the Academy of Arts and Sciences, or writers. The politicization of culture presented direct, practical work on the creation of a greater Serbian state in cooperation with the authorities. The rejection of a double risk—the democratic organization of Serbia as a precondition for its state form, and agreement about a minimal Yugoslav state—as a way of affirming the Serbs' desire to live together as a nation, led Serbia onto the imperial path of the violent seizing and cleansing of territory on which the Serbs had lived together with other peoples for centuries (L. Perović 1993: 63). This also answers the question of why the existing Yugoslavia, but also some other—democratically agreed one—lost value for Serbia.

The tacit and/or open coalition of nationalists and Communists was built on the interests of both parties: anti-reform Communists used nationalistic resentment to preserve and renew their authority; but certain cultural institutions used it to correct their marginal position. 'Connecting extremes'—the far-left and far-right political positions—defined Serbian national-socialism[69] which reduced politics in Serbia to a struggle for 'the survival of the Serbian people'. Thus the whole political atmosphere was pre-structured and radically blended from the field of rational and measurable activity and the field of 'irrational and unclear aspirations of a frustrated national identity' (Schöpflin 1995: 164). The anti-democracy of this kind of reduced politics, by its very nature, allows no discussion and demobilizes rational alternatives since there is no 'guessing' about the nation's fate. Anyone who questioned the politics of 'national salvation' was neither a proper nor a 'good' Serb. Such people were classified as 'anti-Serbian' Serbs and automatically marginalized politically. In such a pre-structured political field, the old power did not need to change essentially. This epochal resistance to change has lasted up to the present day, nine years after the fall of the Berlin wall.

Notes

1 Viktor Zaslavski presents a view of the breakup of the USSR as a positive thing, freeing imprisoned developing forces within multi-ethnic Communist federations. He claims that these positive processes are, unfortunately, necessarily also followed by 'running off the rails', i.e. by nationalism bound to traditions, by territorial wars and the aspirations of national leaders towards the achieving of ethnic homogeneity and the stabilization of new states through discrimination against minorities (1992: 97–122).

2 The American sociologist Rogers Brubaker considers that institutionalized ethnic nations transformed the collapse of the Communist system into the breakup of the Communist federation. To the extent to which

a regime lost its legitimacy, national republics deepened internal divisions right up to the point of immobilization and the collapse of the centre (1994: 61).

3 Regarding the diversity of integration and ability to integrate, see E. Pusic 1995: 2–10.

4 For a long time it has been no secret that Presidents Milošević and Tudjman agreed on the division of Bosnia-Hercegovina in March 1991 at a meeting in Karadjordjevo. In testimony about the Yugoslav crisis before the Committee for Foreign Affairs at the USA Congress, the former secretary of state, James Baker, stated that he knew that the leadership of Serbia and Croatia had held long talks about how to divide Bosnia (*NIN* 20 January 1995).

5 Charles Tilley also posed the question of whether this was the time in which we would be confronted with a process where each ethnic collective would aspire to create its own national state (1992: 329–342).

6 'Switzerland is by definition an a-national state. There is no culture or language, i.e. blood or origin, or naturally previously given Swiss nation... Switzerland is not composed of 26 "national cantons" but rather 26 *people* cantons. In these cantons there is no authoritative belonging to one nation, but rather a *right of citizenship*. Under the rights of citizenship, the Swiss recognize loyalty to Swiss policy, and not to a specific cultural nation. Their loyalty to a cultural nation is not lost at all by the surrounding Swiss rights of citizenship' (T. Flajner 1995: 41–46).

7 This typology was given by Rogers Brubaker at a conference in San Diego in September 1994, at the Institute on Global Conflict and Cooperation of the University of California.

8 I am not using the expression 'Irredentism' in its orthodox meaning, but as it applies to the model presented here.

9 Victor Zaslavski points out this moment of forcing, ideological equality. *Perestroika* and *glasnost* enabled the issue to be raised of why so many different states, as gathered together by the USSR (and analogously Yugoslavia) would live united in one state. Those differences were as great as those between Norway and Pakistan, for example. If they had a choice, why would such different states live in one state? (1992: 105).

10 It is interesting that Milan Kučan, explaining why the breakup of Yugoslavia was unavoidable, said 'you should know that Yugoslavia is an artificial creation' (Nasa Borba [*NB,* a daily newspaper] 9 August 1995; interview with Milan Kucan by the Polish newspaper *Gazeta Wyborcza*).

11 In multinational states, such as former Yugoslavia, loyalty to the nation and to the state were openly or covertly in conflict. It has been shown that loyalty to the 'nation' (the ethnic collective) was stronger (see W. Connor 1994).

12 See Sabrina P.Ramet's research on the Yugoslav crisis, and assumptions about international relations between the Yugoslav republics and the internal balance of power (1992).

13 This mechanism was founded on the theorem of V. I. Thomas: 'If people define situations as real, then they are real in their consequences'.

The first part of the theorem states that 'people do not react simply on the objective characteristics of a situation but also on...the meaning which that situation has for them. When they once attribute a meaning to the situation, their behavior and the results of that behavior are determined by the attributed meaning. A clearly pronounced definition of a situation (prophecy and vision) becomes an integral part of the situation and this produces the following event' (R. Merton 1968: 475–490).

14 This complex period in Yugoslav history will not be analysed in total here since this is not necessary for my subject. I am restricted to my own topic: the coinciding of political and national options.

15 Sabrina Ramit calls this system of 'symmetry', 'a balance of power system' which should have de-polarized Serbo-Croatian rivalry and opened the possibility of a coalition of different interests through the mobilization of other republics and by leaning on them (1992: Chapter 6).

16 V. Vlahović 1964: 141–142. Cited in V. Pešić 1988.

17 The conclusions of the Congress were not completely clear in that view, since more was said about 'national economies', and less about political sovereignty.

18 For example, discussions around what should be developed: north or south (the division obviously implied conflict between Serbia and the two most developed republics–Slovenia and Croatia), an industrial or a raw materials base (again the same division), 'the Danube concept of development' as opposed to 'the Adriatic concept of development' etc. When Serbia agreed with Montenegro on the construction of the Beograd-Bar railway, this was experienced in other republics as a 'great Serb conspiracy', the 'short-term goal' of which was to 'grab the centralized investment fund in advance' (for details see Rusinow: 130–137).

19 This does not mean that 'liberal forces' did not exist in Serbia at that time. Some of the main representatives of this line were committed to the federation and others were prevented by the obstruction of the 'conservatives'.

20 His fall was received in Croatia as a great victory for Croatian national policy under 'Serbian hegemony'. Rusinow says that in Zagreb the euphoria following the fall of Ranković could not be contained (Rusinow: 194).

21 Rusinow considers that the concealed 'counter-reaction' existed in a disorganized union of 'rankovicevci', former Stalinists, information bureauists, students and intellectuals of the 'new left', even of Chetniks (274).

22 Schöpflin points out the danger of making federal power 'empty', something on which Croatia insisted, because it was 'known that the power of the centre was identified with the Serbian national interest' (1973: 138).

23 Ibid.: 142. There was the unavoidable question of what relationship a sovereign Croatia and a Yugoslav federation could have and whether a federation could be possible at all under those conditions.

24 Here, we are not thinking of extreme nationalistic groups which sought the reception of Croatia into the UN, requesting a Croatian

army and special currency, and who expressed clear expansive pretensions towards Bosnia-Hercegovina.

25 This is a reference to Dobrica Ćosić and Jovan Marjanović who spoke
about the unenviable position of the Serbs in Kosovo, the migration of
Serbs from Kosovo and the irredentist purposes of the Albanian minority. They also emphasized that national Yugoslav identity was discouraged as national belonging, while on the other hand the bureaucratic
and narrow nationalistic interests of the republics encouraged it in the
name of a struggle against unitarianism (Rusinow 1977: 246).

26 From the end of the 1960s the influence of the JNA grew. It became
the ninth member of the SKJ Presidency along with the eight republican and provincial representatives at the Ninth Congress of SKJ in
1969.

27 However much Croatian nationalism had been blind to the problem of
the integration of Yugoslavia, which the Serbian national interest supported, Schöpflin considers that it remained in the framework of the
'illirism' variant rather than 'pravastvo' [Croatian political groups], although the line between these variants is blurred. The repression of
the leaders contributed to the myth-making of 1971, to defeat being attributed to Serbian generals and to certainty that resolution of the
Croatian national question could not be achieved within the framework of Yugoslavia. These sentiments opened a possibility for Croatian
nationalism to appear in some future time in the 'pravaska' variant
(Schöpflin 145).

28 V. Gligorov also warns about the same circumstances (46–48).
Gligorov emphasizes that Yugoslavia did not try just one political
form–a liberal federation. This conclusion is confirmed by the fact that,
except marginally, there was no formation of 'liberal federal forces' on
the Yugoslav political scene.

29 1. This metaphysics had no limits in creating fog and naive ideas like:
'self-management from district councils to federation', 'autonomous
agreement and accord', 'free exchange of work', 'pluralism of self-
managing interests', 'association of united work', 'self-managing unions
of interests', 'delegations', 'delegates', etc.

30 See the analysis of the 1974 Constitution regarding its role in the dissolution of Yugoslavia in the contribution by V. Dimitrijević, this volume.

31 Ernest Gellner (1992: 243–254) considers that the lack of political
institutions and civil society in post-Communist countries presents the
main condition for the development of ethno-nationalism, because for
that kind of politics no institutions are necessary.

32 Here I use Renée de Navre's definition of 'moderation' in the context
of democratization: 'Moderation means the avoidance of extremism
and hostility in the creation of a position towards other ethnic groups'
(Renée de Navres 1993: 70).

33 Serbs experienced the disappearance of 'party conviction' as a basis of
Yugoslav integration as being damaging to the Serbian national interest
and as 'treason' by other ethnic groups: 'In each Serb member of the

peoples liberation movement there is a conviction that new Yugoslavia is becoming an inter-nationally founded federation in which...the ideological principle is primarily national.' This confidence 'is testified to in Yugoslavism as a formula of inter-nationalism right up to 1974...with the majority of Serbs as the kernel of national and state consciousness...' (D. Ćosić 1991).

34 The JNA remained in the centre as the only integrated factor. But its existence and function depended on the regime: 'The JNA was at the same time an *instrument* and a *function* of the regime's legitimacy. Its existence depended on the regime's survival, i.e. if there is no regime, there is no JNA' (James Gow 1992: 61).

35 Because of its 'central positioning' on which 'inter-nationalistic' Serbian policy was founded, the Serbs did not have one organized nationalistic movement during the existence of the second Yugoslavia. Other nations, preserving their own 'particularist' positions, passed through the experience of nationalism (the massive Croatian movement at the beginning of the 1970s, the Slovenian *cestna* affair at the end of the 1960s, and the repeated Albanian revolts). 'The Denouement Years' is the title of a book of speeches by Slobodan Milošević. The phrase became a kind of ironic slogan among the opposition.

36 In the article I showed that the Serbian claim that only the Serbs, in contrast to other Yugoslav nations, could not make use of their right to self-determination in fact implied the 'right of the Stronger' and the 'right to unity'. But not one Yugoslav ethnic group obtained this right.

37 W. Connor (1984: 336) claims that the purpose of the KPJ was to create a balance between Croatia and Serbia. By creating provinces in Serbia alone (Connor does not deny the original existence of the provinces in Serbia but not does he deny the possibility that they be created in other republics) the provinces reduced the Serbian community in Serbia by about 1.3 million.

38 For example, neither did the joint state security function (for details see S. Ramet 1992: 76–78).

39 Ramet considers that the provinces were equalized with republics with the whole-hearted assistance of Slovenian and Croatian nationalists who were in power when the amendments were passed.

40 Because of the 'blue book' there was an unlawful confederal agreement by which candidates for the Presidency of the SKJ (League of Communists of Yugoslavia) were automatically accepted on the recommendation of republican leadership. Dragoslav Marković, who, as the representative of the Serbian leadership was responsible for the 'blue book', was not elected into the SKJ Presidency due to sabotage by the representatives from other republics and provinces. Only after the intervention of Petar Stambolić was there a re-vote, and the candidate from the Republic of Serbia 'passed'.

41 The greatest opposition to pressure to reduce the prerogatives of the autonomous provinces came from the provinces themselves. Thus, for example, the struggle between the republic and the provinces is illus-

trated by an incident in 1983 when provincial leaders did not allow representatives of the republic to participate in talks held with Milka Planinc, the then prime minister (S. Ramet: 216).

42 The issue was new struggles which began in the early 1980s over the question of whether the state should be re-centralized or decentralized to an even greater degree ('confederalism'). Under pressure from the IMF and the World Bank towards the re-centralization of the controlling role of the National Bank and an efficient economic system, in 1986 the leadership agreed to start preparing amendments to the Constitution. Certain changes were adopted at the end of 1988. In discussions about constitutional changes, both officially and in opposition, Serbia placed the changes in the status of the autonomous provinces on the agenda. For the pressure exerted by the IMF to re-centralize, see S.L.Woodward 1995, Chapter 3.

43 This meant that they sought the status of 'constitutive people', i.e. the right to self-determination.

44 For the significance of the Battle of Kosovo as the central event of entire Serbian history and national consciousness see the contribution of Olga Zirojević, this volume.

45 In this the church saw a chance to emerge from its marginalized position. See the contribution of Radmila Radić, this volume.

46 The populations of Serbs and Montenegrins decreased permanently, especially from the 1960s. See the contribution of Marina Blagojević, this volume.

47 My research into rapes in Kosovo showed that from 1987 there was not one 'interethnic' rape, that is of a Serb woman by an Albanian, although their was constant talk about this kind of incident. Under enormous pressure from publicity related to the rape of 'Serbian women', a new crime of rape was introduced, where the individuals are 'of different nationality (ethnicity)'. Alongside this, in comparison with other Yugoslav republics, the rate of rape incidents was lowest in Kosovo and highest within the same ethnic groups (see *Kosovski čvor: drešiti ili seći*, 47).

48 It was especially criticized by the Slovenes who did not understand the Serbian problem in Kosovo. 'The Serbs understood the Slovenes when the Germans drove them from their homes during the Second World War, and even provided them with refuge in Serbia'. They did not seek 'proof' that the Germans had really driven them out (Tašić, 1994: 89).

49 In the course of April and May 1986, the Association of Writers of Serbia organized nine protest evenings dedicated to Kosovo. Speakers' platforms about Kosovan literature, and the signing of a petition for the support of Kosovan Serbs were also organized (see the contribution of Drinka Gojković, this volume).

50 This kind of interpretation of the conflict was publicly stated for the first time at the funeral of Aleksandar Ranković, former minister of internal affairs. After his fall in 1966, the situation in Kosovo changed substantially when the governing functions were given to Albanian

party cadres. Rankovic's funeral in 1983 'was transformed into a nationalistic event' in which more than 100,000 people took part. 'His name was shouted, but between the lines was "When Ranković was in power the Albanians were peaceful"' (S. Đukić 1994: 26).

51 The 'Kelmendi incident', i.e. the incident in which an Albanian soldier murdered four soldiers of different nationalities and injured several others while they were sleeping. The Serbian press commented that it was 'shooting Yugoslavia', raising an extremely anti-Albanian mood. Commentators in the newspaper *Politika* implied that the Albanians did not just hate Serbs, but all Yugoslav peoples. The incident was overinflated for days with so much contradiction that the impression was that the massacre in the barracks had been staged (Tasic 1990: 99–100).

52 Charles Tilley considers that the modern epoch legitimized the principle 'that states should suit one homogenous people, that members of a homogenous group owe strong loyalty to the state that embodies their inheritance, and that the world should be composed of nation-states, cherishing the strong patriotism of their citizens' (Tilly, 1994: 133).

53 For an approach to nationalism as a form of politics, see J. Breuilly 1992. His definition of nationalism as a political doctrine and political form includes three elements: 1) the existence of the nation with an explicit and special character; 2) interests and values of the nation have priority over other interests and values; and 3) the nation must hold on to maximum independence, which strictly assumes achieving political sovereignty.

54 By connecting nationalism to the creation of ethnic states and the resolution of the national problem, I have defined this concept with a specific meaning, but omitted its general meaning. Nationalism is a constant form of politics since nation states have been formed, highlighting the modern epoch and separating it from traditional, medieval states. In them the national identity, expressed in terms of national sovereignty as a guaranteed status of all individuals belonging to the nation, presents the greatest value which is permanently protected and in whose name external policy is conducted, as politics of 'national' and 'state' interests. In nation states which resolved the national question long ago, nationalism in the narrow sense of the word (subordinating all interests to the national) practically exclusively appears in external situations, i.e. threat of war. For the general concept of nationalism, see Greenfeld 1992: 3–26.

55 Under nationalism, Gellner assumes exactly this case–establishing congruence between nations and states (Gellner 1983: 43).

56 The literal meaning of 'resentment' includes: 'recalling evil', 'offence', 'hatred', 'bitterness', 'spite'. It would be most precise to say that resentment is a sentiment between envy and hatred.

57 Greenfeld understands this idea of Nietzsche as a psychological factor which determined the form of the identity of individual nations (as most typical examples she analyses Germany and Russia). 'Resentment', or feelings of inferiority, envy and injured national pride, which arise

from lagging behind in the creation of a modern national state of the European type (1992: 15–16), are attributed by this author to certain types of nationalism (here 'nationalism', as already discussed, is understood as a collection of formative characteristics of national identity.

58 Max Weber added to this subjective dimension of nation, by emphasizing that it is for their specific, essential 'belief' or 'feeling' that one group makes a nation. Following a symbolic theory of meaning, Benedict Anderson also defines nation as an 'invented community' (1983).

59 This silence about genocide helped the Serbian leadership to push Serbs living in Croatia into the war, but the propaganda of the nationalistic HDZ (Croatian Democratic Union) helped Serbia confirm its doubts. In this way, fear of Croatian symbols was produced by both sides, especially the infamous chessboard as a symbol of the Ustasha (see B. Denitch 1994: 367–389).

60 This refers to the famous Eighth Session of the SK of Serbia at which Milošević carried the victory over the moderate Serbian leadership, by good organization of local agents and 'Marxist' professors with no standing, gathered together by his wife in the struggle for the introduction of 'integral Marxism' into all levels of education. The motto of the winning stream was 'Tito and Kosovo', old regime plus Serbian national question.

61 For the role of General Ljubičić, one of the most influential people in the army, see Dukić 1994: 35.

62 In the service of nationalistic policy and the creation of the cult of the new 'leader' it was placed in the most influential and reputable daily paper, *Politika*. This paper played a key role in the creation of national intolerance through its offensive column 'Echoes and reactions'. It spoke with the voice of the 'people', attacking individuals, even whole peoples, if they expressed the least doubts about the policy of Slobodan Milošević. Such doubts were identified with hatred towards the Serbian people (see the contribution of A. Nenadović and R. Veljanovski, this volume).

63 'We are faced with the offensive of the opposition, so we must hit hard. The opposition has captured societies, now there will be a struggle for the press. Everywhere that we have not completed differentiation we have a weak offensive' (quoted from: Đukić: 63).

64 General Kadijević, federal minister of defence and chief of Yugoslavian H. Q. from 1989 to 1992, claimed that the reformers in power in socialist countries were part of USA strategy, the goal of which was the defeat of Communism. These 'reformers' had long been prepared 'so that it appeared that the process of destroying the system, in view of the reformers, was led by the internal party forces' (1993: 13).

65 A party army like the JNA could not have objectively defended the state, but could only protect the existing political system and the ideology of the political avant garde. When Communism began to collapse, the army tightened up in an effort to help the system to survive (G. Petrović, *NIN* 6 January 1995).

66 This is what Kadijević called representatives of 'secessionist republics', from which was hidden information and JNA plans for action (ibid.: 95).

67 The subordination of national ideology to state creation was stated by D. Ćosić: 'Slobodan Milošević did not become a politician with qualities or leadership charisma, with nationalism as an ideology, but with *state creation* as a national goal (1992: 141).

68 For closeness between, and the coalition of, Communists and nationalists in Serbia and Russia, see V. Vujačić, 1994.

Yugoslavia as a Mistake

OLIVERA MILOSAVLJEVIĆ

...violence is the midwife in the creation of national states, primarily violence in war. Each nationalism begins with collecting fairy tales or epic poetry, and that is the nationalism of the elite. I tell my students an anecdote from early-nineteenth- century Prague. A group of people met together and were sitting down in the City Tavern at a table, just as we are here. Then someone walked in and asked what would happen if the ceiling of the tavern were to fall down on them. The reply was that it would be the end of the Czech national movement.

M. Ekmečić, *Književne novine*, 1 December 1988

On 16 September 1985, in Ljubljana, at the 'Mrak' restaurant, there was a meeting between the editorial board of the Slovenian *Nova revija*, and three representatives of the Belgrade opposition.

D. Ćosić, *Srpsko pitanje – demokratsko pitanje*, March 1992

In 1918 Yugoslavia came into existence, its founders believing that it would permanently solve the Serbian, Croatian and Slovenian national question. Seventy years later it was permanently shattered, the explanation being that these issues can only be solved without it.

In the vision of its creators, Yugoslavia appeared both as a necessity (in order to gather together the small Slavic nations and thus deny the pretensions of the neighbouring nations), and as an emotional claim (resulting from the closeness of the South Slavic nations and the connections between them). Seventy years later, the elites that shattered Yugoslavia proclaimed these demands to be the misapprehensions of its 'nationally unaware' peoples.

The moment when discussions regarding alternatives to Yugoslavia became legitimate, widely accepted and a dominant aspect of political actions, and when national programmes based on the unique interests of an *ethnos* were defined regardless of the borders of the republics in which it lived, and of the interests of others within the community, marked the beginning of a break with the continued defence of the existence of Yugoslavia. It could be concluded from this that the agents of the immediate action in the break-up of the Yugoslav state appeared only when the national programmes of the intellectual elites had been accepted and put into action by the political elites, and supported by the homogenized masses. External factors (the dissolution of Communism and of the USSR), by supporting their apparently democratic methods, only made these processes easier, while moves made by the European Union and the USA towards the recognition of some of the republics were the effect of the already completed internal destructive processes, and not the cause of the break-up of the Yugoslav state. One of the creators of the idea of delimiting the Serb lands in Bosnia-Hercegovina, Ekmečić, a member of the Academy, had written earlier that 'In 1914 a phenomenon obvious in Yugoslav history was confirmed: the politics of division into spheres of interest makes sense and is truly effective only when it receives support from the Yugoslav region and from Yugoslav national politicians. Borders between the spheres of interest of great powers are not determined by the great powers alone, but by the feuding South Slav nationalisms' (Ekmečić 1990: 442).

Ideological verdicts on Yugoslavia

In 1992 Yugoslavia formally dissolved amid all-out war. This was also the end of a process the ideological foundations of which can be found throughout Yugoslavia's existence, but which began to accelerate in the mid-1980s. At that time, lacking an 'authoritative arbiter', a request for alternatives to the existing state became legitimate, national programmes were made public, and, in the years that followed, these programmes were to be added to and realized through parallel political action.

In analysing requests made after the outbreak of the armed conflict, it is important to identify differences between requests that were given an explicit form, and those made *implicitly*. The explicitly contradictory demands (for 'a unified Yugoslavia', and 'a confederate Yugoslavia') were never followed by adequate political action, which diminished their persuasiveness. In contrast, the implicitly contradictory demands ('all the Serbs in one state', 'an independent Slovenia' and 'an independent Croatia') were realized most directly through political actions and led to the disintegration of the country. It can thus be claimed with certainty that the implicit claims were the real ones, while the explicit claims were used only for rallying public support and acquiring legitimacy, to give the appearance of democratization, and to justify the processes that were already underway.

The majority of those scholars in Yugoslavia who are engaged in analysing the dissolution of the state and the reasons behind it, put the emphasis on the very act of separation of Slovenia and Croatia (Macedonia is mostly forgotten, since it does not fit into the theses on 'separatist' nations), as the result of a long process. The real and immediate factors determining the destiny of the common state—that is, events in Yugoslavia between 1986 and 1990—are mostly neglected, and sometimes are not even known.

A chronological analysis of the ideas, defined in the form of claims, and their realization in terms of political action, reveals several essential points in this process:

1. the publication of the Memorandum of the SANU in 1986, and of the Contributions for the Slovenian National Programme in 1987, which opened up the 'national question' in Yugoslavia in a totally new way;
2. the process of national homogenization in Serbia after 1987, the so-called happening of the people, as a confirmation of the Serb intellectual elite's requests;
3. the relativization of the term 'Yugoslavia', which reached its peak in Slobodan Milošević's interpretation of '*malo morgen Yugoslavia*' between 1989 and 1991; and, finally,
4. the referendums in which people voted 'for' the war option, between 1990 and 1992.

The Memorandum of the SANU and Nova Revija

The overt negation of Yugoslavia began in the mid-1980s through the Serb and the Slovenian intellectual elites' dissatisfaction with their nations' status in the common state. Although objectively the Serbs and Slovenes had different starting positions (Serbs were relatively the most numerous, and Slovenia one of the nations with fewest inhabitants; Serbs lived in several republics, Slovenes in just one; Serbia was a relatively heterogeneous republic, unlike Slovenia, which was mostly populated by Slovenes), their national elites denied the existing state with equal zeal. The former felt threatened by the 'confederate' division into autonomous provinces, while the latter felt threatened by unitarism and 'Yugoslav nationalism'. Serbs rejected Yugoslavia because of the policies of Tito and Kardelj (a Croat and a Slovene), while Slovenes rejected it because of 'Belgrade small-town talk'; Serbs rejected the Anti-Fascist Council for the National Liberation of Yugoslavia (AVNOJ) because of internal borders, and Slovenes because of being put into 'care'; Serbs rejected the solutions of the first Yugoslavia due to the economic domination of the Slovenian and Croat bourgeoisie, while Slovenes rejected it because of the political hegemony of the Serb bureaucracy; the Serbs saw the solution in the Yugoslav People's Army (JNA), the Slovenes in denouncing the JNA ... All of these apparently irreconcilable differences between the Serb and the Slovenian intellectual elites concealed an agreement, invisible at first glance—neither of the elites supported the existing country. Yugoslavia was either to be founded on completely new national principles, or should not exist at all. All efforts to prove that the claims put forward were nothing other than democracy in action were denied by a constant return to separate Serb or Slovenian national interests. Nor could their 'democracy' be confirmed through the frequently iterated claims that, understood in this way, special national-democratic interests at the same time represented democracy for everyone. Although both Serbs and Slovenes started by denouncing the existing Communist authorities and demanding democratization, these requests were merely a cover for the real aim—the denouncing of Yugoslavia. Democracy on the level of the *ethnos*, the neglecting of the interests of other ethnic groups sharing the same territory, the mutual denunciation of motives for living in a common country— none of these were prerequisites for a democratic transformation of the common country, whether 'unified', 'federal', or 'confederate'.

The proposals made by the Serbian and Slovenian intellectual elites for the national programme were not mutually negating in terms of the legitimacy of outlining and defining 'national interests'. Just as the Memorandum stated that 'all the nations within Yugoslavia must be given the opportunity to voice their intentions and wishes', in the Contributions for the Slovenian National Programme also, the requests of 'legitimate Serbian nationalism' received support. The confrontation would arise only on the practical-political plane, when it became all too obvious where the 'legitimate' nationalism of the Yugoslav nations had taken the common country–all in the interests of keeping their hands 'clean' of the (un)expected dirty outcome.

The publication of the Memorandum of the SANU in September 1986, and the events that followed, had a direct influence on the

Contributions for the Slovenian National Programme that was published later in Issue 57 of the review *Nova Revija* in January 1987.
Just as the starting point of the Memorandum is the non-existence
of the Serbian national programme and requests for its definition,
the editors of *Nova Revija,* in explaining their motives for publishing the Contributions, noted that 'it is not by accident that at this
very moment publications dealing with the history of the Slovenian national programme are being issued'. According to them 'the
topic was "hot" and controversial, as proved by the efforts being
made in other national communities (the SANU Memorandum)
and the harsh (although mostly superficial) criticisms of the
"nationalists" '. The editors stressed that the Contributions were
not a new national programme, but only contributions towards a
programme, the formulation of which exceeded the competence of
the review and its contributors. It is here that one reaches the basic,
formal rather than substantial, difference between the Memorandum
and the Contributions. The Memorandum was created in the most
important and the most prestigious Serb national institution, and
thus carried much greater weight than the individual contributions
(notwithstanding the personal reputations of their authors). Both
texts were the result of the work of sixteen authors—the Memorandum began as the collective work of a sixteen-member commission selected by the Presidency of the SANU following the unanimous decision of the General Assembly of the Academy.[1] This was
not a signed document, and the number of members of the Academy involved in it rose to twenty-three. The Contributions were
formulated with more modest ambitions. They were published in a
special issue of the review, and the name of the author, both sur-
name and first name, was given for each contribution (as well as for
the request within it).[2] Unlike the Memorandum, which was conceived with the aim of shedding some light on all sides of the multi-
dimensional crisis in Yugoslav society and only in its second part
reduced the crisis to the Serbian question, the Contributions almost
exclusively dealt with the Slovenian question, with minor remarks
about the Yugoslav crisis as a motive for the emergence of the programme. Both documents are incoherent—the Memorandum because it also aimed at providing an objective analysis of the Yugoslav
crisis, as well as proof that only the Serbian nation was endangered;
and the Contributions, by the very nature of the selection of the
authors' contributions and their dissimilar views on the 'national
interest', and especially on the future of the Yugoslav state.

Yugoslavia belongs to no one nation, all the nations within it are
endangered, and no decision or article of the constitution on

which it is based, is legitimate. This is the first conclusion that one reaches after reading both the Memorandum and the Contributions. The same points have been expanded in both documents as the basis for arguments regarding the danger posed to each nation, and although frequently introduced in a different way, they usually imply the same thing—the denial of the legitimacy of the existing Yugoslavia as a state that did not satisfy, and had never satisfied, Serb and Slovenian national interests. One cannot help feeling that the Contributions were intended by the Slovene intellectual elite as a reply to the authors of the Memorandum, a feeling supported both by the timing of the publications (the Memorandum was published first, and the Contributions include a reference to the Memorandum—in principle, with some general criticisms, the Memorandum is supported by the authors of the Contributions, insofar as it represented 'legitimate Serbian nationalism'), as well as by the compatibility of the two documents and similarities in their style. Those points appearing in both documents, whether with the same or dissimilar introductions, are discussed below.

The Kingdom of Yugoslavia

The need to prove that dangers were posed to one nation alone necessarily led to the selective representation of the shared past, that is, to giving emphasis to those points in which a confirmation for the theses advocated could more easily be found. Thus, the Memorandum does not even mention interethnic relations within the Kingdom, nor does it mention the formation, constitutional regulations or form of government of the Kingdom. This is an important point, since this document looks far back into the past when it explains the Communists' attitude towards the national question and when it seeks arguments for their anti-Serb feelings, even in the pre-Communist period. The ideology of a marginal, dependent party, without the later experience of the NOB and mass popular support (dubiously interpreted along the way), is usedto explain the state of interethnic relations, and is though to be stronger than the twenty-three-year existence of the Kingdom of Yugoslavia (1918-1941), and its immediate practical political influence on these relations. In contrast, the Contributions pay much greater attention to the Kingdom than they do to the creation of the post-war Federation, since it is here that they find more powerful arguments for the danger posed to the Slovenes. It is argued that the Slovenian people would not have made the deci-

sion to be included into the Kingdom of the Serbs, Croats and Slovenes, but for 'the conditions of foreign occupation'. Slovenia paid
more into the centrally regulated finances than it got back from
them; military affairs and education were also centralized; and 'the
whole state apparatus represented and advocated the interests of
small-town Serbia'. Referring to the break-up of the country in
1941, it was argued that 'the Serb military clique had put in most
"efforts", and because of its "heroism" the occupation lasted two
years longer' (France Bučar).

The AVNOJ

The denouncing of Communist Yugoslavia was directed towards
its foundations, not just towards the existing form of government.
For the authors of both the Memorandum and the Contributions, the
legitimacy of the 1943 decisions of the AVNOJ was in doubt. According to the Memorandum, taking into account the basic tendency of
this document to prove that only the Serbian nation was in danger,
the AVNOJ was legitimate when it came to others: 'For the Second
AVNOJ Council, delegates were selected from Serb military units and
members of the Supreme Headquarters who happened to be in the
territory of Bosnia-Hercegovina, unlike the delegates of some other
republics, who came to the council from their own region and had
behind them national and political organizations with coherent attitudes and programmes.' Thus the Serbs, 'without prior preparations
and without the support of their political organizations, found themselves in a position to accept, under conditions of war, solutions that
opened wide possibilities for their break-up'. Some of the authors of
the Contributions also remarked on the 'illegitimacy' of the AVNOJ
decisions, but, in keeping with their basic lack of interest in the
destiny of the other Yugoslav nations, they saw this illegitimacy
only as it affected the Slovenes : 'From the legal point of view, and
from the point of view of natural law, the Slovenian nation was put
into a political order, about which it has so far had no possibility to
express its will in free elections' (Bučar).

The 'home' Communists

Because of their weakness, the 'home' Communists shared some of
the responsibility for endangering their own nations, but the main
responsibility lay with the governing federal institutions. Accord-

ing to the Memorandum, this was due to the fact that these institutions were dominated by Croats and Slovenians, while according to the Contributions it was because they advocated 'Yugoslav nationalism'. Serb Communists were guilty (according to the Memorandum) because they 'capitulated'; they were 'defensive', because they were responsible for the 'greatest defeat in the liberation struggles between 1804 and 1941', all because of their 'subservience', and 'hardened opportunism'. Slovenian Communists were guilty (according to the Contributions) for the 'political impotence of the Slovenian nation', which arose from the 'opportunism of the Slovenian political bureaucracy in relation to the etatist dominant federal state on the one hand, and the republic's etatism and bureaucracy in relation to their own Slovenian society on the other' (Ivan Urbančič).

Yugoslavia

Yugoslavia satisfied the interests of neither the Serbs nor the Slovenes: it was a country in which the Serbs were threatened, unequal and denied, while for the Slovenes it was someone else's country. According to the Memorandum, 'the establishment of the full national and cultural integrity of the Serb people, irrespective of the republic or autonomous province in which they live, is their historical and democratic right. The achieving of equality and independent development has wider historical implications. ... If the Serb people envisage their future as being part of the family of cultured and civilized peoples of the world, they must be given a chance to rediscover themselves, to regain awareness of their historical and spiritual being, to see their economic and cultural interests clearly, and to draw up a modern social and national programme that will serve as inspiration for both the present and the future generations.' According to the Contributions, 'since so far we have known foreign countries only, countries which were not ours, for us, these were transcending countries, we have a country which is the expression of force. ... Among many Slovenes, there is a growing wish that the Slovenian people, following their liberation from foreign nations, should finally become independent from those peoples that are related to them' (Tine Hribar). The threat to the Slovenian nation arose from 'artificial (synthetic) Yugoslavism' (Urbančič). Slovenes should ask themselves 'Who are we? Where are we going?'; they should draw up a national programme (Spomenka Hribar). The relationship between this small

nation and the other bigger, more powerful and richer nations was
a source of difficulties for the Slovenes in Yugoslavia. 'In short, we
are different, so whether we like it or not, above all we have the inalienable right to be and to remain different, for as long as we want'
(Jože Pučnik). 'Whatever the name of that country—the Austro-
Hungarian Empire, the Kingdom of Yugoslavia, DFY, FNRY, or
SFRY—it was never completely identified with the homeland or the
people. It was never a homeland. The country from which they (the
Slovenes in exile) left was never called Slovenia' (Drago Jančar).

Who dominated Yugoslavia?

The essential difference between the Memorandum and the Contributions can be seen in their attitudes to the causes and inspirers of
the 'threat' to the Serb and Slovenian nations. Listing proofs of the
general threat faced by Serbia and the Serb people in Yugoslavia, the
Memorandum lays the blame for all the troubles, both past and present, on others—on the Austro-Marxist class ideology, on the Comintern, on Slovenian and Croatian Communists, on Tito and Kardelj,
Croatia and Slovenia, on balists and neo-fascists in Kosovo, and on
the anti-Serb coalition of everyone within Yugoslavia. The authors of
the Contributions (with the exception of Bučar) look for the causes
in the Yugoslav political system and government. According to the
Memorandum, Yugoslavia is dominated by Croatia and Slovenia.
Almost all the authors in the Contributions take as their starting
point the inequality of the Slovenian language (the unilateral bilin-
gualism of the Slovenes is 'objectively pushing them back into the
position of the Yugoslav national minority, which leads to a gradual
denationalization' [Urbančič]; some languages in Yugoslavia were
guaranteed first-class status, while others were relegated to a second-
class status—'in Yugoslavia, Slovenian is a second-class language'
[Dimitrij Rupel]). However, the majority of the authors negate (e.g.
Urbančič) or do not explicitly identify, any Yugoslav nation as the
dominant nation. On the contrary, nationalism sprang from the political system, and 'inter-republic arguments are the specific effects
of the ruling political system and its bureaucracy' (Urbančič).

The 1974 Constitution

Although both the Memorandum and the Contributions take as a
starting point the new relations established by the 1974 Constitu-

tion, there was no agreement between them about the degree of confederalization of the political system. According to the Memorandum, the Constitution enabled 'the affirmation of the statehood of the republics and the autonomous provinces, with the simultaneous disappearance of the original, co-ordinating functions of the Federation', leading to the 'realization of wide possibilities for satisfying particular interests at the expense of universal ones'. According to the authors of the Contributions, 'despite the federal republic regulation of Yugoslavia, and despite claims about the importance of the 1974 Constitution in the break-up of the country's unity, the federal state establishes its supremacy in politically homogenizing the whole society'. In contrast to the critique in the Memorandum, which claimed that the Constitution established confederacy, the Contributions disputed those competencies given 'to the nations of the republics and the autonomous provinces'. 'The governing unifying force now springs from the dominant federal state, from the political system, and not from the recognized autonomous will of the "nations" of the republics and autonomous provinces, since the 1974 Constitution does not give them the right to secede' (Urbančič). 'An important example of the half-way political reform was the considerably strengthened status of the republics, and the increase in their political independence. This positive idea remained unsuccessful, since it took fright and ended in compromise' (Bučar).

The Fund for the Development of Undeveloped Regions

This fund endangered both the Serbs and the Slovenes in the same way. According to the Memorandum, one of the basic reasons for the Serbian economy lagging behind was the contribution that it had to pay into the Federation Fund for the Undeveloped Regions. 'It [Serbia] was the only real victim of the development of the three undeveloped republics and the Socialist Autonomous Province (SAP) of Kosovo, paying the price of its aid to others by lagging behind the others. This was not the case with the three developed regions. ... Although it helped the development of the undeveloped regions and lightened the load of the developed ones through its contribution, Serbia did not find in any of them any understanding for its lagging behind. A mutual interest directs two types of regions to a coalition in order to maintain the existing state of affairs in which they satisfy their interests at the expense of Serbia'. According to the authors of the Contributions, Slovenes were alone capable of being an independent national system of power, 'we are strong enough ... we do not live at others' expense. Quite on the contrary, Slovenia even has to "help" the undeveloped republics. In the present etatist circumstances in the Yugoslav existing socialist system, our national advantage is turned into our national disaster. Statistics show that Slovenia, with approximately 8 per cent of the country's population, contributes 15 to 17 per cent of the whole federal budget for the "development of the undeveloped regions", which results in a loss of privilege among the more developed regions of the country' (Urbančič).

The national versus the class principle

The supremacy of one or the other principle within Yugoslavia was seen in diametrically opposite ways. Although both the Memorandum and the Contributions called for the drawing up of national programmes, they gave differing evaluations of the supremacy of one principle over the other, due to differences in the openness of the claims that they put forward. In accordance with its controversial denunciation of the Anti-Fascist Council for the National Liberation of Yugoslavia (AVNOJ) as the cause of the break-up of the Serbs, and at the same time its pragmatic reference to them in the demand for the formulation of a Serb national programme, the Memorandum's dissatisfaction with the existing Yugoslavia lay in the fact that 'the national has defeated the class [principle]'. 'The main reason for the multidimensional crisis lies in the ideological defeat of socialism by nationalism. ... Its roots can be found in the Comintern ideology and in the national policies of the Communist Party of Yugoslavia before the [Second World] war.' In contrast, in the Contributions, in which demands were openly stated, it was claimed that the advantage of the class over the national principle lay in that 'which is expressed as a negation of the autonomy of the "particularly" national. ... A unitary nationalist "Yugoslavism" appears as opposed to the "nations" that it unifies through its political power in the single state'. That is why it is 'problematic and imprecise to claim that the the particular interests and discrepancies of the republics and autonomous provinces are the source of the original nationalism, or that they are immediately transported into their "separatist" nationalisms' (Urbančič).

The individual versus the universal, or: Where is the state in the individual-*ethnos*-democracy relationship?

At first sight, human rights were the starting point in both proposals for national programmes. However, the nature of these
documents limited human and individual rights to national rights,
or, more precisely, to ethnic rights. In other words, it made the
very possibility of the realization of civic rights conditional on the
primary realization of separate ethnic rights. While this identification (of human rights with ethnic rights) was hidden in the Memorandum, it was made explicit in the Contributions. According to
the Memorandum, 'in order to execute the necessary changes, one
should get rid of the ideology that stressed nationality and territo-
riality. While integrative functions are getting stronger in contemporary society, with the full affirmation of civil and human rights ...
disintegrative forces are getting stronger in our political system,
along with local, regional and national egoism.' The reply to this
would be 'to create for all the nations within Yugoslavia a possibility to declare their wishes and intentions, in which case Serbia
could also make a decision and determine its own national interests'. According to the Contributions, 'the desire that the individual, as a member of a nation, should himself determine the laws
that shape national institutions through the people as a subject,
that is, the nation, is not a nationalist demand' (Tine Hribar). 'The
Slovenian national programme must be based on personal autonomy' (Spomenka Hribar). 'We should soberly and thoughtfully expose the myths of Slavism, Yugoslavism, shared history (which we
never had), shared destiny (which might yet come), and shared
spilling of blood (which is spilled individually, just as each life is
individual) ... in order to care primarily for the interests of the
Slovenian people' (Jože Pučnik). 'The autonomy of Slovenia as a
nation-state in relation to other states must be supplemented by
the personal autonomy of every individual Slovene' (Alenka Goljevšček).

Solidarity

If the slogan 'brotherhood and unity' was rejected as an ideological
Communist mistake, the issue of elementary solidarity was also
blurred in the national vision. In the request for the establishment
of full national integrity for the Serbian people regardless of the
republics' borders, and in defining the Serb national programme
for the inspiration of all generations, the similarly understood
'national interests' and potential 'urges' of other Yugoslav peoples
were completely ignored. In the same way, but with an awareness

of the better position of Slovenia, which was ethnically homogeneous and where the 'expression of national aspirations has a high degree of legitimacy' (Gregor Tomc), Slovenian independence and sovereignty were demanded in the Contributions with no apparent concern for the destiny of other Yugoslav peoples. While the Memorandum mentions, in a single sentence, 'concern' about the destiny of other nations, reflected in their right to declare their intentions when it came to Yugoslavia, some parts of the Contributions openly denied any interest in their destiny. 'How other nations and nationalities regulate their relations is their problem only, and their decision: it is in no way a Slovenian problem' (Pučnik).

Frustrations

Both Serbs and Slovenes were frustrated with the existing country, the difference being that, according to the Memorandum, others were to blame for this 'fact', while according to the Contributions, it was the result of internal Slovenian motives. According to the Memorandum, Serbian people had, for half a century, carried 'the blame and burden of being the prison guards of other South Slavic peoples'; 'a feeling of historical guilt' had been forced onto them; and 'it is the only one [nation] which has not solved its national question'. Serbian people also suffered 'under an imposed guilt complex'; they had been 'intellectually and politically disarmed', 'exposed to temptations that are too strong not to leave their mark deep in their spirituality'. All this had resulted in the 'depressed state of the Serbian nation'. According to the Contributions, Slovenes had, both on the individual and on the collective level, 'the inherited fear which causes us to react traumatically to some words. We are afraid of our own sovereignty, since it implies complete self-reliance and self-responsibility. ... Furthermore, we are afraid of statehood, since we fear even the image of a state' (Tine Hribar).

Secession

There was one topic which was only hinted at in the Memorandum, in the request for the 'establishment of the full national integrity of the Serbian people, regardless of the republic or the autonomous province in which they live'. The same topic was the basis of all the Contributions–that is, the right of the nations to secede. It has been described as inalienable, as a right 'which belongs to the very essence of subjective independence', and which 'cannot be substituted in any way, and will never be out of date' (Tine Hribar). The constitutional legalization of this right was demanded, since 'we tend to completely underestimate the positive national-psychological effect of the constitutional legalization of such a possibility' (Urbančič). Instead of Yugoslavism, the right to self-determination should be recognized, 'since only with an awareness of that right is it possible to establish sovereign relations at the interethnic level' (Spomenka Hribar)

What to do with Yugoslavia?

The Memorandum offered two mutually exclusive proposals for Yugoslavia. In the first part, it offered a democratic integrative federalism and the rejection of the behind-the-screen scheming of the 'self-proclaimed protectors of the special national interests'. The second part contained the demand that Serbia should define her national interests, and the Serb people their national programme. When it came to this issue, the Contributions were less consistent, shifting from a demand for changes within Yugoslavia, with the legalization of the right to secession, to the full realization of this right. 'If Yugoslavia is to remain as a community of equal and sovereign nations, great changes are needed. "Yugoslavism"[3] proclaimed as brotherhood ... must give way as a principle of our cohabitation' (Spomenka Hribar). 'Whether, at the end of that development, Slovenia lives within the confederacy, or whether it becomes an independent state, or whether it manages to struggle for some other form, is of secondary and terminological importance only, if our inalienable right to national sovereignty and statehood is fully respected and realized in everyday life' (Pučnik). 'If we draw the conclusion that Yugoslavia as a unitary state is not possible ... it clearly follows that Yugoslavia is not possible as a federal country either, since federalism is just one form of unitary state. ... In both cases, it has so far been an artificial construction. So far, Yugoslavia has failed precisely because it was artificial and had no real foundation' (Bučar).

From such a national-ideological foundation, devised and publicly announced in 1986 to 1987, which would later become the basis for political action (in Serbia, towards the end of 1987; in Slovenia, in early 1989), a dominant and generally accepted pattern of the 'national interests' of Serbs and Slovenes eventually emerged. The Memorandum and the Contributions for the Slovenian National Programme were only the first step towards the shaping of such national interests. In the following years, Serb intellectuals recognized their own national ('democratic') task in putting themselves at the service of the Serbian political authorities, as well as in providing professional, moral and intellectual support for all demands made by the Serbian political authorities. Making use of the situation in Serbia, Slovenian intellectuals have increased their influence over the Slovenian public, and, following the Communists' defeat in the 1990 elections, Slovenian intellectuals themselves presented new policies. Although national interests (defined as 'all the Serbs in one state' and an 'independent Slovenia') excluded the survival of the existing state, for some time their creators pragmatically continued to refer to Yugoslavia as a frame in which these interests could be realized.[4] The realization of the first demand was seen in the changing of internal borders (erasing them in Serbia proper, and establishing new ones in Croatia and Bosnia-Hercegovina), and the realization of the second, in true confederalization (a Slovenian army and language) and the legalization of the right to secede. While the fight within the Serbian regime, and the general agreement between the intellectual and the political elite about the nature of 'the national interest', was concluded at the Eighth Session of the Serbian Communist Party's Central Committee in 1987, in Slovenia this happened much later. The Slovenian Communist authorities rejected the demands of its national intellectual elite,[5] and a full agreement between the politicians and the intelligentsia (which even became predominantly personally identical) was only reached after the United Slovenian Opposition (DEMOS) won the 1990 elections. This difference is particularly apparent in the fully explicit and exclusive demands for independence made after 1990, which the Slovenian Communist authorities had not previously put forward, and which are proportionate to the differences in the ways for solving the Kosovo question in Serbia before and after the Eighth Session of 1987.

All aspects of dissatisfaction with Yugoslavia, made public between 1986 and 1987 by the Serbian and the Slovenian intellectual elites in their demands for the determination of separate national interests, were to find their expression in Croatian pretensions in 1990.

Ideology as a material force

During the 1980s the Kosovo problem and the constitutional provisions, particularly those relating to the issue of autonomous provinces, were top-priority political questions in Yugoslavia. However, the publication of the Memorandum in 1986, and of the Contributions for the Slovenian National Programme in1987, imposed a completely new direction and time-table for their solution. From that moment on, the Kosovo problem was exposed as only the first step towards the solving of the Serbian question, which was later posed in Vojvodina, Croatia and Bosnia-Hercegovina, while the Slovenian request for independence in a confederate Yugoslavia only confirmed the legitimacy of the Serb demands for a national, 'third Yugoslavia', since it supported the relativization of the term 'Yugoslavia'.

Slobodan Milošević's book *The Years of Solution* (*Godine raspleta*), published in 1989 and advertised in Serbia as the 'Bible' of the new Serb movement, is the best illustration of the Serb political elite's demands, wholeheartedly supported and promoted by the intellectual elite. In the Foreword, Mr. Milošević states three of his motives for 'writing' the book (which actually consists of speeches made on various occasions between 1986 and 1989): the struggle for the equality of Serbia in the South Slav Federation; solving the Kosovo question; and putting an end to 'the last exodus in the territory of Europe'.

The 'solution' of the Yugoslav crisis, which, according to Slobodan Milošević, started between 1986 and 1989, had not ended by1996. Up to that date the results had included: the dissolution of Yugoslavia; the declaration of a state of emergency in Kosovo; a new—and for the Yugoslav peoples so far the most difficult— exodus in the territory of Europe.

These speeches by Slobodan Milošević always have two clearly distinguishable levels of content. The first, acceptable to the masses which followed him, and a second one beneath it for 'the other' side. On the face of it, he was advocating 'equality', 'brotherhood and unity', 'justice', 'reforms', 'dignity'. ... Beneath this, Milošević was making threats—threats involving his angry and hot-headed followers, non-negotiable and non-statutory solutions to the questions being discussed, arbitrary definitions of what could and could not be 'considered', victories against 'the enemy' secured in advance, and armed battles...

At that time an unknown functionary in [Mr. Ivan] Stambolić's team of politicians, in 1986 Slobodan Milošević advocated the solution of the Yugoslav crisis, using language fully in accord with the moderate terminology of the then Serbian authorities, the 'removal of the inconsistencies in the constitutional position of Serbia' (*The Years of Solution*: 120). In April 1987, at Kosovo Polje where his ascent and prominence began, Milošević still employed a general social terminology, but he also used the opportunity to define his own position, asking for the separation of 'the forces of socialism, brotherhood and unity, and progress', from the forces 'of separatism, nationalism, and conservatism' (145). Unlike 1986, when he advocated 'courage and determination', in 1987 Milošević claimed that only 'the educated and the angry can move things forward', and defined his own future policies in contrast to the appeals for 'cool heads', claiming that 'cool heads, as we can see today, did not stop, but actually encouraged rape, humiliation, emigration ...' (160). His predictions were correct: 'the Serb nationalists would inflict the greatest harm on the Serbian people through what they offer to it today as allegedly the best solution, to practically isolate itself through the hate and suspicion of others' (172).

By solving problems in Serbia through the defeat of Stambolić's group (September 1987), followed by bringing down the political authorities of Vojvodina (October 1988), Kosovo (November 1988), and then Montenegro (January 1989), Milošević stepped onto the Yugoslav political stage. Political events in Serbia soon outgrew the problems that had created them. From his previous discourse, mostly related to Serbia, Milošević changed in 1988 to a discourse exclusively dealing with Yugoslavia and changes within it.

In 1988 Milošević was mostly considering three questions:

1. Which sides are in conflict in Yugoslavia?
2. What do the 'masses' want in Serbia?
3. What is 'negotiable' in the future ordering of the Yugoslav state.

Who would get whom?

Milošević saw the axis of the conflict in Yugoslavia as the demand for 'changes' and opposition to them. In favour of 'changes' were, according to him, members of the Communist Party and 'the majority of the citizens of Yugoslavia', while against them were 'some political leaderships'. By identifying his authority and the demand for 'changes' with the will of the people of Yugoslavia, and demagogically separating the Serbian leadership from the others in Yugoslavia (as vehicles of bureaucracy, nationalism, etc.), Milošević proclaimed the Serbian authorities to be the embodiment of the people themselves, the instrument of the popular will. Defining the political elite outside Serbia as not of the people and as using 'traps', 'tricks', 'cunning' and 'intrigue' (333), and by defining it as 'the enemy of the Serb people', Milošević made its removal from power a primary demand—'all Yugoslav peoples need the reform of society. ... But the main preconditions for this reform are the so-called personal changes in all areas and at all levels, from work organizations to the Federation' (323). These words, spoken in January 1989 after the removal of the leaderships of Kosovo, Vojvodina and Montenegro, could mean only one thing, and that is exactly how they were interpreted in other parts of Yugoslavia. If Milošević, intoxicated by his support in Serbia, really believed that he would be greeted in the same way throughout Yugoslavia, it was the result of a narrow view of events and of a false identification with Tito, whose charisma he did not have. Even if Milošević's evaluation of the other leaderships was correct, and even if the people of the other republics were totally dissatisfied with their leaders, the events in Serbia, mass rallies, nationalist slogans, demands for arrests, the call for arms, a nationalist campaign and the daily production of new Serb enemies—all of these—only created in other parts of Yugoslavia fear and opposition, which also meant national homogenization and the formation of groups (later political parties) in which the ability to oppose Serbian nationalism was recognized. By identifying the 'conclusion' of the crisis with the removal of the leaders of the Yugoslav republics and the federal leaders, and at the same time singling out the Serbian leadership as 'honest and humble people in their private lives', as 'educated', 'determined' people 'who already know many answers and eagerly wait for the right moment to offer them' (227), Milošević raised the structure that he led (that is, the Serb leadership) to the level of the only real, authentic political elite in Yugoslavia which was able to solve the Yugoslav crisis. This resulted in the national homogenization of the other Yugoslav nations, in total chaos in the political system, in the shaping of national programmes, and, finally, in the defeat of the Communists as incapable of confronting Serbian nationalism, and in the victory of the national and nationalist parties in the 1990 multiparty elections. War was the immediate consequence of this 'solution'.

'What the masses want'

While Milošević was still using social terminology in July 1988—'where the working class in Serbia is concerned, it has recently demonstrated clearly enough and determinedly enough that, when it comes to Kosovo, it will not make any concessions, nor tolerate any injustice' (255)–he switched to national terminology in September 1988. When making a distinction between the 'mass gathering of the people' in Serbia, and the 'counter-revolution in Kosovo', Milošević described the former as multi-national, and the latter as uni-national. Arguments that the gatherings in Serbia were uni-national were opposed by the claim that both Serbs and Montenegrins took part in them ('so the question is, which one of the two should be deprived of their right to nationality by describing these rallies as uni-national'). Milošević found an additional argument maintaining that there were 'members of all nations and nationalities' at the gatherings in Vojvodina. In contrast to this, 'if there is anything uni-national, it is counter-revolutionary' (260). Using this argument in connetion with the multi-national character of the gatherings, which extended the legitimacy of their demands as being 'generally Yugoslav', Milošević also defined 'what the masses want'. 'It all depends on what the masses are in favour of. In this case, they are in favour of a unified Yugoslavia, the socialist system, brotherhood and unity, the equality of Serbia with other republics, the fight against the counter-revolution in Kosovo, and just and dignified lives for all people in Yugoslavia' (260). In October 1988 the masses were still 'for' a unified Yugoslavia, socialism and equality, but were by then 'against some present leaderships' as well (268). By giving the term 'street' a positive connotation, and by equating it with the whole range of other terms through which he aimed to please all the ideologies he stood for at one time–national, social, democratic–hence, with terms like 'people', 'working class', 'citizens'–clearly preferring the 'street' to the 'procedure', Milošević opened the door for the possibility that all the fundamental questions of Yugoslavia could be solved using the power of the strongest, that is , the most numerous within the Federation and the republics: 'But that solution will not be brought about by the procedure, its smaller and greater tricks, its smaller and greater treacheries, intrigues and cunning. The solution will be brought about by policies supported by the majority of the people of this country, institutional and extra-institutional, statutory and non-statutory, in the streets, and in their homes, in a populist and in an elitist way, with or without arguments, but in any case so that it is clear that this is a policy for a Yugoslavia in which we shall all live united, equal, richer, and more cultured' (333).

The vision

By switching from the discourse on Serbia to the discourse on Yugoslavia, and by making indisputable claims on what kind of Yugoslavia he wanted, Milošević provoked a direct confrontation with the leaderships of other republics. Although verbally advocating federation, rejecting the extremes of both unitarism and confederalism as being 'out of the question' ('neither a centralized bureaucratic state, nor confederacy', 190), and demanding the strengthening of the unified functions of the Federation, Milošević practically negated the existing Federation both politically (by the abolition of the autonomous provinces and the severing of all relations with Slovenia), and economically (by the economic blockade of Slovenia and by breaking into the monetary system of Yugoslavia). At the same time, he made extensive use of the provisions of the 'confederate' 1974 Constitution, which had previously met with widespread opposition, in addressing questions related to the representation of the autonomous provinces in the Federation. Serbia became unified, but representatives of the autonomous provinces remained in the Presidency of the SFR Yugoslavia and the Federal Parliament.

Combining social and national terminology, Milošević easily switched from the struggle against 'bureaucratized leaderships' to the struggle against 'enemies of the people'. In stating that 'the order of the day is not discussion, but history' (244), he moved from the 'criminals among our own ranks', who 'have to go both because they stole from us and because they brought shame on us' (255), to the 'struggle for freedom' which 'this nation is winning'. Supported by over a million people, according to the official media estimates, at Ušće in 1988, Milošević claimed that 'we shall win, regardless of the fact that today, just as in the past, Serbia's enemies outside the country are uniting with those inside the country ... there is no battle in the world which the people have lost. The leadership has no choice. Either it puts itself at the head of the people and listens to the voice of the people, or it will be swept away by time' (276). In June 1989, at Gazimestan, supported by an even bigger crowd, Milošević gave a clear indication of the kind of battles he had in mind: '...today, we are again in battle and facing battle. These battles do not involve weapons, although such battles are not yet excluded' (*Politika*, 29 June 1989).

In spite of all attempts to pass the rallies off as spontaneous multi-national gatherings, as 'wonderful popular get-togethers', and to give them a character essentially different from the similar events taking place among the Kosovo Albanians (which were 'counter-revolutionary' and 'uni-national'), or later, in 1990, in other republics, it was already clear in 1988 that these rallies, because of their very magnitude, their everyday occurrence in various cities and towns in Serbia, and the slogans heard at them—ranging from demands for the protection of Yugoslavia to demands for the killing of members of other nationalities—caused only fear and rejection in other Yugoslav republics.[6]

Gatherings

The slogans used at the 1988 gatherings can be divided into several groups, and all arose from the political demands dictated by the Belgrade regime. If Milošević spoke of a 'unified Yugoslavia', the masses shouted 'We want a unified Yugoslavia!' (Gnjilane); support for the Serbian authorities was mostly expressed with reference to Milošević: 'Long live the Central Committee of the League of Communists of Serbia (CK SKS), headed by Slobodan Milošević', 'An attack on the Serb leadership is an attack on us' (Kruševac), 'Slobodan is a heroic name' (Raška), 'Keep going, Slobo, the people are with you', 'Help, Slobo!' (Novi Sad) ... but there were also some other rare 'heroes'—'We won't give you up, Kertes!' (Novi Sad). When Milošević called for the removal of the leaderships in the Yugoslav republics, the masses shouted 'Down with Krunić', 'Down with Dolanc', 'Down with Matić', 'Down with Vllasi', 'Down with Kaçusha Jashari' (Gnjilane, etc.), 'Azem, prepare a blanket, there is a cell waiting for you', 'This is the last goodbye, Krunić, Vllasi, Vrhovec' (Nikšić), 'Serb autonomists, go to Croatia and Slovenia, you will get an autonomous province' (Kraljevo), 'Vllasi and Smole are oxen' (Titovo Užice), 'Krunić is a thief' (Novi Sad), 'Vrhovec, Vllasi, Smole—down with them all', 'Hafner, keep your finger', 'Janez, shame on you' (Belgrade) ... Anti-Albanian and anti-Slovenian sentiments were reflected in moralistic slogans, such as 'Albanian mothers, do you love your children?' (Gornji Milanovac), 'Slovenes, remember Serbian bread' (Kraljevo) ... Threats were included in slogans such as 'We are the army', 'We will kill the balists, the people should judge them' (Gnjilane), 'Let the trees grow, let the flowers blossom, Montenegro is going into battle, it will no longer be a slave', 'We will fight' (Peć), 'If necessary, we will all join the struggle for freedom' (Nikšić), 'Strike the devil, and leave no trace' (Kruševac), 'We won't give you away, land of Obilić, we won't give you away without bloodshed' (Putinci), and, in 1990,

'We are ready to organize volunteers' (Svetozarevo), 'We don't want appeals, we want action', 'We are going to Kosovo' (Studentski grad, Belgrade). There were also demands for military rule in Kosovo, and for taking Slovenia to court (Niš). One should bear in mind that these slogans represent a selection from the daily *Politika*, while the more extreme ones could have been seen and heard on television. Milošević himself said in his book that the slogan 'Death to Shqiptars' was unacceptable (the *Politika* reporters did not hear it, just as they did not hear the slogans 'We want weapons' and 'We want the Russians').

Even though Milosevic at first tried to portray the rallies as a social revolt, and even though both those who defended and supported him (believing that in doing so they were defending Yugoslavia), and those who later criticized him for nationalist reasons (thinking that he had abandoned the programme for unified Serbdom) saw in him a Communist leader, there was only one type of slogan absent from his gatherings—those with social content. At one demonstration in front of the Yugoslav Parliament, when the Rakovica workers called on him, claim that their demands were only social, and asking for their salaries, Milošević himself turned this into a demand for a solution to the national question. He dismissed the workers, ordering them to go back to their workplaces, making no mention of their social problems. Once again, it proved that the appearance of a determined national leader, supported by the national authorities, easily shifted social dissatisfaction onto the national level. It was enough for the leaders to claim that the reason for the economic crisis lay in national subordination and disunity, for the dissatisfied masses unanimously to demand weapons instead of increased salaries.

Slobodan Milošević was right when he called 1989 'the year of the solution'. All the preparations for the solution, if Yugoslavia was to be treated as a knot that could not be untangled, and that is exactly how it was treated,[7] were completed during that year. Thus, the events of 1990 to 1992 are merely a logical continuation–the victory of the nationalist parties at the 1990 elections in most Yugoslav republics, the breaking up of Yugoslavia along national seams, and, since those seams were nowhere 'neatly sewn', war, killing, the 'exodus' or 'evacuation' of the population (depending on whether it was 'ours' or 'theirs'), and overall genocide, although this term has been used so much that it has become worn out.. The frequent contemporary debates on whether Slobodan Milošević was a nationalist or a Communist who was playing 'the national card', on whether the Yugoslav People's Army (JNA)

was defending Communism or the borders of Greater Serbia, and
on whether the remaining national leaders were 'Tito's generals',
people from the Communist nomenclature or nationalists, were
totally meaningless. Ascribing to the 'spectre—which had long
stopped haunting Europe—all the credit for later events provided a
safe haven for those who believed that nationalism could be benevolent (especially if it was 'ours'), and that evils done in the
name of nationalism were not an integral part of it; all of this ob-
scures an undeniable fact—Yugoslavia was shattered because of
nationalism, and the first accomplished aim was the 'cleansing' of
the taken/liberated territories, not of anti-Communism, but of
other nations. And, as always, in that work that was carried out so
thoroughly, anti-Communism proved to be the most faithful ally of
those to whom today it is so difficult to give a name.

Steps towards disintegration

The preparatory actions for the break-up of Yugoslavia were the
following:

a) the recognition of the Kosovo Serbs' dissatisfaction as the
   main trigger for the general dissatisfaction of the Serbian
   people (end of 1986 to beginning of 1987);
b) the directing and manipulating of this dissatisfaction, not just
   in order to 'solve' the question of Kosovo autonomy, but also
   to settle accounts with those people with different opinions
   in the Serbian leadership, those who were not ready for radical changes and who believed that the crisis had to be solved
   gradually and without any major breaks (end of 1987);
c) the formidable and unified propaganda activity of the media,
   aimed at heightening to an extreme level first anti-Albanian,
   and later anti-Slovenian, emotions (1988);
d) the exploitation of dissatisfaction among the Kosovo Serbs
   in order to realize the fight against the 'autonomists', that is,
   mass gatherings in Vojvodina, organized by the Kosovo Serbs,
   aimed at bringing down the Vojvodina leadership and denying Vojvodina autonomy (autumn 1988);
e) the exploitation of dissatisfaction among the Kosovo Serbs to
   bring down the leadership of Montenegro through mass
   gatherings (January 1989);
f) the amending of the Serbian Constitution on the same day as
   twenty-two demonstrators and two policemen were killed in

Kosovo, and after special measures had been put into force and the Kosovo Albanian leadership arrested (March 1989);

g) the start of the anti-Croatian campaign, along with the anti-Albanian and anti-Slovenian campaigns already underway (early 1989);[8]

h) Serbia's predominance in federal government institutions in 1989 after the de facto (Vojvodina) and formal (Kosovo) abolishment of the autonomous provinces within the republic, and the retaining of their competencies in the Federation (Presidency of the SFRY);

i) the organizing of the Serbs in Croatia and Bosnia-Hercegovina, with decisive help from Serbia (1989);

j) informing Slovenia, which most ardently and persistently opposed Milošević's policies, that unless it accepted the 'happening of the people' from Kosovo in its republic, it could leave Yugoslavia through the official severing of all ties.[9] Slovenia refused, and ties were severed. The economic blockade was merely the most obvious aspect of the break-up, in which the manipulated population of Serbia had its 'patriotic' role (end of 1989).

Between 1986 and 1989, a parallel process can be observed only in Slovenia:

a) after the publication of the Memorandum, the Slovenian review Nova Revija published the Contributions for the Slovenian National Programme (January 1987);

b) the Slovenian public gathered around the trial of Janez Janša and others, and at the same time media attacks on JNA began, primarily focusing on the exclusive use of the Serbo-Croatian language, and stressing that Slovenes should not serve in any army outside their own republic;

c) the events in Kosovo and Serbia united the Slovenian intellectual and political elites (until then in conflict because of the Nova Revija) in support of Albanians and in rejection of Milošević's policies at the meeting in Cankarjev dom in Ljubljana (early 1989);

d) the amending of the republic's constitution (September 1989);

e) the firm rejection and banning of the 'meeting of truth' in Ljubljana (December 1989).

There were no parallel processes in Croatia, Bosnia-Hercegovina and Macedonia between 1986 and 1989, but they are reflected on the level of national homogenization, directly helping the newly formed nationalist parties to win the 1990 elections.

Preparatory activities between 1986 and 1989, and the reactions which such activities evoked, meant that by early 1990 all the important elements necessary for the destruction of Yugoslavia were present:

a) the dissolution of the League of Communists of Yugoslavia (SKJ) at its Fourteenth Congress, and the breakdown of the Yugoslav Communist option (January 1990);
b) the pre-election campaign in all the Yugoslav republics which brought to the surface nationalist parties, and the pre-election gatherings and nationalist euphoria, especially in Croatia in early 1990, both of which had all the characteristics of the 'happening of the people', merely with a different motive; the unstoppable overflowing of nationalism across the republics' borders and the homogenization of the nations, not just through propaganda, but also as a result of party activity—the Serbian Democratic Party (SDS) in Croatia, Bosnia-Hercegovina and Serbia; the Party for Democratic Action (SDA) in Bosnia-Hercegovina and Serbia (Sandžak); and the Croatian Democratic Union (HDZ) in Croatia and Bosnia-Hercegovina (February 1990);
c) the victory of the United Slovenian opposition (DEMOS) in Slovenia (8 April 1990, with 55 per cent of the votes), the HDZ in Croatia (22 April 1990, 41.5 per cent of the votes), the Internal Macedonian Revolutionary Organization-Democratic Party for Macedonian National Unity (VMRO-DPMNE) in Macedonia (11 November 1990, 37 seats in the Parliament), the SDA, SDS and HDZ in Bosnia-Hercegovina (18 November 1990,SDA: 86 seats; SDS: 72 seats; HDZ: 44 seats), the Socialist Party of Serbia (SPS) in Serbia (9 December 1990, 45.8 per cent of the votes or 77.6 per cent of the members of Parliament) (Kovačević and Dajić 1994). The formula for the 'Third Yugoslavia' in Serbia meant the concept 'all Serbs in one state', with the denial of the AVNOJ borders, and the appropriation of the JNA and its being used for the realization of separate interests; in Slovenia, it meant a policy of exclusiveness when it came to establishing independence, the rejection of the JNA, and the arming of the territorial defence; in Croatia, it meant a demand for independence and the constitutional definition of Croatia as the state of the Croatian people only, and the creation and arming of the Croatian army; in Bosnia-Hercegovina

it represented a confrontation of two mutually exclusive concepts–a unified and indivisible Bosnia-Hercegovina, in contrast to the Serb Bosnia-Hercegovina joined with other Serb lands; Montenegro followed Serbia in all points, and Macedonia just moved along (1990);

d) federal elections were made impossible and the reformist federal government of Ante Marković brought down, with the all-out support of engaged intellectuals;[10]

e) the new national-political leaders were not prepared to make agreements, and maintained mutually exclusive positions, in the belief that the moment had finally come to realize 'historical dreams' through the break-up of Yugoslavia–that is, Greater Serbia, an independent Slovenia, an independent Croatia;

f) the years between 1990 and 1992 were years of referendums. The results of these were cited as the main argument for beginning the war. That is how all came to an end. In the referendums people opted for war, everywhere in the belief that they were giving their voice for peace and security.

Ideology realized through force

The breakup of Yugoslavia was brought about with reference to a 'global civilization of informatics'. Yugoslavia was shattered in the name of the new society, 'wisdom, harmony, beauty, humanity'; in the name of the 'national, democratic future'; in the name of the 'inalienable right of the people to self-determination'; in the name of the 'free, open, modern society'; in the name of securing a 'better, more creative, more moral society'; in the name of 'just state borders which will not cause interethnic hatred and wars'; in the name of 'political pluralism, a social-democratic society, and social justice and equality...'.

Yugoslavia was destroyed in the name of the 'informatic revolution'; in the name of 'the end of the nation'; in the name of the 'endangering of humanity by de-humanization'; in the name of 'modern society', a 'civil nation', 'natural right'; in the name of 'a positive liberal tradition'; in the name of 'mother–homeland–God...'.

In the late 1980s, Serb and Slovenian intellectuals referred to every possible democratic, progressive, civilizational aim in order to prove that the existence of Yugoslavia as a common country was not possible.

In considering the reasons for the break-up of Yugoslavia, many scholars believe that the answer is very simple and clear-cut. Some start from the obvious fact of the secession of some republics, and explain the break-up in this way; others find in the psychological structures perennial evidence of 'anti-Yugoslavism' or 'Yugoslavism' as an immanent characteristic of a collective 'national being', and see in the endless conflict between those 'for' and 'against' Yugoslavia the reason for its dissolution; a third group of scholars believe that all the factors necessary for the disintegration of the state are to be found with the Communists who, by definition, are 'guilty' of everything; a fourth group seek for an explanation in an international conspiracy involving America and Germany, the comintern and the Vatican, 'the Fourth Reich' and the 'new world order'.

We reject the idea that the declaration of independence of Slovenia, Croatia, Macedonia and Bosnia-Hercegovina was the *cause* of the break-up of Yugoslavia and the war in its territory, simply by looking at the succession of events. Even if we accept the explanation that under the term 'secession' we should understand the defining and realization of national aims under national names, unlike other examples of the defining and realizing national aims under the 'Yugoslav' name, and thus mark it as a struggle for 'maintaining' Yugoslavia, we cannot overlook the fact that this took place in mid-1991 or early 1992 when all the factors leading to the break-up of Yugoslavia and the start of the war had already been completed, that is, the definition of national aims, the creation of homogenized nations around national leaders, the formulation of national programmes—none of which 'envisaged' Yugoslavia. To be for or against Yugoslavia cannot be seen as a national characteristic—it is merely a matter of defining what 'Yugoslavia' was, and of stating the amount of fear that had to be provoked through various definitions of the content of 'Yugoslavia'. Only the simple power of great numbers determined what would be called 'defence' and what would be called the 'breaking up' of Yugoslavia. In either case, it ceased to exist.

The second Yugoslavia disappeared through the disintegration of Yugoslavia, but a great deal more disappeared as well. The idea of Yugoslavia as a state community of the South Slav peoples was destroyed, and the belief that any one of those peoples could tolerate in its vicinity anyone who did not share its identity was shattered.

Ethnically pure states have been created, as never before in history, on the ruins of Yugoslavia. The time is not yet 'ripe' for them to introduce democratic systems, and almost all the objective elements of dissatisfaction with the previous state still trouble their citizens, along with a new, irretrievably lost advantage of Yugoslavia. Never in its history has it been so vitally dependent on its surroundings, nor as non-independent as the states created on its ruins are today—without hope of changing this situation in the near future.

Under the slogan 'protection of the people', 'ancient hearths', 'the saving of graveyards and churches', a war for the territories started, out of the anachronistic belief that a big ethnic state is proof of a successful state. Any consideration of the creation of such states also involved the possibility of either the assimilation or removal of groups of the population. When Yugoslavia existed, such a demand was civilizationally regressive, regardless of all the hedges on future democracy and the rights of minorities, and opened the question of why Yugoslavia could not be the frame in which everybody would be given all such rights. By promising respect for minority rights in the future ethnic states, while excluding the possibility of Yugoslavia's existence as a state of equals, the nationalist belief of the intellectuals—that the Yugoslav nations could be free only if they were a 'majority' or, that democracy was possible only where one could say with certainty who was 'the boss'—was confirmed. The reduction of demands for democracy and freedom to the demand for the ethnic state is nationalism, since it implies that the *ethnos* alone is capable of democracy, or that it represents a unique organism, a unique understanding of democracy and freedom free of internal ambivalence and conflicting interests. Every plea to solve the national question 'once and for all' as an ethnic question, ignoring all the historical changes and in the belief that historical heritage can be erased; every such plea which understands by the ethnic space and name everything that at some point belonged to it (to the *ethnos*), regardless of the fact that it belonged to someone else at some other moment and that it lies within territory that is mixed both ethnically and in terms of religion, advocates the cutting up of the country's territory into small pieces to the point of absurdity, and necessarily justifies the domination of the bigger over the smaller, and of the more powerful over the weaker.

The elites tried to solve the intermixing of the population through its removals towards the ethnic 'motherlands'. In the absence of any foundation for their demands on the ethnic level, they found arguments in history; in the absence of any foundation for the borders in history, they found arguments on the ethnic level;

where there were arguments in neither history nor *ethnos*, there were graveyards or churches; for denouncing Yugoslavia as a Communist product they used 'national reconciliation' (Nedić and Mihajlović in Serbia, Bleiburg in Croatia, Kočevski rog in Slovenia). Pointers to the recognition of national identity were found only in the pre-Yugoslav past, and were primarily symbolsthat were as old as possible: flags, coats of arms, hymns, the journeyings of the relics of saints, the removal of the relics, the return of national monuments, the tearing down of monuments that symbolized any common struggle...

Even today there are intellectuals ready to speak of the 'necessity' and 'inevitability' of the war, and even of the positive changes brought about, the aims achieved, the 'biological injections', the good sides of the war and the break-up of the country. Even today, some are positive and full of optimism when they speak of the 'contribution' of the Yugoslav intellectual and political elites towards the better and more just lives of their peoples. For what are the deaths of hundreds of thousands, the displacement of millions, the irretrievable destruction of a cultural legacy, incalculable material damage and spiritual regression ... compared to the realization of the 'centuries-old dreams', 'two hundred years of struggles', visions of 'little Switzerland' or 'great Sweden' ... 'Patriotism' has become a race to break up the shared country, and 'treachery', rare examples (among all the nations) of its protection. There is a conscious effort to hide the fact that the shared country, by the very fact it existed, was accepted by the majority of its citizens for seven decades, regardless of the situation of crisis it was in, and regardless of the international environment. There is also an effort to hide the fact that there was still potential for positive transformations. Its break-up from the inside was the easiest and quickest solution; it demanded least intellectual effort from its intellectual and political elites who were impotent in the face of civilizational questions .

Notes

1 The General Assembly of the SANU, 23 May 1985. For more details, see the contribution of O. Milosavljević in this volume.
2 Tine Hribar, 'Slovenska državnost'; Ivan Urbančič, 'Jugoslovanska "nacionalistična kriza" in *Slovenci v perspektivi konca nacije*'; Dimitrij Rupel, 'Odgovor na slovensko narodno vprašanje'; Spomenka Hribar, 'Avantgardno sovraštvo in sprava'; Veljko Namorš, 'O vprašanju sloven-

skega jezika v JLA'; Alenka Goljevšček, 'Arhaičnost: civilnost'; Jože Pučnik, 'Politični sistem civilne družbe'; Gregor Tomc, 'Civilna družba pod slovenskim socializmom'; France Bučar, 'Pravna ureditev položaja Slovencev kot naroda'; Peter Jambrek, 'Pravica do samoodločbe slovenskega naroda'; Janez Jerovšek, 'Slovenska univerza včeraj, danes, jutri'; Veljko Rus, 'Slovenci in intergeneracijska socialna politika'; Marjan Rožanc, 'Nekaj iracionalnih razsežnosti'; Jože Snoj, 'Moderni kristjan in absurd slovenstva'; Drago Jančar, 'Slovenski eksil'; and Niko Grafenauer, 'Oblike slovenskega samomora'.

3 In the original text: *Jugoslovenarstvo. 'Jugosloven, jugoslovenar*—someone who supports integral Yugoslavism, Yugo-raven' (Jurančić 1981).

4 On the attitude of the Serb intellectuals in more detail, see the contribution of O. Milosavljević in this volume.

5 According to the reporter of the Belgrade daily *Politika*, with the exception of Jože Smole, all members of the Advisory Board of the *Cankarjeva založba* (publisher of the *Nova Revija*) agreed to confirm Boris Novak as the new editor. As a condition for his acceptance of this position, Novak requested the continuation of the work of the Editorial Board, as well as retention the Contributions for the Slovenian National Programme. Jože Smole objected to this, saying that 'a continuity which means undermining the heritage of the socialist revolution and the constitutional order' was unacceptable (*Politika*, 6 April 1987).

6 Great political and media pressure was exerted on those places where someone tried to prevent a rally. Rejection in other places of the events in Serbia could be discerned through the following quotations taken from the Belgrade press: the Presidency of the Municipal Committee (OK) of the Socialist Union of the Working People (SSRN) Titov Vrbas—'the rally is not acceptable' (*Politika*, 25 August 1988); after a meeting with people from Kosovo, it was decided that the rally would take place (*Politika*, 26 August 1988). The day after, *Politika* published a letter—'We support your trip to the rally in Titov Vrbas'—from the Home for War Invalids in Sokobanja (*Politika*, 27 August 1988); Cazin refused the invitation to attend the rally in Bela Palanka (*Politika*, 22 September 1988); after a rally, Sremska Mitrovica refused to host a 'forty-year anniversary of the start of the building of the Brotherhood-Unity highway', giving as his reasons the desire to prevent it 'from turning into something else' (*Politika*, 23 September 1988); a polemic in the press on whether Split made a mistake in not sending a delegation to the Kragujevac rally (*Politika*, 6 November 1988); the severing of all relations with Slovenia because it rejected a rally in Ljubljana (*Politika*, 1 November 1989); following the request of four Serb villages—Trpinja, Bobot, Pačetin and Brsadin near Vukovar—to organize a 'truth rally', the SSRN Vukovar replied that 'it does not accept informal mass gatherings. We estimate that the situation would be uni-national (...) it would only worsen a relatively stable situation' (*Politika*, 10 February 1990). In the 18 February 1990 *Politika*, the following question was posed: 'Will there be a gathering "for a unified Yugoslavia" in Vukovar?'

7 G. Đogo, at the Serb intellectuals' Congress in Sarajevo: 'If you cannot untangle the knot, cut it' (*Politika*, 30 March 1992).

8 It is interesting to note that the anti-Muslim campaign was not prepared—even the 'Agrokomerc' affair did not bring it to the level of the other three. This fact leads one to presuppose that Muslim resistance to the 'Third Yugoslavia' was not expected. The anti-Macedonian campaign began late, when the war was already raging in Croatia and Bosnia; it soon stopped, and the 'endangering' of Serbs in that republic was left to wait for some better times.

9 On 1 December 1989 the following banner headline appeared on the front page of *Politika*: 'Serbia breaks relations with the Slovenian regime'. The text contained a statement to the effect that, on the occasion of the banning of the truth meeting in Slovenia, 'the peoples of Serbia ... refuse to be further humiliated and beg Slovenia not to secede from Yugoslavia, and not to carry out anti-Yugoslav, anti-Serbian and anti-human policies'. For this reason the Presidency of the Socialist Union of the Working People (SSRN) of Serbia 'calls upon all institutions and all work organizations and offices in Serbia to sever all ties with Slovenia'. On that day, and on the days that followed, the newspaper was full of attacks on Slovenia.

10 D. Ćosić: 'We are the country of schisms and lies—national, religious, social lies. We still do not shoot and do not kill each other because we are convinced that death is not the greatest evil that we can inflict on each other. It is hard to understand why President [of the federal government] Marković is ignoring Yugoslav political reality, and it is even more difficult to believe that it could be superseded by [multi-] party elections' (*Politika*, 4 August 1990).

V. Šeks: '... Marković's concept has no future and, in the final consequence, the republics must become independent in relation to it, and seek their own solutions. ... It is my belief that his project cannot be realized: awareness of the republics' sovereignty is so deeply embedded that Marković cannot compensate it with his programme. In short, Marković is still too much a non-nationalist, and the price for that is very high today' (*Da*, 2 October 1990).

Traumatology of the Party State

NEBOJŠA POPOV

This paper deals with the production of traumas in the party state. The historical background of the production of trauma is dealt with first, and the preventing of catharsis is discussed later. The underlying assumption is that three series of factors led to a 'synthesis' of all traumas in the victim-nation, while a liberation from trauma was looked for in a revenge-nation. Only the populist movement ('happening of the people') was able to bring to the surface many traumas that had previously been suppressed and hidden, not only because of the repression of the party state, but also due to a trust in its anti-fascist legitimacy, as well as to the fact that Yugoslavia was more open than all other countries of 'existing socialism' and that people lived much more freely and more comfortably there than in those other countries. In the midst of the horrors of war, many remembered that time with nostalgia, but this cannot deny the facts of the character of the previous political movement.

War as a way of life

War has a very important place in the collective memory of the Serbs; it is part of the way of life, not just a myth, a legend and an epic. The Balkans are a metaphor for continuous divisions and clashes and for ceaseless confusion, although it is also the cradle of different cultures. For hundreds of years, wars have been raging in the Balkans, in which the main roles have usually been played by Turkey, Austria and Venice, as well as by the great powers: Russia, England, France and Germany. These wars have usually included the Serbs. Exceptions are extremely rare (the Crimean war, for example, when Serbia stayed neutral, traded with all sides in the conflict, and became economically stronger). Serbs also took part in wars outside the Balkans, all around Europe and usually on the side of Turkey or Austria (for example the Thirty Years War, 1618–1648).

When war is part of everyday life, it is hard to have a distanced attitude towards it and to regard it as an exceptional or even traumatic event. That becomes even more difficult since, in the states of that time, *the vocation of warrior* was very highly regarded. According to sociologists, that profession was the most convenient channel of vertical mobility for both individuals and their families, even regardless of religious and ethnic allegiance (except for the highest military ranks and government positions). Turnarounds in the life of whole nations were also connected with the results of wars. Whoever was on the winning side consolidated their position (or even expanded it) on a certain territory, while the losing side shared the destiny of the defeated army, retreating even from those territories in which it had lived many years (the Great Serbian exodus of 1690, for example). More permanent ties to one higher military command or another influenced religious or even ethnic allegiances.

The warrior lifestyle also affected significant segments of the civil population that dealt with crafts related to the maintenance of the army, and that supported themselves with war booty. A military *krajina* ran along the northern edge of the Balkans, from the Adriatic to the Carpathians, the best and most lasting organized by Austria. This was a permanent war zone, a fortification from which Austria, Venice and Turkey were attacked or defended. It was common to see this barrier as *ante murale Cristianitatis*, with the expected reward for the defence of Christian Europe from the Islamic intrusion and the Asian onslaught.

This warrior lifestyle was dominant not only at the front, but also at the rear. As stated by the *Istorija srpskog naroda* (*The History of the Serbian People*), war and looting was, for many, the only craft they knew, a profession for life (Vol. III–1, 1993: 283). War and looting created a special *war economy*, both during longer military campaigns and during occasional intrusions into enemy territory, regardless of whether members of the same people lived in that territory. Thus Serbs were frequently both the looters and the looted (228).

Instead of idealized images of chivalric competitions, 'manhood and heroism'—celebrated by the *guslars* and talked about by the ordinary folk—historiography presents us with images of 'mutual hatred' (40) and 'general bloodshed' (97) which also took place among members of the same nation. It was not enough for an enemy to be disabled or removed, even wounded or killed, to make him concede defeat and retreat from the battlefield, he was also subjected to torture, massacre, torment, dismemberment. To this day, all this is preserved in the oral and written folk culture, mostly in epic poetry, but also by a ruling ideology which glorifies war and warriors through a system of education (Čolović 1993, 1994).[1]

In such circumstances, there is hardly any difference between a time of war and a time of peace. Peace merely appears as a deceptive break between clashes and fierce battles. In the *History of the Serbian People* mentioned above, it is written that 'The ordinary folk hit on its former beys, neighbour on neighbour, cousin on cousin, only to make peace within that overall bloodshed, stop the fighting and make ties of blood brotherhood' (337–338).

'Mutual hatred' and 'general bloodshed' were not reserved only for periods of great confusion, but also for many dynastic clashes, rebellions and uprisings. The mutilation and killing of rivals for a throne or some high-ranking position in the army, party or state, features throughout the Nemanjić era, recurs in the time of uprisings (Karađorđe killed his own father and brother; Miloš hired Karađorđe's assassin and afterwards sent Karađorđe's head to the Sultan in Istanbul), and continues right up to the present , from the brutal crushing of resistance to a despotic government, to the assassination of Duke Mihailo and the massacre of Draga Mašin and Aleksandar Obrenović (Jerotić 1993). Violence against political opponents, even going as far as murder, is not rare even at the beginning of parliamentarism in Serbia.

National romanticism inspired rebellions and liberation wars, lowering the level of tolerance of violence. The use of violence on the part of the rebels was justified by sacred national aims, as well as by the goal of liberation from their suffering at the hands of others . That trend was opposed by a sober realism. For example, at a session of the National Assembly (Kragujevac, 1876), the idea of stirring up Serb rebellion in Bosnia-Hercegovina was criticized as putting the future of Serbia at risk. During the Balkan wars, when the mood of hostility reached its peak, there were critical voices in the National Parliament opposing the growing militarization. Such critics included the respected intellectual Jovan Skerlić, a deputy of the Independent Radical Party (1964: 297–417). War adventurism was even more fervently opposed by the Serbian Social Democrats, both in the National Assembly and more generally. They led a campaign against war credits and ran the risk of having their patriotism questioned, or even of being labelled as national traitors.

The advocates of war were stronger and had a decisive influence on public opinion. Thus, the military profession gained a more important role in Serbia, both during the preparations for the war, and, to an even greater extent, after victory. For example, the officers' society 'Unification or Death' (better known as 'The Black Hand') was extremely influential throughout Serbia at the very time when efforts to establish a parliamentary democracy were increasing (Vasić 1990; Popović–Obradović 1995). The military authorities represented serious competition to the civil authorities, primarily in the newly liberated countries where the local population did not see the new government as liberators, but—due to its militarism, cruelty and corruption—as occupiers. This was particularly true for areas such as northern Albania (1913), where 'punitive expeditions' were undertaken, which included massacres of the local population (Tucović 1914).

If a war is evaluated positively, or glorified as the correcting of the results of a previous war, or even seen in terms of collective vengeance (bearing in mind such popular slogans as 'For Kosovo–Kumanovo', and 'For Slivnica–Bregalnica'), then the likelihood of experiencing war wounds as traumatic is very limited. On the contrary, such wounds are a reason for congratulation, the 'honourable wounds' of heroes.

War and government

A positive image of war and of soldiers dominated the public scenc. The victorious Serb army was glorified as the decisive factor in 'the liberation of its brethren', from whom unconditional gratitude was expected. If the non-Serb population showed insufficient respect, or if it 'created problems' for the new regime, violent 'pacification' was carried out by the police, gendarmerie and army, bringing with it new traumas. The use of force brought pain to some, but was fruitful for others. Participation in the victorious side in the war went together not only with ideological support, but also with social promotion, allowing people to escape from joblessness and poverty to guaranteed work—in the army, the postal service, the railway service, the police and gendarmerie, all the way to careers in diplomacy and the highest positions in the state.

The army had basically the same position in the second Yugoslavia. As a result of a set of historical circumstances (i.e. having been subjected to Ustasha crimes and genocide after the military defeat of the first Yugoslavia), Serbs were the first to start the uprising and were the most numerous in the victorious army, especially among the higher ranks, promotion to which was based on length of war experience and military achievements. In the *meritocracy*, a place in the nomenclature was achieved by a proven readiness to use force and violence, not only in war but in peace as well, when an incessant struggle against various 'enemies' continued. A successful career was therefore considered *a kind of war booty* (Popov 1990: 106–108). The emphasizing of war merits implied certain benefits. Diligent work on a farm or in a factory was considered unworthy of a soldier, although socialist-realist folklore for some time insisted on competition at the 'work front'.

War traumas were even more deeply suppressed by the state's *legitimization of* the war victory. In some circumstances, such legitimization might fade or be replaced by some other in the second or third generation (just as war profiteers usually become popular benefactors only from the second generation on), but this kind of evolution was halted suddenly by a new war. The rush for booty sometimes became so widespread that it actually threatened to compromise the legitimacy the order had gained by the war. This occurred following the war, when there was an increase in the number of soldiers waiting in queues to cash in their war merits, or when whole cities, otherwise subservient to the occupation force, were declared 'hero cities'.

The *legitimization* of the political order by war was dynamite at the very foundation of the state. Such legitimization was followed by the slogan 'We came to power through blood, we will not give up power without it'. There was no place for tolerance, either of those who had lost the war, or of political adversaries and opponents. Nor was there any room for democratic reforms. Political changes were tied to new violence, just as the order being disputed had originated in, and was based on, force. Thus, the continuity of the traditionally patriarchal society ('war communities', 'war economy') looked like being extended *ad infinitum*. This situation was furthered by a cultural ideology, from the revitalization of epic poetry to the new heroics of class and national revolution (Popov 1993).

Although, objectively, war endangers the lives of all people, it is not traumatic for everyone–not only do the winners (and their supporters) experience it as something positive, but neither the losers nor those trying to remain outside the sharpest divisions and conflicts have any opportunity to articulate the wounds inflicted on them or to experience an adequate catharsis. In conditions of endemic poverty, widespread illiteracy and lack of education, authoritarian government and weak aspirations towards democracy, an interest in individual traumas and their cathartic resolution does indeed appear a luxury.

Militant anti-modernism

The discussion of trauma becomes relevant only from a different perspective—that of *modernism*, where the individual becomes central. Traumas come to be seen as the endangering of the identity or of the sovereignty of the subject. However, in the part of the world under discussion, modernism is a marginal phenomenon, with very limited initial effects and weak results in politics, the economy and culture.[2] However, in terms of culture at least, European standards with respect to the value of the individual, human rights and freedoms, are not unknown as starting points for the study of traumas and catharsis. Despite the patriarchal tradition, the 'warrior lifestyle', the cruelty of both world wars, and the disasters brought about by totalitarian ideologies (fascism, Nazism and Stalinism), the vision of a free and balanced individuality did not disappear. Such a vision is present in persistent efforts to establish a balance between external, national, and internal, civic, freedom; this current is noticeable in Serbian cultural and political history, but has not brought about any significant results (Popov 1989, 1990: 49–66). Various forms of *individualism*—Christian, liberal and socialist—will go in the same direction.

Taking into account general living conditions, an investigation of traumas and the search for catharsis belong to a parallel history which remains hidden for most, not only because modernization has not prevailed, but also because it was never strong enough to allow people realistically to hope that there was some sense in working towards the developing of a personality and a society. This resulted in a clearly apparent passivity, even widespread apathy, in people waiting for someone else, either the government or someone outside the government, to solve their problems. A detailed understanding of this situation would require a concrete examination of traumas, or at least an examination of the objective events that resulted in wounds, both physical and mental, which remained hidden for long periods only to be reopened at some point through new violence.

Failure to keep up with the developed world is usually interpreted as the consequence of a lack of understanding on the part of the powerful (regimes, states) of the problems of the small (nations, countries), or as a consequence of various conspiracies (of the Freemasons, the Vatican, Comintern, the West). Thus, a people may appear as an *object* of external action. The 'home' players are usually seen as the leaders and the political elite.

At the historical moment when the collapse of the *ancien régime* seemed to be opening up a horizon of modernization and democracy following the fall of the Berlin wall, 'ordinary people' expressed their attitude of militant anti-modernism in a concise and convincing way. It became apparent only when the surface layer of the patriotic pathos (the defence of the 'ancient hearth' from the vicious enemy) was moved aside.

Thus, a Serb soldier (from the large Urukalo family) clearly explained his motives for fighting. First, the army guaranteed a minimal but reliable source of food and clothing, especially to poor people in poor areas. 'If it wasn't for this war', said one member of the Urukalo family, 'we would have nothing to wear! My brother, we are being clothed by the army, and since time immemorial we have preferred the uniform to any other clothes.' Secondly, the army and the war legalized the possession of weapons, and, according to tradition (valid both in the Wild West and in the warmongering East), only an armed man is a free man. Thirdly, and most importantly, the war did away with the dependence of 'ordinary people' and their everyday life in the factory (and elsewhere) to which they were 'called' every morning by their alarm clock. 'Before this war,' said Urukalo, 'the alarm clock was what we hated the most, since it rang at dawn to force people to work in the fields or in the offices, something which every noble man hates.' In the war, the armed 'noble man' stepped from the modern to the archaic age, from various 'artificial creations', such as the alarm clock, the factory, the institution, into the 'organic life' and 'natural state'. Since the alarm clocks no longer rang, the soldiers triumphed: 'You go where you want and do what you want' (Kalajić 1994: 76–79; 1993: 24–25).[3]

The city, as the centre of modern life, is one of the places which 'free warriors' have always hated the most, both in the past and in the present. Regardless of religion or nation , there were frightening traces of barbarism in this war (Vukovar, Mostar, the siege and destruction of Sarajevo). The military leaders and 'ordinary' soldiers did not hide any of their envy, fear and hatred of the city and of citizens, and used such feelings as a motive for destruction (urbicide) (Bogdanović 1994).

From Vukovar (1920) to Vukovar (1991)

Vukovar is a symbol of the cruelty of this war. The city was destroyed. The dead, the wounded and the displaced have not yet been counted, but it has already been called by many the Hiroshima of our days. The main destructive force was the army of the party state (JNA). Just as in ancient tragedies, through a strange set of circumstances the party state was conceived in the city in 1920, only to be destroyed by the army of that same party state in 1991. In 1920 the Second Congress of the KPJ was held in Vukovar, during which the 'Bolshevik current' was victorious and imposed on the Socialists and Social Democrats the famous twenty-one conditions for joining the Comintern, without any discussion having taken place. This marked the defeat of the strategy of the parliamentary struggle for socialism advocated by the Socialists and Social Democrats (Jakšić 1986: 127–181); the doctrine of the Bolshevik revolution had won. Seventy years later, at the last congress of the Yugoslav Communists (1990), a weak attempt to separate the Social Democrats from the Communists failed; a once united party disintegrated, and from its remains the Union of Communists—Movement for Yugoslavia was formed, popularly called 'the generals' party'. The war that was to rage in Yugoslavia started in the same year.

The government, as a holder of power, has a key place in the Bolshevik theory of revolution. Lenin and Stalin transformed Marx's idea of force as 'the midwife of history' into a militant concept, the realization of which required a special breed of cadres. The distant end—the harmony of a classless society—justified all means. The avant-garde embarked on revolution with that idea, spreading a certain practice of government in concentric circles of traumatization.

All against all

The ruthless settling of accounts was conditioned not only by a warlike patriarchal tradition and a particular concept of revolution, but also by more immediate antecedents, such as the world war and the civil war. Not only survival and the realization of certain projects, but the support of the allies, too, depended on militancy.

The violence of the occupation forces (especially the system of 100:1 retribution in Serbia) was followed by the violence of quisling regimes, Ustasha genocide against the Serbs, Jews and Romas, and

Chetnik genocide against the Muslims (especially Foca, 1942), clashes between Chetniks, supporters of Ljotić, and Partisans, as well as among themselves and quite often extremely brutal (killing from ambush, executions, throat slitting). In the prevailing atmosphere of hostility, the slogan 'who will get whom?' became a condition for survival. The stronger the background, the greater the brutality.

The uprising started spontaneously, as defence against the terror of 'wild Ustasha' and the quisling creation of the Independent State of Croatia (NDH) in May and June 1941, before any party directive, when, following tradition, the civil population fled to the forests and hid in refuges under the protection of the people's army.[4] In early June, these formations resisted the Ustasha in Hercegovina and Bosnia. Only when the uprising became more widespread was there a 'differentiation' among the rebels into Partisans and Chetniks, and some bitter internal fighting. The KPJ leadership and the Chetnik leaders around Draža Mihajlović attempted to place their own people in command of the rebel units. The rivalry between them was suppressed until November 1941 while they led a joint struggle against the occupiers. After that, however, it exploded into a vicious civil war. Between autumn 1941 and spring 1942, rival leaderships organized 'coups' in the rebel units, killing their opponents and replacing them with their own people (Šakota 1954; Bajić 1965; Hurem 1970). In parallel with their fight against the occupiers s, the Partisans destroyed the previous forms of government (liquidating the gendarmerie, burning the municipal archives, etc.), while the Chetniks remained loyal to the old regime.

As happens quite often in civil war, points of conflict and the number of participants multiplied. Mutual destruction was carried out between the Partisans and the Chetniks, the supporters of Ljotić and the Chetniks, the Ustasha and the *'domobrans'*, the Chetniks and the Ustasha. ... More people perished in these fights than in the struggle against the occupier. The spiral of violence was so intense that it continued even after the capitulation of the Third Reich when, with no trial (rather according to the 'justice of the victors'), Partisans killed not only members of the enemies' armies, but also members of the civilian population retreating with them (Bleiburg, 'circular road', Kočevje, etc.).[5]

The road to power

Conceptual preparation for the revolution found its practical confirmation in the move to 'the second phase of the revolution', when the struggle widened from that against the external enemy to an internal struggle for power. As soon as the German army was stopped at Moscow in December 1941, the rebels' Communist leadership decided to start the 'second phase' of the revolution—destroying the old forms of government and creating a new one. Both the open opponents of Communism, as well as potential opponents (according to the maxim 'whoever is not for us is against us') were targeted (Petranović 1971). Such people were killed secretly and buried in isolated areas (in 'dogs' graveyards'). The exact number of victims of this 'internal front' is unknown, but this wave of terror led to the defeat of the Partisan movement in Montenegro, and even the Communist leadership itself had to condemn it as 'leftist errors', although it did not give up on the goals of the revolution.

The manufacturing of subjects

Apart from ideological reasons, that is, the creation of a classless society, there is a more immediate motive for the taking away of all property: those who have no economic independence from the government are much easier to rule. It was for this reason that the new government took property not just from wealthy owners, including the Church, but also from the majority of the population–including the peasants, who were limited to owning ten hectares. Despite convincing Western allies and the public at home that a new government would not introduce Communism, in the first days after the war a significant proportion of the population's property came into the hands of the 'revolutionary authorities'.

State terror was hidden beneath the magic formula 'expropriate the expropriator' (or, popularly, 'steal what has been stolen'). Besides 'revolutionary' laws on the abolition of large farms and the confiscation of the property of enemies, there were also fixed court proceedings followed by the confiscation of the property of convicted 'enemies' ('bourgeois', 'kulaks'). Among the better known are the 'Dachau processes' (Krivokapić 1986; Torkar 1984), during which the whole arsenal of Stalinist procedures (torture, denouncement spreading the circle of participants, permanent fear) were employed.

Both those whose property was taken, and those to whom property was given, became dependent on the new government which became the main job provider for a work-force devoid of any (union) protection. From the powerless peasants a new 'work army' was formed, vital for the planned industrialization. Thus, among residents of the growing cities, mostly on their periphery, a 'servant' mentality existed for a long time: workers were unable to behave as free citizens.

Forced collectivization

The chaotic collectivism of the patriarchal tradition was neither widespread nor strong enough to support the new government. The new authority tried to dominate the whole society and to transform citizens into obedient servants. This was achieved through mass colonization, the moving of people from poor areas loyal to the government into the villages in Vojvodina and Slavonia. Colonists in these areas, like the traditional Krajina men, were to have the permanent role of the Praetorian guard of the regime.

Certain 'oases' of 'civil society', independent at least to some extent, disappeared during the clash between Tito and Stalin, the SKP(B) and the KPJ. In order to remove the 'Big Brother's' doubts about 'going astray from the revolutionary line' (and from their own selfish motives), a wave of nationalization of small industries, craft shops, taverns and inns, and the forced collectivization of villages, resulted in total devastation in villages and in agriculture. 'Voluntarily' created village *zadrugas* were characterized by low productivity and general coercion. Along with collectivization came forced atheization, a kind of 'cultural revolution' marked by the 'exorcism of God' (Markov 1984). Nor was there much room for private life. 'A revolution that flows' became a torrent that broke opposition and swept away obstacles, destroying everything in its way. This force had important support from the newcomers, who expressed all their anger towards the 'enemy', proving loyalty to the new government and ascending the ladder of the newly created hierarchy of power (Popov 1983: 78–79).

This 'phase of revolution' lasted from the end of war (especially after 1948) until 1952, almost as long as the 'armed revolution', but left behind more lasting traces.

'Re-education' camps

Solzhenitsyn described the Bolshevik empire as the Gulag Archipelago, as a system of prisons, camps and building sites in which the regime punished its real or imagined opponents and, at the

same time, as an important part of the centralized planned economy (Solzhenitsin 1985). Yugoslavia was not a Communist empire,
nor did it have a vast Siberia, but throughout history it has been at
the very edges of empires (the Roman Empire, for example) where
the holders of power have been the most brutal.

When the anathema was thrown at the KPJ from Moscow in
1948, a counter-anathema followed, along with a rarely seen attempt to prove to 'the first country of socialism' the rightness of its
beliefs, primarily through a grand-scale collectivization of the
economy and the liquidation of even the most modest forms of
parliamentarism. Those who were not quick enough to follow the
government's new course soon became its victims. This wave of
terror engulfed many who had no ties with Communism and no
Communist past (Ježov made use of the saying 'When a forest is cut
down, splinters fly').

Many people disappeared in the darkness of the terror, some
forever.[6] Sentencing was sometimes carried out by a municipal
court ('sending to a certain place of residence'), sometimes by a
military court, and less frequently by a regular court. Old and new
gaols were filled at Glavnjača, Gradiška, Mitrovica, Zabela, Spuž,
Bileća, Zenica, and new camps, also, the most notorious of which
was Goli otok (1949–1963). That was how the 'little Gulag', a copy
of the great Gulag, came into being, a permanent torture (Popović
1988; Jovanović 1990; Pekić 1987, 1989)[7] which produced 'living
corpses': 'I was dead, but I did not die', said one of those who suffered there (Jovanović 1990: 432).

Not only party members who had come under suspicion, but
their families as well, were subjected to repression (coerced di-
vorces, the stigmatizing of children), as were friends and neighbours and all those who did not co-operate with the authorities
(mostly through being denounced). Denouncing spread by
geometric progression, threatening to engulf the whole party and
a significant part of the state and society. What was happening was
'almost a civil war' (Mihailović 1995: 79–80).

The 'Exporting' of the civil war

A network of Comintern (Soviet) informers and agents, in which
Yugoslav cadres had an important place (Mustafa Golubić, Vlajko
Begović, Mirko Marković, et al.), was being developed throughout
the world (in the service of the 'world revolution'). Various tasks,

including the (physical) liquidation of opponents, adversaries and 'enemies' were carried out through this network. Besides rival agents, targets included members of the opponents' groups and organizations (factions, parties), and, relevant to this discussion, the Ustasha, Chetniks, Bali Kombtar and others. There was no shortage of material means. In that regard, apart from public and secret police services (OZN, UDB and SDB), an important role was played by export companies with secret funds. The network of firms with such funds spread after the war through, among other things, the legalization of 'useful malversations' (a term used for the founding of private companies abroad from public funds).

Organizations defeated in the war employed terrorist methods against representatives of the Yugoslav government abroad, as well as in numerous showdowns among themselves, so that one might say that the civil war continued abroad. Members of the classic underworld participated in these showdowns, both at home and on the international scene with the involvement of the notorious 'Mafiosi'.

Of course, the connection between the holders of power and the criminal underworld cannot be determined for certain, but, as time went by, it became increasingly visible. It was made public in spectacular court trials and in the later confessions of the 'heroes of our time', such as that made by the greatest of them all, Bata Todorović (1993: 42–48). Magazines were filled with descriptions, bordering on the romantic, of the 'life and work' of what were called the, 'black pearls' (Vujasinović 1993: 16–21; Bulić 1993: 82–85; Jovanić 1994a: 89–94). Non-state-owned television (TV Politika, and later the Karić Brothers Television) devoted regular shows to them. The war made them, according to the magazines, 'undecorated heroes' (Jovanić 1994b: 28–29). More recently, that connection has become a subject of systematic study, the study of the 'great robbery of the people' (Dinkić 1995) and of the criminalization of the whole of Serbia (Knežević and Tufegdžić 1995). According to researchers 'Belgrade summed up in itself the Chicago of the 1920s, the economic crisis of Berlin in the 1930s, the espionage intrigues of Casablanca in the 1940s, and the cataclysmic hedonism of the Vietnam of the 1960s' (ibid.: 3). Under sanctions, this connection became more visible on home turf, since it was much more difficult for the 'black pearls' to act abroad; under the worn excuse of performing 'patriotic tasks', a permanent civil war continued, with afflicting visible and invisible wounds to a wide circle of people.

'Cases' and 'purges'

Titoism, as Stalinism 'with a human face', avoided mass terror (favouring instead selective terror), and murder, especially of better-known figures. A 'political case' was opened from time to time, with the aim of politically assassinating certain high-ranking party and state functionaries, and, along with them, a number of political and intellectual groups, to be followed by a 'purge' of all their declared supporters or all those who were denounced and labelled as such by the authorities.

One of the first of these cases was the 'Hebrang case' (in 1948) which ended in the mysterious death, the circumstances of which remain unclear, of Andrija Hebrang, the leader of the Croatian Communists before and during the war, and after the war the minister for industry and a member of the Politburo of the KPJ (Ivanković 1988).

The 'Đilas case' (in 1954) had wider implications, although the main figure here remained alive, sentenced to an extended term in prison. This case not only removed one of the most powerful members of the KPJ Politburo, but also removed many real or alleged supporters of Đilas' criticism of Stalinism and Communism in general. Many candidates for expulsion from the party and the workplace, and for prison sentencing or 'internal emigration', were labelled as 'Đilas supporters'. The 'Ranković case' (in 1966) not only removed from the public scene the 'second man' of the regime, the vice-president of the country and of the party, but also shook the foundations of one of the strongest institutions of the regime—its political police (Lukić 1989). The police themselves were subjected to torture, with or without trial (Numić 1989). The 'purge' covered a large proportion of the party hierarchy, although the institution of the political police as such was not questioned. The biggest showdowns were with the Croatian *'maspok'* (after 1971), and the Serbian 'liberals' after 1972 (Đukić 1990). Several thousand cadres were removed from the party, economic and cultural hierarchy, and many supporters of the *'maspok'* were sentenced to several years in prison. Even more numerous in the prisons were the Kosovo Albanians, among whom Adem Demaçi ('our Mandela') was sentenced to a term of around thirty years.[8]

Critically oriented intellectuals were often targeted by the regime. A real witch-hunt followed the student protest of 1968: critical intellectuals, mostly those around the journal *Praxis*, were accused of inciting the protest, along with some students. They were 'blacklisted', their passports were taken away, they were dismissed from their jobs, prevented from getting work, followed, arrested and sentenced. (Among them were Vladimir Mijanović, Lazar Stojanović, Danilo Udovički, Milan Nikolić, Jelka Kljajić and Pavle Imširović).

Crawling repression (TO, ONO, DSZ)

A party state counts on brute force only in extreme cases. The threat of force makes manipulation effective. Contrary to the classic Stalinist terror, Titoist terror was more selective, and it also counted more on corruption than on physical force (to 'care about the people' was a phrase commonly used by functionaries of the regime). A different standard of living and openness towards the world has its other face: it makes it easier to accept collaboration.

Despite all the advantages compared to other regimes of 'existing socialism', the Yugoslav regime displayed signs of growing fear of various enemies, thus it persistently widened its social basis through the militarization and police-ization of the whole society. A parallel army was created within the armed forces—the Territorial Defence (TO), which covered factories, institutions and schools, down to the local level. (The TO was to be the core of the national armies in the war). The General People's Defence (ONO) system covered the whole society. In parallel with its practical activities—occasional military drills, permanent training (under the slogan 'Nothing should surprise us')—the ONO system also became part of regular education at all levels, from elementary school to university. Students were taught how to recognize and fight with the 'enemy'. Social Self Protection (DSZ) was a general system of police surveillance and denunciation of suspicious persons, permanently in force, but particularly intense in so-called crisis situations. Although in the official ideology there was no admission of crisis, the more obvious symptoms of crisis, which included workers' strikes, student movements (1963–1974), nationalist movements in Kosovo (1968–1971) and in Croatia (1970–1971), made the militarization of society more obvious. With the alleged spreading of self-management, the regime started to carry out a more rigid re-Stalinization which included political trials and bans on newspapers, books and journals, and the 'personality cult' reached its peak (Popov 1983: 167–203, 225–248).

Even the mobilization of individuals into the services carrying out the repression had a coercive character, although those mobilized should have felt privileged to be trusted by the holders of power. The ambivalent status of participants in mass events was especially obvious during the mass farewells or welcomes on the frequent occasions of trips made by 'the dearest guest'.[9] Citizens were forced to participate in such events, and at the same time to display great joy and happiness.

The death of the Highest Authority

Due to the unlimited power held by Tito, and the deepening crisis in Yugoslavia as a common state, fear was spreading beyond the increased activities of the official ideology and propaganda, the fear of what would happen 'when Tito leaves' (even the word *death* was avoided, since it was reserved for ordinary people, not for mythical heroes). During the months which Tito spent in hospital in 1980—especially when the daily publication of medical reports became a regular feature—the nation was in a very tense mood. Institutions and organizations were on coustant alert, as if a revolution or a disaster could happen at any moment. When Tito died on 4 May 1980, the coffin was transported, in a ceremony rarely before seen, from Ljubljana to Belgrade. This was followed by an even greater spectacle, as distressed citizens, forming queues kilometres long, filed past the coffin night and day . The ceremonies were concluded with a funeral which remains one of the greatest spectacles of the modern era, attended by representatives of almost all the countries of the world.

Even after his death, Tito's authority was untouchable; a commission for the protection of his name and work was formed. Attempts to criticize that authority were strongly opposed by the regime for years. Here we have the case of authority as the cause of multiple traumas: authority as self-preservation, as the beheading of order and the announcement of chaos, but also as the subject of an increasing conflict between those nostalgic for, and those who blasphemed, the 'personality cult' (the latter even tried, following a pagan belief, to use a hawthorn post in order to destroy a vampire).

A populist roar

The disappearance of the supreme authority brought great insecurity to many people. This insecurity was magnified by an unknown future, especially with the deepening crisis in the USSR and the breakdown of the system of 'existing socialism' at its centre, the fall of the Berlin wall and the end of the Cold War. Amidst the growing insecurity and uncertainty grew a need for a new authority. This need would be satisfied in the cult of the nation and new national leaders. The rise of the new leaders brought a real outburst of nationalism in all parts of Yugoslavia.

Serbia and the Serb people outside Serbia were caught in the populist roar. 'Serb evil-doers' were cursed at the mass gatherings, and 'Serb heroes' glorified, in particular the 'new Tito'–Slobodan Milošević. Populism undertook a new 'purge' of inadequate functionaries ('armchair politicians' and 'national traitors'), legalized the extra-institutional violence of the 'anti-bureaucratic revolution', and glorified force as the principal means of liberation and unification of 'overall Serbdom' (Popov 1993). All proponents of nationalism and chauvinism have recourse to violence. That is how people get into new wars. Supporters of the democratic process were few and had a very limited influence, thus they were unable to stop the torrent of violence and new traumas.

Of course, life for the citizens of Yugoslavia was not totally dominated by coercion and violence. For many of them, life changed when they left the poor areas and villages and moved to the cities, obtained jobs and apartments, and advanced both professionally and socially. Life was not gloomy; on the contrary, there were many mass events, expressions of popular joy, victory parades.

All the sources and mechanisms of coercion and violence which affected large numbers of people (natural disasters, migrations, material and spiritual poverty), or simply individuals, have not been covered here. Instead, the focus is on the repressive apparatus and the party state, and their work. These spread and covered increasing segments of society, and, as time went by, became a *systematic source of violence*. What other function was there for repressive apparatus, especially in an order lacking any public control of the government or any opposition that could limit it effectively? Thus, the limitless power of the party state resembled Bechemot, who is everywhere, more than it did Leviathan, whose abode is known. One could even speak of the symbiosis of victims and executioners, since many people were members both of the repressive apparatus and targets of its work.

The destruction of Vukovar (and of other settlements, known and unknown) in 1991 was probably the result of the long fermenting of the 'negative energy' of envy, fear and hate. Although it is assumed that the war was started by Tito's and Pavelić's colonists as a result of the long-standing tensions between them, Vukovar was destroyed by the Yugoslav Party Army, with Tuđman's army as an accomplice, which, in sacrificing Vukovar ('the Croatian Stalingrad') found an incentive for the continuation of war. Both armies originated in the party state–the party conceived in Vukovar.

Trauma and catharsis

Continuing waves of violence make even more difficult the study and understanding of certain completed experiences of violence, although an attempt at such an understanding will be made here. Although no definitive opinion can be given regarding the extent, and all the consequences, of the long reign of the party state until the archives of the secret police, the mental institutions and other relevant institutions have been opened and studied, some insights are still possible.

Before discussing the results of research so far, mention should be made of some general conditions relevant to that research. First of all, there is a reluctance on the part of those people who were hurt to approach the question of trauma. Simply put, the individual's need to define his or her own problem is rarely noticed. This is probably furthered by a lack of any need to develop a *personal* identity. Research has shown that the syndrome of the authoritarian personality is more prevailing in Yugoslavia than anywhere else in the world (Biro 1994: 19–20). Research also shows that the party state (Communism) produces mass passivity, even apathy. 'The whole economic system', wrote Mikloš Biro, 'functioned on the principle of *receiving*, not *earning* ... Everything was received–salary, apartment, position, credit, money ...' (14–15). The standard of living attained was more the result of a person's place in the hierarchy of the party state and their loyalty to the regime, than a result of personal abilities and actions—improving one's own personality was not highly valued. The 'universities boom' was followed by a 'brain drain' and widespread illiteracy (and functional illiteracy)—around half of the citizens of the 'third Yugoslavia' were illiterate (Biro 1994: 108; Ivić and Perazić 1994: 5–6).

Even when the people resisted the regime, there was a lack of persistence in the search for an alternative. If the peasants complained, they were on their own and the result depended on the will of the holders of power alone (Kržišnik-Bukić 1991). A similar thing happened with the student protests in 1954, 1959 and 1963–1974 (Popov 1983). Even workers' strikes after 1958 failed to produce autonomous unions and the workers themselves did not become a really influential factor, although in the official ideology they were glorified as the ruling class (Jovanov 1979). National movements were the most persistent and the most successful both in the destruction of the common state—Yugoslavia—and in the creation—through war—of the new, national states.

There were certain structural factors which promoted the effectiveness of the party state, and brought about changes in the surroundings. The low level of structuring in society, along with the almost endemic poverty of a population affected by war, was reproduced by the power apparatus which crushed any attempt at the formation of stable social classes, economically independent of the arbitrary government. With constant 'reorganization', almost any attempt to build an autonomous society (civil society in particular) was prevented (Lazić et al. 1995).

The de-structuring of society, the dis-organization of the state, and the depersonalization of the personality, are three inseparable aspects of Yugoslav modernity. Increasing chaos in the economy and in society helped the arbitrary government. This process was enhanced by changes in the rest of the world. The crisis and breakdown of the system of 'existing socialism' brought increasing insecurity with regard to the global 'balance of powers'. A possibility for modernization and democratization was opened, but along with it came a possibility for 'escape from modernization', as well as a possibility for an increase of violence and totalitarianism.

In the following, we will return to a discussion of the extent of traumatization, attempts at catharsis, and general possibilities for escaping the torrent of fear, hatred and violence.

The diffusion of violence prevents a fusion of resistance

As shown in the previous section, different people are, at different times, the objects of different forms of violence. Firstly, at the time of preparation for revolution, several thousand people practised on themselves and on others in order to acquire insensitivity to pain and to become 'a special kind of people', 'soldiers of the revolution', 'dead men on leave'. After that, tens and hundreds of thousands of people were consumed by the revolution, and millions by the 'building' of a new order.

It is unlikely that the distant goals of such projects could be so intoxicating as to justify (legitimize) the use of violence . It is more likely that the violence was so great that its victims were overwhelmed and lost any hope of offering effective resistance. The executioner's authority was given as an explanation for the lack of resistance in concentration camps, even in situations when thousands of prisoners were controlled by only a dozen guards (Caruso 1969: 143-146). However, an understanding of the underlying psychological mechanisms does not provide a satisfactory explanation, nor does the structure of society provide sufficient reason for the 'acceptability' of violence, although it seems that the illiterate or semi-literate masses in less structured societies are more susceptible to violence. Nor can any concrete situation—war, revolution, crisis—provide a complete explanation . It is probably the case that all the circumstances mentioned increase the force of the systematic factors—apparatus of the party state—to such an extent that they have the most important role in everything, including the traumatization of people.

A system of selective terror, with a combination of the 'stick' and the 'carrot', became more successful through the careful planning of action, as well as through avoiding the creation of a critical mass. When repression was directed only towards unreliable party members, it looked like a 'family feud' which was of no one else's concern; when peasants were affected, workers remained aside; when intellectuals were targeted, everybody else remained aside. Those who escaped a wave of violence were pleased for themselves and indifferent to others. And when it was their turn, former victims were also indifferent towards (and to some extent even pleased about) the sufferings of new victims. In this way the apparatus of government appeared increasingly powerful, and its objects increasingly powerless. This situation did not arise simply because of psychological reasons, the system itself prohibited any alternative political organizing. People were allowed to achieve scarcely any degree of economic independence with regard to the regime, it was even unacceptable not to display total loyalty at all times to the ruling ideology, and any political activity outside the ruling party and its transmissions was out of the question. The government looked omnipotent, its subjects impotent. Fear of the government was expressed by, among other things, a distancing from it, as well as from any political activity. The government and politics were equated, and excuses such as 'I'm' not interested in politics', or 'I don't get involved in politics', could frequently be heard, a sure sign of the totalitarian tendencies of the government which were destroying any form of community among free citizens.

In such an order, techniques for the stalking, searching and punishing of 'enemies' were cultivated, as if in an endless evil game in which the hunters become the hunted. Even more paradoxical—and deadly—was what happened at the time that the system, which for years had looked omnipotent and eternal, was destroyed. As if in a general nightmare, almost everyone felt and behaved like victims—of party clashes, war, revolution and various campaigns against the 'enemy'. Since there was nothing either in tradition, in the actual structure or in the new situation, that had its foundation in the universal position of, for example, the free citizen, a deadly synthesis of victims on the national level was created. The fusion of groups and classes was replaced by a chaotic desire for an 'organic unity' of blood and soil. The whole nation was declared to be the victim of another nation. From there, collective vengeance was just one step away.

Mere dreams of collective catharsis

Spiritual creativity in the fields of art, philosophy and science, from time to time inspired cathartic effects, but the barrier of the ruling ideology and the party state was too strong to be breached. It was probably in the student 'counter-culture' that most had been achieved in that direction, especially during the 1960s when the youth and student magazines and journals (for example *Perspektive* in Ljubljana; *Danas, Student, Susret, Vidici* in Belgrade; *Lica* in Sarajevo) with determination and humour, some of it carnivalesque (the *Paradoks* in Zagreb and the Belgrade *Frontisterion*, which was shut down immediately), addressed 'taboo subjects', and were gradually and systematically banned and 'shut down', thus transforming the youth 'counter-culture' into a carefully cultivated regime 'subculture' (*Dokumenti*; Popov 1983, 1988). At the same time, the regime supported, or even pushed, some forms of 'mass culture', a 'show-down' with elitism in all places, except in the highest ranks of power (if it was elite at all—a 'lumpen-elite'?).

Hints at the need for catharsis with respect to the tragedies of the recent and more distant past were drowned out by the wave of new tragedy. For example, instead of catharsis for the crimes of the previous war came calls for revenge. According to psychiatrist and Orthodox Christian thinker Vladeta Jerotić, we have been witnessing a very slow departure from 'cruel, pagan retributions' ('an eye for an eye, a tooth for a tooth'). Genocide against the Serbs from the NDH, according to Jerotić, 'was not an example of Christian oblivion, rather there was a defence-suppressing mechanism. This mechanism was described precisely, and supported with proofs, by Sigmund Freud with respect to his neurotic patients; the experience could be transferred (although with some caution, as Freud himself warned) to situations among nations. Thus, "the return of the suppressed" occurred among the Serbian people in a dramatic, but not cathartic way. Out of their long restrained and forcibly suppressed aggression, vengefulness suddenly boiled over' (1994: 12).

From a coherent personalist position (Christian, liberal or social), the projection of the individual onto the collective psychology is excluded. However, it is possible to see factors that influence reason, spirit and soul among a number of people. If, for example, the Church itself should neglect the spirit of the Gospels and fall into philetism, it would then influence not only real believers, but also others who care only about the authority of the Church.[10] A similar thing happened with the authority of national institutions, namely, even people who did not care very much about the arts and sciences could look for support (and an alibi) for different behaviour with the excuse that it served a murkily defined 'national interest' in the activities of the highest national institution in that area—the Serbian Academy of Arts and Sciences. A similar thing could be said about the *Politika* newspaper, which provided the model on which generations of journalists were formed. What was 'written in a newspaper' was considered as a directive for thought and actions (see the contribution of Aleksandar Nenadović). This is even more true of state television, which, as all the research shows, has the greatest effect on the population.[11]

Weak personality–strong nation

It was already mentioned at the beginning of this chapter that nationalism (unlike national belonging) is connected with the feeling of injured dignity. We have also mentioned that various injuries found a common denominator in national wounds (and vengefulness). Even a moderately informed reader knows about the role of the media and national institutions in stirring up feelings about national wounds and inciting people to violence. However, within the wealth of data there is no trace of the main event—the transferring of actions from the personal to the collective level. It is even more difficult to trace *how* this was done. Let us try to outline it here briefly.

Radovan Karadžić, psychiatrist by vocation and subsequently national leader and 'healer' of collective Serb traumas, explained his endeavour in simple terms. As a person who knew the individual and the collective soul, Karadžić said that for decades something had been 'expelled and was crouching somewhere at the bottom of the human being', and it turned out that this was actually a collective soul: 'Our people as a whole, the Serbs, were exiled to villages. There was such pressure in the cites that only the brave and the fearless displayed their soul and their spiritual allegiance, while other Serbs hid it within themselves and suffered greatly ... A Serb could dedicate himself to his God and his own soul only in his own home, and alone' (1995).

The 'crouching soul' was relieved of its suffering by the national movement and war, so that a 'new soul' could reach its full expression in the creation symbolized by Karadžić himself. 'Destiny had decreed that the centre of events and tremors, but also of the revival of the Serbian people , should move to us. At one time it was in Serbia, at one time in Montenegro, Kosovo and Vojvodina. It moves, but it is in the same body, and the part of the body where the centre is now is Republika Srpska and Republika Srpska Krajina', according to Karadžić. The need 'to hide and appear smaller' stopped there, the freed collective soul acquired strength 'to bridge the river Drina ... from the left bank to the right'. Support for that mission was found in the Church. In Karadžić's words, 'there was not a single important decision that we made without the Church'. There was therefore a true miracle—'a resurrection of the crouching soul'.

Despite his fervent messianism, Karadžić looked for an excuse for all the violence employed in this mission in the guilt of others, who resisted the realization of the mission as the word of God: 'In Croatia and in the former Bosnia-Hercegovina, the enemy made so many mistakes that it led us straight to the path of the complete renewal of the Serb kingdom, the renewal of the Serb state; so our way was actually a reaction to the challenges set for us, and to the need forced upon us by our enemies, and actually it all came out the way God commanded' (ibid.).

Another psychiatrist and national leader of the 'Western Serbs' (as 'a new upholder of overall Serbhood'), Jovan Rašković, looked for a theological-ideological foundation for 'the Serb mission' through the identifying of the historical destiny and mission of Serbs and Jews, in the course of which he crudely plagiarized the Russian philosopher and Orthodox Christian thinker Berdjayev (Žanić 1993: 197-202). The identifying of the historical fate and mission of the Serbs and Jews had as its aim both to provide a theological basis for the Serb mission, and to provide it with an excuse in advance for all the violence and victims, referring to the tragic destiny of Jews under fascism and Nazism (Brikner 1995), as if everything was allowable for the victim.

The Kosovo myth was particularly successful in the inflaming of the masses and the elevation of the 'ordinary people'. Troubles faced by Serbs in Kosovo under Albanian domination (1966–1981)—in the course of history the 'domination model' changed hands between the two national 'political elites'[12]—were used to incite Serb nationalism and chauvinism. Kosovo—a 'holy land' both for Serbs and for Albanians—was used for evoking the feeling of wounded national dignity and as a starting point for the demonstration of force and the use of violence that has been going on in Kosovo for years, now against the Albanian population. It turned out that the Kosovo legend was convenient for the inflaming of the masses because it included an intertwining of pagan, Christian and lay motifs, so that everyone could find in it inspiration for thinking and doing, singing and shooting.

Ironically, the main support for the healing of the wounds from the *ancien régime* period was the military-police apparatus which had itself inflicted those wounds and which continued the spiral of violence. When it turned out that it was not powerful enough to realize the 'new mission', it resorted to calling for even stronger support from 'mother Russia'—as long as it could also have in power a similar elite, led by Zhirinovski or some similar 'messiah'.

A weak personality obviously looks for refuge in a collectivity which is as strong as possible, in the Serbian case the nation, with desires for even stronger support from 'general Orthodoxy'.

The war was not unavoidable. A real choice existed: a democratic process of change, or the violent destruction of society and the state. Everyone had certain motives for their choice—leaders, the political elite, intellectuals and the 'ordinary people'. Motives for the choices made are clear to any careful observer and cannot be hidden forever beneath conspiracy stories, or excuses such as fate, the national interest, or some other non-personal higher force.

In just the same way, peace depends on the choices made by people and on the motives for their thinking and behaviour.

Notes

1 On the way in which the educational system is embedded in warrior mythology, see Rosandić and Pešić, 1994.

2 See the collection *Srbija u modernizacijskim procesima XX veka*.

3 The values of the 'free warrior' are systematically cultivated in 'patriotic' journalism.

4 See G. Polovina, 1988. Even KPH (Communist Party of Croatia) functionaries sometimes thought that the Ustasha terror was only a revenge for the previous Chetnik terror, and that it was better not to get involved in these conflicts (41).

5 According to Ekehard Felkl's study 'Obračuni u Hrvatskoj', around 100,000 members of the Ustasha army and civilians were killed (*Nasa borba*, 5 May 1995: 8).

6 According to the estimate of Dragoslav Mihailović (1990), between 200,000 and 250,000 people were imprisoned in the campaign against the 'Informbureau supporters', and around one million were affected by the violence. The same author estimates that nine out of ten people were sentenced for 'verbal offences'. Torture was not limited just to the prison or camp, the convicts had to sign an obligation that they would denunciate after they come out of prison.

Detailed documentation on the suffering of the 'Informbureau supporters' can be found in the three volumes by Milinko B. Stojanović, 1993 and 1994.

7 A permanent inquiry was conducted in prisons on political prisoners, both after sentencing and after they left prison (Pučnik 1986).

8 Translator's note: 28, in fact.

9 Translator's note: Josip Broz Tito.

10 Jerotić 1995: 15; Radić 1995. 'The Serb Orthodox Church', wrote Jerotić, 'has another very difficult task: to avoid being manipulated by the noisy Serb nationalists, which were neither Orthodox in the past, nor have they become so today' (1995: 19).

11 Research shows that 60 per cent of the population in Serbia listened to the main evening news on state radio-television, while just 2 per cent read newspapers (Biro 1995: 84). On the turn of state television away from 'existing socialism' to nationalism, see the contribution of Rade Veljanovski.

12 See *Kosovski čvor—drešiti ili seći?*, 1990.

ROOTS OF THE TRAUMA

The Flight from Modernization

LATINKA PEROVIĆ

Many nations collapse before they become conscious of their mistakes

Alexis de Tocqueville

What can be used today as the basis for an analysis of Serbia's attitude towards Western Europe? It is an attitude that has not always, or necessarily, been explicit, nor has it been linked to only one institution—whether political, scientific or cultural. It has rather been implicit, and may be detected through an analysis of the course of internal development—particularly through the role of the elite in orienting this development. In essence, it has been a spontaneous and formulated response to the challenge placed before the Serbian elite by the unification of Western Europe leading to its further economic modernization; and the disintegration of the Eastern European system and the need to select paths to overall development in the future. In the past decade it has become increasingly evident that in Serbia, too, a long-term programme was coming to an end.

If, within the framework of Yugoslavia, Serbia had taken a position in between the East and the West, in the past decade it made a definite choice. There are a variety of sources that can be used in order to trace this decision.

Numerous investigations are necessary in order to approach an answer to the question of what position Serbia has taken towards Western Europe in the past decade and a half, towards Western society and cultural standards; and the extent to which this position presents a problem for Serbia, that is, the problem of its own Europeanization?

The criteria for establishing representative sources for such investigations are the following: their critical mass; the possibility of continuously monitoring this position during the short but crucial period; the variety and quantity of social factors, above all the Serbian elite whose attitude towards Western Europe, directly or indirectly, is reflected in these sources; and, particularly, sources through which this attitude is formulated, suggested and even imposed as a social orientation, as a choice and programme.

Uniting the national elite

The position and role of the Serbian elite in the period after the death of Josip Broz Tito, which, for several reasons, was decisive in the choice of orientation that would either bring Serbia closer to, or distance it from, Europe, can and must be traced through sources of different provenance. However, nowhere was the position of the elite expressed as unequivocally and in such a concentrated form as in the daily newspaper *Politika*, particularly in the column 'Reverberations and Reactions'.

Contributions by many experts and doctors of science, previously little known even in their narrow professional fields, were presented in this column. For such intellectuals, this represented an opportunity to come out of anonymity and experience social, if not professional, advancement. They created the impression of a broad and united 'front' of 'learned' individuals. The circle of those expounding their simplified views in an extremely arbitrary manner, intent on helping to solve the problems of the Serbian people, expanded, and as it did so, it became increasingly obligatory, and at the same time simpler and easier, to appear on the pages of *Politika*.

The tone was given by academicians, eminent scholars and artists, well-known writers, painters, philosophers, lawyers, economists, physicians, engineers, architects, journalists, actors, generals and politicians. Although by definition wide open to the public, almost none of the contributions to the 'Reverberations and Reactions' column rectified personal injustices or settled individual accounts. Global problems were discussed and solutions forwarded, the authors of the contributions spontaneously uniting around them. For this very reason, the column is an excellent illustration of the spirit of the time—a time when Serbia extolled itself, becoming intoxicated with self-sufficiency, and gradually closed itself off, isolating itself from Europe and the world. Every differing opinion was crushed and disappeared under the weight of populistic attitudes.

Traditionally highly valued among national institutions, *Politika* was given a central place. What it was expected to provide, and what it did provide generously, went beyond the function of a newspaper, even a great and long-established one. *Politika* was not just an authoritative tool in the hands of powerful and ideological mechanisms. It became an institution with a special mission, a kind of holy book, every last word of which was to be believed. *Politika* was said to be 'more powerful than the law'; 'a torchbearer and leader'; 'the spiritual bastion of truth, justice and progress'; 'a true source of inspiration'. The people's *Politika* would be immortal (see the contribution by A. Nenadović, '*Politika* in the Nationalistic Storm'). It is a source through which the development of Serbian national socialism can be precisely monitored.

The newspaper as a whole, and particularly 'Reverberations and Reactions', contained expressly and unmistakably anti-European views and statements. But in this crucial decade, in order to recognize the deep-seated commitments of the newspaper and of Serbia, of far greater importance than the arrogant, often tasteless and primitive statements full of provincialism and hatred, are judgements regarding the vital internal questions of the country's development: the inevitable modern and democratic reorganization of the common state; reforms in the political system; a multiparty system and parliamentary government; private property; a market economy; the status, rights and freedoms of individuals and ethnic communities; relations and co-operation with other peoples and states; and numerous similar matters.

Consequently, for researchers of the general mood and of Serbia's attitude towards Europe and European civilization, it is more suitable to analyse distinct tendencies and orientations regarding these vital, real matters that determine not only current behaviour but also the far-reaching future of Serbian society.

Academicians lent greatest weight to the 'Reverberations and Reactions' column (see the contribution by O. Milosavljević, 'The Misuse of the Authority of Science'). The column and the newspaper as a whole provided them with a platform from which they authoritatively questioned the 1974 Constitution and explained the necessity of countermanding autonomy–contrary to the civilized and democratic European tendency towards further affirmation of the independence and sovereignty of peoples, and from their anachronistic, narrowly nationalistic and simultaneously centralist viewpoints. Every proposal regarding reform of the Federation was declared to be secessionism; they resolutely rejected the idea of a confederation and demanded the right to self-determination for the Serbian people alone.

The academicians claimed that the position of the Serbs in Croatia was worse than during Austro-Hungarian rule, and they announced to the public, without however providing proof, that the genocide carried out against the Serbs in Croatia had been going on for forty-five years. They did not view the position of the Serbs in Bosnia-Hercegovina as being any better, claiming, without argumentation, that their conversion to Islam presented a real danger. Unable to impose a strong unitarian federation under the domination of the most numerous people (one person–one vote), they accused the north-western republics of separatism while speaking openly about the separation of the Serbian people. 'We Serbs', wrote the vice-president of the Serbian Academy of Arts and Sciences (SANU), Antonije Isaković, 'should think about the fact that we can live alone. We have the experience of being an independent state, we developed a state on our own, unlike others who acquired one by various agreements' (*Politika*, 11 June 1989). Academician Miodrag Jovičić said 'Serbia is big enough and rich enough to survive alone, or united with republics that so desire' (*Politika*, 28 June 1990).

Supporting the programme of the 'new Serbian leadership', when the new Constitution of the Republic of Serbia was declared that rescinded the autonomy of the provinces, the academicians announced that the proposed changes were inevitable, but that things should go further (*Politika*, 4 October 1988). And while others in Yugoslavia were terrified by such statements coming from representatives of the Serbian elite that were identical to the overt imperialistic and warmongering cries heard at mass meetings throughout Serbia, the front spread menacingly from Kosovo towards Slovenia, Croatia, Bosnia and Macedonia. Academician Dejan Medaković, receiving the July 7th Award (one of the highest awards presented on the day commemorating Serbia's uprising in 1941), announced that the process of reviving the Serbian people's deadened historical consciousness, that is, the anti-bureaucratic revolution, was marked by 'dignity and refinement' (*Politika*, 10 July 1990).

The Academy of Arts and Sciences based its social role on an awareness not only of its scholarly, but also of its national, mission—and also on its reputation among the people. In the words of its president Dušan Kanazir, at the end of 1989, after the Memorandum, that is, 'after the Academy's vigorous request to rectify the errors committed against the Serbian people and to resolve more effectively the socio-political problems in Kosovo and the entire country, the Academy gained even greater moral esteem'. The Academy's leaders felt that this reputation imposed an obligation on it. Its president announced that it would 'watchfully monitor and critically evaluate events in our society in a scholarly manner' (*Politika*, 28–30 November 1989). To remain silent regarding the position of the Serbian people would bring into question the Academy's moral integrity. It 'must turn towards the Serbian people as a whole, regardless of where they live today'. The Serbian Academy of Arts and Sciences was at the forefront of other national institutions in its concern for the interests of the Serbian people as a whole.

The presence of the Serbian Orthodox Church on the public scene up until the death of Patriarch German (1991) was considerably more discreet. However, the views expressed in its publications were identical to many of the Academy's views.

Extolling the anti-democratic movement

In accordance with their notion of the role and mission of the Academy, the academicians expressed their views on the nature of society in Serbia and on the characteristics of economic and political relations within it. In spite of powerful trends in Europe towards transformation and change, academician Mihailo Marković announced that the Republic would remain socialist as long as the form of socially owned property was in effect, 'at present valued at 300 billion dinars'. The reasons for this—the unifying of isolated Serbia, surrounded by a hostile coalition and threatened by a world conspiracy—were used to contest the need for Serbia to move towards political pluralism and, in fact, to defend a one-party system. Academician Marković felt that 'the political situation in Serbia is such that most serious people do not want to become involved in other parties, even when they are critical of the League of Communists. These parties would remain small and would not be able to play an essential role in the political system... Most important of all is the fact that the political system designed by the present reform is not, and cannot be, a multiparty system' (*Politika*, 16 August 1989).

Owing to this and similar theories on no-party democracy as a higher form of real democracy, contrary to the centuries-long experience and fundamental political principles of Western Europe— a multiparty system and free elections were introduced, under great pressure, considerably later than in the other republics in Yugoslavia. This only happened when the autocratic regime had become entrenched through the anti-bureaucratic revolution.

'Finally', continued Marković, 'the forms of direct democracy established and fostered by our system are different from those in an indirect, party-based democracy. Consequently, political organizations that exist in such a system are not, in fact, parties, even though that is what they are called. They cannot gain and hold power, which is the basic goal of every true party.'

Academician Marković had in mind the document Views of the Presidency of Serbia's Commission on Reforming the Political System. As one of those who participated in its elaboration, Marković said that it was a 'radical programme that would democratize and modernize the political system'. The key principle of this document was 'one person–one vote'. Based on this principle, the document had no chance of being accepted in multiethnic Yugoslavia. Also, contrary to the strongly expressed wishes of the non-Serbian ethnic groups in Yugoslavia and to democratic convictions in Europe, it offered the projection of a unitarian and centralist federation; this would mean not further progressive democratic evolution, but regression, even in comparison to the situation that had been achieved among the peoples of Yugoslavia. However, the document did have the broad and undivided support of the Serbian elite. It was judged historic; Professor Miroslav Egerić called it nothing less than the 'Magna Carta' of Serbian democracy (*Politika*, 28 July 1989). Although it was one in the series of bureaucratic documents with the guideline title of *Views...*, it was elevated to a special status. According to *Politika* it 'announced the end of the great deceit'; it 'sprang from the power of the people' and was the 'logical ... result of events in Serbia in the past two years'. It was seen as an expression of the resolve to be 'ahead of the times' and as proof that 'Serbia ... is turned towards the future'.

The academicians had a conspicuous role in both the creation of the document and in public support for it. In the first case they gave it a scholarly demeanour, and in the second, their goal was to relativize in advance, and completely invalidate, any questions, doubts and open reservations regarding the document's basic principles.

Thus academician Nikša Stipčević said that no one had any reason to be afraid of Serbia, for the principle of 'one person—one vote' was the 'beginning of every democracy'. Without contesting the existence of the Serbian question, he negated the existence of a national (ethnic) question in Yugoslavia. 'Those in Yugoslavia today', he said, 'who are for a federation of states and against a federal state, are in favour of a special social feudalism, national bureaucratic fiefs, which are the greatest evil in Yugoslavia.' And he found the instructions on 'how to dispose of the future' (*Politika*, 10 August 1989) in the above document.

Academician Radovan Samardžić felt that 'with this document the Serbian people and the commission of scholars who presented it have not enabled Serbia's revival through a return to Europe, but have shown that the country and its people are actually speaking from the heart of Europe'. In his opinion, the Serbs were one of the rare peoples whose right to fight for their own unification was being denied. 'The notorious 1974 Constitution has finally disclosed the intention to reduce Serbia to the narrowest confines, to put it in a position of constitutional inequality and semi-colonial economic dependence ... The return of the Serbs to their historical traditions and their spiritual identity cannot be considered a step backwards, since from the Middle Ages to the present this step has been the basis of transformation and progress' (*Politika*, 11 August 1989). This renewal of the past became the programme for the future.

The Academy openly supported the Serbian leadership in its intentions to re-establish Serbian statehood, and, with this goal in mind, immediately became the representative of the interests of the Serbian people as a whole. On their side, the leadership showed that they cared about this support and, within this framework, gave the Academy the freedom to act. In October 1989 the president of the Republic, Slobodan Milošević, announced that, 'As far as the Serbian Academy of Sciences is concerned, I really don't see why it should not influence policies in Serbia. What people in the world, what sensible country in the world is ashamed of its academy of science. If ideas appear within it that are not in the interests of the democratic, socialist development of our country, this does not mean that such ideas prevail and that the members of the Academy share them. But the Academy does not play the key role here. The key role in this tumultuous time is played by the citizens of Serbia' (*Politika*, 10 October 1989). In other words, the services provided by the Academy were welcomed, but it did not play a leading role.

On the same occasion, Milošević had a similar message for the Association of Writers of Serbia and for the Church. Thus, from the beginning, *they were all together, under conditions that were indisputably politically and ideologically formulated by an already recognized leader.*

Contributions to the 'Reverberations and Reactions' column provide an invaluable basis on which to analyse events during a period that, even viewed at only a short remove, seems to be over. This was the preparation period for what was to come. However, almost unexpectedly for the researcher, these contributions reveal that although certain material prerequisites—elements of a market economy, Yugoslavia's openness towards the world—for transition and rapid Europeanization did exist, Serbia was not mentally and psychologically ready for essential changes within social and political structures, let alone to redefine relations within the country. There was a lack of readiness among the masses and among the elite, which was particularly important. Serbia, of course, should be compared to other parts of former Yugoslavia and other countries in Eastern Europe. Even if there are still places where one can say that profound changes have not taken place, the destruction of the old structures and power mechanisms in Eastern European countries is certain, and this is an essential prerequisite for fundamental changes. Where did Serbia stand in this regard?

It is true, as Ralf Dahrendorf says, that 'with all the noise and uproar, not a single new idea came out of Eastern Europe in 1989'. However, with the slogan 'Europe here and now', an alternative was articulated. For some Eastern European peoples this meant continuing the violently interrupted (1945) movement along the paths of Western European civilization; for others it meant duplicating the path taken by Western European peoples in their development.

Self-isolation

Generally speaking, in the 1980s Serbia did not take an openly hostile position towards Western European civilization. The views of Serbian theologians with regard to Western Europe—that it had abandoned the path of Christ and had become a great evil, a 'poisonous environment' in which the European part of humanity was dying, and that Western Europe, having based its culture on man, had made man a slave to things—did not go outside the bounds of the Serbian Orthodox Church. It is only in more recent times, characterized by the Church's extreme politicization, that this attitude has found its place among broader social-cultural structures. However, from the beginning of political conflicts in Yugoslavia, and particularly from the moment they grew into conflicts of war, Serbia has built its relationship towards Europe on one single need: the need to convince Western Europe of its 'truth'.

While refusing to consider how others saw them was an increasingly reliable sign of inwardness, self-isolation and the loss of the ability to compare themselves with others as the first imperative for realistic self-examination, the Serbian elite was expected to play a key role in spreading 'the truth about Serbia'. This was considered their patriotic duty.

It must be acknowledged that the Serbian elite, not only in *Politika* and not only through 'Reverberations and Reactions', did indeed join the battle for a 'breakthrough of the truth about Serbia', its 'tragedies', and the battle for the 'biological salvation of the Serbian people'.

The problem of Serbia's attitude towards Europe was not denied by the highest political position in the country, but the conditions for Serbia's inclusion in Europe were firmly set. In May 1989 Slobodan Milošević sent a message to advocates of Yugoslavia's Europeanization within Yugoslavia, supporters of 'Europe here and now', that this was possible only if internal solutions were chosen 'that benefit the new socialism, as a richer and democratic society, a society that will belong to Europe'. And he continued, 'But we will not enter such a Europe as lackeys fawning over Europe by mocking our own state and its institutions, even the army, and by mocking other, ostensibly uncultured peoples with whom we live in this state; rather we will go into Europe on an equal footing and, it goes without saying, in our own Yugoslav, socialist way' (*Politika*, 24 May 1989).

Milošević had previously formulated his basic socialist tenets even more specifically. 'We should reach the developed countries of Europe and the world not by returning to private ownership and a parliamentary system, not as a civil society, but as a socialist society' (*Politika*, 13 December 1985). After all, 'the agreement as to whether a society is civil ... or socialist ... has not been made anywhere to date without blood' (S. Milošević 1987: 24).

Socialism, cleansed of bureaucratic deformations, but also elements of capitalism and liberalism, therefore *remained, both in practice and as a social ideal.* This choice was made in Serbia before the crisis of Yugoslavia as a state became evident. More exactly, this choice was one of the essential elements of Yugoslavia's crisis and disintegration. 'At the Eighth Session of the Central Committee of the League of Communists of Serbia,' said one of those who put this course into effect, 'the left wing of the League of Communists of Serbia won'. And this was not the choice of the Serbian regime alone. The leading Serbian national ideologist Dobrica Ćosić wrote that 'The idea of a Bolshevist-Leninist, Stalinist, and if you wish Titoist, variation is certainly worn out in the historical sense. That idea has collapsed historically. But the idea of socialism, in my opinion, is a living idea... by personal conviction I remain an advocate of utopian socialism, for my entire ethos is such that for the rest of my life I will not cease to strive for such an ideal, even if it is utopian' (D. Ćosić 1990).

Politika's headlines reflect the same: 'The press should state the socialist truths of the people and the workers and put them into practice'; 'We are sticking to high-efficiency socialism'; 'It is a question of reforms, not of abandoning socialism'; 'Building socialism can only be the joint work of all progressive social forces'; 'Not the end, but the springtime of socialism'.

Through the anti-bureaucratic revolution, the regime in Serbia became consolidated and offered resistance to real political and economic changes. Since the need for such changes was already ripe, their rejection inevitably led to a negative evolution and even to the degeneration of the regime. This was the starting point of divisions in Yugoslavia, a fact that is often lost sight of, and they were soon manifested as a *conflict of national (ethnic) interests*. War was only the most drastic expression of these divisions.

'The populist movement in Serbia and Montenegro had a social component in the beginning ... Parallel with the socially defined "voice of the people", their ethnic voice was also being heard. Already at the meetings in 1988 and 1989 the people's voice was loudest when it was identified as the voice of the Serbian people ...'. 'Members of other ethnic groups easily become opponents and enemies' of the ethnically defined Serbian people (I. Čolović 1993: 150–1951).

The period from the mass meetings to the first multiparty elections in Serbia can be described as a time in which the leading structures stabilized and consolidated the existing mechanisms of power. In this regard, Serbia was a phenomenon not only in former Yugoslavia, the leading structures of which, if nothing else, were shaken by the war, but particularly in Eastern Europe where the old power structures had been seriously undermined and even destroyed. Viewed in this context, the anti-bureaucratic revolution was a negative anticipation of what followed in Eastern Europe. Collectivism was strengthened during the revolution: it started with social collectivism and ended with ethnic. Even the predominant part of the Serbian elite failed to see this as one more removal from the basic principle of Western European civilization: individualism. On the contrary, the Serbian elite encouraged the 'enthronement' of the people as a united political and social entity and made decisive contributions to it.

Hundreds of thousands of people in the streets of Serbian towns, more than a million at the meeting in Belgrade and two million at Gazimestan, were the chosen form of democracy, a permanent state that even required the adjustment of town plans (an initiative was launched to change the town plan in Niš, and this example was expected to be followed by other towns in Serbia. Every town was to have space for mass gatherings, from around 300,000 in Niš to a million people in Belgrade).

The atmosphere of 'happenings of the people' was an incentive to adjust town plans to the spirit of the anti-bureaucratic revolution: people needed space for meetings and manifestations. But 'the idea of squares for mass meetings of gigantic proportions', as one town planner wrote, 'unfortunately does not contribute to the humanization of man's space, rather it does the contrary—it subjects individuals to the psychosis of the mass culture. The larger the space left undeveloped in a town, the smaller and more helpless people feel in it. Except, of course, in the case of meetings when a person identifies with the masses *volens nolens.*'

That identification of the individual with the masses, the individual's melting into the masses during the anti-bureaucratic revolution, left a trace that was deeper than appears at first glance. Not only was it expressed by attacking the urban culture during the war, it also relativized the meaning of ostensibly accepted Western European values: private enterprise, a multiparty system, parliamentarianism, freedom of the press. They were not the goal. 'For the democratic future of Serbia', wrote Dobrica Ćosić, 'at this historic moment the contents and quality of the proposed constitution are much more important than adequate democratic procedures' (*Politika*, 1 July 1990).

What was also lost sight of, as Slobodan Jovanović wrote, was the fact that 'as soon as a man rises somewhat above national egoism, it becomes clear to him that a nation in itself does not represent what philosophy calls "value". It can only be given value by the general cultural ideals that are put at its service.'

Serbia was removed from Western European civilization even before the outbreak of war. The war only made the process faster, and its end made the distance drastically visible. In addition, it was the victory of a cultural model the mainstay of which was a semi-intellectual, a man whom Slobodan Jovanović described as having a diploma from school but no cultural and moral education. During the anti-bureaucratic revolution he spread hatred and laid the grounds for the policy of war from the pages of *Politika*. For the first time he broke off the Western European orientation that, while never dominant, had always been present in Serbia's political culture, and proclaimed Serbia's self-sufficiency.

The force of traditional collectivism

The attempt to reconstruct the role of the Serbian elite in events during the last decade is not an appeal for its condemnation but an attempt to understand its history and impact on the development of the Serbian people. During the country's relatively short history it has been torn between East and West, between patriarchal views and modern views. Originating from a rural people, in the middle of the last century the numerically small Serbian elite emanated the collectivist democracy of the people from which it had sprung. And then, particularly after Serbia gained independence—in the decade from 1878 to 1888—they institutionalized this system. All the movements that the Serbian elite inspired in the second half of the nineteenth century—the youth movement in the 1860s that pitted 'real, genuine Serbs' against the 'decadent West', the 'positivistic' movement in the 1870s, and the radical movement in the 1880s—'suffer from a spiritual, intimate need for collectivism'. This incontestable need is seen as proof that 'our social life is not deep enough to be able to accept a larger culture which is at heart highly individualistic'. However, using Western phraseology, 'our superficial political intelligentsia', consciously and unconsciously made it impossible to understand 'that we are not a democratic people in the Western sense of the word', and that 'there is an essential difference between our democracy and Western democracy' (D. Nikolajević, 1910: 5).

In the history of social ideas in Serbia it is easy to note that the economic and political dimensions of social development are viewed more in terms of their confrontation than their causality. There has always been dispute over which should be given the priority: politics or economics. It was hard to find a political party in Serbia with a coherent political and economic programme. They all strove for national and social liberation and unity, as well as for political freedom, and not a single one had a clear programme of economic development, or modernization, along with the inevitable price that had to be paid for it. Until the Second World War, Serbian society was agrarian, with a surplus rural population, and without the roots for parliamentary democracy in its social structure.

At the beginning of the twentieth century, Serbia became a parliamentary state, but the influence of the royal court and the military factor was always important. Serbian society moved between anarchy and autocracy, and Serbian statesman Milan Piroćanac was not far from the truth when he wrote in his *Diary* that the Serbian temperament was 'humble when under someone's command and unruly and ungovernable when given freedom'.[1] Viewed from the historical perspective, the meaning behind the words of Serbian scientist Jovan Cvijić, spoken after the wars of liberation against the Turks, becomes clear. The Serbian people, wrote Cvijić, are a democratic people. But theirs is a natural democracy, 'without institutions and a democratic type of rule' (J. Cvijić 1987: 316). Without economic modernization and without democratic institutions, the Serbian people, together with the other Balkan peoples, risk staying on the margin of historical development. Cvijić pointed out the primordial patriarchal views of the Balkan peoples, including the Serbs, which gives rise to their proclivity towards leaders who easily turn into dictators.

The idea of a *people's state*, as opposed to a state based on law, is the general position of Serbian political and social thought. Such a state has a social function since it stimulates and controls economic development, but also guarantees a just distribution. The idea of a people's state has, in fact, never been abandoned. It emerges from the impoverished Serbian society. Only the focus has changed. It has shifted from the social to the national, but it still has the people as a whole in mind.

In Serbia the idea of populism was an answer to the social and political question raised by Western Europe. That ideology embodied the patriarchal mentality of the people, which is why it was able to have such an essential influence on their social history. A fundamental, non-ideological study of history should be undertaken as a prerequisite, not only in order to explain the people's past but also to understand their present; society developed industry but remained undivided into classes and under powerful pressure from 'agrarian mysticism'. The notion of state and the notion of society coincided in these people.

Europe was not a trauma for the Serbian masses. It was a trauma for the Serbian elite and was manifested as the complex of unsurmounted backwardness. The attempt to accelerate history through political revolution had failed. And communistic modernization had reached its limits. But the Serbian elite once again gave a patriarchal answer to the new challenge of modernization. What are the prospects?

More than one hundred years ago, after Serbia obtained independence, Serbian scholar and statesman Stojan Novaković made the following comment: 'What is left now? What is left is to look each other in the eye and find out where the danger lies. Is the danger in staying or in going further? It was up to us ... to choose: either to see the level of education of the Western world as an enemy from whom we should flee, or to see it as an old friend and teacher, who is worthy of our friendship and with whom we must associate ...'[2].

Basically speaking, the question he posed still stands today. Except that Serbia has dropped out of development and its society is in a state of anomie. What we have is more than the failure of a policy, of a regime, of a nationalistic chimera. It is a historical failure. The development of an awareness in this regard would be the beginning of a way out of the vicious circle of social-national-social collectivism. Without this, the Serbian people will confirm that de Toqueville was right.

Notes

1 Milan Piroćanac, *Diary*, SANU Archives , No. 9989.
2 Stenographic records of the National Assembly of Serbia for 1880 and 1881, Belgrade, 1881: 1601.

An Uneasy View of the City

SRETEN VUJOVIĆ

The best lack all conviction, while the worst are full of passionate intensity.

W. B. Yeats

The reason for interest in the urban question in Yugoslavia's war drama is tragic, based as it is on the rarely seen forms, and the violence, of urban destruction, ranging from the renaming of towns, ethnic cleansing, pillaging, blockades and civilian casualties to urbicide and necropolises.

The issue is whether the exact figures for the human victims and material loss will ever be known, either overall or for each side individually. 'Croatian authorities claim that 63 Catholic churches were destroyed along with numerous other buildings. The Serbian side has counted 243 damaged churches. According to rough estimates by experts, 70 per cent of cultural monuments and various religious buildings no longer exist in Bosnia-Hercegovina. Paintings, icons, libraries ... have been destroyed or pillaged' (Igrić 1995: 28). The tragic situation in former Yugoslavia is also shown by the fact that exact figures still have not been established for human and other losses on Yugoslav soil during the Second World War.

The number of destructive factors is large and varied. In this paper we are primarily interested in socio-psychological factors, both those of long duration and those of medium and short duration: historical socio-psychological, systemic socio-psychological and situational socio-psychological. Of course, all the social factors of Yugoslavia's disintegration during the war are interconnected and can be categorized . Our intention here is merely to draw attention to them, and to continue *searching for an answer to the question of the socio-psychological and political meaning of the stereotype of the city in terms of nationalism and war.*

Among the important historical socio-psychological factors considered as destructive is *authoritarianism,* which can be spoken of as a historical constant in the Yugoslav environment. The results of several sociological and socio-psychological investigations bear witness to widespread and very distinct authoritarianism, particu-

larly in Serbia, Montenegro, Croatia and Bosnia-Hercegovina
(Kuzmanović 1994, 161). Authoritarianism was a very fertile background for the 'wide-scale mobilization of the population behind
the nationalistic programmes of the political and intellectual
elite' (Lazić 1994: 160). Authoritarianism is primarily shown as
the uncritical bestowal of trust in, and submission to, a supreme
leader. At the end of the 1980s and the beginning of the 1990s,
after nationalistic-chauvinistic programmes were legitimized,
republican leaders strengthened their power and led the masses
to the ruinous creation of national (ethnic) states, and into 'lost
battles'.

Stereotypes are rigid and biased opinions, views or beliefs about
individuals, groups, institutions or situations, including views
about territorial collectivities or local social communities—the village and the city and their inhabitants—and about rural and urban
populations. They are more often negative than positive and are
created before, or without, the availability of objective data about
the subject in question. As with most prejudices, stereotypes are
rigid and resistant to change. They are passionately expressed and
defended because they activate strong emotional affinities: hatred,
rage, fear, scorn, etc.

Stereotypes are often connected with ethnic distance and then
become ethnic stereotypes or ethnic prejudices. Gordon Allport
distinguishes between the following types and degrees of prejudice: 1) disparaging and stereotypically appraising an ethnic
group; 2) avoiding contact, that is, maintaining social distance; 3)
discrimination, discriminatory behaviour (limiting different
rights); 4) physical attacks (shifting from verbal to physical aggression); and 5) extermination (genocide). All these types and degrees
of ethnic stereotypes are in effect in ethnic relations in the Balkans
and Yugoslavia, including the current civil and ethnic warfare discussed here.

Therefore, in this paper we are primarily interested in *whether
and how stereotypes connected to the city, particularly ethnic
stereotypes, were used in preparation for the physical and spiritual destruction of towns, both internally and externally, and for
the justification of such destruction.* Secondly, we are interested in
the ideological background of prevailing negative stereotypes
about the city, that is, their ideological roots in the past.

Stereotypes about the city

Our experience is provincial.

R. Konstantinović

The question to be explored is whether the ideological roots of negative stereotypes about the city, especially large cities, can be found in domestic folklore, and, above all, in social ideas.

The dislike of the city among recent advocates of militant nationalism certainly had nothing to do with eminent scholars; some of these advocates were uneducated and primitive and did not even know of the work done by such scholars. Their hatred was founded upon conscious and unconscious stimuli based on the collective memory, traditionalism, a patriarchal view of the world, on national romanticism and populism as a stubborn and powerful spiritual orientation.

The invasion of the Slavs destroyed the traditions of Roman and Byzantine urban civilizations in the interior of the Balkans. There was a gradual renovation of some ancient towns (Belgrade, Niš, Skoplje, Prizren) in the eastern part of the Balkans. However, even though these towns existed in the same place and preserved their names, there was no continuity of life from Antiquity (Kovačević-Kojić 1991: 16).

From the mid-thirteenth century, the development of mining led to the creation of mining settlements in Serbia and there was a rapid development of Serbian and Bosnian towns in the first half of the fifteenth century. With the arrival of the Turks, contrary to some opinions, urban life did not come to an end; in the first years of Ottoman rule urban life in Serbia and Bosnia primarily continued in existing towns rather than in the small number of towns founded by the Turks (Sarajevo, Nova Varoš) (ibid.) The Ottoman influence prevailed in small towns. This is also shown by the fact that at the end of the sixteenth century the 'Muslims comprised approximately 27.4 per cent of the overall Balkan population, while registries in the Istanbul archives indicate that they were more numerous than the Christians in town centres' (Beldiceanu 1991: 28). Based on the Turkish words he collected (141 entries) Beldiceanu shows that the new conquerors influenced the 'lexicon of the Balkan towns and centres in Romanian principalities (Vlaška, Moldavia)' (ibid.).

In terms of urban development, the most important part of the town was the downtown area or *čaršija* (a word of Persian origin that reached Serbia through the Turks, meaning four directions or four sides; in a freer translation it is the place where people meet from all four corners of the world); it was primarily the business district of the town and then a street or square with commercial and artisan shops. Later, in the nineteenth century and afterwards, the idea of the *čaršija* took on a new meaning and implied something between 'public opinion' and the 'cultural climate' leading to the 'deep connection between last century's towns and the complex state of the social spirit that was formed within them and that also formed them' (Macura 1984: 7).

The structure of the Balkan downtown was formed in the seventeenth century: it had commercial and artisan areas and was divided by religions and by the manufacture and sale of special goods. Laws and administrative measures established the positions of different downtown areas and the conditions for their operations (Popović 1991: 65). That is when two groups of merchants arose: 1) domestic merchants, Muslims, Christians and Jews; and 2) foreign merchants, with those from Dubrovnik having the principal position until the beginning of the seventeenth century.

'The critical stamp and culture, in a word, the atmosphere in Serbian towns in the eighteenth century, was given by the Vlachs' (Antonijeviić 1991: 162). In the nineteenth century, the Serbs living in areas under Turkish control, unlike their countrymen north of the Sava and Danube rivers, 'had a low level of urban culture. Their settlements were villages, or isolated neighbourhoods within Turkish towns, lacking an urban identity' (Manević 1991: 216).

There were three periods in the process of transforming the *čaršija* into a modern city centre:

First, after the end of the Second Serbian Uprising, the inherited Turkish downtown areas and the towns themselves were in a pitiful state, depopulated and burned for the most part. During the first reign of Miloš Obrenović town centres were recreated and renewed and new centres were formed.

Second, from the fourth decade of the nineteenth century—from the Constitution of 1839 and the Guild Decree of 1847–until almost its end, the *čaršija* continued to develop and gradually brought together the forces that would change it into a city centre ...

Third, at the turn of the century modern industry appeared and capitalism expanded, thereby creating the social, economic and cultural conditions to transform town centres from the substance and form of the *čaršija* into modern city centres. (Macura 1984: 10)

Be that as it may, in the part of the Balkans in which the Serbs lived there were no autonomous and enterprising towns such as those in Western Europe, with the exception of Dubrovnik. What prevailed were trading centres, mining settlements, court palaces and small towns...

Several opinions about the city from the pens of older scholars are given below. These opinions cannot be called 'pro-city' but are rather ambivalent or stereotypical expressions of fear of, or disdain for, the city.

Vuk Karadžić (1849: 11–16) writes about the 'upper class', the town dwellers. He considers the core of the people to consist 'entirely of peasants and farm-hands'. Town dwellers had Turkish and Roman laws. In Montenegro, Hercegovina and Bosnia where the law was Greek, 'one cannot even imagine that other people exist except for peasants and farm-hands, and in Serbia they are the most prevalent'. Karadžić, in essence, has an ambivalent attitude towards town dwellers. On the one hand he is critical of them, for the following reason: 'The upper class should speak the language better and more clearly, it should be more learned than the people, wiser, more courteous, agreeable and patriotic ... but in our upper class everything is upside down.' They prefer 'themselves and their life' to the people and what benefits the people; they have forgotten how to 'think Serbian'; their science, if any, 'does not reflect the principles of the people's common sense'. Vuk Karadžić concludes that 'The simple class of our people ... is not inferior to a single one of the five or six nearby peoples either in terms of their *intellect* or their *integrity* or in any other good deeds; and the *upper class* is the way in which it is brought up and the state in which it lives. Even if they do nothing shameful, they are not excessively honourable either.' Thus, the peasants and -farm-hands were entirely and in all respects hardworking, while this was not the case with the townsmen. In another text, Karadžić writes that the Serbs did not consider townsmen as being 'among the Serbian people, and even scorn them'. However, Karadžić realizes the necessity of an 'upper class' and this is where his ambivalence appears. He writes that 'if at least fifty years ago our people had had men to manage affairs in accordance with present times they would have been their own keepers long ago, and today this deficiency is also the greatest hindrance and misfortune that is all the greater for us owing to the fact that it is easier to manage an orderly and ready-made house than to build a new one and manage it' (1960: 146).

Jovan Cvijić expounds the following views: 'Some peoples and some cultural circles take greater advantage of those positions that are convenient for large settlements. This can be established in particular for the Turks, Vlachs and Greeks, and our people seem to have the least propensity to found cities and towns.' The 'Byzantine Greeks' were the most cultured element as townsmen, and together with the Vlachs were the main merchants and artisans. The type of the *raj* (non-Muslim subject) was created in conditions where the people were longest under Turkish slavery and where, solely in the Balkans, the Turks made up the greater part of the population in towns. According to Cvijić, therefore, the Dinaric ethno-psychological type for whom 'stability and absolute faith in the national ideal was the main component of their history' did not develop a propensity towards town life, and particularly not towards city life. Describing the *čaršija*, Cvijić expresses his anti-city opinion: 'This *čaršija* had a destructive influence on all Balkan peoples, and still has today, particularly owing to the fact that during peaceful times the *čaršija* led society and produced the first intelligentsia with its petty morals and enormous egoism that was completely perverted' (1966). For a better understanding, it should be noted that Cvijić wrote these lines when only 16 per cent of the population of the Kingdom of Serbia was urban. Stressing these facts, our intention, inter alia, is to show that hostility towards the *čaršija* is understandable since it was a foreign, rather than a domestic, stronghold.

Slobodan Jovanović sees nineteenth-century Serbia as an extremely 'simple and uncomplicated country' whose population was ethnically, religiously and linguistically homogeneous: 'There are practically no social differences between the topmost layer of the peasant masses, a thin layer of administrative-clerk intelligentsia, and the wealthy merchants. The clerks and merchants have peasant blood flowing through their veins: many of them came from the village and those who were born in a town had peasant grandfathers and fathers' (1990). Jovanović distinguishes between two prevailing types of Serbian politician: the intellectual parvenu and the village boss. 'The intellectual parvenu was usually born in a village or small town; he completed secondary school there and went to university abroad. He is reproached for having been mentally and morally corrupted by the great learning that was rapidly stuffed into him. ... An educated primitive, he is not able to restrain his ambitions and holds that his diploma from Paris or Heidelberg gives him the right to everything' (ibid.).

Jovanović agrees with Cvijić that nationalism is the only 'firm and solid' tradition in the Serbian people. It should be noted that owing to historical circumstances, nationalism in the nineteenth century had a positive role.

An intellectual, maintains Jovanović, is a 'nationalist and partisan, and so is a peasant'. Both are obsessed and full of 'unbridled personal ambitions'. The conclusion is sombre: 'With such rulers, such an intelligentsia, such peasant masses, it is no wonder that our nineteenth century was full of conflicts and catastrophes' (ibid.).

Karadžić, Cvijić and Jovanović all share a negative opinion of the Serbian intelligentsia, although Jovanović is also critical of the peasants. However, in spite of this, Jovanović writes, 'The rural population is protected against the bias and abnormality of the town culture that mechanizes life and gives rise to that overly prosaic and rational view of the world that is called narrow-minded' (1940: 186). Jovan Dučić thinks in a similar way: 'It seems to us that with the genesis of towns and the growth of the intelligentsia the creative genius of the village and peasant is slowly disappearing'.[1]

Vladimir Velmar-Janković presents the 'mental alignment of the Belgrader' in 1938 as follows: 'Christianity through Orthodoxy, the national church of St. Sava, a patriarchal-heroic perception of life, respect for one's ancestors and the ideas of the old Serbian state, integrity contained in folk poems and other oral traditions preserved in the family and the rural household and fostered by the national language. Among the great historical influences woven into the people's mentality that strongly affect it: Byzantium and the Turks' (1991: 58). Most of this Belgrade view of the world deals with a mental alignment characteristic of the rural or possibly small-town view of things; it shows little or nothing of the vision of the Belgrader as a representative of the city that, when Velmar-Janković wrote this, had a population of around 300,000 people.

Velmar-Janković shows one more interesting dimension of the problem, which is his anti-European opinion. 'That new Serb, that first man with a Belgrade alignment, was his own man, his own in terms of himself and the fact that—he was not a European' (1991: 82). Furthermore, 'of all the corners of Europe, the Balkans are the least European. And among the Christians in the Balkans, the Serbs and Bulgarians are the least European' (1991: 82). Velmar-Janković not only comes to this conclusion about their mental state but also considers it correct. Unlike him, Gerhard Gezeman merely points out the Montenegrins' opinion of the citizens of Europe: 'Whoever is acquainted with the Montenegrins will understand their deep loathing of the citizens of Europe hidden behind ... the word *lacman* (foreigner), someone who dresses in the French manner and does not wear a revolver at his belt—and who can dance on a rope' (1992: 139).

Acquiring an urban status in the sense of obtaining and being part of a middle class was, and still is, a 'transition phase' in Serbia, something second rate, provincial. Velmar-Janković wrote some excellent essays on this transition as a pattern of behaviour and a mental state, analysing this process in Belgrade between the two world wars. He realized that the transition phase created 'its own category of transitional people, transitional types and those in the transition as a profession' (1991: 35). Those in the transition phase as a profession well understood the transitional time and used it very selfishly: 'speculators, professional politicians, punished and unpunished criminal types, profiteers, those fishing in troubled waters...' (1991: 40). The gallery of transitional types is even richer and contains: 'salon Communists, armchair opposition members, nationalistic profiteers, government toadies and small-town dwellers, revolutionaries until their first job, separatists until the first policeman, democrat-sadists, fascist-"liberators"' (1991: 43). The writer Boško Tokin had the following opinion: 'Belgrade was semi-provincial, demimondaine, primitive, immoral, secretive, brutal, inconsiderate, intimate, hypermodern and anarchistic. Raging and wretched at the same time' (1932: 38).

The thesis of transition also indicates that Serbia's city dwellers, who should have been the main actors in modernization, were not constituted as a class between the two wars, nor were they later as the middle class, including the 'new entrepreneurs', and their instability and incompleteness were one of the reasons behind unfinished or deformed modernization.

The views expounded in the important contemporary book by Radomir Konstantinović *Filozofija palanke* (Small-Town Philosophy) are relevant to our topic. Defining the small-town mentality, Konstantinović writes: 'Between the village and the town, forgotten as it is, the world of the small town is that of neither a village nor a town. ... A small-town mentality is one of uniformity, the mentality of ready-made solutions, patterns, very defined forms. ... In the small-town world it is more important to hold onto established customs than to be an individual. ... The spirit of traditionalism is one of the basic expressions of a small-town mentality' (1981: 7, 10, 11, 16).

Owing to the activities of the 'new Serbian right' and several political parties from the extreme right wing, which should be neither overestimated nor underestimated, Konstantinović's thesis that 'Serbian Nazism was not an "import" from the German national-socialism that it served and supported, but the ultimate expression of a small-town mentality' (1981: 366) is of particular interest.

In the service of militant nationalism

The principle of ethnic cleansing, the most terrifying thing our century
has devised, is becoming a guiding principle.

D. Snaper

Ever since the civil war began in former Yugoslavia, the diversified
arsenal of war propaganda, as a component part of the war strategy, contained negative stereotypes about the city. On suitable
occasions, the warlords and their apologists among national ideologists publicly announced through the media their views on the
malignancy and depravity of the city, on the unnaturalness of interethnic coexistence, on the rotten cosmopolitanism of the city,
on the need to 'Serbianize' towns, etc. The images and metaphors
that were used in this regard belong to the realm of *déja vu*, but
there were also some 'epic innovations'.

The creators of the statements and views about the city that will
be quoted do not have the importance and intellectual superiority
of the scholars cited above. Their statements were often 'off the
top of their heads', but they had weight and were menacing owing
to the fact that their speakers were the oppressors who determined the fate of people and towns, or proponents of war propaganda, favoured in the regime-controlled media which included
the greatest number of media with the greatest number of viewers,
listeners and the greatest circulation.

Dubrovnik and its surroundings were the victim of one of the
most senseless undertakings in the civil war under discussion. For
centuries this city was unique in the Balkans; its civilization had a
European glow, and not only during its 'great century'. To make
matters even worse, Dubrovnik, Mostar, Sarajevo and Vukovar are
among the prettiest and most picturesque historical cities with
clearly expressed identities. The case of Dubrovnik might be called
paradigmatic with respect to the current topic.

In mid-July 1991 Mihailj Kertes promised 'a great Serbian state
from Montenegro to the left bank of the Neretva River with Dubrovnik as the capital city' which, if this intention were carried out,
would be called Nikšić on Sea following the wishes of the
'Montenegrin neighbours in charge of renaming' (*V*, 13 September
1993). Božidar Vućurević militantly announced that 'It is only a
matter of days or hours before the JNA (the Yugoslav People's
Army) enters Dubrovnik. If the fascist army finds resistance in the
Old Town it will be destroyed (*B*, 5–6 October 1991). Confronted
by protests from abroad and isolated domestic complaints,

Vućurević made his famous 'off-the-cuff' remark: 'If need be, we will build an even prettier and older Dubrovnik' (*V*, 16 December 1991).

Vućurević's images and metaphors with respect to the city are of a medical, organic, geo-deterministic and ethnocentric nature. He is from the village of Zubci; in his collection of poems he recognizes in Trebinje 'urban pestilence', 'imposed obligations and misfortune', 'disloyalty' (Čolović 1994: 31). In order to get rid of these pernicious diseases, he performed vengeful surgery as the commander-in-chief in January 1993 and expelled all the Muslims from Trebinje before destroying the town's mosque. He applied a selective eradication of the 'urban pestilence'. But Dubrovnik remained his main 'mental' preoccupation. The metaphors remain the same: 'Dubrovnik is neither a Serbian nor a Croatian town but a Latin town built on Serbian rocks. Life within it was always whorish and there was never room for an honest Serb. Zero elevation produced a zero category of people. So-called Dubrovnik gentlemen even sold their children into white slavery to all sorts of worldly good-for-nothings, both male and female. That is how Dubrovnik truly came to an end as Serbia's spleen knowing perfectly well what it is–the mausoleum of red blood cells' (*B*, 1993).

At the beginning of October 1991, at the news that fighting was taking place around Dubrovnik, a group of Belgrade historians–Ljubinka Trgovčević, Sima Ćirković, Andrej Mitrović, Mirjana Živković and Ivan Djurić–sent an open letter to JNA forces and armed formations in Croatia in which they warned and begged them not to allow any part of this historical city to be destroyed. They stressed that Dubrovnik was part of the history of both the Serbian and Croatian peoples and part of the world cultural heritage. 'The entire civilized world would never forgive you for that; not a single goal or any boundary is worthy of destruction...'. It was an isolated voice of self-consciousness from the ranks of the Serbian intellectual elite. It reverberated, but there were also 'reactions'. Art historian Dinko Davidov, in an open letter to Ljubinka Trgovčević (9 October 1991) wrote that '...your concern for the fate of Dubrovnik is touching, except that you made one mistake: you should not have sent the *same* letter to the armed forces of the JNA and the conspiratorial neo-Ustasha units. You have thereby equated something that cannot be equated. That is already deceit. Our entire history is the history of different false parallels... And finally, I would like to ask how it is possible that, along with the concern shown for the fate of Dubrovnik, you did not show a little concern for the Serbian Orthodox churches and monasteries that were catastrophically destroyed by the Ustasha during the genocide against the Serbian people in the Second World War. As far as Dubrovnik is concerned, and our army in front of its walls, I hope that you muster the strength to apologize to the army for addressing it improperly. It is bleeding and you compare it to the worst scum of recent political and military history.' Davidov was not alone in these views. The implication was that the time had come to avenge the suffering of the Serbs in the Second World War. On the other hand, the looting of cultural and other riches from the Dubrovnik area and the officers mixed up in this affair, let alone other things, did not give the JNA any reason to expect an apology.

In a speech at the Second Serbian Unity Congress in Chicago (5 November 1991), Matija Bečković said that '...the mourning towns that were not destroyed show an indifference towards the thousands of people who were killed. It seems that if Hitler had sought refuge in Dubrovnik he would have been protected by UNESCO'.

Radovan Samardžić, who spent a lot of time in the Dubrovnik archives and wrote knowledgeably about the city, took part in this 'dialogue' and expounded views full of xenophobia, ethnic stereotypes and Serbian self-sufficiency. 'The situation is not dangerous for Dubrovnik. It is a prostituted city of hotel keepers visited by American grandmothers, British queers, stupid Frenchmen and German typists... We don't need the Allies because the US is corrupt, the English are stupid, the French are right-wing and the Russians are poor' (*V*, 21 November 1991: 38).

Ratko Dmitrović, a commentator on RTS news, condemned the 'ugly' political views of Bogdan Bogdanović, Filip David and Mirko Kovač, stating, 'And when it comes right down to it, should the dilemma arise, or even the possibility of a dilemma, that either ten Serbs be killed or part of the old Dubrovnik walls be destroyed, I would not hesitate for a moment. No stone is worth more than a human life. In any case, these walls were built by men, the Lord God did not make them descend from heaven' (*V*, 23 December 1991: 54). The false dilemma, that of men dying or 'walls' being destroyed became popular. It was 'forgotten' that both one and the other should be protected from barbarism. Men built the walls, of course, but men, that is, states, also signed international conventions on protecting the cultural treasures of whichever people they belonged to. 'Liberating' towns, as was done in this civil war, meant destroying both people and towns. The examples of Vukovar and Mostar give convincing proof of this.

Unlike contemporaries who participated in the 'mocking' of Dubrovnik, it is interesting to note that Karadžić and Cvijić, although basically anti-urban in their views, singled out Dubrovnik and valued its urbanity. Cvijić wrote the following about it: 'Almost the entire population is distinguished by a mildness and courtesy, tact and judiciousness. These are the characteristics that should be acknowledged for the fact that they succeeded in founding a republic, unique of its kind, and finding the way for it to advance even in the most difficult circumstances.' 'In other words', says Cvijić, 'Dubrovnik's intellectual and moral laboratory' showed 'harmony and docility', but also 'reason and calculation' (1966: 333–334).

The fate of Sarajevo, a town which underwent one thousand days of siege from 28 January 1995, is much worse than that of Dubrovnik. More than ten thousand people died in that siege and around fifty thousand were wounded; in 1994 alone some five hundred children were orphaned (*B*, special issue, 4 January 1994).[2] Many books have been written in the world (around 300) and in our country about the 'tragic paradox of our times' known as 'the siege of Sarajevo'. The composition and contents of the book by Miroslav Prstojević, *Sarajevo–ranjeni grad* (Sarajevo-Wounded City), conceived as the nine circles of hell, gives a convincing presentation of Sarajevo as a place of torture. Prstojević writes: 'An enormous red-hot cloud of hate stands over my city. The city, in which for centuries four of the five largest world religions have lived in parallel, is melting under a burst of heat. I see the gradual destruction of apartments, temples, streets, museums, monuments, factories, people... Cultural values are disappearing' (1994: 115).

On the occasion of receiving the Ratković award for poetry in 1993, Radovan Karadžić made a statement for the newspaper *Pobjeda*: 'We from Durmitor Mountain arc a free people, we have very often felt that towns are like prisons.' In the poem 'Vuksan', dedicated to his father, the second stanza reads: 'Go down to the city / to beat up the filthy / Vuksan, holiday / what a nice name'. And in other poems by Karadžić, fragments can be found that indicate hostility towards the city and foreboding with regard to Sarajevo. Although indicative, this is still poetry. What is significant for our topic, however, is how Karadžić interprets why he kept Sarajevo, the city in which he lived and worked, under siege and in agony as though it were the Middle Ages. Explaining why he had chosen Pale over Banja Luka as the capital of Republika Srpska, Karadžić said: 'Pale does not exist. Pale is a small place and currently the seat of the government bodies... The reason we are staying there is that we have to be on the front line. We have to be on a prominent place of command and I must say that it is very important that we have held Sarajevo and still do. *If we did not hold Sarajevo, there would be no state ... Never hold a snake by the tail, but by the neck: that's what we had to achieve that'* (author's italics) (*B*, November 1994, and almost the same words in *NIN*, 10 February 1995: 13). The metaphor of the city as a 'snake's neck' is rare indeed, probably original. The worst thing is that he treated Sarajevo as one might treat a snake's neck. In the name of megalomaniac national programmes, it was renamed, ethnically cleansed, divided, tortured and destroyed. From genocide to urbicide.

When asked by journalist Branka Ańelković, 'What is the sense of holding Sarajevo the way the Serbs are holding it? The part of the city that is considered urban is in Muslim hands', Karadžić replied, 'We'll see about that. We have an opportunity to divide the city by the river. The international community would approve this idea. Two-fifths of the urban part, the heart of the city would belong to us, and three-fifths to Muslims. There might be some justice in that, although we would be sorry to leave the old church there. However, it is clear that the Muslims cannot have all of Sarajevo. We will never allow that. Either it is ours or it will be two cities' (*NIN*, 10 February 1995: 13).[3] Further on in the interview, Karadžić, just like earlier dictators, goes into urban, architectural and regional planning, but with a strict ethnic stamp. Ghettoization on the city level, then on the state level, was the goal he set.

Momčilo Krajišnik, in a statement in the Serbian newspaper *Oslobodjenje*, shows even greater radicalism. 'All assertions that the war can end somewhere outside of Sarajevo are illusory, and the inhabitants of this city of ours must understand that it is their fate to be involved in the beginning and the end of this war. Sarajevo is of great importance for our fight. Here it is shown that a common state is out of the question. Here we are dealing with two cities, two states. That is the first phase. For the first time I will say publicly what I truly think, here in *Oslobodjenje*. Sarajevo's prospects are to be a united city in the future, but completely Serbian. The Muslims will have to look for their capital outside of Sarajevo, somewhere else. That is the natural course of things. This city will belong completely to Republika Srpska. Maybe it seems too optimistic right now, or too radical, but I am certain that is how it will be' (*V*, 28 November 1994: 55).

The human and social cost of such an undertaking does not seem to worry the founders of mono-ethnic states. In 1986. out of 170 independent states in the world only a small number were ethnically homogeneous. Mono-ethnic states can only be envisaged at the price of breaking up the world into minute communities.

On the occasion of the Spanish civil war, Orwell wrote something that also pertains to the civil war in Yugoslavia: 'one of the worst characteristics of war is that all the war propaganda, the shouts, lies and hatred, are always the work of people who are not fighting' (in Stoyanne 1992: 120).

Momo Kapor writes that Sarajevo was an 'unnatural creation', and that the city 'collapsed by itself' from malice and hatred. Radicalizing such a view of things, Dragoš Kalajić publicly stated his 'Neronian' joy that Sarajevo was in flames. Both of them were bothered by Sarajevo's multiethnic and multicultural coexistence. They were for homogenization, segregation and ghettoization. This stereotypical chauvinistic perception did not take into account, or refused to acknowledge, that the creation and development of every historical city in Europe is the result of interculturalism, and that every city is a mixture of civilizations and ethnic groups. It was a view that overlooked the fact that diversity is the basic characteristic of the city as such.

Nationalisms nourish each other and act just like communicating vessels. Thus, representatives of all three sides in the conflict, including the representatives of religious leaders, condemned mixed marriages and the children born to such marriages. In 1981, a total of 15 per cent of children in Bosnia-Hercegovina were from ethnically mixed marriages. If we consider the extended families of ethnically mixed and other couples, then 'half the population of Bosnia-Hercegovina has interethnic relations' (Bogosavljević 1992: 40). The proportion of mixed marriages was highest—up to 40 per cent of all marriages—in industrial settlements with an extremely mixed ethnic structure, such as Vukovar, Sarajevo and Mostar. In spite of everything, ethnically mixed marriages were still taking place, in Sarajevo for example. It is impossible to organize an ethnically pure life. There will always be 'mixed love', merchants who disturb an ethnically pure situation ('commerce might fall sick, but it will never die'), travellers who arrive, and then stay, in 'pure' areas, etc.

Sarajevo was being destroyed by fire, sword and words; Belgrade, for the moment, was only being destroyed by dangerous words and sporadic acts of extreme nationalistic violence.

In a programme on NTV Studio B (1992), Sonja Karadžić, the daughter of Radovan Karadžić, said: 'I am very disappointed with Belgrade and the "liberalism" that is emphasized in my people's capital.' The first reason for her disappointment was that the city contained people from all the ethnic groups that had fled Sarajevo, while their counterparts were still committing genocide against the Serbs; and the second was that Belgraders were contemplating political changes in Serbia. In the interior, according to Karadžić's daughter, young people were much healthier and less burdened and did not think about such things.

Dragoslav Bokan declared that, 'We should all show that Belgrade is the Serbian Hong Kong. It is not part of the Serbdom, it has betrayed the Serbdom! We should give it, and not honourable Podgorica, the name of Titograd' (*D*, 23 December 1992: 12).

Isidora Bjelica and Nebojša Pajkić, the 'commissars of political art' wrote about the 'anxiety of a sick and run-down Belgrade', a city then truly facing 'stagnation'. Belgrade's stagnation consisted of 'civic commotion', 'peacemaking' and cosmopolitanism. When asked what message he would send to Belgrade, Miroslav Toholj (RS minister of information), speaker of the commissars of the 'new Serbian right wing', replied, 'I feel compassion for them and am discovering the good fortune that here, in the forest, I can scream to my heart's content. I can be completely free, while those in the middle of Belgrade cannot...' (*T*,19 October 1994: 21-24).

The magazine *Srpska reč* (Serbian Word) (No. 89, 1994: 15) contained the following comment: 'Belgrade is Tito's whore. It considers itself Yugoslav, cosmopolitan, democratic. The only thing it does not want to be is what it is: Serbian.'[4] The leader of a 'patriotic party' explained this briefly and clearly: 'Belgrade is an anti-Serbian dustbin.'

At the time of the political conflicts between the leadership of Serbia Proper and that of the Serbs on the other side of the Drina River (autumn 1994), threats came from Pale that Belgrade should be made Serbian by hook or by crook. With this same desire to make Belgrade Serbian, the above-mentioned 'commissars of political art' contrasted Pale and Belgrade. According to them, Pale did not deserve the 'ambivalent attribute of the "largest Serbian hick town" given to it by Crnjanski in his *Apoteozi Kekendi* (Apotheosis to Kekenda)'. They agreed with the statement by Aleksa Buha that Pale was the 'Serbian Bonn, as opposed to the spiritual wall that today divides Serbian Belgrade from non-Serbian Belgrade, just like East and West Berlin' (*T*, 19 October 1994: 21).

Brana Crnčević examining the role of Belgrade as the capital city stated for the daily *Javnost,* in the city of Višegrad, that 'The Serbs here live severely blockaded on all sides. Belgrade is rather indifferent towards it all. It has its own idea about cosmopolitanism, its real and false art, people who want to believe they are right and those who are not right. Geographically speaking, Belgrade is the capital of Serbdom but capital cities have a habit of changing places. It might happen one day, for one reason or another, that Serbia's capital is Kruševac or a small town in Vojvodina; it might be a small town in Republika Srpska or Krajina. Serbia's capital is always where Serbian ideas are the strongest' (V, 1 October 1994: 59).

At the national conference on 10 December 1994 in Belgrade's Sava Centre, during discussions on whether it was feasible and realistic to unite all Serbian lands, consideration was given to the capital of that new state. Belgrade was contested in this regard. Momo Kapor said something very similar to Brana Crnčević. In his opinion the matriarch of Serbian national feelings, which was acting like a step-mother, should be punished by having the capital moved elsewhere.

Momir Vojvodić proclaimed Pale the capital 'since it is Serbia's Cetinje today'.

The reasons for moving Serbia's capital were religious, moral, and even biological. Rastislav Petrović saw 'the two newly created Serbian states (RS and RSK) as fresh blood that would strengthen the two (Serbia and Montenegro) already rather elderly Serbian states'. Aleksandar Drašković agreed: 'Real Serbian national feelings are being tempered and hardened across the Drina River, and I don't see that here'. Threatening both intellectuals and civic circles, Rajko Djurdjević concluded that 'The lurching city of Belgrade, with its intellectual circles that only care about ingratiating themselves to the West, has ceased to be the capital of its own volition. It is no longer the capital in spirit' (R, 16–31 December 1994: 9).

During moments of the greatest iniquity, when the worst breaches of human rights and war rights were taking place, and particularly at the time of widespread crimes against the civilian population and crimes against the cultural and architectural heritage, all of which were protected by international conventions, barbaric threats were made not only against Yugoslav cities outside the theatre of war, but also against the cities and metropolises of neighbouring countries. General Ratko Mladić, in a fit of ambition, announced that, 'Through this war I have broken away from Communism and Yugoslavia and have become the greatest Serb. Sooner or later I will liberate the Serbian city of Zadar, an undertaking that was prevented by the disloyal JNA General Staff. Trieste is an old Serbian city, too, and will be ours in the end. The Serbian army will finish this war, just like the previous two, on the Trieste–Vienna line' (B, 1993, article by M. Marić). Željko Ražnatović Arkan (in the capacity of 'political thinker') 'considered' urban themes as well. He announced that 'Zadar, Šibenik, Dubrovnik and Split are Serbian cities where the Catholics settled by force. The time has finally come to expel them', and 'I am convinced that entering Zagreb is the only way to settle accounts with the Ustasha ideology—then I certainly will open a pastry shop on Jelačić Square' (*B*, 1993, same article).

It might be said that not many authors used ethnic stereotypes about the city to produce 'cultural hatred', although not all of them have been mentioned. In addition, the urban question was not a central point in nationalistic ideology and current political mythology. It 'turns up' by happenstance and was 'inserted' into the propaganda of militant ethnic nationalism. Nonetheless, there are more than enough authors of ethnic stereotypes of the city, since 'civil war does not come from without, is not some sort of imported virus, rather it is an endogenous process. It is always started by a minority: probably one out of a hundred is enough to ruin civilized life together ... When civil war reaches a climax, it turns out that most did not want it' (Enzensberger 1994).

Unlike national ideologists and apologists of ethnic cleansing and Russell-esque cartographers, who for historical, ethnic or any other reason, or sometimes withhout reason, divided the country and towns with the explicit or tacit support of the regime and of a good deal of the opposition political parties, individuals and civic associations active opposing the evil; for this they were stigmatized as traitors, 'anti-war profiteers', cosmopolites, deserving of 'complete disdain' and similar epithets. They had intellectual and moral strength but insufficient political power, and survived on the margins of social and political life both within the country and abroad.

Owing to the fact that he deals with the urban question in the civil war, which is the subject of our analysis, a brief outline of the contents of Bogdan Bogdanović's book *Grad i smrt* (The City and Death) will be given here.

Bogdanović's approach is skilfully to unite views from the field of urban anthropology, urban psychology and the history of civilization. The best indication of the topic and its coherence are the essay titles, and particularly the title given to the book as a whole. For an architect whose charnel house monuments have recorded 'war and death, victors and vanquished', but above all the 'indestructible joy of life', the loss of the civilian population and the destruction of cities are tragedies that stirred his emotions and sharpened his awareness. Bogdan Bogdanović, who comes from Belgrade, speaks frankly, bravely and movingly about the horrible fate of his 'parallel homelands', Vukovar, Mostar and Sarajevo. He cites reasons for and against the city and opts for the city; he wonders about the roots of fear of the city and disdain for the city, about the motives of city-haters and city-destroyers, about the nature of the chauvinists, that is, the ethnic hygienists and warlords who wanted to use violence to wipe out any trace of human and material variety, interculturalism, the permeation of civilizations, urbanity, and, last but not least, the joy and beauty of life. Bogdanović wants both to understand and condemn: morally, politically, culturally. In order to be convincing and relentless, his picture of things is sometimes Manichaean: a division into city-haters and city-lovers. There are also those who are ambivalent and those without an articulated opinion about the city.

The campaign to collect signatures for the Declaration on a Free and United Sarajevo brought together those who did not look at the city through ethnic stereotypes. This campaign, and the Sarajevo Declaration itself, deserve attention. The Declaration was signed by 6,500 Belgraders and 1,500 from Novi Sad, Subotica, Kraljevo, Smederevo, Niš and Novi Pazar. The relative success of the campaign, considering the number of signatures, was due to the Serbian Renewal Movement, the Civic Alliance of Serbia, the Labour Party, the Belgrade Circle, the Centre for Anti-War Action, Women in Black and the Vojvodina League of Social Democrats. The media's help in this campaign was invaluable, particularly that of *Borba, Vreme, Republika,* the *Monitor* and the *Liberal.* The Declaration reads as follows:

> A free, open and undivided Sarajevo is the expression of our everlasting will and therefore we will not allow anyone to divide Sarajevo, on any basis whatsoever, at a time when the entire civilized world aspires towards mutual co-operation and integration.
>
> We are firmly convinced that living with diversity and in a state of tolerance is the inestimable heritage of our past and the sure foundation of a peaceful and happy future for each and every inhabitant of Sarajevo and Bosnia-Hercegovina.
>
> We demand the just and timely punishment of all war criminals and the safe return of all exiles and refugees, which is a prerequisite for the normalization of life and the continuation of the tradition of coexistence.
>
> We completely accept the Charter of the United Nations and the General Declaration on Human Rights as the criteria for our own practices and the organization of social relations, and ask the international community, on the basis of these principles, to undertake the resolution of the future of Sarajevo and Bosnia-Hercegovina, convinced that only a democratically organized political government can

assure the dignity and interests of every free inhabitant of Sarajevo and of our communal state.

At this moment we are responsible for the fulfilment of these civilized principles.

What is Cathartic in Urban Civilization?

We have already stressed that in addition to economic and political transformations, the emergence of the city also meant changes in people's mentality. With the appearance of the Greek *polis*, the discovery of a new intellectual horizon meant

> the promotion of words whose secular use in free debate and discussion provides contradictory evidence, becomes a first-class political tool, the means to supremacy in the state; the character of broad public opinion that is given both by the phenomena of social life and the products of the intellect—written laws and decrees—which are made available for the inspection of all citizens, and the actions of individuals that are subjected to criticism; replacing the old hierarchical relations of domination and submission with new types of social relations that have their origin in symmetry, reflexivity and reciprocity, between 'similar' or 'equal' citizens; abandoning old attitudes towards tradition that is no longer considered an immutable truth that must be respected and repeated, with nothing changing within it, rather each person's efforts to detach himself from it, to confirm his own originality by establishing a distance with respect to his predecessors, whose assertions are taken over, corrected or completely rejected; all these show that the secularization, rationalization, geometrization of thought, as the development of an inventive and critical mind, take place through social practice. (Vernant 1990)

Regarding the expansion of Western European cities, Werner Sombart noted the creation of a new society, and, to an even greater extent, a new mentality. 'If I am not mistaken, it is in Florence, somewhere near the end of the fourteenth century,' he writes, 'where we first encounter the perfect burgher.' The concept of the burgher as opposed to the peasant arose in the municipalities of the medieval West, those autonomous territorial collectivities. Burghers are members of a group of 'men equal before the law'. Max Weber showed that Western European cities strongly encouraged the development of capitalism since they broke up social groups created on blood ties and a common local origin, something which did not happen in populous Asiatic cities. Therein lies the originality of Western cities. Owing to the disappearance or suppression of blood ties, taboos and magic, the city became a confederation of individuals whose social position depended only on structural factors and personal characteristics. Thus the prerequisites were created for the city population to be transformed into a group of citizens founded primarily on the basis of personal interest. Contrary to the widespread belief that modern democracy has its historical roots in ancient democracy, it is Weber's opinion that it has precursors in the democracy of medieval towns in which the basic actor is the burgher in the form of *homo oeconomicus* oriented towards peaceful gain. In Weber's words, the class of burghers is the mainstay of the process of rationalization, and this implies both modernization and democratization.

According to Habermas, ' "The City" is the vital centre of civic society, and not only in economic terms; in its cultural–political opposition to "the court" it denotes above all an early literary public that finds its institutions in the English coffee-houses, French salons and German café societies (*Tishegesellschaften*). Encountering bourgeois intellectuals, the successors of that humanistic-aristocratic society with its social conversation that rapidly developed into public criticism, established a bridge between the backward form of the court public that was disintegrating, and the preliminary form of a new bourgeois public' (Habermas 1969: 41). Habermas investigated the genesis, structure and function of the liberal model of a civic public. In his opinion, 'public opinion' can only be spoken of 'in late seventeenth-century England and eighteenth-century France' (1969: 4).

However, the city is a necessary but insufficient condition for the formation of a middle class. In Serbian society, as a distant province and semi-colony of Ottoman Oriental despotism, entrepreneurship and the middle class, as the mainstays of a liberal orientation, could not be properly developed and consolidated. The social structure did not change essentially, even after the 'village-bourgeois' revolution. The class in power was not the middle class but the merchant bourgeoisie that was originally from rural areas; their cultural–ethical and political value orientations did not provide a favourable atmosphere for economic and political modernization. In the whirlwind of the First and Second Balkan Uprisings and the First and Second World Wars, the small number of bourgeois was reduced even further. Oriented towards the autocratic state, and very dependent on it, the thin layer of the pre-socialistic bourgeoisie was not, for the most part, prone to liberal ideas. Dissident or opposition groups that operated more or less publicly after 1945 often had a Marxist orientation, meaning that it was either directed against the middle class, or ambivalent towards it. 'When the advocates of liberal ideas emerged from the underground where they had been pushed, their rhetoric was primarily anti-Communist (extremely intolerant and therefore anti-liberal in itself); immediately afterwards it merged with nationalism that further cut off its roots. Liberalism thus turned into a set of ritual phrases that appear as fashionable formulas but do not have a deeper foothold in either current social processes (in the social class whose interests it would represent) or in the broader intellectual tradition' (Gredelj 1994: 256).

Let us return to our outline of the development of cities and the rise of urban civilization. Fernand Braudel shows what free cities achieve when they wrest themselves away from the iron embrace of the state, and even the ethnic group. Braudel writes that there are two great rivals on European soil—the state and the city. The state usually wins and the city then becomes subjugated and is placed under a heavy hand. The miracle that appeared in the first great urban European centuries is that the city was the complete victor, at least in Italy, Flanders and Germany. During that rather long period of time it experienced a life all its own, which is a colossal event the genesis of which cannot be defined with certainty. Based on this freedom, great cities and others on their borders and following their example built an original civilization and spread new skills that had either been revived or rediscovered after several centuries. They were allowed to gain quite exceptional political, social and economic experience.

Social thought in the nineteenth century aspired to replace the rationalism and individualism that prevailed in the seventeenth and eighteenth centuries with Burke's return to history and a sociological approach that put the emphasis on traditionally formed communities. But as John Stuart Mill judiciously warned, the shift was all too easy from the accepted principle of individual rights and freedoms to the rights and freedoms of nations, neglecting the fact that the insatiable appetite of the latter might swallow the former (Emerson 1994: 47).

Twentieth-century totalitarian systems were fatal for many cities. Cities were destroyed by bombing, terrorism, prohibitions, absurdity, even by plan (necropolises such as Dresden, Berlin, Hiroshima, Nagasaki, etc.). Gods and power-holders had difficulty putting up with anything that might have had the same importance as they did.

The modern city can only attain civic society, urbanity and culture within the framework of an open society. In this vein, it is wrong to reduce the city to a city planning or political concept. Such an approach to the city usually generates conflicts and great misfortunes. Both town planners and politicians look at the city as a blueprint for intervention, and when reality throws obstacles in their way, they either hate the city or destroy it.

The memory of historical cities is often destroyed when modern city planning undertakes the task of simplification. The same thing occurred in politics when cities such as Vukovar, Dubrovnik, Mostar and Sarajevo became obstacles to the eradication of memory and were therefore disliked. For power-holders who wanted to recreate a homogeneous and closed society, Sarajevo was the symbol of an odious, open and pluralistic city. For proponents of the rigid state model of an ethnic-based state, Sarajevo was the symbol of a hostile city in the true sense, for it was Aristotle who showed that the goal of the city is not unity and homogeneity, but rather diversity.

The city is, simultaneously, organized memory and consented construction, nature and culture, the past and the future. Salmon Rushdie said that 'Sarajevo exists as an idea, a fictitious Sarajevo, whose destruction and suffering make exiles of us all. This Sarajevo represents something like an ideal, a city in which the values of pluralism, tolerance and coexistence created a united and elastic culture. People from Sarajevo do not define themselves as members of a clan or religious group but, simply and honourably, as citizens. If that city should disappear, then we all become its refugees. If the culture of Sarajevo dies, we all become its orphans' (Rushdie, 1994: 218).

The philosophical concept of the city as 'the experience of differences' surpasses the pre-eminence and claim-laying of town planners and politicians. Politics and town planning have transformed the government into a rigorous controller of the city's social space. An open city, as a place of urbanity, is most meaningful if it prevents the realization of this type of manipulation and domination. Diversity, that specific feature of pluralism, is what distinguishes the modern city from other forms of institutionalizing of the political community; such forms always symbolize the dominant factor (the state, ethnic group) and as such generate exclusivity.

In addition to other human rights, people today have the right to the city as a place preserving the 'experience of differences'.

Notes

1 Quoted from Peća J. Marković, 1992. See, in the same book, comments regarding the psychological resistance to industry and the city, 46–47.

2 'In the First World War, 5% of the casualties were civilians; in the Second World war 45%; in the Korean War 85%; and in the Vietnam war 95% ... The percentage in Bosnia is close to that in Vietnam.' From a declaration by the organizers of the protest meeting in Belgrade on 28 January 1995.

3 The very systematic technique of the siege, and Karadžić's abundant flow of words to justify it, indicate the singularity of his motive. The attacks were not intended merely to hammer Sarajevo, 'to kill the city in it', and to punish it for its former spirit of tolerance and cosmopolitanism, but also to cleanse it ethnically and regenerate it nationally. Radovan Karadžić proposed that Sarajevo be divided into ethnic units that had never been either units or ethnic' (see Bogdan Bogdanović 1994: 57).

4 Biljana Plavšić considers 'cosmopolitanism to be a luxury that can only be practised when the national (ethnic) question is resolved and a state is set up' (V, No. 51, 26 December 1994).

The Unresolved Genocide

SRĐAN BOGOSAVLJEVIĆ

Yugoslavia was, according to its pre-Second World War borders, one of the countries with the highest number of war victims, the greatest amount of war damage and the worst effects of genocide. The question of indifference with respect to the war victims therefore arises[1]—while there may be political motives for this indifference, there can be no justification. The fact that in the only register of the victims of war no attempt was made to collect data on the perpetrators of crimes as well, reveals something of the motives of the then leadership of Yugoslavia: there was an unwillingness to stir up and bring into the forefront the barely pacified intolerance among nations that had reached its peak during the war. Thus, the delay in carrying out a serious analysis of the war victims, in compiling lists of victims, as well as in identifying those responsible for the suffering, even at the lowest level, and, naturally, delays in their sentencing, have created room for manipulation and exaggeration.

At worst, it is not impossible to view the present conflict as a continuation of the 1941–1945 war, since the highest numbers of victims and the most brutal clashes occurred in more or less the same areas. Retaliation for what had been done earlier, and fear of a renewal of genocide (irrespective of whether this fear was justified or not), were, at the same time, if not the moving force behind the war, then certainly an important element in motivating the masses.

Launching an investigation now, or even a few years ago, at a time when it served as an overture to the dissolution of Yugoslavia in the war, rather than at a time when many of the facts could have been checked, is in many ways a futile undertaking. Today, one can carry out a critical review of the estimates and appraisals given in previous years, and perhaps by establishing some irrefutable facts one can manage to ascertain the minimum number of victims. Naturally, most disputes regarding the war victims are based on easily recognizable ideology and propaganda, and thus do not merit more serious analysis. If one were to fall into this trap, the discussion on war victims might easily be transformed into a statistical essay which would yield conclusions contrary to those desired and bring to the forefront questions as to who is lying, how much and why, instead of questions concerning crimes and sufferings. In that respect, exaggerating the number of victims—the Serbs—especially in Jasenovac, is just as offensive as minimizing the numbers. Such exaggerations most frequently come from Serbian and Croatian circles that can be regarded as nationalistic, and even warmongering, and as such they will not be taken into account in this paper.

The discussion on the estimates of the number of victims in the Second World War will focus on three aspects: a survey and appraisal (of the more serious)[2] existing estimates; a survey and appraisal of the registration of war victims from 1964; and an estimation of the minimum number of victims.

The existing estimates

In this paper we will discuss the estimate published in the Report of the Reparation Commission of the Government of the Federal People's Republic of Yugoslavia (FPRY) in the document *Human and Material Losses in the War Effort 1941–1945;* the estimate of Dragoljub Tasić published in the foreword to the *Population Census 1948*, Volume I; the estimate of Ivo Lah, published in the *Statistička revija* (Statistical Review) in 1951; the estimate of Dolfe Vogelnik, published in the *Statistička revija* 1952; foreign estimates[3] (Princeton University and Frukman); the estimate of Bogoljub Kočović in the study *The Victims of the World War Two in Yugoslavia* from 1985, and the estimate of Vladimir Žerjavić in the study *The Losses of the Population of Yugoslavia in the Second World War* from 1989.

A general appraisal

There are significant differences among the estimates of war victims quoted here, although the available documents and the methodological approach are more or less the same. In this respect the only official estimate, that of the Reparation Commission of the

FPRY, was carried out on the basis of extremely scanty material (data on the number of inhabitants after the Second World War were lacking) and with very little time available for systematizing the material and statistical and demographic calculations.

The majority of these estimates were calculated by using very similar methodological approaches based on differences between the results of the censuses from the years 1931 and 1948. Different authors compared the results of these two censuses in different ways as regards the territory included, and by starting from different hypotheses on birth rates, mortality and migration they came to different conclusions as to the potential number of inhabitants in 1948. Finally, different authors reached different estimates as to the possible drop in the birth rate due to the war, and as to the number of people who left the country during and immediately after the war.

Table 1

Estimate	Victims	Demographic loss
FPRY - 1947	1,709,000	N/A
Tasić - 1948	1,400,000	2,428,000
Princeton - 1948	N/A	1,200,000
Frukman - 1948	1,500,000	N/A
Lah - 1951	1,000,000	2,100,000
Vogelnik - 1952	1,800,000	2,854,000
Kočović - 1985	1,014,000	1,985,000
Žerjavić - 1989	1,027,000	2,022,000
min.	1,000,000	1,200,000
max.	1,800,000	2,854,000
average	1,350,000	2,098,167
SD	315,347	500,897
average–2*	1,330,000	2,133,750
SD–2*	271,700	174,883

* without minimum and maximum

The first post-war estimates

The first published estimate of the number of victims of the Second World War in Yugoslavia was presented as a finding of the Reparation Commission of the Government of the Federal Peoples' Republic of Yugoslavia (FPRY). The figure 1.7 million was used by Yugoslav officials and was regarded as the 'official' estimate, that is, it was the number given in most textbooks, if any mention of the subject was made at all. It is mainly for this reason, rather than the methodology used in the calculations, that this figure deserves comment.

First of all, the estimate of the government of the FPRY was reached before the first post-war census, which means that it was based on estimated population trends. In most other approaches, the shortcoming lies in the remoteness of the census years from the period for which the demographic loss should have been calculated, that is, the size of the population had there been no war. In the case of the first estimate, there were no even partially reliable data on the size of the Yugoslav population after the war.

The author responsible for this calculation, Vojislav Vukčević, Ph.D., in his text published in the magazine *Naša Reč* (Our Word)[4] presented several additional details, starting from the bizarre fact that he, as a student of mathematics employed at the Federal Bureau of Statistics, was given only two weeks to complete such a complex task, together with the instructions that 'the figure must be significant and based on science and statistics'. What is more important is that Vukčević stated that he had estimated the number of inhabitants by comparing the statistical sources of neighbouring countries with the results of some sample investigations that were available to him in 1947. However, most important of all is his statement that he had calculated demographic losses,[5] and that they were turned into 'victims' in the final version of his text. If this statement is accepted as true, it could be concluded, on the basis of a comparison of the relationship between demographic and real losses presented by other authors, that Vukčević could have come to an estimate of between 800,000 and 950,000 war victims. As he himself stated that he had not taken into account losses on the fronts of Srem and Bosnia, which, according to him, amounted to about 100,000 human lives, it appears that his estimate could have been very close to the estimates of Kočović and Žerjavić, calculated much later.

No appraisal of the methodological value and shortcomings of this work can be given, as there are no original papers showing the way the work was done; at the same time, the author's testimony does not offer sufficient data, beyond the fact that his results are very close to figures in the Kočović study, which was very highly valued by Vukčević.

The next estimate we shall touch upon here was published in the foreword of Volume 1 of *The Census of 1948*, by Dimitrije Tasić. As he was a well-known expert on demography and on the population of Yugoslavia, and as the book was written at a time when data were available which made possible a correct methodological approach, this paper certainly merits attention. Compared to all the other studies, Tasić estimated a higher percentage of real losses within the demographic losses—that is, 58 per cent. Lah gives only demographic losses, and immediately after him, Vogelnik estimated both demographic and real losses.

A comparison of these four estimates places the number of real victims at somewhere between 600,000[6] and 1,800,000, and demographic losses at somewhere between 1,200,000 and 2,854,000. Such a difference is astonishing, especially when one knows that all four authors were employed at the same institution—the Bureau of Statistics—that all of them were well-informed about the work of the other three regarding estimates of war losses, and that the lowest ranking among them, Vukčević, published the first estimate, while the highest ranking, Vogelnik, who was director of the Bureau, was the last one to publish. In addition, the last three estimates were based on the same data and the same methodological approach, which leads to the conclusion that these estimates on migration, birth rates and mortality were, at different moments, adjusted according to different political and 'patriotic' motives.

The estimates of Kočović and Žerjavić

The estimates calculated by Kočović and Žerjavić are far more detailed, contain better argumentation, and are presented more fully than the estimates of the four researchers employed at the Federal Bureau of Statistics.

The differences between these two estimates are extremely small and relate not to the total number of victims, but primarily to the regional and national structure of the figures. Kočović's estimate of 1,014,000 and Žerjavić's estimate of 1,027,000 differ by only 13,000, and as it is quite certain that this method of calculation produces a far greater statistical error, these two estimates can easily be rounded to the figure of one million war victims. The estimates of demographic losses by these two authors can be analysed in a similar manner: Kočović gave a figure of 1,985,000, and Žerjavić 2,022,000, which can both be rounded off to two million. Both authors agree, as do all other available sources, that the highest demographic losses were suffered by Bosnia-Hercegovina, followed by Croatia, Serbia and Montenegro, while fewest losses were suffered by Slovenia and Macedonia. It is estimated that both the highest number of victims and the highest demographic losses occurred in Bosnia-Hercegovina and Croatia—namely, in the territory of the then NDH (the so-called Independent State of Croatia). Serbia had a relatively high demographic loss, primarily because of the high loss in Vojvodina, which was almost completely deserted by the Germans who were highly represented there before the war.

Kočović and Žerjavić differ mostly in their estimates of the number of victims by nationality, especially in their estimate of the number of victims among Montenegrins, Slovenes and Moslems.

Table 2

War Victims	Kočović	Žerjavić	Overlapping in %
Serbs	487,000	530,000	91.9
Montenegrins	50,000	20,000	40.0
Croats	207,000	192,000	92.8
Moslems	86,000	103,000	83.5
Slovenes	32,000	42,000	76.2
Macedonians	7,000	6,000	85.7

According to these two authors, the greatest war losses, in terms of the expected number of inhabitants, were suffered by Serbs and Moslems (nearly 7% of the population perished during the war). Between 5 and 5.5 per cent of Croats perished, as well as a little under 3 per cent of Slovenes and less than 1 per cent of Macedonians. The biggest difference is in the proportion of Montenegrins who perished: according to Žerjavić this was around 4 per cent, and according to Kočović over 10 per cent.

It should be pointed out that these two authors calculated estimates of the losses of non-Slav peoples in Yugoslavia during the Second World War. Particularly high losses were suffered by the Jews (according to Kočovič, 60,000 or 77.9% of all Jews in Yugoslavia) and Romanies (27,000 or 31.4%).

The Serbs as Victims

All available data and research point to the fact that, expressed in absolute figures and by percentage, the number of Serbs who perished in the Second World War was extremely high. Kočović and Žerjavić compared the number of Serbs who died with the potential number of Serbs in the whole territory of Yugoslavia. However, if one looks at the territorial distribution of the war victims, their concentration in the area covered by the NDH, particularly the part in which the Serbs formed the majority of the population, is clearly visible. Accordingly, if the Serbs are divided into two groups—those who lived under the authority of the NDH and those living east of the river Drina—then the percentage of losses changes considerably: whereas relatively few Serbs perished in the area of central Serbia (where the majority of Serbs lived), in some parts of the NDH whole settlements were destroyed. According to Kočović, 16.3 per cent of Serbs from Croatia and 14.6 per cent of Serbs from Bosnia-Hercegovina perished as war victims—which means one in every six.

Demographic losses among the Serbs were similarly estimated: 380,000 in the territory of the NDH, more than in the territory of the Serbia proper.

The registration of war victims (carried out in 1964)

The methodological bases and the shortcomings of the registration

The registration of war victims was carried out in November 1964, almost twenty years after the war had ended. Preparations for this registration started seven years earlier, motivated by the idea of submitting a reparation request to the Federal Republic of Germany. The original idea that the registration be carried out by the War Veterans' Union was changed after a trial registration was effected in June 1963. According to a decision of the SIV (Federal Executive Council) of 10 June 1964, the Federal Commission for the Registration of War Victims was founded, which, in co-operation with statistical institutions, elaborated methodology and organized the collecting of data. These commissions were formed at all levels, from federal to republican to district and county levels. The commissions were made of representatives of the war veterans' unions, socio-political communities, the army and statistical institutions.

Along with the shortcomings that were only to be expected due to the so-called memory effect,[7] the composition of the commissions gives rise to suspicion concerning the objectivity of registration. It can easily be seen that more details were given in the registration of innocent victims in the civilian population and the victims who were either on the victorious side or totally neutral than for victims among members of the local population who were linked to, or recruited into, the Ustashi, Domobran, Chetniks and other formations, which were treated as enemies and quislings by the partisan movement and by the new Yugoslav authorities.

Although this registration gives a list of indisputable war victims, it can in no way be regarded as final. The total number of registered victims should be supplemented by 'ideologically unsuitable' victims and victims about whom there was no one to submit data[8]. Compensation should also be made for the so-called memory effect.

It was planned in the registration methodology to collect data on the following victims of the war and of the fascist terror:

a) those interned, imprisoned, deported, taken to forced labour camps or taken as prisoners of war, regardless of whether they were assassinated or killed, or whether they died, disappeared or survived the terror;

b) members of the Royal Yugoslav Army killed in the period from 6 April to 7 June 1941;

c) members of the National Liberation Army and Partisan Detachments of Yugoslavia and the alllied military formations killed before 15 May 1945, or who died as a result of war wounds before 15 May 1946;

d) civilians killed during the bombardments in the period from 6 April 1941 to 15 May 1942; and

e) civilians who lost their lives as victims of direct terror by the enemy and the enemy's collaborators in the period from 6 April 1941 to 15 May 1945.

It was obvious, even from the formulation of the task of registration commissions, that the registration would not be complete, as it was not planned to collect data on the victims who were not affected by direct terror by 'the enemy and the enemy's collaborators' or on the victims in the armed forces of 'the enemy and the enemy's collaborators'.

Immediately after the registration, field control of inclusion was effected. The strictest control was in Croatia, where it was found that the rate of non-inclusion varied from 2 per cent in Split, 4 per cent in Zadar, 5 per cent in Rijeka and 6 per cent in Karlovac, to up to 12 per cent in Osijek. It was established that in Banjaluka there were as many as 28 per cent of households not included, while in Serbia and Macedonia supplementary registrations were carried out.

All republican commissions, save the Macedonian one, deemed the registration successful. The registration data were processed in the Federal Bureau of Statistics, and the whole documentation was stored in 2,800 crates in The Archives of Yugoslavia.

The Federal Registration Commission, in the introduction to its report (marked 'for limited distribution' and printed in 1966), gave its own estimate of the number of victims and the demographic losses, in order to be able to estimate the response to the registration. The difference between the estimate of the number of inhabitants for 1948, based on demographic model designed by Dušan Breznik, Ph.D., and the actual data for 1948, was 2,056,510, which would represent the estimate of demographic losses, accepted by the commission. The commission was of the opinion that 500,000 Germans and 100,000 Italians and others left Yugoslavia during and immediately after the war. The result is a shortfall of 1,456,000, which should be further lessened by the effects of increased mortality and a lower birth rate during the war, and therefore the commission concluded that the registration included between 56 and 59 per cent of actual war victims. This calculation has no methodological deficiencies and leads to the conclusion that the number of actual victims could have been about 1.1 million, which was contrary to the widespread belief that in Yugoslavia there were 1.7 million war victims.

The results of the registration of war victims—processed, but marked for 'limited distribution'—were treated as a state secret. Except for a small number of copies distributed according to a special list, the remaining part of the press run was kept separately and then destroyed in the early 1980s. The Federal Executive Council lifted the embargo on these data in the late 1980s. The Federal Bureau of Statistics renewed the entry of all data and the processing of data, and created a database on the registered war victims. The list of almost all 600,000 registered victims was printed, as well as a book on the war victims in the NDH and Jewish war victims, but only in ten copies. The limited press run of the published list and the psychosis caused by the dissolution of Yugoslavia in the latest war, again gave a stamp of official secrecy to this material, although without a formal decision. [9]

The results of the registration of war victims

The final result of the registration provided a summary review of the registered war victims: 597,323 assassinated, killed, dead and disappeared, and 509,846 surviving war victims. The distribution by republic is shown in Table 3.

Table 3

Republic	Non-survivors	Survivors
Bosnia-Hercegovina	153,449	41,080
Montenegro	14,423	11,450
Croatia	185,685	103,377
Macedonia	18,745	29,816
Slovenia	41,597	104,008
Serbia	183,424	220,118

Currently, interest in the distribution of war victims by nationality is far greater than interest in their distribution by region.[10]

Table 4

	Total	Bosnia-Hercegovina	Monte-negro	Croatia	Mace-donia	Slovenia	Serbia
Serbs	58.0	72.3	3.4	50.2	6.9	0.6	80.5
Croats	13.9	4.1	1.3	37.4	0.2	0.8	1.6
Slovenes	7.0	0.1	0.3	0.5	0.2	97.9	0.4
Macedonians	1.1	0.0	0.1	0.0	3.3	0.0	0.2
Montenegrins	3.1	0.2	89.3	0.1	0.6	0.1	1.7
Moslems	5.4	16.7	4.6	0.0	0.2	0.0	1.1
Jews	7.5	6.0	0.1	5.8	50.4	0.1	8.9
	100	100	100	100	100	100	100

Statistical limits to the number of victims

It is not possible to give a sufficiently reliable estimate of the number of victims of the Second World War in the territory of former Yugoslavia on the basis of available statistical materials, for the following reasons:

a) the pre-war census was taken ten years prior to the war, and the post-war census three years after the end of the war;

b) there are no reliable war records on civilian victims (from German, Ustashi, Chetnik, Partisan etc. sources),

c) the registration of the war victims was carried out late—twenty years after the war—and was never offered for public review in order to be supplemented while there were still a relatively large number of witnesses;

d) a partial correction of the borders of Yugoslavia was made in such a way that the pre-war and post-war Yugoslavia differed by 8,262 square kilometres, as the territories of Istria, the Slovenian littoral, Zadar and the islands (according to the Peace Treaty with Italy of 15 September 1947) and of Zone B, namely, the counties of Kopar and Buje (according to the London Agreement of 5 October 1954) were added to Yugoslavia;

e) after the Second World War a completely new territorial division was effected, so that the data from the 1948 and 1953 censuses of the newly established republics and counties within them are not directly comparable to the data of the 1931 census, carried out according to the territorial units of the Kingdom of Yugoslavia; and

f) during and immediately after the war a mass emigration took place—of Germans, Italians and Hungarians on the one hand, and ideological opponents of the new regime on the other.

All these factors introduce a high degree of uncertainty into the calculations on demographic and real losses, which increases if we look for more detailed answers by territorial classifications or categories of victims. However, the first lower limit was set by the registration of war victims carried out in 1964, which put the number of victims at almost 600,000. It is highly probably that this registration did not include (or included only some) 'ideologically'[11] unsuitable persons, those about whom there was no one to supply data, and those names which were omitted by accident. The victims of the other side—in the Ustashi, Chetnik, Domobran and similar formations, or those shot by partisan authorities or on their orders—were not registered at all. The number of victims among the Jews was enormous, so that in the case of a great number of victims there were no surviving members of the family to supply data. The situation was similar with the Romanies, as well as with some other, smaller isolated groups of various nationalities. Finally, in the wave of post-war migration, many witnesses moved to other parts of the country. It can be stated that the registration set a lower limit, which was certainly considerably surpassed.

By a rough estimate based on the registration of war victims, the results of the 1931, 1948 and 1953 censuses, statistical records, hypotheses on migrations and on the proportions of the population directly engaged against the partisan movement, one can reach an approximate figure for the actual number of war victims. A figure between 890,000 and 1,200,000 is in accordance with the estimates of Kočović and Žerjavić which are within this range. The report of the Federal Bureau of Statistics also estimates that the registration of the war victims from 1964 enompassed 56 to 58 per cent of the total number of victims, so that this estimate would also fall within the range calculated here. Finally, the Federal Commission for the Registration of Victims in 1964 stated in its report that the registration encompassed 60 to 65 per cent of the expected victims. Therefore, according to this estimate the it could be expected that a little over 800,000 victims would be recorded. Since according to this methodology it was not intended to record the victims of the 'opposite' side, it can be considered that this figure fits into the range calculated.

Table 5

	Registration 1964	minimum non-recorded	maximum non-recorded	minimum (rounded)	maximum (rounded)
Serbs and Montenegrins	365,016	100,000	230,000	460,000	590,000
Croats	83,251	110,000	190,000	190,000	270,000
Moslems	32,300	40,000	60,000	70,000	95,000
Slovenes	42,027	1,000	8,000	43,000	50,000
Macedonians	6,724	300	3,000	7,000	10,000
Jews	45,000	15,000	20,000	60,000	70,000
Romanics/ Gypsies	10,000	10,000	25,000	20,000	35,000
Hungarians	2,690	2,000	5,000	5,000	8,000
Albanians	3,241	1,500	6,000	5,000	9,000
Germans	–	20,000	30,000	20,000	30,000
Others	9,996	6,000	13,000	16,000	23,000
Total	597,323			896,000	1,210,000

Naturally, it is not difficult to find a number of calculations, particularly in the press of the emigrant pro-chetnik and pro-Ustasha population, or in the opinions given on the basis of statements by witnesses, about much higher or sometimes much lower numbers of victims. Politicized or emotional exaggerations can be expected and were particularly likely in the immediate post-war years. However, time has shown that the victims had to be recorded, and as high a number as possible of those guilty for their death punished, or at least identified. Had that been done without delay, one huge disaster could not have been used as an instrument for the preparation and implementation of a new, similar disaster, but this time with a different national structure of victims.

Notes

1 The term 'war victims' in this context refers only to those who were killed or who died during the war. 'War victims', 'victims' and 'real losses' are used as synonyms and do not refer to the wounded or otherwise physically injured (although these are also, indisputably, victims of war).

2 Serious—in a mathematical and statistical sense. Only those papers which deal with estimates based on demographic or other mathematical and statistical analyses are taken into account. A number of papers which rely on historical proofs, testimonies or subjective estimates have not been taken into account.

3 These two estimates are not sufficiently well founded to be classified as 'serious', although they are frequently quoted, and therefore taken into account in this paper.

4 *Naša Reč* was a magazine published in London until 1990, within the Oslobođenje (Liberation) Association which acted as an organization of emigres of republican and democratic orientation. The first edition of the study by Bogoljub Kočović, Ph. D., was published within the series 'Naše Delo' (Our Work) launched by Oslobodjenje.

5 Demographic losses encompass those killed and those who died during the war, the drop in birth rate due to the war, and emigration, that is, the migration balance.

6 If one supposes that at least half of the demographic losses are real victims.

7 The 'memory effect', i.e. the effect of errors in memory, or of oblivion, was not studied particularly in Yugoslavia, but it is a known fact that it must exist after a certain period, even with respect to the most memorable events. On the other hand, one cannot neglect the effect of *pogibeljomanija* (catastrophe-mania), as, according to Desimir Tošić, the painter Mića Popović called the passion among Yugoslav peoples to exaggerate the number of victims in story-telling. However, if it exists, the joint effect of these two effects would have to be negative, i.e. it is most probable that there is a number of 'forgotten' victims.

8 In some cases, whole settlements were wiped out and there were no survivors who could provide information about the event. It is espe-

cially characteristic for the Jews and the Romanies, and sometimes for some urban families. Finally, in some areas no witnesses of war sufferings could be found because of the high rate of migration which took place immediately after the war.

9 Only about ten copies of this set of books, together with the list of the war victims, were distributed and they are not available either in libraries or in the market. The database is not accessible to the public.

10 The table lists only those nations which had over one percentage point of the total losses, while the others can be found in the difference of the sum of seven listed nationalities and the figure 100.

11 In the already quoted methodological guidelines for the registration of war victims it was clearly stressed which categories of victims were to be registered, so that some of the victims of the population not intended to be registered can be considered as ideologically unsuitable victims.

Who Exploited Whom?

LJUBOMIR MADŽAR

In all the republics that made up the Socialist Federal Republic of Yugoslavia (SFRY), there is a prevailing belief that they suffered economic losses as a result of the arrangement of the common state. The devastating effects of the system combined—according to both widely held popular belief and professional economic scholarship—into an indivisible amalgam that allowed weaknesses to be ascribed to what was widely perceived as the exploitative nature of common life. Compromised by such a structurally defective system, the ultimate consequence of the idea of community was the firmly held belief in each individual republic's abuse at the hands of all the others.

Each republic's emphasis on its own losses, and its equally vehement stress on the exploitative strategies and policies *of the others,* were politically instrumentalized to the end and became the most efficient means for the amassing of political capital, both before the breakup of the country and in the first year following its disintegration. This alleged exploitation, whether or not it had any foundation in real movements and relations, became a specific catapult for the launching of new, or renewed, political elites.

One of the major weaknesses in the old economic system was its lack of transparency. Whenever key currents of production and (re)distribution become a matter for political bias and overall voluntarism, a lack of transparency becomes unavoidable. It is the immediate effect of the arbitrariness of political mediation: that which is not based on any objective or predictable factors cannot be understood, let alone meaningfully articulated. As Hayek explained several years ago (1979 [1944]: 42–53, 79–81), there is no way politically to regulate numerous economic issues without destructive conflicts, nor can there be any decision that does not leave the majority—often all—of the participants bitter at the absence, or even loss, of their rights. Thus lack of transparency in the system inevitably leaves participants feeling exploited, and when this lack of transparency becomes an active instrument in political manipulation, it is clear that destructive effects in many parts of the system, as well as in the system as a whole, are inevitable. It was hard for any participant in the politically orchestrated game of creating and distributing revenue, to avoid the trauma of exploitation.

General frames for relations between the republics

The frames within which the relative position of certain republics could be altered depended on an apparently trivial, but nevertheless important, arithmetic fact. Relative position was measured by appropriate levels of revenue per capita and, in particular, by the relative relationship among these revenues defined throughout certain republics and regions. If the revenue of one republic was twice the size of that of another—which, before the disintegration, was approximately the relationship between Serbia and Slovenia— any given transfer would produce in the smaller republic proportionately twice the change produced in the larger one. When revenue flowed from the larger into the smaller republic, the resulting percentage increase, in terms of both total and per capita income of the smaller republic, would be twice the proportional decrease in the larger republic.

The results described here can be well illustrated in the concrete empirical evidence. Based on the detailed picture recently presented by Marsenić (1992: 10–11, 13, 22), it turns out that the present FRY contributed approximately 38 per cent to the social revenue of the SFRY, of which 36 per cent came from Serbia, and just under 2 per cent from Montenegro. Taking into account the fact that levels of development were below average, participation in the SFRY population was significantly higher, for the three areas mentioned they were (around) 44 per cent, (over) 41 per cent, and (less than) 3 per cent. If the equivalent of 1 per cent SFRY social revenue were to flow from Serbia to Slovenia, it would increase Slovenia's social revenue by 5 per cent, and reduce Serbia's by 2.8 per cent. The same relations would exist if the transfer were to be made in the opposite direction: social revenue (total and *per capita*) would have to decrease in Slovenia by 5 per cent in order to be enlarged by just 2.8 per cent in Serbia.

The following conclusion can immediately be reached according to these calculations. In a community such as the Yugoslav community, big republics could not, through transfer or analogous flows—in the obviously relevant sense of the relative changes of total and *per capita* income—either gain much, or lose much. However, the small republics faced exactly the opposite situation: they could gain and lose a lot. The resulting inter-republic exploitation would not be manifested in the same ways, nor would it appear in the same light in the small and large republics.

Three conclusions may be drawn from this. First, the motivation for finding ways to influence the direction and intensity of transfer *varied* in different republics, and depended on their (economic) size. The large republics were less interested either in securing the flow to their advantage, or in taking preventive measures to stop flow to their disadvantage. Secondly, relying on the standard attitude to the declining liminal usefulness of revenue, smaller republics were in a less favourable position than larger ones: for a given average level of social revenue, precisely because of the potential for big deviations in both directions, their security equivalent was obviously smaller. Thirdly, in the perspective of possible economic changes through transfers (and different flows) of revenue, the position of Serbia and Montenegro was significantly different; among the SFRY republics, Serbia was the largest, and Montenegro the smallest.

It is worth noting that the larger republics (and peoples) were better protected in a strictly political sense. Many things which influence a republic's economic position are decided upon, directly or indirectly, through differently formalized majority ruling. On many fronts, the larger republics can outvote the small ones. Thus the non-democratic nature of the (real) socialist order in the SFRY, until its dissolution, disabled democratic voting because there were no authentic procedures for democratic decision-making.

In scholarly discussions and popular presentations, the possibilities of inter-republic exploitation were perceived as the logical and operative consequences of three different mechanisms. *Firstly,* revenue flowed illegally and undemocratically through differences in prices. In most cases, differences were not defined clearly or precisely. They were usually determined as deviations from relative prices with regard to the relevant world standards. Flows were possible only if the economic structures were different throughout the republics and if, in some of them, the structure was superior in the sense of above-average inclusion of the sectors that were privileged when it came to prices. Thus, the republics and the regions which had a high participation of sectors with artificially reduced and depressed prices, were exploited. If, through the depressed prices, agriculture paid for industrialization, agricultural areas were exploited—that is, peasant Serbia, the lowland grain producing areas of Vojvodina and Slavonia, parts of Bosnia and Kosovo. *Secondly*, through specialization towards higher or lower phases of processing, some regions exploited others. The assumption was that the greater revenue was made in higher phases. This may be because they are characterized by a lower capital coefficient (giving the advantage of a greater potential expansion with lower investment), which offers wider possibilities for the mobilization of the complementary (in relation to permanently scarce capital) production factors, or because they enjoy advantages of relatively low prices. The first two reasons for the advantages of higher phases of processing are similar, and the third one is closely related to disparity in prices, covered by the previous (*first*) mechanism. *Thirdly*, the closing of one's own markets and making as much use as possible use of the markets of other was strongly emphasized, especially more recently, as a powerful, and in many ways harmful, factor of exploitation. Here we have a significant increase in the degree of mobilization of the available economic potential, at the expense of other republics/regions, by way of using their demand and through fencing off their own markets in order to prevent them reciprocally using the advantages of markets benefiting from this. This relation is equivalent to the famous export of unemployment, which, in international trade theory, is termed a 'beggar-your-neighbour' policy. At least one scholar (Aghiri 1972) has built a well-rounded and very radical theory of international exploitation of global proportions precisely on this mechanism.

Fiscal mechanisms and institutional determinants of inter-republic economic relations

The mechanisms described above are strictly tied to the market. All three of them were, almost without exception, emphasized in the undeveloped republics and in Serbia, which in the last years emphasized attributes of its own underdevelopment, and even managed to institutionalize them to a certain extent.

On the other hand, the developed north-western republics emphasized the mechanism of non-market distribution. Great expen-

diture on the federal apparatus, especially the Yugoslav People's
Army (JNA), as well as proportional taxation of the social revenue
(a principle of taxing force), meant that these republics participated much more in the immediate financing of the federal bureaucracy and the military establishment. There were serious preoccupations and more hidden doubts than open discussions about
the (always to some extent mysterious) flow of primary money,
through which a vast amount of real resources were expropriated,
including, of course, the resources owned by the developed republics. Contributions were also made towards the development of the
underdeveloped regions. Despite the fact that these never exceeded 2 per cent of the social revenue, they were politically irri-
tating, since they required a direct outflow of cash which was inef-
ficiently used and irrationally spent, and over which the donors
had no control.

Despite the fact that the total funds for the underdeveloped regions—via the Fund for the Underdeveloped Regions, and in the
form of additional budget resources—were usually just over 1.5 per
cent of Yugoslav national revenue, they shook the Yugoslav political structure. The percentage is not, in fact, all that small. One
should remember that the burden on Germany of war reparations,
which caused incredible hyperinflation and destroyed the economic and social life of Germany, was equivalent, after it was re-
programmed, to payments of 2.5 per cent of the GNP between
1925 and 1932 (Sachs and Laraine 1993: 706). In some, albeit rare
years contributions to the subvention of public spending in the
undeveloped regions, and for stimulating their development,
reached as much as 45 per cent of the reparations which burdened
Germany and significantly contributed to its fascisization. In international circles and organizations, Yugoslavia was regarded as a
special country because it cared so much about its undeveloped
regions, and proved it by large financial contributions.

The levels of dissatisfaction, and of feelings of being exploited
because of these contributions, varied greatly from region to
region. Of course, those that had contributed the most felt most
exploited, and there were rumours and accusations from Serbia,
which, with extensive and critically neglected regions of its own,
had contributed much to the undeveloped regions in other republics. Thus, contributions for undeveloped regions caused widespread feelings of severe, and of course unjust, economic abuse,
and Serbia very noticeably shared those feelings, despite the fact
that it was, through Kosovo, one of the main users of the funds for
the undeveloped regions!

A distinctively academic, but never seriously understood, idea regarding the exploitation of the undeveloped regions by the developed republics and wider regions was circulated for a long time. Serbia found its place in that version of threat through exploitation. Almost all productive capital in the SFRY was state-owned. Both the economists and the wider public had understood for a long time that capital is productive, and, most importantly, that with more capital one could, and usually did, realize more revenue. The proprietary status of the social means of production in its normative aspect had to lead to a situation in which part of the revenue that came as a result of the capital ('the social dividend') was equally (strictly speaking, to the same amount) given and used by *all* Yugoslav citizens. However, the operational arrangements of the economic system, as well as existing practice, led to a situation in which the capital revenue accumulated and remained where the capital itself was located. Whoever had more capital was in a position to amass more revenue from that capital, and an empirical connection was established between the technical equipment available and (total) per worker revenue. Those who received a relatively greater sum of the 'social' capital to 'manage' was in a position to appropriate more, and to secure greater individual and public ('general and common') spending. From a normative point of view, this resulted in exploitation. Since the Slovenes, in relation to the number of employees and citizens, received more of the *common* capital to 'manage', they were able, for example, to realize greater expenditure. They secured part of their spending by illegitimately appropriating revenue arising from the 'common' capital as well, which they received for managing *only* as a mere precondition for the organization of work processes. Of course, if implicit proprietary rights are adopted, and if they are ascribed to those on whose territory the capital is located—and this was presupposed to a great extent and was expressed both in the economic policies and in the legal system—then that argument becomes invalid.

A subtle interpretation of the exploitation idea was based on the empirically based, theoretically cleared, and institutionally conditioned insufficient mobility of the social capital. The analysis of low mobility and its unfavourable economic effects goes right back to the 1960s (cf. Madžar 1965). Unsatisfactory mobility was conditioned by the unsettled property status of the social means of production. Capital-based revenue, investment, and enterprising were institutionally disabled, and companies therefore had neither the motivation nor the ability to invest in the expansion of other companies, or to establish new units. They *could not* reap the resulting effects of eventual investment beyond the circle of alternatives tied to their own expansion. Moreover, when a new enterprise was formed, or when an existing one took control of capacities financed through external investment, the investor inevitably lost not only its share, but the capital as well. What remained was investment in one's own expansion as the only one possibility, which, if not attractive, was at least more or less acceptable. That, however, meant the reproducing of the existing structure of production, the very limited possibility of using development opportunities through corresponding changes in the assortment, and, quite simply, the absence of the highly needed mechanisms for the structural adjustment of economy.

How could this consideration be tied to (possible) exploitation? The emphasis is on the disparities between (relative) prices. If some prices were particularly high, and if, through them, since they had in their own structure a high proportion of the price-privileged sectors, some regions were extremely favoured, the question naturally arises as to why all the other areas did not economically re-structure so that they too could use the possibilities of extremely high prices. That would also have provided a precious offer pressure, which would have acted as a factor for eliminating disparity. Moreover, those hit by unfavourable prices could themselves be blamed for their own unfavourable economic position, because they were inert and insufficiently successful in structural readjustment. A response to the eventual counter-arguments such as these would be mechanism of insufficient capital mobility described above: producers in price-discriminated regions were unable to adjust their production structure in order to secure advantages from the disparity between prices, because it was made institutionally impossible. Low mobility froze the given structure, and such general circumstances enabled some areas to be favoured through deformed and unbalanced prices.

Among the general mechanisms of exploitation and the theoretical models that appear as their conceptual superstructure, one should also mention regional differentiation in the degree of monopolization of the economic structures. Here, only the markets engaged in inter-regional exchange will be considered. A monopoly is universally characterized as exploitative. When monopolists from region A sell (buy), at forced high (low) prices, goods and services from the competitively positioned producers (or consumers) in region B, then, obviously, A exploits B. The problem is simply that this mechanism, no matter how conceptually clear, cannot be operationalized.

The question of intensity and of the direction of the currents of revenue and wealth distribution will forever remain without an answer. Results of investigations in this delicate area will be partial, conditional and hypothetical. Those who enter discussions on inter-republic exploitation without extreme caution and many reservations, will reveal more about their own lack of education and objectivity, than about the subject of their insufficiently reasoned considerations.

The redistributive effects of the fiscal mechanisms

Fiscal mechanisms have traditionally been an object of bitter debate when it comes to the economic relations between areas within the same country, especially if these areas are institutionally defined, and if they possess attributes of statehood. Conflicts are possible, and universally present, in all types of countries, including unitary states, but they naturally develop most dramatically in federative countries. Where areas are equipped with adequate institutional structures, and where they have independent political and administrative executive bodies, it is natural that clearly formed interests also arise, and that interactions within these interests influence the political dynamics of the federative community as a whole.

It is generally known that budgets, among other things, act as powerful instruments of revenue redistribution and as correctors of market mechanisms, which are, in the phase of primary distribution, defined by the processes of decentralized allocation and evaluation and via the accompanying mechanisms of a spontaneous, autonomous decision-making. Approaching redistributive processes from the perspective of the undeveloped republics, interested in improving their relative position through one-way transfers, Bogoev (1989: 262–265, 272) points to significant redistributive effects of budgets in international relations, claiming that the corresponding redistributions in Yugoslavia were of modest scope. Among other things, he points out:

a) the insufficient direct transfers (gifts) that the developed regions directed towards the undeveloped ones;

b) the unequal regional structure of federal expenses, more favourable for the developed than for the undeveloped regions;

c) the transfer of too large a proportion of public spending to republic level, which significantly diminished the redistributive and equalizing effect of the federal budget;

d) the insufficient regional configuration of budget incentives in the economy, which were mostly directed to the developed regions;

e) the excessive reliance on indirect taxes, which had a regressive effect, and resulted in a situation where '... less developed republics and autonomous provinces participate relatively more than the developed ones in providing the overall means of the federation budget ...' (269); and

f) the fact that, besides the Fund for the Undeveloped Regions, which directed revenue to their advantage, there were also other funds which acted strongly in the opposite direction and cancelled a good many of the beneficent effects of the financial aid to less developed regions.

Some ten years earlier, the same point was made and strongly emphasized by Kiril Mijovski (1980: 23-24). He pointed out that besides the Fund for the Undeveloped Regions, there were three other 'funds', which all acted in favour of the developed regions, redirecting revenue flows towards those developed regions. The first of these was the fund for export credits, which indeed allocated most funds to the developed regions because of their orientation towards exports and the superior structure and quality of production on which that orientation leaned. Mijovski wrote that in 1970, funds redistributed through the fund for export credits with respect to the export of machinery and ships, reached 76 per cent of the funds redistributed through the fund for insufficiently developed regions and the province of Kosovo. This meant that through just one 'fund for the developed regions', a vast proportion of the effects of promoting the development of the undeveloped republics and the province of Kosovo were cancelled out. The other 'fund' was a consequence of the controlling of prices, which, due to differences in economic structure, affected different areas unequally. Because of the high proportion of agriculture and resources sectors, a much higher proportion of production in the undeveloped regions was hit by the price control: the undeveloped regions exchanged their cheap, control-affected products for much more expensive products, mostly located in the higher processing phases, which were valued in the free market. One could add that a surplus of demand, which always appears in the controlled segment of the market, flowed into the uncontrolled segment, which acted as an additional factor in deepening the disparity in prices. The third 'fund' was the high customs protection of products from the higher processing phases, which were markedly present in the structure of the developed regions, and the low protection, or the complete absence of protection in the case of raw materials and agricultural products, which dominated in the structure of undeveloped regions. Many empirical studies (for example, Kovačević 1973) have indeed pointed to marked interference in customs protection: it was kept at a very low level at lower processing phases, and increased with the increase in the processing level—systematically, predictably, and legally. One should note that the two latter flow mechanisms—price control and customs protection—belong to the area of relative prices and their disparities.

What is the importance of these considerations for the traumatic experience of exploitation which engulfed Serbia? Serbia *was not* an undeveloped region, and only in the late 1980s did it manage to obtain the status of a less developed area. Inasmuch as the results quoted reflect real relations and tendencies—and both Bogoev and Mijovski were experts in both Macedonian and Yugoslav economic scholarship, members of the Academy and specialists in relevant areas of expert analyses, Bogoev in public finances and Mijovski in regional development—Serbia had no basis for its belief that it was exploited by the undeveloped Yugoslav republics. Proving exploitation from that side would have to begin by disproving the results quoted above. The elements of the eventual exploitation should be sought in relations with the developed republics, which narrows the circle to only two republics: Croatia and Slovenia. Of course, one might say that Serbia was disadvantaged due to poor treatment of Kosovo, an undeveloped region which was an integral part of Serbia. That conclusion could be suggested by the argumentation of both scholars quoted above, and especially by their conclusions: viewed with respect to funds, the proportion is 3:1 in favour of the developed regions (Mijovski 1980: 24), and the desired redistributive effects of the fiscal mechanism in relations between republics and provinces 'have been reduced to a relatively small measure' (Bogoev 1989: 272). However, these statements could be answered by the counter-argument that the greatest part of the overall funds for the development of undeveloped regions was allocated to Kosovo. Between 1971 and 1975, Kosovo's share in the total net receipts was 39.6 per cent; and the next highest share went to Bosnia-Hercegovina, which recieved 26.1 per cent; for the next two five-year plans, the corresponding figures were 46.6 per cent and 22.3 per cent, and 55.4 per cent and 17.4 per cent (in this last case, Macedonia was in second place; Dimitreva and Stošić 1989: 425).

The position of Serbia (and its provinces), and the appearance of the eventual exploitation, could be viewed through three mechanisms. The first one relates to the federal budget—that is, the relationship between what Serbia paid into the federal budget and the amount it received from it, and, in particular, the part of the common expenses it had to cover itself. Was Serbia's per capita load below or above the average, or, likewise, how was its participation in the financing of the total federal expenses related to its share of the total population? Secondly, the same question can be put in relation to its contribution to various extra-budget funds—the fund for the undeveloped regions is relevant here—and its share of the resources which arrived through those funds. The third question is Serbia's position in primary distribution. In order not to elaborate too extensively, only a few general, partly illustrative, consideration will be provided about all three aspects of Serbia's position.

Primary distribution as a potential area for exploitation

Exchange is a frame for possible exploitation through prices. There is no exploitation without exchange. In 1987, a sufficiently representative year, Serbia exchanged 40.3 per cent of its social product with the other republics (all the figures in this paragraph are taken from Petrović and Cvjetičanin (eds.), 1991: 10–14). However, that figure also includes exchange with less-developed republics, and even the most fervent fighters against economic injustices could not determine that Serbia was exploited by them. The frame is narrowed further if one takes into account that exports to Slovenia and Croatia, potential exploiters of Serbia, were 21 per cent of its social product, while imports from those two republics amounted to 26 per cent of its social product. Calculating the exchange with the two republics as the average of exports and imports—in the same way as the total exchange of 40.3 per cent, mentioned above, was calculated—it appears that Serbia exchanged 23.5 per cent of its social product with Slovenia and Croatia. This participation implies that, in order to justify the claim of exploitation, prices would have to have diverged from their balanced level much more than appears at first sight.

In order to further narrow the area of the eventual (and, for Serbia, disadvantageous) asymmetry in exchange and to achieve the necessary clarification of conclusions, one must resort to additional, detailed information. Of total Serbian exports, 3.1 per cent went to Slovenia and 4.7 per cent to Croatia, a total of 7.8 per cent (figures are taken from Bazler-Madžar 1993: 13-15). With a share of 3.7 per cent of total exports, Bosnia-Hercegovina was for Serbia a more important market than Slovenia. Together with Montenegro and Macedonia, it absorbed 7 per cent of total exports. Measured according to share of total exports, the undeveloped regions were, for Serbia, a slightly smaller market than the combined Croatian-Slovenian market. On the other hand, Serbia received 10.8 per cent of its imports from Slovenia and Croatia. Asymmetry in trade—not necessarily exploitation—was reflected in the fact that the sum of imports from Croatia and Slovenia was, for Serbia, relatively greater than the sum of exports to them. It was difficult to substitute for imports: the Serbian economy needed trade co-operation with Slovenia and Croatia. When the shares of 10.8 and 7 per cent mentioned above are averaged out, 8.9 per cent of total Serbian trade was with Slovenia and Croatia. This does not appear to be too large a frame for eventual exploitation. If one accepts the claim that, in exchange, a developed region always exploits a less developed region, then 1) the quantitative frame noted here does not offer much space for such exploitation; and 2) with around 6.6 per cent exchange with undeveloped republics, Serbia could, through 'exploiting' them, compensate for almost all the 'damage' inflicted by trading with the more developed regions. This conclusion should not come as a surprise. With regard to all the important development indicators, Serbia was around the Yugoslav average, or just below it. In by far the greatest part of the events and changes, Serbia was able to compensate in the other direction. It is difficult to find reasons for expecting a different outcome in the area of exploitation, or supposed exploitation.

When it comes to the exploitation of Serbia, Slovenia is the most serious candidate for the role. It sold 8.1 per cent of its total exports to Serbia, and bought from it 6.5 per cent of its exports. From the Serbian perspective, the percentages are smaller: Serbia sent to Slovenia 3.1 per cent of its exports, and received approximately 3.9 per cent ([3.1/6.5] x 8.1%) of its imports (Bazler-Madžar 1993: 11-15). The frame is narrowed again. If we suppose that in terms of acquisitions and sales it had, on average, 10 per cent more favourable prices (i.e. sold more expensively and bought more cheaply), the total effect would be 1.46 per cent of its trade, or, taking into account that trade is around 2.7 times greater than the social product, the effect would be 3.94 per cent of the Slovenian social product. Since the Slovenian social product was at around 55 per cent of the social product of Serbia, the same effect for Serbia would be 2.15 per cent of the social product. Since trade with Serbia was just above one-quarter of Slovenia's total trade, in non-equivalent exchange with all other republics Slovenia would, through disparities in prices, gain 15.1 per cent of its social product.

This represents a high percentage, but the presuppositions for it are quite extravagant: enormous superiority in buying and selling with *all* Yugoslav republics. Such a belief is inconsistent with the often mentioned, and for a long time predominant, tendency towards increasing autarky in the republics, and even in municipalities (Mijovski 1980: 21). Why would any federal unit—especially among the developed ones—close itself off if exchange brought such profit? The only possible motive for closing off is a rise in the level of the mobilization of resources and the use of capacities, but the above-mentioned participation of Serbia and Slovenia in mutual exchange suggests that the effect was not big. Apart from that, the closing of the market, at least with respect to imports, clashes with the idea of exploitation through exchange; exploitation on both tracks is simply not possible. Moreover, Slovenia traded more with Croatia than with Serbia. Hence, it exploited Croatia more. Or could it be claimed that only Serbia was exploited in trade? Perhaps the Croats were not lucid enough to realize they were being exploited, while the Serbs realized it, even if belatedly?

The upper estimate of 15.1 per cent of total gains through non-equivalent exchange, of which 3.94 per cent was at Serbia's expense, is therefore totally wrong. Again, what is relevant has been emphasized in another context. In order to acquire gains in exchange, goods need to be produced, attractively packaged, placed on foreign markets, and, finally, sold. Gains in exchange cannot be compared with pure, cash transfers that flow automatically, without any need for the securing of other preconditions.

A register of typical complaints and a methodology of conditional revenue

In a system which does not usually include objective and objetivizing market mechanisms, which is burdened with political voluntarism and the corresponding numerous arbitrary interventions, it is natural that each part should acquire a feeling of lack and of long-term exploitation. Currents of revenue flow, and ways of establishing economic relations in these systems are multiple and reflect the whims of political will rather than objective measures for evaluation, costing and allocation. It is in the nature of both an individual and an organization to perceive more readily and more precisely the mechanisms which work against them, that is to say, the channels through which their revenue *flows away*, than those instruments and measures which benefit their economic position. Moreover, since the economic position of both the economic units and the wider segments of an economic system depends to a large, often predominant, extent on the relations of political power and allocations decided in the purely political sphere, the various parts of the system are not interested in any objective review of their own position, let alone the position of the other parts. Economic interests push them to stress those aspects of mutual relations by which they are harmed, and to neglect or suppress those that are beneficial to them. The truth becomes instrumentalized in the service of promoting and protecting one's own economic interest. Hence, it is no accident that, in many cases, each one of the eight Yugoslav republics and provinces emphasized its alleged exploitation, and 'proved' that the system was set specifically against its interests. There was a science to these exercises in proving one's own disadvantageous position. After all, what followed from these assumptions was a firm, not exactly simulated, belief that everyone was a victim of political games and manipulations of the economic system. Things that are repeated often enough become objects of genuine belief. Perhaps it is not too much to say that in building those beliefs there was a specific self-traumatization on the part of all the Yugoslav republics and provinces.

Any recognizable tendency towards change in a regional structure of revenue was observed closely and used for political purposes. Republics whose share of the Yugoslav social product decreased, readily interpreted such changes as a manifestation of exploitation. The character of exploitation did not have to be, and most often was not, clearly articulated. The fact that a region's share could change due to a variety of exogenous, uncontrollable factors, or, more importantly, that it could reflect relative changes in regional levels of effectiveness—independent of exploitation determinant changes—was never, or hardly ever, taken into consideration. A slightly more refined approach was the diachronic comparison of the participation of certain republics in the Yugoslav social product in current and permanent prices. If the first ones were tendentiously higher that the latter ones, that was inter preted as exploitation. It was interpreted that the 'handicapped' republics in that case exchanged their otherwise sufficiently large or sufficiently rising amounts of products with other republics under increasingly worsening conditions. 'Handicapped' republics were treated as efficient in production and, generally, in economy, but as victims of worsening economic positions due to an increasingly unjust exchange. It was forgotten that structural adjustment is an important dimension of efficiency, and that those who are more efficient are the ones who, despite the institutional rigidity, manage to follow price changes more quickly, orienting, of course, to the most profitable sectors. It would often be forgotten that the results of an analysis depend on the choice of the base year, the prices of which are used to express 'real' participation compared to participation calculated on current prices.

Exploitation and illusion

It was noted many times, and almost always correctly, that similar or identical products were being sold at very different prices. Slovenian goods were much more expensive: citric acid sold in Slovenian packaging as *limontos* was several times more expensive than the Belgrade product *limuntus*. This was characterized—and experienced—as exploitation. Several things were forgotten here. Firstly, the determining of optimal prices requires skill, and some are more successful than others in evaluating markets. Secondly, selling similar products at markedly higher prices can be done only by those who have established their position with respect to the consumers, that is, who have gained a reputation thanks to high quality, persistence and the guaranteed providing of a good selection of the range; the privilege of selling at above-average prices is acquired through the quality of services, efficiency and the reliability of servicing in guaranteed and exploitation terms. This requires long-term and persistent investment in the market, and what at first sight appears as a range of unjustified differences in prices actually represents the dividends of past investments, not only through capital, but also through business solidity, good organization, successful marketing and the cultivation of good relations with consumers. It is no mere coincidence that Serbs bought Slovenian goods far more frequently than Slovenes bought Serb goods. Thirdly, developed republics also had an objective advantage in that they bordered developed Western industrialized countries, which enabled them more successfully to innovate their production and naturally monopolize the transfer of new knowledge and technologies; of course, this brought with it market advantages as well. Fourthly, for various reasons companies from these developed republics simply appeared first in different markets, and primacy is a very important factor in long-term market advantage. All these are factors contributing to the greater market successof some regions, and the market inferiority of others; the differences were experienced as exploitation, although there was no real basis for this.

A strong illusion of exploitation was created in relation to the acquisition of raw materials, especially agricultural raw materials. Slovenes bought raspberries, apricots and grapes. Afterwards they processed them minimally, packaged them, wrote on the packaging '*mleko z bregov*', and sold them on at prices several times higher. This does represent exploitation. However, if it was so easy and simple to organize the purchase of raw materials and, in particular, the selling on of the resulting products, the question arises: Why did the local population not do the same? Why did the locals leave to someone else something that was so simple and profitable? As it happens, a more careful analysis reveals in the necessary chain of operations links that are far from simple. Involved in the buying, and especially in the selling, are certain components which, as Marx said, represent the 'death jump' of the goods. The fact that a large proportion of these agricultural raw materials would just have rotted had they not been bought by businesses from other republics is of no less importance. Moreover, looking at relations with developed areas in a long-term dynamic context, and taking into account that this kind of expanded and facilitated selling gave a big impetus to production, much of what was sold to buyers from the north-west would not even have been produced without the necessary and precious incentives from that side. There were many accusations regarding competition from the north-west in the buying of wheat from Vojvodina and other wheat-producing regions. It was forgotten how much the destroying of local monopolies meant, not just in terms of improving the peasants' economic position, but also for the advancement and development of production itself.

A simple lack of understanding and a remarkable slowness in adjusting mentally to new events, led to the creation, in the southern parts of the SFRY, of a belief in exploitation through financial transactions. Due to non-existence of a capital market, especially of its financial currents and instruments, various surrogates were developed, through which banks and companies from the developed republics financed many economic processes and ventures in undeveloped republics. Although it was not formalized by capital transactions in the financial market, capital brought revenue. There were many companies in Serbia which acquired up to 90 per cent of their total income through financing. These important revenue flows, achieved through financial transactions, have simply been ignored, thus, based merely on naturally defined figures, that is, physical indicators, it was *wrongly* concluded that the same configuration would be followed by the revenue currents! Again, it is important to remember that a cascade structure was predominant in inter-republic trade balances, that followed development levels: Slovenia had a positive exchange balance with respect to everyone else; Croatia had a positive balance with everyone except Slovenia, etc. (Petrović and Cvjetičanin 1991: 12–13). Surpluses in the inter-republic exchange of goods and services had their equivalent in the accumulation of corresponding cash funds. These funds, of course, did not remain static, but were invested, and brought revenue. That important characteristic of the economic system as a whole was ignored, so relations were perceived as exploitative, even though they had a completely different background.

Three examples of possible exploitation

It is, nevertheless, important to point out three examples of irregular and illegitimate disturbance of economic currents, which could contain, and probably did contain, elements of exploitation. The first involves the buying of agricultural products, mostly fruit, at prices below the production cost, although higher than the prices producers could get from their local organizations. Those organizations, through credits to producers and otherwise, invested in the development of agricultural production. Instead of making investments on a purely economic basis and charging users the full costs of the capital, they forewent capital revenue and a part of the investment (due to inflation), in order to obtain, as compensation, lower (*unbalanced*) prices of products and a secure trade base. This kind of arrangement was unstable and technically inefficient. It combined needlessly, and with huge losses and risks, two economic transactions into one. When a raw material base was created and a new product went on the market, the advantages of previous investments were already being used, but it was difficult to sustain the agreed unbalanced, lower prices. Competition from buyers from other places, who had not previously made any investment and who claimed no right to lower prices, pushed the prices, as in any other market, towards a higher, that is, balanced, level. Offering a balanced price, the buyer from outside had a competitive advantage, and those who had invested (the local *zadruga* or agricultural combine) remained both without the capital and without the raw materials. There were elements of illegitimate flow, or exploitation, here, but they were the result of a clumsily agreed arrangement between the financier and the producer, as well as of the inefficiency of the state in securing properly concluded contracts.

Another important element to be considered is corruption. There was a widely held belief that firms from the north-west placed corrupt business personnel all around Serbia and elsewhere. Of course, we are talking here about suspicions, impressions and partial insights, not firm and statistically documented evidence. There are no statistics and no published data on corruption. Hence, due to corruption, unfavourable contracts were probably concluded and asymmetric business deals made which put local businesses at a disadvantage, but which were to the advantage of companies from other regions. This situation could, indeed, be said to have the attributes of exploitation. However, the question immediately arises as to why, within the same legal order and economic system, 'their' business practices should disadvantage 'us', and not the other way around. In questions of pronounced differences in business morals, it is natural, even perhaps justified, that those whose ethics are on a 'lower level' should fare worse. Morality in general, and business morals in particular, represents some sort of production force, and greatly enhances economic efficiency. Morals are a component of comparative advantages. Those with higher moral are more successful in creating revenue, just like those with larger amounts of capital. It was no accident that Serb public opinion was traditionally so markedly honest. Among other things, honesty was extremely important from the point of view of profit. Trust greatly facilitates transactions and increases their efficiency. Many business deals would not be possible without trust. Thus, can deformities in distribution currents, those caused by corruption, be described as exploitation? The reply will essentially depend on whether corruption is represented unequally, for example, in Serbia and Slovenia, and whether it reflects differences in business morals and, finally, in morals in general. If, because of the differences in size of certain republics, there are different *technical possibilities for corruption*–if it is, for example, *technically* easier for the smaller republics to corrupt the larger ones, than vice versa, or, which is more probable, if republics with higher revenues can buy off earlier and more easily republics with lower revenues–then there is an exogenous element, independent from morals, which could produce an exploitative effect. This would be a textbook example of the misuse of an objective advantage. However, that question demands further consideration and research. Part of the responsibility certainly falls to the (republic) state, which was 1) notoriously inefficient in preventing corruption; and 2) through its stiff economic policies and literal interpretation of quite often absurd regulations, practically pushed business people into various forms of deviant behaviour, thus contributing to the creation of a general environment appropriate for the spreading of corruption.

The third example of a possible exploitative attempt to gain another republic's revenue is the (one-sided) closing of markets. The great importance of using someone else's demand in the mobilization of one's own productive potential has been theoretically explained, and the enormous repercussions of this aspect of the foreign economic policy of some countries in international economic relations has been demonstrated (Aghiri 1972).

It should be noted that this form of exploitation is not only possible, but also potentially extremely dangerous. It does not lead to revenue flow, but demobilizes and devaluates a great part of the economic potential of some countries. Disabling an economy in order to use part of its potential, including depression, due to which a large number of people are deprived of any chance to work and create revenue, is more damaging, than revenue flow through non-equivalent exchange.

However, it is one thing to allow the possibility of exploitation through a mechanism, and quite another to demonstrate that this mechanism really worked. For example, Serbia bought from Slovenia 8.1 per cent of its exports, and the corresponding proportion from Croatia was 9.4. At the same time, Slovenia bought 6.5 per cent of its total imports from Serbia. With Croatia, the percentage is even higher. Serbia sent to Slovenia and Croatia 7.8 per cent of its exports, and acquired from them 10.8 per cent of its total imports (Bazler-Madžar 1993: 11–14). A three-point difference does not seem high enough to support the claim of the one-sided use of demand and the export of unemployment to the south. Furthermore, an analogous question arises once again—why was the closing of the market, to the extent it had become apparent, not turned in the opposite direction? Was it not because of differences in quality, design, marketing, business reputation, customer service and previous investments? Taking into account the—again—narrow frames within which particular examples of the usurping of demand took place, and bearing in mind the possible effects of many other factors, rash claims of exploitation in this domain can be characterized as unproven and one-sided, although not a hundred per cent false.

The SANU Memorandum: the expression of traumatization in economic relations

Even if viewed only in terms of its economic content, the *Memorandum of the Serbian Academy of Arts and Sciences (SANU)* (*Duga*, special issue, June 1989), is a wide-ranging document of above-average complexity. A detailed analysis of its contents is beyond the scope of this article, thus only its most characteristic points will be mentioned (see the contribution of O. Milosavljević in this volume). Due to its programmatic character, its generalized tone and style, and its treatment of wide-ranging, global themes, it is not easy to provide a rigorous and analytical criticism of the *Memorandum*—at least of all aspects of it. Many claims have been put forward without being accompanied by argumentation, and only partly substantiated by the necessary facts. In order to disprove arguments that are only hinted at, those arguments must firstly be clearly articulated or explicitly formulated, with the usual risks. Thus part of the claims can be disputed by calling into question the relevant argumentation, and the other claims can simply be criticized for their lack of argumentation.

The *Memorandum* was characterized by a critical approach to everything that happened—and there was hardly anything that did not deserve criticism—from positions of a strategy and a theory of social action, which led to a breakdown that was already easy to see. Starting from the correct premise that the deep roots of the economic decline lay in a multiply deformed political system, the *Memorandum* looked for ways out not in a determinant and definitive emancipation of the economy from politics, and in the transferring of the economy onto a consistently market track, but in a reform of the political system, which would condition it to relate to the economy in a radically different way. Instead of isolating and protecting the economy from the immediate meddling of politics, the *Memorandum* demanded that the economy as a whole be put at the top of the list of political priorities, and called for a return to the tried and tested methods of the strong and overall political mobilization of all forces and resources towards economic renewal and long-term guaranteed prosperity. The text does not mention a single important element of the political organization, such as, for example, the unconditional abolition of the monopolies of any, even reformed, political organization, or the introduction of a multiparty system. The *Memorandum* looked for solutions to the numerous troubles of both the economy and society in a return to authentic socialist values, and in the principles of political and economic organizations conditioned by them.

The *Memorandum* completely misses the point in the part which deals with development strategy. In several places (20, 22), tight spots in economic development are mentioned, resulting from the insufficient production of energy and raw materials. Approximately contemporary research, with a firm analytic base (Nikezić [ed.], 1987: 52–55), shows without any doubt that the problem experienced by both Serbia and Yugoslavia was completely the opposite: these production sectors were hypertrophied; a politically inspired investment policy was still generating above-average growth rates, and, in terms of international comparisons, both the Yugoslav and the Serbian economy had, due to the hypertrophy of these sectors, jumped out of world standards. A wrong diagnosis of the structural discrepancies, just like a wrong evaluation of the real and alleged potential role of the political factor, obviously contributed to the traumatization of the public in the Republic of Serbia. Problems were located where there were, in practice, none; real difficulties were not identified; and the diverting of attention from real to pseudo-problems led to the misunderstanding of Serbia by others, and by itself. Therefore, traumas could not be limited to Serbia only: reciprocal traumatization, in numerous return reactions, could only deepen and amplify as a result of the unavoidable negative energy.

The *Memorandum* contains similar errors of judgement when discussing smaller tendencies in economic or general societal development or institutional changes. In several places (21, for example), there is criticism of decentralization as being marked by etatism and as deeply deformed; and of an initially highly centralized and bureaucratically monolithic political, and conditioned by it, economic system. Nothing else could have been expected: from an etatist egg only an etatist chicken could hatch, and an excessively centralized, mostly despotic, system of political domination over society as a whole could break and decompose only into similar, authoritarian systems at the republic level. It is not unnatural, through an evolutionary development, for democratic mechanisms to grow out of the undoubtedly authoritarian—and in important dimensions even totalitarian—structures. No one should be surprised by the naïveté of a theory of social development that, in the course of work on the *Memorandum,* was used as a sort of intellectual infrastructure and conceptual basis.

The economic policies of the 1980s are one-sidedly evaluated as unsuccessful. There is a lament over the loss of economic-political independence, and at the same time it is acknowledged that some difficult correct moves have been made under pressure from international financial organizations (20). A more far-reaching oversight is the fact that the authors lamented over the sudden slowing of the growth rate, without realizing that this was part of the price for the financial curing of the economy. The creators of the *Memorandum* did not see that a good deal of previous and actual growth was unhealthy, in the sense that it was realized at the cost of losses and the financial exhaustion of the economy, thus decreasing its ability to mobilize resources in the future. This necessarily led to a considerable and long-term projected slowing of growth, without any possibility of a much needed turn-around. The authors of the *Memorandum* did not realize that the regulations which narrowed the autonomy of the companies were a predictable necessity in a decentralized system in which, due to unsettled property relations, right motivation was not secured (31), even though the growing interdependence of countries was already becoming a planetary mega-trend; far from assuming that the importing of foreign capital means falling under foreign domination, such imports are today regarded as one of the main areas of competitiveness: a country is more *successful* in a competitive game if it manages to attract more foreign capital. Great concern was expressed about the politically inspired and arbitrary disintegration of companies, and there was an insistence on reintegration (21). The authors did not realize that both integration and disintegration are economically useless here, since neither of them is put on a market basis. They forgot that, with all the politically inspired disintegration, one of the main structural problems of the Yugoslav economy was the lack of small companies (World Bank 1981). In short, the key diagnoses and evaluations contained in the *Memorandum* were diametrically opposed to the intellectual trends and the latest findings in world economics.

The explanation for Serbia's economic sluggishness was given one of the central places in the *Memorandum*. It was stated that Serbia had many reasons for insisting on being released from its obligation to contribute to the Fund for the Undeveloped Regions: those who formulated these demands did not allow themselves to be confused by the fact that most of the funds involved–which were, in proportion to social revenue and thus well over the proportion determined by the population structure, also paid by the developed republics–were returned to Serbia, albeit to the undeveloped province of Kosovo. It was noted (37) that only Serbia really helped the undeveloped regions, and that Slovenia, Croatia and Vojvodina did not pay their fair share. According to the authors of the *Memorandum*, the best solution would be a *progressive* contribution.

One can only note that a contribution proportional to social product is automatically transformed into a differentiated burden when the contributions are viewed per capita. The contribution by federal units varied greatly, and by introducing a progressive contribution, differences would increase. However, it should also be noted that high fiscal burdens, especially the perspective of their enlargement—combined with the fact that they were in part transformed into ever-painful cash flows directed towards other members of the federation—greatly increased the attractiveness of the alternative way of contributing and independent state organization. The hint of an increased contribution for promoting development in the undeveloped regions, as well as the possible freeing of Serbia from that contribution, was probably not a meaningless figure in the sum of the elements which led to the disintegration of Yugoslavia.

Within inter-republic relations on the verge of the political democratization of society, there is a surprising and intriguing paradox. In the economically heterogeneous and developmentally unequal federation, appeared a strong legal pressure towards a fiscal levelling, even towards an abuse of the fiscal system in order to decrease as much as possible the differences in *per capita* revenue. On the other hand, it was natural that a reaction to that pressure appeared among the developed regions, as well as an attempt to reduce fiscal redistribution to a minimum. The paradox is that the developed regions could better protect their revenue from improper fiscal attempts in some version of the authoritarian political order in which there was no danger of being outvoted. In a politically pluralized system, if it includes various decision-making processes at the level of the federation as a whole, a poorer majority could easily outvote a richer minority and acquire gains through strictly political means. This invariably happens in rudimentary, institutionally unfinished systems, which are quickly built at the beginning of a democratic transformation. Such systems are far from containing useful constitutional and other mechanisms through which minorities can be protected, on various bases, from constituted majorities. Democratization without refined constitutional arrangements and corresponding limitations, simply because of the danger that it might evolve into democratic totalitarianism, is more than a serious threat to federations in that stage of democratic development. The Yugoslav federation did not overcome that threat. It seems that the developed republics clearly saw the danger of democratic totalitarianism, and in due time left the federation. Finally, there is a paradox in the fact that various secessionist tendencies looked for an excuse in the need for democracy, and timed their leaving of the common state exactly when democratization was visible with a naked eye, when it appeared inevitable, and when it had made its first decisive steps through the first multiparty elections.

One contributing factor to the deep, and this time completely justified, traumatization of Serbia, was the ruthless–totally voluntaristic and appropriate for the Communist government–disassembling of significant industries throughout Serbia and Vojvodina, and their dislocation to the less-developed regions. The *Memorandum* strongly insists on this factor (36), this time with good reasons, although adequate argumentation could not be developed due to the nature of the document and the lack of space. A sizeable research project has now been completed in the Economic Institute in Belgrade, dealing with the moving of industry from Serbia and Vojvodina, and Z. Đorđević (1992) has skilfully summarized the most important consequences of the project. Particularly badly hit were industrial areas in Belgrade, Kragujevac and Leskovac. Accompanying this, there was long-term discrimination against Serbia in investment policy, owing to the strategic threat from the East. Industries were located in the centre, and towards the west of the country. Following the logic of bureaucratic inertia, this policy was continued for years, even after the threat was long past.

The explanation for Serbia's economic sluggishness has not been empirically tested in a rigorous or satisfactory way. It is usual—and quite appropriate—that the status of some federal units is measured through the relationship between their per capita revenue and that of Yugoslavia, with—again, quite appropriately—both figures expressed in terms of current prices. In the long post-

World War II development, that pointer varied in many ways, thus, by an appropriate choice of periods observed almost any conclusions chosen in advance can be supported.

In order to illustrate this, the Table 1 provides pointers to the relative position of selected regions for several selected years.

Table 1

Relative position of the selected regions, measured according to the relationship of the social product per capita (SFRY = 100)

Year	Serbia	Central Serbia	Vojvodina	Kosovo	Developed regions	Undeveloped regions
1952	83.1	89.5	84.2	45.1	100.0	69.2
1953	87.1	90.3	95.3	52.5	110.3	71.3
1959	92.7	95.7	110.5	41.3	116.4	66.2
1960	90.4	94.5	108.0	35.7	117.2	64.9
1966	96.4	98.6	124.1	38.2	118.6	63.8
1980	89.9	94.4	121.4	31.7	122.1	59.7
1988	85.1	90.0	124.0	27.9	127.1	56.7

(after Bazler-Madžar 1991: 147)

The relativity of conclusions on economic sluggishness can clearly be seen. It is true that between 1960 and 1968 Serbia lost around 5 points in its relative status, and the same is true for Central Serbia. However, it is also true that in 1960 Serbia was around five points above the level in 1952–1953. If the period is seen as a whole, both Serbia and Central Serbia more or less kept the same relative position at which they entered the long period of post-war development. The fate of the provinces differs significantly: while Vojvodina markedly improved its position by around 50 per cent, the position in Kosovo worsened by almost the same percentage. This is the main reason behind the remarkable parallelism in the tendencies in the economic position of Serbia and Central Serbia. The economic structure markedly influences the measure of the position. It is easy to see from the table, and a detailed analysis of these figures provides even better proof, that the position of the undeveloped regions improved in good agricultural years and worsened in less productive ones. In conclusion, one could say that

1. any judgement on the changes in relative status is, due to the influence of the way the period is chosen, completely conditional;

2. from 1960s onwards, the status of Serbia has, with major oscillations from year to year, undoubtedly worsened; and
3. that Serbia's worsening position was not so much engineered 'nor' taking into account the annual oscillations, so systematic, as to justify the force with which it was presented to the public.

Bearing all this in mind, it is one thing to make statements about the eventual lagging behind of a region, and something quite different to describe its causes, and especially to prove that among those causes a visible place was taken by conscious policies, or even a conspiracy on the part of other republics. However pronounced, one republic's lagging behind the others could not be a justified excuse for the inflaming of national passions, if there was no convincing proof that it was the result of a conscious and negatively directed policy against a concrete region. That feature—a clear proof that Serbia was a victim of antagonistic policy—was absent in the fervent discussions in the late 1980s, thus numerous accusations (and the complete absence of any self-criticism) remained, without any real scientific basis and even without serious logical foundation.

What conclusions can be drawn from these considerations? *Primarily*, the deeply irrational economic system, founded from the beginning on a wrong basis, inevitably had numerous, far-reaching and devastating flaws. Among the most important, which are at the same time among the main causes of its destruction, was the fundamental inability of the system to correlate rewards in the distribution process with real and full economic contributions. Inability to co-ordinate awards and contributions inevitably and automatically led to a number of different deviations from the economically reasonable, and even morally acceptable, configuration between the price of the products and the price of the materials. These deviations hid dangerous factors generating political instability. It is in the nature of things that participants should keenly and precisely perceive the mechanisms which work to their disadvantage, taking those favourable to them granted. Pressed by factors that trouble them, and blind to what speaks in their favour, sooner or later the participants activate some kind of negative political energy and turn against the others. The integrity of a community whose economic system is being questioned then quite seriously becomes an issue.

Secondly, the advantages of deviations from economically based evaluations and the accompanying effects of permanently upset mutual accounts *were not* restricted to just one category of participants, or exclusively to one participant only. On the contrary, with all the risks inherent in such notoriously immeasurable matters, one could say that both advantages and handicaps were widely spread and almost equally distributed. The developed regions gained some advantage from the disparity in prices and, partly and occasionally, from the asymmetric approach to the market, although it should be noted that these two categories of advantage are mutually exclusive. The undeveloped regions had the advantage that a highly disproportionate—taking into account the regional population structure—part of the burden of the enormous and hypertrophied state was put on the developed regions. Among the developed regions, this contributed to the inflammation of the at first hidden, and later openly stated, desire to leave Yugoslavia, even though they too, at least based on the economy of the perimeter, must have obtained some benefit from the common state. Expenses for services on the level of the system as a whole are characterized as fixed expenditure, and these are smaller for each participant in proportion to the size of the whole served by those common organizations. The questions of whether the effects of communality were greater than the effects of this or that form of flow is a huge and difficult one, which will probably never receive a reliable and generally acceptable answer. In any case, a more modestly dimensioned and cheaper state would have made the Yugoslav community more attractive to all the participants, especially the developed ones, and would certainly have reduced the probability—and might even have removed the possibility—of its disintegration.

Thirdly, Serbia was permanently, in almost all respects, at the level of the Yugoslav average. According to the criteria relevant for Yugoslavia, it was certainly not undeveloped. It was clearly not developed either, although it was regarded as such in the official statistics. Located in the middle of the developmental ladder, Serbia could enjoy neither the advantages of the developed regions, nor the benefits of the undeveloped ones, just as it was not excessively exposed to either of the two distinctive kinds of handicaps. Besides, as the biggest republic, Serbia could—in an obviously relevant *relative* sense—neither gain nor lose much on the basis of various redistributive currents. In short, by its size and by its (relative) developmental level, Serbia was predestined *not to be* traumatized. Despite that, it *was* traumatized, and to a very large degree. Causes of the traumatization of Serbia should not be looked for in the objective characteristics of its economic and demographic position, but in the defects of the political system and, especially, in the intensive and not very wise political use of the accumulated dissatisfaction.

Fourthly, even though in every deformed, institutionally defective system, every exchange, including inter-republic exchanges, could contain the elements of exploitation, it is impossible to give any scientific proof of this, and it is simply wrong to treat exchange as primarily exploitative and to claim *a priori* that exploitation is necessarily turned in one direction. As an act of good will , exchange mostly benefits both sides, since, exactly because of this good will, both sides have, in every transaction, the alternative of not entering the exchange. This reminder is especially important in relation to the frequent claims that Serbia was being exploited. Positioned somewhere in the middle according to many economic pointers, Serbia traded with both the more and the less developed regions. If it 'lost' in the exchange with the developed regions, Serbia recovered at least part of that loss through exchange with the undeveloped ones. The idea that Serbia carried out a policy of fair and equivalent exchange with respect to the undeveloped regions, and that it was a victim of exploitation in relations with the developed ones is so close to the absurd that it hardly merits any serious consideration. Related to that is the fact that in Yugoslavia, like anywhere else in the world, the developed regions traded to a much greater extent among themselves than with undeveloped regions. How was it that the possibility of exploitation did not drag them in the opposite direction? All of this illustrates the fact that beliefs in the exploitation of Serbia had very little foundation in economic facts. Most of what was said in public about exploitation had the characteristics of myth, which was more damaging than useful both to Serbia and the others.

Fifthly, there was outflow, although damages and benefits on various bases to a great extent compensated for one another. Independently of this, but therefore more important, is the fact that the unfortunately missing knowledge that *all* the members of the Yugoslav community, including Serbia, which was more traumatized than it should have been, based on its location and size, lost much more because of a deeply irrational economic system that was opposed in many respects to human freedoms and rights, than the cumulative sum of net flows of revenue in any direction. That knowledge could have inspired a radically different pattern of thinking and action. Instead of directing obstacles so fiercely against each other, Yugoslav peoples and republics could, in solidarity, have taken notice of the *general* great loss and tried together to leave behind, as soon as possible, that human and civilizational prehistory. Perhaps this was the last great defeat of solidarity, which had lost many other battles in this part of the world.

Kosovo in the Collective Memory

OLGA ZIROJEVIĆ

In the national consciousness of the Serbian people the Battle of Kosovo was, and still is, the central event in its entire history. 'It is where, according to general but unjustified belief, the Serbian state perished and its independence was buried; it is the place where the Serbs were enslaved by the Turks' (S. Ćirković 1987: 560).

The date of the battle is indisputable: St.Vitus's Day, 15 June (28 June according to the new calendar) 1389. On the Serbian side, along with Prince Lazar Hrebeljanović, fought his son-in-law Vuk Branković (who would, in a legend which arose much later, be accused of treachery) and the Bosnian Duke Vlatko Vuković. The Turkish side was led by Sultan (Emir) Murad, along with his sons Bayezid and Jakub Celebi. If Murad's *turbeh* [tomb] (still standing today) was indeed built on the exact spot where the Turkish sultan lost his life, then the battle must have taken place on thet part of the Kosovo plain at the confluence of the rivers Lab and Sitnica, in the vicinity of Priština. It is also certain that both rulers lost their lives on the battlefield. Murad was knifed to death by a Serbian feudal lord, identified in later sources as the Prince's son-in-law Miloš Obilić (or Kobilić).

Such is the data that contemporary historical science has at its disposal. Despite the efforts of numerous researchers, we still do not know the number of either the Serbian or the Turkish troops, the time of death of either ruler, the number of casualties on either side, or even the outcome of the battle. In other words, as Sima Ćirković writes, the battle of Kosovo 'attained fame as the greatest defeat of the Serbs, although today we have reasons to doubt that it really was so' (Ćirković 1987: 560).

The greatest difficulty in ascertaining even the most basic facts regarding this Serbian-Turkish clash does not lie in the scarcity of contemporary sources (sources which are, at the same time, con-tradictory), but in the creation of the legend of Kosovo at a very early date. A whole cycle of epic poems and a series of legends about this fateful battle were created, and, sooner or later, recorded. Regardless of whether it concerned sainthood or martyrdom, the victims or the war, heroic deeds or great courage, the legend of Kosovo always had a certain political, religious and, finally, national symbolism (Ljubinković 1989: 127–164).

The legend of Kosovo

There is no single, uniform legend. Immediately after the battle and the Prince's death, a Kosovo legend was created with a distinctly religious character, with Prince Lazar at its centre, to serve the needs of his heirs, the Lazarević dynasty. The existing ten cycles of ballads on Kosovo, created between 1390 and 1419, were written in order to preserve the cult of the dead Prince Lazar, who, soon after the Kosovo catastrophe, was proclaimed a saint by the Church (Mihaljčić 1989: 140–157). The legend of Lazar was renewed twice in later times. The first time was in Russia under Ivan IV (the Terrible), as a result of the Russian autocrat's wish to make Russia into the Third Rome; the second time during the Great Migration (1690), when the relics of Lazar[1] were transferred from the monastery of Ravanica, via Szentendre (Hungary) to Vrdnik, which then obtained the name of Sremska Ravanica (Ljubinković 1989: 127; 1991: 159–160; Redžep 1992: 527–588). The relics remained there until 1942, when they were transferred to Belgrade and kept there until St.Vitus's Day in 1988, 'when the honourable Prince embarked on his great journey, once more to Kosovo, finally to rest in the first Ravanica. In addition to these two Ravanicas, there is a third one—in Detroit, USA—the creation of which speaks clearly of the growth of this cult and its continuation; the same applies to the churches called "Lazarica", from the one in Kruševac, which served as the royal court church, to new ones—in Belgrade, Birmingham, etc.—dedicated to God in honour of the prince-martyr Lazar' (Kalezić 1989: 287–288). The cult of the historical person of Prince Lazar—along with the remains of his body, the holy relics or *Sanctorum reliquiae*[2]—is still present in our times, representing the continuity of a living tradition.

Parallel with the legend of Lazar, the legend of the knight Miloš also existed among the people of those times and their descendants. However, it had developed in a secular atmosphere, maybe in other regions (probably in western parts) and as part of folk tradition (Schmaus 1970: 312). Slandered in the same way as the brave Roland or Tristan, Miloš was also forced to prove his heroism and loyalty by his deeds. He made a vow to kill the infidel ruler, which he actually did, but he was himself slain in the act. Murad's assassin was identified as Miloš Kobilić (i.e. Kobila and Kobilović)[3] a hundred years after the battle of Kosovo (Redžep 1991: 86). As the years passed, his chivalrous feat was enriched with an ever growing number of additional details.

On the opposing side, the Turks also created their own legend of Kosovo, not totally independent from Serbian influence. Turkish chroniclers looked upon this battle as an event which opened the door wide to the Turkish onslaught on Europe, depicting the Sultan's very death as a conscious sacrifice (the sultan-martyr) built into the foundations of the future Turkish empire and state.

Also, at the very site of the battle of Kosovo, on Kosovo Field, the local legend of Kosovo (both the Christian and the Turkish one) was created and maintained for centuries (Ljubinković 1991: 160). In the late nineteenth century, over thirty folk legends were found there which, according to Milovan Bovan, show beyond any doubt that in the first days of the creation of the Kosovo legend and epics, Miloš Obilić was, as he still is, the main character in the oral tradition, particularly in Kosovo itself (Bovan 1991: 311).

In these and other areas, the names of towers and the ruins of former fortresses are associated with Miloš Obilić, thus these legends offer a new substitute for a mythological heroic predecessor.[4] In the region of the river Vardar, as well as in Mount Athos (Khilandar), Miloš Obilić was considered to be a saint ('without the proscribed and customary manner').

Along with the motif of heroism, at the roots of the Kosovo legend is another motif, that of betrayal. It was elaborated in the legend, almost in every detail, according to the well-known form found in the New Testament. The comparison between Christ and Prince Lazar 'was depicted with astonishing precision'. The main order of events also coincides: both betrayals were discovered at table (Christ's supper with the apostles and the Prince's with the Serbian lords). Both betrayals were discovered on the day preceding the death of Christ/Lazar (Mihaljčić 1989: 224). The motif of betrayal, however, had been developing over many years and centuries. In the Chronicle of Peć (1402), in discussing the outcome of the battle betrayal was mentioned only as a possibility and not as an event which actually took place. In the late fifteenth century, in the famous *Turkish Chronicle* (by Konstantin Mihailović from Ostrovica), the motif of betrayal was associated with a group of persons (the author discusses discord and disloyalty). The motif of betrayal was associated for the first time with the name of Vuk Branković in the *Kingdom of the Slavs,* written by Mavro Orbin, a monk from Dubrovnik, who made use of existing works and written legends, as well as of those which he incorporated directly.[5]

In the early eighteenth century, an unknown writer from Boka Kotorska (or Montenegro) compiled the *Hagiography of Prince Lazar, Miloš Obilić and Other Lords Who Were in the Field of Kosovo.* This late *Hagiography of Prince Lazar* retained the final and complete form of the Kosovo legend and was, therefore, named by academics as *The Story of the Battle of Kosovo*[6]. This work is a well-designed compilation[7] and depicts events from the death of Dušan's son Uroš to the death of Prince Lazar, its historical axis being enriched by the legend of Kosovo. The two main motifs of the Kosovo legend, the motif of betrayal and the motif of heroism, are brought together in this story. The story is preserved as a manuscript, and numerous details are logically well connected. The same as the legend, the *Story of the Battle of Kosovo* also suggests that the medieval Serbian state was doomed due to betrayal and disloyalty, but also due to discord, disobedience and disunity. In the *Story* Vuk Branković was Prince Lazar's son-in-law (married to his daughter Mara—which is a historical fact) and he slandered Miloš Obilić in order to avenge himself. After a quarrel between their wives (Lazar's daughters) Miloš threatened Vuk, who then accused Miloš of being a future traitor of the Prince in the battle of Kosovo[8], whereas he was a traitor himself. During the meal, Vuk sat at the Prince's knee and constantly fed him with insinuations regarding Miloš's treachery. He fled the battle with his troops, which numbered, in the existing variants of the manuscript, between seven hundred and one hundred thousand. The compiler of the *Story* paid particular attention to the personality of Miloš Obilić. He was also Prince Lazar's son-in-law (not confirmed in relevant sources), just and impulsive, and a great hero. He was accompanied by his two blood brothers, Ivan Kosančić and Milan Topličanin (who are not historical persons). He attended the Prince's supper with them, went to the Turkish camp with them (the 'spying on the Turkish army' motif), and all three of them fought bravely against the Turks. While talking with the Turks, Miloš made threats and behaved haughtily and overbearingly. In the *Story,* as well as in the folk poems, he is given some mythical attributes (as the Fire Dragon). Obilić is, at the same time, a loyal vassal, who demonstrates his loyalty at his hour of death, wishing to be buried by Lazar's feet (in order to serve him posthumously as well). In this way, Vuk Branković, a negative character, a slanderer, defiler and traitor, is contrasted with a proud and a just hero and loyal vassal, Miloš Obilić. The story of the quarrel between Lazar's daughters served as a motive for Vuk's slander, so that the motif of heroism was associated with the motif of betrayal; the legend of Kosovo, which already had a certain form as early as the late sixteenth and early seventeenth century, was given its final form in the *Story of the Battle of Kosovo*. All the elements of the legend are bound logically, and, in addition to the main motifs of the legend, the *Story* preserved a series of details (some of which are not found in the folk poems). The *Story* also contains the local Montenegrin legend on the heroes who did not participate in the Battle of Kosovo, but who, in a later period, fought against the Turks (Redžep 1991: 79–80). Migrations brought the *Story* from the old Hercegovina region to the coastal area, and it echoed powerfully among Serbs living in Hungary.

The poems on the Battle of Kosovo

Serbian epic poetry is closely associated with Kosovo; pre-Kosovo poetry foretells the defeat, Kosovo poetry depicts it, while post-Kosovo poetry mourns it, occasionally raising the greatness of an individual feat or of a vassal's sacrifice to a mythological level. The epic folk poems devoted to the battle against the Turks are the best known and the most beautiful. The 1389 battle is a favourite subject of poems (and story-telling), revolving around two essential motifs: the feat of the positive hero (Miloš Obilić) and the treachery of the negative hero (Vuk Branković). The subject is complemented by many international motifs, present in the epic poetry of other nations: the conflict between sisters regarding precedence, the slandered hero and his oath to perform a heroic act, supper on the eve of a decisive event, spying on enemies, a promise to do a good deed, the tardy hero, etc.

According to Miodrag Maticki, 'it was certainly the system of archetypes, accepted and active in the collective consciousness of the people long before the battle of Kosovo, which made it possible for the system of poems on the battle of Kosovo (the Kosovo cycle as an epopee) to last so long and which helped make it truly the longest lasting memory of our people' (Maticki 1991: 176; Đurić 65–66). It is for this reason that in all the poems about Kosovo there are two layers: a mythical-heroic, and a purely Christian one. However, according to Mircea Eliade, the historical traits of the characters and the action of the heroic epic could not defy 'the corrosive action of mythicization'.

In this way, the comparative mythicization of the legend of Kosovo in folk stories, as well as in decasyllabic poems, undoubtedly contributed to the creation of the Kosovo myth and its dissemination among the masses (Popović, 76–77).

The poems on the battle of Kosovo were probably recited immediately after the battle, both by the people living at the time of the battle and by the participants themselves. These poems changed both in content and in form with the passing of time, but their main topic has been preserved until the present day. Based on the motifs of slander, Miloš's feat and betrayal (deviations were temporary and insignificant), they have maintained this line persistently to the present day (Krstić 1958: 97).

The poems (as well as the stories) annihilated the reality of slavery and became not only a substitute for reality, but also the iron fist of revenge. By identifying with the hero of the epic, who, together with the people, carries the load of historical hardships during long centuries of foreign oppression, the people were able to experience catharsis. Identification with mythical or epic heroes is a well-known phenomenon in traditional societies (the folklore-mythical consciousness).

The Kosovo choice and/or the Kosovo testament

Passing into eternal life after death on the battlefield, as a kind of heroic transcendence, was the mythical nucleus of many heroic epics from the pre-Christian era. Narratives about heroes who lost their lives bravely in order to live forever were, in ancient times, not only stories, but the true reality of mythical people: 'they truly experienced death on the battlefield as a passing into eternal life', writes Miodrag Popović. The choice between spiritual values and material goods was at the very heart of dramas originating from different religions and cultures. In Christianity, this dilemma was always dramatized as the making of a choice between 'the heavenly and the earthly kingdom'. In a similar way to Christ, the Serbian Prince Lazar, on the eve of his death, made a choice between the earthly and the heavenly kingdom.

Inducement to battle and the encouragement of warriors is also common both to oral heroic narratives and epic folk poetry. Heroic transcendence, as a poetic theme, also existed in Serbian medieval literature, even before the Kosovo writings on Prince Lazar. It came from the *Alexandrida*, the most popular work in the translated Serbian literature of the fourteenth century: '...better an honourable death than a disgraceful life'. In his speech on the eve of the battle, Prince Lazar says: '...it is better for us to die by a heroic act than to live in shame'.[9] Lazar's words are accepted by his warriors who reply in the form of a chorus; the idea of death is elevated to a heroic feat through which they will pass to eternal life.[10] Through their sacrifice, the Serbs earned freedom, but not in the usual sense of the word. They earned freedom in the heavenly kingdom, and that kingdom was within them, in the spirit and the consciousness of the people, that is, out of the reach of any conqueror. Although defeated, they were never enslaved (Bandić 1990: 41). In this way the Kosovo choice became 'the deepest engravedtrait which characterizes the common character of the Serbs' (Samardžić 1990: 30). According to Novak Kilibarda, 'the engraving of the Kosovo oath into the collective consciousness of the Serbian people as a whole, that is, even in those regions which were not subjugated by the Turks, was performed by Njegos's work *The Mountain Wreath*' (1989: 68). 'To make the Kosovo choice', writes Zoran Mišić, 'means to renounce everything that stands for illusory gain and covetous fame, to desert what is attainable for the sake of the unattainable, to wish, in Njegoš's way, for things to be the way they cannot be. It means to accept the rule of the game that "he who loses, wins", to reach for victory through death on the battlefield, to wager on the impossible, the only thing which cannot fail.' It is, in short, 'the choice of the most difficult, the most perilous road, which is the only true road' (Ðurić, 197). Atanasije Jevtić points out that the Kosovo choice became the historical destiny of the people, as it decisively determined the attitude of the people as a whole at crucial moments of Serbian history (1989: 25). The events in connection with 27 March 1941 also demonstrate that the idea of the Kosovo choice is permanently present in the historical and spiritual destiny of the Serbian people. Gavrilo Dožić, the then Patriarch of the Serbian Orthodox Church, made the following announcement on Belgrade radio: 'We have opted once more for the Heavenly Kingdom, that is, for the kingdom of God's truth and justice, people's unity and freedom. This is an eternal ideal, buried in the hearts of all Serbian men and women, preserved and kept alive in the sanctuaries of our Orthodox memorials.'

After the collapse of Serbia in World War I, Prime Minister Nikola Pašić declared, 'It is better that we all die as free men than live
as slaves' (Bishop Nikolaj 1988: 87). During the most recent celebration of the battle of Kosovo (1989), it was also pointed out that
the Kosovo myth and the oath to liberate Kosovo were so strong
that they had determined the whole history of Serbia and of the
Serbian people for centuries, all the way through the Balkan Wars
and the liberation of Kosovo. This was true even later, during
World War II and the clash with the Cominform (1948). Finally,
even in more recent times, it has been an important force associated with the position of the Serbian people in Kosovo and in the
rest of Yugoslavia (Lukić 1989).

The Kosovo myth (cult) in Montenegro

Deeply embodied in the national consciousness of the Montenegrins is the belief that they are the descendants of those men who,
after the Battle of Kosovo, escaped the Turkish yoke and fled to the
unreachable mountains, which themselves were increasingly becoming a symbol of resistance and ceaseless struggle. One can
therefore say, with no exaggeration, that Montenegrins were born,
lived and died with Kosovo. 'As in the most ancient legends, which
are actually the greatest human reality,' writes Ivo Andrić, 'every
individual personally felt the historical anathema which turned
lions into farmers, leaving in their minds the terrible thought of
Miloš Obilić, to live their lives split between their agricultural
peasant reality and the chivalrous thought of Obilić.' This is, in
Andrić's opinion, the root of Njegoš's drama, and without it it
would be difficult to realize the tragedy of his life. The prototype
of the Kosovo warrior, this poet and ruler ('the Jeremiah of
Kosovo') was, at the same time, an active and devoted fighter for
the 'lifting of the anathema' and the bringing to life of the memory
of Obilić (Andrić, in Đurić 1990: 486).

Although one can really only discuss the Kosovo myth in Montenegro after the appearance of Njegoš, it is quite certain that it
was present among the people; it was transmitted and spread in
folk legends, in folk and church feasts of patron saints, and particularly in folk songs (sung to the accompaniment of the *gusle*, a Balkan musical instrument). Only in the period of the liberation wars
in the eighteenth and nineteenth centuries, and the Romantic return to 'the old glory and greatness', was the myth more clearly

characterized by a number of symbols. Two of them are heroism on the one side, and betrayal on the other. Miloš Obilić and Vuk Branković represent permanent symbols of these characteristics. The former is glorified forever and the latter is cursed and damned. And both of them serve as examples, thus becoming the weapons of the indomitable force of the people. It was therefore necessary to incite passion for revenge against the Turks, to organize the Obilić-type heroes, and to liberate Montenegro from the Turks who, at that time, were hated with a vengeance.

The annihilation of the converts to Islam—which took place in the early eighteenth century (on Christmas Eve)—is considered to be a direct consequence of the battle of Kosovo. In other words, it was an attempt to prevent another division, since division, as the people understood it, was one of the crucial reasons for defeat in Kosovo. Thus, the annihilation of the converts to Islam is a symbol of the post-Kosovo oath: not to let national tragedy occur by keeping and cherishing 'a plague among the sheep'. By accepting the conquerors and their religion, the converts to Islam had chosen treachery, and that, according to popular belief, was a road leading to national destruction and the loss of independence (Čupić 1991: 111).

Heroism as a positive moral category (although it is 'the lord of all evil') was given priority in Montenegro over all other positive features. The model for all kinds of heroism was the feat of Miloš Obilić in Kosovo. This is why Njegoš, in his *Mountain Wreath*, gave such grandeur to Miloš and made him a model of all chivalrous traits. 'He is awarded the first place on the national Olympus, he is like some godlike creature in the temple of some heroic-mythical religion', says Alois Šmaus (1970: 317). His name is used to reprimand degenerates ('what will you have to show to Miloš once you appear before him'); his name is called on in the most difficult hours; dreaming about him is a privilege; and Duke Batrić Petrović swears to the converts to Islam, 'by the faith of Obilić', that the members of both religions will 'swim in blood' if the converts do not return to the religion of their ancestors. This was something the converts to Islam were not able to understand; they said that 'Miloš makes some people dizzy and some overly exhilarated'. The expression 'by the faith of Obilić' is, according to Miloš Babović, only conditionally a religious idea, and even less a religious feeling. It does not accept the kind of forgiveness expressed in Christ's symbolic turning of the other cheek (this is the only motif of the Kosovo myth which is not present in the *Mountain Wreath*. Contrary to Gospel ethics, 'the faith of Obilić' not only pleads for defence from evil, but also for revenge, which in the epic is on three levels: personal, tribal and popular (Babović 1990: 108; Gezeman 1968: 130-131).

Njegoš wanted the everyday life of Montenegrins to be pervaded by symbols of the Kosovo myth.[11] He designed a cap (in fact, he merely added some elements to the already existing Montenegrin cap) featuring black silk in mourning for Kosovo, and red fabric to represent the Serbian soil soaked in blood. One part of the cap, representing Montenegro, with the coat of arms of the Nemanjić dynasty at its centre, was encircled with five golden threads, symbolizing five centuries of the Montenegrin struggle against enslavement. He designed the Obilić gold medal for courage, the ideal of every Montenegrin warrior, awarded only to the most courageous among the brave. For the Montenegrin soul he wrote the *Mountain Wreath*. 'In this way the Montenegrins, both in their minds and hearts, lived with the Kosovo myth, from their first cap and their first rifle, to the first battlefield or to old age, reciting the verses by Bishop Rade (i.e. Njegoš), which they knew better than the hymn for the patron saint's day, and even better than the Lord's Prayer' (Babović 1990: 111).

This romantic tradition had been developing intensively particularly since 1878, when Montenegrin poets frequently chose Kosovo as the motif of their poems. These poems called for the final 'revenge of Kosovo'[12], preparing the Montenegrins in this way for a new historical act. Particularly outstanding among them was the Montenegrin ruler Nikola Petrović Njegoš, whose poems, although inspired by the Kosovo tragedy, had a clear political message and reflected his political programme. His cult was growing, and Montenegro itself was frequently referred to as the 'Piedmont of Serbdom'. Prominent Serbs from different regions looked up to Prince Nikola, and his ambitions were thus strengthened. His aspirations to the 'first place' among the Serbs were clearly seen in his poem 'O'er there, o'er there' (written in 1867), in which he described the Emperor Dušan's medieval capital, Prizren. The people accepted this poem as their battle song, as a call to liberate those Serbian people still under Turkish occupation, as a great national duty which had to be accomplished. The explanation given on the occasion of Prince Nikola's crowning as king (1910) showed that the Kosovo cult was one of the constitutive elements in the people's consciousness.

Literary works by numerous poets were inspired by the Kosovo myth and contributed significantly to the preparation of the Montenegrins for the 'final hour'. And this hour came in 1912, when the Balkan states made an alliance against the Turks, with the intention of driving the Turks out of the Balkans.

The cult of St. Vitus

Who exactly was St. Vitus, whose cult has continued to develop right up to the present day, in parallel with the Kosovo myth?

According to Veselin Čajkanović, Vitus or Saint Vitus ('the strong Vid') is a well-known Slav god of war. Vitus is the name of the supreme god, and possibly also of the oldest Greek chthonian god Avides. It is not impossible that one name, or one hypostasis, of the great chthonian god was also Vitus. In Kosovo, on the eve of St. Vitus's day, the head of the household would give every member of his household, as they left to participate in the square dancing, a peony, saying: 'I want you to be as red and strong as this flower'. In reply, the recipient would say 'I shall be as those who shed their blood on the Field of Kosovo '.

There were some tiny flowers growing on the field of Kosovo, bleeding tiny drops which, according to folk legend, were 'the tears of the wounded in the Battle of Kosovo who mourn for their lost kingdom'. The very name of this saint—Vid or Vitus[13] (Vid meaning sight)—determined, for the most part, the nature of the ritual performed on the day devoted to him. For example, what one saw on that day was of particular importance. One could see one's future on St. Vitus's Day, and so, even to the present time, St. Vitus's Day has been considered as a day for predictions and fortune-telling, done mostly with the aid of certain kinds of plants the names of which contain the name Vid (*vid, vidac, vidovčica, vidova trava*). The plant known as *vidovčica* is used for curing eye diseases, as are 'Vid's waters', where certain cultic acts are performed.[14] Finally, on St. Vitus's Day the cuckoo stops mourning for the slain Kosovo heroes.

It is possible that, due to the homonymous names of the ancient Slavic god Svetovit or Svetovid and a lesser known Christian martyr from the third century (Vitus Vit), who died on the same day as Prince Lazar was slain, the older cult was replaced by a new one (Nodilo 1885: 77–78; Kulišić 1979: 185). It is possible that the Church tried to push aside the pagan saint Svetovit and replace him with St.Vitus (Sveti Vid).

Prior to the battle of Kosovo, in the Orthodox church the 15 June (or the 28 June, according to the new calendar) was dedicated to the Old Testament prophet Amos. However, after the battle this date was dedicated to the canonized Prince Lazar. St. Vitus's Day became a red-letter day for the first time in church calendars in the late nineteenth century.

In the fifth decade of the last century, alongside the triumph of the ideas of Vuk Karadžić and the strengthening of the national consciousness, there was a growing interest in all things old, both historical and mythical. In the atmosphere of the ever-growing popularity of the Kosovo tradition, St. Vitus's Day was mentioned more and more frequently. The main political-literary magazine in Belgrade, called *Vidovdan* (St. Vitus's Day), also contributed to the spread of the cult.

In the state calendar, St. Vitus's Day was recorded (in regular letters) in Serbia after 1864 and in Vojvodina after 1869. Vit (the martyr) was replaced by Vid, and the following year the day was marked in the calendar as St. Vitus's Day (in brackets) (Popović: 120–121; Durković-Jakšić 1989: 365–367).

In 1879 in Belgrade, an article on St. Vitus's Day appeared, in which it was stated that 'St. Vitus's Day should become a day of general penitence, fasting and prayers. We remember our heroes, but we remember God as well.'

At the time of the five hundredth anniversary of the battle of Kosovo in the then independent Serbia (1879), the government made a decision to hold several memorial services to Prince Lazar and the heroes slain in Kosovo on St. Vitus's Day. Two medals were designed for the occasion, one of them devoted to St. Vitus. In the state calendar for 1890, for the first time *St. Vitus's Day was included as a national holiday, and it was written* that 'on 15 June ... memorial services will be held for the Serbian soldiers who gave their lives for their faith and their homeland'. In the calendar for 1892, the same text appeared, but 15 June, St. Amos's and St. Lazar's Day (St. Vitus's Day) was a red-letter day for the first time.

Church celebrations of St. Vitus's Day and public memorial services for the heroes of the battle of Kosovo were strictly forbidden by the Turkish authorities in Kosovo. Nevertheless, the memory of the so-called *isprijas* who used to carry candles and incense on St. Vitus's Day around local churches or church walls, lit in memory of the 'heroes of Kosovo' was preserved (Vukanović 1986: 407). In the late nineteenth century there were vivid stories circulating in Kosovo about the rivers Sitnica, Morava and Drim, which would turn red as blood on St. Vitus's Day. This would be repeated until 'the revenge of Kosovo and its complete liberation from the Turkish yoke' (Bogosavljević 1897: 99).

In 1905, in the reconstructed church of Gornja Gušterica (devoted to the holy martyr Lazar), a mass popular gathering was organized and St. Vitus's Day was celebrated openly for the first time. On the pretext of celebrating the local church feast, the day of the Kosovo martyr was celebrated thereafter in that village, in the presence of a great number of worshippers from the region of Kosovo and Metohija (Bataković 1991: 126)

Only in the late nineteenth and the early twentieth centuries, did St. Vitus's Day, as a symbol of Kosovo, become the focal point of the final settlement with the Turks. The Kingdom of Serbia used all political means to annex the then Turkish territories of Kosovo and Macedonia. The idea of the revenge of Kosovo was becoming more and more prominent, and the Kosovo myth was gradually turning into the cult of St. Vitus's Day. This day, as the day of the heroic battle and victory over evil, became a symbol of the bloody, merciless revenge over everything that stood for Turks or Moslems. Expressing the state-constituting climate of that period, the cult of St. Vitus's Day, in the first decades of the twentieth century, was admired and followed by the great majority of Serbian people (Popović 1976: 129–130).

However, in the early twentieth century there was some hesitation about proclaiming St. Vitus's Day an official national and religious holiday. Only in the 1914 calendar (i.e. after the battle of Kumanovo), did St. Vitus's Day become a red-letter day (i.e. marked as a church holiday), and after that it became one of the nine official holidays of the Kingdom of Serbia. 'So, only after the definite victory over the Turks, in which the Serbian warriors, in the same way as the archaic people of bygone times, proved that they were worthy of their heroic predecessors, was St. Vitus's Day officially proclaimed a national, religious and popular holiday. Starting with 1913, on the day celebrating St. Vitus, memorial services will be held for the slain warriors[15] and food and drinks will be distributed for their souls, as in the mythical times' (Popović: 122–123).

Some two decades ago M. Popović uttered the words which sound as a warning and a prophecy, 'The cult of St. Vitus's Day, which combines historical reality with myth, a real fight for freedom with pagan tendencies (revenge, slaughter, the offering of sacrifice, the revival of a heroic ancestor), potentially has all the characteristics of a milieu with untamed mythical impulses. As a phase in the development of national thought, it was historically indispensable. However, as a permanent state of mind, the St. Vitus cult can be fatal for those who are not able to free themselves from its pseudo-mythical and pseudo-historical snares. Caught in these snares, contemporary thought and the human spirit can experience another Kosovo, an intellectual and ethical defeat.'[16]

That St. Vitus's Day is popular in the twentieth century can be seen in the fact that some crucial events in the life of the Serbian nation are associated with this holiday. On St. Vitus's Day in 1914,

Gavrilo Princip (a member of the Young Bosnia Society) killed the Austrian archduke Franz Ferdinand in Sarajevo. In 1921, the Kingdom of Serbs, Croats and Slovenes adopted the unpopular St. Vitus's Day Constitution. The action of the JNA (Yugoslav People's Army) in Slovenia also took place near that day (27 June) in 1991, and the Serbian opposition organized the St. Vitus's Day gathering in 1993.

The use (or abuse) of the Kosovo myth

Folk poems, particularly the poems about Kosovo, in the richness of their mythical consciousness and ethical principles, represented a support in the struggle for liberation and the preservation of the national character. Vuk Karadžić saw the uprising and the epics which accompanied it as a revival of the Kosovo heroes.

Christian symbols from the time of the uprising made use of pagan vocabulary. The 'boiling blood' is not only the blood shed under Turkish oppression, but also the blood shed in the battle of Kosovo; when the blood of the slain starts boiling, it calls–according to ancient myths–on the avenger to avenge ('everyone to avenge his ancestor').

In his studies of Serbian political myths, Jovan Skerlić uses the terms 'religion', 'cult', 'idol', 'fetishism', 'messianism', and 'mysticism', finding the source of such myths in European Romanticism, mostly in its French and German variants. Most of these manifestations were found by Skerlić while studying the period of Serbian political and literary history between 1848 and 1871, which he described as the time of 'national and literary Romanticism among the Serbs'. The political images and beliefs of Serbian Romanticism were limited to a number of commonplaces, the repertory of which Skerlić described as a series of cults around particular idols—Kosovo, Montenegro, outlaws, the *gusle*, Serbdom, homeland, the historical past. All of these cults, taken individually, derived from the central general cult–the cult of nationality, the adoration of the nation perceived according to its Romantic meaning. Or, in Skerlić's words, 'belonging to a nation became the ideal of the new generation, the only god before whose altar they burned incense and before whom they fell down on their faces' (in Čolović 1994. 367).

Describing the national and liberation enthusiasm of the generation of 1860 and its 'patriotic mood', Skerlić wrote about 'the cult of Montenegro' and its antithesis, the 'hatred for the Turks'. He tried to understand this 'exaltation of the national feeling', but did not fail to present the expressions of hatred against the Turks from an ironic distance: 'the Turks were described in the darkest possible colours, and all vices and crimes were attributed to them ... The young poets behaved like cannibals towards the Turks.'

Brought up under the influence of the Kosovo myth, the leaders of the Youth Movement, according to Slobodan Jovanović, accepted as a historical fact that the defeat of the Serbs in Kosovo was the result of internal discord. Accordingly, the new war against the Turks required, in the first place, unity among the Serbs, and the Youth Movement was founded specifically to provide an example of this unity.

According to Slobodan Jovanović, there is no doubt whatsoever that the Youth Movement was successful in awakening and strengthening the national consciousness and in creating the moral atmosphere which made possible the 1876 Serbian-Turkish war (550).

The legend of Kosovo, preserved through religious tradition and centuries-deep layers of epic heritage, lay at the very foundations of Serbian national consciousness in Kosovo and Metohija. It was one of the spiritual sources which contributed most to the survival of the Serbs in the territory of the former state of the Nemanjić dynasty. Not many intellectuals, aided by the Serbian consul in Priština,[17] tried 'with the help of narratives in the Kosovo legend and moral lessons from the heroic poems, to consolidate the struggle for survival and to talk the people out of migrating, reminding them all the time that in Serbia and Montenegro the new breed of Obilić was preparing to start a war against the Turks in order to liberate them. The final settlement had been eagerly awaited since the times of the uprising of Karadorde' (Bataković 1991: 121–130). Those who succeeded in staying in their centuries-old homes until the Balkan Wars, remained there primarily due to an awareness that they were prisoners of the 'traditional Serbian ideal' and that, without them, the sacred mission of the liberation of Kosovo could not be achieved.

In the newly proclaimed Kingdom of Serbia (1882), the celebration of the five-hundredth anniversary of the battle of Kosovo was an event of utmost importance. 'Taking into account the fact that the Serbian people had not yet been liberated completely, the celebration had an actual meaning as well', writes Mihailo Vojvodić. 'It was a kind of test' of Serbia's relations with those states in which the Serbian people was still waiting for the hour of liberation. This refers primarily to relations with Turkey (1992: 483).

The Serbian government intended the celebration to contribute to and strengthen the reputation of the Obrenović dynasty (and primarily that of King Milan); the signs were becoming more certain that King Milan would abdicate from the throne in Serbia, so that the Kosovo celebration—and the transfer of Prince Lazar's relics into the country—as well as his annointing in the monastery of Žiča, were meant to strengthen the King's authority.

The celebration started several days before St. Vitus's Day. The president of the Royal Academy, the historian Čedomilj Mijatović, spoke about the battle of Kosovo and its significance. The key message was that the death of Prince Lazar was a testament to the Serbian people to preserve its unity; it was a symbol of the sacrificing of one's life for freedom, an inspiration for young generations to patriotism and heroism. The older generations had continued the fight and, according to Mijatović, the struggle went on.

A solemn ceremony was held in the Officers' Club as well. Colonel Jovan Mišković, the Chief of Staff, appealed for the establishment of a strong military organization in Serbia, with well-equipped troops, which, at the right hour, would bring about the unification of the Serbs.

On St. Vitus's Day, the liturgy and memorial service for the slain in Kosovo was held in the Cathedral; the Stanković choir sang and three-gun salutes were fired by the army. However, the main celebration of the Kosovo anniversary was held in Kruševac. On St. Vitus's Day, in the Lazarica church, the liturgy was performed in the presence of the king, invited guests and the people, and was accompanied by several choirs and gun and rifle salutes. After the liturgy, a memorial service for the Kosovo heroes was held in the churchyard, followed by an appropriate speech given by Metropolitan Mihailo.

In the afternoon, the king (accompanied by his regents) laid the foundation for the Monument to the Heroes of Kosovo. On the following day he laid the foundation for the new Serbian gunpowder factory on the river Rasina. On a parchment built into the foundations it was written that 'the gunpowder factory is raised in memory of the Kosovo heroes, as it will produce arms to be used for the liberation of the Serbian people' (Vojvodić 1992: 497–498).

The celebrations in Kruševac were not officially attended by Serbs from the parts of Serbia still under Turkish occupation, although they were very keen to attend. Respecting the authorities' wish that the celebrations should not be taken as a sign of demonstration against the Turkish rule in the Balkans, no official representatives of the Serbian people from Turkey attended.

The Hungarian Ministry for Internal Affairs, in order to avoid political demonstrations, forbade all celebrations in Hungary, with the exception of church celebrations. There were articles in the Serbian press about boats on the Sava and the Danube being under surveillance in order to prevent people from crossing over to Serbia. Other measures were also undertaken with the aim of preventing the celebration. Nevertheless, a liturgy was held in the monastery of Ravanica (in Srem), attended by thirty thousand people.

In Zagreb, at a meeting of the Yugoslav Academy, Franjo Rački ('a true friend of the Serbs') read his paper on the battle of Kosovo, and the religious service in the Orthodox church was attended by many citizens, scientists, professors and writers.

The authorities in Bosnia-Hercegovina managed to fulfil their aim in a very cunning manner. By making some small concessions to the Serbs with respect to the organization of the celebration, they managed to stifle any demonstration of national feelings and keep the celebration within church boundaries. They also ensured that the number of individuals who went to Sremska Ravanica and Kruševac was negligible.

Finally, this anniversary was marked by an important event in Serbian historiography. On the eve of the celebration, Ilarion Ruvarac wrote a treatise on Prince Lazar, while Ljubomir Kovačević wrote a treatise on Vuk Branković. Both of them, through a scholarly analysis of the sources and by applying existing principles of historiographical critique, ruthlessly omitted anything that was not verified by well-informed sources close to the event under study. In this way, the story of the Battle of Kosovo was stripped of many picturesque details, the most important among them being the betrayal of Vuk Branković (Ćirković 1990: 115–116). These two scholars, independently of one another, came to the conclusion that Vuk had not been a traitor in Kosovo (Mihaljčić 1990: 23–24). According to Sima Ćirković, their work represented the most valuable result of this anniversary, although it was met with resistance and denial by many contemporaries, by patriots and romantics, as well as by historians and lovers of history. Some were convinced that the national spirit would be weakened and undermined by doubting the popular tradition.

After 1889, the legend of Kosovo in Hungary was given a fresh impetus; calendars, almanacs and theatre performances (this topic was very suitable for presentation on the stage) featured poems, stories, critiques and papers on the heroes of Kosovo (Pejin 1991: 156–165).

Folk poems, particularly those about Kosovo, were a driving force and support in the liberation wars of the Serbian people in the twentieth century as well. Even the 'simplest peasant was imbued with faith in our national mission and expected the day of the revenge of Kosovo. This popular perception of the Dinaric type', writes Slobodan Jovanović, 'went even further then the observations of Cvijić and led to the revival, in a somewhat different form, of old beliefs as to the heroic character of the Serbian people.' Therefore, 'this Dinaric psychosis did not pass without practical consequences. Serbian feats in the Balkan Wars and in World War I can, to a certain degree, be explained by this psychosis '[18]

After the battle of Kumanovo, a new slogan was created—'For Kosovo-Kumanovo'. Although Kumanovo is not located in Kosovo, the victory at Kumanovo meant the liberation of Kosovo. In preparation for the liberation of Kosovo, the ethics of duty and the status of victim was born (with the emphasis on 'duty'); later on, in World War I, while losing territories (even the newly liberated regions) and during the retreat of the Serbian army and people through Albania, the Kosovo ethic was being developed with the emphasis on 'victim'. However, in the period of the Thessaloniki front, both ethical principles were once again cherished equally.

Generally speaking, the first quarter of the twentieth century was characterized by a wave of literary treatment of Kosovo, to which many poets contributed. Milan Rakić, Dragoljub Filipović, Miloš Vidaković, Rastko Petrović and Miloš Crnjanski wrote special cycles of the Kosovo (St. Vitus's Day) poems, while others—Aleksa Šantić, Jovan Dučić, Vladislav Petković Dis, Sima Pandurović, Veljko Petrović, and Milutin Bojić (together with some Slovenian and Croatian authors)—wrote more about current events associated with Kosovo, in the spirit of fulfilling the Kosovo testament. Branislav Nušić (the Serbian consul in Priština) wrote a comprehensive and detailed description of the tragic position of the Serbs in Kosovo, while Jovan Cvijić produced a condensed evaluation of their 'slavery which is equalled by none in Europe'.

In 1989, the six-hundredth anniversary of the battle of Kosovo, as well as in the years preceding it, the Battle of Kosovo, that is, the subject of Kosovo in the broadest sense, again reached a peak of popular interest. The motif of betrayal, one of the two key motifs of the Kosovo legend, was once more becoming immediately relevant. The motifs of Kosovo are also present in recent Serbian drama (Ljubomir Simović), painting (Mladen Srbinović, Miloš Gvozdenović), music and cinema. In the period of the so called happenings of the people, in 'meetings for truth' (July 1988-March 1989) the symbols of Kosovo were widely used.[19]

Preparations for the sixth-hundredth anniversary of the battle of Kosovo began a year earlier and were accompanied by numerous articles in the media, pointing out that the celebration of the Battle of Kosovo took place, as a rule, 'in decisive years of our history'. Just as they had in 1939, the celebrations were held in Gazimestan, in the presence of two million people[20], including about seven thousand immigrant Serbs (from the USA, Canada and Australia).

While the speech delivered in 1939 was composed of quotes from history, the 1989 speech was placed in the context of the political idiom of the more recent post-World War II history of Yugoslavia. These were the expressions most clearly remembered by the participants: 'Kosovo is the heart of Serbia', 'the heroism of Kosovo', 'the vassal position'. Slobodan Milošević made the following remarks in Gazimestan: 'There was discord among us in Kosovo six hundred years ago', and 'discord and treachery in Kosovo would follow the Serbian people as an evil fate throughout its history'. Even today 'discord among Serbian politicians has held Serbia back and their inferiority has humiliated it'. As a result, 'now, six centuries later, we are again in battle and facing new battles. They are still not armed battles, but even battles of that kind cannot be ruled out. Regardless of how they are fought, however, the battles cannot be won without determination, courage and devotion.'

The daily *Politika,* bearing the date of St. Vitus's Day, was devoted entirely to the Kosovo myth; the editorial headline read 'Six centuries from the battle of Kosovo, the time of Kosovo', with the subtitle, 'The Serbian people has glorified and still glorifies its heroes and recognizes its traitors'. This was followed by the claim that 'we failed to defend Serbia, but we saved Europe'. Further on it was stated that 'even now there are disputes about the betrayal of Branković. But, regardless of the historical facts, the Serbian people, from time immemorial to the present day, has been cursed by some Branković or other, as an unavoidable destiny'. Thus, 'we are once more living in the times of Kosovo, as it is in Kosovo and around Kosovo that the destiny of Yugoslavia and the destiny of socialism are being determined. They want to take away from us the Serbian and the Yugoslav Kosovo, yes, they want to, but they will not be allowed to.' The words of Prince Lazar delivered on the eve of the battle of Kosovo were also recalled: 'it is better to die honourably than to live in disgrace' (*P*, 28 June 1989).

In the texts written in 1989 the word *boj* (an archaic expression for battle, or fight) is used twice as often as compared to the texts describing previous celebrations, that is, 90 per cent more frequently than the word *bitka* (battle). On the other hand, the expression 'St. Vitus's Day' was much more frequently used in 1939 than at the time of the latest anniversary.

Finally, the six-hundredth anniversary of the battle of Kosovo was characterized by some expressions which stand out when compared to the 1939 texts. These are: 'consciousness', and 'coming to one's senses' (nationally, spiritually, religiously and morally), as well as the antonyms 'memory' and 'oblivion'.

Part of the celebration was also the evocation of myth, history and present-day reality, while the Battle of Kosovo was characterized more than once as a clash of 'two mankinds', 'a clash of two civilizations', of Moslem and Christian, in which Serbia, in 1389, was 'the last rampart against the onslaught of Islam'.

Exactly two years after this celebration (on 27 June), the Yugoslav People's Army's action in Slovenia marked the beginning of the end of the Socialist Federal Republic of Yugoslavia. Soon after that war erupted, first in Croatia and then in Bosnia-Hercegovina; the opponents were not the Bosnian Moslems, but the Turks, that is, the mythical enemy. A new mythical hero also emerged— Slobodan Milošević (in lieu of the late mythical father Tito)—who 'came to put an end to these banal times of misery and suffering, of disunity and lack of faith, and to announce the beginning of a new time of freedom, welfare and happiness' (Čolović 1994: 25–26).

Television screens and newspapers continued to glorify the feat of Miloš Obilić, a feat that was being imitated literally[21], while the name of Vuk Branković was applied, not as a metaphor, in the service of daily politics, to various personalities, even including certain foreigners ('Van den Broek is Branković Vuk!'). Militant speeches were adorned by quotes from folk poems and proverbs and citations from the works of Vuk Karadžić and Njegoš. The epic decasyllabic line was brought back into writing as a stratagem of propaganda which Ivan Čolović calls 'war-propaganda folklore' (1994: 8–9). The shrewdness of this folklore, according to the same author, 'is embodied in the presentation of war under the guise of eternity, that is, in transferring the conflicts from the sphere of politics, economy and history into the extrapolated sphere of myth' (96). And, 'in the temporality so conceived, the present-day wars fought by the Serbs are only a continuation of the former ones, or, to be more precise, their repetition, while today's leaders are incriminated ancestors (109). As a result today we are in danger of answering the call of demagogues, false prophets and politically ambitious and crazy priests, and of succumbing to myth and religion as the only plane of our existence, as the measure and the content of life in its entirety' (78).

Notes

1 The monks from the monastery of Ravanica led the column of several tens of thousands of families headed by Patriarch Arsenije Čarnojević, carrying the reliquary with the relics of Prince Lazar, as the Israelis did with the Ark of the Covenant in their exodus through the Sinai desert.

2 In the opinion of Leontije Pavlović, the main reasons for the creation of the cult of Prince Lazar are his role in the reconciliation of the Serbian and the Istanbul patriarchies (anathema had been placed on the Serbian church after Emperor Dušan proclaimed the independent Serbian patriarchy), his life, which ended in martyrdom, and the preservation of his relics (1965: 126).

3 The legend of Miloš Kobilić (*kobila* = mare) points to the matriarchate era, when heredity was matrilineal and when mares, and not stallions, were still holy animals (Matić 1976: 136–137)

4 M. Popović 1976: 61. Other heroes of the battle of Kosovo also lent their names to mountains, rivers, settlements and regions in the Serbian land where they had either lived or left various traces. (The most numerous are the stories surrounding Prince Lazar and Miloš Obilić.) Also, many Serbs believe that the heroes of the Kosovo battle are their true, blood predecessors, as, for example, the families of Orlović, Jugović, Banović and Kosančic (V. Đurić 1990: 53).

5 M. Orbin writes that, 'Vuković, with a small number of his warriors, fled after the battle, which took place on the Field of Kosovo, on 15 June 1389. However, Prince Lazar's son-in-law, Vuk Branković, saved himself and most of his warriors by conducting (some people say) secret negotiations to betray (which he actually did) his father-in-law in order to seize his state. Thus, after Lazar's death, he become the ruler of a part of Raška, while the other part went to Lazar's wife Milica and his two small sons, Stefan and Vuk' (Redžep 1991: 85).

6 The great number of preserved variations of the *Story* (36) goes to show that it had been copied and spread for a long time (from the early eighteenth to the mid-nineteenth century), in a wide belt from Boka Kotorska and Moscow to Budapest and Sofia. The absence of any prototype—the oldest known manuscripts date from the early eighteenth century—would lead to the hypothesis that the text originated in the late seventeenth century (Redžep 1991: 77).

7 In addition to the work of Mavro Orbin, the unknown writer compiled in his work the old Serbian chronicles and hagiographies, orally disseminated legends and folk poems.

8 The motif of conflicts among the lords who accuse one another of future disloyalty to the master is very frequent in literature (it is full of

dramatic tension), it is found in many medieval legends, but is also based on real relations in which loyalty to the king (or to the prince) was one of the foundations of the whole hierarchical order of those times (the epic *Poem of the Nibelungs*; Shakespeare's *Richard II*. See M. Pavlović, *The Epic poems of the Battle of Kosovo*; Đurić 1990: 539-540).

9 Milošević-Đorđević 1989: 324. Vuk Karadžić also recorded the following proverbs: 'It is better to die honourably than to live shamefully', and 'Better a grave than a slave'. In a folk poem we find the verse: 'The earthly kingdom is but for a while, while the heavenly kingdom is forever'.

10 Trifunović 1975: 262. The idea of the conscious choice of the heavenly kingdom (in Danilo's 'Sermon on Prince Lazar') was so exaggerated in the course of time that in the Kosovo legend it becomes—in addition to the treachery of Vuk Branković—one of the most important reasons for the defeat on the battlefield and the fall of the Serbian Empire (Redžep: 541).

11 'They mourn for Kosovo', says Ljuba Nenadović about the Montenegrins; they do not use any ornaments (not even a flower), women wear black scarves on their heads, and 'when you talk to them you get the impression that the battle of Kosovo took place only yesterday' (in: Đurić 1990: 372). The dirges acquired the importance of 'a living chronicle of the area, its history and its memory', so that 'until some forty years ago it was not unusual that the shepherdesses, in groups, high in the hills, mourned the Kosovo heroes and the soldiers who were killed at Scutari in 1912 (not their relatives, but in general)' (Mikitenko 1991: 272). Later on, the Partisans were also compared to the Kosovo heroes: 'Another Obilić sleeps here, the Montenegrin hero Sava' (275-276).

12 A collection of poems written on the occasion of the Montenegrin–Turkish war (1876-78) was called 'The Revenge of Kosovo' (Rakočević 1989: 391).

13 Preserved in many personal names: Vidoje, Vidosav, Vidak, Vidojka, Vidosava, and later on, Vidovdanka (Grković 1977: 52-53; 230-231).

14 According to the testimony of Felix Kanitz, at the foot of the mountain Vidojevica (near Prokuplje) 'on 15 June, St. Vitus's Day, which, as the date of the Kosovo battle, is "a black day" for the Serbs, the people gather there around a spring, whose water flows into a big rocky basin; a priest blesses the water, the people throw coins into the basin and wash their faces with healing water which protects them from every illness throughout the year. These semi-pagan customs ... are very frequent in Serbia' (1985: 326).

15 In Montenegro, memorial services were also held later on for the victims of genocide in the former NDH (Independent State of Croatia) (Bojović 1989: 398).

16 Popović: 151-152. Recently a similar warning came from the German Slavist R. Lauer: 'National myths, which are positive in times of peace as they enrich art, turn in times of conflict into potential militarism, in-

humanity, cruelty and intolerance, which act as a mass madness and can turn people into beasts. Regardless of whether it is a matter of *furor teutonicus* or *furor serbicus,* the victims suffer just as badly' (1994: 7).

17 The consulate was opened on the five hundredth anniversary of the battle of Kosovo.

18 Jovanović: 553–554. 'During the Great War', writes Jovan Cvijić, 'I used to meet Serbian officers and soldiers who asked to be told what was the most useful way to die, as they wanted to give their lives for truth and justice; they would look foolish to anyone who was not aware of this popular trait—the need for self-sacrifice—as a heritage of long generations' (in: Đurić: 183).

19 The popular slogans were: 'The plain of Kosovo, our bleeding wound', 'The peonies are withering in Kosovo, mourning the Serbs who had to move away', 'Let us not give away Kosovo, let us not give away the grave of Miloš', 'Janko was too late for Kosovo, but we won't be', 'Emperor Murad, you fell in Kosovo, and so will the traitors of today', 'What shall we show to Miloš once we face him', 'Miloš, rise from the grave', 'Kosovo is sacred Serbian ground', 'Kosovo is the soul of the Serbs and their unhealed wound, their blood and their prayer, their memory and their cradle' (Nedeljković 1989: 266–278).

20 In 1939 there were 100,000 persons present. Other celebrations, such as the ones in Knin or Dalmatian Kosovo, were attended by 10,000 persons in 1939 and by 100,000 persons in 1989 (Polovina 1991: 73–74). Reuters news agency estimated the number of participants at the Gazimestan manifestation at 300,000 (*P*, 29 June 1989).

21 'One should not neglect the importance of military tradition in the Serbian culture', warns Miklos Biro. 'Heroic deeds in wars were glorified in epic poems, and heroes praised extravagantly as a supreme educational ideal.' An analysis of elementary school textbooks (carried out in 1990) shows that these textbooks conspicuously favoured war heroes (65% of personalities), while outstanding persons in the fields of culture and history were mentioned only in passing. The freedom-loving tradition of ancestors was emphasized, while crises were settled in blood and by chivalry, without relying on reason. Willingness to suffer and sacrifice oneself for national ideals was emphasized as an important element of the national character (1994: 32).

The Migration of Serbs from Kosovo during the 1970s and 1980s: Trauma and/or Catharsis

MARINA BLAGOJEVIĆ

The migration of Serbs from Kosovo in the 70s and 80s is one of the deepest traumas felt by the Serbian population.[1] This article focuses mainly on the real roots of this trauma, and partially on the ways it has been interpreted and manipulated within the Serbian nationalistic movement.

This analysis of the migration of Serbs from Kosovo in the 70s and 80s has been deliberately restricted in many ways. In the first place, it deals only with migrations in a limited historical period. Secondly, the focus is on migration, not on overall Serb-Albanian relations in Kosovo: the migration of Serbs and Montenegrins is treated as one aspect of these relations, probably a key aspect in the Serbian trauma over Kosovo in the late 80s and early 90s, with the assumption that relations in general have been traumatized on both sides. Thirdly, analysis is based on different sources (statistics, surveys, content analysis) which due to their number and scope, have not been used systematically to the same extent. Fourthly, the emphasis is on a sociological interpretation of relationships between the two ethnic groups. A historical, and perhaps more importantly a demographic, approach is necessary, but is still insufficient for an understanding of the social implications of migration.

In the mid 90s the problem of Kosovo had lost nothing of its immediacy, simply because it had not been solved. However, the text was written in a good faith that behind every good solution there is an understanding of the problem in all its dimensions and at different levels. The problem of Kosovo, like others of the former Yugoslavia, has been subjected to one-sided, simplistic interpretation, fabrication and mystification, by all sides involved. The aim of this paper is to throw light on the migration of Serbs and Montenegrins in the 70s and 80s as a specific aspect of the Kosovo problem, an aspect which can contribute essentially to understanding the emergence and growth of Serbian nationalism and current Serbian entanglement in Kosovo.

In the case of Kosovo, and indeed of the former Yugoslavia in general, from the late 80s and especially in the 90s the conflicting sides were competing for the status of victim, with the ethnocrats making a tangible contribution to pushing their own people towards national suicide and, in fact, war.

The international political and professional public never took the problem of Serbian and Montenegrin migration seriously. This was largely due to the fact that the Serbian side, politically represented by the regime, never articulated an adequate explanation acceptable for the outsiders. Instead of a human rights problem, which the Serbian Kosovo issue was in the 70s and 80s, it was presented as a purely ethnic conflict embedded in history. In reverse, that was strengthening the Albanian argument along the same lines. The result was that exactly because Kosovo was not treated as a human right problem and a problem of undevelopement, the interpretations offered by either side had led to radicalisation of the conflict. As a result, the whole of the painful issue of interethnic relations in Kosovo was moved away from the idea of a civic state as the ideal model, and closer to that of an ethnic state as solution. Besides, the Serbs brought the problem to the attention of the international public too late, when the international community had already formed an opinion as to who was the victim and who the culprit. Later events in the 90s and especially genocidal acts of the Serbian regime made Albanian claims a self-fulfilled prophecy.

In addition, the migration of the Serbs is laden with a symbolism which harks back to the Kosovo myth (see O. Zirojević: 201–231) and has extraordinary traumatising power while fostering an irrational approach to reality. The migration of Serbs from Kosovo was a trauma not only because of the factual basis which produced it, but also because of inadequate attempts to solve problems of economic growth and ethnic co-existence. In the case of Kosovo, as in other parts of the former Yugoslavia, it was in fact the intensification of the conflict to the point of war which led to *post factum* arguments supporting its inevitability. The disclosure of this mechanism of *rationalisation-with-hindsight*, the goal of which was to *justify* the conflict, not to resolve it, is an element important in bringing about a rational and constructive attitude towards the Kosovo problem. This paper analyses the problem of migration on different levels—individual, group, political and social—in order to provide a better understanding of the complex deterministic strands that shaped it.

Facts—the terror of figures

Understanding and explaining any part of the Kosovo problem, including the migration of the non-Albanian population, is impossible without *figures*. Figures, in Kosovo and about Kosovo, have not only been the facts, they have always been the facts *within* the agenda of one or the other side. Not only have they often differed, but they have been differently interpreted and frequently used as arguments to prove opposite points.

On both sides in the of Kosovo conflict figures have most often been used to back arguments. Kosovo seemed to engender a sort of *hysteria* which was coupled with a fear of figures; the player not in possession of the right figure to use as an argument or counter-argument seemed to drop out of the game. In fact , the extensive use of numbers showed the weakness of both sides in the debate. In a very telling way, it also pointed to the domination of the collective over the individual, collective rights over individual rights, the over-simplification of problems and a vulgar nationalism.

On the other hand, at the macro level, numbers offer persuasive proof of on-going processes, of trends, and can even suggest appropriate solutions. Numbers are unavoidable, because in Kosovo they have been important *political category*. The facts of Kosovo's demographic structure can, to a major extent, be held to be the cause of ethnic conflict, not merely its rationalisation. *The migrations of Serbs and Montenegrins from Kosovo in the 70s and 80s have been both cause and consequence of the change in the ethnic structure and the quality of interethnic relationships.*

The population in Kosovo following World War II grew exponentially, from 727,820 in 1948 to 1,956,196 in 1991. This growth can be clearly divided into two periods: the first—from 1931 to 1961—in which the ratio of the Albanian to Serbian population was fairly balanced (27% as against 60–67%), and the second—after 1961—in which the balance totally collapsed (Krstich 1994). The fastest growth rate among the Albanian population was between 1961 and 1971. It should, however, be said that Albanians consider the figure of 2,171,433 (the estimate for 1991) to be an underestimation and that they claimed to be about 3 million in the former Yugoslavia, although there was no reliable source cited for this (Pula and Beqiri 1992).

The drop in the size of the non-Albanian population in Kosovo was the consequence of two factors: the differences in population growth between the two ethnic groups and the migration of Serbs and Montenegrins. Migrations from Kosovo, therefore, should also be considered in terms of accelerating the reduction of the non-Albanian population.

Differences in birth rates are the source of major contrasts in population growth as could easily be seen from the following data: the rate of termination of fertility among Serb and Albanian women in Kosovo (45–49 age group) in 1953 was 5.92 per cent for Serbian women, and 6.32 per cent for Albanian. In 1991 it was 2.78 per cent for Serbian women, and 6.16 per cent for Albanian (estimates from data processed by the Centre for Demographic Research, 1995). This shows that in the same undeveloped social environment, there was a clear drop in fertility among Serbian women but no such a fall among Albanian women of the same 45–29 age group.

Differences in birth rates meant distinct differences in population growth between the two ethnic groups, which especially became pronounced in the second half of the twentieth century. A young Albanian population with high acceptance of marriage, in combination with generally low mortality rates and high birth rates, produced a rapid increase, in fact an exponential growth unique in twentieth-century Europe. Huge contrasts in the level of population increase between Kosovo on the one hand, and central Serbia and Vojvodina on the other, have made Serbia unique among the countries of the world. It is the density and intensity of the population reproduction differences that made them so dramatic and encouraged political conflict.

In the period following World War II, Yugoslav Albanians differed from other Yugoslav and European populations in having the highest birth and fertility rates combined with the least spatial mobility. Up to the middle of the 1980s, the Kosovo population grew in ways more closely resembling the demographic development of Albania than Yugoslavia. However, in recent times the reproductive pattern of Albanians in Albania has begun to diverge from that of the Yugoslav Albanians: a fall in fertility and a slowing down of population growth has been more marked in Albania than in Kosovo (Avramov 1994).

Due to its surge in population growth, Kosovo, in 1921 the most sparsely populated part of Serbia (40.3 inhabitants per square kilometre), became in 1991 the most densely inhabited (179.7 inhabitants per square kilometre; DS 1991: 29). However, this did not result in any corresponding migration of the Albanian populace towards the more developed parts of Serbia or the former Yugoslavia. The closing down of the Albanian school system in

Kosovo, combined with an education system geared mainly to-wards white-collar occupations, considerably reduced the mobility of the Albanian work-force in the former Yugoslavia and Serbia (Petrović and Blagojević 1989).

These demographic factors contributed to the fact that after World War II Kosovo alone in the former Yugoslavia saw an in-crease of the majority, Albanian, population, in fact an increase of ethnic homogeneity. In all other areas it was heterogeneity rather than homogeneity that increased. Following the recent civil wars in the former Yugoslavia, however, it was clear that the situation would change utterly and that the newly created states would each show a considerable increase of the most numerous nation present.

The high birth rate among Kosovo Albanians, combined with low mobility, formed the *framework* within which the migration of Serbs and Montenegrins occurred. There was a connection be-tween *domination, number and emigration* of both ethnic groups which has repeatedly occurred at various times in history.

The picture of Serb and Montenegrin migration from Kosovo may easily be perceived by comparing percentage figures for Serbs in the Kosovo population before migration intensified (1948–23.6%; 1953–23.6%; 1961–23.5%) and after the process of inten-sive migration had begun (1971–18.3%; 1981–13.2%; 1991–9.9%) (Bogosavljević 1994). Between 1941 and 1981, over 100,000 Serbs and Montenegrins left Kosovo.

The figure of over 100,000 migrants can be best evaluated if the size of the entire Serb population of Kosovo is taken into account: (1948–171,911; 1953–189,869; 1961–227,016; 1971–228,264; 1981–209,498; 1991–194,190) (Bogosavljević 1994: 23). The Serbs who left, therefore, represented approximately half of the Serb population in Kosovo, while the Montenegrins who left (over 17,000 in the post-war period) represented almost half of the Mon-tenegrins that lived in Kosovo.[2] Similar data were given by the Albanian demographer, Islami: 'It is estimated that ... from 1966 to 1981, due to direct migration, around 52,000 people left Kosovo, and since 1981, around 20,000 Serbs' (Islami 1994: 47).

The migration of Serbs and Montenegrins from Kosovo contin-ued throughout the 1980s and first half of the 1990s, but with less intensity. Regular, systematic records of migrations began to be kept only as the most intensive period came to an end and popula-tion movement among the Serbs began to fall off. There was a negative migration balance among Serbs for each of the four years from 1990 to 1993, whereas Albanians had a negative balance for the first three years, and a positive balance in the last year. This was result of the migration of Albanians from Macedonia to Kosovo. From 1989 to 1993, over 6,000 Serbs, almost 1,200 Montenegrins and around 9,700 Albanians emigrated from Kosovo (source: SZS).

Albanian demographers frequently explained the migration of Serbs from Kosovo as a 'return' to the places they came from as colonists between the two world wars. However, the data suggest differently.Records show that between 1919 and 1930, a total of 5,795 families were brought in to colonise Kosovo, followed by a further 11,383 between 1931 and 1941 (Nikprelević 1989: 9). If the average family had, say, five members, that would mean around 86,000 people. The figures are, of course, only approximate. What they add up to, however, is not. After many intervening decades, the descendants of these Serbs would result in a number far greater than 100,000.

Also, the connection frequently referred to between later migrations of Serbs from Kosovo and their previous arrival there as colonists has not been confirmed by studies of Serbian and Montenegrin migration. A comparatively high number of migrants were born in Kosovo. About 85 per cent of the heads of migrating families were Kosovo-born and about 50 per cent of their fathers were colonists, whereas about a quarter had bought land there (Petrović and Blagojević 1989). It is worth mentioning that Kosovo, at the beginning of the century, was not only attractive from the agricultural point of view but also less populated than central Serbia, another strong element of attraction.

On the other hand, Albanian demographers claimed that in the same period no less than 300,000 Albanians from Kosovo were moved out by force. 'It is estimated that between the two world wars about 50,000 Albanians were moved to Albania and about 250,000 to Turkey' (Islami 1994: 43). Although at this point it is not possible to delve into the problems of historical demography or prove any facts, the conclusion seems to be that in view of the number of Albanians in post-war Kosovo, the Kingdom of Yugoslavia uprooted about 40 per cent of the Albanian population.

Albanian demographers also argued that the second wave of colonisation after World War II was extremely intensive.

A considerable number of Serbs and Montenegrins arrived from Serbia and Montenegro to take up positions (although with low or medium qualifications or barely literate), and with families. They found employment mostly in the civil service, in the administration, in social, health and cultural institutions, in the municipal services etc. ... today, having completed their working careers and become wealthy, they are returning to their places of origin, where their property is. The number of Serb-Montenegrin immigrants from 1945 to 1966 was as high as 500,000 people". (Islami 1994: 45)

The absurdity of this is clear from the following facts—the number of Serbs in Kosovo in the post-war period never exceeded 230,000, and questions put to migrants showed that not only had the absolute majority of heads of families been born in Kosovo, but also that only about 10 per cent of their fathers had came to Kosovo after World War II (Petrovic and Blagojevic 1989: 119).

Towards the middle of the 1990s, Albanians began to migrate to Kosovo from the adjoining areas: Montenegro, Macedonia and central Serbia. This became more pronounced following the opening of Priština University. 'It can be estimated that from 1966 up to today about 45,000 Albanians came to Kosovo' (Islami 1994: 46).

One of the basic characteristics of ethnic structural change in Kosovo has been its *spatial aspect*. Data from the censuses of 1961, 1971 and 1981 showed that 'the lower the number and comparative percentage of Serbs and Montenegrins in the population of a municipality, the steeper the drop in numbers and the earlier this became manifest. Simultaneously with this overall fall in numbers, a *reduction in territorial distribution* appeared throughout the province, with a growing concentration of smaller numbers into fewer municipalities, that is, over an increasingly narrow area' (Petrović and Blagojević 1989: 90).

These statistical data are closely related to a survey of migrant Serbs and Montenegrins which showed that the proportion of non-Albanians in the overall population of an area or municipality was crucial in *explaining the level of discrimination* and thus emigration from the area. The proportional representation of Albanians and non-Albanians played a key role in determining interethnic relations at local community level. This link between the proportion of ethnic groups, their mingling, and the quality of interethnic relationships is logical and exists in all multiethnic communities. What differs is the way in which it makes itself apparent.

It was this concentration of Serbs and Montenegrins over a diminishing area which gave rise to *parallelism* as a form of ethnic coexistence in the early 90s; this culminated in a parallel state, parallel school system and other parallel institutions. Together with the shrinking percentage of Serbs and Montenegrins in Kosovo, the number of mixed areas decreased. Between 1961 and 1981, the number of settlements without a single person of Serb nationality rose from 410 to 670, and areas without Montenegrins from 243 to

760 (Petrović and Blagojević 1989: 93). A town or village which at the time of one census was 90 per cent Albanian, had become 'pure' Albanian by the time of the next census. An 'ethnic homogenisation of settlements' had taken place in Kosovo. Some 94 per cent of the settlements were dominated by one ethnic group. Settlements were no longer multicultural, which had been their basic characteristic for a long period (Krstić 1994). What this meant was that the majority of Albanians *had no contact* with Serbs in the course of their daily lives, and vice versa.

The pattern of movement among Albanians within the province was also unexpected, as they tended to move much more to mixed-population municipalities than to Albanian-only ones. Between 1961 and 1981, twice as many people moved into the nine mixed municipalities than into the other fifteen. The lower the percentage of the Albanian population, the higher the rate of immigration into the area (Krstić 1994: 156). Internal resettling by the Albanian population made it dominant not only in the areas where it was in the majority in the 1960s, but throughout the province. An analysis of the directions in which movement took place shows that the end effect was that the 'major part of the Province became predominantly Albanian' (Krstić 1989: 161).

The expansion of the Albanian population was linked to three processes: 1) an ethnic take-over of settlements; 2) ethnic territorial expansion; and 3) occupation of land by ownership (Krstić 1994). This last process is hardest to document, as there is no way of examining land registers and the sale of land largely took place outside the law (introduced in late 80s) which banned any inter-ethnic traffic in property. All these processes, like the population growth itself, had an effect on the migration of the non-Albanian population from Kosovo.

Interpreting the demographic processes

Interpretations of demographic movements in Kosovo—like the facts—differed widely between the two sides. While the Serb side insisted on the political aspect, treating the high birth rates as a *political strategy*, the Albanian side insisted on *undevelopment* as the main reason. Perhaps the greatest consensus existed on the link between high birth rates and the status of women: both sides agreed that the unfavourable position of women was a substantial cause of high birth rates. More subtle analysis, however, shows that even the unfavourable position of women is subject to different interpretations. An understanding of the complexity of the determinist blend which led to the exceptionally high birth rates in Kosovo is essential also for the understanding of the determinist blend that shaped the migrations. In other words, the common denominator in both processes was the reduction in the percentage of the non-Albanian population in Kosovo. Ignoring this connection would mean failure of understanding the situation and, as a result, failure to find a solution.

One of counter-arguments to undevelopment as a determinant of high birth rates of Albanian population are the figures showing the speed at which the birth rate declined between the two world wars in other parts of former Yugoslavia. While this decline continued after World War II in the rest of the country, in Kosovo it was considerably delayed. Many areas at the same level of development had a far lower birth rate, and there were parts of Yugoslavia which, in terms of development, did not differ much from Kosovo but which still had a lower birth rate. One explanation is that 'modernisation' in Kosovo was an import and not the result of indigenous development, which meant that it was unable to effect appropriate changes in institutions which traditionally encourage high birth rates. This situation is analogous to that of Third World countries where a drop in the birth rate has lagged considerably behind the fall in mortality, 'imported' from developed countries. 'Modernisation came from outside Kosovo, and was upheld and subsidised by sources outside Kosovo' (Avramov 1994: 171).

According to some contemporary demographers (e. g. Livi Baci), a change in the demographic pattern is not simply a consequence of modernisation, but rather of the fact that 'bringing fertility under control is a way of preparing society for the changes that lead towards modernisation'. However, birth rates can also be 'controlled' at a higher level, if it has clear objectives for a certain community.

Albanian demographers claim that demographic growth is one of the factors of 'resistance towards assimilation and physical extermination' (Islami 1994: 30). Among the social and political conditions of the 70s and 80s, and even the first part of the 90s, it was hard to imagine the assimilation of such an overwhelmingly numerous and homogeneous group as the Albanian population in Kosovo. The 'baby boom' in the Kosovo Albanian population lasted almost four decades, which, according to Avramov, points to the conclusion that this was a 'cultural option' (1994). In the 1980s, the general rate of fertility in Kosovo–at 4.5–was the highest in Europe. Albanian women in Kosovo had almost one child more than women in Albania, where the general birth rate for the 1980s was estimated at 3.6 (ibid.).

Albanian demographers offer the following explanation of this phenomenon: 'The actual birth rate (about 28%) and reproduction among Albanians as a whole, the extreme youth of the Albanian population (52% under 19 years of age with an average age of about 24 years)–rare in world trends–taken with the stability of marriage and the family, speak of a *vital population with a faster demographic growth*' (Islami 1994: 32–author's emphasis). It is certainly interesting that Islami takes a high birth rate and the sta-bility of marriage as indicators of *vitality*, which sounds like a rac-ist type of argument. It is hardly necessary in contemporary sci-ence to prove that differences among populations in birth rates, apart from the influence of the age structure, are not the result of vitality or a biological capacity for childbearing, but are due merely to differences in behaviour.

'Vitality' may also be considered in the light of the following facts: data from a survey carried out in 1976 showed that only every second Albanian woman knew that fertility could be con-trolled, and only 9 per cent used contraception (Avramov 1994). All women above the age of thirty gave birth to more children than they considered optimal for a family. Women between forty-five and forty-nine, in fact, gave birth to as many as 2.4 more children than they considered a family should have.

Birth rates in Kosovo subsequently began to change, mostly in the segment of younger and more educated women, but most women still accepted, or were forced to accept, the traditional model. One of the arguments in defence of high birth rates is the question of the reproductive rights, which includes the right to decide on the number of children. But in the case of extreme high birth rates the aspect of responsibility towards children already born is completely neglected. In large families, investment in chil-dren is small, and the standards of care and upbringing extremely low (Rapi 1995).

The key to the demographic situation in Kosovo was that 'this area has long ago overstepped the threshold of development be-gun by an impressive fall in birth rates in other parts of Yugoslavia. Its social and economic features show Kosovo society to be in transition; true, it is closer to a modern community in its social and economic aspects and to a traditional one in terms of the repro-duction of the population' (Avramov 1994). In other parts of

Yugoslavia, a reduction of birth rates came about in unfavourable conditions of development. The connection between development and the birth rates level in Kosovo was weakest, compared with the rest of the former Yugoslavia. This gives added point to the question: '*Why was the fall in birth rates not faster in Kosovo?*'

Policies aimed at lowering the birth rate in Kosovo, in the words of Islami, were totally Albanophobic, and Albanophobia is based on counting Albanians. It is interesting to note, however, that Albanians themselves took their number as one of the best proofs of the importance and justness of their national cause (Pula 1992).

Collectivism provides the frame for high birth rates, low standards of nurture of children, and national homogeneity; it is this that assists us in understanding national unanimity and readiness for collective, and consequently individual, sacrifice.

The domination pendulum

Migrations of Serbs from Kosovo in the 70s and 80s must be viewed in a general social and ethnic context. They were only a segment of the migration swings which have characterised the pendulum of Serb–Albanian relations in the province. A glance at these relations alone in the post World War II period, till the mid 90s, reveals three distinct periods.

1. From 1945 to 1966—domination by the Serb group (over agriculture and traditional structures which maintained parallelism in Serb–Albanian relations), within the context of the entrenchment of communes and state property.

2. From 1966 to the end of the 1980s—discrimination against the Serb group, within the context of industrialisation, accelerated development, the zenith of Communism, self-management, and 'socially owned' property. Albanians see this period as a period of 'more equal treatment' (Islami 1994). This was a time when 'minority rights in Kosovo up to 1989 were guaranteed above and beyond international standards' (Vasilijević 1994: 77). 'Albanians were too backward and lacking in political culture, the Kosovo bureaucracy was too mediocre and dogmatic to forego the opportunity of using improved status and weight of numbers in the administration to take revenge on the Serbs or, if this was not open, at least to ignore their interests. At the same time, Albanian nationalism was fed by the unchanged status of the vast majority of Alba-

nians who lived as a minority in Yugoslavia and as a functional minority in Kosovo' (Maliqi 1989: 73).

3. From the end of the 1980s to the mid 90s—domination by the Serb group (complete parallelism of institutions and a parallel state, the breakdown of Communism, introduction of a market economy, privatisation, a grey economy). 'The actual majority in Kosovo feels like a functional minority, and the actual minority wants to have the status of the functional majority' (Maliqi 1989: 71). This period is characterised by discrimination of Albanians best expressed in schooling problems and sacking of over 85,000 working Albanians (Pula and Beqiri 1992).

It should be noted that at different periods, when the 'pendulum of discrimination' swung to one side or the other, as a rule it changed the direction of the migration of the Albanian and Serb populations. As one group attained a more advantageous situation in the province, this attracted (either by plan or spontaneously) members of the same group from areas outside the province. Migrations to and from Kosovo represented, to a certain degree, the *measure of the status* enjoyed there by a certain ethnic group. Especially interesting is the connection between immigrations and emigrations of the Albanian and non-Albanian population. Emigration of one of the two ethnic groups encouraged immigration of the other. As these trends owed nothing to economics, it may be concluded that migrations were shaped by political circumstances. Thus both groups used political, and through them economic, mechanisms to encourage trends in a certain direction. This undoubted regularity shows that, where Kosovo is concerned, numerical presence was truly a political category. Just how strategically important figures and percentages are in the forming of new national states has been tellingly demonstrated by subsequent events in the former Yugoslavia.

The alternation of these periods also meant the taking of *revenge* on the ethnic group which had temporarily 'lost out'. However, in periods of domination by one or the other, the greatest losers were those who were in any case underprivileged: the lower classes and different minority groups.

In these three periods, the *direction of domination* changed, and relations between ethnic groups were placed in a different economic and political context, changing the context of ethnicity itself. The first period, agrarian and early Communist, was marked by a generally high level of repression founded in extreme traditionalism and related authoritarianism. The ethnic groups came second to the division between the 'enemies' and 'friends' of Communism.

In the second period, accelerated industrialisation and urbanisation, coupled with the expansion of education, enabled a more rapid breakdown of traditional norms and the formation of an Albanian elite. New political oligarchies began to *produce ethnicity* all over the former Yugoslavia, including Kosovo. Within the Communist framework, the new 'naciocrats' built their strategies using the institutions of the system, especially the Communist Party. 'Around Kosovo and in Kosovo there was, and still is, conflict about the redistribution of power between national oligarchies formed among the local leaderships of the Communist Party which held the monopoly' (Maliqi 1989: 72). Different oligarchies strove to achieve legitimacy in order to rule. The migration of Serbs and Montenegrins was used to legitimise the Serb oligarchy in the same way as pressure by Serbia on Kosovo from the early 1990s was used to legitimise the Albanian oligarchy. At the heart of all the constitutional and political changes in Kosovo lay an abuse of the position of power. At the same time, there were no appropriate institutional mechanisms to control this abuse. The destruction of institutions, above all of the legal state, began in Kosovo.

It should be remembered, however, that not only national oligarchies but both populations, especially the Albanians, identified totally with Kosovo as their own territory. This was a very natural process, as the latter had a problem in identifying with the South-Slav community, while the extreme backwardness of the province contributed to a high level of autarky. In addition, as shown by data on ethnic distance in the former Yugoslavia, the Albanian population itself exhibited the greatest distance towards other groupings and was held at greatest distance by others (Pantić 1991).

The third period in the 90s features the completion of the process of creating national states by carving up Yugoslavia, and the strengthening of the ethnic economic basis, especially through the grey economy. Throughout the three periods, the international context also changed perceptibly, rendering the problem even more complicated.

The mimicry of anachronism

Migrations of Serbs and Montenegrins from Kosovo were usually explained as *economic* by the Albanian side, and as *political*, ethnic or 'due to pressure' by the Serbian side. In the mid-1980s, public disagreement in Yugoslavia as to the cause of the migrations grew more vociferous; rumours of sales of Serb land at a price far below the market value were rife, and political pressure by the non-Albanian population of Kosovo (petitions and arrivals *en masse* in Belgrade) increased. By way of response, in 1985 the Serbian Academy of Arts and Sciences (SANU) initiated a survey among migrants aimed at discovering the causes of migration. The field work was carried out between 1985 and 1986.

This study was one of the rare attempts to broach an issue still taboo at the time. As the real dimensions of migration and inter-ethnic conflict in Kosovo were still being concealed, the Serbian public of the time was upset only by revelations of sales of Serb land under pressure and below the market value.

The initial theoretical framework, based on the assumption of a major influence of economic factors which 'pushed' people from less developed to more developed areas, proved to be defective and inadequate after an analysis of a wealth of empirical material. Although similar to economic migration in their external charac-teristics, in that movement took place away from an underdevel-oped Kosovo towards a more developed Central Serbia and Voj-vodina, in essence the majority of these migrations were not eco-nomic. In fact, they turned out to be not only ethnic but anachro-nistic, an ominous portent of the *global anachronism* in which Yugoslavia would find itself a few years later. The mimicry of eco-nomic factors contributed to a failure to recognise or admit the real causes. In fact their neglect helped the radicalisation of Ser-bian nationalism. Unfortunately, from today's perspective they seem like a logical introduction to the events that took place in the 90s in former Yugoslavia. Migrations of Serbs from Kosovo were the first predominantly ethnic migrations in the second Yugosla-via. Even though the general flow of migrations, particularly from 1971 to 1981, tended to gather ethnic groups into the territorial centres of their largest concentration (Petrović 1987), migrations from Kosovo appeared to be distinctive, not for the direction they took but for their quality, that is, the proportion of non-economic motives involved.

The main finding of the survey was that only 15 to 25 per cent of the migration of Serbs and Montenegrins from Kosovo in 70s and 80s can be explained by economic factors, while the rest were chiefly due to non-economic reasons.

If the migrations of Serbs and Montenegrins from Kosovo had been entirely inspired by economic factors, migration would have taken place at the level of the individual, not whole households; the younger and working population would have moved out, not

all generations; it would have represented a step upwards on the
social ladder for the majority of emigrants, causing upward and
spatial mobility to converge; a mainly rural population would have
migrated because of overpopulation, not middle class urban population; the migrant population would have been lower on the social scale in Kosovo than the non-migrant population (except in
the case of brain drain), and economic factors would have been
cited as the main reason for migration. Besides, the Albanian population would have migrated to the same degree and to the same
destinations.

However, survey results have shown that none of those was the
case. In fact, characteristics of the migrants (500 households, 3,418
members) differ to an appreciable extent from the theoretical
model for economic migration. Before the migrations Serbs enjoyed a comparatively favourable material and social status and
they were often urban population. At the same time they were
deeply rooted in Kosovo and integrated: as many as 41.5 per cent
of respondents over the age of fifteen spoke Albanian. Migration
for the great majority of the migrants was both painful, traumatic
in fact, and meant a loss in economic and prestige terms.

Forms of discrimination

Analysis of survey results led to the conclusion that there were
three interlined forms of discrimination in Kosovo: 1) indirect or
informal; 2) institutional; and 3) ideological.

Informal discrimination was mainly expressed by social groupings. The discriminators acted on their own behalf or that of their
families. The setting was provided by the town or village. Discrimination was spontaneous and without any institutional guidance; it was not planned or programmed in each individual case.
Spontaneity, however, referred to each individual act of discrimination, to the choice of place, time, method, means and victim, but
not to the spontaneity of discrimination itself as a societal and political phenomenon. The fact that informal discrimination was
spontaneous did not mean that it was not organised, encouraged
and even rewarded on a larger collective level. Its spontaneity
made resistance of Serbs extremely difficult.

Indirect discrimination was unpredictable, employed a variety
of methods and means, was frequently invisible and took place

without witnesses. All this made it impervious to control by society. At the same time, its powers of destruction were great, as it was aimed at the everyday life of the individual, at his or her immediate surroundings. Informal discrimination therefore was the strongest factor in causing migration.

Institutional discrimination existed within the system of social and economic institutions. It manifested itself at secondary group level. Within the institutions, those who were discriminated against and those who discriminated stood in relation to one another not only as members of different ethnic groups, but as players of different roles in society. The essence of this type of discrimination within the institutions was that it became the *hidden* but *real* reason for their existence. The importance of these new discriminatory functions of the institutions was even greater than the original functions for which the organisation was intended. Thus discrimination in schooling was becoming more important than education, and discrimination at the workplace more important than making a profit.

Only the existence of discrimination within institutions enabled its institutionalisation, which gave it structure and endurance. Thus a system of domination and social difference was institutionalised, based on discrimination. Discrimination, even though an illegitimate act, gained a certain legitimacy in general practice by right of custom.

Substituting legitimate with illegitimate goals within institutions was made possible by establishing a parallel structure and parallel system of behaviour, which rested on special rights. Upholding the new rules and respecting this system enabled promotion, while failure to do so drew down sanctions. Discriminatory behaviour meant promotion for the individual and for the group, regardless of which ethnic group they belonged to.

Ideological discrimination was reflected in the unequal treatment of different ethnic groups at the level of social awareness and public discourse. Discrimination became ideology by the process of creating a social awareness that rationalised and justified discrimination, and, finally, made the act of discrimination possible. Ideological discrimination, therefore, provided a basis of norms and values for the actual discrimination which took place at primary or secondary group level. The effects of this discrimination were not direct, but made themselves felt through two other types of discrimination. The basis for this discrimination was the well-known phenomenon of 'blaming the victim' (Rayan), that is, blaming the *Other*, the one who is actually victimised to be responsible for his/her own victimisation.

The object of ideological discrimination, unlike that of informal or institutionalised discrimination, was not the individual, the household or some narrow group, but the ethnic group as a whole. It therefore conferred on discrimination—which, after all, took place as an individual act—a particular weight of its own and the legitimacy of generality. Therefore, the existence of ideological discrimination and the development of such an ideology clearly distinguished interethnic strife at the individual level from discrimination as a global societal phenomenon. Ideological discrimination was based on a wide acceptance of ethnic goals, voluntary or involontary: 'The information system is channelled and there are many restrictions on the free advocacy of various political options among the Albanians' (Maliqi 1989: 133).

Education (curricula and syllabi), the media, cultural institutions, political organisations and public opinion all served as channels of ideological discrimination. The opinions of the group that was the target of discrimination were formed in response to the opinions of the group discriminating against it, and were marked by a feeling of fear and of threat to their cultural and ethnic identity.

Is there a basis for claiming that the various types of discrimination formed a *system?* In the first place, the discrimination had an objective: the result of all three types of discrimination was the reduction of the percentage of non-Albanians in the province. Regardless of whether this objective formed part of the political manifesto of an organised group or not, and regardless of whether it was deliberate and public or spontaneous and hidden,[3] it was being *achieved*. The reduction of the percentage of Serbs and Montenegrins in the ethnic structure of the province was, in large measure, the result of discrimination, that is, migration under the influence of discrimination.

Besides, the methods implied by the different types of discrimination were of the same kind (establishing numerical superiority, segregation and worse), while the means were closely connected and intertwined. All three types of discrimination were *complementary* and acted in *synergy*. Finally, empirical confirmation of an integrated system of discrimination can be found in the fact that *numbers*—the numerical superiority of the Albanian group—are the universal key to understanding the strength of discrimination. Discrimination was all the stronger, its means more repressive and cruel, if the percentage of the Serb and Montenegrin group in the population of the municipality or town was lower. The *critical point* at which relationships between ethnic groups turned in the direction of discrimination was the shrinking of the percentage of Serbs and Montenegrins to between 20 and 30 per cent.

A quantitative and, to an even greater extent, qualitative, analysis of empirical material uncovered a sequence of fairly open, crude and violent means and methods of discrimination.

The analysis shows that in Kosovo, *informal discrimination* included inciting fear and a feeling of danger (on the street, on public transport); restricting freedom of movement (in terms of time and area); endangering children (in school, on the street, even in their own backyards); physical abuse (fights, murder, assault); verbal abuse (bad language, insults, threats); threats of rape and rape itself; and causing financial damage to households (illegal use of property, destruction of crops, the damaging and stoning of houses, arson, the sale of land for less than its market value, manipulation of the transfer of land and tax payments).

Institutional discrimination in the workplace in Kosovo was evident in recruitment policies for employees (according to which Serbs would have to know both languages but not Albanians); the setting of quotas for employment which prevented Serbs from getting a job; staff relationships (quarrels, verbal and physical assault, laying traps, preventing members of the minority group from attaining managerial positions); the use of the Albanian language at meetings without providing translation; according privileges to Albanians in shift work; protecting Albanians from the consequences of idleness, lack of discipline, irresponsibility and destruction of company property, and, on the other hand, unjustly penalising the minority group, transferring them to less congenial jobs, imposing early retirement, making them redundant and subjecting Serbian women to sexual abuse and blackmail.

Discrimination in the Kosovo Communist Party took the form of establishing a negative selection for joining and advancement within the party. Party organisations were blocked from solving interethnic relations. This was especially affected by the change in the ethnic structure of such organisations as, in time, growing numbers of Albanians joined while Serbs increasingly left the party, disappointed by its inability to solve problems of interethnic relations.

Institutional discrimination in government bodies was reflected in the obstruction of any intervention which would help to eliminate it. Here, the methods used were ignoring and covering up cases of discrimination and protecting the culprits, and even incriminating and abusing Serbs who sought protection. The courts contributed by dragging out cases, allowing cases to lapse, imposing inadequate fines, allowing false testimony, punishing the plaintiff instead of the culprit, and making unfair use of language (hearings were held only in Albanian even when the parties involved were Serbs). The police were actively discriminatory, perpetrating violence against Serbs (physical assault), participating in demonstrations on the side of demonstrators and provoking the Serb population. Within the police force, as in the workplace and the Party, the criteria for advancement depended on services rendered in the area of discrimination. The administration also contributed to the unfavourable position of the Serbs by setting up various 'blockades' which made their position difficult—preventing them from regulating pensions and social security or from obtaining various legal rights, refusing to speak Serbian, interfering with Serb housing by urban planning ... The non-Albanian population did not have the right to rebel or react, as 'Dispute or objection raised with respect to the existing [regulations] are placed on a par with criminal acts' (Vasiljević 1994: 78).

Ideological discrimination comprised a host of actions which contributed to producing a distorted picture of Kosovo. The predominantly Albanian media in this period created an extremely one-sided picture of what was happening in Kosovo, to the extent that it could be said with some truth that the media war in the former Yugoslavia was invented in Kosovo.

Ideological discrimination led to a deep division of public opinion along the lines of ethnicity. In opposition to institutionalised public opinion, there was the spontaneous emergence of the opinions of the threatened group. This relied on private, illegal channels of information and fostered feelings of danger and fear; it represented an attempt at rationalising interethnic clashes by resorting to historical arguments. What was especially vital in the opinion of the threatened group was the *collective memory* of hardships suffered, especially in World War II when Albanians were on the fascist side (Petrović and Blagojević 1989: 180–184).

Crisis and trauma

Memories of past hardships were constantly refreshed, endlessly reinforcing the *trauma* together with a feeling of helplessness and a fatalistic acceptance of the 'looseness' of Kosovo. A sense of the *'nowness'* of history was present in the memory, a sense that history and the present did not differ but contained eternal forces of good and evil, so that what was happening became a pattern for understanding what had gone before and what was yet to come.

The methods and means of discrimination described above, applied to the Serbs and Montenegrins prior to migration, acted simultaneously and interdependently. Their interdependence, however, was the strongest proof of the rule demonstrated by this research, that the strength of discrimination depends on the ethnic make-up of the social environment.

Thus, when asked what relations were like in the place from which they had migrated, 71 per cent of migrants said they were not good, or were bad. The most frequently described situations were those related to 'direct verbal pressure' or material damage. Over a quarter of all explanations referred to some form of physical violence. The smaller the percentage of non-Albanians in the area, the worse relations were. Among the migrants from municipalities with a Serb and Montenegrin population of 30 per cent or above, there were noticeably more frequent references to noninterference, avoidance or good relations, terms which rarely appeared in samples from municipalities with a small Serb population. The critical point for a change in relations was a proportion of Serbs and Montenegrins of between 20 and 30 per cent. Anything below that level directly brought about a deterioration in relations.

A very strong motivation among Serb migrants was fear for their children, since, as the survey shows, 28.5 per cent of the children from the respondent households had experienced physical injury and fights, while 23.5 per cent had been exposed to threats and verbal abuse. Children were frequently unable go to school without parental escort, often armed. Here again, the key to understanding these relationships is the ethnic structure of the area or settlement; the rule that emerges is that the threat to children was in direct proportion to a lower percentage of non-Albanians within the ethnic structure. From this, the dynamics of the situation can be deduced: discrimination grew in parallel with the reduction in the proportion of Serbs and Montenegrins in the ethnic structure of municipalities in Kosovo (Blagojević 1991).[4]

In contrast to this approach, in which the emphasis is on 'pressure', the most frequently mentioned reason for migration cited by Albanian scholars and political leaders is usually the following:

> The migration of Serbs from Kosovo after 1966 did not occur because of Albanian pressure as alleged by the post-1981 Serb-Yugoslav-Communist government, but because of a loss of the privileges which they had enjoyed up to then and an unwillingness to accept

Albanians as equals; it was also partly due to insecurity on the part of some Serbs in the state and police apparatus because of the abuse and injustice inflicted on Albanians during the rule of Ranković; furthermore, there was the better economic situation in Serbia and the enormous sums to be earned from selling property in Kosovo; there were also family and personal reasons, as a huge number of the migrants were of colonial descent (first and second wave) etc. (Islami 1994: 47)

The argument that Serbs occupied a privileged position and migrated because of the loss of those privileges is particularly interesting. It appears to place them on an equal footing with the colonisers of the Third World who left as these countries gained their freedom. In Kosovo, however, the arguments and counter-arguments are a great deal more complex. Although Serbs occupied a more favourable position in the immediate post-war period, this was, to a great extent, due to their participation in the People's War of Independence and to the high percentage of Communists among them.

Just after the war and fresh disturbances in the second Yugoslavia, military rule was imposed. Next, as in other parts of the country, an authoritarian system held sway with the ruling Communist Party at its centre. Status among the wielders of power depended on the part one had played in the war, on one's service as a fighter and party member, and on loyalty to the supreme power. As Serbs were most numerous among war veterans and party members in Kosovo, it was they who disposed of the given model of domination. This then came to appear as essentially *Serb* rule over the entire population, including the majority Albanians, not an *anti-democratic movement.* (Popov 1994: 6)

It should be said that similar arguments—that the anti-democratic and authoritarian structure of two conservative ethnic groups lies at the root of Serb–Albanian conflict in Kosovo—may always be used, regardless of which group actually has the upper hand. Besides, at this particular point, the Serbian group was, on the whole, more educated than the Albanian, thus fulfilling two of the main conditions for upward mobility: education and party membership. Serbs simply fitted the conditions better.

Furthermore, any structural comparison along the lines of careers and unemployment between Serbian and Albanian ethnic groups must take into consideration the very great differences in age structure and previous educational levels of the two groups. The younger Albanian generations were vastly more educated than their elders, but sheer weight of numbers, taken with an adverse economic situation, inept development policies and low mobility as a group, resulted in high rates of unemployment.

One particular problem was the inadequate educational streaming of young Albanians. Albanians, for instance, formed the highest number of school-leavers (21%) from high schools (translator's note: classical, general educational establishments) in 1981, the lowest being Romas and Slovenians (5.0% and 6.1%, respectively). The speed at which Albanians made strides in education is best illustrated by the fact that the twenty-five to thirty-four age group out of the entire Albanian population in the former Yugoslavia, in comparison to all other ethnic groups, showed the fastest rate of reduction in the proportion of persons without schooling (Petrović and Blagojević 1989).

Given that a decision to migrate is one of the most complex ever taken in the course of human life, generally speaking it is very difficult, perhaps even pretentious, to attach any precise measure of significance to one factor or another. However, it is indisputable that the change in the status of the Serbs, which ended their domination following the fall of Ranković and which was later reinforced by the Constitution of 1974, resulted in a reversal not only of the concept of what constituted a minority or majority group, but also of the direction taken by discrimination. Ethnic migration by one group and encroachment on the land by the other, which began in Kosovo, was later to become the norm in the tragic war which engulfed Yugoslavia. Ten years ago, Kosovo had all the appearance of an extreme case in Yugoslavia, which only a few years later was to become normality. Kosovo introduced a new paradigm of discrimination into Yugoslav practice: discrimination along ethnic rather than political lines. 'Kosovo was the catalyst of the Yugoslav crisis' (Maliqi 1989).

The situation in Kosovo was also, however, to a great extent, the product of internal Yugoslav conflict, or rather conflict among ruling national elites. 'Violence against the non-Albanian population, the banishment and moving out of Serbs from Kosovo as a drastic historical experience, showed the true face of the system. This was hushed up for fifteen years, then with unaccustomed accuracy presented as a *Yugoslav* problem. It was demonstrated that Serbs were moving out because the problem was really a Yugoslav one, with the result that, in terms of finding a solution to it, it was nobody's responsibility. It did, however, have a certain role to play in competing relations between the Yugoslav federal units. The problem of the Kosovo Serbs points to the firm structuring of these relations' (Samardžić 1989: 165). The system, or rather the prevailing order, was too inert to be capable of solving any real problem, whether economic, social or political. The extent of this inertia and the tenacity of the system, incarnate in the ruling elites, was such that it did not balk at war in order to ensure its own renewal.

A vicious circle

The migration of Serbs and Montenegrins from Kosovo in the 70s and 80s had multiple and complicated consequences, only some of which will be referred to here.

Firstly, migration was a major, if not a decisive, factor in changing the ethnic structure of the province. Its effects were more visible at communal, town and village level. As the data show, changes in percentages (relationships) and territorial distribution were directly related to change in the ethnic structure.

Migration contributed to making both ethnic groups homogeneous. Ethnic identity is a very complex result of the two dimensions of identity: 'we' and 'they'. In a word, identity is formed via the complex inter-relational image that a particular group has of itself and the image that others have of it. The national identities of both Serbs and Albanians have been formed in *opposition* to one another. It was for this reason that migration, the most dramatic aspect of Albanian–Serbian relations in the second Yugoslavia, had an extremely important role in the forming of the Serbian national identity and in 'putting the Serbian national question on the agenda'. In retrospect, it is difficult to claim that migration alone, and the way in which it was interpreted by the media, decided the political scene in Serbia and gave rise to national euphoria. It might rather be said that the real problem and its interpretation fitted neatly into the general trend of stepping up ethnic conflict in the process of transition from Communism to post-Communism.

One of the important consequences of migration is its use or misuse by the media. Any attentive analysis of the press will affirm that the treatment of the Kosovo problem, including migration, was never free of a latent political agenda. Kosovo served to overheat the atmosphere and would unfortunately continue do so in future.

The dismemberment of its institutions and a strong secessionist movement meant that Kosovo greatly contributed to the collapse of the second Yugoslavia. The effects of migration itself and the uses to which it was put in the process are difficult to assess.

The migration of Serbs and Montenegrins from Kosovo provided the main excuse for the repression of Albanians in the 90s. Violence has been justified by violence.

Parallelism—a segmented society

One of the most prominent characteristics of life in Kosovo in the mid-1990s was its total segmentation. This new departure as a model of ethnic co-existence, however, appeared not to bother either Serbs or Albanians. In short, it seemed that neither group wished to live together any more. The speeches, articles and public statements of politicians, academics, even activists, contained no word of integration, of bonding or of a common life. Multiculturalism and interculturalism were not treated as values any more. [5]

The model of parallelism survived and became embedded both in the historic segregation which existed between the two ethnic groups and in new elements such as: 1) the grey economy; 2) the parallel state; 3) parallel systems of education; 4) common law as an alternative to the official judicial system; 5) religion; and 6) segmented public opinion. The Albanian parallel system was based on a widespread and well-organised system of self-help, solidarity and traditional collectivism, which was aimed at eventually uniting all Albanians into one nation (from a divided tribal society). Action taken by the Serbian government in the 90s had only contributed to making the division between Serbs and Albanians complete.

An analysis of different forms of ghettoization shows that it is always accompanied by the creation of parallel institutions. Exclusion by the *Other*, furthermore, is often followed by self-exclusion in the interests of self-protection (Blagojević 1985). Segmentation, in this case, is rounded up to the point of *self-sufficiency*, and is grounded in economics and ideology.

The importance of the grey economy for the economy of Kosovo, and especially the maintenance of the Albanian community, is difficult to ignore. It was the linchpin both of the privatisation process and of economic development. It may be assumed that the accelerated nationalisation of Kosovo helped to hasten privatisation, although private property already existed in the agrarian economy. The first accumulation of capital in Kosovo, as in other parts of the former Yugoslavia, was directly linked to processes of national homogenisation and the consolidation of national markets, and also to the criminalization of society. It may even be said that the idea of creating a national state in the economic sphere is suited to protectionism, the protection which a young national state should provide for the nascent owner class. The basis of this privatisation was the development of the tertiary sector, the service sector, by means of the grey economy: 'Practically all economic activity has moved into the area of the grey economy and takes place absolutely in the public eye, avoiding the involvement or influence of the state' (Bogosavljević 1994: 24).

The grey economy represented a parallel sector, far more elastic, adaptable, tougher and more profitable than the fossilised version provided by the state. Thus, 'while private property in 1990 in central Serbia provided barely a sixth of GDP (an eighth in Montenegro), in Kosovo and Method it provides over a third' (Bogosavljević 1994: 24). It is estimated that the proportion of the grey economy in 1992 was 42 per cent of actual (registered) GDP (Bogosavljević 1994: 26). It is especially important to remember that the flourishing of the entire grey economy in Yugoslavia, including Kosovo, was closely connected to the introduction of international sanctions. Coupled with revenues accruing from emigration, it rapidly became a new and vital source of Albanian self-sufficiency in Kosovo. However, macro-economic factors in Kosovo did not have the same effect as in other parts of Yugoslavia, precisely because the informal elements acting through kinship, interest groups, local or religious communities were so vital to life and the economy.

The Serb and Albanian educational systems in the province were also completely separated in the 90s. From 1989/90 onward, the number of Albanian-language schools, pupils and teachers was radically reduced. Of over 300,000 pupils in primary education, and almost 70,000 in secondary education in the preceding school year (88/89), only about 17,000 remained (Bogosavljević 1994: 27). A parallel educational system is one of the main features of a segmented community such as Kosovo. Parallelism was maintained by sacking Albanian workers from public health institutions, hospitals, clinics and dispensaries. The parallel state in Kosovo united and organised all these types of parallel activities. Unemployed Albanians, for instance, received financial aid from a solidarity network, which naturally helped to make them even more homogeneous.

At the ideological level, it may then be assumed (and probably documented by separate research) that both Orthodox and Muslim religious institutions contributed to feelings of separateness and difference. This, of course, was helped along by completely separated channels of information and totally different interpretations of what was really going on in Kosovo.

The Kosovo situation, from demographic through economic to 'historical' rights, was interpreted completely differently by the two sides in an interesting sort of mirror reflection. Both in the Albanian and Serb collective conscience, each side's victims tended to be viewed as absolutes. The *Other* was never seen as victim, nor was there any *desire* to see it as such . The view that one is oneself the absolute victim excludes any possibility that the victim could be the *Other*. There was a complete asymmetry of rights, complete exclusion, the absolute dichotomy of 'either/or'. Simultaneously, history and memory were continuously selective. The impression was that Serbs and Albanians not only lived in segmented territory in a segmented society, but also in segmented historical time, a time in which they each held the monopoly on victim-hood.

The complete blame attached to the *Other* is obvious from this example: 'The Serb regimes, political parties, cultural and academic institutions incessantly accuse other peoples of ethnic cleansing and crimes of genocide, of crimes, therefore, that they committed themselves. The idea of ethnic cleansing is not new and pertains to none other than Serb governing circles' (Islami 1994: 41).

It is interesting, too, to note the difference in emphasis on aspects of Serb–Albanian relations. For the Serbs, it was clear that the main argument for the rightness of their stand was migration from Kosovo, while for the Albanians it was on-going discrimination.

Perhaps the most striking example of the mirror image is the interpretation of the destiny of the Albanian people. The Albanians claimed that they had been artificially divided as a nation by the Communists into four parts (Albania, Kosovo, Montenegro and Southern Serbia) (Islami 1994: 29–30). Paradoxically, this is very similar to a Serb argument based on territorially divided nations, the different parts of which 'naturally' tended to unite. Both were forgetting that other nations were also living in this region, so that nationalistic manifestos always lead to overlapping territories.

A special type of controversy was that related to the economic development of Kosovo. One of the claims of the Albanians was that 'on the economic level, Kosovo has always had colonial status and today is a textbook example of a colony in classic terms' (Islami 1994: 31). In other words, the Albanians defended their political position by saying that Kosovo was a Serb colony with the Serbs as colonisers. This, however, did not fit with the claim that 'Kosovo occasionally achieved a noticeably high economic growth. Two such years were 1981, when real GDP growth in Kosovo was 5.9 per cent and in Serbia 0.1 per cent; and 1985, when a similar situation occurred—8.1 per cent in Kosovo and 0.2 per cent in Serbia. On the whole, Kosovo's growth rate in the 1980s was double that of Serbia's, but showed greater falls in 1983 and 1987' (Bogosavljević 1994: 24). With regard to resources disbursed by the Yugoslav Fund for Underdeveloped Regions, Kosovo received 43.5 per cent between 1981 and 1985, and 48.1 per cent between 1986 and 1990 (Echoić 1990: 13).

Resources for backward areas in Kosovo were not used to encourage growth. Instead, a large proportion of investment went into the state administration. Investment in capital-intensive industry presented a particular problem, as the final effect was low employment and, importantly, few opportunities for the employment of women. It is almost certain that proper development policies and the employment of women, particularly in process manufacturing, would have hastened the demographic transition in Kosovo (Islami 1994).

The high population growth slowed down development, since it created 'a gap between gross GDP growth and GDP per head of population. This gap was between economic growth and living standards, between investment and results ... The rising population in Kosovo continuously wiped out investment in economic development at the point where it should have translated into social and family standards of living' (Petrović 1991: 176).

Albanians declared Serbs to be the colonisers and Kosovo a colony. They called the situation in the 90s to be 'occupation' or 'annexation'. Serbian politicians and even academics, on the other hand, represented Albanians as 'colonisers' and 'persecutors'. The Serbs in Kosovo, according to them, had an 'historical right' and therefore an 'actual right' to continue to rule Kosovo. The more extreme among them demanded that Albanians be banished by genocide (Islami 1994: 41).

As an agrarian society with a large share of subsistence farming and an increasingly grey economy, Kosovo was really an environment dominated by 'mechanical' as opposed to 'organic' solidarity. For this very reason, Kosovo, more than perhaps anywhere else, should have been homogenised by means of national ideologies. There, as in the rest of the former Yugoslavia, the 'collective owner class' relied on the political legitimacy of its rule. It is important that this was first accorded in line with the class principle and only then in line with the national principle. The change-over occurred in the 1980s, but obviously the dynamic was not the same everywhere.

One particular controversy surrounded the conditions under which Serb and Montenegrin houses were sold in Kosovo. As with other questions, two extreme versions circulated: one, that houses were sold for a song or abandoned under pressure; the other that they were sold for outrageous prices. An interesting interpretation of the high price theory is given by Krstić when he says that :

> the purchase of land became crucial to final possession of the territory. The key significance in changing ownership of land or houses lay in the fact that once done, it reproduced all the rest–from further population expansion, through the entire development of the economy to the wielding of power. Moreover, the new occupant is not a settler; he is the owner of the land... This was the main reason why the sale and purchase of land and houses in Kosovo and Metohija between Albanians and Serbs or Montenegrins fetched prices far and away above the market, higher than the most valuable land in developed parts of Serbia... It was not merely the house and land which was being paid for, but their enhanced value: the value of finally possessing the land (1994: 172).

These apparently contradictory claims about prices appear more logical if we take into consideration other similar experiences, together with the *dynamics* of Serb–Albanian relationships. There is a general rule that any 'breakthrough' by a minority group into the territory of the majority is accompanied by this type of price increase. For example, the purchase of real estate by black people in a whites-only neighbourhood usually means paying the highest possible price. However, the higher the proportion of blacks in the neighbourhood becomes, the more rapidly prices go down. The case of property buying by Albanians was similar. The houses and properties that fetched the lowest prices were those sold in the 1980s. It was subsequently likely that prices would rise again because of the climate—which was generally unfavourable towards Albanians–the ban on the purchase and sale of real estate, and the fact that demand exceeded supply.

It may be concluded that, as the segmentation of Kosovo society became total and absolute in every aspect already in the mid 90s, any future solution would have to take this into account as being the factual state of affairs. To assume otherwise would be naïve.

The logic of inversion

Kosovo introduced into Yugoslav political discourse and practice an inversion which was later to become a pattern—an inversion of minority and majority, cause and consequence, image and reality, means and objective, subject and object, victim and torturer, the discriminated against and the discriminators, rights and lack of rights. Inversion can be captured, analysed and assumed at different moments of reality, but its essence is the inversion of reality into the para-real or surreal. Ethnicity in this new age has all the attributes of para-reality. It is symbolic, ritual; it fights for territory so that by gaining it and overcoming history, it may actually become real. It is this that makes it so feverish.

There are several inversions which confirm the post-modern character of this phenomenon. In the first place is the inversion of the minority and majority group. Even though the Serbs were, from the legal aspect, treated as the majority group, the over-protection of the minority—something which might be called the 'extreme positive discrimination' in favour of Albanians–turned the Serbs into a minority group. The lesson that can be learnt is that any kind of group discrimination, even a positive type intended to compensate the effects of previous discrimination, in the final instance leads to the jeopardising of individual human rights. Human rights are always individual rights. Kosovo also placed high on the agenda the problem of protecting the majority from the minority, no matter how this majority is defined, or of whom it is comprised at any given moment.

Another element which gave Kosovo a post-modern reality was the use of the media. The long years in which the media ignored the problem or accorded a mechanical, symmetric treatment to both Serb and Albanian nationalism during communism, was followed by a period of completely segmented media which created another sort of meta-reality; in fact, conflicting and mutually excluding images of reality produced separate realities for the Serb and Albanian groups. The greater the influence of the media, the stronger the distortion of reality. Kosovo was used from the outset as a symbol by others, and, as such, grew as a symbol in Serbia and served to construct the image of Slobodan Milosević and thus a reality out of that image.

The inversion of reality was contained in the fact that the Kosovo problem was, to a great extent, constructed for the international public. The Albanian side was constantly seen as the weaker side, and as a victim; the indigenous poverty shocked observers and led them to conclude that the province had been deliberately neglected; figures showing its backwardness were easy to prove, and Albanian leaders excited sympathy by insisting on a peaceful solution to the Albanian question, at a time when the Western media saw Serbia's President Milosević as a metaphor for evil. Serbia's behaviour, including the cancelling of the OSCE mission to Kosovo, contributed greatly to the negative image.

The international public, as far as Kosovo was concerned, tended, as in other situations in the former Yugoslavia, to form a black and white picture which helped radicalisation of the conflict between Serbs and Albanians.

> True, the largest nation numerically, which also has the largest army numerically, bears the greatest responsibility for what is happening here. But if all responsibility is thrust on one nation and the collective guilt ascribed to it, this not only fails to correspond to historical truth but also prevents the ending of the war and the finding of a political path to dialogue and negotiation. Nor do sentimental views of small nations, with prior amnesty for their responsibility in fomenting conflict over territory and state boundaries, help in this respect. Even more of a problem is the support, at home and abroad, for identifying the struggle for human rights with the struggle for territory and the changing of state borders by force... and then ascribing collective responsibility for atrocities and crimes, contrary to modern standards of examining responsibility for specific acts (Popov 1994: 7).

The crucial inversion in Kosovo was, however, connected to the functioning of the institutions. These, instead of developing and stabilising the system, contributed to dismembering it. At the same time, parallel ethnic institutions were formed. Paradoxically, these were very centralised and enabled strict control over individuals, the outcome of which was a para-state and new totalitarianism.

The very explanations for the Kosovo problem contributed to inversion. For example, the exceptionally high birth rate was usually explained by under-development, but under-development is essentially due to a very high birth rate, which results in a very young population with a large portion of available work-force.

The consistent application of Western theoretical paradigms to Kosovo in fact ignored the very specific traditional organisational mechanisms within these different ethnicities. This could be seen not only as a mere absence of objectivity, but rather as a 'surplus' of it, which, honed in the study of industrial capitalistic societies, fails to take into account the essential cultural characteristics of premodern societies.

As it became more homogeneous, Kosovo generated more and more arguments for secession, thus fulfilling a self-fulfilling prophecy. In addition, the conflict itself became a pretext for secession (non-participation in elections, for instance, meant clearly opting for a conflict strategy while rejecting inclusion in the political and social life of Serbia—a strategy of maximal demands: i. e. for secession).

Explaining the Serb–Albanian conflict as historically 'eternal' was another useful argument for secession. History was used to define the present, but only the history of conflict, while that of a life in common and the changing political and social conditions within which the conflict took place were ignored. Both ethnic communities were observed out of context, as though fixed forever in their ethnic characteristics and their antagonism towards each other.

The next inversion was that of class conflict into ethnic. All ethnic groups in the former Yugoslavia, including Kosovo, experienced a drastic redistribution of public resources to the advantage of the newly emerging elite, and an equally drastic rise in inequality. Instead of this turn of events leading to increased antagonism between the haves and have-nots, it sharpened conflict between ethnic groups. Ethnic conflict homogenised all ethnic groups, including the Kosovo Serbs and Albanians. The highly possible, expected and logical clash clash between the poor majority and rich minority turned into a battle in which the masses turned on themselves.

Yet another inversion was that by which the non-nationalist, civil opposition in Serbia, understanding the symbolism of Kosovo and the use to which it had been put in forming Serb nationalism, disputed any factual foundation for the pressures produced by the exodus of Serbs and Montenegrins from Kosovo. Retreating behind commonplaces such as human rights and a general nostalgia for the old Yugoslavia, the civil non-nationalist Serbian opposition showed itself unprepared to come to grips with its own intellectual inertia. It seems that wishful thinking on desirable solutions (non-violent, democratic, pro-development) prevented them from seeing the situation clearly or perceiving the inadequacy of progressivist and evolutionist patterns.

Finally, democratic tools such as elections and referendums were used on both sides of the conflict, in fact to justify undemocratic goals. Like the referendums held elsewhere in the former Yugoslavia, if elections and referendums are taken in without open public debate, under the strong pressure of collectives over individuals, without real choices, they are producing counter-effects.

Notes

1 This paper was completed on 29 March 1995. Subsequent events, particularly the huge wave of refugees from the Serb-populated parts of Croatia in August of the same year, were to overshadow any migration from Kosovo in 70s and 80s. On the other hand, events related to geno-

cidal acts of the Serbian regime in the late 90s and during the war with NATO, and the war of Serbia with NATO itself, called for changes of the text in making it more precise and understandable for the outside readers.

2 For the purposes of this paper, 'the migration of the Serbs from Kosovo' is taken to include Montenegrins. However, it should be noted that the number of Serbs who left was far greater (Montenegrins represented about 20% of the emigrants). Both migrated due to the same circumstances, mainly in the same fashion and for the same destinations. Certain differences, not pertinent to the issue here, existed with respect to the speed of migration.

3 'The Albanian nationalist demonstrations of 1981 did a disservice to the Albanian people but were well-suited to the Serb oligarchy and Serb nationalist circles. There are indications, indeed perhaps evidence, that a group of Albanians, trained by the secret services of foreign states, was paid to provoke the student demonstrations of March 1981 in Pristina and give them tone and direction' (Maliqi 1989: 74).

4 It appears that all the findings from this research still hold good even after ten years. The most frequent doubt raised by international academic circles relates to the authenticity of the replies by the respondents. There were claims that those who had left Kosovo felt the need to represent themselves as victims, to justify their action. It is possible that a certain degree of light and shade in the interpretation would indeed improve the quality of the findings. Still, if we bear in mind the generally unfavorable political climate in which the research was carried out, the number of very clear statistical correlations ascertained, the scrupulousness and caution with which the author proceeded and the complete availability and verifiability of the research material, there seem to be many reasons for treating the results of this research as relevant and as having a sound theoretical base, regardless of the Serbian Academy of Arts and Sciences which ordered it. Unfortunately, subsequent events in Yugoslavia only confirmed that what seemed impossible was possible everywhere, including Kosovo.

5 However, in order to fully grasp the model now being established, it should be borne in mind that, mainly due to information technology, *parallelism* is becoming the new paradigm of ethnic coexistence in the post-modern era. In that sense, parallelism in Kosovo should not be too lightly rejected as an anachronism.

IDEOLOGICAL BEARING

The Church and the 'Serbian Question'

RADMILA RADIĆ

In the period between 1980 and 1985, the Serbian Orthodox Church returned to the public and political scene from the social margins where it had existed during the previous forty years.

Church and nation

The relationship between the state and the church in the East has been shaped rather differently than in the West. Unlike the Catholic Church in Western Europe, Orthodox churches never became independent political forces. Because they are autocephalous, Orthodox churches functioned as one of the primary agents of nation–state integration. In Byzantine spiritual and political circles, the state and the church were two aspects of the same phenomenon (Kolarić 1985: 109–110). The situation evolved from the biblical principle 'Render unto Caesar that which is Caesar's and unto God that which is God's'. The Orthodox Christian Church acknowledges that the state is a divine institution and preaches complete subjugation to state authority, condemning every act of disobedience regardless of the religion professed by the head of state. The ideal relationship is conceived as a close tie and mutual support between the church and the state. This principle of co-ordinated diarchy (co-ordination and co-operation on all vital issues but with mutual respect for autonomy) was interpreted by certain theologians as the tactics of yielding and accommodation for the sake of higher ends. The Greeks referred to it as the politics of iconomy. Opposed to this principle was the 'rigorous politics' promoted by monastic orders, advocating strictness on all questions (Samardžić 1988A: 171). On those occasions when the state adopted an adversarial or hostile attitude towards the church, the latter was supposed to focus inward and humbly await the moment when 'God's justice shall prevail', for the Church is One, unchanging and eternal, while states are many and ephemeral (Milaš 1926: 738–743). The close tie between the Orthodox churches and the rulers contributed to a unique development in Orthodoxy as a form of Christianity and as the cult of the 'nation state'. To understand better the close link between confession and *ethnos*, it should be noted that as early as 451 AD, the Holy Synod determined that the territorial boundaries of the church's influence should coincide with state borders.

Among the Orthodox churches, there exist different conceptions of the nation as a domain of church influence, and of the relationship between the church and the nation. Basing his remarks within a critique of New Age rationalism, positivism and materialism, a contemporary Orthodox theologian maintains that

> both in the East and in the West, the Orthodox religion and the Orthodox conception of the relationship between church and nation were observed, often uncritically, through the prism of the concept of 'nation' as defined by the French Revolution. Such an understanding and conceptualization of *nation* exerted considerable influence, particularly in the last century, not only on the awakening of national consciousness among certain Orthodox nations (Serbs, Greeks, Bulgarians, Romanians, etc.), but also on the formation of such consciousness. It also influenced an alternative conception of the relationship between church and nation, to the detriment of the church's ecumenical (universal) self-knowledge. (Radović 1984: 80)

This fact deeply affected the Serbian Church and its position *vis-à-vis* the Serbian nation after the 1804 uprising. One of the consequences is its contemporary name—the Serbian Orthodox Church—where the national affiliation stands in the forefront. The name was introduced only after the creation of the Kingdom of the Serbs, Croats and Slovenes in 1920.

Kosovo—the renewal of the myth

In April 1982, twenty-one priests signed a 'Petition' addressed to the highest Serbian and federal state authorities, the Holy Assembly of Bishops, and the Synod. Three most reputable theologians— Atanasije Jevtić, Irinej Bulović and Amfilohije Radović—were among the signatories. The text of the Petition represented an attempt 'to protect the spiritual and biological being of the Serbian people in Kosovo and Metohija' (see Olga Zirojević's contribution in this volume). This marked the beginning of a new practice in the Serbian Church: the circulating of petitions within and outside the church, which indicated an understanding of the importance of international public opinion. Subsequently, a group of bishops of the Serbian Orthodox Church in the United States paid a visit to the US Congress and the US State Department, seeking an 'intervention concerning the developments in Kosovo'. In June the same year, *Pravoslavlje* (Orthodoxy) published an article by Atanasije Jevtić, 'From Kosovo About Kosovo', in which he stated:

> 'Today one, tomorrow seven, the day after tomorrow every single one!'—this is the uncompromising slogan and the ultimate message of the Albanian irredentists to Kosovo Serbs recently published in the press. It openly discloses their true and ultimate objective: the extermination of the Serbian people in Kosovo and Metohija. Albanian Nazis have been making such threats for decades. There were times when such genocidal slogans were whispered, there were times when they were uttered aloud, but in the past decade they have often been accompanied by drastic acts of psychological and physical terror, even public crimes, against the innocent Serbian population of Kosovo... (*PR*, No. 366, 15 June 1982)

At the beginning of 1985, in an article published in *Pravoslavlje*, Žarko Gavrilović demanded that the church stop being passive and establish a new presence among the people. *Glas Crkve* (The Church Voice), in one of its regular editorials, also called for church activism, particularly in the following domains: personnel, education, the construction of churches and the free practising of religion. Another petition was launched in the same year on St. Vitus's Day[1] by the priests and monks of the Church of St. Archangel Gavrilo in Zemun. The petition reflected a concern for the Serbian and Montenegrin population in Kosovo. The signatories demanded that regular and extraordinary measures be implemented to restore order in Kosovo, and that measures prohibiting ethnic Albanians from handling food be introduced in the narrow territory of Serbia [i.e. Serbia without the autonomous provinces]. At that time, the first arguments for the transferring of the seat of the Serbian Church to Peć also surfaced in public debate.

Kosovo was an unavoidable topic at that time. One would have been hard-pressed to find a church publication without some information about 'Old Serbia'. Heroic poems and elegies on the subject appeared particularly frequently.

At the end of 1983, *Pravoslavlje* started to publish Atanasije Jevtić's series of articles entitled 'From Kosovo to Jadovno' [Croatian concentration camp during the Second World War] that drew parallels between Serb suffering in different regions in Yugoslavia. The series chronicled alleged rapes, attacks on Serbs and everything Serbian, the harassment of monks and nuns, murders, etc. The series also included detailed stories about mass graves and concentration camps on the territory of Croatia where Serbs were victimized during the Second World War (*PR*, Nos. 400, 404 and 405, 1983 and 1984).

Arch-priest Božidar Mijać provided an explanation of what Kosovo means to Serbs in his text 'The Light From Kosovo'.

> Kosovo is not only a physical residence but also a metaphysical creation... This Serbian homeland is composed of heaven and earth. It is the essence of the spirit in time and space. It is the highest proof that the number of inhabitants is not crucial for determining to whom a patch of soil belongs. There is something far more important—the spirituality which has given it its essence and which exists in a higher existential manner. In this case, ideogenesis prevails over ethnogenesis (*PR*, No. 388, 15 May 1983).

Archive documents, prepared by expert historians and bearing compelling titles such as 'Crimes and Violence in Old Serbia' were also published regularly. Those documents, accompanied by appropriate photographs representing atrocities committed against the Serbian people, appeared continually in *Pravoslavlje*, the official publication of the Serbian Patriarchate. They generally referred to complaints made by Serbs from Kosovo during the previous century. A number of those complaints were typically addressed to the Russian tsars. In the spirit of the myth of the 'universal protector of Orthodoxy', the Russian Patriarch Pimen visited Kosovo in 1984 where he was greeted by masses of elated believers. The enthusiasm of the ovations for the patriarch, and the sheer number of Serbs who assembled for that occasion, each represent rich material for a serious political analysis (*PR*, No. 422, 15 October 1984; *GC*, No. 11, 1984).

Using Kosovo as an unresolved problem within Serbia and Yugoslavia, the Serbian Orthodox Church offered itself as the traditional bastion of national security and the centre of national life, as evidenced by its centuries-long role as the single institution that 'never in history betrayed the Serbian people'. The ideological basis for such an assertion emerged from the synthesis of the teachings of Nikolaj Velimirović (d. 1956) and Justin Popović (d. 1979). Since the mid-1980s, there had not been a single issue of a church periodical published without texts by one or other of these two 'enduring examples and models of modern Serbian spirituality', or articles about them. *Glas Crkve* is a particularly prominent example. This review led a campaign against the opponents of Bishop Nikolaj, lobbying for the return of his remains from the United States, and celebrating him as a saint and an exemplary Serbian bishop.

The essence of Velimirović and Popović's thinking consisted of a critique of humanism, European civilization, materialism, etc. Velimirović wrote about the three deadly spirits in the image of Man–God–Darwin, Nietzsche and Marx–who had contributed to the decay of European civilization. He considered Europe a great evil of which one must beware, and warned the Serbian people that

> European schools of thought strayed from God. Since then, Europe has produced poisons which will bring about the demise of European mankind. Pagan cultures never attempted to disassociate science from faith although their faith was wrong and stupid. Therefore, my brothers, let us not listen to those who cry 'in the name of culture', or 'in the name of science', or 'in the name of progress'. They are all assassins in the service of Satan ... Let the Orthodox people rise and be heralds to the heretics, so that they may return to truth and righteousness. (Bishop Nikolaj, 1985)

Serbian people were advised to place their trust in the fact that they are 'Christ's immortal people', a virtue which is stronger than any death. This was evidenced by the Serbian nation's place throughout history, which was not a meaningless coincidence, but disclosed 'some mission in this world, some task in eternity, which it achieves through faith in the eternity of the spiritual world and a higher eternal meaning of human history–through faith in God' (Milin 1982; 1985). Its decline begins when it ceases to cherish its spiritual and national heritage and instead chooses material wealth, because 'atheism and nihilism are reverse sides of the same phenomenon–the godlessness and lack of spirituality that afflicts human beings' (J. Popović 1980: 259; 1978: 832; Velimirović 1931: 130-132). This ideal of 'returning to the roots' recognized as legitimate only two authors based in the European tradition: Gogol and Dostoyevsky.

The Church as a Protector

The new neo-conservative opposition within the Serbian Orthodox Church sought to distance itself from society as much as possible, engaging in dialogue only with certain circles of the 'liberal
national intelligentsia'.

The search for a programme

In 1987, the editorial board of the review *Glas Crkve* openly requested that the Holy Assembly of Bishops, which held its meeting
at the Patriarchate in Peć that year, propose a clear programme of
action for Kosovo. It suggested that the Assembly reach the following decisions: to establish a committee for Kosovo which would
maintain close contact with the Diocese of Raška-Prizren and
which would engage in repairing the endangered religious life in
Kosovo; to create a publication of the Serbian Church in Kosovo
which would report on the religious life there; to organize public
forums on the question of the 'Migration of Serbs from Kosovo' at
the Patriarchate in Belgrade and at the seat of the Diocese of Raška-
Prizren; to resolve the problem of the schism within the Serbian
Orthodox Church; and to begin procedures for the canonization of
Nikolaj Velimirović (*GC*, No. 3, 1987).

The Bishops' Assembly dissociated itself from these statements,
made by the official publication of the Diocese of Šabac-Valjevo.
Many of the requests had already been processed, however, or
were soon to be accorded.

The word 'genocide' was used for the first time publicly to describe what had been happening to the Serbian people in Kosovo
and in parts of south-east Serbia in a statement issued by the Bishops' Assembly after its session in 1987. Commenting on the motives for holding the session in Peć, *Pravoslavlje* wrote:

> The Stavropigija Monastery in Peć remains of interest today. Those
> who want to seize Kosovo—the heart of Serbian lands—also wish to
> seize and destroy the Holy Stavropigial Lavra, the heart of the Serbian
> Church, and the spiritual centre and origin of the Serbian people... Pa-
> triarchs from Peć lead the great Serbian national migrations from
> Kosovo under terrible pressures from conquerors and tyrants, and a
> time may come (perhaps in the not-too-distant future), when, pro-
> voked by the new circumstances, they may lead the people's return
> to Kosovo. This year's session of the Assembly in Lavra might be a
> sign, if only a symbolic one, of such aspirations ... (*PR*, No. 487, 1 July
> 1987)

Another prominent topic in the time of Vuk Karadžić [1787–1864; famous Serbian language reformer], was the urgent need to revive the endangered Cyrillic alphabet so that 'Serbs would not feel as if they were living in a foreign country'.

In addition to the question of Cyrillic, there were an increasing number of stories about Serbian sufferings during both world wars, about the irreproachable ethics of Serbian soldiers, etc. In October 1987 *Pravoslavlje* published an article by Svetozar Dušanić—'Reflections on a Speech'—in which Dušanić wrote

> The world which developed under 'Byzantine influence', ... differs from the world which evolved under the 'Western–Roman influence', not only in its religion, but also in its culture, historical development, ethics, psychology and mentality. The Byzantine world cannot envision a common survival in the same state with the members of the Western–Roman tradition, particularly not after the Second World War. Its path does not lead toward the Karavanke Mountains and the Julian Alps. It does not wish to head towards the north-west of Europe to confront eighty million Germans and sixty million Italians. It has no intention of giving up the sacred land inherited from its grandfathers, nor will it abandon the historical direction designated eight centuries ago by the immortal Nemanjić family. The roads left by the Nemanjićs lead towards warm seas which have always attracted peoples from the North. That is why a community of states of the Balkan peoples is a sacred imperative for the coming times. That future entity is a natural, logical and necessary escape from the 'Versailles Yugoslavia' which is not a complete 'Yugoslavia' in the full sense of the term, as it excludes Bulgaria ... The future community of Balkan states would be freed from the machinations of the superpowers from the East and the West. The common characteristics of the peoples entering into such an association would yield many benefits, which, in turn, would guarantee its future and prosperity ... (*PR*, No. 493, 1 October 1987)

Direct actions

During 1987, the Serbian Orthodox Church prepared for the celebration of the six-hundredth anniversary of the Battle of Kosovo. For that occasion, the Priest-Monk Atanasije Jevtić published in instalments his text 'The Kosovo Oath'. He quoted Bishop Nikolaj, who maintained that the ascent of Prince Lazar (1329–1389) to the celestial kingdom

> was made in the name of the entire Serbian people (like Moses's on behalf of the people of Israel). As such, it represented the strongest expression of the meaning of [Serbian] history and its operative

idea ... Kosovo (i. e. Lazar's choice at the Battle of Kosovo) demonstrates that [Serbian] history was unfolding at the highest level, on the tragic and elevated boundary between the celestial and the earthly, between God and Man. Kosovo testified that [Serbs], as a people, have never fought for meaningless things, nor could [they] ever be sincerely enthusiastic about ephemeral trifles. (*GC*, No. 2, 1987)

Shortly before the massive 'meetings of truth' in towns across Serbia in the summer of 1988, and the fall of the so-called autonomous government in Novi Sad, a conflict erupted between Djordje Radosavljević, President of the Presidency of the Socialist Autonomous Region of Vojvodina, and Bishop Amfilohije. Radosavljević accused the bishop of surrounding himself with Serbian monarchists. The Committee for the Protection of Artistic Freedom, under the presidency of Svetlana Slapšak, and the clergy of the bishop's diocese, all rallied to his defence. Another attack on the church occurred in the same year in Croatia. Bishop Nikolaj from Dalmatia was sharply criticized by the state authorities for initiating the construction of the Church of St. Sava in Split.

During 1988, Prince Lazar's remains began a journey from the monastery at Ravanica, passing through the dioceses of Zvornik-Tuzla, Šabac-Valjevo and Šumadija-Žička, and finally arriving at the monastery of Gračanica in Kosovo where they would rest during the celebration of the six-hundredth anniversary of the Battle of Kosovo. Everywhere they passed, the remains were solemnly welcomed by masses of people. The term 'celestial Serbia' was first used at that time, in an epistle in honour of the sacred remains issued by Jovan, the bishop of Šabac-Valjevo. The term would be heard often in the following years.

Since the time of Prince Lazar and Kosovo, Serbs have been primarily engaged in creating a CELESTIAL SERBIA, which is perhaps the greatest celestial state today. If we consider only the number of innocent victims of this last war, those millions and millions of Serb men, women, children, and the frail who were murdered or tortured in most dreadful ways or thrown into mass graves and caves by Ustasha criminals, then we can begin to imagine the vastness of the Serbian celestial kingdom.

Genocide

Since 1984, one of the topics that increasingly occupied space in the church press touched upon Serb sufferings during World War II in the Independent State of Croatia (NDH, *Nezavisna Država*

Hrvatska) and in the Jasenovac concentration camp. In September 1984, at the dedication of a church in Jasenovac, Patriarch German called on people to forgive, but not forget. During the second half of the 1980s, the theme of genocide was accompanied by stories about the current threats to the Serbian people in Croatia and Bosnia-Hercegovina. In autumn 1988, Atanasije Jevtić and Živko Kustić, the editor-in-chief of *Glas Koncila*[2], initiated a bitter polemic. Jevtić sharply objected to the publication's editorial policy on the question of 'the tragedy of an entire people and its sacredness in Kosovo and Metohija', and to reports claiming that 'genuine ethnic Serbs' originally comprised only 10 per cent of the population of Bosnia-Hercegovina, Montenegro and parts of Croatia (and 'even they were immigrants'), while the remainder converted to Orthodoxy. Jevtić interpreted these reports as the return of Ustasha phraseology. Others also joined in this polemic.

The polemic involving the review *Glas Koncila* continued in the following years. Reports published during 1990 concerning the number of victims of the Jasenovac concentration camp, the massacre of Serbs from Livno, etc., engendered particularly heated debate (*PR*, Nos. 559, 564 and 568, 1990; *GC*, Nos. 1, 2 and 3, 1990). Archive documents about genocide against Serbs in the NDH appeared regularly in *Pravoslavlje*.

At the end of 1988, Dragomir Ubiparipović, a priest from Sarajevo, published in *Glas Crkve* an article under the title 'Cultural and Religious Genocide Against Orthodox Serbs in Sarajevo'. He explained that the cultural genocide was evidenced by the insistence on protecting the cultural monuments 'of the Turks, our oppressors, who for five centuries deliberately degraded the highest achievements of Christian culture in the Balkans', to the neglect of Serbian churches, cemeteries and museums of Serbian history, and by the deliberate promotion of cultural objects from the Turkish period in tourist brochures, while disregarding Serbian monuments. Furthermore, the Sarajevo newspaper *Oslobodjenje* allegedly violated Orthodox rights by refusing to publish announcements of deaths using the Cyrillic alphabet and by editing out Christian terminology from such announcements (*GC*, No. 4, 1988).

Commenting in a church publication on events taking place in Yugoslavia in 1988, Vuk Drašković stated that Yugoslav integration in 1918 represented the beginning of slavery for the Serbian people. He claimed that an entire generation of Serbs was obliterated in order to create Yugoslavia, and that another had been sacrificed so that the state could be reconstructed. He condemned the blocking of Bosnia-Hercegovina's annexation to Serbia after the war, as Serbs were clearly the largest national group. He also asserted that the Muslim and Montenegrin nations had been artificially created to undermine the dominance of the Serbs. Furthermore, he claimed that more than one million Serbs had been expelled from Bosnia-Hercegovina and Croatia, and another half a million from Kosovo, while the 1974 Constitution ultimately deprived Serbs of their state. Drašković maintained that the time had come to end this suffering, that Serbs demanded their freedom, but that these legitimate aspirations inevitably provoked panic among the others. He argued for a fundamental restructuring of the state that would reverse all the 'unnecessary and unhistorical partitions' (*GC*, No. 4, 1988).

Homogenization

The 'closing of Serbian ranks' or 'homogenization', the amendments to the Serbian Constitution which reintegrated the autonomous regions of Serbia into a unitary republic, the six-hundredth anniversary celebration of the Battle of Kosovo, and the repeated celebrations at the monastery of Krka (Croatia), were all hailed within the Serbian Orthodox Church as 'the most important events in recent Serbian history'. The church interpreted these events as a renewal of the authentic spiritual tradition, a recovery of cultural and national consciousness, an 'awakening of the Balkan giant', and a sobering up of the Serbian people. In the pages of the church press, numerous members of the clergy, intellectuals, and various cultural and public figures unanimously praised the actions of the Serbian authorities and demanded that a common future with other Yugoslav nations be reconsidered.

Arch-priest Dragan Terzić wrote that that which had been done in Croatia against the Serbs, against their culture and national identity, was a mere continuation of their past victimization. The Serbs, according to him, were tolerated as long as they were silent and as long as they accepted national oppression, but as soon as they demanded their rights, they were brutally refuted. Terzić then posed the question of whether the rest of the Serbs would stand by and watch disinterestedly as events unfolded, or whether they would come to the aid of their 'defenceless brothers'.

In response to the increasingly heated situation in Croatia, in an interview for *Glas Crkve*, the writer Danko Popović stated that he feared the Croats as they 'may entice [the Serbs] to commit evil, destroy [their] eternal, Orthodox goodness and godliness, expel

[them] from Christ's vineyard, and compel [them] to dangerous vengeance ...'. Popović warned that what might happen was a 'Jasenovac for Jasenovac', because this time the Serbs would not forgive. He characterized the regime in Croatia as Nazi, and maintained that within Yugoslavia there existed a tradition of genocide against the Serbian people. His was not an isolated view, and the majority of such views also maintained that the Vatican loomed behind all that was happening to the Serbs in Croatia, because of the Vatican's 'centuries-long intolerance of schismatics' (*GC*, Nos. 1,2 and 3, 1990; *PR*, No. 568, 1990).

Patriarch German transmitted a letter to Cardinal Kuharić much in the same spirit, in which he asked whether 'the Roman Catholic Church in Yugoslavia [had] abandoned dialogue with the Serbian Orthodox Church'. Earlier, at the end of May 1990, Cardinal Kuharić had dispatched an invitation to dialogue between the two churches. The Bishops' Assembly had accepted the invitation and issued a response at the end of June, but received no further communication from the Catholic Church. The Patriarch's letter re-opened the question of the Catholic Church's responsibility for the victimization of Serbs and the Orthodox Church during the Second World War, and the concealment or minimizing of such crimes. It also reproved the Catholic Church for ignoring the presence of Serbs in Croatia, for its position on the question of Serbs and Montenegrins in Kosovo, etc.

The regime and the church

Anti-Communism

Church circles were disappointed by the fact that the 'new Communist regime ... [which] knew how to exploit the vast democratic energy of the people', did not meet expectations. They identified President Milošević as the greatest delusion and disappointment of the Serbian people: he promised a great deal in the beginning, he seemed to speak about Serbian interests, but he failed to keep his promises–including those he made to the church.[3] Atanasije Jevtić rebuked Milošević particularly sharply, calling him 'unbearably arrogant', while Radovan Bigović claimed that the air in Serbia had become exceptionally 'polluted' thanks to the regime (*PR*, 1 December 1990).

On the other hand, in June 1990, Bishop Simeon Zloković stated that

> Neither Hitler nor Mussolini are at Yugoslavia's borders today. Europe is at its borders. One must bow to it. Tudjman and his followers, even the most extreme ones, must know that. We cannot possibly recreate a Balkan jungle at the end of the twentieth century. Europe does not accept fascism, or Marxism, or any other extreme. I criticize Serbia for fighting so desperately for the Yugoslav Communist Party. That party can no longer exists. One can no longer impose something that the people do not wish. While everyone around us heads toward unification, we are heading for disintegration. This trend is sheer stupidity, because there can be no Yugoslavia without agreement. Neither Belgrade nor Zagreb can impose it. No one can. But we could convince ourselves that it is better to live together. (*D*, June 1990: 9–22)

The church press attacked the Communists increasingly frequently and openly for everything that the Serbian people had endured. While the church continued to advise the clergy against joining political parties, reminding them that they must remain outside political disputes, it nevertheless called on political parties to build the future parliamentary life of the country responsibly. As elections approached at the end of the year, certain church publications openly appealed to voters not to support the Communists and expressed the hope that the victorious party would restore the church to its rightful place in society. It is not difficult to guess to which party such statements referred, considering the strong presence of its members in the pages of the church press (Vuk Drašković, Milan Komnenić, Slobodan Rakitić, and others).

The unavoidable factor

Kosovo remained a permanent topic within the Serbian Orthodox Church. The following April, a delegation was even invited for a visit to the United States by congresswoman Helen Delić-Bentli. During the visit, the Archimandrite Atanasije Jevtić and Arch-priest Milutin Timotijević reported on the situation in Kosovo to the US Congress. Other members of the delegation included the bishop of Raška-Prizren (Pavle), Dobrica Ćosić, Radoslav Stojanović and Slobodan Vučković.

During its May session, the Bishops' Assembly decided to address to the competent authorities a request that the remains of victims from the Second World War buried in mass graves be exhumed and the victims given proper, dignified funerals. Throughout the year, reports arrived from Bosnia-Hercegovina (Bileća, Kupres, Fahovići, Vlasenica and elsewhere) and Croatia, about memorial services held for the victims of genocide, about the excavation of their remains, and about their ceremonial funerals. Graphic descriptions of the manner in which the victims had been killed frequently accompanied such reports. The clergy of the Serbian Orthodox Church warned that 'Ustasha ideology [was] being resurrected' in Bosnia, and that Serbs would have to remain united for the forthcoming elections in their support for those who would protect the Serbs' religious and national values (*PR*, No. 558, 15 June 1990; No. 559, 1 July 1990).

In December 1990, at an extraordinary session of the Assembly, the church selected the bishop of Raška-Prizren, Pavle, as the new patriarch, due to the protracted illness of German Djorić. Amfilohije Radović was also elected the new metropolitan of Montenegro and the Coast (at the time of the debate on the autocephalous status of the Montenegrin Church), while Irinej Bulović became bishop of Bačka. The Assembly also decided to hold a liturgy to honour the fiftieth anniversary of the sufferings of the Serbian Church and the genocide against the Serbian people, and encouraged continued exhumation and reburial of the innocent war victims. Finally, the Assembly urged the people to vote for those who were 'truly faithful to God and to the people', instead of those who made too many promises (*PR*, No. 570, 15 December 1990).

This extraordinary session of the Serbian Bishops' Assembly represented, in many aspects, a turning point in the church's work. It set a precedent for calling extraordinary Assembly sessions, and this practice continued into the following years. The session also established a balance between the two factions within the episcopate, one led by Metropolitan Jovan and the other led by the students of Justin Popović, Bishops Amfilohije, Atanasije, Artemije and Irinej.

One of the first addresses given by the new patriarch, at Easter in 1991, referred to the 'uncovering of the gallows and graves of the new martyrs and the new saints'. The patriarch reiterated the words of his predecessor: one must forgive, but not forget. He particularly emphasized that the past sins and 'unparalleled crimes' had never been atoned for, a fact confirmed by the recent events.

During this period, an increasing distancing from, and dissatisfaction with, the government could be observed. Patriarch Pavle went as far as to publicly deny a report published in *Politika* that he had enthusiastically congratulated President Milošević on his election victory when they met in January 1991. Clearly, the patriarch did not want the public to believe that he and the church supported Milošević and his party. During the period of opposition's that March, the patriarch and the bishops continually appealed to all sides to forgive and to seek reconciliation at any price, regardless of what had come to pass. The patriarch addressed the demonstrating students on two occasions, and he received representatives of the opposition parties in Serbia, expressing a wish for a speedy resolution of the problems to the benefit of all peoples, and particularly the people in Croatia and in Bosnia-Hercegovina. Atanasije Jevtić was the only one openly and severely to condemn Slobodan Milošević for deploying the army in the streets and for 'terrorizing Serbian children' (*PR*, Nos. 572 and 576, 1991; *GC*, No. 2, 1991).

War victims and the diaspora

Funerals for victims of the Ustasha terror campaigns in Bosnia-Hercegovina began as early as January and continued throughout 1991 in Žitomislić, Prebilovci, Ljubinje, Trebinje, Majevica, Banja Luka, and elsewhere.

In May of that year, Patriarch Pavle used the occasion of a liturgy in Jasenovac to announce that a liturgy marking the fiftieth anniversary of this tragedy was not intended to provoke hostilities and vengeance, but rather to confront people with the truth about evil so as to prevent new evils. In Croatia, however, the commemorations were not perceived as Patriarch Pavle intended. On the contrary, they were understood as an attempt to reopen old wounds and to condemn the entire Croatian people. Such reactions prompted Radovan Bigović to comment that the Orthodox Church's actions represented an 'appeal to Croats that their children do not repeat the crimes against Serbs' (*PR*, Nos. 580 and 592, 1991). The polemic involving *Glas Koncila* about the Ustasha crimes against Serbs in the Independent State of Croatia likewise continued.

On 7 March, Patriarch Pavle paid an official visit to the head of the Yugoslav state, Borisav Jović, to discuss the position of Serbs in Croatia. Members of the delegation demanded that the state guarantee the safety and equality of all its citizens. At the same time, Bishop Lukijan of Slavonia condemned the 'brutal attack by Croatian special forces on Pakrac and their intrusion into the episcopal residence', as well as the general anti-Serbian actions of the Croatian state.[4] The clergy of the diocese of Zagreb-Ljubljana likewise met on 22 March to warn of the precarious position of the Serbian Orthodox Church in Croatia, and to deny false information about the alleged relationships between the church and the Serbian authorities. The following statement was issued at the meeting: 'The new Croatian constitution has reduced the Serbs in Croatia to the status of a national minority. This will provoke ongoing unrest until the injustice is rectified.' In response to events in Croatia, Patriarch Pavle dispatched telegrams to the heads of all the autocephalous Orthodox churches. On 7 May, representatives of the Serbian Orthodox Church and the Roman Catholic Church met in Sremski Karlovci in Vojvodina. At the end of the meeting, Cardinal Kuharić and Patriarch Pavle issued a joint statement appealing for peace, non-violence and tolerance. By that time, however, the conflict was already intensifying.

At the beginning of July 1991, the heads of political parties in Serbia and the heads of Serbian national parties active in Bosnia-Hercegovina and in Croatia convened at the patriarch's palace in Belgrade to discuss the essential interests and goals of the Serbian people. At the end of August, Patriarch Pavle and Cardinal Kuharić met again, this time in Slavonski Brod, Croatia. On that occasion, the cardinal declared that the war had been imposed on Croatia, that the war was being waged in order to reach certain specific objectives, and that it was becoming more widespread and more cruel. The patriarch responded that the parties responsible for the war began the conflict under the guise of the highest national and democratic goals. In the end, both sides agreed to form a joint commission which would work on overcoming the differences between the two churches; their joint statement called for an end to the war and for the beginning of negotiations. Despite such statements, observers were left with a strong impression that this meeting, and all subsequent meetings, were little more than necessary rituals, rather than genuine attempts at co-operation.

Somewhat later, Metropolitan Jovan of Zagreb–Ljubljana commented that the Catholic Church had used the meeting to qualify Croatian responsibility by arguing that the war had been imposed, that Serbian terrorism was responsible for the conflict, and that the only solution was to seek assistance from outside. According to the metropolitan, the person ultimately responsible for such a position was Pope John Paul II because of his negative attitude toward the Serbs (*PR*, Nos. 587 and 590, 1991).

In October 1991, Patriarch Pavle transmitted a letter to Lord Carrington, president of the European Union Conference on Yugoslavia, stating that Serbs could not form a part of an independent Croatian state because of the genocide committed in the past and because of the current events in that region; their only option was to join Serbia and all other Serbian regions. 'The time has come to recognize that the victims of the genocide cannot live together with their past and perhaps future executioners.' A similar letter was also sent to the president and the participants at the Peace Conference in The Hague on 4 November. A delegation formed at the extraordinary session of the Bishops' Assembly visited the vice-president of the Presidency of Yugoslavia, Branko Kostić, and the president of Serbia, Slobodan Milošević, to demand that neither the Presidency of Yugoslavia nor the representatives of Serbia and Montenegro permit the 'most tragic solution to their problem' to be imposed on the Serbian people, in The Hague or anywhere else. Kostić praised the church for its efforts to protect Serbs, adding that the church's role had an invaluable significance (*PR*, Nos. 591 and 592, 1991). The Assembly working group also met with the representatives of the opposition political parties in Serbia and announced its position regarding the need for the Serbian people to unite in forming a government of national salvation [a grand coalition].

The state's 'church roof'

A few months prior to the onset of the war in Bosnia-Hercegovina, a delegation of the Islamic Religious Community led by Hadži Hamdija effendi Jusufspahić, the Belgrade *Mufti*, visited Patriarch Pavle. On that occasion, the two sides issued a joint appeal for peace and against the instrumentalization of religion for national–political purposes. A month later, at the beginning of September 1991, Patriarch Pavle received Alija Izetbegović, the president of the Presidency of Bosnia-Hercegovina, who told the patriarch that 'a Muslim would never harm a Serb', and that problems could only be solved through peaceful means (*PR*, Nos. 585–586, 1–15 August 1991; No. 587, 1 September 1991). In October, however, a Memorandum on the Sovereignty and Independence of Bosnia-Hercegovina was adopted, while the Bosnian Serbs decided through a referendum to remain in Yugoslavia. In December, the Bosnian Serbs adopted a resolution on the establishment of the Serbian republic in Bosnia-Hercegovina, the Republika Srpska.

In January 1992, at an extraordinary session of the Bishops' Assembly, the arch-priests formulated a pledge to support the freedom and rights of the Serbian people in Bosnia-Hercegovina and other Serbian regions: 'No pact—not with the Serbian authorities,

who have no mandate to represent the whole of the Serbian people, nor with the institutions of the Yugoslav federation, nor with
the command structure of the Yugoslav army—can bind the Serbian
people as a whole without the approval and the blessing of its
spiritual Mother, the Serbian Orthodox Church.' The statement
also expressed support for 'the demands of the people in Bosnia-
Hercegovina for freedom and autonomous political organization'
(*PR*, No. 598, 1992).

The Orthodox Church had not reacted, however, when in
Gazimestan, at the six-hundredth anniversary celebration of the
Battle of Kosovo in 1989, Slobodan Milošević promised prosperity
despite all obstructions, by all means necessary, 'including armed
battle'.

In April 1992, Metropolitan Amfilohije pledged to support the
integration of all Serbian states into a type of 'united states of Serbia'. In his opinion, the opportunity for such integration had been
missed in 1918, and might be missed once again. At the same time,
with respect to Macedonia, the metropolitan stated that:

> One should keep in mind that both in the Balkan Wars and in the
> First World War, Macedonia received its freedom over the corpses of
> Serbian soldiers. When I say Serbian, I mean soldiers from Serbia in
> particular, but from Montenegro as well. Macedonian soil is strewn
> with Serbian bones, not to mention the churches, the historical
> memory, and the vast numbers of people there who feel themselves
> Serbian, despite the brainwashing. This situation exists from the
> Skopska Crna Gora mountain range all the way to Ohrid ... The Ma-
> cedonian question will not be easy to solve.

Two months later, following the long session of the Bishops'
Assembly, there appeared a Memorandum of the Serbian Orthodox Church. The Memorandum condemned the ruling parties in
Serbia and Montenegro as the heirs to the post-war Communist
system's structures, organs, methods and principles. They were
criticized for preventing an equal, democratic dialogue within
society and an equitable distribution of responsibilities, for refusing to co-operate with others, and for denying the church its
rightful place in society. Therefore, the church 'openly
[disavowed] and [disassociated] itself from such a government
and its representatives'. The Memorandum furthermore condemned the atrocities committed by all sides in the conflict, as
well as the attacks on humanitarian convoys (*PR*, No. 605, 1 June
1992; *GC*, No. 3, 1991).

Justifying the war

At the end of February and the beginning of March 1992, Bosnian Serbs proclaimed their own state and boycotted the referendum carried out to decide the independence of Bosnia-Hercegovina. Barricades went up in the streets of Sarajevo. By mid-March the UN had established its headquarters in Sarajevo, and on 6 April the European Community recognized the independence of Bosnia-Hercegovina. Two days later, Alija Izetbegović declared a state of emergency.

On 9 April, the supreme head of the Islamic Religious Community, Reis ul Ulema Hadži Jakub Selimoski, transmitted a letter to Patriarch Pavle informing him that on 8 April the forces of Željko Ražnatovic, 'Arkan',[5] and Serb members of the Serbian Democratic Party had launched an assault on the town of Zvornik. Selimoski told the patriarch that Muslims were being killed only because of their religion, and that many attackers claimed to be committing the murders in order to protect Serbs and in the name of Orthodoxy. Selimoski had expected the Patriarch to condemn the aggression on Bosnia-Hercegovina much earlier, as both Serbs and Croats were being victimized and Arkan's forces were committing massacres in Bijeljina. The patriarch replied that the Orthodox Church vere doing everything possible to prevent hostilities and that the Serbian people were not the aggressors in the Bosnian conflict, although some of them may have 'acted aggressively in self-defence', and their crimes deserved censure (*PR*, No. 603, 1 May 1992). For several days, in his editorial column in *Pravoslavlje*, Dragan Terzić wrote that Serbs in Bosnia did not wish to live in a *jamahiriyya* like Libya, and that, if governed by the *mujahedins*, they would be reduced to a status typical for Christians in Islamic states, that is, they would be slaves—an experience they had already endured during the five-century-long Islamic occupation.

Somewhat later, another theologian, Božidar Mijač, attacked 'peacemakers' who 'fight against the war by condemning only one side—the Serbian side—which [was] the victim in the war'. Such activity equalled defeatism and desertion. Mijač further wrote that, depending on its content, peace as such could be evil, and war as such could be good. According to him, in the current conflicts, God was taking the side 'of those who defend their soul, soil and religion, and not of those who destroy others' soul, soil and religion, and whose genocide crimes past and present have covered the martyred Serbian soil' (*PR*, No. 600, 15 March 1992).

There were, however, Orthodox theologians like the priest-monk Ignatije Midić, who condemned the war as a means to achieve 'higher aims, either defensive or aggressive', and who thought the war an unacceptable and unjustifiable means from the human point of view, let alone the church perspective (*TP*, Nos. 1-4, 1991). Another theologian who partially disagreed with the quoted opinion on the war was Vladeta Jerotić, professor at the School of Theology.

The saviour

Patriarch Pavle was present at the proclamation of the Federal Republic of Yugoslavia on 27 April 1992. His presence provoked numerous comments which prompted the patriarch himself to respond that the political side of the events remained beyond his scope. The editorial board of the publication *Pravoslavlje* reacted with the article 'The Church is Beyond Parties', explaining that the fact that the church sometimes had to perform its official duty did not mean that it supported the regime (*PR*, No. 603, 1 May 1992; No. 605, 1 June 1992).

'Western Serbs' as an ideal

The representatives of the Orthodox Church continued to attack the regime openly during 1992 (Patriarch Pavle's speech before the Sabor Church on 14 June , his presence at the St. Vitus's Day Meeting organized by the Serbian democratic opposition, editorials in *Pravoslavlje*, articles in *Glas Crkve*, the June letter written by the Bishop Artemije of Raška-Prizren, expressions of support for students' demands, etc.). The basis of the attacks was the church's discontent with the degree of attention and help rendered to the people of Bosnia-Hercegovina by the Serbian and Montenegrin authorities. Gradually, the critiques began to encompass descriptions of an ideal Serbian state. For example, some claimed that 'the century-old Serbian aspiration to unity' had been defeated when the Serbs deviated from the Orthodoxy of St. Sava which had been the sole spiritual and ethical driving force towards liberation and integration; the Serbs were able to begin uprisings only in the name of Orthodoxy and St. Sava's solemn commitment.

Certain conditions must be met in order for Serbs to restore their Serbian state. If the highest government representatives are not Orthodox, that is, if they maintain no spiritual ties with the Serbian Orthodox Church, do not attend religious service, do not take Communion, do not celebrate *Slava*[6], do not invite a priest to bless water, and if they refuse to cross themselves, then they cannot be legitimate Serbian representatives. While they may rule Serbia, the Serbian people cannot accept them as their own, just as the Turks ruled Serbia for centuries without ever being Serbian statesmen ... Fortunately, some Serbian states give full respect to Serbian insignia, like the Serbian republic of Krajina and the Serbian republic in Bosnia-Hercegovina. These states adopted the Serbian Orthodox flag, insignia, and national anthem. Their leaders attend religious service and celebrate *Slava*; they introduced religious instruction in schools; they maintain the administration in Cyrillic; and they regard Orthodox priests as spiritual guides, not as enemies. Only time will tell whether Serbia and Montenegro will ever become Serbian states.

During 1992 the church leadership engaged in limited political activity. Patriarch Pavle dispatched a letter to UN Secretary General Boutros-Ghali, Reis ul Ulema Selimoski and Cardinal Kuharić, regarding the 'criminal aggression of the Croatian Army against Serbs in Eastern Hercegovina'. The patriarch invited all the religious heads for a meeting and called for joint statements and appeals for peace. Shortly thereafter, at the end of July, he dispatched letters to Boutros-Ghali, Hurd, Carrington and others, regarding the tragic position of the Serbs in Sarajevo, as well as the suffering of the population belonging to other religions, appealing for the prevention of crimes and an end to hostilities. In November, the patriarch and Cardinal Kuharić met in Geneva to appeal once again for peace. In October, the patriarch visited the United States, and in December he met with the representatives of the Serbian Orthodox Church, the Roman Catholic Church and the Islamic religious community in Bern. In the meantime, the church press wrote about 'Serbia Under Threat from the Entire West', about non-Orthodox nations not being expected to help Serbs, and about the attacks on Serbs and Serbian homes being led by 'Italy, Austria and Germany, the countries obedient to the pope'. The statement issued following the extraordinary session of the Bishops' Assembly in December 1992 refuted all accusations against Serbs for the rape of Muslim women, and made counter-allegations of violence committed against Serbian women and children (*PR*, No. 618, 15 December 1992; *Glasnik*, No. 12, December 1992).

The church press wrote often, and with unconcealed sympathy, about the regime across the Drina and its relationship with the Orthodox Church. At the end of April 1993, Metropolitan Nikolaj Mrdja, who replaced Metropolitan Jovan in Zagreb, commented in an interview that the army in Bosnia was being deprived of its rights and that General Mladić accepted all of his proposals (*D*, 24 April–7 May 1993). *Pravoslavlje* wrote about the Serbian army waging the war under its national flag, in the spirit of the Orthodox tradition, and looking to national heroes for inspiration. School children from Bosanska Krajina had recently learnt to appreciate a new subject in schools—religious instruction—and soldiers had likewise recently discovered an affinity for army priests.

> The new bond with the religion of their grandfathers [enabled] the proud people of Krajina to realize that, high above the supersonic NATO airplanes breaking the sound barrier in the skies above the villages of Krajina, there resides the Dear, Almighty God and His Justice, with the Serbian saints and Saint Sava beside him, and that they are more powerful than the entire threatening force on Earth (*PR*, No. 631–632, 1–15 July 1993).

In May 1993, at the celebration of *Slava* in the church in Foča, Metropolitan Jovan emphasized in an address to the believers the importance of the support of the Bishops' Assembly for Republika Srpska, particularly its efforts to help the Serbian people obtain their own state (*PR*, No. 633–634, 1–15 August 1993). These efforts were perhaps best described by the daily observations of Dragomir Ubiparipović, a priest from Sarajevo. He wrote that the church had entered too far into politics and that Prosvjeta publishing house had experienced a renaissance entirely thanks to the church's support.

> Church premises and rituals were instrumentalized to promote the leaders of the Serbian Democratic Party and to endorse them before the people. Such overstated support illustrates our inclination to exaggerate. We have gone so far that sometimes the leaders themselves had been dismayed by the attention and the flattering remarks they have received–such as statements that God had entrusted them with a messianic role. This should come as no surprise if one remembers the unprecedented panegyrics the priests devoted to those leaders, reminding them before the people that 'they had been sent by God himself to save the Serbian people' ... Such excessive servility to politics, and the church's assistance in securing the people's support for such politics, that all-too-visible symbiosis and joint action, this will require that they also share both the success and the failure after everything has happened! One can certainly expect that the new government will generously reward the church. However, if the question of responsibility for the consequences of the war, for the destruction and the victims, is ever raised, one should expect that the church will likewise be mentioned (*S*, Nos. 1–2, 1993; *HM*, Nos. 6–8, 1993).

Contrasting the status of the Serbian Orthodox Church within Yugoslavia with its position in the newly formed Serbian states, Metropolitan Amfilohije Radović once said that the church felt like a victim of all three Yugoslavias, but that at that time it was threatened by manipulation, which would be a misfortune greater than the previous ones.

> The church and the people are in danger of being seduced by a false sense of freedom, yet the church's place in society has not been restored, and the conditions that would enable it to assume such a role have not been created. The only hope rests in co-operation between the church and the state which is being born following the immense misfortunes which have struck the newly created Serbian states in Bosnia-Hercegovina and Serbian Krajina. There is a sign of a new beginning there, preceded by the blood of martyrs (*HM*, Nos. 6–8, 1993).

The leader of the Serbs in Bosnia-Hercegovina, Radovan Karadžić, confirmed at the beginning of 1994 that the relationship between the church and the state was excellent, stating that, 'Our clergy are present at all our deliberations and in the decision-making processes; the voice of the church is respected as the voice of highest authority'. Karadžić also added that everything he achieved in life he owed to religion and the church, and that whatever he did, he did 'with God in mind' (*SS*, 1/1994).

Between Pale and Dedinje

The attitude of the church regarding the situation in Bosnia-Hercegovina in the middle of 1994 once again captured the media's attention. An 'Appeal to the Serbian People and to the International Public' sent out by the Bishops' Assembly on 5 July, expressed the church's position on the negotiations in Bosnia-Hercegovina.

> With full responsibility before God, our people and human history, we invite the entire Serbian people to stand up in defence of its centuries-old rights and freedoms, its vital interests indispensable for physical and spiritual survival, and its patrimony.

The bishops rejected the proposed maps and expressed the belief that the people needed to decide their future by referendum.

In June 1994, *Svetigora* published three speeches by Bishop Nikolaj Velimirović, addressed to Serbs in Bosnia-Hercegovina. In the first speech dating from 1912, he called on Serbs to organize themselves, to work, and to endure. In the second one, the bishop claimed that heroism is not possible without faith in God. In the third speech, from 1940, he advised Sarajevo to look to Belgrade and expect the unity of the homeland.

Metropolitan Nikolaj and Bishops Vasilije and Atanasije attended the session of the Parliament of Republika Srpska where the decision was being made on whether or not to accept the peace plan proposed by the Contact Group for Bosnia-Hercegovina. Bishop Atanasije conveyed the church's position that the Serbian people must not be devastated once again. In July, Metropolitan Amfilohije of Montenegro and the Coast sent a telegram of support to the Parliament of Republika Srpska, stating:

> Having restored faith in God's Justice, you have restored the faith of Saint Lazar to the people and restored the dignity of the people. Your decision will expose the false democracy of the so-called New World Order, but it will also expose all those who are hiding their ambition behind an alleged concern for the people. May God help you (*SV*, Nos. 30–31, 1994).

Following the decision by the government of the Federal Republic of Yugoslavia to suspend all political and economic relations with Republika Srpska, the church convened an extraordinary session of its Assembly. Some days earlier, the Metropolitanate of Montenegro and the Coast petitioned the representatives of the Montenegrin Parliament to reject the decision. This address sounded rather militant and much sharper in tone than the Patriarchate's official statement issued at the extraordinary session of the Assembly (*P*, 11 August 1994; *NIN*, 12 August 1994). The statement was perceived in public as aligning with the Bosnian Serbs, which provoked numerous comments both in the country and abroad, and condemnations for publicly expressed nationalism (e.g. from the Ecumenical Association of Churches). In response, the bishop of Bačka, Irinej Bulović, issued a statement claiming that the church had not taken sides (*P*, 22 August 1994).

Patriarch Pavle attempted to negotiate a reconciliation. He first visited Pale, then asked for a meeting with President Milošević (*P*, 9 August 1994; *NIN*, 12 August 1994). His efforts were, however, unsuccessful. The essence of the church's position was perhaps best illustrated by his visit to the Russian Orthodox Church. In the talks conducted in Moscow, the patriarch stated that hostilities must cease immediately and peace talks be initiated, and that these discussions must endeavour to bring about an equal right to self-determination for all sides in the conflict. This meant that the Bosnian Serbs would accept an agreement that 'granted them the right to self-determination, that is, confederation with the Federal Republic of Yugoslavia' (*P*, 11 October 1994).

Conclusion

While the Serbian Orthodox Church has been autocephalous and independent throughout its history, it has nevertheless remained closely tied to the state. It has been financially dependent on the state and thus susceptible to state influence. Since its founding in 1918, political life in Yugoslavia has evolved according to two separate principles: according to the first, Yugoslavia was little more than an expanded Kingdom of Serbia, and according to the second, it functioned as a community of several nations. The church, which viewed itself as the protector of the Serbian people, operated according to the first principle. It did not regard the national question as a separate political problem, but as a form and an aspect of religion; thus it acted as a national, and not solely religious, institution.

Political conditions during the Second World War (the destruction of church organization, genocide of Orthodox peoples, civil war, etc.), and the conditions immediately following it, had particularly tragic consequences for the Orthodox Church, from which it took a long time to recover. Disorganized by the war, reduced in size, with a completely devastated material base, and with the hypothetical burden of being the carrier of Serbian nationalism, the church confronted an adversary who had the power and the ability to exploit its weaknesses. The church did, in fact, identify itself with Serbia as a state and with the Serbian nation. It experienced the creation of a federal Yugoslavia as a loss of statehood, and along with that, as the loss of national identity by the Serbian people. Unable to resist the pressures exerted by the state, because of its structure, centuries-long practice and dependence, it began to develop a character contrary to its spirit.

During the post-war period, religious communities were gradually, but successfully, moved from social and political life towards the margins of society. While on the surface an idealized image of human rights and harmonious social relations in the state was constructed persistently and diligently, not far below there lurked unresolved problems which would return to the forefront at the first opportunity.

The revitalization of Orthodoxy occurred in the mid-1980s, during the period of the collapse of the socialist system and the liberalization of social relations. Movements within the church had already become apparent at the time, with the introduction of the Kosovo question and the entry onto the scene of a group of young theologians who sought a greater involvement of the church and an abandonment of lethargy. As the previous phase of development permitted no 'opposition' on the social scene, the church attracted all those who 'thought differently', for within its structure they could find the only available form of legal 'resistance'. The Orthodox Church thus became a haven for a segment of the political and cultural opposition, just as it conveyed a legitimacy to a segment of the nationally oriented intelligentsia. Within the framework of the church, national continuity was cultivated, as was the cult of national and religious 'greats', along with national history in general, the national alphabet, and traditional customs and values. With the escalation of the general state crisis and the collapse of the system, there was a renewed readiness to trust in traditional answers to existential problems. Orthodoxy became increasingly important for the cultural and national uniqueness of the Serbian people and its homogenization and identification in the face of other national and confessional identities. The conditions under which religion became revitalized, however, also contributed to the instrumentalization of the church towards nationalistic and other ends.

The church continued to maintain that it was the only institution which, throughout history, had remained the protector of the Serbian nation, that it had never abandoned the Serbian nation, that it stood above the state, that it represented the highest moral arbiter, and that its intentions and positions could not be questioned. It rejected every accusation that it was becoming politicized, yet a section of the clergy and the episcopate were among the first to raise questions and offer solutions regarding the national question, the state order, the position of the church in the state, the relationship with the West and with the East, etc. That very process formed the ideology which deepened the crisis and opened new areas of conflict. The church's desire to reclaim its former position in society became increasingly clear and open, and regime or opposition leaders were offered support as long as they offered hope in helping the church reach this objective. It is clear

that political actors could never have accomplished such a successful social homogenization of the Serbian ethos as that achieved by
the church. It is also clear that when their respective visions began
to diverge, a segment of the church representatives showed hostile
and militant behaviour not only toward the Communists, atheists
and other religious sects, but also toward certain creators of the
national idcology.

From the onset of the war in the territory of the former Yugoslavia, the church granted substantial moral and material support
to the Serbian population in the territories where the war was being waged. Contacts with other Orthodox churches, whose representatives conveyed messages of support, constituted an important
aspect of this assistance. The church leadership maintained that
the Serbian people were not the aggressors but the victims of the
conflict, and that they, for the second time in their history, were
confronting genocide. The church defended the war, characteriz-
ing it as defensive. It viewed the unification of the entire Serbian
people as the only and final solution of the national question (it is
important to remember that any other solution would have likewise fragmented the church itself). Crimes were severely condemned, but those committed by the Serbian side were more often
interpreted as 'excesses'. The Episcopate was by no means unanimous, but an important majority of the bishops did come from
areas where, at the time, war was being waged. Appeals for peace,
for negotiations, and for finding just solutions were a constant
activity of all church representatives, although the concept of a
'just solution' coincided with the articulated interests of the Serbian nation. As a national church which served the interests of its
people before all else, the Serbian Orthodox Church remained
faithful to its programme, in contrast to many other parties, groups
and individuals. The question which remains to be answered is
whether the Serbian Orthodox Church's mission in this world consists of being a Christian or a national church, and whether a path
based on the national option leads to the heresy known as
philetism[7].

Notes

1 Translator's note: 28 June; St. Vitus's Day is one of the most important
   saint's days in the Serbian Orthodox calendar.
2 Translator's note: A publication of the Catholic Church in Croatia.

3 At the time of the celebration at Gazimestan there was a lot of talk about Milošević involving the Church in politics, but in the circles close to the Patriarchate, the president of Serbia was condemned for failing to attend the most important church ceremony at the monastery of Gračanica.

4 At the beginning of March 1991, a conflict between the Serb population and Croatian special forces occurred in Pakrac. It began when policemen of Serbian ethnicity refused to affix the new 'checkerboard' Croatian national emblem to their uniforms. The conflict escalated when special forces of the Croatian MUP (Ministry of the Interior) attacked the Yugoslav People's Army (JNA, *Jugoslovenska Narodna Armija*) and ethnic Serbian residents. The first incident occurred at a police station, the JNA intervened, and the following day ethnic Serbs who had escaped to the hills in nearby Kalvarija returned to open fire (*NIN*, 12 August 1994). By the end of the month further bloody clashes between the Croatian police and ethnic Serbs erupted in Plitvice. The JNA intervened there as well. The next conflict took place in Borovo Selo. The Executive Council of the Serbian National Council of the [self-declared] Serbian Autonomous Region of Krajina declared its intention to annex Krajina to Serbia. Serbia never officially responded to this decision. Somewhat later, the Croatian Sabor [Parliament] unanimously adopted the declaration of independence of Croatia. In July, the JNA pulled out of Slovenia, while conflicts in Croatia grew more violent. At the beginning of October, both Croatia and Slovenia proclaimed their independence, and a month later, the Presidency of the Socialist Federal Republic of Yugoslavia invited the UN to help resolve the crisis.

5 Željko Ražnatović claimed that he was a favourite of the Patriarchate and that his superior commander was Patriarch Pavle himself. He had his army baptized by Bishop Lukijan in Dalje, and he carried with him the icon of St. Nikola, signed by the patriarch (*D*, 8–23 November 1991).

6 Translator's note: *Krsna Slava* is the celebration of a family's own patron saint, and is one of the most important rites in the Serbian Orthodox tradition.

7 Translator's note: In Orthodoxy, an overemphasis on national identity over the unity of faith.

The Abuse of the Authority of Science

OLIVERA MILOSAVLJEVIĆ

The focus of this study is limited to the public and political activities of the Serbian Academy of Arts and Sciences (SANU, *Srpska akademija nauka i umetnosti*).[1]

In the article, we will concentrate on the period between 1986 and 1992, on the assumption that the process of politicization of the SANU became known to the broader public only after the Academy had published its Memorandum in 1986 (a document that is still the subject of wide controversy). We nevertheless believe that the process must have commenced earlier. The choice of 1992 as the end of the period under discussion was based on at least four essential factors. Firstly, at the institutional level, this year marked the end of ostensible political consensus, as the defections of certain Academy members and groups throughout 1991 indicated a political rift in the SANU which would mark its activities from that point on. Secondly, Dobrica Ćosić—an Academy member with no official function but who had an immense political and ideological influence on the politicization process within the institution and on the political and ideological content of the Memorandum, and who played an important role in presenting the main underlying ideas of the document to the public—became president of Yugoslavia in 1992. Thirdly, at the beginning of 1992, the Socialist Federal Republic of Yugoslavia (SFRY) formally ceased to exist, halting the process of the multilateral disintegration of the state—which is a prerequisite for achieving the planned national goals. And fourthly, the third phase of the war for the redistribution of Yugoslav territories and the creation of national states began in April 1992.

In any attempt to analyse even a single aspect of such a complex institution as the SANU, one must resist the temptation to identify the whole with its parts. Rather, one must endeavour to distinguish the views that represent the institution as a whole (remembering that an official position may not coincide with the attitudes of all academicians), from the views of individual members. To this end, it seemed prudent to exclude from analysis the positions of individual members which are not contained in SANU documents, and to consider them merely as the political views of particular academicians. The fact that most of the views presented in SANU documents and in the public statements of its leadership have been further radicalized through their the political activities of some members of the Academy, confirms, rather than disputes, the political significance of the institution as the originator of the impulse to formulate a particular idea. Under favourable political circumstances, and through the activities of certain members, this idea developed a different, more radical meaning. Moreover, the fact that there existed different voices within the SANU, certain of them contradicting the official position, hardly undermines the overall content of the Academy's public and political activities— after all, with the exception of a few members who criticized the Memorandum in 1986, there was no dissent in the co-ordinated activities of the politically engaged members of the Academy until 1991.

We have likewise elected to exclude from this article those rare dissenting statements of individual academicians issued since 1991, as these have no real relevance. The carefully designed public opinion, such as it existed at the time, was programmed to ignore anything that did not fit into the predefined pattern of ideas. Conversely, each new affirmation of the pattern, especially when it originated with institutional authority, became deeply rooted in the public consciousness and accepted as a reliable and relevant justification for certain policies.

The 1986 Memorandum

> The body of knowledge that exists within the Academy should not remain confined to the professional disciplines, but should be integrated into wisdom, general experience, and a collective strategic vision.
> (*Dobrica Ćosić,* at the session of the Assembly of the SANU, held on 14 May 1984)

'This year marked the fifth anniversary of the death of J. Broz Tito, the statesman-architect of our socialist society ... Forty years of peace in the Balkans is the longest period of peace in this part of the world. This peace gave birth to substantial material, economic, technological and spiritual developments in the country ...' (*Godišnjak SANU XCII za 1985* [SANU Yearbook XCII for 1985], 1986). With these words, Dušan Kanazir, president of the SANU, opened the infamous session of the SANU Assembly on 23 May 1985, at which the decision to create the Memorandum was made. Yet the tendency within the Academy to take an active role in fields beyond science or the boundaries of the professional disciplines had become apparent even earlier. In 1984, while talking about 'the burdens of the past and the challenges of the future', academician Dobrica Ćosić demanded that the Academy take a stand on 'societal and national issues', while denying that 'the concern of intellectuals for society and its betterment' represented a desire to act as a partner of the regime or an attempt to gain power (*Godišnjak SANU XCI za 1984* [SANU Yearbook XCI for 1984], 1985). A year later, the same proposal, articulated as the need 'to highlight the most immediate social, political, economic, scientific and cultural issues', was unanimously accepted in the form of the Memorandum. In June 1985, the Presidency of the SANU formed a 'Committee for Preparing a Memorandum on Current Social Issues',[2] which began work at the end of 1985, engaging the services of twenty-three full and associate members of the Academy. Work on this document coincided with preparations for the one hundredth anniversary of the existence of the SANU (1 November 1986). The preparations for the celebration stopped abruptly with the unauthorized publication of materials designated at the time as 'the so-called SANU Memorandum'.

Determining how the daily newspaper *Večernje novosti* obtained the document, why they printed it on 24–25 September 1986, and in whose interest this was done, may be relevant in an analysis of developments in Yugoslavia, especially if one wishes to identify the groups which were keen to hasten the process of the disintegration of the state. However, having no possibility to examine these issues, and not wishing to speculate, we will not consider the question in this article.

The Memorandum[3] will be considered as equivalent with other statements issued by the SANU, that is, as an institutional document—even though it was not endorsed by the competent bodies—for the following reasons: 1) the Academy never denied authorship of the document by its committee, despite numerous qualifications that it was merely a working version, that changes had not been included, and that it had not been officially adopted; 2) the Academy never disputed the contents of the document, only the way in which it was released to the public; 3) in later SANU statements, and especially those made by certain members of the preparation committee, the opinions expressed in the Memorandum were constantly reiterated and significantly radicalized; 4) the influence of the Memorandum on public opinion and, with time, its identification with the SANU (both positive and negative) was never denied by the Academy; and 5) in the ensuing years, in statements and public appearances by its leadership, the SANU referred to the Memorandum as an Academy document, emphasizing that the Academy was the first to define the Serbian national programme.[4]

Starting out as an analysis of the crisis of Yugoslav society in general, and ending as a blueprint for a Serbian national programme, the Memorandum met with contradictory interpretations because it attempted to reconcile two irreconcilable motives: it endeavoured to explain the ineffectiveness and the inadequacy of the existing political system which threatened every one of the Yugoslav peoples (this is explicitly stated at one point), and at the same time, it tried to prove the danger inherent in such a system for the Serbian people and for Serbia. Because it examined the entire social and economic crisis exclusively through the Serbian national lens, it did not recognize the perspective of the other Yugoslav peoples. As a result, it identified the ineffectiveness of the political system as the basic cause of the crisis, which it then reinterpreted as national, economic, political and cultural discrimination against Serbia and the Serbian people exclusively. The following examples illustrate the collision of two parallel and mutually exclusive explanations.

a) In the very first paragraph, in an attempt to identify possible causes of the break up of the state, the authors observe that the crisis may well lead to 'social dislocations of unimaginable proportions, including catastrophic developments such as the disintegration of the Yugoslav community', yet they do not explain how and why social disturbances directed against the decision-making centres would lead to the disintegration of a community founded on common interest, be it on the national, republic or community level. In the second part of the text, however, instead of elaborating on the social problems which they identified, they reduce the problems within the Yugoslav community to one national problem—the discrimination against Serbia and the Serbian people (Serbia's economic, political and cultural subordination; the endangering of the Serbian people in Kosovo and Croatia; the disintegration of the Serbian community in Vojvodina). This key problem, if ignored, could have 'serious consequences' for the whole of Yugoslavia.

b) In the first part of the Memorandum, the authors observe that a 'democratically integrated federalism in which the principle of the autonomy of parts is synchronized with the principle of the integration of parts into the larger framework ... where decisions are made through free, rational, public dialogue, and not at behind-the-scenes, "highly confidential" meetings among self-proclaimed and independent protectors of special national interests', would be the ideal alternative to the existing system. Yet completely contrary to this 'true alternative', the second part concludes with the demand that Serbian people 'should arrive at a social and national programme which will inspire the present and future generations'.

c) The Memorandum provides a number of arguments for the democratization of society as a condition for weathering the crisis, except in Kosovo, where a 'political confrontation' should be carried out in a 'revolutionary struggle'. Events in Kosovo are assessed as an 'open and total war', as 'neo-Fascist aggression' which has evaded a 'real resolution', with the conclusion that 'young offenders were punished with intentionally exaggerated sentences in order to incite and to deepen interethnic hatreds'.

d) Serbia is threatened by an anti-Serbian coalition, with Vojvodina as a member of this coalition. One can identify two criteria applied in assessing the motives for 'anti-Serb sentiments'—a national one for Slovenia and Croatia, and a bureaucratic one for Vojvodina. In the latter case, the authors claim that 'anti-Serbian' policies have led to a 'disintegration' of the Serbian community, but there is no mention of the Serbian majority in Vojvodina when discussing three privileged, developed regions in Yugoslavia (Slovenia, Croatia and Vojvodina), which have not only developed normally, but have also managed to 'improve their relative situation in comparison with the Yugoslav average'.

e) Interpretations of the past abound with similar contradictions, especially with respect to the history of the Communist Party and its attitude toward Serbia and the Serbian people. In an attempt to prove the anti-Serbian policy of the Communist Party of Yugoslavia, the Memorandum claims that Serbia did not even participate as an equal partner in decisions reached by the AVNOJ[5], when relations among the Yugoslav peoples were defined. This means that Serbs 'found themselves in the position where, due to the pressures of war, they had to accept solutions that created the conditions for their dispersal'. Later on, the concluding part of the text completely contradicts this interpretation of the AVNOJ. In a passage that emphasizes the need to define Serbian national interests, the Memorandum points to the need to 'support the choices made by the AVNOJ'. It is especially unclear how the observation that, 'the Yugoslav solution for the national question initially represented an exemplary model of a multinational federation, in which the principle of unitary state policy was successfully fused with the principle of educational and cultural autonomy of nations and national minorities' can be reconciled with the conclusion that the AVNOJ introduced the possibility for the dispersal of Serbian people, or with the assertion that after 1980 'the understanding of relations between peoples formulated by the National Liberation Movement was radically revised ...'.

These and other contradictions and inconsistencies prevent us from identifying any consistent ideological and political attitude of the authors of the Memorandum. We will therefore limit ourselves to analysing the theses which, being presented as incontestable truths through their constant reiteration by politically active academics, and by becoming the general topics of political discussion in Serbia, made the greatest contribution to the shaping of public opinion in the subsequent years (1987–1992).

Yugoslavia and Serbia

The SFRY was defined as a state characterized by 'a long-standing discriminatory policy against Serbia', 'a traditional discrimination against Serbia' which resulted in an 'unequal status for Serbia on all levels', 'the politically inferior position of Serbia which has determined all political relations', 'the subordination and neglect of the Serbian economy', ' consistent discrimination against Serbia's economy', interference in its internal affairs and 'dominance over it'. In addition, an 'enduring anti-Serb coalition' had been established in Yugoslavia, characterized by 'chauvinism and Serbo-phobia', and motivated by 'revisionism'. This revisionism did not stop at Serbo-phobia, but 'grew stronger, to find its ultimate expression in genocide'.

Slovenia and Croatia were identified as the principal advocates of anti-Serbian policies, but other republics and provinces were their accomplices, because only Serbia 'suffered real consequences in the development of three underdeveloped republics and the Autonomous Federal Province of Kosovo', while the three developed territories only improved their positions as their 'burden' of assisting the undeveloped regions was 'eased' by Serbia. Both types of territories in Yugoslavia, the developed (Slovenia, Croatia and Vojvodina) and the underdeveloped (Montenegro, Macedonia, Bosnia-Hercegovina, and Kosovo) formed a coalition to promote 'common interests' and 'to perpetuate the existing state order where they could satisfy their interests at the expense of Serbia'. The Memorandum defined the position of Slovenia and Croatia (the leaders of the anti-Serbian coalition) as 'political and economic dominance'; they had organized Yugoslavia 'to meet their needs'; 'they pursued their national programmes and economic aspirations' through political domination, while in the economic system 'they imposed solutions which served their economic interests'. With the help of Tito and Kardelj[6], they had established an 'enduring anti-Serbian coalition' intending to 'dominate' the state. Furthermore, the Memorandum accused them of having 'monopolies over official posts', of harbouring 'sympathies for separatists and autonomists', and of offering 'active and largely unconcealed support' for 'total war' in Kosovo.

The Serbian people in Yugoslavia

In addition to outlining Serbia's subjugated position within the state, the Memorandum also presented the difficult position of Serbian people, evidenced in 'genocidal terror' and 'neo-Fascist aggression in Kosovo'; in 'discrimination, the subtle and effective politics of assimilation and national inequality' in Croatia; and in the aspiration to 'completely destroy the national unity of the Serbian people' through the existing autonomy of Vojvodina. Serbian people in other republics did not have the right 'to use their language and alphabet' or to form political or cultural organizations. They were constantly accused of being the 'oppressor' and of promoting 'unitaristic' policies, and they 'bore the stigma and endured the accusation of being the jailer of other Yugoslav peoples' for over half a century. Serbian history had been brought into question and 'pushed into the background'; 'its cultural heritage was "denied", assimilated, or devalued, ignored or ruined; the language was suppressed, while the Cyrillic alphabet was slowly disappearing'; its 'cultural and spiritual integrity were rudely denied it', as with no other people; its culture and literature were 'systematically disintegrating'; its best writers were 'appropriated'; there was an 'assimilation and parcelling out of the Serbian cultural heritage'; Serbian artists and writers were the ones most censored; school reading lists considerably reduced the proportion of Serbian literature, and certain school programmes 'reduced and subjected to chauvinistic interpretations' the history of the Serbian people; the Serbian people were subjected to 'ideological indoctrination, leading to the devaluation and denial of their own tradition through an imposed sense of guilt, leaving them intellectually and politically disarmed'.

Causes

Contradictions abound throughout the Memorandum, including contradictions in the interpretations of the causes of the Yugoslav crisis, that is, the difficult position of the Serbian people. Each aspect of the general threat to the Serbs was ascribed to 'the interwar attitude of the Communist Party of Yugoslavia to the national question, influenced by the Comintern'. Also responsible for this general situation were the AVNOJ (which had convened without authentic Serbian representation); Tito and Kardelj, as founders of the anti-Serbian coalition, and their followers; the 'capitulation' of the Serbian Communists; Kardelj's 1974 Constitution, etc. This consistent anti-Serbian Communist policy, from the time it was an underground organization to the time of the Memorandum, was allegedly founded on a certain predisposition of the Comintern, and it continued for a half century after the dissolution of the Comintern. Yet this continuity was inexplicably (and without explanation in the Memorandum) interrupted between 1953 and 1965, a period when nearly everything in Yugoslavia was functioning perfectly ('a period of visible material improvement, gradual democratization, and spiritual emancipation', of 'successful development', 'national independence, enviable economic growth', 'impressive cultural ascent of truly revolutionary proportions', 'the celebrated position of the Programme of the League of Communists', etc.). In the mid-1960s, the previous mode resumed, with 'nationalism again gaining prominence in the practices of the

League of Communists' under the influence of the Comintern and the pre-war nationalist policies of the Communist Party of Yugoslavia ('a negative turn of events occurred in the mid–1960s', 'social clashes in the late 1960s', 'the fatal breach in 1965', etc.). Considering that the same Communist Party, with the same leadership, ruled both before and after 1953, after 1965, and even under the influence of the Comintern between the two wars; considering that Tito and Kardelj were the authors of both the 'celebrated position' of the Programme of the League of Communists and the 1974 Constitution; and considering they were the ones responsible both for the 'impressive ascent' and the 'coarse refutation of the integrity of the Serbian people', the Memorandum's position on the causes of the Yugoslav crisis contradicted the authors' fundamental thesis about 'anti-Serbianism' as an enduring feature of Communist policies. A serious analysis might at least have attempted to explain this interruption in the 'continuity' of the single ideological model—anti-Serbianism—which was supposed to be dominant to such an extent that it was responsible for 'persistent discrimination against the Serbian economy' after the 1960s, for the 'greatest defeat in the fight for freedom in Serbia from 1804 to 1941', and for the 'multi-dimensional crisis' in Yugoslavia. The Memorandum did not.

What did the Memorandum propose?

The text of the Memorandum is divided into two sections, with the majority of positions and demands outlined in the second part negating the positions set out in the first. Part one called for: 1) a democratic, integrative federalism (the principle of autonomy of the parts synchronized with the principle of the integration of the parts within a unified whole); 2) a complete reassessment of the 1974 Constitution; 3) democratization and complete regeneration of the cadres, true self-determination and equality for all Yugoslav peoples, including the Serbian people, the full realization of human, civil and socio-economic rights, and the rationalization of the political system. Part two comprised recommendations for a future Serbian political leadership: 1) the unveiling of the political crisis; 2) a decisive end to the post-war practices of replacing politicians who questioned the equality of Serbia and of discriminating against economists, sociologists, philosophers and writers from Serbia who attempted to forewarn society about impending malignant social phenomena; 3) in Kosovo, to 'defeat aggression', to achieve a 'political settlement through truly revolutionary battle' (which, according to the Memorandum, included 'open confrontation, with the right to free expression, even if this means demonstrating opposing positions'); 4) the cancellation of the debt of the Serbian people for their alleged historical guilt—an official refutation of the claim that Serbs had an economically privileged status between the two wars, and confirmation of the Serbian contribution in the history of the liberation and creation of Yugoslavia; 5) the establishment of the full national and cultural integrity of the Serbian people, regardless of the republic or region in which they happened to reside; 6) the establishment of a modern social and national programme for the Serbian people which would inspire both present and future generations; 7) Serbia's open confirmation that its internal organization was imposed; 8) support for the principles set out by the AVNOJ, and, if other alternatives were considered, Serbia's economic and national interests, should be made clear so as 'not to be surprised by the developments'; 9) fundamental reforms in the area of democratic socialism; 10) the 'democratic mobilization of the entire intellectual and moral energy of the people ... in creating a programme and planning for its future'.

In the months following the publication of the Memorandum, the Serbian authorities exerted a great deal of pressure on the Academy to retract the contents of the text. The Academy refused to do so explicitly. Several meetings were held in an attempt to resolve the impasse, including the meeting of the Active Committee of the League of Communists, held on 14 October at the Academy, a closed session of the SANU Presidency on 21 October, a visit by the SANU Presidium to Ivan Stambolić on 29 October, and an Extraordinary Assembly of the SANU held on 18 December 1986. Qualifying the 'so-called Memorandum' as a 'legally nonexistent text', the SANU extricated itself from the obligation to explain and justify its positions, shifting the attention to the problematic way in which the text had reached the public. Certain academicians expressed particularly sharp criticism of the Academy's political engagement. These included Vasa Ćubrilović: 'all this is politics, not science'; Pavle Savić: 'the Memorandum bears all the characteristics of a pamphlet or other propaganda material'; and Sima Ćirković: 'the current situation demands that the Academy not be used for objectives that are contrary to its essence and its mission' (*KN*, 1–15 January 1988).

At the same time, the whole of the Yugoslav media conducted a campaign against the Memorandum. In Serbia, all public statements condemned the Memorandum as a nationalistic text which aspired to the break-up of Yugoslavia, and demanded the resignation of the SANU leadership, particularly its vice-president Antonije Isaković. Criticism of the Memorandum continued into the first half of 1987, with the anti-Memorandum campaign culminating in the publication of the supposedly satirical article 'Vojko and Savle' (*P*, 18 January 1987), then waning, and disappearing altogether in the summer of 1987. After the Eighth Session of the Central Committee of the League of Communists of Serbia in September 1987, that is, after the victory of Slobodan Milošević's 'camp' in the divided Serbian government, there were no further attacks on the Memorandum or the SANU; demands for resignations were forgotten, and the Academy returned to the pages of *Politika* and other government newspapers.

Support for the programme of the new government (1988–1989)

In the year of mass meetings throughout Serbia and Montenegro that occurred almost daily, the new Serbian government and the Academy synchronized their activities rather well. A scientific conference held at the SANU between 17 and 19 March 1988, on the 'Current Problems of the Constitution and Constitutional Changes', marked the first joint project born out of this newly established partnership. At the annual SANU Assembly in May 1988, President Kanazir expressed the Academy's support for the efforts and proposals of the Serbian leadership, 'whose main objective is to find a solution to the crisis' (*P*, 27 May 1988). At the beginning of October, the SANU sponsored a discussion on constitutional changes and adopted a document known as the Opinion of the SANU on Changes to the Constitution of the Socialist Republic of Serbia (*P*, 19 November 1988). On that occasion, academician Radovan Samardžić observed that 'our science and the SANU are profoundly responsible for the process that has been initiated, and for what appears to be an opportunity to make changes' (*P*, 4 October 1988).

The Opinion of the SANU was formulated during a period when the Serbian government was most actively pursuing constitutional changes, when dramatic events were unfolding in Kosovo, in Vojvodina and Montenegro, and when mass meetings were being staged throughout Serbia. On 19 November 1988, the day of a massive meeting for 'brotherhood and unity', when, according to *Politika*, 'peace returned to the streets and squares of Novi Sad' following the resignation of the Vojvodina leadership, the newspaper also published the Opinion. The Opinion was a terminologically diluted, edited, and more concrete selection of the positions set out in the Memorandum. It was much less generalized, and was written with much more decisiveness and self-assurance with regard to the possibilities for the SANU and its position. It presented a brief programme for future policies, punctuated with the repeated demand for 'fundamental changes' that would be more significant than those the Serbian leadership was prepared to undertake at the time. The changes to the Serbian Constitution proposed by the government were deemed insufficient, acceptable only as a 'first, initial step in creating a new constitution'. The Opinion, like certain sections of the Memorandum, identified the 1974 Constitution as the cause of the crisis in Yugoslav society, which was once again interpreted exclusively as a Serbian crisis. The document put forth demands for constitutional changes that would achieve the following: the elimination of scparatism, demands for autonomy, genocide in Kosovo, economic stagnation, cultural drifting, etc.; the promotion of Serbia's equality with the other republics and the return of its forfeited statehood; the removal of the constitutional provisions that established the statehood of the [autonomous] regions; the democratization of elections; uniformity among all scientific and cultural institutions in Serbia; the official use of the Serbo-Croat language and the Cyrillic alphabet in the territories of Serbia, without limiting the rights of other nationalities to the use of their own languages; the devising of a long-term functional demographic policy;[7] and the insuring of the drafting of new Yugoslav and Serbian constitutions immediately following the adoption of the amendment.

The government and the SANU continued and increased their mutual support to the point of creating an image of complete symmetry and harmony between science and politics. Just before publishing the Opinion of the SANU, *Politika* also printed several favourable articles about the Academy (16–19 October 1988), and this was followed by visits and open support, along with joint public appearances. In January 1989, the Presidency of the SANU visited *Politika* to negotiate further co-operation between the two institutions. In a gesture of mutual respect, President Kanazir presented Živorad Minović, the director of *Politika*, with a plaque and a badge from the Academy, announcing that all previous 'mistakes and foul-ups' in mutual relations were the responsibility of 'individual leaders, restrictive structures, and bureaucracy' (*P*, 7 January 1989).

During 1989 the SANU Presidency used every available opportunity to extend verbal support for the policies of the Serbian leadership. In March 1989 its Executive Committee presented the public with a special explanation in response to 'the offensive slander' about the SANU 'in connection with the policies of the current leadership of SR Serbia [Socialist Republic of Serbia]'. It concluded with an expression of the SANU's wholehearted support for the Serbian leadership in its efforts to 'establish the integrity and dignity of SR Serbia ... at this fateful, historical moment, recognizing the full extent of its significance' (*P*, 30 March 1989). At the Grand Assembly, held in Belgrade, President Kanazir proclaimed that 'after two years of impressive battle waged by the people, and the decisive attitude and unanimity within the new party and state leadership, Serbia had regained its sovereignty ...' (*P*, 26 April 1989). In May 1989, under the headline 'The Academy Continues to Support the Programme of the New Serbian Leadership', *Politika* reported on the annual SANU Assembly at which the president made a virtually identical announcement: 'thanks to the impressive unity and struggle of the people, thanks to direct, courageous and honest attitudes, and the unity of the new party and state leadership headed by President Slobodan Milošević, Serbia has regained its sovereignty, statehood and unity, and has become an equal member of our federal socialist multinational community. The Academy has supported and continues to support the efforts and programmes of the new Serbian leadership' (*P*, 26 May 1989).

By the end of 1989, however, there developed an ambivalence towards the Academy's political activities, even among its membership. The annual Assembly in November of that year occasioned the first formulation of a sentiment which would be repeated regularly from that point forward: 'while it is understood that the Academy should not interfere in everyday politics, it nevertheless cannot remain ambivalent with regard to the fate of its people' (*P*, 17 November 1989). In the following years, this statement would become an alibi both for its failure to react when the context was unpleasant, but also for intense activity when it was deemed necessary. Adopted in May 1990, the compromise decision to be politically non-active—or rather, to be active occasionally—relieved the SANU, as an institution, of the obligation to provide support to the government. Throughout 1990 a marked decline in instances of institutional support for the regime could be observed, but also a simultaneous increase in the activities of individual academicians and members. Such activities occurred in waves, reflecting the needs of daily politics concerning current issues.

The academicians limited their support to the Serbian government alone, excluding other governments, as evidenced in their attitude towards the president of the Federal Executive Council [the federal prime minister], Ante Marković. When it suited the Serbian government, and when *Politika* introduced a column which would feature attacks on Marković's reforms in August 1990, among the first contributions to the column were academician Antonije Isaković's negative commentary on 4 August, along with the views of Milorad Ekmečić, Dobrica Ćosić and Ljubimir Tadić, which were originally published in *NIN*, followed by those of Mihailo Marković on 28 August, Miloš Macura on 29 August, and Antonije Isaković on 6 September 1990.

While the SANU unanimously adopted the proposal, submitted by Miroslav Simić on behalf of thirty academicians at its annual assembly in May 1990, to dissolve the Active Committee of the League of Communists and to prohibit the work of political parties within the Academy, certain academicians, including members of the leadership, nevertheless continued to offer considerable support to political parties, especially to the SPS (Socialist Party) and SDS (Serbian Democratic Party). With the founding of the SPS in July 1990, academician Mihailo Marković became its vice-president and Antonije Isaković a member of its main committee, and a number of academics were also enlisted in support of its pre-election campaign.

The Academy is not involved in politics and Serbia is not at war

Prior to March 1991, public statements by academicians did not upset the harmony of the relationship between the Academy and the government. Whenever the government needed assistance, there were enough active academicians available to proffer expert opinion and scientific verification of the inevitable correctness of the policies implemented. While it was always the same small group of academicians (largely from the Departments of Social Science and the History of Language and Literature) who made the majority of public appearances, and while the SANU frequently emphasized that only the Presidency and the Executive Council could speak on its behalf, there was still an overwhelming impression of close mutual support between the Academy and the government. The SANU never publicly disapproved of the government's actions, nor did any academician ever openly criticize the highest scientific institution's open political support for the government. While some dissenting views must have existed, they were never publicly articulated, and SANU public announcements were never challenged by the Academy, even if they were not unanimously adopted.

Events in March 1991[8] in Belgrade marked the first public expression of political disunity within the SANU. Even this initial expression of discord occurred on two levels—on the institutional level and on the level of individual statements. On 12 March, President Kanazir made a public statement in the name of the Academy which maintained the institution's formal neutrality by voicing a general appeal for calm and for the 'silencing of raging passions'. Commencing with the standard formulaic expression of 'deep concern', the statement was limited to an observation that there was no agreement on 'minimal national interests', and to encouraging tolerance and understanding between the government and the opposition in order to 'preserve the unity of the Serbian people's vital interests' (*P*, 13 March 1991). On the same day, *Politika* also published a message by fifteen members of the Department of Language and Literature which, in contrast to the SANU Presidency, voiced explicit support 'for the empty-handed Serbian people and its youth' whose aims were supported by 'the greater part of the Serbian intelligentsia'. The statement also condemned the 'irresponsible use of force' and the deployment of tanks in the streets.

Only a few days later, the SANU issued another statement in response to 'numerous letters from citizens' petitioning it to make its opinion public. Demonstrating its concern for the future of the Serbian people, the Academy explained that, as an institution, it was unable to take positions on political issues, because its duty was only to bring together 'intellectual forces' for solving current problems, and that it functioned 'exclusively through scholarly work'. The Academy judged it to be the appropriate moment to refer to the Memorandum as a document which 'had significant consequences for social development in recent years', and which was 'understood as a unique national programme for the future progress of the Serbian people'. The SANU also announced a new, similar project 'which will consider the problems and paths which the Serbian people should follow into the twenty-first century', and once again dissociated itself from the personal views of certain academicians (*P*, 23 March 1991). This statement represents a particularly interesting shift with regard to the Academy's political activities. The emphasis on its obligation not to interfere in daily politics—after it had prepared the Memorandum in 1985-1986, published the Opinion of the SANU on Changes to the Constitution in 1988 when the question of the constitution was the foremost political issue, signed an announcement of explicit political support for the Serbian leadership and its political programme in 1989, etc.— probably reflects the Academy's inability to continue to appear on the political scene as an institution of like-minded individuals. Relinquishing the obligation to comment on daily politics as an institution, the SANU also emphasized the full right of its members, as private citizens, to participate in political life. The indecision of the institutional leadership proceeded from two opposing motives: on the one hand, from the desire to support the government's policies in protecting Serbian 'national interests', and on the other, by the need experienced by at least one segment of the Academy to distance itself from Milošević. These inconsistencies later produced contradictory interpretations of the position of the SANU leadership on the political activities of individual academicians and on opinions expressed by the institution. Although it constantly emphasized that academicians spoke exclusively for themselves, when it was necessary it nevertheless acknowledged certain individual statements as representative of the institution's position.[9]

The crisis which gripped Yugoslavia during those days did not prompt the Academy to consider possible solutions in a 'scholarly' way. On the contrary, the manifold public political activities of a group of academicians, whose positions on questions relating to Yugoslavia mirrored official Serbian politics, created the impression that there existed absolute agreement between the new national politics and the intellectual elite which had been summoned to decide the fate of the people. In this respect, there was no significant difference between the two sides of the politically active membership of the SANU: the division simply consisted inbeing 'for' or 'against' Milošević. There was no dispute on questions of the alleged dangers that the existing Yugoslavia represented for the Serbian people, nor on the concept of Serbian 'national interests' which would be built in Yugoslavia's ruins, nor on the Academy's position regarding the war.[10]

The academicians' largest group initiatives were the founding of the Serbian National Council (SNS, *Srpski nacionalni savet*) in

March 1991, and the founding of the Serbian Assembly in September 1991. Following the events in March, or perhaps in response to these disturbances, the Founding Committee of the SNS met in Belgrade. According to *Politika*, candidates for the presidency of the body were Ćosić, Bećković and Ekmečić, and the academicians present included Ćosić, Bećković, Rašković and Marković (*P*, 30 March 1991). The SNS was conceived as a 'supreme national institution which will represent the interests of all Serbs, regardless of where they live' (*P*, 31 March 1991). At about the same time, again according to *Politika*, at the founding of the Association of Serbs from Bosnia-Hercegovina in Serbia, academicians Ćosić, Ekmečić, Isaković and Bećković again took the floor, and proposals by Amfilohije Radović and Radovan Karadžić to create a union of Serbian states were greeted with ovations (*P*, 31 March 1991). The speed with which they set out to realize this idea of 'united Serbian states', their fear that the 'historical moment will be missed', and the absence of any doubt that it was their task to realize something that had eluded generations of Serbian politicians and academicians for over two hundred years, all testify to the magnitude of the political ambitions of this group of academicians.

By 27 March 1991, academician Marković had already acquainted the public with the initiative to found the SNS, the mission of which was to promote the formation of a single Serbian state. *Politika* reported that, in addition to a number of political parties in Serbia and beyond, the initiative had been greeted by the Serbian Orthodox Church and 'the most important scientific and cultural institutions in Serbia'. *Politika* reports on 30 and 31 March 1991 indicated that representatives of the SANU would also participate in the SNS. On 2 April 1991, academician Ćosić, as a member of the Founding Committee, promised that the expectations of 'our political people' would be fulfilled by the preparation of the SNS Declaration, while academician Bećković estimated that the Declaration would have to include 'that which is indisputable among Serbs' and nominated Tomislav Karadjordjević for president of the SNS (*P*, 2 April 1991). *Politika* continued to report on discussions accompanying the drafting of the Declaration in subsequent weeks, with the next report in the summer of 1991 announcing the demise of the idea.

The initiative to establish a Serbian Assembly progressed in a similar fashion. In September 1991, a press conference was held at the SANU Historical Institute in order to announce to the public that the founding session of the Assembly would take place on 28 September. The organization would be an association of independent scientists, writers, artists and intellectuals who supported the advancement and protection of Serbian interests. The project's initiator, academician Pavle Ivić, himself emphasized the fact that the Serbian Assembly represented an attempt to substitute for the failed SNS project; he stated that the founding of the Assembly would rectify the error made six months earlier, when the establishment of 'a similar organization collapsed because of personal and party animosities'. He believed that the Assembly was supposed to assemble all 'thinking people'. Special emphasis was given to the founding of the 'Information Centre for Advancing the Truth About Serbia and the Serbian People'. The initiative was launched by the Historical Institute because, the organizers stipulated, few historians participated in the 'struggle for truth' (*P*, 24 September 1991). In October 1991 the Serbian Assembly publicly appealed to Lord Carrington and the Council of Ministers of the European Community, on the occasion of the Hague proposal, demanding that all those 'who wish to do so' should be permitted to remain in Yugoslavia (*P*, 23 October 1991).

Its second public statement was made several days before war broke out in Bosnia-Hercegovina, on 28 March 1992, when its president, Pavle Ivić, saluted the Congress of Serbian Intellectuals in Sarajevo and '*handed over the ethnic maps which were created at the founding of the Serbian Assembly*' (author's emphasis), an event which *Politika* failed to report in September 1991 (*P*, 29 March 1992). Pavle Ivić's statement to *Politika* in August 1991 on the futility of Izetbegović's project for a sovereign and indivisible Bosnia-Hercegovina, confirms the suspicion that ethnic maps and a division of Bosnia-Hercegovina were under consideration much earlier than previously thought. On 9 January 1992, three months before the war and the division of the republic, Radovan Karadžić himself admitted that 'a unitary Bosnia-Hercegovina no longer exists'. The Republic of the Serbian People of Bosnia-Hercegovina (*Republika Srpska*) was proclaimed the same day (*P*, 10 January 1992).

Exempting itself from the obligation to make statements on current political issues by evoking its statutes, while at the same time giving free reign to its members to participate individually in public political life, the Academy greatly contributed to the broad (and seemingly disunited) political engagement of its membership. In the period from July to September 1991 alone, *Politika* published ten unusually lengthy interviews with academicians. It is interesting to note that while cities were burning throughout Yugoslavia, and while huge numbers of civilians were being murdered, *Poli-*

tika published the more important interviews with academicians (those published in instalments) on its front page—a place normally reserved for the most important news of the day.

In contrast with its previous regular statements—on the occasion of the meeting at Cankarjev Dom, the articles published in Zagreb's *Vjesnik* in 1989, the March 1991 events in Belgrade—the Academy offered no official statements regarding the May 1991 events in Croatia, the war in Slovenia, the events of June–July 1991, the fighting around Vukovar, the shelling of Dubrovnik, etc. Its only public statements came on 15 October 1991 regarding threats to cultural monuments, and in the form of a letter to the world-wide public on 16 October regarding the precarious position of the Serbian people in Croatia. The statement was made in response to a letter sent by the Croatian Academy of Science and Art (HAZU, *Hrvatska akademija znanosti i umjetnost*)[11] criticizing the SANU for not reacting to the destruction of cultural monuments in Croatia, as indicated in the statement's conclusion: '...criticizing the SANU for its silence and lack of concern for cultural monuments is an accusation not based in fact. On the other hand, there is plentiful evidence that those who criticize us so loudly today were silent at the time when the Serbian cultural heritage was under threat'. The SANU further appealed 'to all those who control the fate of our cultural monuments to respect cultural heritage regardless of its ethnic origin' (*P*, 15 October 1991).

The following day, *Politika* published a SANU statement directed at the international public—'Several Key Facts about the Position of Serbian People in Croatia'—intended to counter 'the lies and deceit'. The war in Croatia was characterized as 'a fierce conflict between the Serbian people living in Croatia and the Croatian authorities' which was 'turning into an ethnic and religious war'. The Academy once again leapt to the defence of the Serbian government with the observation that 'the Republic of Serbia, its policies, its state and public institutions, are unfairly, incorrectly, and at times maliciously, characterized as the cause and the main culprits in the drama of the Yugoslav state'. It further noted that 'Serbia never declared war on Croatia', and that the conflict had transpired between Serbian people in Croatia and the Croatian state.

Along with some new observations—for instance, that Slovenians and Croatians, dissatisfied with the Kingdom of Yugoslavia, 'without much hesitation contributed to its disintegration and fall when, in 1941, the state was attacked by Nazi Germany and Fascist Italy...'—the SANU largely repeated the positions outlined in the

Memorandum regarding the position of Serbia and the Serbian people: that in Yugoslavia, the leading role was played by Croatians and Slovenians, while 'a minor and marginal' role was reserved for the Serbs; that Serbia was the bread-basket and the source of natural resources for Croatia and Slovenia; that autonomous provinces were introduced in Serbia 'to weaken it economically, socially, culturally and spiritually'; and that 'in Tito's Yugoslavia, the Serbian people and Serbia were culturally, spiritually and materially impoverished'. Considering the fact that the SANU had made these pronouncements on several previous occasions, it is surprising that it elected to identify new enemies of Serbia—this time in Serbia itself—at the time of the fiercest fighting and in the midst of Yugoslavia's disintegration. 'With its anti-Serbian propaganda, the Croatian state strives to direct international public opinion against the Serbian people living in Croatia, and against Serbia itself, and to provoke the disapproval of *ethnic minorities hostile to Serbia: the Albanians in Kosovo, Muslims living in Serbia, and Hungarians living in Vojvodina*' (author's emphasis). As with the Memorandum, torn between the pragmatic need to advocate the continuation of a federal Yugoslavia and the primary desire to define its conception of Serbian national interests, the Academy once again promulgated a contradictory political solution. It further stated that '... the Serbian people have realized that a life within Croatia is no longer possible', that Serbs 'realize that they, like every other Yugoslav people, cannot be unified except within a federal state', and that 'allegations that Serbs want to create a Greater Serbia or a unitary Yugoslavia over which they will rule, are both malicious and untrue' (*P*, 16 October 1991).

The political divisions which beset the Academy in March 1991 deepened during the year. In October 1991, a group of historians published a letter demanding the protection of Dubrovnik, directed to the Yugoslav People's Army [JNA, *Jugoslovenska Narodna Armija*] and to the Croatian military formations. Among the signatories were two academicians, Sima Ćirković and Andrej Mitorvić (*P*, 5 October 1991). In November 1991, eighteen members of the SANU published an appeal for a peaceful resolution of the Yugoslav conflict, which differed in tone from all of the Academy's previous statements in that it did not relativize the demand for peace. While the Academy demanded a peaceful solution in its own letter to the world-wide public, it was merely a conclusion to its observation that Serbia was not waging the war, that the war had been imposed on the Serbian people, and that it was therefore a necessity. The appeal launched by this group of academicians denied the necessity of war, however: 'We do not believe in the usefulness of this war. We do not believe in the people who lead it. We do not believe in the people who support it, whether consciously or unconsciously. We do not believe in victories which lead to new wars.' They demanded a peace 'in which there will be no persecutions or subjugation of any national, political, or religious groups, and in which the propaganda of death will not rule ...'. At its regular session on 23 November, the Academy dissociated itself from this anti-war appeal with Secretary General Medaković's claim that it merely represented the attitudes of the signatories and not that of the institution as a whole.

There is further evidence that growing differences in political attitudes influenced certain groups within the Academy to issue statements. A group of academicians, this time members of the Department of Social Sciences, issued a third statement that was made available to the public. It was a letter addressed to the HAZU in December 1991, signed by the department secretary, Ivan Maksimović. It is interesting to note that the reply to the Croatian Academy was not signed by the SANU leadership, but merely by one department, even though its tone suggested a response from the institution as a whole.[12] In an attempt to demonstrate the many decades of subjugation of the Serbian people in Croatia, this text also abounds with contradictions which will be illustrated here only in citing its conclusion: 'the Serbian people's experience of the common life with Croats—whether they were in Croatia, in Bosnia-Hercegovina, or in Serbia—has been largely negative, even tragic', while at the same time, Serbia *supported and continues to support the continuation and the democratic renewal of the Yugoslav federal state in which all its peoples would live together, as they have done thus far* ... But that is precisely what Slovenia and Croatia do not wish ...' (author's emphasis; *P*, 13 December 1991).

The Academy was more proactive at the Congress of Serbian Intellectuals on 'The Yugoslav Crisis and the Serbian Question', held on 28–29 March 1992 in Sarajevo. According to *Politika*, participants numbered five hundred of the 'most respected Serbian intellectuals'. The Congress was addressed in the name of the SANU by academician Macura and in the name of the Serbian Assembly by academician Ivić, and academician Ćosić forwarded a letter proposing that Serbs, Muslims and Croats divide their populations and the land 'so that [they] can eliminate the reasons for hating and killing one other'. The Congress adopted a Declaration based on academician Ekmečić's introduction and academician Ćosić's letter, concluding that the only solution for Bosnia-Hercegovina was 'a three-part community in which Serbs will take sovereign control of their borders' (*P*, 30 March 1992).

After several months of silence by the Academy as an institution, and, at the same time, of the loudest speeches imaginable by academicians, at the beginning of 1992 the public finally learned about the political rift within the institution. At the 4 June SANU Assembly, thirty-seven academicians submitted a statement demanding Milošević's resignation, an act which provoked a discussion about the relationship between the Academy and the regime. President Kanazir relativized the proposition, claiming that the Academy 'must realize that a part of the responsibility for this entire situation ... belongs with the leadership of the Yugoslav People's Army and even the Serbian people'. His effort failed to preempt a conflict, however, just as his demand to close discussion to the public 'because of the sensitivity of the theme' was rejected. Nevertheless, the request that the Academy refrain from political announcements was approved, while the academicians were given the option to sign the statement individually. The majority of the signatories were academicians who had not publicly participated in political life in the preceding years, but among them were also several figures who had supported Milošević and his policies only months earlier (e. g. M. Pavić) (*P*, 5 June 1992).

By 13 June the first proposals that academician Ćosić become president of Yugoslavia appeared in the press (from the Association of Serbs from Bosnia-Hercegovina, the Association of Serbs from Croatia, SPS Valjevo, etc.). Within a staggeringly brief period, the proposal was taken up, procedures were begun, and by 16 June 1992 it was announced that Ćosić had been elected the president of the state.

However symbolic Ćosić's presidency might have been, it concluded a period of the SANU's political activities. Several months earlier, the second Yugoslavia—which had inflicted so much suffering upon the Serbian people, according to the SANU Memorandum—had disintegrated, while at the same time a third 'domestic' war for consolidating national states had began. Internal disunity prevented further political statements by this institution, while the new questions about a future which needed to be defined, and about a state and borders which needed to be determined, proved less inspiring than reflections on the existential possibilities of a common state.

While it is impossible to establish any consistent ideological position of the Academy through an analysis of the Memorandum, the Opinion, or its announcements of a political nature, its political position has been far more consistent. Differences were expressed only in the degree of satisfaction with the political programme of the Serbian government, but their essential content changed little. More or less openly, the institution officially supported the regime.

While the Memorandum was a hybrid of Communist ideology (planned economy, self management, producers' councils, etc.), democratic principles (civil rights), and nationalist–romantic ideologies, documents which had a political content, produced in direct reaction to concrete events, unequivocally indicated the institution's political position. Not a single political document (announcement) issued by the Academy between 1988 and 1992, nor any statement by its leadership, challenged official Serbian politics either globally or on specific points. On the contrary, the government and the Academy expressed identical positions with regard to political events: in 1988, demanding profound changes to the constitutional order, revoking the 'statehood' of the autonomous regions, reducing the birth rate of Albanians in Kosovo, etc.; and in 1991, claiming that Serbia is not waging war, the Serbian leadership had been attacked unjustly, etc.

One can remark a striking difference between the activities of the SANU in the years before the legalization of pluralism in Yugoslavia, and the years that came after. Until the introduction of the multiparty system in 1989, it steadfastly supported the Serbian government's programme. It is difficult to ascertain whether this political orientation was indeed objectively dominant, or whether a group of academicians with political authority and ambition successfully 'imposed' their convictions on the institution as a whole. What is indisputable, however, is that the years prior to 1989 were marked by a single political orientation, publicly depersonalized, which stood behind the authority of the highest national institution and its unitary public declarations.

The legalization of pluralism, the prohibition of party activity within the Academy, and the decision to abstain from political activities, all contributed to redirecting the politically engaged academicians toward parties which shared their conception of 'national interests' (SPS, SDS). The new circumstances also pushed these academicians to join or establish in Belgrade new national societies of Serbs from other republics, an activity which completed the process of the national homogenization of Serbs in Yugoslavia around a unified political, rather than cultural, programme personified by Slobodan Milošević. A smaller number of politically active academicians defined their place within political parties or movements (e. g. the Party of Democratic Opposition [DEPOS, *Demokraski pokeet Srbije*]) opposed to Milošević's 'Communism', although they nevertheless remained close to his national programme. In general, the academicians eschewed investing the authority of the Academy into parties, movements or citizens' associations with a Yugoslav or an anti-war orientation.

The Yugoslav political and economic crisis was invoked most of ten to justify the 'well-intentioned' decision of individuals and institutions to become politically engaged. Yet even a rudimentary understanding of the fundamental causes of instability in both the first and the second Yugoslavia—the fact that Yugoslavia was a multinational state with a mixed population and with few ethnically homogeneous territories—should have convinced these actors that the state could not be preserved (if that was indeed the intention) through a simple formula, and certainly not through a formula based on defining and implementing national programmes. Considering that such programmes necessarily involve opposing ambitions, every attempt to realize them would lead to conflict, ultimately resulting in war. In a multinational community, the definition of a national programme as a separate ethnic–territorial and political interest of a segment of society can be legitimate only if the people in whose name it is formulated understand and accept the inevitable consequences.

The SANU's engagement in Yugoslav political life was not imposed. Motivated by the conviction that scientific resources should be engaged to find a solution to the Yugoslav crisis (above all economists, lawyers, historians and writers), the SANU expressed the views of its membership when it decided to draft the Memorandum. The question of whether the Memorandum would have differed to any significant degree had it been completed before reaching the public is irrelevant. It was the 'so-called SANU Memorandum' that defined the institution's public political activity in the years to come. The political positions expressed in the Academy's announcements and in statements made by its Executive Council and its president (who were the only legitimate representatives of the institution, according to its statutes) confirm that the Memorandum was, above all, an institutional document. Hence the argument for the institution's immense influence on public opinion, particularly in the widespread conviction that the crisis in Yugoslav society could be solved only through radical measures— through provoking a political crisis, defining the Serbian national programme, and 'if necessary', outlining alternatives to the Yugoslav state. Similar attitudes, even more radical ones, were publicly expressed by other groups or individuals, but none of them were legitimized by the authority of an institution associated with the greatest names in Serbian science and culture, and an illustrious century-long history.

The Academy as an institution appeared on the pages of *Politika* largely in connection with its scientific activities. The greatest number of reports covered its Assembly, scientific conferences, presentations of new books, exhibition openings, etc. The height of its political activity in 1989 corresponded to the largest volume of press coverage. As mentioned previously, with the Academy's retreat from offering unambiguous verbal support to the Serbian government's political programme, there was a parallel increase in the political activities of individual academicians, among them members of the executive bodies of the Academy. Their presence in the pages of *Politika* in 1990 and 1991 cannot be precisely tabulated, as it is difficult to establish criteria for quantifying such activity. Mention of individual academicians appeared almost daily, in various contexts: the paper regularly printed their essays dealing with current political issues, their speeches in various cities in the country and abroad, their political comments and promotions of different parties, and their reminiscences; it reprinted entire interviews given to television stations or other newspapers; they were mentioned in reports on round table discussions, debates and public forums in which they had participated; *there were reports* on their appearances at book presentations concerning current topics (for their own publications or those of other authors); and they made contributions to '*Politika*'s Open Phone' and to the columns 'Echoes and Reactions', 'Current Themes', and 'One Question—One Answer'.

In previous years, a number of active academicians had constituted the so-called critical intelligentsia that primarily promoted the democratization of society and condemned 'uniform thinking' in Yugoslavia. Their actions—their active role in the process known as 'happenings of the people', the immense contribution to the 'resolution' of the crisis as such, the conscious promulgation of a new type of 'uniform thinking' which proved more destructive than its predecessor—indicate a relativized conception of democracy among this segment of the so-called critical intelligentsia. They perceived nationalism as something characteristic of others, and presented it in its extreme ('malignant') forms such as 'chauvinism' and 'fascism'. It was never identified within their own national political and intellectual elite. On the contrary, they judged as democratic every Serbian territorial, ethnic, political or historical demand. Of course, different criteria applied if identical demands were voiced by other national groups. For example, on the question of Kosovo, only the historical claim was judged democratic; in the case of the Serbs in Croatia, only the ethnic; for Serbs in Bosnia-Hercegovina, the claim was based on real-estate registries; for Dubrovnik, its relatively brief history as a part of Croatia was evoked; for Vojvodina, again, the ethnic principle; while for Zadar, Karlovac and Vukovar, etc., no attempts at justification were even made. In this mixture of principles, what was 'democratic' was not universal—it was defined within the limits of national interest.

President Kanazir resigned in 1994, commenting on feelings of disenchantment within the institution, evidenced in the fact that certain writers and artists were 'making waves' (although it was never specified what these 'waves' entailed). His resignation led to considerations about dividing the institution into an academy of science and an academy of the arts (*P*, 27 May 1994). The daily newspapers reported on this rather important news only incidentally, casting a doubt on the institution's insistence in the previous years that conflicts and divisions did not exist and that it operated under the highest democratic principles. At least one part of the institution did not support its political engagement.

The conditions in Yugoslavia in recent years have been particularly propitious for the conducting of an analysis of the shaping and the manipulation of public opinion. A content analysis of the daily *Politika* sufficiently demonstrates an unconcealed, successfully executed and near perfect experiment. The essence of the mechanism lay in the application of basic advertising and propaganda principles: constant repetition of slogans, as short and as clear as possible, simplified and memorable. 'Attention focusing' was done deliberately, in a single direction and with a single meaning; ideas were made memorable through an aggressive approach, communicating a supreme confidence in the fundamental correctness of the articulated demands. The participation of the intellectual elite signalled objectivity and signified a scientific rather than a political perspective—and as such, it was far more influential than the arguments of political propagandists, even though the content of their statements was essentially the same.

Any public speech which aspires to being serious must reject one-sided interpretations and must attempt to address the complexity of the problem at hand (especially if the problem concerns interethnic relations, the soundness of promoting a single state, and the necessity for war). Limiting arguments to the framework of an established model, and interpreting phenomena to fit such a framework, characterizes classic propaganda mechanisms which compensate for the simplification of their particular 'truths' through their constant repetition and reaffirmation. *Politika*'s coverage of the Academy's political activity can be reduced to this essential formula. Having established their 'axioms', which they then followed as if they were proven facts, Academy members authoritatively submitted proposals, offered solutions and defined goals. That their ideas were read and implemented 'incorrectly', was, they felt, certainly not their responsibility.[13]

Notes

1 This article analyses the political activity of the SANU working bodies: the Assembly, the Presidency, the Executive Board, and the full and associate members. Other institutions founded by the SANU (e.g. institutes) are not included in this analysis.

2 Members of the Committee were the following academicians: Pavle Ivić, Antonije Isaković, Dušan Kanazir, Mihailo Marković, Miloš Macura, Dejan Medaković, Miroslav Pantić, Nikola Pantić, Ljubiša Rakić, Radovan Samardžić and Miomir Vukobratović; the associate members were: Vasilije Krestić, Ivan Maksimović, Kosta Mihajlović, Stojan Čelić and Nikola Čobeljić.

3 'SANU Memorandum', *Novosti 8 (osmica)*, 12 February 1991.

4 D. Kanazir: '... this is an occasion for remembering the fact that the Academy was among the first institutions to recognize the long-standing unequal status of the Serbian people, and the eventual consequences which such a situation can cause' (*P*, 26 May 1989); K. Mihajlović: 'I am proud of being a co-author of the Memorandum. I think that it is a brilliant document which diagnosed the situation; the document represented a huge step in comprehending our social reality and it contributed enormously to critical thinking among the public' (*P*, 27 December 1990); Announcement by the Executive Council of the Presidency of the SANU: '...one of the examples of such activity [by the Academy] was represented by work on the Memorandum which, although it was not completed, still had important consequences for social developments in recent years. It was a unique national programme for the progress of the Serbian people into the future' (*P*, 23 March 1991).

5 Translator's note: the Anti-Fascist People's Liberation Council of Yugoslavia (AVNOJ, *Antifasticko veće narodnog oslobodjenja Jugoslavije*) met in November 1943 to proclaim the state of the Socialist Federal Republic of Yugoslavia (SFRJ, *Socijalisticka Federativna Republika Jugoslavija*) and to decide on its future structure.

6 Editor's note: Edvard Kardelj was the chief ideologist of the Communist Party, especially on the national question, and the author of the 1974 Constitution.

7 M. Macura: 'The birth rate must be limited for the benefit of women, the family, and the local community in Kosovo, and in the interests of relations in Serbia and Yugoslavia. I say this because, unfortunately, the contrast between the high and low birth rates is beginning to make an impact on the political and ethnic levels, not only because of the emigration of Serbs and Montenegrins from Kosovo, but also because the great demographic pressures are beginning to extinguish the Serbian and Montenegrin population [there] ... It must be made known that fertility can be controlled, that it is not a gift of God or Allah about which only they can decide, but that it is rather a biological fact which can be regulated through healthy, medical, and socially acceptable means' (*P*, 27 January 1989).

8 Editor's note: March 1991 was marked by vast anti-regime demonstrations; see Bojana Šušak 'An Alternative to War' and Nebojša Popov 'The University in an Ideological Shell' in this volume.

9 The best example is the SANU announcement from 15 October 1991, when in response to criticism that it had failed to call for the protection of cultural monuments during armed conflict, the SANU stressed that it had demanded their unconditional protection 'both as an institution, and through its individual members'. The response of the leadership of the Academy to an anti-war appeal made by eighteen of its members discloses a similar equivocation: at its 1992 Assembly, Secretary General Medaković spoke about the 'noble intentions' of the signatories, while six months earlier (*P*, 23 November 1991), he explicitly stated that the Academy did not sponsor the appeal.

10 The Academy's position towards the war was uniform regarding the question of whether or not the war was 'necessary'. What was disputed was the assessment of its character—whether it was an ethnic, civil, religious or international war.

V. Krestić: 'Those who deny the Serbian people the right to its land despite all the evidence that the land belongs to them, as indicated by history, are ready for a genocidal destruction of that people. Serbs have become aware of this fact, and will certainly defend their rights, their lives and their goods, which also means their land, in a manner commensurate with the aggression' (*P*, 9 August 1991); M. Marković: 'War began when the Croatian police and paramilitary forces attacked the Serbian people' (*P*, 19 February 1992); D. Kanazir: '... the pro-Ustasha government forced the Serbian people to defend their human rights with weapons' (*P*, 22 February 1992), '... at this dramatic moment, when the survival and the future of Serbian people is in question, when the imposed war in Croatia threatens psychological, cultural and biological genocide ...' (*P*, 25 August 1992); M. Ekmečić: 'I did not realize that the civil war, which I had deemed necessary, would be so profoundly destructive' (*P*, 25 May 1992); D. Ćosić: '... a small world war has begun' (*P*,

21 January 1991); A. Isaković: 'The term civil war is not appropriate. A civil war would involve the same people, for instance, a war between the socialists and the opposition. This is an ethnic conflict which began when Serbs were denied their rights in Croatia' (*P*, 9 May 1991); M. Ekmečić: '... here we have more of a religious than a national conflict' (*P*, 19 July 1991); SANU Letter to the World-Wide Public: 'The pointed conflict between Serbian people living in Croatia and the Croatian government is turning into an ethnic and religious war' (*P*, 16 October 1991); D. Kanazir: 'This year's SANU Assembly is taking place at a time of ethnic, religious, and media war ...'(*P*, 5 June 1992).

11 Letter from the HAZU dispatched to the SANU at the beginning of October 1991: '... the SANU, the pre-eminent institution of science and culture of the Serbian people, has remained silent before the horrors and vandalism which have shocked the entire world, and which the world condemns most severely. You failed to denounce the destruction of monuments of the highest artistic value, and you have not demonstrated a readiness to contribute to establishing peace and to ending such crimes. All this prompts the Presidency of the HAZU to discontinue further co-operation with the SANU' (*P*, 11 October 1991). Somewhat earlier, a group of HAZU academicians resigned from the SANU: in August 1991, N. Škreb and V. Majer; in September 1991, M. Herak, D. Grdenić, V. Stipetić, C. Fisković, and K. Prijatelj (*Godišnjak SANU XCIX za 1992* [SANU Yearbook XCIX for 1992], 1993).

12 At one point the letter does speak in the name of the SANU: 'The SANU does not believe that the Kingdom of Yugoslavia was in all respects a flawless state ...'.

13 D. Ćosić: 'Planned resettlement and population exchanges, while most difficult and most painful, but are still better than a life of hatred and mutual killings' (*P*, 26 July 1991).

The University in an Ideological Shell

NEBOJŠA POPOV

Those who are familiar with the history of Belgrade University will have difficulty understanding certain events, such as those that took place on the night of 28–29 February 1989, when thousands of students, led by their professors, gathered in the centre of Belgrade, in front of the Federal Assembly, to celebrate violence and to demand arrests and weapons. This image presents a stark contrast to the familiar image of the University and of Belgrade.

Opening towards the world

One might search for the answer in the absence of a university tradition in an essentially peasant society without a developed economy, without an authentic urban culture, and under an authoritarian regime. The national romantics' fascination with medieval frescoes, monasteries, and the golden cutlery used at noble courts ('while those in the West tore their meat with their hands') cannot obscure the findings of sober historiography: when it comes to the university in Serbia, 'there were no medieval traditions' (Božić 1988: 3). We must also remember that Serbia was governed by illiterate rulers at times, such as the celebrated Miloš Obrenović who toyed with the idea of killing all literate people–who were, allegedly, prone to sedition and uprisings. Yet it is also a fact that uneducated and illiterate rulers such as Karadjordje and Miloš supported the initiatives of educated people like Dositej Obradović who had attended university in Europe, and allowed the founding of the Great School (1808–1813), and of the Lyceum (1838–1863). The later, more educated rulers, from Mihailo Obrenović to Petar Karadjordjević, permitted the renewal of the Great School (1863–1905) and its transformation into a university (1905).

At the outset of the struggle for national liberation, the early institutions of higher education lacked both professors and students, had no regular programmes and curricula, nor any other conditions for normal growth and development. The bases of Serbian university tradition originated 'outside', at universities abroad—first in Harkov, Vienna, Bratislava, Budapest, Graz, Szeged and Pécs, and later in Paris, Berlin and St. Petersburg. The first 'youth associations'—'Illyrian' at first, but later just Serbian—were also founded there (see Skerlić 1906, Vol. I).

Similar associations were also formed in Belgrade. A group of secondary school students, led by the future liberals Jevrem Grujić and Milovan Janković, founded 'Dušan's troop' in 1847 with the political objective of ousting Aleksandar Karadjordjević, bringing to power Mihailo Obrenović, expelling the Turks, and rebuilding the Great Serbian Empire. The same goals (exacting revenge for the Battle of Kosovo and re-establishing Dušan's empire) remained after the group became the 'Association of Serbian Youth' later that same year. As the wave of the 1848 revolutions approached Serbia, the same youth urged the trans-Danubian Serbs to rebel against Hungarian rule and to 'establish Vojvodina' (*Istorija srpskog naroda* [A History of the Serbian People], 1993, Vol. 2: 58).

After a period of tranquillity following the defeat of the 1848 Revolution, these same ideas again gained importance at the beginning of the 1870s, under the influence of 'Young Italy' and 'Young Germany', and after the Austrian military defeats in Italy. The 'impassioned generation', as Jovan Skerlić called them, reorganized as 'United Serbian Youth', which, in the period from 1866 until 1871, sponsored annual meetings, started newspapers and periodicals, and attempted to mobilize the nation for the struggle for 'liberation and unification'. 'The generation of the 1860s', Skerlić concluded in his analysis of their activities during this five-year period, 'threw itself into work, it burned and roared, until it soon exhausted itself and collapsed, leaving behind many good intentions, but few positive results' (ibid.: 110). With conspicuous melancholy, he added: 'For others, the beginning was always difficult; for the Serbs, the beginning was easy, but it remained merely a beginning' (ibid.: 117).

This assessment applies to all the initial thinkers on liberty, observable in the writings of the first advocates of the 'natural right' to individual liberty like Božidar Grujović and Jovan Sterija Popović. The same ideals were shared by the first heralds of liberalism in Serbia. As early as 1848, in his article 'The Horizon of the State', Jevrem Grujić claimed that happiness and welfare could not be achieved if people were 'arbitrarily oppressed' by the ruler and his administration, and if the church taught the people that the government was a divine institution whose injustices and violence must be tolerated (*Zapisi Jevrema Grujića* [Writings of Jevrem Grujić], 30). This was one of the key themes among contemporary liberals and socialists: the relationship between national and civic freedom, and between external and internal freedom.

At the same time as the struggle for national liberation (first against the Turks, and later against the Austrians), and despite the strong influence of European Romanticism, Central European Pan-Slavism and Russian Slavophilia, what also gained in popularity were the liberal notions of freedom of the individual (Jevrem Grujić, Milovan Janković, Vladimir Jovanović and others) as well as socialism (Dragiša Stanojević, Svetozar Marković and others). All these ideas were in constant opposition, as evidenced by the ongoing discord among the youth movements. The fact that Prince Petar Karadjordjević translated the liberal classic Mill, while a close friend of his father, Vladimir Ljotić (the father of the convinced anti-liberal and anti-Communist Dimitrije) translated the *Communist Manifesto*, further illustrates the extent of this conflict. While it is generally true that the contemporary educated youth was 'burdened with the historical past, the state tradition, and an overwrought nationalism' (ibid.: 135), one should not neglect the presence of clearly individualist ideas, and a strong orientation towards the Enlightenment and education for the people—from the earliest school associations, to the organized struggle for liberty conducted by the United Serbian Youth under the motto 'On the basis of truth, and with the help of science', following a strong positivist current.

According to Skerlić, just as the different ideas clashed and overlapped, so the modes of public action differed, from pointed criticism of the political regime, to an enthusiastic enlistment into the civil service(ibid.: 67).[1] Loyalty to the government was also emphasized, only to be eclipsed by an even sharper criticism. It could even be argued that there existed a long-term desire to limit the rule of the *Knez* (king) and his administration. Students and pupils, along with their professors, were ready to demonstrate against the government and to clash with the police. Demonstrations protesting against the abolition of the constitution in 1894 (Vojvodić 1988: 773–786), the stifling of autonomy in 1902 (ibid.), and the autocratic rule of King Aleksandar Obrenović in March 1903[2], all attest to an ongoing struggle for the University's autonomy (L. Petrović 1988: 787–795).

During the rule of Karadjordje and Miloš there could be no discussion of autonomy, but during the rule of Knez Mihailo the idea gained ground, although without noticeable results. At that time the professors were little more than 'ordinary state employees', and it was only after 1896 that the institutional foundations for autonomy were laid down: first, councils to make decisions about the internal organization were formed, and later, with the University Law of 1905, it was stipulated that the 'professors [would be] free to present their science'; although the Minister of Education confirmed their appointment, professors could not be fired without the approval of the University Council (Božić 1988: 9–16).

Religious tolerance and cultural and political pluralism represent the other necessary conditions for the development of a university. While a dominant system of values is implicit even under these conditions, they do guard against a rigid dominant ideology. Within the framework of legal pluralism, professors and students can express their ideas freely, and advocate them publicly through the freedom of the press and in the parliament. These freedoms disappeared in the period of dictatorship (1929–1934), during the occupation, and later, under the one-party state.

Universality of science and education was not guaranteed by tradition, and even less so by the unstable parliamentary system. It could be said that the history of the University is characterized by the constant struggle for—rather than the precondition of—universal ideas, freedom of thought, university autonomy, free public sphere and openness towards the world. Liberals as well as Communists struggled for the autonomy of the University. Police interventions within the University were supported only by the extreme nationalists (Ljotić's followers, for example[3]) who later became ardent collaborators with the occupation forces despite having boasted of nationalism and patriotism. On the other hand, the Communists—internationalists who were dismissed as being 'nationally unreliable'—fought uncompromisingly for the liberation of the country and against the occupying forces and their allies. Numerous Communists and liberals from Belgrade University (Djordje Tasić, Mihailo Ilić and many others) perished in this struggle.

The national composition of the University reflected its openness to individuals of all nations, except in the period just before the war (1940), when a *numerus clausus* for Jews was introduced (ibid.: 25). After the war, the discrimination was ideological and social, informal rather than formal, privileging the 'workers, peasants and the honest intelligentsia', although it was not as rigid as in the other states under 'existing socialism'. Even the 'purges of bourgeois elements' were not as frequent nor as systematic as in those other states. After the 'break with Stalin', the regime developed a tendency to boast of greater freedoms than in the 'socialist camp', especially in the field of culture, hence literature in translation became more readily available, which in turn permitted a lively contact with the rest of the world.

The University expanded rapidly. It grew from eight faculties in 1945 to twenty-four in 1988. Belgrade University also founded new universities in Novi Sad in 1960, in Niš in 1965, in Priština in 1970 and in Kragujevac in 1976, along with special units in all the large cities. The number of students—11,430 in 1945/46—had increased sixfold by 1974/75 (ibid.: 26–28).

During the period of 'administrative rule' (1945–1954), professors were appointed by the Minister, of Education although there existed a University Assembly that elected the rector, and councils at each of the faculties that elected the deans. From 1954 to 1956 there was a period of 'social rule': the University Council and the faculty councils included both members elected by the University and members appointed by the government; students could also take part in the discussions, but without the right to vote. In the phase of 'self-management', after 1963, the powers of the faculty councils and of the University Council increased, and the organization of work was regulated by independent charters. The councils were still elected by the University 'base' (faculties and institutes), while they themselves elected professors, deans and vice-deans, the rector and the pro-rector (ibid.: 33–35).

The real power, however, remained in the hands of the government, especially with regard to financial and 'personnel' decisions– that is, decisions about the 'cadres'. Regulatory initiatives were important for the leverage of power: there were frequent changes to the by-laws, and restructuring. In addition to the positions already secured, the regime continued to expand its influence at the University, which served as the recruitment camp for the cadres within the University and outside it. One of the most far-reaching 'restructurings' that created real chaos in education and that relativized all the criteria of science and education, was the introduction of 'directed education and upbringing' in 1986.

The power of ideology

Paradoxical as it may seem, in a peasant country with a predominantly illiterate population and an autocratic regime, cultural development was given considerable attention in order to afford

Serbia the recognition of the outside world. Many people–not just
the educated–wanted Serbia to be regarded a modern state. As a
result, disagreements and conflicts in the field of culture were less
intense than those in politics and power. Although violent clashes
sometimes erupted between the advocates of different ideas, those
who took part in them seldom adopted exclusive or militant positions with regard to those holding different views; moreover, these
clashes prompted the founding of magazines and periodicals,
translations and the domestic production of textbooks and texts,
and the creation and development of institutions of culture, from
learned societies to the Academy. The development of the University was at the centre of this process. Although the regime intervened in the sphere of cultural affairs–sometimes even by brute
force–it nonetheless permitted the largely unfettered development of the cultural sphere.

The absence of the ideological paradigm

The aim of introducing an ideological paradigm did not come from
the heads of cultural institutions–much less from top-level intellectuals–but from the margins of culture. The pressure of the 'Russian
factor' was especially strong. Apart from direct pressure exerted by
various Russian envoys (deputies, officers, church dignitaries),
resolute demands were addressed by certain intellectual groups to
their 'Serbian brothers'–for example, by the Russian Slavophiles in
1860–to oppose every influence from the West. Although these
pressures failed to leave any significant mark on the highest institutions of science and culture, the connection to 'mother Russia'
was conspicuous among certain intellectual and political circles.
There are indications that this tie was especially strong among the
seditious and conspiratorial groups of middle-school and university students outside Serbia, such as the Young Bosnia group, one
of whose main ideologues, Vladimir Gaćinović, pledged to his Russian friends: 'We are, if you so wish, your ideological colony'
(Dedijer 1978, Vol. I: 295). Yet research has revealed no absolute
fascination with force and assassinations, even among the conspiratorial groups. Cultural renaissance and the importance of
'piecemeal work' (under the influence of Masaryk) were discussed
far more frequently than assassinations–shocks that would move
the inert and illiterate peasant mass towards revolution, 'liberation
and unification' (ibid.: 227). These groups were less interested in

the development of a real, existing Serbia than the abstract 'fate of all Serbs'; they made contact with conspiratorial groups in Serbia (the 'Black Hand') and Orthodox clerics, presenting themselves as the 'opposition both to the government and the opposition' (Dedijer 1978, Vol. II: 79–83).

Revolutionary ideas and ideologies, however, did not become dominant either in Serbia or in the first Yugoslavia; within the University itself they remained one of the marginal tendencies. Militant nationalism had a similar fate—for example, Ljotić's followers, or members of the Serbian Cultural Club on the eve of the war. Far more than the general public, the University was 'obsessed' with autonomy, the critique of authoritarian rule, and, in the period of the rise of Fascism and Nazism in Europe, with anti-Fascism.

Yugoslav and Balkan co-operation facilitated the development of culture, far more than the development of the economy and of society. Belgrade University promoted the founding of the universities in Ljubljana, Sarajevo and Skopje. At times, Belgrade also hosted meetings of students and professors from the whole of Yugoslavia and the Balkans.

The imposition and advancement of the ideological shell

In the second Yugoslavia, life progressed on two tracks in the whole of society and the state. An image of freedom and democracy was created for the world, while the Communist Party instituted a *de facto* one-party state. The new regime 'purged' the University of 'remnants of the bourgeois elements' and installed the 'new cadres'. In general, 'a single truth' was imposed on the arts, science and culture: 'socialist realism'–'Marxism–Leninism'. The purge was less radical than in the other countries of 'existing socialism', however, especially after the famous 'NO' to Stalin, when, partly for the world and partly for the domestic public, the regime showed a certain degree of tolerance for different ideas. In addition, the need to develop the economy and the state required co-operation with the 'honest intelligentsia'. The corner-stone of the new order was the Communists' monopoly over political organization—every other kind of organized political activity was forbidden and punishable. The ideological monopoly and the monopoly of ownership were less rigid: private property was permitted but marginalized, as was the 'pluralism of ideas'.

The above-mentioned aspiration of the regime to present itself in a favourable light before the world (because of foreign aid and credits) allowed for a certain degree of creativity in art, philosophy and science, and even some forms of public activity, through magazines, periodicals, symposia and professional associations. Of course, all the strategically important positions in scientific and cultural institutions were controlled by the 'new cadres'.

Yugoslavia nevertheless became increasingly open to the world in this respect, which was an essential condition for the development of culture. Many students, young researchers and professors studied abroad; educational exchanges with other countries became more and more frequent. In art, and especially in popular art, there was even greater openness. Especially important for the development of culture was the fact that this openness was not limited to the elites, but included the whole of the educational system. This created favourable conditions for the development of critical thinking, especially in philosophy and sociology, allowing these disciplines to regain their academic prestige after their imposed rejection as 'decadent' bourgeois disciplines. Having confidence in its stability in power, the ruling party even refrained from imposing an ideological monopoly, distancing itself from 'socialist realism', allowing for a 'competition of ideas', and giving opportunity for 'all the flowers to bloom'. Only the occasional bans on certain periodicals, journals or books, as well as on authors (cf. 'the case of Branko Ćopić' or 'the case of Milovan Djilas') warned of the real limits of freedom.

The development of critical thought—primarily in philosophy and sociology—which transcended the framework of the University through a growing number of student publications, journals and books, including those produced by people outside the University, encouraged a more independent development of culture, but also provoked concern and resistance among the ruling elite. The critique of the dominant Marxist ideology, though performed in the name of 'young Marx', provoked a real storm, similar to the one engendered by the Protestants within the ranks of the Catholic Church. The proclamation of the 'young Marx' motto—'the critique of everything existing', which included the Yugoslav reality—was received by the political regime and its ideologues and propagandists as a pointed affront.

New ideas and 'schools of thought' became targets of reprisals, including the use of brute force, only after they had become a part of the emerging movements among the critical intelligentsia. More agile 'counter-reformation', in the form of the renewal of the ruling

Marxist ideology, followed the use of force. While a measure of resistance to the new order did emerge as early as the post-war years, it did not take hold (see Pekić 1987, 1989). Student demonstrations erupted in Belgrade in 1954 and in Zagreb in 1959, but they likewise made little impression, except in the private lives of victims of repression. More conspicuous imprints in culture and politics were left by the student protests in Ljubljana in 1963–1964, the demonstrations against the war in Vietnam in Belgrade, Sarajevo and Zagreb in 1966, and, more decidedly, by the 'June events' of 1968 which involved almost all Yugoslav universities but primarily Belgrade University.

The 'June events' were a part of broader world developments, sometimes characterized with conspicuous pathos as a 'planetary phenomenon' of youth rebellion, an occurrence that involved 'all three worlds' (New York, Paris, Berlin and Tokyo; Warsaw, Prague and Belgrade; and also Cairo). Protests against limits on the freedom of speech, even in the most developed democracies, extended to challenging the dominant ideology of production and consumerism. Criticism of the American war in Vietnam was especially fierce.

The 'June events' began in Belgrade on 2–3 June 1968 with student protests against the falsifying of facts by the regime media, and were further fortified by the brutal use of force against students (see Popov, banned in 1983, published again in 1990).

During the seven-day strike announced by the University Council, as well as during the next several years (until 1974), the University became the focus of cultural and political events. A dialogue developed on the ideas of counter-culture and the 'new left' in frequent public discussions, magazines and periodicals, far more so than in the regular classroom sessions. Freedom of the press was not only demanded, it was actually won: although some student periodicals were officially banned, they in fact circulated freely. The freedom of political activity was also not only demanded but actually won, even if only temporarily and with much sacrifice. Autonomy for the University was not only an articulated demand, but also a fought-for and hard-won reality, even if for a short period of time.

The regime was always sensitive about the University, perhaps because many members of the establishment were once 'rebels' at the University. The regime's repressive tactics ranged from preventive censorship, to downplaying conflicts and clashes, to brutal repression. The inclination towards repression grew as the feeling of security diminished, especially after the first workers' strikes in

1958, evidence of economic stagnation in 1961, and the ever more open conflicts within the nomenclature in 1962; Ranković[4] 'fell' in one of these clashes in 1966, but the political police which he personified remained, although it was not as effective in building a 'monolithic' society as before. Permanently fearful of conspiracies, during the 'June events' the highest levels of political power were overwhelmed by the fear that an 'interim government' was forming and that the breakdown of political order was imminent.[5] Although the police surrounded the 'occupied' faculty buildings and the army was on alert the whole time, the regime nonetheless rushed to form its 'parallel structures' ('headquarters', 'guards', 'patrols') in order to isolate the 'rebels' and to protect the factories (the 'faithful working class'), the institutions (the 'honest intelligentsia'), and all the other 'healthy subjects'. Marshal Tito, who himself was upset by the events[6], made use of his authority to calm down the students and disperse them: he appeared in a television broadcast conceding that the students were 'right', only to mobilize all the powers of the regime to silence permanently the whole movement and everything it brought with it.

The party apparatus was mobilized to eliminate all forms of organized political activity by the students (councils, meetings, and the Student Union itself in 1973). The student newspapers were the next to be silenced—*Student, Susret, Vidici* and *Frontisterion*—along with the critically oriented periodicals *Filozofija* and *Praxis*. Criminal trials followed (of Vladimir Mijanović, Milan Nikolić, Pavluško Imširović, Jelka Kljajić, Danilo Udovički, Lazar Stojanović, etc.), along with numerous non-criminal investigations of individuals such as Miodrag Stojanović, Zoran Djindjić, Lino Veljak, Mario Rubio, Darko Štajn and Vinko Zaler. The finale included proceedings against 'ideological offenders'—university professors at various faculties across the country, many of whom were brought to trial (Mihailo Djurić in Belgrade and Božidar Jakšić in Sarajevo, for example).[7] The campaign for the expulsion of eight professors from the Faculty of Philosophy in Belgrade lasted a full seven years; they were finally expelled by a decision of the Serbian Assembly on 28 January 1975.[8]

The fact that the regime persecuted its opponents with brute force without succeeding in making them commit 'hara-kiri' ('admission of guilt'), and the fact that it failed to force the University to introduce repression within its ranks in the form of 'self-management', testifies to the strength of the cultural sphere itself and the budding tradition of the struggle for the autonomy of the University. It became evident, however, and not only in Yugoslavia (de Gaulle, the world statesman, used all available measures against students), that political regimes were nevertheless more powerful than culture, especially in underdeveloped societies which lacked the most rudimentary forms of democracy. The renewal of authoritarian power, the one-party state and the dominant ideology, was accelerated through the showdown with the student movement. 'Moral–political suitability' became the norm of the dominant ideology.

In the years following 1968, after many of the participants had even forgotten what had happened, the campaign against those guilty of damaging the ideological picture of 'self-management socialism' continued. In addition to the artful regime cadres who advanced rapidly in university careers (Fuad Muhić and others), regime/university 'in-betweens' (Stipe Šuvar, for example), and the veterans of ideological showdowns (Dragan Marković, Savo Kržavac, Vojislav Mićović), the evening press and weekly magazines (Sarajevo's *Oslobodjenje* and *Svijet*, Zagreb's *Vjesnik*, *VUS* and *Start*, Belgrade's *Borba*, *Duga*, *Zum Reporter*, and even *NIN*) also played an important role in the developments (see Ž. Djordjević 1972). They helped define a new 'security culture' trained for 'special warfare' which would become a university entrance requirement, as part of pre-military service training or national defence.

It seemed, at times, that the ideological shell managed to stifle just about every 'inappropriate' idea and critical thought, that the ideology of force replaced the power of ideology, and that it was becoming increasingly difficult for the persecuted to find a 'hole' in which to take refuge. The media, which were generally under the control of the regime (with a few honest exceptions), reinforced this perception.

Closing in from the world

In the almost two-hundred-year history of the University, two different and opposite long-term processes can be observed. In the first and more stable one, ideas and schools of thought became more diverse; the number of professors, students and institutions increased; and the communications network linking the University with other scientific and cultural institutions within Yugoslavia and with relevant institutions throughout the world, grew. At the same time, the autonomy of the University relative to the regime increased. This process was at its most successful during the period of parliamentarism, and even for a time during the one-party state when the dominant ideological paradigm was significantly more 'subtle'. However, after the unsuccessful attempt to break out of the ideological shell during the 1960s and the beginning of the 1970s, the reverse process began to unfold: a national paradigm, which replaced the 'class' ('Marxist') paradigm, grew to dominate all other ideas. The number of institutions, professors and students generally did not diminish, but the system lost its former intellectual dynamism. Communications within Yugoslavia and with the world deteriorated and eventually broke down, especially after UN sanctions were imposed in 1992. At the same time, the regime repealed the last traces of autonomy, leading to rapid isolation from the world.

The deterioration of the elite

Entire groups of intellectuals and politicians disappeared from public life in periodic purges in culture and politics. Dozens of intellectuals were eliminated through conspicuous repression, and hundreds more disappeared from Belgrade and other cities via less visible means. Even greater numbers of politicians were 'cleansed'—a few thousand just during the campaigns against members of the Croatian 'mass movement' and Serbian 'liberals'. The criteria for upward mobility were lowered: proof of 'moral-political suitability' was the only condition for advancement. The entire public scene was brutalized by ever more frequent 'political trials'—against the 'new left', against the 'mass movement', against the 'Informbureau', and against the 'liberals'. These developments not only damaged the University's standing in science and culture, but because it was no longer critical that the political order be ideologically legitimized, the University degenerated into a mere accessory of the regime's propaganda machinery.

Paradoxically, the 'involution' of the University was not as rapid nor as profound during the near-absolute rule of Josip Broz (and the rest of the 'old cadres'), when the regime still cared about its reputation in the world, at least to some extent. After Tito's death in 1980, a certain rebirth of culture was observed, especially in the open dialogue about the increasingly conspicuous crisis of society and state that took place within the renewed Yugoslav Sociological Society and in other institutions. During those years, committees for the protection of human rights emerged spontaneously, new magazines and periodicals were started, symposia were held. But the rump of the old political elite and newcomers in the political and cultural elite lacked the necessary intellectual and political power to accept the real developments, or to tolerate discussions about them, therefore a new series of 'cases' ensued, including bans and political trials. This process removed the last obstacle to the rise of the party *apparatchiks* to the highest positions in the party and the state, to eventual confrontation with the remnants of the 'old cadres' during the so-called anti-bureaucratic revolution (1987–89), and to the internecine showdowns of the emerging *arrivistes*, especially during the period of the 'happenings of the people' (1988–90). While the members of the old elite had maintained a certain measure of respect for the previous one (if for no other reason than for the work that was yet to be done and the reputations which could not be dispensed with so easily), and while their ambitions were more long term (they believed they would rule forever), by contrast, the members of the nascent elite wanted 'everything immediately', behaving ruthlessly not only towards others, but also with regard to their internal relationships and their own reputations.

There was an important difference within the nomenclature itself between the higher and the lower strata—those who had already assumed secure positions and therefore supported slow upward movement, and those who were not yet sure of their places and thus wanted to move upward as quickly and directly as possible. Instead of the usual electoral competition, the latter group used certain 'cases' not only to eliminate 'enemies', but also to vacate positions for themselves or for people loyal to them. They used the same methods within the party structure at the University to accelerate ascent in the party and university hierarchy. Thanks to a campaign against 'moral and political' unsuitability, many of those who were 'suitable' ascended both hierarchy ladders towards the peaks of political and ideological power, regardless of qualifications.

The ascent of one group of 'university–party people' through the ranks of the University Committee of the League of Communists (SK, *Univerzitetski komitet saveza komunista*)[9] illustrates this phenomenon rather well. The central figure of the group was a professor at the Faculty of Natural Sciences and Mathematics and a member of the University Committee of the League of Communists, Mira Marković, unknown in academic circles, who with her 'comrades' rapidly ascended to the peaks of power (first through the League of Communists, then the Socialist Party of Serbia (SPS, *Socijalisticka partija Srbije*), then through the League of Communists—Movement for Yugoslavia (SK-PJ, *Savez komunista-Pokret za Jugoslaviju*-the 'generals' party'), and finally through the Yugoslav Left (JUL, *Jugoslovenska udružena levica*-the alleged 'peace' movement). They fortified their positions by promoting 'pure Marxism' as a required subject at the University and in schools (a campaign which brought, along with power, significant financial revenues from the high circulation of textbooks), ultimately settling in strategic positions where decisions about cadres and money were being made.

Long before the Serbian Academy of Arts and Sciences (and its Memorandum) occupied public attention—as early as 1984—this group launched the struggle for the 'Serbian cause', as Marković boasted some ten years later. This circle, she wrote (and she described herself as being 'in the heart of that circle'), played a 'decisive role in those events' (M. Marković 1994: 161-165).

At a 'given moment', they felt themselves powerful enough to settle accounts with their 'party comrades'. The 'case of *Student'* was used particularly effectively for that purpose. The question involved a student journal on the cover of which, on the occasion of Youth Day 1987, was depicted a strange animal biting the leaf of a certain plant. It was proclaimed that the cover was an expression of disrespect for the 'personality and deeds' of the late President Tito. The 'case' was put on the agenda of the top Belgrade party organization. Its president, Dragiša Pavlović, attempted to avoid 'shortcuts' by examining the matter closely and reacting carefully to the question at hand. The members of the University Party Committee (Radoš Smiljković, professor at the Faculty of Political Science, Jagoš Purić, the dean of the Faculty of Natural Sciences and Mathematics, Nebojša Maljković, assistant professor at the Faculty of Political Science, Snežana Aleksić, and others), on the other hand, condemned his indecisiveness, slowness and reluctance to act (*P*, 3 June 1987: 8-9). In the ensuing confrontation, Pavlović was dismissed from his position, and Smiljković replaced him; other cadres from this group (Danilo Ž. Marković, Miloš Aleksić, Slobodan Unković, Dragomir Drašković and others) accordingly found themselves in high positions in the party, state and university hierarchy.[10] The changes in the highest state positions followed shortly thereafter, with Ivan Stambolić, and others who opposed the 'new political course' defined by Slobodan Milošević, being replaced.

The avant-garde of populism

Professors and students had an important role in the appearance, rise and victory of Serbian populism. An important occasion for this process was the meeting of Slovenian intellectuals and politicians who supported the strike by Albanian miners in Kosovo, which was broadcast live on 27 February 1989. The meeting outraged a considerable number of students, who staged a protest in response. They first gathered at the University Dormitory Complex (*Studentski grad*), where the rector, Slobodan Unković (a professor at the Faculty of Natural Sciences and Mathematics who began as secretary of the University Committee, then rose to the position of rector, speaker of the Serbian Parliament, and ambassador), expressed his support and led the crowd to the centre of Belgrade. 'We will go together', the rector stressed before their departure, 'peacefully and with dignity. We, the students and professors of Belgrade University, hereby accept great responsibility and we all have to live up to the magnitude of our task' (*P*, 1 March 1989: 21). On the night between 27 and 28 February, this procession advanced to the square facing the Federal Assembly building, undisturbed by police, who, by contrast, had brutally intervened in the student demonstrations of 1954 and 1968. However, this time the police cleared the way and diverted the traffic so that they could all join in a traditional dance of *kozaračko kolo* once the procession reached its destination.

This was the beginning of one of the largest rallies the populist movement ever organized, along with the protests at Ušće in 1988 and Gazimestan in 1989. The media estimated the size of the crowd at one million. While this was not the largest rally, it was certainly the longest lasting, going on as it did for nearly twenty-four hours. Organized processions of workers from industrial sectors of Rakovica and Zemun soon joined the students and professors in front of the Assembly. The University Collegium convened even within such a mass of people. As *Borba* reported (3 March 1989: 4), 'Rector Slobodan Unković held a mini-meeting with deans and professors of Belgrade University', in order to maintain 'peace and dignity'. The mass demonstration epitomized the harmony between the 'working class' and the 'honest intelligentsia', and stands in stark contrast with demonstrations that had taken place some twenty years earlier, when all contact between the two groups was violently checked, and when students and professors who chanted 'workers–students' were subsequently brutally punished. This time, such cheering was not only permitted, it was rather encouraged. The demonstrators cheered one another, but above all the 'beloved leader', in the form of the clichéd slogan heard at many rallies 'Slobo slobodo'.[11] Speakers who appeared before the enthusiastic crowd ranged from officials from the Socialist Alliance of Working People (SSRN, Socialistički savez radnog naroda) such as Dragan Tomić and Bogdan Trifunović, to Raif Dizdarević from the Federal Presidency.

The crowd patiently awaited the arrival of the Leader. It increasingly generated negative energy which it aimed at the Slovenes' meeting in Cankarjev Dom, but even more so towards the Albanians in Kosovo, at whom rather militant slogans were directed. The crowd demanded weapons and the arrests of the 'troublemakers', especially Azem Vllasi, the head of the ruling party in Kosovo. The Leader indeed confirmed the righteousness of these demands, and echoing the frenzied crowd, promised that the 'instigators' of the miners' strike would be 'punished and arrested'. His remarks were greeted with the wild cheering of a lynch mob, and he added: 'It will be so, and it cannot be otherwise' (B, 1 March 1989: 1). Once they had received this promise, the mass of people dispersed after the speech, as if it had been relieved of a great burden.

A similar event was staged one year later. On 30 January 1990 students again gathered at the University Dormitory Complex in response to the situation in Kosovo. This time Obrad Pejanović, secretary of the University Party Committee and professor at the Faculty of Political Science, outlined 'what the students would say before the Assembly', towards which they once again headed 'to demand that measures be taken immediately to normalize the situation in Kosovo' (P, 31 January 1990: 17). The path to the Federal Assembly was once again cleared and many 'protesters' were transported by taxis. In the report 'The Night of Rebellion for Peace and Freedom', Politika ekspres devoted much publicity to the event, emphasizing that among the ten thousand students there were many professors and political activists, among them Balša Spadijer, dean of the Faculty of Political Science, and Aleksandar Bakočević, member of the Serbian Presidency (PE, 31 January 1990: 2). Overall, this rally was less spectacular than the previous one, and the participants dispersed shortly after midnight.

Incorporating the University, the professors and the students into the populist movement infused the movement with new energy which could not have been provided by the church or the Academy, as these institutions did not have 'at their disposal' tens of thousands of people ready for 'direct action'. The inclusion of the University helped create a populist wave strong enough to intimidate and silence all those who held a different opinion about the current events.

Protests and reprisals

On the other hand, the University remembered its liberal tradition with protests against the political regime in March 1991 and the summer of 1992. (In March 1991, however, the protesters were mainly high school students; university students did not participate.)[12]

During the night of 9 March, the student demonstrations began in response to a television broadcast of the regime's violent reprisals against the opposition which had held a rally during the day to protest against the regime's monopoly over television ('TV Bastille'). Two people were killed amid the chaos that developed, and tanks were deployed in the streets of Belgrade to restore order. As with previous demonstrations that the regime had deemed 'unsuitable', this time the security forces violently attempted to prevent students from entering the city centre. The students nevertheless managed to reach Terazije, where they staged a five-day-long protest against regime repression, demanding the release of the arrested demonstrators and the resignations of police and television officials. Ultimately, their demands were largely met—a rare outcome in the history of student demonstrations.

A truly exceptional event confirmed the importance of the University shortly thereafter. On 19 March the increasingly powerful national leader, Slobodan Milošević, visited students and professors to hold immediate and direct talks. When the pro-rector, Rajko Vračar, expressed 'great satisfaction' that the president had 'found the time' to visit the University, Milošević replied, 'I did not come to deliver a speech and then depart, but to engage with you in open dialogue'. The dialogue was indeed open at times, for example when student Nebojša Milić requested that Milošević resign because of his silencing of parliamentarism, because of violence against the protesters (the regime had treated them 'like animals', he said), and because 'the Serbian national interest is only one: that Serbia and Yugoslavia be a free and democratic state', the president replied that he was not going to kowtow to the students and the professors, nor bow to their demands. He further declared that 'there can be no compromise when the state upholds the law', citing the example of the Italian regime which did not yield to the

'Red Brigades' in the 'Moro case'.[13] On the other hand, he himself was in favour of broadcasting all parliamentary sessions ('so that nothing that goes on in the Parliament remains secret'). He claimed not to know who ordered the use of force, and that he would not succumb to pressure. He also scorned his interlocutors as privileged members of society compared to the workers, who were left 'cleaning piles of [your] garbage on Terazije'.

In response to the request that he resign, Milošević answered, 'You told me here that there are certain groups, certain individuals, who demand my resignation. But there are other groups and other people who demand that I take measures in accordance with my responsibilities, and I am doing my job.' His 'job' was defined by the Constitution and the law. 'Rest assured,' he emphasized, 'that I will not protect my position by force ... [moreover], from the day I pledged my oath of office, I ceased heading the Party.' In closing, he praised the quality of the conversation: 'Where else can people speak democratically like we do in Serbia? We set an example for others.'

Indeed, Milošević was responsible for introducing television broadcasts of sessions of the highest party bodies, at least as long as he, personally, and the populist movement more generally, were on the rise. Those broadcasts, in reality, served more to elicit strong emotions from the viewers, pitting 'one side' against 'the other', than to provide essential information. They depicted the expansion of populist power, encouraging some and intimidating others. The mere fact that events were unfolding before the eyes of the public was supposed to mean that the population actively participated in these events and that democracy was in process ('an example to others'). Of course, while the masses cheered 'Slobo, slobodo', the regime television broadcast the 'happenings of the people'; when at other rallies the crowds chanted 'Slobo, Sadame',[14] these events were reported only by marginal [independent] media.

The swan-song

The new university protest, the longest in its tradition, followed in June and July of 1992. This time it began not only at the University Dormitory Complex, but also at the University itself, as well as in Novi Sad and Niš (see D. B. Djordjević 1992). The catalyst was the introduction of UN sanctions against Yugoslavia (in response to the brutality of the Yugoslav army against the city and the residents of Sarajevo). The original idea of protesting against the UN sanctions soon gave way to a general opposition to the political regime in Serbia. Students and professors demanded Milošević's resignation and new elections.

Like the 'velvet revolution' of March 1991 (named after the peaceful change of regime in Czechoslovakia), the 'Student Protest of '92' ran parallel to the St. Vitus's Day rally (28 June to 5 July) organized by the coalition of opposition parties (DEPOS, *Demokratski pokret Srbije*). The coalition dispatched a delegation for talks with Milošević (who refused to discuss a resignation, but allowed for the possibility of new elections which would be held by the end of the year).

On this occasion, a platform for action was defined in a Declaration that was accepted by the University Council in Belgrade on 8 June 1992. The document stated that the University perceived the current situation as dramatic 'due to the complete international isolation and extremely volatile internal conditions'. In accordance with its 'responsibilities as the highest scientific, educational and cultural institution in Serbia', and 'in keeping with its liberal and democratic traditions', the University announced its position to the public, before the regime and the opposition, and before domestic and international actors.

The starting point of the Declaration was close to the regime position regarding the 'Serbian question'. Others were responsible for the war ('unilateral and violent secessions'), and they were supported by the European Community (EC), despite the EC's original position of supporting Yugoslav unity. The responsibility of the 'Serbian side' was thus offset by the abstract symmetry of the responsibility of others. At one point, the document did mention the responsibility of 'those Serbian formations in Bosnia-Hercegovina that contributed to the destruction of Sarajevo and other cities, and to the suffering of the civilians of all nations', but it never established a connection between this responsibility and the UN sanctions. Therefore, the sanctions were condemned as 'unjust', 'biased and unlawful' because they targeted 'the entire population', and because they functioned under the principles of 'collective responsibility' and 'collective punishment'.

Just as others were responsible for the war, so was the opposition more responsible than the regime, both for the war and the internal situation. 'The regime was not ready fundamentally and thoroughly to democratize political and social life', the Declaration stated. It exhibited 'arrogance and insufficient readiness for constructive co-operation with the opposition and other social factors'. Decisions were made within closed circles, and the Parliament was marginalized. But the opposition was even more responsible: 'Its nationalist wing not only failed to challenge the legitimacy of the regime, but it also often supported its chauvinistic positions. Their calls for war against other nations and national minorities damaged the international reputation of our country; in certain extreme cases, their inflammatory rhetoric bordered on fascism'. Also responsible was the segment of the opposition which used 'putschist' methods in the struggle for power, bringing disgrace to the people and the country before the international community.

The most measured words in the document concerned a subject on which the University should have been most direct: the definition of its relationship with science and culture. Instead of presenting a clearly defined position, the authors delegated the responsibility among the various parts of the intelligentsia: one part was responsible by hesitating to enter the public sphere, staying on the margins and adopting 'indifferent, neutral and apolitical positions'; another segment was condemned for 'contributing, through their public appearance, to the creation of an exalted nationalist atmosphere which facilitated the insufficiently critical individual and collective judgement in political life'; a third segment ('some "independent" intellectuals'), were guilty because 'under the veil of objectivity and impartiality ... [they] pronounced harsh judgements and insulted the Serbian people, contributing to an extremely negative picture of Serbia and the Serbian people in the world'; others still were responsible for expressing an 'excessive infatuation with the past', which 'directly or indirectly supported the romantic–nationalist programmes and political forces'. There was no mention of the causes of the current situation, nor the University's role in creating the ideological shell which surrounded it, and certainly not its acquiescence in serving the ruling ideology and its propaganda.

If one fails to analyse the causes of a given problem thoroughly, one cannot expect to find an appropriate 'therapy'. In this case, the University assigned responsibility to others in an alleged attempt to 'prevent a possible catastrophe'. Its proposed solution was to form a grand coalition government of Serbia and of the Federal Republic of Yugoslavia (FR Yugoslavia), and to hold 'local, republican and federal elections for all the institutions of the system'. The new government and the renewed institutions would end the war and facilitate peace talks.

The University, the document emphasized, 'did not pretend to be a political arbiter; being an autonomous, non-partisan institution, it simply wished to contribute to a peaceful and democratic resolution of the dramatic crisis in which the citizens of Serbia and the Serbian people found themselves'. By relinquishing the status of a particular actor, for which it should have been struggling before all else, the University simply appealed 'to the regime, all political parties, groups and individuals who participate in the political life of Serbia to refrain from actions that can objectively provoke an escalation of conflict and civil war', as this would 'equal a national catastrophe'. As if nothing catastrophic was already under way, the University advocated *improving the quality of continuity*, and the 'further development of freedom and democracy, science and culture, the strengthening of national and intra-national concord, and humanism itself'.

The purpose of this document, it seems, was not to outline a course of action in response to the given circumstances, but to 'save face' before History. 'The public and History', the Declaration concluded, 'will ultimately judge everyone's conduct during these turbulent times.'

During the 'Student Protest of '92', students themselves took the lead, while the professors remained in the background. The student action began on 4 June, before the Declaration discussed above was issued, with protests against the regime in front of the Faculty of Electrical Engineering. It continued for forty days at several other faculties and in the streets and squares of Belgrade. Representatives of many different ideological positions and parties were given the opportunity to speak at the student rallies, including those who advocated nationalistic, chauvinistic and war 'options'. One moment the audience applauded one speaker's position, the next moment, the next one. There was a conspicuous distancing from politics, although explicitly political demands were also emphasized.

Hailed as an unprecedented outpouring of 'positive energy', or at least as an 'oasis of positive energy' (Popadić 1992: 15-16), the 'Student Protest of '92' ended with the symbolic burial of the 'Freedom of the University' in front of the Serbian Parliament (see Djurdjević–Lukić 1992, and Komlenović 1993), which, in the meantime, rejected a new proposal for a University Law that was drafted by university and political officials, and instead passed a law which erased the last remnants of autonomy.

The New University Law was passed despite a petition against it signed by 28,000 students and professors. It augmented state ownership of the University, strengthened the participation of government representatives in university bodies, and diminished the role of the University in the election of the rector and the deans. Within the circles close to the University, this Law was interpreted as retaliation for the protests. According to a professor at the Faculty of Philosophy, Zagorka Golubović, a member of the university senate, the alleged de-politicization of the University masked the abolition of its autonomy (Golubović 1993: 15–18). Despite pressures from the outside, the highest university organs proposed candidates for the existing rector's Collegium (with Rajko Vračar as rector and Dragan Djilas as student pro-rector), a recommendation which was supported by twenty-eight of the thirty-one university units. However, the 'representatives of society' rejected this proposal and installed the 'suitable cadres'.

As the students 'dispersed', and the professors, blackmailed with their salaries, agreed to the implementation of the new law, subsequent university initiatives were averted 'quickly and easily', in keeping with the motto of the increasingly powerful university and political *arrivistes*. Although on 22 January 1993 the members of the University Senate again protested against the violations of democratic procedures, to all intents and purposes the regime had succeeded in transforming the autonomous University into an institution in the 'service of the state and the ruling party' (ibid.).

To make the irony greater, the one-time critic of the repression against science and the University, and member of the Academy, Mihailo Marković, holds a particularly distinguished place in the crushing of the University's autonomy. As vice-president of the ruling party (SPS), he found himself in the position of president of the University Council precisely at the time when—as the dedicated fighter for the autonomy of the University and the former 'commiserator' Zagorka Golubović noted—the government became the 'main actor in decision making', and the Council became a 'pseudo-university organ', a 'veil which masks its pseudo-democratic essence' (Golubović 1993: 6).

In conclusion, we can observe a curious and long-term ironic reversal in history. In the beginning of the process of formation of the modern Serbian nation—in the midst of insurrections, uprisings and wars, and often with merciless rulers—the University assumed an ever more significant place within the state, while after almost two hundred years, during the 'crisis of the nation', the University became a mere instrument of anti-democratic government.

The *criteria* used in this work to evaluate the development and involution of the University are not only universal standards, they are also the works and the public actions of people like Dositej Obradović when the University's foundations were first laid, Jovan

Skerlić during its rise, or Zagorka Golubović in its later years. When these criteria become fully understood, it may be possible objectively to evaluate the real advance and decline of the University, and estimate the possibility for a renewal of culture where force and violence will no longer be publicly celebrated.

Notes

1 Bakhunin (1979: 49) made the same observation; he was also a favourite of the Serbian students in Switzerland.

2 *Istorija srpskog naroda*, Vol. VII: 132–133. See also Dragiša Vasić (1990).

3 Translator's note: Dimitrije Ljotić, leader of the Fascist Party in the 1930s.

4 Translator's note: Aleksandar Ranković was vice-president of Yugoslavia and heir apparent to Tito until his fall in 1966. Ranković embodied the centralist and pro-Serbian course of Yugoslav Communism.

5 The highest police officials, Radovan Stijačić and Slavko Zešević, agreed with Military Police Chief Ivan Mišković's estimation that 'students [were] taking power in Belgrade' and that military intervention was necessary (Vuković 1989: 191).

6 One of his closest collaborators remarked that Tito was extraordinarily angry, especially because of the 'meekness' of the government's response: 'We should have had a "stronger hand", sent those people somewhere—we know where—so that they no longer drift', adding, 'I will be the first to demand most severe sanctions' (Vukmanović-Tempo 1985, Vol. II: 301–302).

7 For more details about the retaliation against the June 1968 offenders, see Nebojša Popov, 1990.

8 Draža Marković, who was president of the Serbian Assembly at the time, considered this decision 'self-defence' in the context of 'special psychological warfare against our country' (see D. Marković, vol. II: 90).

9 Because of the University's strategic importance, the University Committee [or the University Party Committee, trans.] always differed from other Party Committees in having direct links with the top of the party, especially in critical moments such as in 1968. Its connection with the Central Committee of the League of Communists of Serbia (CKSK Srbija, *Centralni komitet saveza komunista Srbije*) strengthened when Slobodan Milošević became the CKSK president while his wife Mira Marković remained a member of the UK. The president of the Belgrade Party Committee, Dragiša Pavlović, himself one of Ivan Stambolić's key people (as was Milošević), noted once that the University Committee's routine side-stepping of the municipal Party Committee interfered with the regular functioning of the party (see D. Pavlović 1988: 48–49).

10 Marković herself boasted in one of the interviews that she, as an official of the university and municipal party committees, was very influential in personnel politics: 'I promoted certain cadre solutions very energetically and very successfully' (see M. Marković 1993: 179)

11 Translator's note: *Slobo* is the vocative form of the diminutive for Slobodan (Milošević), and *slobodo* is the vocative form of *sloboda*– 'freedom'.

12 These events can be reconstructed more reliably than the previous protests thanks to the liberalization of the media. The daily *Borba* earned its reputation as the 'newspaper of truth', precisely during the March events, for its professional reporting. The weekly *Vreme*, and even the electronic media like NTV and Studio B, also demonstrated their professionalism. The events represented a true challenge for investigative journalism. For a more detailed report, see, for example, 'Only War Would Be Worse' (Roksanda Ninčić, Miloš Vasić, Aleksandar Ćirić, Dragoljub Žarković), *Vreme*, No. 20, Belgrade, 11 March 1991.

13 Translator's note: Aldo Moro, president of the Italian Christian Democrats, was kidnapped and killed by the Red Brigades in the late 1970s in Italy, symbolizing a phase of anarchy and left-wing violence in that state.

14 Translator's note: *Slobo* is the vocative form of the diminutive for Slobodan (Milošević), and *Sadame* is the vocative form of Saddam (Hussein).

The Birth of Nationalism from the Spirit of Democracy

The Association of Writers of Serbia and the War

DRINKA GOJKOVIĆ

Follow your fine phrases to the point where they become incarnate...

Georg Büchner, *Danton's Death*

In the short period of only ten years in which the Association of Writers of Serbia (AWS) participated in the political life of Serbia and Yugoslavia, it managed to run the gamut between two completely opposite poles of political involvement. It appeared on the political scene at the beginning of the 1980s, offering resistance to the ideology of the old government. The end of the 1980s found it helping the new government to put into place a new ideology. This was a complete surprise: the energy of democratic changes was replaced by an eruption of nationalism.

First period of politicization: the defence of poetry

The AWS was, for many years, a supporter of the regime under whose patronage it was created. Its veering from 'the path' periodically, *intra muros,* did not cause any great public upheavals; people made amends individually, in the manner not overly dramatic and rather customary at the time–they were removed from their positions or temporarily ostracized. Institutionally, the AWS backed the government whenever, and for however long, it was expected to do so (Radovan Popović 1991). The crossing of swords occurred in 1981, less than one year after the death of Josip Broz Tito, the president-for-life of Yugoslavia. After the backlisting of a collection of poems published under the title *Vunena vremena* (Woolly Times), by Gojko Djogo, in which the court saw glaring disparagement of Tito's character, the AWS, at protest literary evenings, publicly opposed the judiciary's interference in poetry and criticized the regime for stifling artistic freedom.[1]

The protest evenings were the AWS's first great involvement in opposition activities. With the exception of the ten-day strike by the students of two faculties and two art schools in response to the political trial of student Vladimir Mijanović in October 1970, before 1981 no institution as a whole had ever offered resistance to the arrest of any of its members (*Dokumenti jun-lipanj 1968,* 1971: 349, 515–518; N. Popov 1983: 194–199), nor had protests against political dogma gone beyond the framework of private disagreement. The AWS's 1981 gesture set a precedent. 'Francuska 7' (the Association's premises in Francuska Street in downtown Belgrade), where the protest took place, became a synonym for the free expression of critical views.

The two and a half months of rebellion earned the AWS a reputation for dissidence among the broader Yugoslav public. In subsequent years as well, Serbian writers used public protest insistently to draw attention to cases of repression, and took threatened writers all over Yugoslavia under their protection–from Adem Demaqi in Kosovo, Vladimir Šeks in Croatia and Vojislav Šešelj in Bosnia,[2] to numerous others in Belgrade, Dubrovnik, Priština and Novi Sad.[3]

During that first period of politicization, the AWS formed and expressed its political views only as a reaction to illegitimate and autocratic gestures by the existing government. It did not, however, get involved in the more serious development of democratic ideas—a failure that at the time was not greatly noticed. The AWS started to demand freedom of speech because of the trial against Djogo. It questioned the legitimacy of the court's decision and refuted the right of the court to judge art, pointing out that poetic language never alluded to immediate reality in a straightforward way. Yet in defending single-mindedly the freedom of art by separating art from reality, the AWS avoided questioning the controversial reality itself.

Hence, in its most radical undertaking, the AWS stopped halfway: it was proud of its role as iconoclast, but left the icon—the Yugoslav social–political system and its leader—untouched. After much thunder, the 'Djogo case' ended, strictly speaking, with tactical moves on both sides: in order to save the author from jail, the AWS argued the autonomy of art. Following almost two years of tension, the government sent the poet to jail, only to release him well before his sentence had been completed.[4] The state's repression could not be regarded as drastic, nor was the writers' rebellion revolutionary. Totalitarianism in Yugoslavia had been, and continued to be mild, and the writers' reaction to it was equally mild. It was not until the very end of the 1980s that the regime became not so much the subject of genuine controversy, but the target of arbitrary—and thus all the more poisonous—verbal attacks by the AWS's leading members.

Nevertheless, the alternative political scene in Belgrade, with the AWS as its prominent mouthpiece, remained an enduring critic of the regime and a promoter of free thinking. Within this framework, however, its criticism of the leading ideology lacked any analysis of that ideology. The democratic mood condensed, and exhausted itself, in resistance to the government's methods. And when the time came to consolidate the democratic trend into a programme of tangible changes, it turned out that the true idea of democratization, itself democratic at its core, did not exist. Instead, another ideology was upheld, but this time it had a national character.

Digression: the emergence of a crisis, and possibilities for its resolution

In the mid-1980s the nationalism that had been ignited and that was aggressively present everywhere, used for its purposes political, economic and cultural problems. Yugoslav society was crying out for change. During those years almost every issue of *Književne novine* featured articles on the Yugoslav crisis. These articles showed that Serbian and Yugoslav sociologists and philosophers—Branko Horvat, Zoran Djindjić, Silva Mežnarić, Nebojša Popov, Žarko Puhovski and others—had not only noted the existing danger, but were also pointing out the remedy. At the beginning of 1987, Belgrade sociologist Nebojša Popov and Zagreb philosopher Žarko Puhovski wrote more directly about the question of nationalism.

Popov linked resistance to nationalism with the possibility of 'living freely': 'The extent to which this or that nation is truly part of modern civilization is best seen by the level to which democratic aspirations have been developed within them, and particularly whether they have allowed room for opposition to their own national state ... The real risk would be to get "involved" in the "national question" which, for all practical purposes, means opposing everything partial and aggressive and helping articulate universal values and democracy' (1987: 11).

Puhovski (1987: 1, 7) warned that it was too optimistic to say that the system *brought* Yugoslavia into the crisis: 'I feel that it will only get worse ...'—because the government was in the hands of a small circle of politicians who protected their positions not by means of the traditional repressive methods of so-called 'existing socialism', but by—'a priori, preliminarily'—thwarting the 'constitution of the Subject'. The Student Protest in 1968 prepared the way for a 'mass-subject, in the literal sense of the word mass', which during 1971 to 1972 headed 'outside the previous track' in Croatia, Serbia and Slovenia, although: 'no one wanted to notice that the medium of this Subject was strictly national, nor that discussion after that in Yugoslavia on the public level was actually a discussion between 'us' and 'them', 'one federal unit as opposed to another'. Yugoslavia would only escape this 'pressure cooker' if 'rational discussions were allowed regarding the foundations of the political system and fundamental economic problems, and if the trend of constant interventions from above in the political and economic system was interrupted ...'.

Rational discussions, however, were quickly overpowered by the language of irrationality and strong emotion. In spite of expectations, the AWS was one of the first to adopt this language.

Commitment in a new key: from freedom of speech to the freedom of the nation

In May and June 1987, the first evenings devoted to the crisis brewing in Kosovo were held by 'Francuska 7'.[5]

In previous decades the province of Kosovo had been problematic enough, but as of 1981 it became politically the most troubled region in Yugoslavia. The hot-and-cold policy towards Kosovo, with its equal doses of support for autonomy and of repression; the often violently rebellious Kosovo Albanians; and the drawn-out departure of the Serbian—Montenegrin population from Kosovo exacerbated the crisis to such an extent that it seemed less and less possible to 'untie' the knot.[6] The Albanians' dissatisfaction with their minority status and their call for an independent republic clashed with the widespread Serbian belief that the 1974 Constitution[7] had already had the effect of emptying Kosovo of the Serbs. During 1986 the Kosovo Serbs complained more and more loudly that Albanian pressures were forcing them to leave, and through their petitions and appearances before the Yugoslav Assembly they sought protection from republican and federal bodies.

The evenings known as 'On Kosovo–For Kosovo' (see note 5) opened up a new phase of the AWS's politicization. Interest shifted from freedom of speech to the broader and more dramatic field of state politics. This brought fundamental changes to the nature of the writers' involvement in public affairs. In the first half of the 1980s the profession defined its political attitude: the defence of poetry was a defence of the right to free speech. In the late 1980s its political attitude defined the profession: defending Serbian people became the primary task of writers.

This change was, in a certain way, linked to previous activities. Under the old regime (that had shrunk from explaining interethnic tensions and national problems for fear of, among other things, awakening nationalism) discussions on ethnic matters were at best suppressed, and at worst prohibited. Speaking out in 1987 about the position of the Kosovo Serbs therefore meant opening the door to a previously forbidden topic, entering the new realm of free speech. This gave the gesture the appearance of an exemplary democratic act, in keeping with everything the AWS had undertaken since the beginning of the 1980s.

The AWS, however, had taken up the topic of the Kosovo Serbs and Montenegrins when it was no longer proscribed in Serbia. If discussing the problem of the Kosovo Serbs' position (as well as the position of the Serbs living in other Yugoslav republics) was still prohibited in the autumn of 1986,[8] the ban was dropped in the spring of 1987 after Slobodan Milošević—at that time still president of the League of Communists of Serbia—had made appropriate promises to the Serbian-Montenegrin population at a meeting in Kosovo Polje.[9] Milošević was in Kosovo on 27 April. On 1 May, the front page of *Književne novine* featured a poem by Radoslav Zlatanović, 'Hymn in the Wasteland':

> But a handsome young speaker came forth.
> The evening sun set his bristling hair ablaze.
> I will speak with my people even in the wasteland, he said,
> In school-yards, and in the fields...[10]

There was no irony here. The voice of R. Zlatanović was apparently the voice of the AWS. Although the AWS never officially supported Milošević, its ethnic stance fitted that of the president hand in glove.

The protest evenings in May 1987 introduced the 'Kosovo theme' linking all the AWS's actions in the following years: the discussion 'The Serbs and Albanians in Yugoslavia Today';[11] the protest 'on the occasion of the dramatic situation in Kosovo and the meeting in Cankar Centre';[12] and the protest over the arrest of those participating in the celebration of the six-hundredth anniversary of the Battle of Kosovo in Dalmatian Kosovo in Croatia.[13] At a meeting of the AWS in March 1988, the Kosovo crisis served as the basis for a discussion of the political organization of Serbia and Yugoslavia, resulting in the AWS's Contribution to the Public Discussion about the Constitution.[14] The Kosovo crisis ushered in the themes of 'Serbophobia', 'Serbs outside Serbia', 'Serbian cultural space', and 'The white plague (negative population growth among the Serbs)', themes to be discussed during 1989 at the newly formed 'Cultural Forum'.[15]

Regardless of the current events in which the Kosovo-theme became involved, its bottom line was the Serbian national question. No other aspects of this problem were noted, nor were issues that did not concern the Serbian national question. The Kosovo theme became a kind of obsessive metaphor; this obsessiveness thwarted any possibility of criticizing the Yugoslav political system productively.

The Serbian Question: a question of democracy

Of the more than one hundred presentations at the discussion 'On Kosovo–For Kosovo', *Književne novine* published three, including the speech by the novelist Dobrica Ćosić (*'Koliko smo sami krivi'* [How much are we ourselves to blame?], 1987a), which was given a central place in that issue. Ćosić was not merely a writer with a distinguished public reputation, he was also a confirmed dissident who had split with the party in the 1960s precisely because of his views on the unfair treatment of Serbia within the Yugoslav federation.

This time Ćosić advanced three views: that Kosovo was a 'vital question for the Serbian people'; that Kosovo was a 'question of Yugoslavia's fate'; and that the 1974 Constitution, which gave Kosovo autonomy, had to be changed if Serbia and Yugoslavia were to be saved.

According to Ćosić, Kosovo was crucial for Serbia because it epitomized the problem Serbs faced throughout Yugoslavia:

'Everything that has happened in recent decades with the Serbian people in Kosovo and Metohija ... is taking place in a milder and different form throughout the Serbian diaspora.' The Serbian people, Ćosić repeated several times, 'is today in the most difficult position in all of Yugoslavia'.

In Ćosić's view, the Kosovo crisis revealed the 'collapse of Yugoslav ideology and its origin' and indicated that Yugoslavia, such as it was, could not survive. Yugoslavia declared itself socialist and democratic, yet in one of its republics it allowed 'the minority population to terrorize the majority ethnic group and to use persecution to take over their territory'. Yugoslavia's 1974 Constitution allowed the 'total Albanization of the Serbian and Yugoslav national and state dominion' and the 'creation of a second Albanian state on Yugoslav territory'. The survival of Yugoslavia, according to Ćosić, hinged on the capacity of 'those responsible' to put a 'democratic union' in place of the 'active anti-Serbian coalition' that was misappropriating state territory and preventing 'the foundation of a democratic order in Kosovo'.

Ćosić thus saw the untangling of the Kosovo knot as a test of Yugoslav democracy. He reduced the problems plaguing Yugoslav political life to the problem of only one ethnic group, the Serbs. He was convinced that by changing the 1974 Constitution, that is, by reintegrating Kosovo into Serbia, 'the aggression of Kosovo Albanians on Serbian and Yugoslav territory', 'their misuse of autonomy' in order to 'create an ethnically pure Albanian territory' and the 'total Albanization of Serbian and Yugoslav space' would be stopped.[16]

This interpretation went no further than noting the plight of Kosovo Serbs on the one hand, and Albanian violence and federal indifference to the Serbs' anguish on the other. Ćosić overlooked the long-term imbalanced treatment of Kosovo Albanians, the manipulations by the political elites victimizing both sides—Albanian *and* Serbian—and the fact (pointed out by the Serbian writers themselves) that the Kosovo Albanians were the most numerous political prisoners in the country.[17] He left the deviant aspects of the political system (except for the deviant aspects of the Constitution), and the political violations of that system wherever it was not deviant, unexamined. Treating the problem of Kosovo, and of Yugoslavia as a whole, exclusively as the problem of the Serbs, was reminiscent of the old bipolar ideological division in which a distinct line divided the oppressed from the oppressor. In order to prove itself as a multiethnic community, Yugoslavia had, according to Ćosić, to break up the anti-Serb coalition that was playing into the hands of Albanian terrorists in Kosovo.

At the end of his talk, Ćosić specifically emphasized that 'as we fight for the national equality, democratic freedoms and civil rights of the Serbian people in Kosovo and throughout Yugoslavia, we must never in any way jeopardize and harm the national equality, democratic freedoms and civil rights of the Albanian people or of any other people with whom we live.'

Ćosić 's democratic resolve, however, remained rhetorical. Although on other occasions he insisted that 'the Serbian Question is only a question of democracy' ('*Srpsko pitanje–demokratsko pitanje*' [Serbian question–democratic question], 1987b), his obsession with the Serbian national plight drastically reduced the room for democratic action,[18] suggesting that the path to democracy lay in resolving the Serbian problem, not that the Serbian problem could be resolved only by using democratic means.

Ćosić's diagnosis of the political, economic and cultural position of the Serbian people within Yugoslavia was more than dark. It was as if, from his point of view, history did not move and the course of time did not bring change: '... after two uprisings and five wars of liberation [the Serbian people], as at the beginning of the nineteenth century, must fight for their national territory that they liberated three times, and ... for the elementary freedoms and democratic rights that they adopted and established in their Constitution and laws back at the very beginning of this century'.

The threatening cloud that Ćosić perceived hovering over Serbia and the Serbs projected his otherwise favourite theme of the tragic nature of man's history, rather than offering any true political insight and analysis. Used politically, this became an ideological construct which Serbian writers exploited to respond to all aspects of the Yugoslav crisis.

Dialogue turns into monologue

Less than one year after the protest evenings 'On Kosovo-For Kosovo', Serbian writers discussed 'The Serbs and Albanians in Yugoslavia Today' with their Albanian colleagues from Priština.[19] The desire to talk was more obvious on the Serbian side than on the Albanian side. The Albanian writers postponed this meeting for a long time. Finally, at the end of April 1988, a meeting was held in Belgrade's Youth Centre.

At the AWS's Assembly one month earlier, on 27 March 1988, the Serbian writers had demanded the release of all those sentenced to imprisonment for dissent, 'and particularly those in Kosovo, the most numerous in Yugoslavia, including primarily young people and minors'.[20] The demand was made in conjunction with the writers' long-established support of freedom of speech.

In his introductory remarks at the meeting with the Albanian writers in April 1988, Aleksandar Petrov, at that time president of the AWS, said that 'there can be no freedom and peace without Kosovo. Without a free and peaceful Kosovo' (Petrov 1988). Although several sentences later, within the context of the Serbian writers' protests, he mentioned the Kosovo Albanians as the most numerous prisoners in Yugoslavia, he nonetheless presented the problem of freedom only in relation to the Kosovo Serbs. He concluded that life 'in Kosovo and Metohija for individuals and members of some peoples has become worse and more difficult than imprisonment'. The metaphor of imprisonment, jail, bondage was the crux of Petrov's address to his colleagues from Kosovo: 'Maybe it would be easier for us if we were in a courtroom and they were waiting for us with shackles on the other side of the door. But this is not a trial. And what awaits us on the other side of the door is worse for many than prison. For the sentence is being served without a judgement and a term, and everywhere—at work, in the street, in the field, in our own homes.'

Somewhat less emotionally than Petrov, other Serbian participants used a similar approach, presenting the Serbs as the sole victims of the Kosovo conflict. The historian Radovan Samardžić spoke about the long history Serb persecution in Kosovo (1988b: 4); professor of law, Radoslav Stojanović (1988: 3), spoke about the development of an anti-Serb atmosphere; linguist Pavle Ivić (1988: 3) emphasized the fact that Serbia, although impoverished itself, was financially assisting Kosovo, where the 'Afro-Asian birth rate' was nullifying any effects of this assistance.

The Albanian writers spoke in a similar key. Ibrahim Rugova (1988: 3) stressed the 'anti-Albanian strategy' and emphasized that the Albanians, and not the Serbs, were under repression, while Redžep Ćosja (1988: 5) underscored the negative relationship with respect to the Albanian historical tradition, the Serbian–Montenegrin–Macedonian agreement on a joint hard line towards the Albanians, and Kosovo's limited autonomy. The basic characteristics of this 'discussion with no discussion', this dialogue of monologues, were opinions that did not extend beyond the problems of each speaker's own ethnic group. According to the texts published in *Književne novine*, the basic tone of the meeting was calm, but both sides completely side stepped each other's position.

The only one to abandon this oblique and uncommunicative attitude was Albanian writer Agim Mala (1988: 5) who calmly uncovered the gulf between the two sides: 'It is bewildering that neither has the slightest understanding of the other's problems. Each is totally indifferent as to how the other feels and what he is going through. Each has his own burden, pain and tears, and looks at the other as the cause of his misfortune; he sees everything that is bad in the other, and nothing, not a single bad thing in himself.'

When he spoke of the position of the Kosovo Albanians, Mala was also the only one to use concrete arguments regarding the current situation in Kosovo:

> The notion has been created that this ethnic group has solved all its existential problems in Yugoslavia, that it has nothing else on its mind other than how to pressure the Serbs and Montenegrins. ... It is completely forgotten that we are nonetheless talking about Kosovo and its population, which has the smallest per capita national income in the country, ... the lowest socio-economic and cultural development rate, 200,000 people who are illiterate and 150,000 waiting for employment; that this is an ethnic minority whose political criminals have made up half the total number of prisoners throughout the country in recent years. ... The fact is forgotten that we are talking about members of an ethnic minority with a high rate of migration in and out of the country, people who leave the country to work at third- and fourth-class jobs, in order to live like citizens of the lowest class ....

Neither the Serbian nor the Albanian side, however, spent any time on the particulars of Mala's words: instead, historical retrospective and generalized statements took the place of an analysis of the immediate Kosovo reality. Milan Komnenić (1988: 4) was the only one whose tone varied from that of formal propriety. Komnenić's speech was characterized by the very 'maelstrom of the irrational' mentioned by Mala; Komnenić not only eliminated any consideration and control from his address, but also replaced existing harsh facts with naked aggression:

> As far as I am concerned, you can talk from here to eternity, I don't believe a thing you say. You don't believe that story either, because you are intelligent, because you know that it is simply a contest in telling tall tales. You have imposed a tautology of evil as a figure of speech in bloody rhetoric. You know the percentage, but will never admit it. Let me remind you: the modern world knows of no greater atrocities per capita than in Kosovo. Perhaps you really believe that you will become a cultured people through violence. We thought

otherwise. We left a trace of spirit behind us and not of wild animals. ... You consider our essence to be a myth. In your opinion the spiritual support of our tenacity regarding Kosovo is the chimera of priests. ... Your are sick from history-destroying aggression and we from historical melancholy. ... What renaissance can there be at the price of exterminating and driving out the people whose first step into civilization was taken from Kosovo ....

This non-meeting, this dialogue without dialogue nonetheless ended with an agreement to continue, next time in Kosovo. Soon afterwards, however, information was received from the Association of Writers of Kosovo that the continuation of the discussion would be 'postponed indefinitely'.

The apex of the Kosovo triangle

The impetus for a new, large-scale protest in the AWS was linked to Kosovo once again, although this time it happened in Dalmatian Kosovo, near the city of Knin in Croatia. After his speech at the six-hundredth anniversary of the Battle of Kosovo, Jovan Opačić, the founder of the Serbian cultural society 'Zora', was arrested in Šibenik in July 1989. [21]

This arrest was illegal, and at that time was not the only one of its kind directed at Serbs in Croatia. In front of probably the largest public in the history of the protest evenings, the poet Matija Bećković, the new president of the AWS, said that for 'Francuska 7' it both was, and was not, of particular importance that this time it was the Serbs who were involved: 'We have taken a stand defending the freedom of those who suffer because of their name, their religion, language and alphabet, regardless of which ethnic group is involved' (1989c: 3). It was not so crucial here that the AWS's previous battle for freedom of expression was transformed into the more trendy battle for name, religion, language and alphabet, which also meant defending elementary democratic rights. Of greater importance was that the AWS interpreted Opačić's arrest and the Croatian reaction to the celebration as a political attack on Serbia and as a new attempt to destroy the Serbs.

The administration of the AWS issued a Communiqué with reference to events in Dalmatian Kosovo: 'The six-hundredth anniversary of the Battle of Kosovo served to ... spread fear of the Serbs, to frighten and silence the Serbs in Croatia, as part of the long-prepared retaliation against Serbia',[22] and Dobrica Ćosić (1989: 1) pointed to the 'anti-Serb mood from Djevdjelija to Triglav, from Kotor to Subotica, from Zvornik to Velika Kladuša'.

The belief that both Dalmatian Kosovo and Serbian Kosovo symbolized the fate of all Serbs in the Yugoslav federation was also expressed in the letter of the AWS to the president of Yugoslavia at that time, Janez Drnovšek. The judicial experiment to be carried out against Jovan Opačić, a citizen of Knin, in the district court in Šibenik, could indicate that through Jovan Opačić the trial is beginning in our country of the entire Serbian people, their language and alphabet, their right to anniversaries, tradition and history ...'[23]

Opačić's arrest produced enough material radically to question the elementary democratic precepts of the Croatian judiciary within the Yugoslav legal system, and thereby begin a discussion about what was standing in the way of democracy. But the rational question of the 'independence and objectivity of our judiciary and the equality of citizens and peoples before our courts' was raised only by poet Ljubomir Simović (1989: 4).[24] Instead of his more finely reasoned argument, the AWS's protest in August and September was dominated by negative generalizations and drastic analogies with the past.

In accordance with the claim that events in Dalmatian Kosovo were an explicit indication that Croatia was once again establishing a policy similar to that of the pro-Ustasha Independent State of Croatia during the Second World War, the AWS's Communiqué demanded 'a stop to the mistreatment of people carried out recently along the tarmac roads of Dalmatian Kosovo, which is reminiscent of the worst times when people perished for the sole reason that they were Serbs', and warned that: 'hatred cannot ... be justified by fear of those who have always been only victims'.[25]

The comparison with the genocide of the Serbs by the Croatian Ustasha state was made by almost all participants. Dobrica Ćosić wondered whether 'the fate of man and of peoples was, truly, an eternal repetition of the same thing' (1989:1).

Poet Aleksandar Petrov commented that those present at 'Francuska 7' could meet 'in any other place in the city or go to the banks of the Sava River, for the citizens of Belgrade once went there to await the results of the trials against Serbs in Croatia' (1989: 20).

Poet Žarko Komanin announced with passion that 'the Serbian people, even with their throats cut, are ready to love ... that is where they get their strength, and thus with an honourable brow they may enter into the horrendous chronicle of eternity' (1989: 4). Poet Milan Komnenić said that 'in a country in which pastures were turned into graveyards during both wars, and where pits became monstrous dramas, the Serbs ... as the victims, are now portrayed as the culprits. Those who avoided being thrown into their graves, ended up later in jail' (1989: 4).

This most straightforward linking of current events with one of the greatest Serbian tragedies and one of the most traumatic periods of Serbo-Croatian history found its most extreme expression in Matija Bećković's line 'The Serbs in Croatia are the remains of a slaughtered people' (1989c: 3).

The arrest of Jovan Opačić, and his sentencing, were no banal or insignificant political act by the Croatian judiciary. There was every reason to react resolutely to this unlawful act, to defend the individual and collective civil and national rights of the Serbs in Croatia. What was more disputable, however, was linking this case with the Ustasha terror of the Independent State of Croatia. If the AWS members truly believed that there were similarities between the two, they should have abandoned any alarming predictions and should have rationally addressed the specifics. This did not happen. The extreme rhetoric, persistently repeating that the Serbian people were victims, seemed to provoke, rather than prevent, the course of events.

The same 'pits' alluded to by Milan Komnenić in September 1989, had been spoken of in the AWS several months earlier in connection with another Kosovo-related incident, the meeting in Ljubljana's Cankar Centre, where the Slovenian writers gave their strong support to the striking Albanian miners.[26] The Slovenian meeting was by no means held in the spirit of impartiality and linguistic neutrality. Just as the Serbian writers, in speaking about Kosovo, refused to see the Albanian side, so the Slovenian writers refused to see the Serbian side. In response, the AWS suspended relations with the Association of Writers of Slovenia because of the latter's 'organization and participation in the Assembly of Hatred towards the Serbian people and their siding with Serbia's enemies'.[27] In terms full of indignation and protest, the AWS wrote to their Slovenian colleagues: 'Just as a rope is not mentioned in the house of a hanged man, so pits should not be mentioned to the Serbian people. The Serbian people did not go to the pits willingly, nor could they return from them' (1989a: 1). [28]

Using the same reference, Matija Bećković said in his presentation at the AWS's Special Assembly in mid-March: 'The first

Albanians thrown into the pits were volunteers who came out of them safe and sound. In Ljubljana they were declared Jews that had been thrown in pits by the Serbs. They forgot that the pits were the sole ethnically cleansed Serbian settlement and that somewhere underground the kinship between the Jews and Serbs was sealed forever' (1989a: 1).

Language

In addition to the thematic single-mindedness, the language of the AWS during this period was characterized by lexical homogeneity. Almost all official and personal announcements were structured around three main, closely connected motifs: *the Serbian people*; *degradation*; *fate*. Used a priori abstractly and emotionally, these concepts created a monochromic, rigid para-literary projection of reality.

At the evenings convened in response to the Kosovo crisis in 1987, one writer asked: 'How can we live in such a deprived and *degraded* national and civil situation' (author's emphases) and how could we heed for so long 'those who deceived us, subjugated us, verbally denigrated us, *degraded* us, and shamed us before our children and the world' (Ćosić 1987a). Another concluded that 'the Serbian people in Kosovo are deprived, defeated and *degraded*' (Simović 1987: 4). A third stated in an interview that '... they [the Albanian nationalists] do not understand that without Kosovo the Serbian and Montenegrin people would be historically and spiritually robbed, *degraded* and dishonoured ...' (Petar Sarić *KN* No. 731, 1 May 1987: 15). On the occasion of the six-hundredth anniversary of the Battle of Kosovo, M. Bećković wrote that neglecting the Kosovo tradition '*degraded* [the Serbs] in the eyes of their enemies who have set out to deprive us of our birthplace and national self-awareness' (1989b: 1).

The events in Dalmatian Kosovo led to talk of 'insulting the Serbs, underrating and *degrading* their holy places'.[29]

On the occasion of the meeting in the Cankar Centre in Ljubljana, it was heard that the interests of the Serbian people within Tito's Yugoslavia were 'completely trampled on and *degraded*' (V. Drašković 1989); that it would be impossible 'to create democracy and pluralism on the *degradation, humiliation* and negation of the Serbian people'(B. Crnčević 1989); also that 'the decades-long loss of political rationality has led Serbia and the Serbian people into a state of permanent *degradation*',[30] and to 'national *degradation*' and the 'political *passiveness* of the Serbian people'.[31]

The notions of *fate, ordeal,* and *survival* do not have the same value charge, but do have an equal emotional weight. Thus, Kosovo is a 'matter of Yugoslavia's *fate*'; and untangling the Kosovo knot is a '*portentous ordeal* for the Serbian people' (Ćosić 1987a). Once again in connection with the meeting in the Cankar Center in Ljubljana, writers referred to the 'events that concern the *survival* of our community, *the fate of the Serbian people and their culture*' (Bećković 1989a). The special AWS assembly, convened on this occasion, was to consider events 'that are perhaps decisive for the *future of the Serbian people and their culture*'—therefore the Serbian writers 'in the days of *portentous ordeals*' expressed solidarity with all those 'in Kosovo who are suffering *genocidal persecution* and all kinds of violence'.[32]

The notion of *fate* was the main topic at the protest evenings for Jovan Opačić: 'Today, in 1989, politics has attained such power that it has become *human fate* ... Politics, those of yesterday and today, are mistreating and destroying not only the *fate* of Jovan Opačić, but, through him, the *fate of the Serbian people in Croatia*' (Komanin 1989). It was also the main topic of the platform document Serbia and Democracy, Yesterday, Today and Tomorrow: 'In the days when the Serbian people are once again making decisions about their *social and national fate*, the AWS Administration hereby submits to the public its views and proposals for the establishment and development of democratic political rights and freedoms in our country'.[33]

The Croatian government's reaction to the celebration in Dalmatian Kosovo raised the question: 'Since they are bothered by each and every thing related to Serbia, how can we help but think that they are bothered by the *mere existence* of the Serbian people?'.[34]

The use of superlatives expressed the same thinking in extremes. The situation of the Serbs in Kosovo was 'in terms of hopelessness, our *worst* national defeat since 1813', and the Serbian people in Yugoslavia was a 'people that is considered with *the greatest* political suspicion among neighbouring peoples' and 'that is hated *the most*'. Kosovo is the '*last warning*', but 'our *greatest* enemy [is] within us' (Ćosić 1987a). Life in Kosovo for the representatives of different peoples has 'become *worse and harder* than a prison sentence' (Petrov 1988); and 'the modern world has *never* seen as many atrocities per capita as in Kosovo' (Komnenić 1988). In the same vein there are '*countless* examples of collective pathology, of individual and wide-scale madness, when it is a question of relations towards *everything* that is Serbian' (Vukadinović 1989). The meeting in the Cankar Centre in Ljubljana was a '*unique* event in the history of Slovenian–Serbian relations' and a '*fateful defeat* of the truth and morality of modern Slovenian culture'.[35]

This language of hyperbole painted the Yugoslav system in the darkest colours. The standard slogan of nationalists throughout Serbia was that in Yugoslavia, the Serbian people were 'incarcerated'.[36] Opačić's arrest was 'an *absurd* act in an *absurd* country, whose political *demonism has destroyed* reason' (Ćosić 1989). Yugoslavia was a country with '*evil and portentous* politics' (Ćosić 1987a). The Yugoslav regime was routinely called Communist *despotism*. One writer spoke of the '*general anathema, of the occupation of the Serbian intelligentsia*' (Puslojić 1989). The October 1990 International Writers' Summit, dedicated to 'the end of the utopia', was opened with the following words: 'Mankind will not stop dreaming after the collapse of the utopia. But do not let this dream contain norms on universal happiness. We have barely awoken from such a dream, although it was not a dream, but a *living nightmare*' (Perišić 1990: 3). Foreign and domestic guests were also greeted with the words: '... By the end of the utopia we mean the *end of Communist despotism*, and we know that poetry, the weapon of the soul, the empire of freedom, of *universal justice,* is also to be commended for this end ... We are witnessing a great sigh of relief in the world. That which *no one* believed would *ever* happen has already happened. *No one* believed that *anyone* could be saved, and now it already seems that *everyone* can be saved' (Perišić 1990: 3).

The same welcoming address contained this sentence: 'A *worse* order has *never been paid a higher price*, but *neither has a more colossal coup* ever been executed with *fewer victims*.'

Following the style of the last quoted sentence one could say: never has such fatal verbosity been more bitterly contested by the terrible reality to which it helped give birth. Yugoslavia's bloodshed began less than a year later.

National vs. democratic: platform documents

During the second half of the 1980s, the AWS published three platform documents on matters dealing with ethnic groups and democracy. The first, in chronological order, was the Contribution to the Public Discussion on the Constitution, in 1988.[37]

The AWS joined the public discussion on the Federal Constitution initiated by the Serbian government with a text composed by the writers together with the Association of Sociologists and Philosophers of Serbia. The text's introductory remarks spoke of the absence of elementary democracy and the wave of repression in Yugoslavia, and asked for a 'move towards democracy' by discontinuing the ruling party's monopoly on power, by introducing freedom of the press and pluralism in forms of ownership, by confirming self-management as a direct democracy and by providing the citizens with true freedoms.

The Contribution concluded that 'the borders between the federal units established by the leadership of the Yugoslav Communist Party in 1943 and 1944, without the real contribution of the National Anti-Fascist Liberation Council of Yugoslavia, the subsequent Constitutional Assembly, and a relevant plebiscite of the people from the territories under dispute, are not, for the most part, ethnic borders.' To correct this, far-reaching changes were recommended. It was necessary—by 'institutional and other means'—to enable the political, cultural and spiritual integration of large numbers of different peoples located outside their home republic. National and cultural identity and spiritual affiliation to the ethnic matrix must be achieved through—constitutionally guaranteed—'independent political and cultural associations and organizations'.

Only the idea of political parties based on ethnicity was meant to give ample support to 'establishing the full national, spiritual and cultural integrity of each Yugoslav ethnic group individually, independent of the republic and province in which it is located'. However, this idea had in fact very little to do with the search for democracy. How this democratic nationalism—or national democracy—was supposed to function remained unclear. The AWS Assembly accepted this awkward symbiosis almost unanimously; only four writers opposed it.

The remarks made by these opponents were clearly articulated and solidly founded. The poet Borislav Radović (1988: 5) pointed out that ethnic political organizing had brought about heinous repercussions. The examples, he said, 'are too well known, parti-cularly those from the war years 1941–45, and we should also not lose sight of bitter experiences from the mass movement in Croatia in the 1970s and the counter-revolution in Kosovo in 1981'. Poet and novelist Oskar Davičo (1988: 6) saw the request to form ethnic associations as 'drawing out the dagger again, so to speak'. Poet Boško Bogetić (1988: 6) asked 'in our support for a different social organization, how can we accept the possibility of national states, or ethnically pure national communities? ... I think just the opposite, that the mixing and intertwining of ethnic groups is the basis of a healthy, unfettered, free and democratic community'. Djoko Stojčić (1988: 6) expressed the fear that 'trends and processes would head towards the division of ethnic groups into their own partics and opposing each other' and explicitly rejected the idea of republic borders being ethnic borders: 'I wonder what Bosnia would look like then. Who would be able to draw ethnic borders in Bosnia?'.

Such criticism remained on the periphery of the discussion,[38] although it raised a vital question: should a political pluralism which is achieved through national political parties be regarded as nationalism or democracy? The AWS, which in the second half of the 1980s tried relentlessly to prove that involvement in the national question was a shortcut to democracy, did not tackle this question in the other platform documents, either.

Views voiced in the Contribution to the Public Discussion on the Constitution received their radical expression in the document *Uspostavljanje države* (Establishing States)[39] in June 1990. In this document, Serbian writers maintained that the 'battle for freedom, democracy and the return of the Serbian people to the historical scene' had produced initial results which, however, were being slowed down by the 'hesitancy of Serbian official policy'. Writers pressed for multiparty elections, which had already been held in all of Eastern Europe, and the 'decisive and urgent introduction of full political democracy and the unobstructed work of all political parties'. To ensure that 'full political democracy' would see the light of day as soon as possible, the AWS proposed that the Serbian Assembly should '...abandon its attitude advocating the 1974 Constitution and, without beating about the bush, *without public discussion and agreement, without waiting for a new constitution*, immediately suspend the provinces'.

At the end, the text bitterly advises abandoning the 'futile seventy-year advocacy of a single Yugoslav state' and announces that 'the Serbian people do not want to prevent other peoples from creating their own states, but want to, and must, bring back and establish their own state within its realistically possible natural, historical and ethnic borders, with strong protection for all the Serbs, regardless of where they live.'

Two things appear for the first time in Establishing States: criticism of the Serbian government because of the delay in organizing free elections, and the notion of ethnic borders.

Elections were held at the end of 1990. The gallop of democracy came to a halt at ethnic borders.

Summa ideologiae

When the war broke out in Bosnia in the summer of 1992, the AWS received a telegram:

> Dear colleagues, for days a merciless civil war has been raging in Bosnia-Herzegovina that today, by all judgements, has reached the very limit of tolerability. Information regarding the real nature, causes and effects of this war is having a hard time reaching the ears of your republic's citizens, moreover most of the information belongs to the arsenal of false war propaganda. We assure you that we, the writers of Zenica of all faiths and nationalities, and the majority of all the ethnic groups in the Republic of Bosnia-Herzegovina do not want this war. The will of a small number of power-hungry extremists is hiding behind the current bloody events in Bosnia-Herzegovina. We call on you, respected colleagues, to raise your voice and help us spread the truth so that the peace-loving citizens, particularly the children and all other vulnerable segments of the population of our beautiful Bosnia-Herzegovina will be spared from further suffering and destruction. We ask you to address your readers and the citizens of your republic so that they are not taken in by false messages and propaganda tricks, and will help the citizens of Bosnia-Herzegovina in these crucial times. Time will show that your efforts are not in vain. In this spirit we, a group of Zenica writers, thank you and invite you to continued fellowship, just as we have always done before, in all situations. We are sending telegrams with the same contents to our colleagues in the Association of Writers of Croatia and Serbia.
> The Writers of Zenica (stamped: Belgrade, 11 April 1992)[40]

The telegram was not published in Belgrade either in daily or weekly publications, nor in the *Književne novine*, the newspaper of the AWS.[41] The AWS had long since ceased to have anything to say on the topic addressed by the Zenica writers.

After 1990 the Association did not speak out much; a period of low intensity commenced. At the beginning of 1991, however, the AWS Administration and Serbian PEN issued a communiqué with respect to a documentary film on the secret arming of Croatia,[42] commenting on it as a 'special military programme on the preparation of a new genocide against the Serbs'. During the summer the AWS Administration formed a Committee for the Protection and Development of Democracy. However, both were merely ritual gestures. The statement warning of preparations for a new genocide belonged to the worn-out rhetoric: in the standard manner, instead of calm political analysis (increasingly imperative as the situation became more dangerous), the statement offered a prophetic judgement based on an overstrained historical analogy. The Committee for the Protection and Development of Democracy was founded at a time when it was already perfectly clear that nationalism had upstaged calls for democracy, in the AWS and in society in general. In this respect there was nothing left to 'protect' or 'develop'.

* * *

In the increasing number of discussions about the Serbian writers' responsibility for the war, their role is usually either overestimated or underestimated. If the political circumstances and the objectives of the political elites are borne in mind, it is clear that war would have broken out even without them. This, however, is not the crucial issue.

Had it not become part of the consummate price that the ideology of nationalism cost the former Yugoslavia and Serbia itself, the Association of Writers of Serbia's involvement in the second half of the 1980s would have been merely grotesque. Its entire contents consisted of the unremitting idea that the Serbs, without exception and for all time, were only victims. In this context, nationalism, according to its caricatured romantic nineteenth-century model, was stylized into a force for democratic transformation, and the writer into a standard-bearer of the people's interests. This outdated concept drained the remaining strength from the earlier potential of dissidence. Dissidence shrank to its most elementary form—opposition to the regime but the regime was already dead.

Instead of apportioning blame, it is more useful to talk about responsibility for the public word. The anti-modern, anti-intellectual, anti-literary trend in the AWS[43] increased, by means of its victim ideology, the field of irrationality, in which various forms of aggression became psychologically acceptable and politically 'inevitable' and 'justified'. That this did not happen in Serbia alone does not diminish the damage done by its main cultural institutions. They are a salient part of the picture of Yugoslavia's collapse.

Notes

1 In February 1982, the Supreme Court of SR Serbia sentenced Gojko Djogo to one year in prison. In May 1982 the AWS founded the Committee for the Protection of Artistic Freedom (see: Miroslav Josić-Višnjić 1984). Djogo was finally summoned to serve the sentence in March 1983, and the AWS began a series of protest literary evenings with the goal of having the sentence repealed. At the beginning of June 1983, the authorities decided that 'for reasons of health, Djogo's sentence would be temporarily interrupted'. The last protest evening was held on 6 June 1983.

2 Changes in the ideological-political convictions of the individuals mentioned is beyond the scope of the current article.

3 Data on these activities for the period after 1983 can be followed in *Književne novine* (hereinafter *KN*), the literary magazine published by the AWS. Data up to1983 are systematized in M. Josić-Višnjić, 1984.

4 Different treatment was accorded, for example, to the representatives of the Student Protest in 1968, who were sentenced in the early 1970s to between two and four years in jail, and who did not deny their convictions. Lazar Stojanović, Danilo Udovički, Milan Nikolić, Vladimir Mijanović, etc; or Faculty of Law professor Mihajlo Djurić, who spent two years in jail for his commentary on the 1974 Constitution.

5 This massive event known as 'On Kosovo-for Kosovo', in which more than one hundred people participated, was conceived 'as an expression of Serbian writers' support for efforts to resolve the foremost problem in Yugoslavia-the problem of Kosovo' (see: R.K. 'UKS-O Kosovu, za Kosovo' [AWS-'On Kosovo, for Kosovo'], *KN* No. 733, 1 April 1987: 4).

6 The book *Kosovski čvor-drešiti ili seći* [The Kosovo Knot-Untie It or Cut It?], Belgrade 1990 (joint authors: S. Popović, I. Janković, V. Pešić, N. Kandić and S. Slapšak) discusses the failures of the Kosovo policy that roused interethnic tensions rather than calming them.

7 The new Constitution of the Socialist Federal Republic of Yugoslavia, passed in 1974, gave republics rights that made them states within a state, and the provinces (Kosovo and Vojvodina) became republics within a republic.

8 The Memorandum of the Serbian Academy of Arts and Sciences, the unfinished version of which was made public in autumn 1986 practically by illegal means, is considered to be the first platform document of Serbian nationalism in post-Tito times.

9 At the meeting in Kosovo Polje, Slobodan Milošević sided unequivocally with the Serbs and Montenegrins. He responded to their protests

against Albanian violence with the famous sentence, recited in his well-known demagogic-populist style: 'No one dares lay a hand on the people'.

10 *KN,* No. 731, 1 May 1987: 1.

11 The discussion was held between 26 and 27 April 1988, in Belgrade. The most important presentations were published in *KN,* No. 753 dated 1 May 1988. Previously, at the end of 1987, a similar discussion was held with Slovenian colleagues, 'Slovenci i Srbi danas' (The Slovenes and Serbs Today); for the latter, see *KN,* No. 743, 1 December 1987.

12 At the meeting in the Cankar Centre in Ljubljana in February 1989, Slovenian writers, together with Slovenian authorities, gave their support to the strikers in the Kosovo mine of Stari Trg; in Serbia, this was understood as a direct anti-Serb gesture: it was felt that solidarity was being shown with the oppressor and not the victim. Embittered by this Slovenian attitude, the writers in Serbia protested in March 1989.

13 In July 1989 a celebration was held in the Knin Krajina celebrating the six-hundredth anniversary of the Battle of Kosovo. 'The official policy from Croatia considered this celebration to be nationalistic; the celebration was followed by arrests and persecution of the more prominent Serbs' (S. Kovačević and P. Dajić 1994: 24). In late summer and autumn 1989, protest evenings were organized in the AWS at which attendance was greater than at any of the meetings since their initiation.

14 See *KN,* No. 751, 1 April 1988.

15 The AWS, the Serbian PEN and *KN,* the founders planned for discussions to be held in 1989 on 'A Democratic or a One-Party State', 'Black Lists', 'The Concept and Position of the Citizen', 'The Public and Freedom of the Press', and 'Political Crimes and Rehabilitations'. Of those planned, two discussions were held: on 'Serbophobia' and 'The White Plague'.

16 Belgrade sociologist Zoran Djindjić (later the leader of the Democratic Party), at that time still clearly an antinationalist, wrote: 'Nothing would be more mistaken than to believe the official interpretation of that relationship in which the problem of Serbia's Constitution is resolved by returning Kosovo under its state–political wing. ... Then we will be able to declare with considerable certainty that in every future Serbian state Kosovo will be a permanent source of repression. ... On the contrary, Serbia can only be constituted as a political community if its borders are established by the free will of its (actual and potential) inhabitants'; *KN,* No. 756, 18 June 1988: 3.

17 See: 'Apel jugoslovenskoj javnosti' (Appeal to the Yugoslav Public), communicated on 27 March 1988 from the AWS Assembly. It is quoted by A. Petrov, the chairman of the discussion 'The Albanians and Serbs Today' that was held in April 1988, and published in *KN,* No. 753 dated 1 May 1988.

18 The intellectual elite in Slovenia and Croatia also cited national vulnerability as the main objection to 'Communism', and an objection

to Communism, regardless of what it contained, was considered a priori to be a sign of democratic leanings.

19 See note 11.

20 'Apel jugoslovenskoj javnosti', *KN*, No. 753, 1 May 1988: 'Releasing people who were found "guilty" only because of thinking differently, releasing them even if they think wrongly, would create considerably better preconditions for open, lucid, tolerant discussions, the only meaningful alternative at this extremely critical moment.'

21 See note 13.

22 Communiqué from the Administration of the Association of Writers of Serbia with respect to events in Dalmatian Kosovo, archives of AWS, No. 677/I, 18 July 1989.

23 'Osloboditi Opačića' (Release Opačić), letter from the AWS Administration to the Presidency of SFRY/President of the Presidency Janez Drnovšek, dated 31 August 1989, *Jedinstvo*, 2–3 September 1989.

24 'Finally, on the occasion of the charges against Jovan Opačić, I would raise one question which summarizes all questions regarding the objectivity and independence of our judiciary, and the equality of citizens and peoples before our courts: How could anyone be brought before the court for the charges against Jovan Opačić, before that person is judged who said that perhaps Yugoslavia should not have been defended in 1941?'. Simović had in mind a sentence uttered by Croatian politician Stipe Mesić.

25 Communiqué, see note 22.

26 See note 12.

27 In a similar fashion, the Serbian leadership suspended relations with Slovenia somewhat later: organized by the 'Božur' association from Kosovo, a 'meeting of truth' was scheduled for 1 December 1989, at which the Kosovo Serbs and Montenegrins intended to inform the citizens of Slovenia about events in Kosovo. The Slovenian leadership prohibited this meeting and announced that, if needed, it would be prevented by force. At this, the Presidency of the Republic Conference of the Socialist Alliance of the Working People of Serbia issued a proclamation to the citizens of Serbia seeking a severance of economic relations with Slovenia. 'This was followed by a wide-scale boycott of Slovenian goods in Serbia, sanctioned by secret decisions in the Serbian Assembly' (S. Kovačević and P. Dajić 1994: 24).

28 Reply from the Administration of the AWS to Slovenian Writers with respect to the letter from the Society of Writers of Slovenia dated 25 February 1989, and the Assembly in the Cankar Centre of 27 February 1989. Archives of the AWS.

29 Administration Communiqué No. 677/I, Archives of the AWS .

30 P.P. 'Vanredna skupština UKS' (Special Assembly of the AWS), *KN*, No. 772, 15 March 1989: 4.

31 'Srbija i demokratija, juče, danas i sutra' (Serbia and Democracy, Yesterday, Today and Tomorrow), *KN*, No. 776, 15 May 1989.

32 'Zaključci' (Conclusions) *KN*, No. 772, 15 March 1989: 1.

33 'Srbija i demokratija, juče, danas, sutra', *KN*, No.776, 15 May 1989: 1.

34 Administration Communiqué No. 677/I.

35 'Zaključci' (Conclusions), *KN*, No. 772, 15 March 1989: 1.

36 'Uspostavljanje države' (Establishing States), *KN*, Nos. 801–802, 1 and 15 July 1990: 2.

37 The full title reads 'Prilog javnoj raspravi o ustavu, usvojen na skupštini UKS 27. marta 1988' (Contribution to the Public Discussion on the Constitution, Adopted at the AWS Assembly on 27 March 1988). The text was published in *KN*, No. 761, 1 April: 1988.

38 Partly because all four of the opponents belonged to various committees of the Communist Party, which was anything but sympathetic towards the idea of political pluralism.

39 The text was adopted by the AWS Assembly held on 15 June 1990. See *KN*, No. 801–802, 1 and 15 July 1990: 3.

40 The telegram is in the AWS archives and does not bear a number, which means that it was not recorded.

41 A similar fate befell the protest letter that poets Milovan Danojlić and Miodrag Pavlović sent to the Association Assembly on 6 January 1992: 'We call for renewed confirmation of allegiance to the principles of freedom and truth that we once supported at "Francuska 7" ... We would remind you that representing national narrow-mindedness is a destructive temptation for the Serbian people and their culture ... No such higher goals exist that would allow us to repudiate our obligation to critical thinking, to make concessions to a reign deprived of freedom.' The letter was not read at the Assembly since its authenticity was doubted.

42 On 25 January 1991, several television centres broadcast a documentary programme by the Ministry of Defence about Croatia's illegal imports of arms. Prior to that, on 20 January, at an electoral assembly of the Croatian Democratic Community, Stipe Mesić, the vice-president of the Federal Presidency, announced that Croatia had armed its police for the purpose of defending itself, and on 24 January the Yugoslav People's National Army's military police arrested a large number of people suspected of having participated in the arming of paramilitary units. (See S. Kovačević and P. Dajić 1994: 31 and 32.)

43 Many young writers stayed outside this trend. The texts of Albahari, Velikić, Pavković, Pantić and others revealed completely different viewpoints.

Populist Wave Literature

MIRKO ĐORĐEVIĆ

Contemporary literary studies tend to abide by one fundamental principle which applies equally to both literary criticism and literary history as disciplines, to the extent permitted by their methodological possibilities. Contemporary literary studies seek to uncover the 'individuality' or 'uniqueness' of a work, an author, or a national literature (Wellek and Warren 1956: 6–7). In this context, 'uniqueness' refers to the necessary specificity of a literary work and, additionally, it assumes a methodological principle which would accommodate this definition of specificity. Distinguished theoreticians René Wellek and Austin Warren emphasize this uniqueness as the starting point for research into all literary phenomena, but they also consider a number of other criteria in the analysis of specific works, specific periods or other broad categories, one of which we shall define here as a 'wave'.[1]

Of course, it is difficult to ascertain the 'deepest meaning', or the 'essence' of a work of art (or an artistic 'current', or, in this case, 'wave'). The task is far from simple because the universe of human emotions and the unexplored realms of human sensibilities cannot be easily accessed with the tools of exact scientific methods. In short, the problem is far more complex than one might think, and one can never determine with absolute certainty a theoretical model that would be broadly valid. In one explanation that is extremely important for the purposes of this research, the aforementioned theoreticians remark that a work of art is an enigma the meaning of which can be interpreted in numerous ways, yet never fully or completely. The meaning of a work of art 'is not exhausted by, nor even equivalent to, its intention' (ibid.: 31.). This remark is especially important in analyses of phenomena such as the one before us here—the populist wave in a segment of Serbian literary production during the 1980s. In this investigation we shall be concerned with the sphere of literature, but also with all that is found 'around' literature. By this we refer to the enigmatic relationship of literature in the broadest sense and literature in its most narrow designation, but also to the no less complex problem of para-literature, the literary value of which, as traditionally defined, is seriously called into question.

These wider theoretical explications are required for an alternative reading of works such as Danko Popović's well-known novel, *Book About Milutin* (*Knjiga o Milutinu*). In the case of Serbia, this kind of work—and Popović's especially—was used in a way that distinguished it from all others during this period, and guaranteed it not only repeated publication, but extraordinary success. While analysing this work, or the phenomena related to the wave mentioned above, one should keep in mind that 'the graph of a book's success, survival and recrudescence, or a writer's reputation and fame, is, mainly, a social phenomenon' (ibid.: 89). This kind of assessment—seemingly simple and without particular theoretical weight—is actually extremely important, and it should not be contested nor overly relativized. One must also add the simple observation once made by Boris Tomashevskii on the subject of literary works–they are to be understood as strictly 'fixed speech', which simply means that every analysis and every new reading must stay close to the text, to the work (Tomashevskii 1972: 4).

High literature versus popular literature

Traditionally, much of the thinking on the subject of literature argues that literature should liberate us from trauma, because the principal purpose of all art is to generate a catharsis. But within the broad category of 'art' there exist works, even entire 'waves', which induce trauma, because the ideas they present traumatize both on the individual and on the collective level. And that is precisely where one can locate the nexus of elements needed for interpreting the aesthetics and poetics of a populist literature, and for analysing and evaluating its essential characteristics. In this case, we are concerned with the elements characteristic of the 'wave' of Serbian populist prose, and of Serbian literature more generally, during the 1980s.

In general, populist literature is not evaluated as a separate theoretical category, which is perhaps the reason why it has been left out of more serious theoretical thinking. Populist literature has been viewed—perhaps correctly—as being inferior, below a certain level of literary merit or artistic value. French scholars use the term *images d'Épinal* to designate populist art, or any artistic production which does not have an authentic mark of creative imagination, which is intended for the broadest possible audience, and which is literally intended for popular reception. This term does not, however, encompass all forms of literary production that could be considered, to some extent, populist literature. Moreover, populist art is not produced by real, authentic authors, but by 'accidental poets'. Populist literature also appears in many variations; it can occupy many different levels. This very idea was formulated by Laza Kostić at the beginning of this century in one of the best polemical essays in Serbian literature. The essay, which has been neglected for decades, appears in his *Book About Zmaj* (*Knjiga o Zmaju*). Kostić left us some important observations essential for examining populist waves in literature. It is not an exaggeration to claim that Kostić explained their very genesis, their very essence. Kostić also reached two conclusions that deserve particular attention because of their theoretical weight and precision.

> When a people finds a voice, when a whole people becomes carried away as they were during the French revolution, for example, it traps everyone in this zeal. One person might seize his weapons, another might incite others, but each one in his own way indicates that he has been carried away in the euphoria. Another one begins to sing, and he sings about that which has captivated him and the entire people. Yet when the uproar reaches the people who were already enraptured, who were already carried away in their own separate and different ardour, this new voice of the people fails to enthral them. They are immune. For these are the bards from time immemorial. (Kostić 1984: 113)

Having identified very precisely the origin of populist 'bards', Kostić's literary–theoretical 'anatomy lesson' further elaborates a thesis on the very value of populist wave literature which warrants at least one additional citation. Kostić's remarks help us to understand the essence of every populist wave of this sort, even the one under consideration in this analysis. 'For the difference between these two types of raptures,' he continues, 'between the passing euphoria of the people, between this ephemeral voice and the eternal, immemorial inspiration of the poet, or more precisely the aptitude for experiencing such poetic inspiration, is a difference which I have only begun to understand of late and something that

Zmaj Jova has not yet comprehended, nor wishes to. Therein lies the origin of his aesthetic, of his tragic literary quality' (ibid.: 114).

These remarks by Laza Kostić point to several essential theoretical assumptions, some of which are worth enumerating here.

If a literary work of art is indeed rooted in a creative effort in the form of an inspired individual act, it is then intimately tied to the very wonder of creation, and in that sense it cannot be reduced, rationalized or used. It is then an act of a real, authentic creator who differs from the 'accidental' folk poets, bards and other creative artisans precisely in that respect. In other words, as long as the system of meaning in the work is formulated to communicate an authentic universalism, as long as the whole of the meaning of a work addresses the broadest range of humanity and crosses the boundaries of time, thus escaping determination, it will be better, more precious. Of course, the converse is also true: as the system of motifs and meanings of a work converges on a recognizable representation of the objective material world, it can more easily be used for purposes which are not immanent to literature. More precisely, populist literature has always emerged from the currents of 'folk life' while distancing itself from the field of literary abstraction.

No matter which theoretical position we take, or which system of methodological 'keys' we apply, every analysis, including the analysis of specific time periods or 'waves', should seek to avoid two important pitfalls of literary analysis. Generally speaking, it is advisable to avoid every positivistic reduction which does not yield real results, as, for example, the well-known neo-Kantian reduction of works to a system of signs and signification. Each creative endeavour, including works from the realm of populist literature, has its unique idea in the literary sense of that term. While it may seem simpler to interpret a populist work for the reasons mentioned above, one must not lose sight of the fact that such works are necessarily something more than the sum of the elements which can be distilled from them, including the 'excess' consisting of the difficulties 'around' such works. In this sense, even the simplest works like Popović's *Book About Milutin* are subject to this assessment. These works also contain elements which must be considered carefully, taking into account the theoretical implications mentioned above.

It is precisely in connection with that point that one must note another difficulty encountered in the analysis of these types of works. The question was identified by a well-known literary theoretician, Viktor Vinogradov, as a type of 'figure of the author'. This question has seldom been elaborated in literary studies, although it is a problem that inevitably surfaces in every discussion about ideology and literature, for example. The author's 'intention', or the 'figure of the author', represents an ongoing difficulty for literary scholars, as well as for sociologists. The 'intention' of the author is a difficult concept: the classic example is Balzac, who did not hide his royalist intentions, but whose works 'eludcd' these intentions and developed in an entirely different direction. One can also cite instances where authors did not have 'populist' intentions, but whose works nevertheless acquired such dimensions. Followers of a strictly sociological method would have a slightly easier time interpreting these phenomena, for they would be able to use the 'diagram of social success' to identify almost all the elements they might need.

It should also be borne in mind that the 'figure of the author', both in the work and 'around' it, is not only something that the author himself creates, but it is also something influenced by time and the reception of the reading public. In the case of Popović's *Book About Milutin* and works similar to it, one should consider both the work itself and its immanent system of meaning, and also the broadest possible context in which such works are created. One could then claim that Popović's novel is a 'sign' of a particular wave and of a period in more recent Serbian prose, a work which came into existence on the rising tide of populist agitation first felt at the beginning of the 1980s. The book was published one year before the infamous Memorandum, written by a number of Serbian 'intellectuals', that incited a strong political wave and fuelled the advance of nationalism, which, in turn, deeply traumatized the nation's consciousness. In that sense, Popović's work—published in 1985—is a valid 'sample' sufficient for an examination of the essential characteristics and 'markings' of the populist wave in literature under consideration.

Yet one could not claim that the phenomenon under consideration is completely new and that it is without tradition. We have already mentioned past reflections on the phenomenon such as Laza Kostić's, and at this point we shall turn to other valuable and timely reactions. Slobodan Selenić, for example, remarked that contemporary literature was increasingly besieged, 'shaded over by reality', while Nebojša Popov recalled the words of Isidora Sekulić on the mentality of small nations who are 'one minute the heroes, the next, slaves of an ascetic mentality', referring to the representation of the nation in recent literature. Popov also gave an important explanation for what was becoming noticeable in literature.

'In addition to the psychological incompleteness of the hero in works that nevertheless have important artistic innovations and represent real intellectual achievements,' Popov remarked, 'in more recent literature we also find "collective heroes" who sermonize about the victimization of the Serbian people, who incite hatred and yearn for revenge, like Vuk Drašković's novels *Knife* or *Prayer* (*Nož, Molitva*), and who neutralize the catharsis that had been reached earlier, like Dobrica Ćosić's *Divisions* (*Deobe*), or who simply appropriate the literatures that are unprepared to generate catharsis.'[2]

This was the time when literature wanted, once again, to serve as a substitute for philosophy, science, i. e. for culture in general. Moreover, there is a particular intellectual disposition in our society: people believe the Writer.

Of course, in order to be better able to follow the relevant signs of the populist aesthetic that was applied to poetics at that time, let us consider the essential elements of the wider context from which Popović's work emerged.

Limited in scope, Popović's novel, or 'narrative'—the latter designation will help us to avoid some of the difficulties of more precise genre definitions—became the most widely read book of the period. It was literally in the hands of the widest possible reading audience, being read by the most experienced critics and academics, by ordinary people, and by politicians who either attacked or defended it. And even before the literary critics handed down their assessments and informed judgements, the work assumed a function which real literary works seldom have, especially not in times of populist frenzy and political upheaval. This was a sure sign that Popović's 'fixed speech' defined its place from the start with its thinly veiled political agenda. Thus the literary problems that arose became inextricably linked with 'para-literary' ones. Yet whatever the intention, Popović's work carried a certain usefulness which ultimately determined its fate. Within a very short period, the novel was printed in more than twenty editions, it was translated into foreign languages, and a vast amount of criticism on it was produced (more pages have been written about the novel than make up the work itself). In short, it became the representative specimen of Serbian literature at the time. Moreover, it very quickly started to be referred to not by its complete title but by an abbreviation which was universally used—*Milutin*. The name was also used to designate the author, which happens only rarely but is a characteristic populist sign entirely appropriate to the work. Within such a massive and typically populist reception one could discern certain features from the sphere of collective intuition, but others that were strictly and discernibly political and topical. The connotations of just one of the elements from the title–the word 'book'–point to something that goes beyond literature, imply some sort of 'truth of a higher order', and suggest a type of publication which surpasses a literary work in the usual sense of the term. In other words, the work was received as a type of programme, or as the sum of national truths of the highest order–as something that existed outside the individual experience in which the reception of literature and literary works is ordinarily situated. Even without a thorough theoretical investigation, it is clear that Popović's work easily blended into the great wave of Serbian populism that was being transformed into aggressive nationalism during those years. Its applied poetics follow a tradition best exemplified by Dobrica Ćosić's populist poetics and literary mythology.

The *Book About Milutin* revived a tradition within a segment of Serbian prose that in analogous moments in history also offered a privileged place for a type of 'collective hero', the 'voice of the people', the 'embodiment of the people'. Popović's work evokes Ćosić's often reiterated aesthetic-populist motto: 'In each of my works I see the people'. The applied aesthetics of such typically utilitarian provenance–largely derived from the Russians–are well known, and the question does not require theoretical explication. Nevertheless, among a small people, in rural collectives, where one does not encounter a more refined level of consciousness (not to mention the more recent literary culture), such an aesthetic takes hold very naturally. Danilo Kiš, who in the book *Anatomy Lesson* (*Čas anatomije*) continued where Laza Kostić left off, addressed this question most astutely. 'In these kinds of communities,' Kiš wrote, 'a literary work is not an individual production, but a collective one, like the folk song.' Even more importantly for our considerations, Kiš asserted that 'a work born in a certain socio-political climate cannot have an individual stamp, but only a collective and collectivizing, generational one' (Kiš 1978: 58.). Leaning on tradition, most often inspired by epic form, often with political and programmatic intonations, populist literature lacks the approach typical of more contemporary prose. For example, it lacks the smallest trace of what the Russian formalists have called 'making strange' or 'defamiliarization'. Occurrences are not described with a spirit of invention, as if the author was seeing them for the first time; they are not made unusual in order to achieve the effect of seeing something new or experiencing something deeply. On the contrary, in these works everything is derived from the sphere of the visible, or lowered to the level of the easily recognized, which requires that its essential elements be reduced to the level of the commonly known. The newer novels, Ćosić's especially, lack the necessary distance between the literary character and its historical prototype, according to which one measures the degree of inventiveness. The followers of the theory of so-called national realism which is crafted in the spirit of the well-known utilitarian aesthetic, firmly believe that in a novel one can wholly express reality in all its dimensions, forgetting the essential credo of modern aesthetics and poetics which maintains that a novel can be only a model but not a true depiction of reality. That kind of applied aesthetic is easily discernible in the structure of Popović's *Book About Milutin*, which thematically and in other ways follows Ćosić's applied poetics. Furthermore, populist literature lacks inventive metaphors in the sense of the 'omnipresent principle of language'. It remains in the realm of the objective material world, it is 'anti-metaphoric' by definition, and it exhausts itself through attempts to express some sort of 'folk spirit'. *Habent sua fata libelli*—one can say for Popović's *Book About Milutin* that its fate was determined precisely with the application of that kind of poetics and that kind of approach. The 'folk spirit' is a type of doctrine which the populist–utilitarian aesthetic elevates to the level of dogma, although it is not particularly valued in the domain of modern theoretical judgements, nor does it represent a novelty.[3]

In the literature of the populist wave there is a strongly articulated need—and this is the dominant essence of that type of aesthetic—to express not an individual, but a general, most often national, folk truth about people and life. The well-known thinker and literary theoretician Lev Shestov once remarked that books are not written in order to say something, but to conceal something. If we apply this paradox in a typological sense, which the work itself guides us to do, and if we apply it to the poetics of populist literature, we would conclude that Popović's *Book About Milutin* was written not only to say something, but to say it loudly, and with programmatic intonations. Its hero is conceived as a seemingly quiet, sympathetic and spontaneous teller–preacher, for whom it is important that his sermon be heard by everyone, especially those around him. He addresses others—the plural collective. From beginning to end, on all structural levels of the work, the hero seems to stand at a distance from the others, but in reality he is a part of the collective. When he makes critical judgements about everyone and everything, including 'his people'—and in that respect he is particularly privileged by the author—he is only communicating the 'national truth' and never his own in a strictly individual sense. In each segment of the structure, his word is literally the last. Such a position in the structure of the work, along with an accordingly favourable distribution of thematic units confirms his role as the hero–preacher. In that respect, the book is truly Milutin's. Moreover, the truth which the hero offers is not only his, but that of 'the people' as a whole. To be fair, his voice is not the 'thundering' voice of the oracle, but nonetheless it is a voice which must be heard because it is the great 'voice of the people'. In that respect, Popović's book positions itself as a book from 'the head of the whole people'. This is the context in which we must search out an explanation of the complex problem defined by the Russian formalists as the 'figure of the author'. This is also the specific ideological subtext present in the poetics of the work.

There has been a great deal said about the relationship between ideology and literature. Nonetheless, all the new problems that arise with respect to the literature of the populist wave indicate that thinking on the subject has not been fully exhausted. Populist literature operates under the banner of a national, or more precisely, nationalist, ideology. One could not properly examine the phenomenon of Serbian populism in the 1980s without remaining mindful of the 'effect' brought about by the populist wave literature in existence at the time. Furthermore, depending on the 'intention' of the author, that kind of effect was not insignificant. Literary heroes—especially the kind of collective hero who has remained far too long on our literary scene—are endowed with the power to traumatize the consciousness in its individual and collective dimensions. It is conceivable that a collective hero can also have the opposite function, as an agent who assists in releasing the reader from trauma. The difficulty lies in the fact that while catharsis occurs on an individual level, traumatization is possible both in individual and collective dimensions. One of the effects of the trauma is paranoia of the broadest scope imaginable which can progress to nationalistic madness. Populist literature always contains a healthy dose of that type of 'opium'. According to the Russian thinker referred to above, Lev Shestov, there was never any dispute about the fact that in a philosophical sense—as thinkers—Lenin and Trotsky were simply 'cheap, market-bought candles', yet they were nevertheless candles that ignited an inferno that swallowed up a portion of the world and its culture. As remarked by a well-known critic in a recent analysis of Popović's work—a remark that has been repeated often, and almost ritualistically—Milutin inaugurated the 'process of re-examination of the entirety of our historical conduct over the past two centuries'. An assessment formulated in this manner indicates more than an ordinary literary–critical evaluation; it points to the very ideological subtext which we addressed earlier. Literary heroes seldom occupy such important roles, or at least not so explicitly, yet this critic's assessment is generally correct—namely, that this particular book with this particular hero portrayed in this particular manner actually marks the moment that initiated this process. Collective heroes in populist literature do not have the right to a personal, individual fate, and in that respect Popović's *Book About Milutin* has assured its place as a paradigm in the research on literary and para-literary phenomena in the most recent wave of populist Serbian literature.

The influence of these kinds of books and these kinds of literary heroes does not depend in any way whatsoever on the level of their artistic accomplishment. Artistic merit is paradoxically relativized–what is valued is something else altogether.

Literary hero—national programme

An analysis of Popović's book must follow this 'fixed speech' with all its literary and para-literary references and meanings. In the book, one can discern aesthetically indifferent elements relatively easily, just as one can distinguish their transformation into aesthetic value, to the extent that such values exist in the work. According to Wellek and Warren, aesthetically indifferent elements are those elements that can be classified as 'materials', while 'the manner in which they acquire aesthetic efficacy may be called "structure"' (Wellek and Warren: 129). In these kinds of works, the distinction is best illustrated in examples of so-called extra-literary elements, and those are—according to Tomashevskii—'the range of themes which have a real meaning outside the realm of artistic production' (Tomashevskii: 215). It is easy to note that in Popović's work the 'materials' have a privileged place, and that extra literary elements lie immediately beneath the layer which is built—or which is supposed to be built—by the narrator's imagination. It is even easier to notice if one locates the difference between the *fabula* ('story') and *syuzhet* ('plot' or 'narrative structure') without which one cannot encompass the wholeness of a literary work's structure. In the case of Popović's book, it can be accomplished using methods employed by classical philological criticism, with a presentation synopsis of the elements that comprise the structure of the work. This is also the best way to determine the typology of a work.

According to the most commonly used typology of the genre, Popović's *Book About Milutin* can be classified as a type of *skaz*—a work with a relatively simple structure, easily recognizable in its emphasis on authentic, 'living', dynamic language that comes close to colloquial expression. One cannot pretend that this language represents real literary innovation, except in cases when such language is used in certain parts of the structure as functional 'ornament'. The theme of the *skaz* is likewise easily recognizable, easily reduced to dimensions indicated by an entire range of extra-literary meanings. Yurii Tynianov once remarked that in those cases, especially in works of the populist wave, readers themselves communicate relatively easily with the work: they 'play it out', or 'live it out' collectively, because in such works everyone recognizes himself as a participant, as the 'hero'. This also explains the experience of the work—its reception—as something collective. The collective experience is characteristic of works of this genre, and it is particularly prominent in places—at specific moments—where refined taste and an appreciation for literary creations of a higher level are not a consideration. It is not a strict rule, but it is often the case that a *skaz* of this type encounters an echo, or a massive reception, in rural communities where it propitiously overlaps with the preserved tradition of oral communication which resists the spirit of modern civilization, and which becomes reduced to its archaic essence in times of populist surges.

It is hardly necessary to mention political manipulation which is always possible. In that sense, a *skaz* of this type is a common occurrence in the literature of small nations that frequently and easily enclose themselves within their national myths, the myths of the tribe. This type of literature is often fed by this kind of mythology, which it then regenerates in new variations. Needless to say, this type of *skaz* leans on tradition which helps maintain a continuity according to the principle of 'selection by recognition'. The phenomenon in question, which we can note quite easily in Popović's *Book About Milutin,* was easily understood by the ideologues and the critics who designated for themselves the role of ideologues. In small, closed communities, away from the main roads of civilizational and modernizing processes, such roles are most often assumed by writers and critics—ideologues—of precisely these kinds of works. It must be conceded that they played their roles exceedingly well.

In populist wave literature, motifs from the narrowly defined sphere of national myths stand in the forefront. That sort of literature distances itself quickly from the sphere of universal motifs and universal meanings, which are, by contrast, signs of literary novelty and represent an attempt to reach more lasting values. It has been asserted in the past that these works have an easily recognizable 'thesis' that is present to the detriment of literary value. These were considered tendentious works. In Popović's novel one can discern a type of thesis, but tendentiousness is far more present. This assessment applies to the works of this 'wave' in general. It is demonstrated most readily by the loss of artistic spirit in Ćosić's newer novels—this is a topic discussed increasingly frequently, and with very good reason. His novels—especially the ones from the last big cycle—increasingly encompass historical reality. They 'portray' it more and more precisely in a realist sense, and are less and less novelistic models abundant with material at a more complex metaphorical level in the modern sense. The spirit of artistic innovation wanes in proportion to the growing strength of the voice of the national ideologue–narrator. In Ćosić's novels one increasingly detects a 'settling of accounts with history' which lowers the value of the work to the level of a banal tirade and a peripheral place in historiography which cannot substitute for creative ingenuity.

At this point, let us situate Popović's *Book About Milutin* within the literary milieu of the period. During the 1980s, one part of Serbian prose—precisely that part which comprises the populist wave—witnessed an uncreative regeneration of an archaic range of motifs, applied without innovation. One can easily recognize the inability to distinguish between fiction and historiographic 'feuilletonism' or 'essayism' of questionable calibre (which was supposed to replace the 'historisophical' reminiscences present in great literature) among the writers in question. Overwhelmingly present were so-called patriotic motifs, picked from the category of the less-than-creative apotheoses of 'blood and land', 'faith and nation', and especially 'the glorious past'. Of course, this phenomenon is not characteristic of Serbian prose or poetry on the whole, but only of the one segment which did not resist the populist wave. This segment of literature had a considerably lower level of artistic achievement, clearly below the standard of the best of Serbian literary tradition in the modern sense of the term. The motifs in question were most often applied functionally, or more precisely, nationalistically, made banal to such an extent that they became tasteless. Tribally regionalized idioms—'the languages of the village or tribe'—began to be held up as models for poetry. In fact, a significant portion of Matija Bećković's poetry functions according to this principle. Analyses of this phenomenon are only just beginning, and very cautiously at that. Bare political slogans were ideologically semanticized and cultivated as if they had artistic value, but one could nevertheless easily recognize in them the vulgar political principle of 'gathering the flock' of one's own *ethnos*, and purging it of all others. The poetry of Milan Komnenić stated this literally, archaically and uncreatively. The individual's own nation and its history were endowed with a metaphysical, cosmic dimension. Reincarnated classical odes (which traditionally celebrate the Leader—in this case, Slobodan Milošević) could also be found, brutally appended to the body of masterpieces that had truly earned their place in the *Anthology of Serbian Eulogistic Poetry*. It is within this climate that Popović's *skaz* about Milutin distinguished itself. In that sense, it truly represents a paragon of that literary period.

On the whole, as a literary composition, Popović's *skaz* is organized monotonously and monolithically, seemingly without authorial 'intervention'. Such is the first impression of the work as the reader encounters it. The telling—'telling' in the classical epic sense rather than 'narration' in the modern sense—is left to the hero, and largely only to the hero, with other characters having only episodic roles within the structure. Further evidence of the hero's privileged position is found in the placement of the so-called extra-literary elements—they are present in part in ordinary footnotes, but they spill over freely into the whole of the structure of the *skaz*. These footnotes are insubstantial, both technically and in terms of content. There are twelve of them, and they remind one of philological remarks that do not ordinarily belong in literary works, that do not ordinarily constitute an aspect of narrative technique, at least not in such a manner. It is interesting to recognize that such footnotes seem extraneous even as extra-literary elements since they lack a justified and well-conceived artistic function. But everything is subordinated to a certain goal—Milutin is conceived as a hero who must usher in a process of national awakening and instigate a re-examination of the last two centuries of Serbian history as a collective past. Ideologically invested to such a degree, he loses the individual characteristics of a literary hero.

This point is perhaps best demonstrated by the author's 'solutions' with respect to space and time in the work, as well as the other elements that constitute the natural structure of this *skaz*.

Time and space are historically recognizable–possibly too much so. The very year of the publication of the work, in its own way, fits into the scheme of that same recognizable, physical time. The work opens in both times–first, the physical, historical time, and second, the hero's time, the temporal planes literally converge. Stated differently, the time of the story and the time of its telling overlap–in fact, the very 'idea' of the work is conceived and actualized with this goal in mind. The action begins in 1945 but goes back as far as 1914, to the time of the Great War when the 'fatal error' which represents the principal content of the hero's consciousness first occurred. That is the primary 'idea' of the work, and that error is easily 'read' as the historical futility of creating a common state of the South Slavs–Yugoslavia. Of course, this is not the only 'idea' that we are to identify in the work. Yugoslavia occupies a specific and emphasized position in the work. The circles of narration open and close–when this opening stops at the year 1941, the reader is confronted with suggestive prose passages and systems of narration, along with successfully executed details about fatal Serbian 'divisions'. It is decidedly the most successful aspect of Popović's work, although even these well-executed details (successful as prose) do not contribute to a conception in which catharsis may be possible. Everything crumbles as the hero experiences the time of the Second World War as a repetition of the fatal 'mistake'. The action then moves to the post-war period–to the moment when the hero is in prison because of 'unmet obligations'–but the principal characteristic of the time of action in general is perfectly clear: time passes only so that Serbs can repeat the fatal mistake. The hero's personal problems affect him scarcely more acutely than this 'error'. Everything evolves within the essence of the national idea.

The system of narration in Popović's work is not particularly complex. Within the structure one can clearly identify three types of narration that are semanticized to conform to a central idea, or the principal motif which dominates the entire work. The first system of narration is in the first person, and the tone is pronouncedly confessional, with a string of details from the narrator's personal life that are developed neither sufficiently nor originally. Many of these ideas are suggestively developed in the final portions of the book, among them one expressing an anti-war position in line with a worthy tradition of classical Serbian prose. In this passage, Milutin discovers that war is imminent, and because he knows that war always brings evil among people and that everyone falls victim regardless of faith or nation, he is overcome with feelings of human compassion. Some parts of these narrative passages are quite promising, such as the following one which encapsulates one of Milutin's great truths: 'We must take care so that we do not sin against the Turks.' Unfortunately, these motives remain undeveloped and largely unrealized in the work, and they are therefore quickly subordinated to motifs of an entirely different order. In the consciousness of the hero we can discern a truth that applies to us: 'It is easy to kill one prince and one woman', but that truth is quickly subordinated to the general, *assigned* goal which always supersedes the sphere of the hero's strictly individualized consciousness. Similar narrative passages exist, but are likewise overshadowed by others with broader implications.

The second circle of narration engages the unclouded and ever-alert consciousness of the Serbian peasant with the question of the Serb's perpetual task to 'liberate our brothers'. This question is the principal topic in the *Book About Milutin*, and it is presented as problematic from a basic, human, common-sense point of view. At a certain moment, while Milutin listens as 'educated people' discuss the problem—the hero frequently finds himself in the company of intellectuals—he begins to doubt. 'I am silent. I tread carefully, taking care not to lose him and Pavle. I expect that from the other side where one finds our churches, our brothers might greet us with hot lead. And they should. Who asked us to liberate them? If they wanted to be liberated, they would have liberated themselves' (Popović 1986:14). This scepticism, as 'content' of the hero's consciousness, exists elsewhere in the work and reappears at other moments, but is eclipsed by other sentiments exactly opposite in tone. This is perhaps best observed in Milutin's relationship to all that is different from his own experience: 'I have nothing against people from Srem, I know people from Srem, but I ask myself what benefit they derive from our foolish demise' (ibid.: 16). At a certain moment, nevertheless, while Milutin's interlocutors argue about the future state where all of their 'liberated brethren' will live together, and claim that they will 'arouse all of Bosnia to join [them]', the hero is ready to challenge them with his own suspicion about that type of future state unity (ibid.: 22-25).

These kinds of statements indicate a convergence of motifs that move to the third circle of narration, shaping the final meaning of the whole *skaz*. Here one discerns the fundamental purpose of Milutin and his interlocutors, the essential 'message' of the work.

From that moment on, the hero speaks less about his own bad fortune at being a soldier, and less about his personal life, as he slowly transforms into a sort of proselytizer who, among his learned interlocutors, holds to his own idea about the state. This motif is clearly dominant and can be followed through numerous details and 'scenes' which the hero generally narrates himself. Conceived as an ordinary Serbian peasant, he has his own 'human truth' with which he suddenly transforms into a peer of high officers, party leaders, ministers and other persons of the state. That is what makes him far more an omniscient narrator than a hero with an individual consciousness. That is why he is capable of discussing Macedonia, 'old Serbia', 'the left bank of the Vardar river'. To him it is clear that 'Serbs are dying only because they are Serbs'.

An entire string of such syntagmata exists in the circle of the hero's narratives, and they belong to the realm which we have defined as extra-literary material, or the domain of the national political mythology and ideology. They could not represent the real 'content' of the conscious thought of a literary hero who is, in a narrative sense, successfully individualized as an ordinary Serbian peasant. Furthermore, Popović's hero moves in a circle of people who, with little regard for the war and its perils, discuss at the height of the war the fact that the Allies will give 'us Serbs all the regions where South Slavs live' afterwards, and that the future state will be embellished with cities 'such as Novi Sad, Osijek, Vukovar and others' (ibid.: 25 *et seq.*). True, such statements are qualified by the hero's scepticism, as his own 'commentaries' accompany all that unfolds. At times these evolve into separate narrative strands, yet these passages are also characterized by the conflict of motifs. The peasant's suspiciousness and traditional caution stand in the shadow of his singular idea. He does not confront his interlocutors, he often even stands aside, because–and this is important for understanding the character–he has his vision, and he owns the transcendent knowledge of the legendary traditional Serbian peasant, symbolized by the *opanak* and the *Šajkača*.[4] That is why he is the only one who sees the mistake which is being historically repeated in the hope of creating a state where 'we Serbs' would live together with others. This proposition is reiterated in a series of heavily ideological passages, intended to confirm to the reader Milutin's only truths—that concord among the Serbs is paramount, that it is even more essential than freedom and democracy, but that it cannot be achieved, just as a common life with others cannot be achieved. In a famous scene where the author introduces the character Raka, nicknamed Trotsky, Popović's hero displays compassion toward others: the 'Arnauts', his designation for Albanians. Yet he cannot accept their truth, nor the possibility that another, alternative truth may exist. While such passages are significant, they are ultimately subordinated to a greater number of sections with strongly articulated programmatic qualities that eclipse the individual consciousness of the hero. In that sense, these narrative passages slowly degenerate into little more than excerpts from an articulated national programme that is nevertheless subject to Milutin's revision, for even the 'learned people' fail to see the 'error' which they fatally repeat in their ill-fated desire to live with others who are different from them. These others–Slovenes and Croats–may be their brethren, but they should not build a common state with them because 'it will be costly'. Milutin's 'position' extends farther, however. It is deeper and more far-reaching than the intentions of the 'learned men', and it springs from a sphere far beyond the experience of an ordinary Serbian peasant. This idea is the real 'intention of the author' or the fundamental meaning of the novel. The hero enters the action precisely as someone who must present a specific programme, and in that, the voice of Milutin as 'sage' drowns out all others.

The latter aspect also highlights the shortcomings of Popović's work. Introduced into the narrative in this way, the hero is sufficiently defined but insufficiently individualized as a literary character. This represents a textbook example of a literary flaw characteristic of populist literature. The approach is often intended as a functional device, which, along with the large number of programmatically intoned narrative passages, actually undermines the artistic coherence of the work as a whole. In other words, as the narrative unfolds, the hero is less and less an individual, and increasingly an embodiment of the collective, the people. He is increasingly convinced that he speaks the 'national truth'. The most essential scenes convey the message that the nation must finally 'wise up'. The speeches, both those made by the hero and those by other characters, add up to the essential programmatic conflict between those who advocate the formation of a common state, and others who endorse the position that it is time to stop repeating the 'error' once and for all.

Every aspect of Popović's narrative is subordinated to that single goal, including his treatment of the space within which the action unfolds (geopolitically demarcated as the space from Soča in Slovenia to Djevdjelija in Macedonia), and the treatment of the timeframe, as already discussed.

Isolated, privileged as the principal narrator, Popović's hero has a carefully planned function. In the closed circle of the dilemma in question, alone and pitted against everyone else, Milutin manages to maintain a balance in the development of the action. He does not harbour petty resentments or deep hatreds, he does not reject others, but he stands apart because he has his own political, historical truth—unconditionally his because he recognized it and adopted it—which asserts quite simply that 'Serbs should finally learn'. Milutin embodies the logic of the Serbian *domaćin*,[5] which Popović establishes as the highest level of consciousness. The very term *domaćin* becomes a key for interpreting certain essential situations in the work. The word is used some twenty-seven times throughout the novel, and by that fact occupies a structural place and role of a specifically semanticized expression. Its primary meaning is someone who creates a home, and it follows that it can also symbolically designate someone who creates a state, in the sense that a state is a symbolic home. The word is elevated to a higher level of meaning as a specific idiomatic expression. Other idioms have a similar function in the novel, words such as 'house', 'household', 'bulls', '*šajkača*', 'brothers', 'neighbour', and a number of others. In this sense, and judging from other characteristics of its idiomatic structure, Popović's tale resembles, and is closely related to, the literary mythology of the populist wave which emerged as the ruling fashion in one part of Serbian prose during the 1980s.

The meaning of Popović's work is not strictly singular, however, nor can it be reduced to a single dimension. As a literary character, Milutin is created in the tradition of a well-known literary method derived from the poetics of classical realism, and especially the realism of the nineteenth-century Serbian folk tale. The hero does emerge as a 'typical' representative of the people, for it is through him that the 'entire nation' speaks. It is also a question of the paradigm of Ćosić's aesthetic, the belated echo of a utilitarian aesthetic the ineffectiveness of which was defined by Laza Kostić. The aesthetic ideal derives from well-known folk–populist literature of Russian origin, which was redefined during the period of so-called social realism only through the change of prefix. Popović's hero cannot communicate personally lived experience. Concepts such as evil are understood only in a single–historical–dimension. These concepts do not draw on real human experience. Rather, everything is interpreted from the realm of 'post-history' and utilized for yet another 'settling of accounts with history'. When writers define their role in this manner, when they 'invest' their heroes with this kind of task, it should hardly be surprising if the artistic achievement fails to reach an enviable level.

Of course, neither in terms of modern methods, nor of specific thematic approaches, does populist wave literature offer a great deal of innovation. It is 'traditionalistic' according to its own inner logic, and its essential aesthetic concepts are hardly worth a mention.[6] Several moments in Popović's work demonstrate this. While in prison during the period of post-war forcible requisitioning of peasants' agricultural goods, for example, Milutin is not someone who has been broken, but remains the 'master of the house'—*domaćin*—preoccupied with the organization of the state. Drawing parallels with Tolstoy's Platon Karatayev, as critics tended to do, is a mistake since Tolstoy's hero saves himself 'through faith alone', which is the enduring content of his character. With Popović's hero one cannot pretend any such similarity. His is rather a type of literary medium that expresses a certain national programme, while in literature proper one finds 'protagonists' rather than 'programmes'. Ironically, such treatment was once deemed a defect of socialist realism, while more recently, the very same approach has been hailed as a virtue in works of 'national realism'. Sadly, just when it seemed it was behind us once and for all, we again find ourselves confronting the old problem of ideology in literature.

Mass euphoria

The difficulties associated with the reception of Popović's *Book About Milutin* evoke the half-truth that 'books also have their fate', but such difficulties also point to another type of literature which develops 'around' populist literature. The reception of this book was extraordinary by any measure. Given the atmosphere surrounding it, which we have briefly described already, it could not have been otherwise. In the overheated atmosphere of mythomania which was already unfolding in the early 1980s, many works of art were received on a massive, literally populist, scale. Some of the examples will always remain characteristic signs of that unsettling time.[7]

The English critic L. A. Richards once remarked that a book is a machine with which one thinks, which does not mean that it should assume the role of a locomotive (Richards 1964: 23). Within the body of populist literature, the *Book About Milutin* and its author were not the only ones that consciously accepted such a role. Richards added that there do indeed exist works that engender massive acceptance, just as there exist those which are accepted only under specific circumstances (ibid.: 203-204). Richards' typology applies to Popović in both aspects, but Popović's novel primarily accentuates its programmatic side. Wellek and Warren also noted a simple, often forgotten fact which is crucial in these cases: a study of a work of art is 'inextricably bound up with a study of the audience [the author] addresses and upon which he is dependent financially' (Wellek and Warren: 88). True, in this case it is less a question of a literal financial dependence—that issue could be a topic for sociological research. One thing is clear, however: a writer who meets with mass acceptance must have intended such a reception. In the case of *Milutin*, the work was created with a certain intention and its poetics were adjusted in order to realize that intention. For example, another novel published at approximately the same time failed to achieve the same massive reception despite a positive response from critics at home and abroad: Branimir Šćepanović's micro-novel *A Mouthful of Earth*, which approached almost metaphysical topics such as the eternal evil among people. Arguably, this author's intention and approach were markedly different from Popović's.

Immediately and without any interpretation from the literary establishment, the public itself understood the meaning built into Popović's novel, which can be summed up in the following manner: an ordinary man, Serbian peasant and *domaćin*, a man of the people—in this case, the embodiment of 'the people itself—understands the meaning of the new history in the South Slav lands better than the intelligentsia. The wider reading public accepted Popović's work, discovering it before the critics made their pronouncements, and found in it a blueprint of its own conscious and unconscious thought. At the moment of the collapse of the state, the already traumatized public consciousness responded collectively as an echo, since what had been predicted by Popović's hero was actually beginning to happen. Popović's work was accepted and 'played out', as Russian formalists would have phrased it. Its reception further points to a phenomenon that has nothing to do with literature strictly defined. The *Book About Milutin* was read widely and collectively, in the literal sense of the word. There are documented cases of the memorizing of the work in groups, along with ritualized recitation of passages from it at public gatherings—especially in local political meetings—a phenomenon typically occurring in small, closed tribal communities. In the press, whole narrative passages were used as titles in extra-literary contexts, for example. Politicians used the novel to compile an entire new lexicon of literary–political phraseology. Again, this is a phenomenon characteristic of closed communities and undeveloped societies, and it cannot be ascribed to Popović's work alone. In the moment of a painful historical break, the collective consciousness, as much as the individual consciousness, desperately needs some sort of collective hero.

The reception of Popović's *Book About Milutin* by the literary establishment is a separate story, and it holds few surprises. A segment of the critical establishment itself, on the wave of strong political populism, greeted it as the sum of truths that are revealed only in rare historical moments of national life. Such truths can be analysed and elaborated, but in no way challenged. Thus, this line of critique remained on the level of untempered enthusiasm for the 'racial hero', 'a typical man of the people' who embodies the paradigm of 'Serbianness'. This praise included no special effort to judge and evaluate the work. Danilo Kiš, following Laza Kostić, observed that literary criticism, in moments of strong tides of populism in small, closed, tribal communities, itself becomes a type of power. 'The fundamental characteristic of our criticism', asserted Kiš, 'is its anti-individualistic tendency which explains its preference for a generational approach' (Kiš: 58). In the same essay, Kiš was even more precise: 'Our literary–critical establishment is actually a literary government which does not serve literature, but literature serves it. The grey mass of literature is merely the justification for its existence' (ibid.). The literary ruling elite must subordinate itself to the political ruling elite, however, and the branch of the critical establishment in question found itself in a difficult situation—every attempt to approach Popović's work from another perspective was in itself a risk of being 'aligned' in the strictly ideological sense of the term. One could thus only talk about the novel's ideological perspective in positive terms. The final evaluation of Popović's work remains to be carried out, but it cannot be denied that the *Book About Milutin* remains a sign of the literary (and not strictly literary) period that came into existence and rode out its fate on the wave of political populism of the 1980s.

Notes

1 This study addresses a wave in Serbian literature that emerged in the early 1980s, rather than analysing specific characteristics such as periods or trends, which one ordinarily sees in studies in the field of literary

history. The term 'wave' is most often applied in this sense in film theory, but we feel that it applies equally well to the object of this research. This research will not consider a number of other writers, nor will it approach the topic chronologically: rather, it will focus on one set of examples characteristic of the phenomenon in question, which in our judgement represent a sufficient 'sample'. The wave in question—Laza Kostić referred to it as an 'epidemic'—traumatized the national consciousness. This spiritual state continues still.

2 See appendix: *Novija Srpska književnost i kritika ideologije* (More Recent Serbian Literature and a Critique of Ideology), 1989.

3 This aesthetic principle gained currency at the time of the early realists; Russian Slavophiles emphasized it even earlier, and it was revived again much later in aesthetic theories of socialist realism as the famous problem of the 'party line' in literature. In segments of the populist wave, it was revived and theoretically explicated as 'national realism'.

4 Translator's note: the *opanak* is the traditional Serbian peasant moccasin, and the *šajkača* is the traditional Serbian peasant head covering for men.

5 Translator's note: *domaćin* indicates the 'head of the household', 'master of the house', or 'host'.

6 One possible source of aesthetic dogma which stands at the foundations of 'national realism' can be found with the old Russian slavophile K. Aksakov, who clearly defines the 'character of the nation' (rather than the 'image of the nation'), which he contrasts with the character–individual. According to him, the character–individual is 'only an atom' lacking all significance without the collective. Ćosić used the same formulation, substituting only the prefix, in his own quasi-theory of national realism.

7 Aleksandar Milosavljević described an example of a typically populist reception of a work of art in the publication *Kultura vlasti* (The Culture of Rule), 21–28. A play which presented an image of St. Sava was prevented from being performed. Curiously, the interdiction was not official but 'informal', as 'the people' broke into the theatre in order to prevent the actors from going on stage. 'The people' here assumed the classic role of the censor; leaders of certain opposition parties participated as well. The event demonstrated that 'the people' rejected the claim that a work of art 'in its unique way, creates an authentic, autochthonous reality which may be based on historical facts'. The event reminds one of the nineteenth-century anecdote of an incident when the theatre audience literally intervened when someone on stage attacked the character of Miloš Obilić.

Football, Hooligans and War

IVAN ČOLOVIĆ

The story of the collapse of Yugoslavia, in a frenzy of hatred and war, in honour of the gods of ethnic nationalism and pre-modern militarism, may also be described as the story of the evolution of violence in Yugoslav sport, especially among football hooligans, and of the gradual transference of that violence, at the end of the 1980s and the beginning of the 1990s, into the domain of inter-ethnic conflicts and 'greater-nation' politics, and thence onto the battlefield. It is a story of the ostensible opposition of sports reporters to overt nationalism among supporters, of the consecration of the Red Star football club in the role of one of the most important symbols of 'Serbdom', of the 'spontaneous' organization of the supporters of that club into a group under the name of 'The Warriors' and, subsequently, of their transformation into volunteer soldiers and their being sent to war. It is an, as yet, unfinished story, but one of its possible ends may be glimpsed: the victory of the hooligan tribes and the founding of a new, vandal-warrior tribalism.

At the gates of hell

Judging by articles published in the sports press from the mid–1980s on, the violent behaviour of supporters in Yugoslavia (football fans, above all) was increasingly manifested in the form of insults, incidents and conflict on a so-called national basis. Through the expression of adherence to their club, or independently of any such adherence, supporters increasingly demonstrated a sense of national allegiance, just as the greatest aggression was shown towards teams and supporters from different national centres. In the years which preceded the outbreak of armed conflict in Croatia, supporters at sports stadiums, and most of all at football grounds, began carrying placards bearing political messages, portraits of national leaders and saints, national coats of arms and flags; they also began chanting Chetnik songs and using the Ustasha initial and greeting.

Such an increasingly obtrusive and increasingly radical transformation of the supporters' enthusiasm into nationalistic hatred and aggression was met with the unanimous condemnation of the sporting press of former Yugoslavia. Between 1989 and 1991 the Belgrade press printed a large number of commentaries full of dramatic warnings of the danger presented by the spread of chauvinistic passions in sports stadiums, and appeals that something be done to put a stop to such a development.[1] The titles of some of these articles convey the tone in which they were written—for example, the titles of commentaries published during 1990 and the first half of 1991 in the organs of the Red Star (*Crvena zvezda*) and Partizan clubs include 'Politics as pollutant', 'Nationalistic war games', 'Spectators outplay politics', 'The championship and war games', 'No politics in the stadium!'(*ZR*); and 'At the gates of hell', 'Distorted support', 'Demons of evil', 'Love instead of hate', 'The abuse of sport', 'Falangists among sportsmen', 'Supporters turn wild', 'National warriors', and 'Threat to the principles of decency and strength of spirit' (*PV*).

In these texts, the sports journalists' tone ranges from moral indignation, to didacticism and ideological judgement. 'Nationalism', writes one of them, 'is the greatest ill that could befall a multinational community' (*PV*, 3 March 1990). Another considers that the word 'chauvinism' is more appropriate, describing it as 'an expression of impotence, behaviour which has nothing to do with education and intellect. But it is precisely with that vice that young men arm themselves when they go to the stadium with the desire to break, burn and beat.' They are 'destroyers of everything progressive' (*ZR*, June 1990). A colleague laments that 'we are living at a time of the unbelievable raging of almost all the irrational delusions of the past, in which—in our Yugoslav space—the "vampirization" of national chauvinism has become so rife that we are threatened not only with general civilizational disintegration, but a return to a time when the guillotine, the knife and harassment were in everyday use' (*PV*, 3 February 1990).

In these articles, both sportsmen and sports officials were accused of nationalism, because 'in all of this the people who occupy positions of responsibility in sports organizations are by no means innocent' (*ZR*, September 1990). What is more, some sports commentators did not refrain from criticizing political leaders, that is, 'the nebulous politics of Nazi chauvinists and the ruling political bureaucracy'. For this dangerous 'cry of the blood of the nation ... is launched by no small number of the current holders of power in our country' (*PV*, 3 February 1990). What was at stake was the 'bestial abuse of sport on the part of people who are powerless to respond to the challenges of the contemporary world, exchanging creativity for the callous struggle for bare power, based on intrigue and international manipulation' (*PV*, 17 February 1990).

As a rule, in these texts the main cause for sounding the alarm about 'the demons of evil' and the 'bestial abuse of hatred' was the behaviour of supporters outside Serbia. Thus in one article, examples of the 'aggressive and fascistic behaviour of the spectators' occurred exclusively in Trogir, Mostar, Dubrovnik, Split, Zagreb and Ljubljana (*PV*, 17 February 1990). 'Pro-fascist cries' were loudest in the stadiums of Maksimir in Zagreb and Poljud in Split, and there was even a reference to 'the twilight of Maksimir nationalistic rampaging' (*ZR*, June 1990).

Belgrade sports commentators generally found examples of the worst 'rampaging' among supporters of Dinamo (Zagreb) and Hajduk (Split). According to one journalist, at the Dinamo–Partizan match in Zagreb on 25 March 1990, the supporters of Dinamo were overcome by a real 'bestial madness'. 'Like beasts, they smelled blood in the air, they wanted blood to be spilled so that their basest instincts could be satisfied' (*PV*, 9 June 1990). The picture painted of Hajduk supporters is no better, since 'in them the instinct of the wild beast has superseded human reason' (*PV*, 6 June 1990).

Among the sportsmen cited as bad examples of abandonment to nationalistic passions there is not a single one from a Belgrade club in the corpus we are analysing here. The worst offenders are the Cibona basketball player Arapović (*PV*, 31 March 1990) and the Dinamo footballers Boban, Šalja and Škerjanc (*PV*, 26 May 1990).

In the unanimous opinion of Belgrade sports commentators, the cause of the distortion of support for sport into nationalistic outbursts and conflicts occurred first, and in its most extreme form, in 'the northern republics', above all in Croatia: 'For the sake of their egotistical aims, obsessed with nationalistic hysteria and unbridled hatred of everything Yugoslav, the holders of power in Croatia and Slovenia have finally reached out to sport, too.' In the same place, the commentator attacks 'the organic national arousal and nationalistic blustering of the leadership of the ruling parties—DEMOS in Slovenia and HDZ in Croatia' (*PV*, 24 August 1990). At the end of a commentary devoted to 'nationalistic raging' after the Dinamo–Red Star match of 13 May 1990, the author also mentions 'an element among the Star supporters, who did not lag behind their Zagreb peers in their chauvinist delusions and actions'. However, these were not real Red Star supporters (as suggested by the title of the article 'They are not all Warriors'), but are described as '... groups of varying size which demonstrate that they do not come to football grounds in order to watch a competition, but in order to compete themselves—in hooliganism' (*ZR*, June 1990).

When the nationalism of Belgrade supporters was not an imitation of others' nationalistic 'raging', then it was the work of provocateurs from the ranks of some Serbian nationalistic opposition parties. As the author of 'They are not all Warriors' writes, 'In Serbia too there are parties which threaten with daggers, which seek to erect monuments to war criminals on Ravna Gora,[2] which respond to nationalism with nationalism.' These parties endeavour to shift into sports arenas 'political marketing, particularly of an ill-fated and bloody spirit that once raged through Serbia. In the Second World War the Chetniks were the national disgrace of the freedom-loving Serbian nation ... Red Star has taken on a difficult task. It has publicly distanced itself altogether from such mad political ideas and political marketing' (*ZR*, September 1990).

Among the politicians whom the commentators of *Partizanov vesnik* and *Zvezdina revija* accuse of chauvinism in 1990 and 1991, in addition to Tudjman, Rupel and Rugova, one Serbian politician is also mentioned: Vuk Drašković. There is not the slightest allusion to the role of the ruling SPS party or its leader (Slobodan Milošević); there is no attempt to connect the atmosphere in sports stadiums with the similar atmosphere at political rallies in Serbia and Montenegro between 1988 and 1989; nor is there any mention of the striking similarity between the slogans, songs and placards that were appearing both in the stadiums and at political rallies, the main focus of which—in both cases—was Slobodan Milošević, to whom supporters in the stadiums and participants at rallies would frequently chant: 'Serbian Slobo, Serbia is with you'.[3]

Serb-haters and football-haters

When armed conflict began in Slovenia and Croatia, the sports journalists took over from their colleagues, the political commentators, the main topoi of war-propaganda discourse. The reasons

for the collapse of Yugoslavia, the outbreak of war and the consequences of such a situation in the realm of sport, can be explained
with the help of 'arguments' offered by the state media. One article
devoted to the cancellation of the start of the football league
championship in Yugoslavia in 1991 began 'The national football
championship did not begin as expected on the first Saturday of
August. In Croatia, with the Ustasha-like policies of Tudjman's HDZ
party, vicious war games are being played, in which the Serbian
population is suffering. Suffering precisely because it is Serbian.'
The article also mentions 'Croatian fighters in Slavonia and Krajina'
who 'keep attacking the Serbian inhabitants ... who are defending
their homes' (*ZR*, August 1991).

Similarly, the decision of UEFA, made in August 1991, to ban
matches in European competitions from being held in stadiums in
Yugoslavia, was interpreted as part of 'the general hypocrisy towards Yugoslavia, and, it seems, particularly towards Serbia' (*ZR*,
September 1991). It was explained by one commentator in *Sport* as
'the whim of a Serb-hater and football-hater'. He attributed the
main role in dismantling Yugoslav football to 'the German lobby'.
'UEFA, obviously German-led, is doing all it can to destroy Yugoslav
football' wrote this author, adding that this was increasingly reminiscent of a return to 'the rallies of 1933, 1939 and 1941'. The fundamental idea behind his commentary is suggested by its title: 'A
slap in the face of the Germans' (S, 14 December 1991). In another
place, the role of the 'fiercest and most frenzied destroyers' was
attributed to Austria (*ZR*, January 1992). This 'anti-Serb lobby' also
included Hungary, which, in an article about the Red Star–
Anderlecht match, played in October 1991 in Szeged instead of
Belgrade, was referred to as 'a country which is, in any case, ill-
disposed to the Serbian nation in Croatia' (*ZR*, November 1991).

The exclusion of Yugoslav teams and clubs from international
competitions was also interpreted with reference to the international isolation of the Serbian regime as described by the state media. According to their interpretation, Milošević's Yugoslavia was
exposed to international isolation and was under economic embargo and other United Nations sanctions because the main voice
in the international community was that of enemies of the Orthodox Serbian nation, and above all the influential German and Vatican lobby. The enemies of the Serbian nation, it was argued, hated
Serbia because Serbia was in every way better and more righteous
than they were, and so, in accordance with this logic, they imposed
sanctions in sport in order to disable a nation that was far in advance of all others in this field. The author of the article 'Europe's

petty spite' put it succinctly: they want to spite us because we are
the best' (*SŽ*, 21 December 1991).

Such an explanation for the introduction of sporting sanctions
against Yugoslavia was put forward by Milan Tomić, the general
director of Red Star, in a statement to *Zvezdina revija* (September
1992): 'We represented a particular kind of danger for world sport
... We would have found ourselves in the centre of events at the
Olympics, and that means that we would have been on the victors'
podium in every team sport. The world could not bear that. Especially those who have pretensions to power. For example, in team
sports Germany means nothing. And nor does Great Britain. And if
individual sports represent the civilizational premise of a nation,
team sports are its spirit—a spirit which those nations lack ... For all
of these reasons, I am convinced that many of the pretentious sporting nations could not tolerate our increasingly obvious domination
in sports ... and that it is nothing other than the desire to deliver a
blow to Serbian sport where it has attained the highest international
achievements. That is an appalling strategy.'

This ostensible endeavour on the part of Western sport to eliminate Serbian competitors was, it was claimed, only the latest episode in a war that had lasted for two millennia. 'Besides,' Tomić
continued, 'as early as the time of Cornelius Sula in the first century AD, the West had already reduced the Olympic spirit to its
lowest, circus level, to the level of gladiators and blood. The nobility of Athenian athletes and Olympic victors was lost for a long
time thanks to the Latin need for games in blood.'

The coming of footballers as refugees from Croatia into Belgrade
clubs was also an opportunity for sports newspapers to reach for
imagery from war propaganda. Thus one former player from Osijek was quoted as saying 'I could not remain in a city where people
were killed just because they were Serbs and Orthodox.' According
to the journalist conducting the interview 'all the evil suffered by
the Serbian nation in Slavonia could be seen in his eyes'. Another
of the footballer's statements was chosen as the title of the article:
'I always crossed myself with three fingers' (*SŽ*, 5 December
1991).[4]

Their adherence to 'Serbdom' and to the Orthodox Church was
also cited as the reason why Serb trainers suffered innocently in
various Catholic countries. At the end of 1991, the football club
Espagnol in Barcelona broke off its contract with the trainer
Ljupko Petrović, and at the same time the basketball trainer Božidar Maljković also found himself out of work. 'Both of them', explained the author of one article, 'paid the price for their adher-

ence to Orthodoxy. The Catalonians could forgive them all their successes and failures but not their origin. Is that the reason why, even today, yet another Serb, Radomir Antić, is working in Real with a knife at his throat' (*SŽ*, 31 December 1991).

Serbian Star

When faced with the international isolation of war, involvement in sport—playing and supporting football, particularly abroad—acquires an exceptional patriotic value. In the opinion of sports journalists, Red Star and its fans were participating in the defence of 'Serbdom' and Serbia whenever they went to matches played by the Serb cup-winners outside Belgrade, in Szeged or Sofia. In one report of a match between Red Star and Panatinaikos, played in Sofia in March 1992, the fans were praised for their exemplary patriotism, comparable to that shown by the Serbian army in the most glorious moments of Serbian history. 'The Army of the Warriors', stated the report, 'was as numerous as the Serbian army led by the Mrnjavčević brothers into battle at Marica[5] ... A team persecuted and damned by UEFA did something which no one else has ever succeeded in doing ... In the international 1991–92 football season, the miracle called FC Red Star can be compared only with the Serbian army in the First World War. That army, also despised and humiliated by its allies, and driven out of the homeland by a more powerful opponent, survived and was victorious on a front that was "always out of town" ... There is no hope for us, we must win. The sentence spoken by Nikola Pašić[6] in 1915, appears to have become the way of life of FC Red Star.'

To follow Red Star on this thorny road represented the supreme act of patriotism: 'Star's supporters display unparalleled patriotism. They clutch that one bright national and internationally acknowledged phenomenon, FC Red Star, as a drowning man does a straw, regretting neither time nor expense, neither effort nor unjustified absences from school nor the reprimands of their bosses or threats by the directors of their firms.' To be with Red Star in those difficult times was the real education for the young, far more important than that imposed on them by their teachers. The author of the article quotes several examples in support of this opinion, including the following: 'One father from Belgrade took his eleven-year-old son to the Star–Panatinaikos match in Sofia. The child missed two days of school, after which the father went to see his son's teacher and said: "Madam, I took my son to the Red Star match in Bulgaria in order to give him some practical lessons in patriotism, and it is up to your conscience to decide whether to consider those lessons administratively justified or not'" (*Te*, 25 March 1992).

In the sports press, in the course of 1991 and 1992, particularly in *Zvezdina revija*, the idea became firmly established that the greatest value of this club was its Serbian identity, and that supporting Red Star meant, in fact, supporting 'Serbdom' and Serbia. Thus one article in *Zvezdina revija* in August 1991 claimed that Red Star was 'a European club in its results, but in its origin and through the allegiance of its fans, supremely Serbian'. Particular emphasis was given to the fact that 'For Serbs from Croatia, Red Star is practically a part of their national identity! They did not dare to say out loud what they were by nationality until recently, but they could say who they supported—always! "Red Star is more than a football club, it is a symbol of the Serbian being" is a quotation from one of the last issues of *Nasa riječ* (Our Word), the newspaper of the Serbian nation in Croatia. "In Cetina, near Knin, every single child and young man knows the Red Star anthem, but few of them know the Orthodox Lord's Prayer", was recently reported in *Slobodna Dalmacija* (Free Dalmatia). In the reception centre for refugees from Tenj, Borovo, Mirkovci, Bršadin and Vukovar, some fifty youngsters, boys and girls, housed in Kula, asked for footballs as they chanted "Zvezda, Zvezda!" directly into the television cameras.'

In addition to the journalists, the club's officials also participated in the definitive shaping of the Serbian character of Red Star, its consecration in the role of one of the most important symbols of 'Serbdom', that is, the Serbian national identity. Thus Vladimir Cvetković, the general manager of FC Red Star (later also a minister in the Serbian government), in an interview published in August 1992, was at pains to deny any connection whatsoever between his club and Communism and the previous Communist regime in Serbia. 'First of all,' said Cvetković, 'the Star is not a symbol of Communism, we have no hammer and sickle in our coat of arms ... If we were to roll the film back a little, it would be clear that we were never a club that was closely connected with the government' (*Te*, 12 August 1992).

Had Cvetković really been inclined to 'roll the film back' he would have found in the monograph *Crvena Zvezda*, published in 1986 at the time when he was secretary of the club, information about the fifteen political and military leaders who were presidents of the club between 1948 and 1992. He would also have been reminded that the introduction to this official publication was written by Dragoslav-Draža Marković, one of the most influential people in the Serbian government of the time, and he could have read in that introduction that the name of Red Star 'was associated with the five-pointed star, under which we spilled our blood in the course of the revolution'.

Politically inclined writers also appeared to bear witness to the Serbian identity of Red Star. The literary critic Petar Džadžić recalled in 1989 that 'In the seventies, my friends and I identified only four such representative institutions of recent times in the current social life of the Serbs: the Serbian Academy of Arts and Sciences, the daily newspaper *Politika*, the publisher "Prosveta", and *Red Star*' (P, 30 January 1989). In an interview in *Sport*, the writer Brana Crnčević gave apparently contradictory information about himself, that is, that he was 'a Partizan fan, who supported Red Star'. In fact, there was no contradiction, because for Crnčević, too, Red Star was a symbol of Serbian identity. 'Star's successes', added Crnčević, 'meant a great deal both to Serbs in the diaspora and to Serbs here' (S, 26 December 1991). The poet Matija Bećković once explained that he had begun to support Star because 'national allegiance was expressed through support' for that club (*ZR*, March 1992).

Hooligans or patriots?

Before the crisis in Yugoslavia, the collapse of the federal state and the outbreak of armed conflict in some parts of the country, the most fanatic Yugoslav supporters, especially of football, belonged to the great international family of hooligan fans. For them, as for groups of other European fans who were beginning to attract public attention through their violent behaviour, their models were English and Italian fans. Following their example, Serb fans also chose provocative names, gathered around belligerent leaders, attended matches equipped with the requisite props for supporting their club and, more importantly, for fighting. They threw firecrackers onto the pitch, lit flares, made enormous flags, and, above all, aimed to settle scores with the supporters of opposing teams and to cause havoc in the towns where they went to encourage their club.

What is striking is the attitude of these hooligan fans and their hostility to society and its official representatives–an attitude which usually extended to the club's officials. Defying the established order and overturning the hierarchy of official social values, the fans developed a kind of subculture. They practised, or at least praised, alcoholism, barbarity, vandalism, madness, sex and a pornographic vocabulary.

Above all, it seems that the real target of the hooligan fans' provocations was the ruling authority in their immediate social environment. When they were aggressive towards visiting supporters, they provoked the local community leaders and organs of public order above all, and when they behaved destructively at away matches, they were competing with the local hooligans rather than currying favour with the chauvinists back home.

A substantial proportion of the supporters' 'folklore' consisted of songs of a 'hooligan' character, that is, songs in which, in order to be provocative, the fans consciously took on the role of antisocial types, social drop-outs, alcoholics, madmen. This hooligan defiance on the part of the 'Gypsies' (Red Star fans) and 'Gravediggers' (Partizan fans) is expressed in the following lines:

> As long as the Earth revolves round the Sun
> Star's hooligans will never die.
> Thousands of Gravedigger hooligans
> will give their lives for Partizan.

Following the example first of English, then of Italian fans, they usually gave themselves names which emphasized that role: Vandals, Maniacs, Bad Boys, Evil Hordes. One group of Red Star supporters called themselves BAH (Belgrade's Alcohol Hooligans). Their anthem was:

> Alcohol, alcohol, that's the real thing,
> If you don't like alcohol, you're not all there.

Hajduk (Split) favoured this verse:

> The dawn breaks, the day grows light,
> the whole north is blind drunk,
> eveyone drunk, eveyone drugged,
> we are Hajduk supporters.

Taking on the role of social outcasts and rebels, the fans developed forms of 'warlike' behaviour and discourse. One group of Star's supporters called themselves 'Zulu Warriors'. The fans were 'at war' not only with foreigners or their neighbours, or with 'other nations', but most readily with rival local clubs. Partizan and Star supporters exchanged threats full of death, blood, axes and slaughter. When the first group shouted 'If you're happy, kill a Gypsy', the 'Gypsies' had a ready response:

> Axes in hand
> and a knife in the teeth,
> there'll be blood tonight,
> Gravediggers' blood.
> Oh Gravediggers, Gravediggers,
> you're nothing now,
> you'll be like the Frogs
> against Liverpool.
> 38, 38 died then,
> hurry home, hurry home,
> there'll be dead now too.

The vocabulary and phraseology of confrontation used by the hooligan fans consisted equally of elements from the repertoire of the language of violence and death, and from the arsenal of obscene, pornographic words and phrases of abuse. Here, if 'slaughter' and 'fuck' do not mean precisely the same thing, they are at least equally offensive. In the following example there are two characteristics of the hooligan fans which became unacceptable at the time when inter-nation hatred and preparations for war began to flare up: abuse directed at a 'same nation' opponent, combined with solidarity with a club of a 'different nation', and a pornographic vocabulary unworthy of a disciplined national fighter.

> Oh Star, you fucked-up tart,
> Let Hajduk fuck you, let them all,
> especially the Gravediggers.

For the fans, going to the stadium and supporting their team meant 'release', liberation, throwing off restraints and rules—at least that is how some of them answered the direct question when asked what they got out of supporting their teams at matches. 'Dad started taking me to matches as a kid,' says Mihaijlo (a Partizan supporter, aged 22), 'and I simply began to like that experience of a crowd; it's a special kind of release. There's a kind of beauty in hating the others, those who don't support the team you support. Also, you can shout your head off ... I like that, everything else in life has rules' (Questionnaire, 20 January 1990).

But, in Serbia and Montenegro, there began increasingly to appear among the supporters those who looked for a kind of patri otic justification for their provocative and aggressive behaviour, especially at matches where their team was playing against a club from a 'different centre'. Thus Goran, twenty-three, the leader of the 'Vandals' gang of Partizan supporters, said that 'one should give the fans due recognition, because they were the first to support Serbia in these changes'. 'I think', he added, 'that it all began in the stadium. People always knew that Star and Partizan were Serbian teams, and Hajduk and Dinamo Croatian, and that's all there is to it. End of story' (Questionnaire, 8 May 1989).

In the supporters' folklore in Serbia (songs, slogans, placards, flags, coats of arms, etc.), the theme of ethnic identity, until then sporadic and illegal, became the predominant content from the mid-1980s, at the same time as the theme began to appear in political communication and propaganda, especially at the populist mass political rallies which set the tone of political life in Serbia and Montenegro in the course of 1988 and 1989. The supporters wanted, above all, to present themselves as belonging to 'their nation'—Star and Partizan supporters as Serbs—and at the same time to see opposing clubs as representatives of different nations, inimical to them.

According to one Red Star fan, preparations for going to Zagreb for the Star–Dinamo match of 21 May 1989 included one feature, obligatory for all. Every supporter, including Partizan fans, had to have tattooed on their arm the four letter 'S's from the Serbian coat of arms.[7] 'Imagine the scene,' he said, 'when we all roll up our sleeves and begin to wave our arms!' (Questionnaire, 7 May 1989). At the same time, there was a similar evolution towards the national self-determination of supporters in Croatia, too, also under the influence of the development of political circumstances there, that is, the establishment of a nationalistic regime.[8]

Star supporters, especially when they found themselves in the stadium of their opponent's team, emphasized above all their allegiance to Serbia and its leader Milošević:

> We are the Warriors from proud Serbia
> Come onto the terraces, greet the Serbian race
> From Kosovo to Knin, Serbs stand shoulder to shoulder
> Serbian Slobo, Serbia is with you
> Who says, who lies, that Serbia is small?
> It's not small, it's not small, it gave us Slobodan!
> *Manastirka, manastirka*, Serbian brandy:
> that's what warms the Serbian army, Slobodan!

At the beginning of 1990, Star supporters would also on occasion shout the name of Vuk Drašković, as this example shows:

> Star, Star, in one voice now,
> Vuk Drašković supports us.

But equally, Star's greatest urban rival, Partizan, and particularly its supporters, did not want to stand aside from this movement towards national identification. Among the supporters' slogans and songs the following lines could be heard:

> Partizan, Partizan, that's a Serbian team.
> Slobodan Milošević is proud of them.

> The whole of Yugoslavia dances rock-and-roll,
> Only a true Serb supports Partizan.[9]

Nor did Partizan fans want to leave the name 'Warriors' to Star supporters:

> Partizan loves only warriors,
> warrior heroes of proud Serbia,
> may their name shine forever,
> long live Partizan and mother Serbia.

The Star fans would not have that, and responded to such words from the 'Gravediggers':

> Partizan, Partizan, well-known Muslim team,
> Azem Vlasi, Azem Vlasi, is proud of them.[10]

Nevertheless, this folklore bears witness to the overriding endeavour among supporters of both these clubs to establish ethnic solidarity, so that at some matches they chanted 'Serbia, Serbia!' together. The equivalent in Croatia was the sense of fraternity between Dinamo and Hajduk supporters, who were able to forget their internal conflicts and sing together:

> Dinamo and Hajduk are of the same blood
> it doesn't matter which of them is first,
> Dinamo and Hajduk are two brother clubs,
> the whole of Croatia is proud of them.[11]

In the years preceding the outbreak of war in Croatia, Star and Partizan supporters often found their inspiration and material for slogans and songs in Chetnik folklore, which reappeared in general circulation at that time, especially in the form of records and tapes which were freely sold by street vendors in Serbia. Since one of the main demonstrative functions of supporters' folklore is to achieve the maximum degree of provocation and to touch the 'opponent' with the worst possible insult, in the supporters' variations on the lines of Chetnik songs there is more blood and slaughter than in the texts of the 'originals' on which these variants were based. This is confirmed by these examples:

> The emblem on my beret
> is shaking, shaking,
> we will murder, we will kill
> all who are not with the Star.

> Prepare yourselves, Gravediggers,
> it will be a fierce battle,
> heroic heads will fall
> well slaughter our Ustasha (Gypsy) brothers.

> The Serbian army is on the move
> heading for Zagreb, heading for Zagreb,
> we will murder, we will kill
> all who are not with us.

These examples show that the Chetnik folklore from the Second World War offered suitable material for creating supporters' slogans and songs. For this purpose, bellicose, threatening cries were particularly useful, as was the theme of sacrifice.

The departure of the 'Warriors' to war

At the end of 1990 the sports press, and particularly *Zvezdina revija*, began to write about positive changes in the behaviour of Red Star supporters, changes that were attributed to the influence of their leader—Željko Ražnatović Arkan—a man who was increasingly forcing himself onto the attention of the broader public. He was credited with reconciling the management of Red Star with a section of the unruly supporters, with establishing order and harmony between the mutually antagonistic groups of fans, and, most importantly, with succeeding in separating support for the club from political passions and interests.

In the first article about Ražnatović, published in *Zvezdina revija*, he is described as 'a man close to Star, with an excellent understanding of events in the "Marakana" stadium, who was helping "The Warriors" to leave politics in the political arena.' It also said

that 'Star's management proclaimed him its saviour when he succeeded, through his personal authority, in reconciling the warring
factions' (*ZR*, December 1990). Beside this article there appeared a
photograph of a group of supporters, 'The Warriors', with Željko
Ražnatović who was wearing, like all the others, a supporters' cap
and trainers.

With the coming of Ražnatović among 'The Warriors', it appears
that the danger of their displaying 'political intoxication in general,
particularly of the Chetnik type', to which *Zvezdina revija* had
previously drawn attention, receded (*ZR*, September 1990), because from that time on the paper wrote about Star supporters in a
different way, praising their behaviour. The club itself hurried to
repay 'The Warriors' for their obedience to the supporters' com-
missar Ražnatović, by paying for some eighty of the most passionate supporters to go to Glasgow for a match against Glasgow Rang-
ers, with Ražnatović as the leader of the expedition (*ZR*, December
1990).

Another commentary in *Zvezdina revija* from December 1990,
'Spectators get the better of politics', was devoted to 'The Warriors'. Here it stated that in Belgrade there had been 'aggressive attempts to politicize sport', although 'significantly fewer than in
other places', for the simple reason that 'Belgraders were traditionally great lovers of true sporting contests'. There was, nevertheless,
a danger, since 'it is not difficult to poison the souls of these young
people' and 'party leaders, with the aim of winning at the elections
at any price' (meaning the parliamentary elections of December
1990) 'most frequently try to imitate only what is worst in the arsenal of Western democracy'. Thus it happened that 'Belgrade did
not escape the attempt to introduce national paraphernalia, and at
one time relations between a section of the misguided young men
and the Red Star management became strained.' But then Ražnatović came on the scene, or rather, as it stated here, '"The Warriors"
reorganized themselves'.

There is no doubt that in these articles the introduction of
'national paraphernalia' and everything else that the supporters
took with them into the stadiums was not so much in dispute as
those in whose hands such paraphernalia were found, that is, those
who had control over the aggressive chauvinistic passions, and
therefore a monopoly over their use for political or military ends.
And the war in Croatia and Bosnia was on the horizon.

Ražnatović made the decision to begin preparing Star supporters for real war, as he said himself, after the Dinamo–Star match of
13 May 1990 in Zagreb. 'The match took place on the thirteenth,'

he was to say some years later, 'we began to organize immediately after that ... I could see war coming because of that match in Zagreb, I foresaw everything and I knew that the Ustasha daggers would soon be slaughtering Serbian women and children again.'[12]

At the end of 1990, Ražnatović came to public attention as a man who was arrested in Dvor on the Una (in Croatia) and spent six months in prison accused of going to Krajina[13] in order to help the Serbs there, who had begun to offer armed resistance to the new Croatian government in a protest known as the 'log revolution'. Just before his arrest, Ražnatović had founded the Serbian Volunteer Guard, although not much was known about it publicly.

When he came out of prison, the leader of the 'Warriors' and commander of the Serbian Volunteer Guard became involved in armed conflicts in Slavonia, which, in the course of the summer of 1991, turned into real war. The core of his volunteer army consisted of Red Star supporters. In an interview for *Srpsko jedinstvo* (November 1994), recalling those days of war in Slavonia, Ražnatović talked about the way he and his fighters had prepared: 'Well, remember that, as supporters, we had trained first without weapons ... From the beginning I insisted on discipline. You know what football fans are like, they're noisy, they like drinking, clowning; I put a stop to that at a stroke, I made them cut their hair, shave regularly, stop drinking and–it all took its own course.'

In December 1991, *Zvezdina revija* published a short 'note from the front' about 'the legendary Zeljko Ražnatović Arkan, the leader of the Star "Warriors" and commander of his "Tigers" who distinguished themselves in the liberation of Vukovar', but it was only after the March 1992 issue that this paper began to write more extensively about the Star supporters on the Slavonian battlefield. A report 'Rifles in their hands, flags in their thoughts', accompanied by a photograph, described 'a day with the Warriors in the Serbian Volunteer Guard'.

> All with neatly cut hair under their black military berets, they set off to the song 'We are the Serbian Army, Arkan's tigers, all to a man volunteers, we'll let no one have Serbian land' The beat of their foot steps seemed to give rhythm and strength to the melody. They disappeared into a wood, but it rang with the words: 'To battle, to battle, to battle, rise up my Serb brothers, do not leave your hearth, Serbs are protected by glory and God!'. I wind back the film of my memories and distribute these brave boys through all the stadiums of Europe. I know exactly where each of them stood, who first started the song, who first unfurled his flag, who first lit the torch. Arkan's warriors ... They occupy every line of the new issue of 'Star'. The best

supporters in the world ... The 'Warriors' have left their supporters' props somewhere under the arches of our 'Marakana' stadium and have set off to war with rifles in their hands. Fearless fighters, heroes to a man. (*ZR*, March 1992)[14]

The Red Star footballers did not forget their supporters at the front. The captain, Vladan Lukić, was praised in one issue of *Srpski žurnal* (Serbian Journal) for having gone 'in his Mazda 323 four times to Erdut to visit the wounded', and for the fact that he was planning to spend New Year's Eve with them. He was quoted as saying: 'Many of our loyal supporters from the north end of "Marakana" are in the most obvious way writing the finest pages of the history of Serbia.' (SŽ, 25 December 1991). His team mate Siniša Mihajlović complained that thinking about the war stopped him from concentrating on football: 'Our supporters are at the front ... my people are dying and bleeding, and how can I play. I even caught myself thinking that it was actually indecent for us to play and enjoy ourselves when there are so many victims' (*Te*, 11 December 991).

The fighter-fans did not forget their clubs or their songs. It turned out that between supporters' songs and war songs, themes and component elements could easily be exchanged. Many of the supporters' songs, which had come into being as improvisations on the basis of Chetnik and patriotic folklore, were simply restored to their original form. However, there were some 'authentic' supporters' songs, that is, those for which external models were not identifiable, which featured only supporters, their antisocial violent behaviour and the requisite props. These 'hooligan' texts were the shared heritage of various groups of supporters, who adapted them to their needs in 'performance'. They included the following two verses:

> Tonight there's going to be trouble,
> tonight will be a madhouse,
> the hooligans are moving
> through the streets of Belgrade (Zagreb, Split).

> Let axes ring out,
> let chains rattle,
> here come the Gravediggers (Gypsies)
> the greatest madmen of all.[15]

As they went to war, in paramilitary volunteer units, supporters from Serbia adapted their 'hooligan' songs to their new function, turning them into patriotic and war folklore. That is how this song, published in the Pale weekly *Javnost* in October 1993, came into being:

> There will be hell again,
> there'll be a madhouse again,
> the specials are on the move,
> from the streets of Foča.

> The Chetniks are on their way,
> the fighters are on their way,
> Cosa's men are on their way[16]
> Serbian volunteers.

> They do not fear Allah,
> they do not fear the faith
> they do not fear Alija
> and all his Turks.

Sport as military training

The example of the organized departure of a group of supporters to war, combined with the fact that they did not lose their supporters' identity in the war, sheds new light on the question of the relationship between violence, sport and society. Over the last two decades, this question has usually been posed as the problem of the antisocial, destructive and violent behaviour, but often also the criminal behaviour, of extreme groups of hooligan football fans. In peacetime, in countries faced with the growth of aggression among groups of supporters, appropriate (political, police, sport-related, educational, etc.) measures are sought to put an end to what is seen as 'a social evil', that is, attempts are made to 'pacify' the supporters.

However, the episode of the 'Warriors' going to war demonstrates that in one country, as in many others, in which hooliganism among supporters was obtrusively present, in wartime the fans' aggression became for the state a valuable 'capital of hatred',[17] and the fans became welcome 'cannon fodder'. The state did not have any need to repress the violent behaviour of the fans, partly because in wartime there was little opportunity for it to be manifested in the usual way. On the contrary, it was in the interests of the state that this 'capital of hatred' among supporters should be conserved in order to use it for the realization of war aims.

Those who study the state in the twentieth century have already noted that it is interested in sport and physical culture on the whole as a kind of military training. That is particularly true of states which show features of a totalitarian order, and states preparing for war.

In Communist states, too, the main motive for the great interest in sport was the conviction that sport was an important means of political propaganda and preparation for potential war. That was how sport was perceived in former Yugoslavia. In a paper prepared for the founding meeting of the Red Star Sports Club, held on 4 March 1945, Zora Žujović defined two main tasks for sport in the new Communist state: 'First, to strengthen the body for the forthcoming reconstruction of the country, and secondly, accessible to all, it should gather and unite all our young people, regardless of their age or position. Its greatest and most sacred duty is to provide wholehearted and fraternal help to the front' (Ršumović, 37).

The idea that support for sport was a preparation for war (should it be necessary) can be found in Yugoslavia also in the time after Tito's death. In a book of patriotic sports songs by Nedeljko Neša Popadić, *Srce na travi* (Heart on the Grass), which was published in 1982 by *Sportska knjiga* (Sporting Books) in Belgrade, there is a poem called 'The Fan'. The character of the fan includes the following features:

> I am one of those
> who sings far into the night after a victory.
> And who will punch the nose
> of my opponent's supporter,
> one of those who will go tomorrow to the front
> and swap my club's flag
> for a rifle in my hand...

These patriot-fans, together with their favourites—footballers— make up Tito's army:

> And therefore ... Before the well-known whistle blows
> and the signal to start the match is given,
> remember the land of the Partizans
> and know: now it is you
> who are Tito's army!
> ...
> Forward for the homeland ... for the House of Flowers ...[18]
> Forward for the tricolour ... Forward, forward, for Tito!

The hooligan revolution

On the eve of the outbreak of armed conflict in former Yugoslavia, war propaganda on the Serbian side, above all through sports journalists, succeeded in directing the aggressive energy of the supporters towards the battlefields, giving to the new forms of its manifestation the meaning and value of patriotic sacrifice, if not for Tito and the House of Flowers, then certainly for the new or renewed symbols and ideals of the national collective. In other words, unlike peacetime endeavours to pacify gangs of hooligan supporters, here was an example of their militarization.

The well-documented significant presence of hooligans from sports stadiums and others, seen in conditions of peace as antisocial and criminal groups, among the 'heroes' of the wars on the territory of former Yugoslavia, is one reason why these wars can be described as the vandalistic, destructive campaigns of hooligan-fans, taken over by the state for the aims of its war policy, disciplined, supplied with 'props', that is, armed, and sent to fight with the 'enemy' as though it were a question of inter-supporter confrontation at some football match.

But how is it possible to transform unruly hooligan–fans so quickly into disciplined soldiers ostensibly fighting for the state and nation? Is the essence of the behaviour of hooligan–fans, as some believe, their testing of unbridled, excessive freedom, 'rampaging', chaotic abandonment to 'their basest instincts'? In that case, the transformation of fans into soldiers (though military drill, cutting their hair, getting them to come off drugs and limiting alcohol) would mean their undergoing a fundamental metamorphosis in order to be transferred forcibly from the chaos of unbridled freedom to the cosmos of military order.

There is reason to dispute such an explanation. Thanks to some new sociological and ethnological research, we know now that in the apparently ungoverned, chaotic world of extremist fans there is order. Their behaviour is, in fact, governed by unwritten rules, codes, protocols, hierarchy and discipline.[19] With this in mind, it is possible to explain logically why it is precisely some groups of supporters who lend themselves most easily to being transformed into volunteer military units: such groups are already imbued with the spirit of organization and subordination. The transformation of fans into soldiers is only a reinterpretation of the already existing structure of the supporters' group, and that is why it is possible for the essential identity of the group, as fans, to be retained (Arkan's volunteer 'Tigers' did not cease to be 'Warriors') and also, as in the example quoted, for the supporters' folklore to be preserved.

However, even if that were not the case and one accepted that, as they themselves said, hooligans really did celebrate crime, drunkenness, chaos and madness, their involvement in war would not have to entail any fundamental change. There was nothing to say that short-haired, disciplined supporter-volunteers were forbidden from hating the enemy passionately, nor did anyone prevent them from revelling in that hatred and in destructive and murderous revenge to their hearts' content. And that means that the taming of the unrestrained behaviour of the hooligans, now soldiers, could merely be illusory, that it was perhaps only in war that they could taste the full pleasure of the free transgression of fundamental human prohibitions imposed on them in peacetime, including even the most aggressive behaviour in the stadium. The grim stories that emerged from the war in Croatia and Bosnia, of sadistic orgies orchestrated by people in military uniforms engaged in military actions, suggest that the freedom of abandonment to the most gruesome forms of violence offered by war cannot be compared to that tasted by sports fans even at their 'wildest'.

The phenomenon of fighter-fans in the war in former Yugoslavia calls into question the thesis of the positive socio-psychological functions of supporters' violence. Authors who promote this thesis seek to distinguish between the ritual, symbolic, carnival manifestation of violence, and 'real' violent behaviour, explaining those instances when supporter violence becomes real as isolated incidents, extreme phenomena. According to this interpretation, by deflecting the manifestation of mass aggression onto a symbolic plane, and by transforming it into a spectacle, a ritual, an image of violence, sporting events, and especially football matches, have the prophylactic function of catharthis. A football match is a war, but a 'ritualized war', and not only because journalists describe it using military vocabulary but because the supporters' props, flags, drums and uniforms suggest that it is a kind of symbolic warfare. According to Alain Ehrenberg, it is, in fact, only a 'desire for show' (Ehrenberg, 1986: 148–158).

Michel Maffesoli attributes to contemporary sport the function of the ritualization of violence, that is, the channelling of intensity and a way of expressing it, analogous to the function of ancient bachanalia and medieval tournaments and duels. In his opinion, ritualized eruptions of violence in sport 'help to prevent the social body as a whole being contaminated by the aggression which in

fanaticism or other forms of integrism acquires a dangerous direction. These eruptions of violence–favouring fusion, and confusion,
around one ephemeral god, that is,some sporting star or emblem-
atic team–prevent violence crystallizing around some clusive god
with truly bloodthirsty demands ... in any case it is less damaging
than slaughter on the field of honour in the name of the nation-
state' (Maffesoli 1990).

Some authors consider the phenomenon of ritually controlled
violence in sport and among supporters as a product of modern,
industrialized society. Starting from Herbert Spencer and his followers (for example Norbert Ellis), according to whom, by contrast with pre-modern, militaristic society, modern society is characterized by the constant transformation of open, uncontrolled
violence into regulated and controlled violence, P. Marsh came to
the conclusion that violence in sport appears in just that modern,
controlled, ritualized form, and that it is a matter of an illusion of
violence, of apparent violence. In the words of Krešimir Popović,
whose review of this 'Spencerite' approach to the problem of violence in sport: we adopt, 'In the behaviour of contemporary football supporters, Marsh sees at work a certain humanizing trend ...
He suggests that the ritualization of violence is beneficial' (Petrović
1990: 35).[20]

Our example reveals, however, that it was in fact one group of
hooligan fans that showed itself particularly susceptible to recruitment and re-qualification into a war unit, and that had no difficulty in exchanging the stadium and conflict with the supporters
of different teams for the battlefield and slaughter in the name of
the nation-state. The ritual, symbolic warfare of aggressive fans in
sports stadiums, which after all sometimes becomes bloody confrontation between groups of fans, does not appear to offer effective protection from the flaring up of violence 'in real life'.

Does this mean that war could be the real solution to the problem of hooligan violence? It does certainly create the possibility of
transfer, that is, it offers a good opportunity to channel that violence so that its target is no longer authority and established social
values, against which the aggression of hooligan fans is usually
directed in peacetime, but external enemies of the nation. The
regime in power acquires fighters, demonstrably fierce and fanatical, who, according to a widely held belief, are better able to carry
out the 'dirty' business of war than the regular army, and at the
same time it offers an opportunity for such hooligan-fan-fighters to
redeem their peacetime transgressions and, sacrificing themselves
for the Fatherland, to return to the fold and earn the love reserved

for the penitent prodigal son. This would mean that, thanks to war, the state redeems the aggression of hooligan-fans (and, on the same model, other antisocial groups) by giving them a chance to become socially useful, or, as it would be put today, to contribute to 'positive energy', the foundation of post-war life.

Or is it perhaps closer to the truth that war—particularly the kind of warfare in which the Red Star supporters stood out, becoming first 'Warriors' and then 'Tigers'—is an opportunity for the ultimate victory of the hooligan revolt, a continuation and conflagration of destruction directed, in the final analysis, against the fundamental values of civil society? For the hooligan subculture, as B. Perasović would say, by transforming the leaders of hooligan fans into national heroes, seeks to become the dominant culture of the social elite. History knows of several examples of the successful realization of such projects, the creators of which, whether on the left or the right, are usually called revolutionary. We are today on the way to granting history yet another fine example of the realization of the hooligan-revolutionary dream.

Notes

1 The examples quoted here are taken from the following sports papers: *Sport* (hereafter *S*), *Sportski žurnal* (Sports Journal, *SŽ*), *Tempo* (*Te*), *Partizanov vesnik* (Partizan Herald, *PV*) and *Zvezdina revija* (Star Review, *ZR*).

2 Translator's note: A reference to the monument to the Second-World-War Chetnik leader, Draža Mihailović, erected at the instigation of Vuk Drašković.

3 '*Slobo Srbine, Srbija je uz tebe!*'. On S. Milošević as a hero of folklore dating from the time of mass political rallies (1988–1989), see Čolović, 1993: 28–37 and 1994: 23–27.

4 Translator's note: The Orthodox way of making the sign of the cross.

5 Translator's note: The Mrnjavčević brothers are historical figures who have taken on a new life in the traditional oral epic songs. Both were killed at the Marica in 1371(?), at a battle that was decisive in the Ottoman advance into the Balkans.

6 Translator's note: Political leader and prime minister of Serbia between the wars.

7 The Serbian coat of arms consists of four Cyrillic letters 'c's ('s's) arranged in a cross.

8 A brief history of sports support and hooligan supporters' groups in Yugoslavia was written by the Split sociologist Dražen Lalić. Particularly interesting for us are the places where the author reconstructs the

changes which took place in the early and mid-1980s, when the behaviour of the supporters became ever more openly violent, 'losing its earlier symbolic character' and turning into serious mutual conflict and confrontation with the police, that is, ever since that kind of support 'virtually lost any connection with playing ball'. According to the author, that trend continued also at the end of the 1980s, with the difference that 'the basic model of excess became political' (1990: 124–129).

9 This couplet, a variation on the text of a famous hit by the Belgrade rock-group 'Electric Orgasm', was also taken up by supporters of Hajduk: The whole of Yugoslavia dances rock-and-roll, only a true Dalmatian supports Hajduk' (Ivo, 23, Hajduk supporter, Questionnaire, 14 May 1989).

10 Translator's note: Azem Vlasi, ethnic Albanian; in the late 1980s, member of the Presidency of the Central Committee of the League of Communists of Yugoslavia. Previously President of the Committee of the League of Communists of Kosovo.

11 Quoted from Perasović, 18–19.

12 *Srpsko jedinstvo*, the organ of the Serbian Unity Party (*Stranka srpskog jedinstva*), No. 1, November 1994.

13 Translator's note: Part of Croatia where there was a large Serbian minority.

14 After Slavonia, in the summer of 1992, Arkan and his 'Valiants' participated in the military campaign in Bosnia. Rade Leskovac, one of the commanders of the Serbian paramilitaries, remembers those days nostalgically: 'Always now in my dreams about what once was, I see a dusty village road and the Serbian flag carried by Ražnatović and his boys together with the Star supporters' flag. They always trumpeted their way through our villages, shouting one after another "Arkan, Arkan!"' (*Svet*, 6 September 1993).

15 The variant 'Tonight there's going to be trouble, tonight will be a madhouse, the hooligans are moving through the streets of Zagreb' is quoted in Perasović: 19.

16 Translator's note: Brana Ćosović, 'Ćosa', leader of a unit of specials.

17 For the 'capital of hatred', see Čolović, 1993: 93–98.

18 Translator's note: Tito's mausoleum in Belgrade.

19 This is one of the conclusions reached, among others, by the French ethnologist Christian Bromberger, studying the behaviour of supporters of Olympic (Marseilles) and Juventus (Turin) (1987: 13).

20 The ritual aspect of football and its support has been discussed in Serbia by, among others, Ivan Kovačević and Vera Marković. V. Marković quotes some interesting examples of the ritual behaviour of supporters at Belgrade stadiums, taken from observations in the spring of 1987: singing the club anthem, greeting the state flag, waving flags and passing them from hand to hand across the stands, greeting groups of supporters, throwing live hens onto the ground, kneeling and bowing (1990: 142–143).

POLITICAL MOBILIZATION

The 1974 Constitution as a Factor in the Collapse of Yugoslavia, or as a Sign of Decaying Totalitarianism

VOJIN DIMITRIJEVIĆ

The situation immediately preceding the adoption of the 1974 Constitution

The Constitution of the Socialist Federal Republic of Yugoslavia, promulgated on 21 February 1974, has often been quoted as one of the reasons for the civil war in that country, or at least as one of the contributing factors leading to Yugoslavia's disorderly and bloody dissolution. In fact, it has such a poor reputation, even among those who have never read it, that it is not surprising that no one claims to have been its author.

'Socialist' Yugoslavia was famous for its social and legislative experiments and for the frequency with which it changed its constitutions and its official name. After the 1946 Constitution, which was, together with the national emblem (something not subsequently changed), a rather unimaginative replica of the 'great' Stalin's Soviet Constitution of 1936, new constitutions, in a new 'self-management' vein, were adopted in 1953, 1963, and 1974. These constitutions were extensively amended in 1967, 1968, 1971, 1981, and 1988.[1]

The framework for the Yugoslav federation had already been determined by 1946, which means that the 1974 Constitution cannot be held responsible for it. However, there were developments immediately preceding the drafting of that document that were probably the main concern of its drafters and which could explain the specific features of this constitution.

In the 1960s there were strong indicators of a crisis in Yugoslavia, manifested through economic difficulties, social tension and sometimes overt nationalism. They were mostly beyond the comprehension of the Partisan ruling elite, but inspired the reform-minded younger generation in the Communist Party to look for new solutions. They essentially tried to modernize self-management (nobody dared mention capitalism) by giving it real substance in terms of some kind of market economy and by freeing it from the constraints of statism. In 1966, two important events took place: the political police was weakened and its conservative chief, Aleksandar Ranković, was removed by Tito himself[2]. At the same time, an ambitious economic reform was announced in order to do away with rigid central planning and most of the state and party tutelage.

The economic reform was not acceptable either to Tito's immediate conservative entourage or to Marxist intellectuals, who, in June 1968, inspired and led a curious revolt of students in Belgrade and in some other university centres, which was an imitation of similar leftist outbursts in Paris and elsewhere in that its thrust was against the 'red bourgeoisie' and in favour of a truly Marxist education and full egalitarianism. The students themselves were generally against the regime, but some of their most influential intellectual leaders were neo-Marxists, concerned with the purity of the doctrine and with social justice, and who perceived the new 'middle class' as the greatest danger to society. While his less clever lieutenants panicked, Tito calmed the crisis quite simply, by making a conciliatory and paternalistic speech praising the young generation and inviting students to go back to classrooms and libraries. Nevertheless, the regime immediately seized the opportunity to scrap the 'socially unjust' economic reform and to strengthen the police, with the excuse that the student revolt had been inspired by foreign agents.

It was at this point that the reformers within the party (no other channels were available at the time) shifted the centre of their activity to the more economically developed republics in the hope that the managerial elites there would be stronger in the absence of the federal dogmatists and their primitive supporters from the backward areas. In some ways, this was a resistance against the centre, essentially similar to that of Tito against the Comintern, but this time an association with nationalism was more inviting. This became quite clear in Croatia, where the reformist Communists, headed by Miko Tripalo, appealed to the population and almost immediately got unwanted and vociferous support from Croat nationalists, some of them invoking the memory of the puppet Nazi state in Croatia and the imagery of the Ustasha, which was extremely disquieting to the local Serbs.

At the same time, the Serbian Communist Party was in the hands of reformists gathered around Marko Nikezić, who were better at handling Serb nationalism, in spite of the vulgarity of the nationalist 'mass movement' in Croatia and the formidable challenge of rising Albanian nationalism in Kosovo[3]. In Slovenia, the reformists, led by Stane Kavčić, were most concerned with economic development, which they primarily envisaged within the boundaries of that republic. Nevertheless, they could not seriously have been accused of being nationalists.

After some hesitation Tito did away with all the reformist party leadership. The purge, initiated by a circular letter countersigned by Stane Dolanc[4], had the makings of a cultural revolution. Directors of the most successful enterprises were sacked (irrespective of self-management), the ablest editors and journalists were dismissed, university professors were removed (in clear violation of the laws), senior civil servants were demoted etc., to be replaced by docile and incompetent *apparatchiks*, obedient to the new federal and republican party leadership, which now included a considerable number of aged Partisans, recalled from retirement or semi-retired. Without satisfying the newly introduced criterion of 'moral-political fitness', even junior posts in the administration, schools and enterprises could not be held. Marxism was (for the first time!) introduced in the obligatory part of the curriculum in all schools at all levels. In many cases, but not as a rule, criminal prosecution followed.

It is very important to note that, at the time of the gestation of the 1974 Constitution, Communism (in its 'existing socialism' version) looked quite alive and well universally, and that the West was perceived as being in moral, economic and strategic disarray. As a number of randomly selected examples will demonstrate, this was the time of the end of the Cold War, which resulted in some grandiose arrangements with the Communists and in the increasing relevance of the non-aligned movement: In 1970, the Soviet Union consolidated its grip on Czechoslovakia, and West Germany normalized its relations with Poland by recognizing the Oder–Neisse border. In 1971 China was represented at the United Nations by the Beijing government, and the Soviet Union and India signed a treaty of friendship and mutual co-operation. In 1972 President Nixon visited China and the Soviet Union, and the two Germanies recognized one another. In 1973 the Western powers recognized East Germany, and West Germany received Brezhnev, as did the United States and France; West Germany normalized relations with Czechoslovakia, and after the Yom Kippur war oil-exporting Arab countries declared an oil embargo against the West. In 1974 Willy Brandt had to step down because of the presence of East German spies in his entourage, India exploded its first atomic bomb, and

President Nixon was forced to resign over the Watergate scandal.

In the light of these events the regime in Yugoslavia had no reason to believe that the prevailing interpretation of Communism was historically doomed, nor that there was any challenge to the Yugoslav government's comfortable international position as a tolerable socialist entity and one of the leaders of non-alignment.

The 1971 constitutional amendments and public debates

The 1974 Constitution cannot be studied in isolation from the preparatory work already undertaken in 1971 in the form of amendments to the 1963 Constitution. Draft amendments were formulated early in 1971 and, as usual, 'public debate' was held. This invitation was accepted in good faith in some intellectual quarters, with results reminiscent of Mao's 'thousand flowers' campaign. One of the liveliest discussions was held at the University of Belgrade and resulted in the arrest and sentencing of one professor of Law, the outright dismissal of several other members of the Faculty of Law, with still others being relieved of teaching assignments. The issue of the faculty journal containing the papers and a summary of the discussion was banned and destroyed [5].

The amendments were perceived by liberal critics as further complicating the political process with the result that decision making in state organs became all but impossible without the extra-constitutional intervention of the party and its guidance, which was again formally acknowledged. There had already been a tendency to atomize self-management so as to have it cover only trivial affairs, thus diverting the interest of the population from crucial political issues. Another clear tendency was to weaken the federation in favour of the republics by delegating more power to the legislatures of the latter and by preventing the federal Parliament from making a decision if it was vetoed by members from a federal unit. This, in addition to the quasi-independence of the autonomous provinces, was again an argument in favour of the further deterioration of the position of the Serbs, many of whom believed that the nationalists in Croatia had been compensated for their apparent defeat. A truly decisive shift was to be observed, generally, in the strengthening of the party leadership in the republics and their transformation into semi-independent feuds of the republican Communist elite.

The 1974 Constitution as Law

After another series of empty public debates the new constitution was promulgated on 21 February 1974. It was an unusual, enormously long (406 articles), verbose and confused text, leaving the reader with the inescapable impression that its purpose was rather to hide than to reveal. Nevertheless, it was praised as original and non-legalistic by apologists in Yugoslavia, as well as by some observers abroad (see, e.g., J. Djordjević 1984: 12; Zečević 1978: 5; Flanz 1986: 6). Mystification was intensified by new jargon which was difficult to comprehend in the original Yugoslav versions, and almost impossible to translate.[6] The old dogmatic Communist tendency to rename in order to change here reached new heights.[7]

An excursion through the new terms is probably the least tedious way of introducing this constitution.

The delegation system

'Delegate' was one such new term, not only to indicate parliamentary deputies but also members of intermediary 'delegations' that elected them after being themselves elected by inferior delegations. This concealed a system of multiple indirect elections, where the population had the chance to choose only at the lowest possible level, whereas the delegates had a fully bound mandate and were easily replaceable if they did not follow the instructions of the delegations (which, naturally, were convened only when the party found it opportune). In its jargon, 'delegates were responsible to their delegational basis'. Federal decision making was thus made even more remote than in the past when there was at least an illusion that elections presenting one candidate offered a real choice and that the deputy was answerable to his or her electorate. At the microscopic local level, voters were unfamiliar with the names of the proposed candidates for the basic delegations, so that the symbolic presence of slightly more candidates was meaningless. This charade was called the 'delegation system' and was praised as a major departure from 'bourgeois parliamentariansm' towards direct democracy (Lovrić 1974: 3).

The inherent inequality of citizens

The population was divided into the 'working class', 'working people' and 'citizens'. The 'working class' was not clearly defined but it was there to indicate the source of power (e.g. Art. 1), in accordance with Marxist theory. 'Working people' were, for all practical purposes, men and women employed in state ('socially owned') enterprises and institutions. They were also 'citizens', but others were 'citizens' only, and could not fully benefit from the electoral process as being outside 'self-managing organizations and communities', which, through their particular delegations, sent delegates to the federal Parliament. Ordinary citizens were theoretically able to act, together with 'working people', in 'socio-political communities', which was the new name given to territorial units, from the federation to the commune. Their real participation, however, was in 'local communities' of their immediate neighbourhood, where their electoral powers ended with the selection of a 'delegation'. Only the 'working people' had the right to join 'socio-political organizations'. Such organizations masqueraded as belonging to civil society but were firmly controlled by federal statute, which made their creation and activity dependant on the approval of the largest of them all, the Socialist Alliance of the Working People (a successor to the National Front, without even token participation of any political party but the Communists, who were the guiding force in the Alliance and formally appointed members of the Alliance's leading bodies).[8]

The mystique of self-management

The Constitution devoted most of its provisions to self-management in the public sector, which was designated as 'associated labour' and included all activities performed with 'socially owned' (i.e. state) resources. The whole structure was atomized to the extreme. Self-management became fully universal and covered non-economic activities, such as the state administration, schools and theatres. Former enterprises or institutions became 'organizations of associated labour' and were divided into several 'basic organizations of associated labour', which were supposed to be rounded technological units, although in the frenzy of the implementation of the Constitution became ridiculously minute and artificial, such as, for example, schools divided along the lines of classes or groups of subjects, typists representing a separate basic unit from accountancy etc. 'Organizations of associated labour' could then further associate in 'composite associations of associated labour' (e.g. railways) or co-operate with individuals in 'contractual organizations of associated labour'. The whole self-management system was protected by 'social attorneys of self-management' and 'self-management courts'.

A conscious effort was made to dislodge the legislative functions from the parliaments and transfer them to self-managing bodies, which, instead of laws, created 'self-managing agreements', 'social compacts' and 'inter-republic compacts'.

The 'classic' political provisions of the Constitution

In contrast to the self-managing parts of the Constitution, which account for most of its length and which were augmented in 1976 by the still longer accompanying Law on Associated Labour (671 articles!)[9], classical constitutional matters were dealt with using less jargon and appeared to allow for a better insight into compromises made in the party leadership. While the ideas of Kardelj and his associates about the ramifications of integral self-management were not opposed by anyone in the party, either because they were irrelevant to the exercise of real power, or too difficult to follow, or appeared as attractively but innocuously learned and original departures from 'bourgeois parliamentarianism', articles relating to the structure of the federation, its competencies and relevant decision making were easier to understand and became increasingly important as it became obvious that the republican parties were gaining more independence and that their arrangements should be protected from the intervention of a federal parliament, which could not be relied on to rubber-stamp them unless the parliament was not an exact replica of the relationships within the League of Communists. It is therefore certain that the important (closed) debate in the supreme quarters of the League was about these matters, and that it was there that some divergence of opinion emerged, denounced as 'unacceptable' by Mijalko Todorović, who introduced the draft as president of the Constitutional Commission, but who failed to identify the relevant controversies (Todorović 1974)[10].

The principal message was that, in spite of class oratory, the federal state was based on national arrangement, where even nations not originally considered to be the 'titular nations' of Yugoslavia came to play a full role. The Slavic Moslems, principally inhabiting Bosnia-Hercegovina, had been promoted into a fully fledged Yugoslav people under a religious name in 1971, which was not only a misnomer for the non-religious majority among them, but proved later to have dreadful consequences. Others, like the most numerous Albanians and Hungarians, obtained a better status under another new euphemism for national minorities, *narodnost*, meaningless in Serbo-Croat and poorly translated into English as 'nationality'[11].

> Article 1 defined the Socialist Federal Republic of Yugoslavia as: '... a federal state having the form of a state community of voluntarily united nations and their Socialist Republics, and of the Socialist Autonomous Provinces of Vojvodina and Kosovo, which are constituent parts of the Socialist Republic of Serbia, based on the power of, and self-management by, the working class and all working people; it is at the same time a socialist self-management democratic community of working people and citizens and of nations and nationalities, having equal rights.'

Self-determination and secession

In Article 3 the republics were referred to as states, based on the 'sovereignty of the people' and '... communities of the working people and citizens, and of nations and nationalities having equal rights'.

This was a clear indication of a drift to a confederate structure of the Yugoslav federation. The republics were states, but the federation was a 'state community', in the context of which, unlike the republics, the term 'sovereignty' was not used.

All this was accompanied by an ominous statement, in the Introductory Part of the Constitution:

> The nations of Yugoslavia, proceeding from the right of every nation to self-determination, including the right to secession, on the basis of their will freely expressed in the common struggle of all nations and nationalities in the National Liberation War and Socialist Revolution, and in conformity with their historic aspirations, aware that further consolidation of their brotherhood and unity is in the common interest, have, together with the nationalities with which they live, united in a federal republic of free and equal nations and nationalities and founded a socialist federal community of working people – the Socialist Federal Republic of Yugoslavia ... (Basic Principles, I)

Without referring to legalistic squabbles as to whether the rights to self-determination and secession were or were not 'consummated' by the creation of Yugoslavia or by the adoption of this or some other constitution, it should be noted that not only self-determination and secession were legitimized in this, albeit inoperative, part of the Constitution, but that it remained unclear whether the subjects of this right were ethnic nations or peoples in the sense of inhabitants of a state or territory[12]. Furthermore, it was also unclear whether it applied also to 'nationalities' (minorities). The procedure by which these rights were to materialize was not regulated by the Constitution, nor anywhere else. After 1989 this was a complicating factor of extreme importance. The remaining federal authorities tried to declare the decision to secede, made by some republics, unconstitutional, but the latter opposed it with the argument that Yugoslavia was dissolving[13]. The seceding republics claimed, however, all the territory which had been theirs as constituent parts of Yugoslavia, thus indicating in this respect that they believed 'people' to be understood in the territorial sense. This was generally opposed by the Serbs, who maintained that the right to self-determination belonged to ethnic nations, encompassing Serbs in Croatia and Bosnia-Hercegovina[14]. The mention of 'nationalities' was used by some Albanians in Kosovo to support claims for a separate republic, an independent state, or even unification with Albania. The vagueness and incompleteness of the Constitution made the process of secession (or dissolution) even more disorderly, to say the least.

Autonomous provinces and minorities

The indication that the autonomous provinces were parts of Serbia was meant to appease some Serbian Communists, as was the definition, contained in Article 4, of the autonomous provinces not as states, but as 'socio-political communities'. However, this could not conceal the fact that the autonomous provinces were, for all practical purposes, promoted to the full status of federal units. According to the same article, this was the place where nations and nationalities realized their sovereign rights. Furthermore, the Constitution gave a clear indication of the autonomous provinces' participation in federal affairs and their own affairs, while their role within Serbia was envisaged as facultative participation in its state affairs without mentioning their subordination to the organs of the whole republic. In Article 3 the autonomous provinces were listed, together with the republics, as constituent parts of Yugoslavia. According to the widely accepted designation, invented by the masters of the jargon, the autonomous provinces were 'elements of the federation' (Fira, 1974: 4).

Parity in the federation

The already existing tendency toward confederation was cemented in the provisions of the 1974 Constitution relating to the set-up of the organs of the federation and of decision making within them, and the hierarchy of legislative acts. As in most federations, the federal Parliament (the Assembly of SFRY) was bicameral. The chamber representing federal units (Chamber of Republics and Provinces) was composed, as usual in federate states, of an equal number (12) of 'delegates' of all republics, elected by their respective assemblies, with the important addition that the autonomous provinces would also be represented, although by a smaller number of representatives (8) (Art. 292). The 'lower' chamber (Federal Chamber), which, in federations, normally reflects the size of the populations of the federal units, was constituted according to the same principle: it was to be composed of an equal number (30) of 'delegates' from each republic and of twenty representatives from each autonomous province. They were not directly elected by the population, but were selected as a result of the previously mentioned cumbersome 'delegation' system, the nominations being controlled by the Socialist Alliance of the Working People (i.e. the local League of Communists) (Art. 291). This arrangement was criticized both by liberals, who objected to discrimination against more populous federal units, and by most Serbs, who found it to be detrimental to Serbia, as a state in the federation, and to Serbs, the most numerous nation. Fear of Serb domination, traditionally shared by Communists and non-Serb nationalists, was undoubtedly the principal concern[15].

Consensus and paralysis in the federal Parliament

The essentially unequal composition of the Federal Chamber had only symbolic significance. The real and fatal flaw of the Constitution was that it prevented any decisions from being adopted if opposed by one federal unit (including the autonomous provinces). The size of its 'delegation' was irrelevant in this respect. To begin with, the Chamber of Republics and Provinces was unable to conduct business unless all republican and provincial 'delegations', as well as the majority of delegates, were present (Art. 295), which enabled one delegation formally to paralyse the Chamber. Furthermore, highly important statutes and other decisions, such as the adoption of social plans, the regulation of the monetary system and the total volume of budgetary expenditure, the ratification of international treaties and even of the Chamber's own rules of procedure, could be adopted by that Chamber only after it had ensured the 'adjustment of stands' of the assemblies of the republics and autonomous provinces (Art. 286), which not only meant long delays but also that, in such cases, the vote in the Chamber was by delegation rather than by individual members. This meant that each delegation, including the smaller ones of autonomous provinces, could prevent a decision from being made (Art. 295). This was a step further from the 'distributed majority' which had been introduced by the 1971 amendments, and which had required majorities *within* each delegation (Dimitrijević 1971). Consequently, in this house of eighty-eight members, the only majority possible was eight to none! The grip of the republican and provincial party elites was thus made even stronger: by instructing the whole delegation they destroyed the individuality of the 'delegates' and were fully insured against federalist and liberal mavericks or supra-republican alliances.

The result was that in the Chamber of Republics and Provinces there was gradually less and less deliberation. The 'delegates' waited in the corridors or in the quasi ex-territorial premises of their delegations for the republican and provincial powers to send in their agreements and, if there was no objection, proceeded to confirm them by delegational vote. Debate took place only if some of the less rigid republican or provincial authorities had given conditional consent to a decision, allowing the same liberty to its delegation to come to a compromise with others. Even to a casual visitor to the Parliament it was abundantly clear that things happened elsewhere.

In Part IV, Chapter I, 3 the 1974 Constitution provided certain rules relating to the possibility of impasses caused by a lack of consensus among the republics and provinces. These rules involved new consultations with the federal units, whereupon the Federal Executive Council (the government) could propose to the Presidency to pass a decree on temporary measures which had to be confirmed by the Chamber of Republics and Provinces, this time by a two-thirds majority of all 'delegates' (Arts. 301 and 302). If such a majority could not be achieved, a simple majority was sufficient for the Presidency itself to adopt a temporary measure, pending the final approval of the statute (Art. 302). Given the composition of the Presidency[16] any dominance by a single nation was excluded.

The Chamber of Republics and Provinces was the more important house of the Parliament and became increasingly so with time.

Most matters of relevance were either decided by it, or with its consent (Arts. 286 and 288). To be sure, the Federal Chamber had a number of formal competencies that appeared important, such as its right to adopt amendments to the federal constitution, to decide on alterations to the (external) boundaries of Yugoslavia, to adopt the federal budget or to decide on war and peace. Its other assignments were either outright pomposity, such as to 'lay down the foundations of internal and foreign policy' or to 'formulate the policy of enforcement of federal statutes or other regulations enacted by it', or were trivial items such as to 'discuss the reports, opinions and proposals of the federal social attorney of self-management' (Art. 285). Even then,

> if a bill, draft regulation or draft enactment or any other issue concerning the general issues of a Republic or Autonomous Province, or *the equality of the nations and nationalities* is on the agenda of the Federal Chamber, and if so requested by the majority of delegates from one Republic or Autonomous Province, resort shall be made to a special procedure to consider and adopt such a bill, draft enactment or issue ... (Art. 294, italics added)

This special procedure was laid down by the rules of procedure and again involved seeking consensus from powers in the republics and provinces. Thus each federal unit or 'element of the Federation' was at liberty to claim that the issue on the agenda was nationally sensitive and again reduce the lower chamber to a forum for negotiation of practically sovereign states. In the Federal Chamber, consisting of 220 deputies, eleven votes (the majority of the delegates from an autonomous province) were sufficient for that purpose. Nobody had any doubts as to whether the majority of the delegates of one republic or province (there were no formal 'delegations', as in the other house) would in fact present the views and attitudes of their mentors who, it should again be stressed, until 1990 belonged to the politburos and central committees of the only existing political parties, that is, the relevant leagues of Communists.

In this light, the whole controversy about the number of deputies was irrelevant, since the true members of both chambers of the Federal Assembly were republican and provincial delegations, each of them, irrespective of its size, able to obstruct work or prevent a decision from being taken. On the other hand, there was no chance for any majority to play a meaningful role: even a larger number of delegations could not outvote a minority. It was even less likely that this could be achieved by a majority of individual 'delegates', who by definition were not independent but fully controlled either by their assemblies or by their 'delegation base' (Arts. 291 and 296). The only exception was with respect to temporary measures, where a two-thirds majority, or even a simple majority, could play a role, but this was only a theoretical possibility dependant on the attitude of the Presidency, which was again constituted on the basis of strict parity.

The Presidency as a negotiating place of constituent states (parties)

There were in fact two versions of the Presidency incorporated in the 1974 Constitution. One was with Tito, the other without him. It was fairly obvious that the position of president of the Republic was created only for Tito who was to be elected 'for an unlimited term of office' (Art. 333)[17] Given the whole logic of the Constitution, it was inconceivable for a significant federal office to be exercised by an individual, there being no 'delegate', or even person, not belonging to a federal unit. People who declared themselves as 'Yugoslavs' were not represented anywhere as a group, although, in 1981 they constituted some 6 per cent of the whole population[18]. The only trusted Yugoslav was Tito, in spite of his Croat and Slovene ethnic origins. While the president of the Republic was there, he was at the same time president of the Presidency (Art. 335). Curiously enough, there was no provision making him a member of that body: in the case of Tito that problem was solved by the fact that the president of the League of Communists of Yugoslavia was *ex officio* a member of the state Presidency (Art. 321) and this was, of course, Josip Broz Tito. Otherwise, the Presidency was equipped to act without the president of the Republic, and this is the only instance in which the Constitution implied that Tito was mortal and that he could not be replaced by anyone. In fact, the relevant article (321) determined the composition of the Presidency without mentioning the president: in addition to the president of the League of Communists, it consisted of one member from each republic and autonomous province, elected by the respective assemblies. After Tito's death Article 321 was amended to accommodate the abolition of the position of the president of the Party. Amendment IV of 1981 stipulated that the League of Communists would be represented by the president of its organ 'specified by the by-laws of the League ...'. This was a unique case of a constitution of a state explicitly depending on the statutes of a supposedly non-governmental organization, and brought Yugoslavia closer to the African model of the one-party state—with the important difference that, in Africa, the party was wider than the state.

Members of the Presidency were not independent. They, as everyone else in the organs of the Federation, were 'delegates' of the federal units. This was clear from Article 324, which implied a very easy way for the assemblies of the federal units to remove 'their' representatives from the Presidency, as well as from the provision, contained in the same article, that members of the Presidency would, in case of incapacity, be deputized by the presidents of the collective heads (presidencies) of the republics or autonomous provinces. On the other hand, there was no control by the organs of the Federation over the composition of the Presidency. Its members could not be impeached in any manner. This became fully clear at the height of the crisis, when the Serbian-controlled group of members of that body tried unsuccessfully to prevent a new member, Stipe Messy, delegated by the non-Communist and nationalist majority in the Assembly of Croatia, from becoming its chairman according to annual rotation. Members of that body rotated as chairman not on the basis of any personal criteria but, as in the Security Council, depending on the alphabetical order of the republics and provinces (Art. 327 in conjunction with the Rules of Procedure of the Presidency of 1975[19]).

In the context of the Presidency there was not even token differentiation within the republics and the autonomous provinces: each had one full member, with automatic entitlement to be chairman. This went further in making Serbia equal with the autonomous provinces, nominally its constituent parts. Sinan Hasani, a member of the Albanian minority, representing Kosovo in the Presidency, thus acted as its chairman from 1986 to 1987, a phenomenon experienced in already nationally agitated Serbia as humiliation.

An autonomous but ineffective executive: the Federal Executive Council (government)

The only federal organ which was not based on strict parity was the government, that is, the Federal Executive Council. Its president, elected jointly by both chambers of the Federal Assembly, was, of necessity, an individual from a federal unit and he was under the obligation to observe 'the principle of equal representation of the republics and corresponding representation of the autonomous provinces' in.nominating members of the Council, who had to be approved by the Assembly (Art. 348). For a long period, the candidate for president of the Council had been determined by the top of the hierarchy of the federal League of Communists and was known long before the indirect elections for the Federal Assembly even started. As a rule, the new 'prime minister' was not from the same republic as the preceding one, but the rotation was not rigid as in other bodies and was free of ethnic considerations[20]. After the adoption of the 1974 Constitution the presidents of the Federal Executive Council were Džemal Bijedić, a Moslem from Bosnia-Hercegovina; Veselin Djuranović, a Montenegrin; Milka Planinc, a Croat from Croatia; Branko Mikulić, a Croat from Bosnia-Hercegovina; and Ante Marković, a Croat from Croatia.

The Federal Executive Council was heavily constrained by other federal bodies and the republics and autonomous provinces (Arts. 352–362), as witnessed by its frequent failure, especially in the last years of the existence of Yugoslavia, to have its draft statutes adopted by the Assembly or to effect meaningful change. Constitutional limitations were compounded by the unwritten rule of every Communist system whereby it is the task of the government to deal predominantly with the economy, leaving essential political matters, including foreign policy, to the party or the head of state. Nevertheless, there were some opportunities for initiative and action which, paradoxically, increased with the intensification of inter-republic and inter-nation squabbling. The last 'prime minister', assisted by a number of federally minded colleagues in his cabinet, was probably the most enterprising: mainly through government decrees an important economic reform was successfully introduced in 1989. He was soon to realize that he had no true political backing in the existing set-up: his unsuccessful attempts to create an independent political basis among the population do not belong to constitutional history, except as a reminder that federal units (Serbia and Slovenia, in the first place) refused to back a constitutional amendment, proposed by the Federal Executive Council and adopted by the existing Assembly on 8 October 1990, which would have permitted direct elections to the Federal Chamber of the Federal Assembly[21].

The allegedly crucial question: which nation was the most disadvantaged?

There is a general impression that it was the Serbs who were most frustrated by the symmetrical consensual set-up described above. This belief is based on the prevailing assumption that the Serbs identified themselves with the federal state in order to dominate it, as they did before 1941, and is due to vociferous complaints by the Serb nationalist elite. Closer scrutiny of the legal terms of the 1974 Constitution reveal that, *per se*, it further weakened the Federation through its confederate elements, but that it was not necessarily disadvantageous to the Serbs under all circumstances. The position of the Serbs rather depended on the play of political forces which gave substance to constitutional provisions. The best example was the partition of the Serb people into several federal units with the over-representation of the autonomous provinces. In the original Titoist political climate, which prevailed for quite some time after Tito's death, this in fact meant that only Serbia proper would be represented by 'true' Serbs; Montenegro would be represented by those who believed themselves to be more Montenegrin than Serb; Kosovo by the Albanian majority; and Vojvodina, if not by Hungarians or members of another minority, by an 'autonomist' Serb of dubious nationality[22].

From another perspective, the proliferation of 'Serb' federal units offered a chance to the Serbs, or to the leagues of Communists dominated by them, to appear in the organs of the Federation under various hats. This opportunity was in fact seized by the populists around Slobodan Milošević, who, in the wake of their 'anti-bureaucratic revolution' deposed the leadership of the leagues of Communists in Montenegro, Vojvodina and Kosovo, and replaced them with persons loyal to the League of Communists of Serbia and its paramount leader (Pešić 1995: 49). This had happened before political pluralism was gradually introduced in 1990 and, as a matter of course, resulted in changes in the supreme state organs of Montenegro and the autonomous provinces and in the replacement of their representatives in federal organs. At the peak of the crisis, the regime of Milošević thus controlled 4 out of 8 members of the federal Presidency, 100 deputies in the 220 member Federal Chamber, and 40 'delegates' in the 88-member Chamber of Republics and Provinces (4 our of 8 delegations).

This was not sufficient for a majority, but it resulted in deadlock. Because of the built-in consensual decision making, even a majority would not be sufficient for any kind of domination. Nevertheless, this was another reason, or excuse, for the (now mostly non-Communist) regimes in Croatia and Slovenia to opt out of the Federation, after which other non-Serb entities reluctantly followed suit, not from fear of Serb constitutional domination, but disturbed by the fierce nationalist rhetoric of the recycled dogmatic Communists who came to represent Serbia and the Serbs.

The constitutional arrangement in Serbia

None of what has been said above denies the fact that Serbia, according to its own constitution, adopted in accordance with the federal constitution, was not itself in an abnormal constitutional situation. Suffice it to say that Serbia proper ('Serbia outside the autonomous provinces'[23]) had no organs of its own but was governed by the all-Serbian Assembly, Presidency and Executive Council and Court, where both autonomous provinces were guaranteed influential representation. These organs had no jurisdiction in the autonomous provinces, which had their own assemblies, presidencies and governments and supreme courts. In some important matters, such as social planning, defence and education, legislation was possible only on the basis of the consensus of the supposedly Serbian legislature and the legislatures of the autonomous provinces, with the result that some indispensable Serbian statutes were not enacted until the very end of Yugoslavia or, to be more precise, until the League of Communists of Serbia under the new populist leadership removed the party elite in the provinces and then proceeded to abolish their autonomy by unilateral acts of the all-Serbian legislature, which they now controlled.

Liberal and dogmatic 'Yugoslavism': the government and the army

Only the Federal Executive Council remained basically unchanged, creating the illusion that the crisis could be overcome by the actions of this only remaining truly Yugoslav body. It soon became clear that the government was powerless without the loyalty of the army. However, the Yugoslav People's Army (JNA) was never able to forget its late commander-in-chief, and was never comfortable with his replacement by a collective Presidency, which after 1990 came to include non-Communists. The 'technocratic' reformers in the Federal Executive Council, bent on privatization and pluralism, appeared utterly unreliable. The military used the constitutional stalemate to elevate its 'Staff of the Supreme Command', a body recognized neither by the constitution nor by law, to a position whereby it applied its own criteria as to the trustworthiness and 'political correctness' of individual members of the Presidency and the Federal Executive Council (Kadijević 1993: 6, 109). In fact, this was a natural attempt by the army to make the formal constitution correspond to the reality of the party state. In the real centres of power the army had been the 'ninth federal unit': its personnel was organized within a separate system of the League of Communists, not submitted to any republican party but corresponding directly with the federal League, in the organs of which the organization of the League within the JNA had its independent representation. The army elite eventually joined Milošević and his associates, not because, as has often been suggested, the majority of the officer corps were Serbs and Montenegrins, but for reasons of ideological closeness. The leading generals in 1990 to 1992 were later retired by the now openly nationalist authorities of the new Federal Republic of Yugoslavia. None of them continued to be active as declared Serb nationalists, while most deplored the fall of Communism, in the USSR and elsewhere. Had the Communist party prevailed in some other republic and not in Serbia, it is quite conceivable that many of them would have led the army in another direction[24].

The hierarchy of federal and state norms

Inherent confederalism was to be observed in the 1974 Constitution in many other areas, the most important of them being the hierarchy of federal and republican (provincial) norms. There was an interesting message to be gleaned from the wording of the Constitution, insofar as Article 207 states that the acts of the federal authorities had to be 'in conformity' with the federal constitution and federal statutes, which applied also to 'socio-political communities' and 'organizations of associated labour' (Art. 206), but not to constitutions and other acts of the republics and provinces which should only 'not be contrary' to the federal constitution and statutes (Arts. 206 and 207). This distinction had wide implications since it made it possible to argue about the extent to which departure from federal norms without crossing the threshold of 'contrariness' was tolerable.

However, even if a republican or provincial statute was contrary to the federal law, the inferior, republican statute had to be temporarily applied pending a decision by the constitutional court (Art. 207). According to Article 384, in such cases the Federal Constitutional Court could rule that the inferior statute was contrary to the federal one, but this ruling was without immediate effect: it had to be submitted to the relevant assembly, which had up to one year to remove what was contradictory in the statute. Failing this, the Constitutional Court had to declare that the contested statute ceased to be valid.

Another growing problem was related to the administrative action necessary for implementing federal statutes (Kambovski 1991: 3). Except in the limited field of the competencies of the federal administration, this was to be done by the administrations of the federal units, which frequently failed to act. The problem gained such proportions that in 1990 a constitutional amendment was introduced to deal with such cases: the Federal Executive Council was to be empowered to undertake any necessary action, after the republican or provincial executive had been alerted but had again failed to act. The amendment was not approved by the federal units[25].

The misery of human rights

Republics and autonomous provinces thus became very powerful states. If it was not the Federation, what was their counterweight? For the drafters of the Constitution, this was the vague experiment with decentralized 'associated labour'. Their Marxist–Leninist upbringing forbade them from looking toward the individual and his or her rights. Chapter III of the Constitution, devoted to 'the freedoms, rights and duties of the citizen', mostly repeated the unsatisfactory provisions of the 1963 Constitution, together with its inherent repugnance towards 'bourgeois individualism', reflected in the incessant reminders of duties, solidarity, socialist community etc., and in the unusual order of the rights, with economic rights close to self-management at the top. The only innovation was the 'inalienable right to self-management', which was defined in terms of the new *langue de bois*:

> [It] enables each individual to decide on his personal and common interests in an organization of associated labour, local community, self-managing community of interest or other self-managing organization or community and socio-political community, and in all other forms of their self-management integration and mutual linkage.
> Each individual shall be responsible for self-management decision making and the implementation of decisions. (Art. 155)

Even this inspired vagueness had to be coupled with a 'socialist' duty:

> Everyone shall be bound conscientiously and in the interest of socialist society based on self-management to exercise self-management, public and other social functions vested in him. (Art. 158)

As in other 'socialist' constitutions, traditional human rights were granted only grudgingly and were generally submitted to a restrictive socialist *ordre public* (Dimitrijević 1990: 73). Thus, for instance, freedom of the press, freedom of public expression, of association, of speech, of gathering and of public assembly were lumped together in a short sentence in Article 167, coupled immediately with the duty of the media 'to inform the public truthfully and objectively' (Art. 168), which was then the 'constitutional basis' of criminal law and practice prosecuting 'false information', 'the disquieting of the public', and, most famous of all, 'inimical propaganda'[26]. All rights listed in the Constitution were, in spite of the use of the word, only conditionally 'guaranteed' and were made wholly dependent on simple statutes and haunted by the typically 'socialist' obsession with the prevention of the 'abuse' of human rights (e.g. Art. 203).

The most disquieting feature of this part of the Constitution was what it failed to provide, in spite of the fact that in 1974, Yugoslavia was a party to both International Covenants on Human Rights and an impressive number of other international treaties (Dimitrijević 1987). The best testimony to what was missing and incomplete in the 1974 Constitution's 'bill of rights' was to be found in the draft Amendment LX, adopted by the Federal Assembly in October 1990 but never ratified by the republics and provinces. Its drafters found it necessary to suggest improvements to the principle of non-discrimination (which conspicuously allowed for discrimination on the basis of political opinion), to ban torture, to safeguard privacy and protect personal data, fully to guarantee the freedom of conscience and religion, to establish the right to organize in political parties, to safeguard trade union rights, including the right to strike and the right to collective bargaining and to secure a fair income from work for 'everyone', not only for 'working people'.[27]

Conclusion: the 1974 Constitution as a piece of constitution-making

If the 1974 Constitution were to be taken seriously as a transparent normative act reflecting reality and being truly and conscientiously implemented and implementable, the following observations would have to be made about its main characteristics:

1) it further weakened the Federation by paralysing the decision-making process and removing real authority from federal decisions;

2) it promoted the federal units into sovereign states and the only real centres of power: the Federation was run by their consensus;

3) in the form of autonomous provinces, it tolerated a duality of two federal units, which at the same time were constituent parts of another federal unit (equal and subordinate);

4) as a check on state power, concentrated in the federal units, it attempted to create a parallel social system of autonomous self-management, atomized and incomprehensible, and as such unable to influence political decision making;

5) it created an artificial division of the population into 'working people' and 'citizens' and deprived all of them of the right to vote, except at the lowest level of government and 'self-management';

6) it totally neglected the individual by denying and restricting his or her rights and allowing him or her to act only within the framework of a collectivity, as a part of it, and fully controlled by it;

7) it did not leave room for political pluralism[28] by preventing the creation of any political organization which was not a 'socio-political organization' controlled by the League of Communists, the leading role of which, together with its transmitter, the Socialist Alliance, was constitutionally recognized;

8) in addition to its inherently illiberal spirit, manifested in some of the previously mentioned features, it was openly undemocratic in that it allowed political discrimination and assured the League of Communists the right to nominate all candidates for office and to appoint its own representatives as members of the Federal Assembly and Presidency;

9) it included provision for a president-for-life, applicable only to one person;

10) in the sensitive field of inter-nation relationships, it provided for the right to self-determination and secession without, however, envisaging the corresponding procedures;

11) it made constitutional changes impossible, except by some kind of inter-nation (confederate) agreement.

A true conclusion: the 1974 Constitution as a monument to pseudo-ideology, false legitimacy and bombastic mediocrity

To rest on the above conclusions would be highly unrealistic and naive and would fail to make the most important point, namely, that the 1974 SFRY Constitution was an ornamental piece of rhetoric and a justification for dictatorial (largely totalitarian) rule, and that its main deficiency, which became quite apparent in the late 1980s, was that it was not meant as a supreme legal and political text, nor was it intended to be seriously put into practice in the political sphere, and that it was impossible to implement in other fields.

In spite of its official descriptions Yugoslavia has, in fact, never been a true federation. Even with the 1974 Constitution it was, until the death of Tito, a unitary state governed by its centralized Communist Party. Top party officials, and above all Tito, were able to make the most important decisions and enforce them, regardless of the statutes of the party, not to speak of the constitution. Party members were submitted to the strict discipline of 'democratic centralism' and were removable by the decision of the superior party organs, a decision which was obeyed even if it violated the constitution and laws and which could always take the shape of 'resignation'. This is not to say that the party itself was devoid of infighting and an internal struggle for position (and for the ear of the supreme leader), but this took place according to the murky rules of the game, which had nothing to do with the constitution and laws.

The 1974 Constitution came at a moment when the party structures, cadres and morale had started to decay owing to the prolonged possession of absolute power. The majority of members and functionaries were opportunist careerists who gradually forgot the Marxist origin of their philosophy and, faced with the lack of enthusiasm in the population, started to seek for sources of support and legitimacy which for them were more comprehensible and natural. By necessity, these sources were parochial and provincial, with a tendency to become nationalist. This was to be countered by the largely artificial constructions of integral self-management, but they were not supportive of any broader unity, relying as they did on minuscule 'basic associations of associated labour' which could not stand up to the meddling of party committees and secretaries, from the municipal to the highest levels.

With respect to its handling of ethnic matters, the political system in Yugoslavia, behind its constitutional *façade*, was that of consociationalism, to use the term employed by McGarry and O'Leary (1993: 35). However, as correctly observed by Schöpflin, 'consociational arrangements were never formalized, and with the demise of the party there were no institutional mechanisms to establish democratic consociationalism' (Schöpflin 1993: 182). The 1974 Constitution, as well as all the others, failed to provide such mechanisms, even as a fall-back position.

When Tito disappeared, both as commander and arbitrator, the system continued to function for an amazingly long time: there was even a morbid pretence that he was still alive. Inertia was strong enough to overshadow serious economic problems (when the bill for the borrowed life of luxury in the 1970s had to be footed) and ethnic unrest (especially in Kosovo). With the departure of the few stronger Partisan personalities[29] the party was governed by conservative non-entities who had been recalled by Tito from retirement, in conjunction with the obedient apparatchiks who had replaced the liberals and technocrats ten years earlier and who had been promoted on the basis of the criteria of obedience and faithful repetition of current slogans. This 'negative' selection produced power hungry but insecure personalities, who, in search of legitimization, became the first converts to populist nationalism, and in fact its leaders (Denić 1990: XV). Even the politically and administratively gifted party cadres, especially if they were young, realized then that they had no future outside the nationalist context.

One can only speculate as to the extent to which the 1974 Constitution was responsible for the collapse of the federal state and the non-viability of the democratic option. The safest answer is that it could not save something that did not exist. The Constitution itself had made it possible for the real government to change directly from a unitary party state to a confederation of party states. As for democracy, the 1974 Constitution did not contain any democratic ingredient, neither did it pay any respect to human rights, which meant that most of the successor states started life with problematic human rights law and still more problematic human rights practice.

The 1974 Constitution was a reflection of its time. Given the internal and international situation and the background of its drafters, it could not have been different. These factors combined to produce a genre of constitutional experts, political scientists and jurists who do not seem to have made any effort to provide constitutional solutions for real political difficulties, to secure alternative decision making in the case of the failure of the party system and thus not to save Yugoslavia if it was not wanted, but to increase the chances for a reasonable transition into explicitly confederate arrangements and the peaceful dissolution or separation of the constituent units. For the creators of the 1974 Constitution, real difficulties were not even a theoretical worst case scenario: they were simply unthinkable. In their arrogance, the constitution makers were whistling in the oblivion of self-management.

Notes

1 It is to be noted that the main architect of all constitutions and amendments adopted until his death was Edvard Kardelj, a close associate of Tito and the chief ideologist of the Communist Party (later League) of Yugoslavia. He was always at hand to justify 'scientifically' changes in Tito's policies and has therefore been compared to an ideological tailor (Schöpflin: 186, 189). Kardelj was an ethnic Slovene. While I dislike referring to the ethnicity of former Yugoslav political actors, I find it necessary to do so in view of the deplorable tendency of many writers on Yugoslavia to explain the motivations of the former predominantly by their national origin. I shall therefore indicate ethnicity whenever it can be established without doubt.

2 Tito acted principally for personal reasons and not in order to liberalize the system. Ranković was a Serb and for some Serbs his deposition (including criminal charges, later dropped by Tito's decision in his capacity as president of the Republic) was another anti-Serbian gesture.

3 It was at that time that the famous national writer and later (impeached) president of the new Federal Republic of Yugoslavia, Dobrica Ćosić, lost his position in the Serbian Communist Party for warning against the Albanian threat, and thus gained most of his political popularity.

4 At that time secretary of the federal League of Communists. This close associate of the ageing dictator remained very powerful after Tito's death. A Slovene.

5 A reprint was published in 1990. *Anali Pravnog fakulteta u Beogradu,* 3/1971 (1990).

6 I shall be using the valiant translation into English by Marko Pavičić, published in A.P. Blaustein and G.H. Flanz, *Constitutions of the Countries of the World*, Dobbs Ferry, N.Y.: Oceana, 1986.

7 After the adoption of the Constitution, 'newspeak' permeated legislation, public discourse and administration. There were no wages and salaries anymore: 'working people' had 'personal incomes', schools became 'educational centres', peasants and farmers were replaced by 'agricultural producers', tenants were promoted into 'bearers of tenant rights', etc.

8 One of the features of Yugoslav 'legal totalitarianism' was the extreme legal obstacles facing the founders of any non-governmental organization. Laws on 'associations of citizens', passed in all republics after the adoption of the 1974 Constitution, imposed on them a rigid uniform structure, including the duty to have certain unusual organs, such as, e.g., boards of self-managing control and councils on general people's defence. Another interesting feature was that pan-Yugoslav associations had to be reorganized on a strictly federal basis, with the central organs composed of delegates of republican associations.

9 A. P. Blaustein and G. H. Flanz, *Constitutions of the Countries of the World*, Supplement, Dobbs Ferry, N. Y.: Oceana, 1979.

10 Todorovic is a Serb.

11 The intended meaning was probably closest to the German 'Völkerschaft'.

12 The word 'narod' conveys both meanings in many Slavonic languages.

13 Cf. the Decisions of the Federal Constitutional Court regarding the constitutions and declarations of independence of some republics adopted in 1991. *Borba*, Specijalno izdanje, November 1991: 21.

14 Some of these disputes were later brought before the Arbitration Commission of the Conference on Peace in Yugoslavia (the Badinter Commission), which advised that Yugoslavia was engaged in a 'process of dissolution' and that Serbs in Bosnia-Hercegovina and Croatia were minorities without the right to self-determination. Opinions, No. 1 (1991) and 2 (1992).

15 That this was a complaint of the Serbian leadership was demonstrated by the proposals for constitutional amendments stemming from them in 1990 and 1991. A compromise, which would make the number of deputies correspond to the size of the population but within a maximum of 30 and minimum of 10, was, however, flatly rejected. *Borba*, Specijalno izdanje, November 1991: 34.

16 See above.

17 This wording has been sarcastically interpreted to mean that Tito remained president even after his death. One of the reasons was that in Slovene, the language of Edvard Kardelj, the notion of a 'life term' cannot be expressed without referring to death ('dosmrtni' meaning 'until death'). In the 1970s the cult of Tito's personality reached its peak and he was treated as immortal.

18 *Statistički godišnjak Jugoslavije 1988*, Beograd: Savezni zavod za statistiku, 1988: 122. Contrary to the prevailing opinion that 'Yugoslavism' was promoted by the Communists (e.g. Schöpflin: 186), such allegiance has been discouraged since the late 1960s, which was evidenced from the instructions given to the census-takers (Liebich: 36). Yugoslavs were not a nation, even not a 'nationality'. It is often forgotten that the first Yugoslavia of 1918 was not created, but opposed, by the Communists. The greatest promoter of supra-national Yugoslavism was King Alexander, a staunch anti-Communist (D. Djordjević: 316).

19 'Sluzbeni list SFRJ', 6/1975.

20 In practice, special attention was given to the distribution of the posts of greatest political significance. Thus, as a rule, the presidents of the Presidium of the League of Communists, of the Federal Assembly, the Presidency and the Federal Executive Council, were not of the same nationality.

21 Proposed Amendment LXV. *Borba*, Specijalno izdanje, November 1991: 29.

22 Autonomist ('autonomaš') became a frequently used invective in the late 1980s for those Serbs favouring strong autonomy for the Province of Vojvodina.

23 Commonly ridiculed as 'Serbia beside itself' (Srbija van sebe).

24 For a considerable period Milošević was actively protecting the cult of Tito's personality primarily to please the army (Pešić: 48–49). The memoirs of the last federal minister of defence, Veljko Kadijević (born in Croatia of mixed Serbo-Croat parenthood), who was also the head of the Staff of the Supreme Command in 1990 and 1991, are extremely revealing (Kadijević). In 1993 he still remained convinced that the collapse of Yugoslavia was the result of a devilish plot by the 'actors of the new international order ... Bush's administration and Germany' (7), that 'the destruction of the regime in Yugoslavia was only a segment of the unified plan to topple all "Communist" regimes in the world, above all the Soviet Union' (31), and that Gorbachev was a traitor who led the way to the 'classical restoration of capitalism' in all former socialist countries, with China remaining the only hope (55). In the Federal Executive Council, of which he was formally a member, Kadijević trusted only the minister of the interior, a retired general (109).

25 Amendment LXX. *Borba*, Specijalno izdanje, November 1991: 30.

26 On this, see the symposium volume *Misao, reč, kazna* (Thought, Word, Punishment), Beograd: Institut za kriminololoska i sociološka istraživanja, 1989.

27 *Borba*, Specijalno izdanje, November 1991: 29.

28 According to Kardelj, this was to be substituted by the depoliticized 'pluralism of self-management interests' (Kardelj: 112).

29 Apart from Kardelj, the most important was Vladimir Bakarić, a Croat.

The Ruling Party

MARIJA OBRADOVIĆ

One day you will regret this,
You loud ones, yelling, and you who are quiet, the silent!
If such a day were not to come, I would cry for you today,
If only because of your children.

Bertolt Brecht

This examination of the ideology and technology of power of the Socialist Party of Serbia (SPS) is intended to establish the main historical and social traumas used by this party in order to formulate public opinion and to legitimize its power.

The task of this paper is to establish which political formulas were successfully used by the SPS to persuade part of Serbia's population to *resist modernizing changes* and social transition. We will study the political mechanisms whereby the SPS transformed the fear of losing acquired social rights and the fear of capitalism, which had been systematically encouraged by the Communist Party since the end of World War II, into the fear of losing national identity and of jeopardizing the Serbs' national interests and Serbia's statehood.

The fact is indisputable that the SPS and its leader Slobodan Milošević had support from the Serbian plebiscite for their rule and for the decisions they made, and even for the war. The goal of this paper is to reconstruct how this support was obtained and amassed.

Party of continuity

The Socialist Party of Serbia was the only former Communist party of Eastern Europe that managed to hold onto power after the 'glorious revolution' of 1989. The fall of the Berlin wall on 10 November 1989 marked the collapse of the Communist systems in Eastern Europe. In the free, multiparty elections held soon after this symbolic historical event, democratic forces emerged the victors and began the transition process in Eastern European societies with the privatization of state-owned property, the entering of human rights and freedoms into the law, and the formation of multiparty parliamentary political systems (Stokes and Gale 1993).

The Socialist Party of Serbia, formed at the congress that united the League of Communists of Serbia and the Socialist Alliance of the Working People of Serbia (Belgrade, 17 July 1990), maintained the historical, ideological, organizational and personal continuity of the League of Communists of Serbia. Not even the technology of power changed.

The decision to form one party was made at a joint meeting of the presidencies of the Managing Committee of the Socialist Alliance of the Working People of Serbia and the Central Committee of the League of Communists of Serbia, held on 8 June 1990 (*P*, 9 June 1990). In his closing statement at the Unity Congress, Slobodan Milošević, previously the president of the League of Communists of Serbia Central Committee who was elected the first president of the SPS, stressed that 'a good mobilizing programme has been adopted not only for the members of the party but for all the citizens of Serbia', and 'the left wing's time is before us'. Milošević underscored that 'the new Socialist Party of Serbia is a barrier to the right wing' that was active in propagandizing 'extremely destructive political orientations', and that 'the party itself is fighting for a better life with the *united left*' (author's emphases) (*P*, 18 July 1990).

The ideology of the SPS gravitated around two basic points that were also used by post-war Eastern European Communism to formulate its political legitimacy. The first was fundamental, representing a social–historical goal: the establishing or maintaining of socially owned property as the basic social relationship. The second was related to mobilization and dealt with the so-called national question. When formulating the national interests of Serbia and the Serbs in Yugoslavia, the SPS inaugurated a collectivist, traditionalist formula of nationalism with the intention of winning over the traditional section of society. The society that emerged under Communism was mobilized by the ideas of socially owned property, social security and the creation of the illusion, through clever political tactics, that the SPS supported the preservation of the Yugoslav federation, equality among ethnic groups, social rights, and the peaceful resolution of interethnic conflicts in Yugoslavia.

The middle class was not the SPS's 'target group'. Since this section of society was oriented towards the market, private initiative, risk taking and technological innovation, it served as the social basis for recruiting opponents and critics of the anti-reform and war policies of the SPS and its leader Milošević.

The collectivist nature of egalitarian–Communistic and traditional–nationalistic ideologies enabled their symbiosis in the SPS Platform of Basic Tenets and its political operations. This was owing not only to the political volition of the SPS, but also to the previous historical development and social structure of society in Serbia. The political activity of the SPS constantly moved with the Communistic–nationalistic pendulum, where the range of movement depended on concrete internal and external policies, and economic and social factors and circumstances.

The political technology of the SPS was typically populist by nature (Popov 1993). It was based on the principles of mobilizing and homogenizing the masses while atomizing society at the same time. Thus the SPS succeeded in narrowing the space in which to form and organize interest groups, trade unions, non-governmental social organizations, etc.

The concrete instruments of the SPS's power included, first of all, the wide-scale mobilization of the people through supervised 'national movements of the people' (the so-called national happenings). During this process the energy of a society confronted with the historical necessity of transition and the collective fear of change and an uncertain future was transformed into nationalistic and political social hysteria. This process was most evident from the summer of 1988 to the demonstrations in Belgrade on 9 March 1991 which denoted the beginning of greater widespread political activities by the opposition.

The second feature was the instigation of civil war in former Yugoslavia, that is, in Croatia and in Bosnia-Hercegovina. The surrounding hostilities and Serbia's involvement in the war in former Yugoslavia were used by the SPS to hinder internal social differentiation, democratization and modernization. The war policy of the SPS was accompanied by a policy of creating poverty among the citizens of Serbia through hyperinflation, while simultaneously creating the illusion that the country was pursuing a suitable social policy since it was impossible to dismiss employees (compulsory leave from work was introduced during which employees kept their job and continued to receive part of their salary).

Both of the techniques employed by the government were based on the use of political myths (the 'Kosovo myth', Yugoslavia as 'an error of judgement by the Serbian people', the 'exploitation of Serbia by other parts of Yugoslavia', etc.) and traditional socialist-populist formulas legitimizing the government ('national unity', 'external menace', 'enemy of the people', etc.).

In autumn 1990, the SPS established operational headquarters in order to increase membership. The local organizations of the former Socialist Alliance of the Working People of Serbia located in urban and rural areas were particularly important in recruiting new members and spreading the party infrastructure. The most important way in which the party's infrastructure was spread was through meetings between municipal SPS committees and the directors of larger state-run enterprises, at which the directors would join the SPS, since the socialists would remind them that 'they had received their position as director because they were Communists'. A large number of the newly registered members came from rural areas. However, before the SPS victory in the 1990 elections, membership rose slowly. Only between 15 and 20 per cent of SPS members had been in the League of Communists of Serbia.

In terms of building its horizontal party infrastructure, the SPS was a relic of the Communist party's organization. The SPS had two important mechanisms that enabled its network of organizations to cover all of society. The first was the presence of active members of the SPS in economic activities (enterprises), social activities (institutions) and at the University, even though party organizations were not allowed there by law.

The second mechanism was the use of socio-political organizations (the Independent Trade Union, League of World War II Veterans Associations, the Association of Reserve Army Officers, etc.) and certain parties (the League of Communists–Movement for Yugoslavia), 'left-wing forces' in SPS vocabulary, as a means of *transmission* to implement SPS policies, but primarily 'against meetings with a political hue, strikes, protests and demonstrations'.

The SPS has won soundly at all multiparty elections held in Serbia to date. The first multiparty elections in Serbia were held on 9 December 1990 (with a second round on 26 December). Owing to the majority electoral system, the SPS with 45.8 per cent of the votes won 77.6 per cent of the seats for deputies (190 out of 250) in the Serbian National Assembly. Slobodan Milošević, as the presidential candidate, won 65.35 per cent of the votes cast. Early federal, republican, provincial and local elections were held in FRY on 20 December 1992, along with elections for the president of the republics of Serbia and Montenegro. The elections were held according to the proportional representation voting system. In elections for the Citizens' Chamber (lower house) of the FR Yugoslavia Assembly, the Socialist Party of Serbia received 31.4 per cent of the votes and 47 seats. In elections for the Serbian National Assembly the SPS won 101 seats out of 250. In the presidential elections, Slobodan Milošević was elected president of the Republic of Serbia with 2,515,047 votes or 56 per cent of the votes cast. Early elections for 250 seats in the Serbian National Assembly were held on 19 December 1993 and the SPS won 123 seats.

The SPS pre-election campaign for the first multiparty elections in Serbia in 1990 began immediately after the Unity Congress. Both in its Platform and in the pre-election campaign, the SPS presented itself as 'Serbia's salvation', a 'modern left-wing party' of the people. It particularly stressed its success in establishing a 'united Serbia'. In addition, it endeavoured to emphasize its 'progressiveness', underscoring that the opposition represented 'dark forces' that would lead to a sombre future for Serbia should they win.

In his election campaign speech in Niš on 21 November 1990, at a huge meeting attended by 250,000 people, Slobodan Milošević spoke of the elections as 'a test for all the citizens of Serbia' and stressed the determination of the people of Serbia 'to be on the side of work' and that 'Serbia can go forward: to peace, freedom and better days. And it can also go backward to war, dependence and underdevelopment. I am certain that Serbia will not hesitate greatly as to which way it will go.' And he continued 'we can be proud of our past ... It is no coincidence that these dark forces think that everything that the Serbs have done for as long as they have existed until now has been good, and that the only bad thing was that they were Partisans, that they went to war for freedom and for socialism. According to them we should have served Hitler and the occupying forces, we should hate all other Yugoslav ethnic groups that are not Serbs, and that the Serbs, divided into the few rich and many poor, should be kept all together and backward, at the tail-end of history and the world ...' (*P*, 22 November 1990).

The basic pre-election strategy of the SPS in 1990 was to present itself as a force that would provide Serbia with *peace and prosperity*, unlike the opposition whose victory might lead Serbia into *war and poverty*. However, *it was the electoral victory of the SPS that marked the beginning of war in Yugoslavia, Serbia's economic collapse and the pauperization of the overwhelming majority of the people.*

The number of SPS members and the election results achieved indicate that in the 1990 to 1993 period, Serbia's one-party political system had been transformed into a *ruling party system.*

Ideology

The SPS Platform was adopted at the Second Congress held from 23 to 24 October 1992 in Belgrade, two months before early elections in FR Yugoslavia. Freedom, social justice, creativity, solidarity and peace were determined as basic values.

All of the SPS's political propaganda during 1991 and 1992 was intended to emphasize that the Serbs in Croatia and Bosnia-Hercegovina had been 'forced' into war by the separatism of these former Yugoslav republics and the threat of genocide from the Croats and Muslims. However, two years earlier, according to the writings of Borisav Jović, one of the SPS leaders, this party had discussed with Yugoslavia's top military commanders 'the concept of using military operations to resolve the crisis'. Slobodan Milošević had suggested to Jović 'that we undertake action as soon as possible, but only against Croatia, we'll leave Slovenia alone; and in Croatia we'll only act where the Serbs live, should conflicts arise, and they will. Let's limit things territorially in order to avoid operations on all of the "democratized" territories, but we'll incapacitate them to prevent them fighting against the Serbian people who do not want to tolerate an Ustasha government.' According to Jović, in the summer of 1990, together with the federal secretary for national defence Veljko Kadijević, they created a strategy to 'expel the western republics' from Yugoslavia in order to preserve the socialist system in the other parts of Yugoslavia (B. Jović, 1995: 218, 160, 161).

SPS declared itself to be a party maintaining continuity with the League of Communists of Yugoslavia, endeavouring to be its successor, just as they demanded that the Federal Republic of Yugoslavia be the successor state to the SFRY. They did not therefore acknowledge that the social system of 'existing socialism' was historically exhausted. They did not consider that the obvious entropy in Yugoslav society was the result of the inability of the given system to enable social growth and development. 'Bureaucratic deformations' were to blame for this, and not the system itself. The ideology of the 'anti-bureaucratic revolution' was based on these very principles, so the unconstitutionally overthrown provincial leaderships of Vojvodina (replaced after the meeting in Novi Sad on 5 October 1988), Kosovo (17 November 1988) and Montenegro (9 January 1989), were accused by the League of Communists of Serbia of 'political voluntarism, etatism, bureaucratism and particularism'. This had led to a 'standstill in the development of self-management', an economic crisis in society and the 'weakening of the unity and communal spirit in the Socialist Republic of Serbia', that is, the republic's power throughout its territory. According to SPS ideologists, the basic problems in achieving 'socialist structures in post-war Yugoslavia were due to the fact that the idea of socialism was carried out in a primarily authoritarian and not a democratic manner'.

> The Communist Party had established a complete monopoly of power over all of social life. The political self-will of the leadership produced many erroneous systemic solutions, such as administrative direction of the economy, blocking business initiatives, establishing the economy by mutual agreement, constituting socially owned property without a specific subject of ownership rights, splitting up large economic systems into 'organizations of associated labour', joining states into confederations and forming independent states and national economies. The 1974 Constitution definitively destroyed Yugoslavia by declaring the republics to be sovereign states, introducing general agreement for all decisions on the federal level and allowing republican laws to have priority over federal laws. This system did the greatest harm to the left itself with its undemocratic, authoritarian characteristics, poor personnel policy, the compromising of its great liberating ideas (e.g. the idea of self-management), hypocrisy and the great gap between proclaimed ideas and practice. However, both the system and the policies that were pursued all along have harmed Serbia and the Serbian people in particular. The Serbian people is divided into five republics, and the Republic of Serbia itself is divided into three separate parts, of which Serbia 'Proper' had the least rights. Those parts of the Serbian people in other republics, and even in the provinces of their own Republic, were deprived of their rights and left unprotected. Certain economic policy measures (such as moving enterprises into other republics, the pricing policy, shifting the great burden unevenly with the help of undeveloped areas) put Serbia in a subordinate position and its development was slowed down compared to the more developed republics, particularly Slovenia. (*Basic Tenets of the Platform...* 1993: 8, 9)

This defined the basic political myths and legitimate political formulas upon which the League of Communists of Serbia/SPS based its activities in the period from the Eighth Meeting of the Central Committee of the League of Communists of Serbia (23–24 September 1987), a meeting that is considered to be a turning point in the ideology and policies of Serbian Communists, to the 'St. Nicholas' elections in 1993. The political view that Serbia's statehood was threatened, that it had been economically exploited and kept undeveloped in Yugoslavia, and that the Serbs in Kosovo, Croatia and Bosnia-Hercegovina had lost their national (ethnic) rights, became the framework of the new social–integrative formula with which the Serbian Communists mobilized the masses and held onto power during the historical process of the fall of Communism in Eastern Europe. The Serbian Communists' rhetoric calling for state political unity, an economically strong Serbia and the preservation of the Yugoslav federation equated *Serbian national interests with the preservation of socialism*; first of all throughout SFRY by trying to make the League of Communists of Serbia the dominant force in the League of Communists of Yugoslavia, and the Socialist Republic of Serbia the dominant force in the Yugoslav federation, and subsequently, as of the end of 1990, in Serbia, Montenegro and parts of Croatia and Bosnia-Hercegovina where the Serbs constituted the majority population.

Opting for nationalism, the Serbian Communists wanted to prevent the opposition from legitimizing itself as the defender of Serbian national interests at a time when interethnic conflicts were intensifying in Yugoslavia owing to the entropy of the system of socialism at the end of the 1980s.

Until the Eighth Meeting, the Communist Party of Serbia tried to use doses of nationalism to hinder the political articulation of the opposition. Afterwards it incorporated the traditional political formulas of Serbian nationalism into its ideological corpus and made contact with the social institutions and individuals that represented them (the Serbian Academy of Arts and Sciences, the Association of Writers of Serbia, Dobrica Ćosić and others). In this manner, the Communist Party of Serbia prevented the opposition in Serbia from using slogans on Serbian national interests to articulate a new principle of social integration politically, that is, to use national interests to oppose class interests.

Associating national interests with class interests, the League of Communists of Serbia continued the 'national–democratic' tradition of the Communist movement and formulated its strategy of the 'national path' to socialism, countering the 'new world order'. The League of Communists of Serbia/SPS endeavoured to present itself as a 'people's party' that represented the interests of the Serbian people and Serbia, but also as the 'protector of the interests of potential "social losers" in the process of economic transition'. The goal of the leadership of the League of Communists of Serbia was to maintain the 'unity of the Serbian leadership', that is, not to allow the formation of liberal factions; to link writers, artists, academics and others to them; and to prevent the workers from turning against them owing to social problems. 'Sloba says that almost all academics, writers and artists are with us and that we have to include them more in joint actions domestically and abroad' (B. Jović 1995: 131).

In the Basic Tenets of the SPS Platform from 1990, the party is described as advocating a united Serbia, and it is noted that Serbia is constituted as a socialist republic based on 'the rule of law and social justice'. It is emphasized that the autonomous provinces in Serbia cannot be states, but can only have a form of territorial autonomy, and that authority in the hands of the state should be carried out by bodies of the Republic of Serbia over the whole territory (*Basic Tenets of the Platform and Statutes of the Socialist Party of Serbia*, 1990: 34). At the time the Basic Tenets were published, the republic's Constitution had already been revised. The amendments to the Constitution of SR Serbia were declared on 28 March 1989; the provinces' possibility of vetoing constitutional changes in Serbia was removed, as was a part of their legislative, administrative and judicial functions. The SR Serbia Assembly passed the 1990 Constitution of the Republic of Serbia on 28 September 1990. Unlike the Basic Tenets, the Constitution defined the Republic of Serbia as a 'democratic state of the citizens who live within it, based on the rights and freedoms of men and citizens', but also, as in the Tenets, on the 'rule of law and *social justice*' (author's emphases). The provinces lost their attributes of statehood and were given a form of territorial autonomy. The local governments became centralized.

In its 1992 Platform, the SPS saw the solution to the crisis in Kosovo in preventing the activities of militant Albanian separatists, and it rejected the possibility of Kosovo breaking away from Yugoslavia. 'Kosovo and Metohija are an inseparable part of Serbia; their natural resources, cultural monuments and history give them not only great immediate political importance but also extreme symbolic importance for the Serbian people. Indeed, over a long period of time this area had been occupied and settled significantly by ethnic Albanians, but it was finally liberated and permanently attached to the Serbian state. Owing to historical circumstances, the ethnic Albanians have become the majority in Kosovo and Metohija, but they are a national minority in Serbia. What constitutes a national minority is not a larger or smaller number, but the fact that they belong to a people that has its own state outside the borders of Yugoslavia' (Basic Tenets: 81, 82). Condemning all forms of ethnic cleansing, the Serbian socialists advocated the return of the displaced Serbs and Montenegrins and the settling of citizens who wanted to live and work in Kosovo.

The war in former Yugoslavia, Croatia and Bosnia-Hercegovina had already been under way for a year and a half when the Platform of the Serbian socialists defined their position towards the Serbs living outside Serbia:

> The Socialist Party of Serbia is convinced that the principles of international law were breached when the Serbs in Croatia and Bosnia-Hercegovina, who spent seven decades united with their brothers, were prevented from exercising their right to self-determination and from remaining in a common Yugoslav state. The socialists of Serbia will continue to support their right in this regard and offer them moral and material assistance. ... In the situation in which the Serbian people are being forced once again to fight for their survival, all national forces must be gathered together and all types of solidarity and assistance to the fatherland should be encouraged from Serbs in the diaspora. Serbs in the world are a force upon which we can depend in the fight to spread the truth about the position of the Serbian people in the areas of former Yugoslavia and about the efforts peacefully and justly to resolve the Yugoslav crisis. (ibid.: 85)

With the collapse of the SFRY, the SPS emphasized that the same right of a people to self-determination according to which the Slovenes, Bosnian Muslims and Macedonians had decided to break away from Yugoslavia, allowed the Serbian people, on the territories where they constituted the majority, to decide to remain within the common Yugoslav state.

On Serbia's political scene, the SPS launched a slogan about the 'new world order' which, according to its ideologists, had arisen with the collapse of the Soviet Union and the system of 'existing socialism' in Eastern Europe, and the unification of Germany, thereby making it possible for the USA to dominate in the world and Germany in Europe. This ideological argumentation found its place in the SPS Platform: 'the new world order has an extremely imperialistic nature; its goal is the domination of the West over the East and South; unlike the totalitarian type of imperialism, established through invasion and occupying territory, this liberalism-based imperialism has a specific feature whereby economic interests (petroleum supplies, conquering markets, issuing loans and controlling debtor countries) are primarily achieved through political means; however, the ultimate arguments are used–the arguments of force. One of the first victims of the new world order is Yugoslavia ...' (ibid.: 74, 75).

Although the SPS, according to the Platform, accepted representative democracy, a market economy and respect for human rights (and human socio-economic rights: the right to strike, to free basic health care, to old age and disability pensions, to social assistance in case of social hardship and to free education), the SPS did not abandon a 'regulated market economy based on the equality of forms of ownership'.

The ideologists of the SPS were convinced that a 'mixed economy' was the optimal solution in the circumstances. The solution advocated by the SPS 'includes a market economy, but also a certain degree of government regulation, transformed socially owned property, but the possibility of its unhindered transformation into private, co-operative and state-owned property'. However, the Serbian socialists were 'fighting against the unrestricted domination of capital over people and against the conversion of economic power into political power' (ibid.: 33). The SPS saw a regulative role for the government in the economy in the area of monetary and tax policies, foreign trade and customs policies and policies dealing with the environment. In addition, the SPS felt that the state should directly manage certain public enterprises.

Emphasizing the equal footing of different forms of ownership in its Platform, the SPS first cited socially owned property, which it defined as 'social joint-stock capital'. The SPS saw the transformation of socially owned property in the direction of state-owned or private property, but when enumerating the forms of ownership in the Platform, first state-owned property was mentioned, then co-operative, and finally private property at the end. Their attitude towards property and the concept of the economic development policy most distinctly expressed its continuity with the Communist government. Insisting on socially owned or state-owned property, the SPS wanted to maintain control over the country's economic resources. Their concept of an economic policy contained some elements of the 'five-year plan', for example industrialization as the goal of economic development. The construction of extensive traffic facilities could be associated with 'key facilities of capital construction', and their readiness to use the cheap work-force could be equated with Communistic political accumulation at the price of the population's low standard of living. The goals of economic development were unreal and megalomaniac, which is characteristic of the Communists' 'five-year plans'.

The SPS Platform also fastened onto the old socialist system with its policy towards workers' trade unions. The SPS did not advocate union pluralism and independent trade unions, rather Trade Union was written with capital letters in the Platform. By emphasizing that the Trade Union's fight for the workers' interests was 'at the same time the fight of the Socialist Party of Serbia', the SPS indicated that it viewed the Union as its own transmission organization. 'We are convinced that the interests of the working class are best served by a united non-party trade union organization and that these interests are jeopardized by a plurality of politically opposed organizations' (ibid.: 91).

The SPS also considered the World War II Veterans' Association and the association of veterans from the 'recent liberation war in Croatia and Bosnia-Hercegovina' to be its transmission organizations.

The SPS's role as the political continuity of the League of Communists of Serbia is indicated by an analysis not only of its Platform, but also of its Statutes, that is, the form and principles of the party's organization. Any citizen who accepted the party's Platform and Statutes, and who was over the age of sixteen, could join the SPS. According to article 10 of the Statutes, SPS organization existed on the level of municipalities, universities, towns and autonomous provinces. The basic form of organization and operation of the SPS was at local community level, or in parts of municipalities, in enterprises, institutions and faculties. A special youth organization was also anticipated within the Socialist Party of Serbia.

The technology of power

War was the most important means by which to legitimize the regime inaugurated by the SPS/League of Communists of Serbia. Through it, the political technology of populist mobilization and the homogenization of the masses produced perfect results. War was the most effective mechanism to compensate for the 'lack of legitimacy' of the old system's political oligarchy which, although superseded and worn out, had no desire to step down from the historical stage. In addition to war, the Serbian socialists used different mechanisms to legitimize their political power, and a number of instruments to mobilize political support.

The SPS played an important role in inciting, organizing and waging war. However, the SPS did not consider war as simply the means of accomplishing national or state interests. *Confrontation* was part of this party's ideological nature. The socialists needed conflict so that they could perform the *role of arbiter* on the political and social scene and thereby legitimize their monopoly of power. The SPS's political ideology was constructed towards the conscious and organized instigation of social tension and high intensity crises ('anti-bureaucratic revolution', 'spontaneous meetings'), with the goal of eroding all social institutions. Thus, institutions lost their function as catalysts and instruments for resolving social conflicts, and this role was taken over by the SPS and its leader Slobodan Milošević.

The collapse of the League of Communists of Yugoslavia occurred at the Fourteenth Special Congress, held between 20 and 22 January 1990 in Belgrade, when the Slovenian and Croatian delegations left the auditorium, symbolically denoting the beginning of the end of Yugoslavia and the outbreak of civil war.

Two irreconcilable factions were clearly formed at the Congress: the Slovenian and the Serbian. The Slovenian faction was silently supported by the Croatian wing in the League of Communists of Yugoslavia. Although the conflict formally involved the question of federation versus confederation, the essence of the dispute had to do with deeper institutional changes.

According to the testimony of Borisav Jović, the Serbian Communists felt that the main battle would take place at the Fourteenth Congress of the League of Communists of Yugoslavia and that their task was to preserve the integrity of the League of Communists of Yugoslavia and democratic centralism, 'at least statutorily (formally)'. At the end of 1989, the League of Communists of Serbia launched a slogan about 'democratic non-party pluralism' while the League of Communists of Slovenia advocated a multiparty system. The League of Communists of Serbia was not prepared to accept the liquidation of party organizations in enterprises and the depoliticization of the armed forces and security forces. The Serbian leadership justified their ideological position by 'reasons of state', emphasizing that a multiparty system would lead to the disintegration of Yugoslavia owing to its multiethnic composition. Slobodan Milošević felt that the League of Communists of Slovenia had considerably weakened its position in Slovenia and had practically excluded itself from the League of Communists of Yugoslavia. 'They have almost liquidated their party, they have no right to talk about us. In any case, we're not asking them and we won't listen to them—we'll ignore and spurn them. We have the moral right to do so' (B. Jović 1995: 62). The League of Communists of Serbia considered itself to be the only part of the League of Communists with 'the people's support' and believed that it would be the only one not to lose power in a multiparty system.

The strategy of the League of Communists of Serbia at the Fourteenth Congress anticipated 'strong ties and co-operation with the

army' and the 'isolation' of the Slovenes 'so that Croatia and Macedonia, and possibly Bosnia-Hercegovina, did not join them. The
banner was to be carried by members of the Yugoslav People's
Army (JNA) and we were to support them, so that we were not at
the head, for that would have had a negative effect on the Croats
and Macedonians. The army accepted such a role' (ibid.: 88). The
party organization in the JNA and the federal secretary for national
defence Veljko Kadijević shared the ideological convictions of the
League of Communists of Serbia.

It was clear to the Slovenian section of the League of Communists of Yugoslavia that socialism had collapsed as a world economic and political system. They felt that the economic system
should be changed as soon as possible and adapted to what existed
in the Common Market. Within this framework, the role of the
League of Communists had to change, too. They were willing to
have free elections, even though they knew they would not win.
This would be a painless way for the Communists to descend from
power. At the same time, they felt that these changes would go
much more slowly in the rest of the country, and that Slovenia
should enter Europe immediately. They supported institutional
changes, but not all the constitutional changes proposed by the
federal government headed by Ante Marković who was elected at
the SFRY Assembly on 17 March 1989. In the autumn of that year,
Ante Marković publicly declared on television that he was in favour of a multiparty system.

The Serbian wing of the League of Communists of Yugoslavia
was against fundamental institutional changes in the economic
system, believing that some kind of reforms to the socialist economy were still possible. At the same time, the Serbian Communists
were great advocates of Yugoslavia as a strong federation and were
not prepared to yield power voluntarily to other parties in free
elections. Using the wave of national populism, they carried out
constitutional reforms in Serbia, revoked the autonomous provinces and substantially suspended the institutional changes set in
motion by Marković's government. The League of Communists of
Serbia believed that their views would prevail at the Congress and
that this would also be the case with the new SFRY Constitution.

The opinion of the party's military leaders was that 'inter-
republic agreement on constitutional changes cannot realistically
be achieved since there are great conceptual differences, and there
are anti-socialist and anti-Communist external factors working
against any agreement; nor will the foreign factor allow agreement
to be reached on a socialist orientation, since their goal is to de-

stroy socialism with the introduction of at least a Western type of social democracy'. The JNA party organization felt that Yugoslavia must 'survive as a state with a socialist orientation' (ibid.: 67, 68).

The League of Communists of Serbia judged the League of Communists of Yugoslavia Congress to be the critical moment at which to change the SFRY Constitution. Before the Congress, they tried to do everything they could to establish the principles upon which constitutional changes would be made, then have them confirmed at the Congress and implemented. They were ready to take strong political initiatives up to, and during, the Congress.

The Congress was interrupted when the Slovenian delegation walked out. The League of Communists of Serbia expected that the Congress would take a position regarding the need to pass a new SFRY Constitution, and new republican constitutions. Milan Kučan's opinion was that a new Yugoslav Constitution should not be passed before the republics passed theirs. 'Irritated' by the rejection of their numerous amendments to congress documents, the League of Communists of Slovenia delegates left the Congress.

In the discussion that followed, Slobodan Milošević proposed that the Congress establish a new quorum without the Slovenian delegation and that it continue its work, since the tactics of the League of Communists of Serbia delegation were to 'isolate' the Slovenes. However, Ivica Račan, president of the Croatian League of Communists Central Committee, informed the Congress that if work were to continue, the Croatian delegation would not take part in the decision making. In such circumstances, the Congress broke off work indefinitely. The strategy and tactics of the League of Communists of Serbia had failed.

General confusion and uncertainty arose concerning the party leadership of Serbia. Delegates from the JNA party organization were 'completely disappointed', feeling that many of the Communists felt frightened and lost in the face of the anti-Communist hubbub. 'They're not fighting, not reacting, as if they don't care what happens ...'

Military party leaders and Veljko Kadijević did not feel that a multiparty system was as much of a problem, 'as the fact that some Communists have agreed to break up their united organization; and second, they believe that a multiparty system will preserve Yugoslavia's unity and lead it into civic (Western) Europe. The tragedy is that they do not understand that they are breaking up Yugoslavia this way and leading it into civil war. They do not understand that such parties will not resolve the problem of Yugoslavia, since they do not understand the national (ethnic) question in

Yugoslavia. *For Yugoslavia, its survival and renewal, a united League of Communists of Yugoslavia must remain and be renewed along with competition from other parties'* (ibid.: 94. Author's emphasis).

Thus, the League of Communists of Serbia and military party leaders identified Yugoslavia as a state with a socialist system and the League of Communists of Yugoslavia's monopoly of power. For them, Yugoslavia was only possible as a Communistic party state.

After the suspension of the Congress, Ante Marković announced that Yugoslavia did not need the League of Communists of Yugoslavia in order to function.

At the beginning of 1991, military party leaders and SPS leaders began considering the possibility of resolving the Yugoslav crisis by introducing martial law. They jointly believed that the West wanted 'left-wing forces' to descend from power in Serbia and Montenegro. The military leadership was of the opinion that the conspiracy (external and internal enemies) aimed against JNA and Yugoslavia had to be thwarted. They characterized the political views and propaganda of the 'anti-Communist and anti-socialist front' as being 'anti-Serbian'. The military leaders endeavoured to accelerate the creation of the League of Communists–Movement for Yugoslavia (LCMY), while at the same time, like the Serbian socialists, they opposed the creation of the Yugoslav Alliance of Forces for Reform (YAFR) organized by Ante Marković's federal government.

Judging that the leaders of Slovenia and Croatia were pursuing a 'policy of *fait accompli*', the military leadership felt that 'the reaction must be according to the law, including *martial law* if there is no other way' (author's emphasis) (ibid.: 189, 238).

With regard to solving the Yugoslav crisis, up until war broke out military and SPS leaders stressed that peoples, not republics or minorities, had the right to self-determination. They emphasized that the Serbian people had its united federative state within Yugoslavia and wanted to decide about its future from that position. According to them, the entire Serbian people wanted to live in one state, with equal civil rights, with internationally recognized borders, with one army, currency and market. For them, the state could be unitary or federative but they stressed that a confederation was not a state and that the Serbs as a people did not want to consider it. A federation with minimum functions, they argued, was the optimal form for Yugoslavia. This practically meant that republics were denied the right to secession while peoples were acknowledged this right.

The SPS leadership's plan was for the army to 'cover Serbian territory in Croatia'. The military leaders had judged that the country's situation could not be resolved without the appearance of force and the use of force to the extent required to end the crisis without civil war and in a democratic manner. Plans were therefore made to overthrow the governments in Slovenia and Croatia. According to their estimates, Serbia, Montenegro, the army and the Serbian parties in Croatia and Bosnia-Hercegovina were in favour of Yugoslavia. The army's basic idea was to rely on the 'forces that are for Yugoslavia' and 'to use a combination of political and military measures to destroy the government in Croatia first, and then the government in Slovenia ...'

The army felt that governments in republics it considered 'uncertain' should be overthrown by demonstrations and uprisings, that is, in the way that the League of Communists of Serbia carried out its political putsch in Serbia and overthrew the leaderships in Vojvodina, Kosovo and Montenegro.

According to Borisav Jović's writings, the military leadership proposed to 'organize mass meetings in Croatia against the HDZ, bring Bosnia-Hercegovina to its feet with a "For Yugoslavia" meeting, and in Macedonia use the concept of meetings to overthrow the pro-Bulgarian leadership. Use widespread meetings of support in Serbia and Montenegro. Prohibit any assemblies in Kosovo' (ibid.: 277).

The military leadership and the SPS developed a partnership based on the interests of preserving the socialist system. However, the relations between them were rather complicated and multi-layered, filled with mutual distrust and occasional smaller conflicts.

The SPS leadership supported the military leader's plan with respect to the introduction of martial law. Jović bears witness to this: 'I consulted Slobodan Milošević about the army's plan ... He thought that everything was all right, except that Slovenia should be left alone. Only Croatia should be given the treatment' (ibid.: 281).

In mid-March 1991, Veljko Kadijević advocated a military *coup d'état* throughout SFRY, changing Ante Marković's government and the SFRY Presidency, and hindering the convocation of the Federal Assembly. The army was to determine a specific period (six months) within which to reach an agreement on the country's future. On 15 March Borisav Jović resigned from the position of president of the SFRY Presidency after a Presidency meeting at which the majority refused to support the military leaders' proposal to introduce martial law, 'to give them [the army] a free hand to act in the four days since they had informed us of their decision to execute a military coup' (ibid.: 307). During the demonstrations by the opposition on 9 March 1991 in Belgrade, army tanks went into the streets and blocked different buildings, in particular Serbian Television.

The JNA plan to introduce martial law was intended institutionally and politically to strengthen Srpska Krajina in Croatia and support its secession from Croatia.

The SPS policy relied on support and assistance from the army to preserve its monopoly of power. Jović writes that Slobodan Milošević openly asked the army leaders 'whether the army would protect the government in Serbia if the opposition resorted to violence again. They said they would' (ibid.: 310).

At the beginning of the 1990s, the most noticeable characteristics of the population's political mood in Serbia were highly expressed feelings of *worry and fear*, considerable indignation at all that had happened in Yugoslavia since the end of the 1980s, and a *feeling of deception* owing to the contradiction between the great promises that had been made (a just society, prosperity for all) and a reality that was the exact opposite. People were overcome by fear at a future that promised poverty, conflict and war. According to the results of an empirical investigation of political public opinion conducted between 20 and 29 October 1990 by the Institute for Political Studies in Belgrade on a sample of nine hundred people throughout Serbia, 27.5 per cent responded that they were frightened for themselves and their families; 66.4 per cent were worried, but felt that the crisis could be overcome with an intelligent policy (messiah syndrome); and only 3.9 per cent said they were not at all worried about the situation.

When asked how they felt about what had happened to socialism in the world and in Yugoslavia, 49.8 per cent answered that they *felt they had been deceived*, 'they told us fairy tales and the exact opposite happened'; 26.2 per cent did not feel deceived because they had never believed what had been said and promised regarding socialism; 10.3 per cent did not feel deceived because they thought that socialism would win sooner or later; and another 15.8 per cent did not feel deceived, this time since they thought that socialist self-management was well founded and would be achieved one day.

This political mood was accompanied by great feelings of *powerlessness*—some 52.2 per cent felt that the individual could not succeed in society simply by work and ability; 30.5 per cent were convinced that the individual could only succeed if he were 'his own man'; 9.8 per cent believed the individual could succeed only if he was lucky; and 11.9 per cent thought that the individual was completely powerless to do anything further for himself. Even so, 45.6 per cent felt that capable and hard-working people could succeed in spite of everything.

Research into views about the nation showed that nationalism was not the prevailing ideology among the inhabitants of Serbia in spite of three years during which nationalistic euphoria had been incited and spread by the League of Communists of Serbia. Only 18.5 per cent of the citizens of Serbia considered their nation (ethnic group) sacred (compared to 57.4 per cent in Kosovo and only 5.4 per cent in Vojvodina); 8.4 per cent considered it important, but were not ready to turn it into something sacred. The answer 'I respect my nation, but I am aware of how I earn my living' was given by 5.5 per cent; 5.6 per cent had cosmopolitan views; and 8.8 per cent had no national feelings.

Proof that traces of the authoritarian regime were still present in the value structure of the Serbian populace was given by the rather high percentage of those who felt that society should be authoritarian, that is, power and government in the hands of one man. Thus 27.4 per cent believed that 'in the state, as in a family, everyone must know who is the oldest, that is, there must be one commander who is listened to by everyone'. The response that 'The state should be governed by a minority of the most competent and most intelligent individuals who will be followed by the people' was given by 13 per cent. Nevertheless, the greatest support was given to the democratic view that 'the state should be governed by individuals elected by the people who can be dismissed by that same people if they do not act according to the people's will'. This view was shared by 48.5 of Serbia's citizens.

Research into people's value systems and political orientations indicated that the ruling political stereotypes of many long years were deeply rooted in the cognitive value structure of Serbia's citizens, particularly regarding the concept of *social justice*. Thus, in spite of the evident collapse of the Communist system, 30.3 per cent of people supported the Communistic understanding of justice ('the state should ensure that everyone in society has the same and lives the same way'). This number was even greater in Kosovo (44.4%), while it was noticeably smaller in Vojvodina (18.4%). Among the believers, Muslims had the greatest sympathy for the communist type of justice (38.9%) and the proportion of Orthodox was somewhat above average (35.6%). A liberal understanding of social justice ('the state should not set limits on people's work and on the accumulation of wealth, that is, each person should be given the possibility to work and accumulate wealth in accordance with his capabilities and how much he has earned') was the choice of 18.3 per cent of the citizens of Serbia. The greatest number of respondents (43.8%) chose a type of justice between these two 'pure' models that corresponded to the social democratic concept of social order ('each person should be allowed to work and accumulate wealth without restrictions but society should ensure that all its citizens have the basic means to live, social security, health care and other protection'. Around 30 per cent were in favour of socialism.

Research into value systems, ideological orientations and social awareness in Yugoslavia showed high support for authoritarianism among the population. This was accompanied by a tendency towards conformism, *resistance to change* and an unwillingness to take risks, lack of tolerance, and feelings of alienation and helplessness.

Authoritarianism is deeply rooted in the traditions of Yugoslav society, and during the post-war Communist rule it became petrified. Political promotion in the Communist nomenclature was achieved by obedience: 'Obedience towards the party leaders and obedience towards the ideology.' This resulted in the formation of an 'authoritarian post-Communist individual', as rightly stated by Novi Sad psychologist Mikloš Biro (1994: 22).

The authoritarian type of individual who prevailed in the system of 'existing socialism' had suitable socio-psychological characteristics for nationalistic identification in Yugoslav society's post-Communist era. Nationalism as an exclusive identity appears when the individual's confidence is endangered, and this personal insecurity is compensated for by the size of one's own nation. The appearance of social changes in Yugoslavia at the end of the 1980s, particularly ownership transformations, increased the feeling of insecurity and resistance to change that already characterized the social awareness of a large proportion of the population, particularly the important social layer of the workers/peasants, or the 'fringe population' of large cities.

The SPS based its propaganda and its techniques for mobilizing political support on authoritarianism as the predominant trait in Serbia's social character, a trait that accompanied people's fear of uncertainty regarding changes in the social system and social transition. In addition, in order to preserve the socialist system and its power monopoly, the SPS endeavoured to use the ruling social stereotype of social justice, and the authority of the 'leader' Slobodan Milošević, and the cult surrounding him created by the media from 1987 to 1990.

The chapter on social equality holds a special place in the Basic Tenets of the Platform adopted at the SPS founding congress. This chapter emphasizes that the SPS 'attaches special importance to achieving solidarity, equality and social security', and to the principle of solidarity, particularly with respect to impoverished members of society. The SPS saw social equality as 'creating the same material, political and cultural possibilities for all people', and the right to work and create conditions for full employment.

The socialist party declared itself *'against the widespread dismissal of workers and against policies that produce social insecurity*. The problem of technological surplus must be resolved primarily with new development programmes, with corresponding employment that will enable the expansion of production in existing or new enterprises. At the same time, special attention will be given to the employment of young professionals' (author's emphasis).

SPS ideologists emphasized that *'social differences must be restricted* within a reasonable and socially acceptable range' (author's emphasis). They would also fight for 'greater social security expressed in the broadly based right to old-age pensions, health care and social security, education, and culture that is accessible to the citizens' (*Basic Tenets of the Platform and Statutes* ... 13, 14, 15).

SPS tactics for amassing political support and increasing the party's political capacities included affirming the Communistic-egalitarian model of social justice, and using recognizable political formulas that were intended to create among the citizens (voters) the feeling that the SPS alone was capable of assuring a prosperous future for all of Serbia's citizens. The target group was the social classes that had arisen under Communism, who had achieved their social advancement under that system and who were socially and politically favoured.

Owing to the SPS's war policies, on 30 May 1992 the UN Security Council adopted Resolution 757 introducing economic sanctions against FRY. Subsequently, UN Resolution 787, dated 16 November 1992, intensified the sanctions against FRY in such a way that the international transit of important raw materials and products was prohibited across FRY territory. In the summer of 1992, petrol coupons were introduced:

Shortages, smuggling and the illegal (grey) economy gained momentum. The standard of living dropped sharply. Almost an entire month's salary was needed to buy a bag of washing powder ... In the socially owned sector, 40 per cent of the factories had stopped working. At the proposal of the Serbian government, the Assembly adopted a package of measures 'that should mitigate the effects of the sanctions'. The most important among them was the law that guaranteed workers a salary and job during the period in which the international community's sanctions were in force. In addition, the government limited employees' salaries and froze the prices of around 50 per cent of products. To top it all, it was stated that 'public consumption in future must be financed from real sources'. Those days saw the beginning of private exchange offices and savings associations. Annual vacations were followed by the season of 'compulsory' vacations (when employees were laid off while continuing to receive a salary). Around 300,000 employees were already out 'on the street' at that time. They supplemented their guaranteed wages with income from smuggling, buying and selling foreign currency and reselling a whole variety of things. The streets of Belgrade were filled with improvised, often unsightly stands, and with merchants and dealers from all social levels ... Dafiment Bank offered monthly interest of between 100 and 200 per cent for long-term dinar deposits, and from 15 to17 per cent for long-term foreign currency deposits. Jugoskandik also raised its foreign currency interest rates. The number of depositors at these banks is greater than ever. (ibid.: 37, 38)

In spite of everything, the Socialist Party won at the elections held on 20 December 1992. After the SPS's new election victory, a new Serbian government was constituted in February 1993, headed by Prime Minister Nikola Šainović. The government's economic programme contained three basic goals: 'to stop the decline in production and bring about growth, to eliminate hyperinflation, and to undertake public works in order to encourage economic activity'.

However, the government's programme was merely empty demagogy. In 1993, the SPS war policy provoked one of the greatest instances of *hyperinflation* in world history. At the end of December, one German mark on the black market was worth one billion dinars. During December, the National Bank of Yugoslavia put four new notes into circulation, the largest with a nominal value of 500 billion dinars. At the end of 1993 the dinar was completely suppressed in terms of practical use. Hyperinflation reached a peak in January 1994 when the inflation rate was more than 313 million percent.

Hyperinflation was accompanied by shortages of a large number of consumer items, and the population's purchasing power was extremely low. In August 1993 coupons were introduced for rationed supplies of flour, oil, sugar and detergent, as part of the government's 'programme to supply the population in an organized fashion'. In addition, the Serbian government froze the prices of vital foodstuffs and municipal services, which resulted in great shortages. The standard of living fell drastically; three-quarters of the population were not able to provide for their basic subsistence.

Describing the SPS 'economy of destruction', or the ruling party's 'great robbery of the people', Mladjan Dinkić cites the following data that illustrate the population's standard of living that year: '... in the middle of November 1993, two average monthly salaries were needed to buy a simple electric plug, while a baby's push-chair cost ninety-seven average salaries. However, one single average salary was enough to buy four ordinary ball-point pens. In December 1993 the largest pension (which only some 300 people in Serbia received) was barely enough to buy one bar of soap or one-third of a tube of toothpaste on the day it was paid' (M. Dinkić 1995: 243). Seen on the annual level, retail prices rose by 352; 459; 275; 105; 197 per cent (ibid.: 43). Early parliamentary elections, in which the SPS won once again, were held at the time of the worst hyperinflation.

In analysing the enigma of the SPS electoral victory, Vladimir Goati used Županov's formula of the coalition at the 'top' and the 'bottom' of the social pyramid that had been effective in the old regime; however, owing to the suppression of technological structures and the middle classes to the benefit of the 'bottom of the pyramid', it hindered economic development.

The SPS assured support from the working classes, particularly the most numerous and poorest paid (unskilled, semi-skilled), at the first free elections in 1990, promising social security, and above all job security. Explaining the 'secret' of the SPS's success at these elections, one writer noted that the SPS '... succeeded in creating an image of itself as the protector of the social classes comprising a massive voting army. At the same time, it has confrontations with the intelligentsia (the University, culture, media). It therefore favours classes that comprise the massive voting army, but disfavours classes that are the promoters of social and cultural development ... Electoral calculations and the future development of society are very much at odds' (Pečujlić 1992: 198). The SPS did not change the social strategy described, even after civil war broke out in Croatia (1991) and Bosnia-Hercegovina, or after the UN economic sanctions against Serbia (30 May 1992) when Serbia's economy was on the brink of collapse. Before the 1992 and 1993 elections, the SPS promised voters that they would not be fired from their jobs as a result of any decrease in production. This did not remain an empty campaign promise; on the

SPS's initiative, the Serbian parliament adopted a law that made it impossible to fire an employee while the sanctions were in effect ('Law on the Special Conditions for Hiring and Dismissing Employees During the UN Security Council Sanctions', *RS Official Gazette*, 30 une 1993, no. 47). In short, at all parliamentary elections held up to that time, and in political life in general, the ruling party appeared as the representative of the interests of potential 'social losers' in the process of economic transition. In other words, from the viewpoint of the immediate interests of the disfavoured classes, the SPS acted as a socialist party. But from the viewpoint of their long-term interests and those of society as a whole, it was a conservative party, since the effects of such actions slowed down or blocked transition (V. Goati 1995: 204).

The Socialist Party of Serbia is undeniably an important political entity in Yugoslavia's post-Communist era. It bears enormous responsibility for the tragic and brutal civil war in parts of former Yugoslavia and for the pauperization of huge numbers of citizens of Serbia. With its policy of defending its own rule at all costs, it hindered the further modernization of society in Serbia. It severed the historical flow of social reforms and the transition of the political and economic system that would open the path to Serbia's progressive development and its entry into the community of European peoples.

The Traumatic Circle of the Serbian Opposition

DUBRAVKA STOJANOVIĆ

> While the whole world over political struggles are being
> sorted out and canalized, they still remain in a state of
> chaos here, where there are no incentives other than stub-
> bornness and appetite, where everything is considered al-
> lowed: political auctions, overnight changes in thought,
> most unnatural unions, and the selling of consciences.
>
> *Jovan Skerlić, 1906*

By all normal criteria,[1] Yugoslavia was one of the states of 'existing socialism' until 1990. However, the distinctiveness of Yugoslav Communism influenced its specific 'implosion' and unique post-Communist[2] development. In Yugoslavia, the political system of existing socialism was not demolished by a mass uprising of the population as occurred in other Eastern European countries, where the existing regimes were rapidly brought down and 'power' and 'opposition' given equal positions in round-table discussions. In Yugoslavia there was no uprising, and the impression is that the rhythm of political transition was determined more by the pressure of change in Eastern Europe than by the influence of otherwise deep economic and social crises. These special circumstances, combined with the state crisis, influenced the position of emerging political parties, their character, type, and political or ideological organization. It is therefore important at the outset to refer to the specific political situation in Serbia and Yugoslavia at the end of the 1980s.

The preconditions for pluralism

The Communist regime in Serbia and Yugoslavia was more deeply rooted than in other East European countries, and enjoyed incomparably greater support in society than in the other peripheral countries of 'existing socialism'. In these regions it was not introduced by Russian tanks, but rather by authentic revolution in the form of a peoples' revolutionary movement arising from victory in the civil war and World War. Mass support for a revolutionary transformation had *social* roots in a socially weakly stratified, predominantly agrarian society, which only saw the possibility of imposing an egalitarian model in the destruction of its initial social division. This confirms the thesis that a society undeveloped because of a long interval from the beginning of reform (industrialization, modernization and the creation of a just state) to the first satisfactory results, tends towards a return to a pre-modern social model, ideologically formulated by the radical elite as 'a project to accelerate history and shorten the path of development', producing the model of twentieth-century revolution (L. Perović 1993: 157). The idealogical roots of that political project are deeply embedded in the history of political ideas in Serbia. This trend, continued without interruption from the time of Svetozar Marković (1846–1875), formulated the folk concept of revolutionary transformation, the task of which was to impose a past model of social equality in the name of the future and to establish the 'new' on this, as an anachronistic system (L. Perović 1993: 157). The duration of these concepts in the history of political ideas in Serbia is most certain proof of their deeply social, historical and political foundation.

In 1987 the regime, already overthrown in Eastern Europe, experienced complete regeneration in Serbia with the coming to power of Slobodan Milošević, and was again firmly established. In the name of 'an anti-bureaucratic revolution' the old regime would present itself as new and create a united whole in the emergence of a politically impossible situation: a party which had been in power for forty years succeeded in being both government and opposition through this 'cleaned-up' leadership. Maintaining its continuation in power, SK Serbia (the League of Communists of Serbia) at the same time filled the opposition gap in the manner of a maelstrom, presenting itself as a political opponent of the former Serbian leadership, which it would change by storm, thus creating the impression that great changes had come and introducing the 'new power' of fresh ideas. At the same time, this new, strengthened SKS would become the opposition in the framework of the SKJ (the League of Communists of Yugoslavia), and through conflict with all remaining republican leadership in Yugoslavia, promote collective, national homogeneity and almost completely absorb the potential opposition existing in Serbia. The political conflict within the SKJ (leading to the final destruction of the organization at the Fourteenth Congress in January 1990) directed the

SKS towards union with the existing political opposition, united in the battle to protect Serbian national interests at Yugoslav level (Goati 1991: 20). Thus, instead of conflicts, the government and existing opposition in Serbia met together, thwarting the interests of the other Yugoslav nations and their elites.

The third important component for understanding the relationship between power and opposition in Serbia is the fact that the Communist system in Serbia received a transfusion, whitewashing itself with the Serbian national question which had been an area reserved for demonstrating opposing views in Serbia before Milošević came to power. Importantly, during the 1970s and 1980s, with the exception of narrow liberal and civilly oriented circles, resistance to the ruling regime had been largely based on national arguments and ideas about the conceived exploitation and endangerment of existing nations by the regime, but even more, and more importantly, by other Yugoslav peoples. Thus the new Serbian leadership, announcing the defence of Serbianism as its most important task, seized the programme from the hands of the opposition, leaving it with no ideological identity. The opposition never recovered from that first blow.

The fact that the strengthened totalitarianism in Serbia after 1987 offered strong resistance to all forms of pluralism, whether in other Yugoslav republics or in Serbia alone, is also important in an understanding of the relationship between power and opposition in Serbia. The daily newspaper *Politika* is rich in examples demonstrating the force of resistance shown by the Serbian ruling party towards any vision of alternative organization, including co-operation with peace, anti-nuclear or even feminist movements.[3]

The emergence of the opposition

Under pressure from the opposition, the events in Eastern Europe, and the establishment of a multiparty system in the other Yugoslav republics, the government in Serbia was compelled to pass the necessary laws legalizing parties and announcing the first multiparty elections in December 1990. There are many signs that this was done more as a tactical concession, at a moment when the power of the Socialist Party in Serbia fully permeated state and society, than as a real acceptance of the course of parliamentary democracy. The government did not facilitate institutional assumptions of political pluralism, as can be seen in the serious deficiencies in the law on political parties, elections and public voting; in the ruling party's inheriting of all the assets of the SK and the Socialist Alliance; in its preventing the passage of a law on the financing of political activity; and in its undermining equality in the most powerful media. Thus, in assessing the efficiency of the Serbian opposition, one must take into account that the established political system basically did not suit a system of parliamentary democracy, but rather one of a transitional, hybrid nature.

By such a system of rule, the opposition was pushed into a political struggle outside parliament. However, at the first demonstrations (13 June 1990) at which the opposition sought the passing of a law on political parties and the announcement of a multiparty election, the thesis that a ruling party brought to power by bloodshed would not admit defeat without bloodshed was confirmed. The demonstrations were terminated when a police cordon assaulted a peaceful group of demonstrators led by Dragoljub Mičunović and Borislav Pekić, who were protesting outside the studios of Belgrade Television. The full extent of the government's brutality was shown particularly clearly on 9 March 1991 at the strongest opposition demonstrations, when there was bloody confrontation and tanks were sent onto the streets of Belgrade. There was nothing more brutal than the arrest and beating of Vuk Drašković on the night of 1 July 1993, after which he was kept in prison for six weeks.

By pushing the opposition into activity outside parliament, and by physical confrontations between the military and citizens oriented towards the opposition, the ruling party continued clearly to show its essential non-acceptance of any form of political competition. At the same time, by its brutal conduct it radicalized the opposition, who by means of the massive gathering of frightened citizens could easily press for drastic political demands. In return, the government used the behaviour of the opposition as propaganda, presenting them on television screens as a destructive and anti-civilian phenomenon, or, as was often stated, as a 'chaotic, mindless force'.

The overbearing, arrogant conduct of the Serbian government differed from the pre-election conduct of powers in other Eastern European countries. Political analysts commented then that the issue was an expression of Slobodan Milošević's weakness, but time proved that it was a question of the expression of power, force and thoughtlessness. These characteristics arose from the nature of the ruling political system and type of Milošević's regime, but they were also deeply historical and part of the traditional political culture and idiosyncrasies of Serbian rule.

Historical analysis has shown that the modern history of the Serbian state is distinguished by the extraordinary force of its political struggles. The struggles of rival dynasties, the murder and persecution of rulers as well as frequent rebellions and conspiracies, made nineteenth-century Serbia a politically unstable country. At the beginning of the twentieth century Serbian parliamentarianism was continuously under the shadow of political terrorism—especially before elections—political assassinations, and the conspiratorial activity of the 'Black Hand' (a group of officers who led a conspiracy from 1911–1917). Legally guaranteed elections were completely out of the question considering the attitude of the minister of internal affairs in the pre-election campaign and before voting itself (O. Popović and Obradović 1994: 333–339). The best testimony to the atmosphere in Serbia at the time is contained in the words of Ljube Davidović (the opposition leader) in 1906: 'Political opponents are considered as enemies of the state; all possible means can be used against them'.[4] The leaders of the Kingdom of Serbia, Croatia and Slovenia had a similar attitude. Political confrontations with a national component were also widespread, filling the pages of daily newspapers without limit, leading to a political assassination in Parliament in 1928, and a royal dictatorship.

This short, superficial historical overview shows that the current political system in Serbia need not be considered as an isolated phenomenon, but as one which corresponds to one of the long-lasting cultural models of this region.[5]

The roots of the dominant model in Serbia can be sought in the revolutionary nature in which the Serbian state was created during the nineteenth century, and in the continual attempts at national unity, which lasted for more than a century. This historical development of the Serbian state created a need for strong, centralized leadership, leaning on repressive means of authority, especially the army. One important role of the army was to secure a constant desire for national liberation in military competition with neighbouring kingdoms. Besides this, in undeveloped countries the army appears as the best organized and integrated institution, always being the surest support for authoritarian rule (D. Djordjević 1989: 66). From such historical and political roots was created a dominant authoritarian cultural model of power, both a product and an instrument of a strongly bureaucratic centralized state. Although originating from the special historical development of the Serbian state, it was inseparable from the wider, authoritarian cultural model of Serbian patriarchal society. Belonging to the same model, both society and government created a particular kind of alliance. Identical in their authoritarian essence, they supplemented and 'nourished' each other.

However, since the government and state were also at the same time autarkic, they did not assume bilateral communications. Society became an abstract object to be governed, and government grew into an abstract necessity which was above question. The relationship between ruler and subject was united in certain para-religious traits, especially recognizable in that this type of rule most frequently offers no rational, political undertakings, but rather a system of moral values. Sanctified rule also receives power from a persecuted opponent, that is, anathema and judgement of 'unbelievers'. Joined to citizenship of the same long-lasting cultural model, massive support was received in this anathema, on which was based a system of political relations.

Regulated by this historical tradition and concrete political conditions, the relationship between government and opposition in Serbia was different from that assumed in other Eastern European countries, and in other Yugoslav republics. The nature of Serbian authoritarian rule, partly totalitarian, controlled the character of the opposition. As there existed no sufficiently strong alternative cultural and political model on which to lean, the opposition parties became part of the same model represented by the ruling party, in their internal organization and ideological identity.

The historical similarities between the current leadership and the previous forms of political activity is an expression of a deeper model regulating modern Serbian political history. The fact is that neither at the beginning, nor at the end of the twentieth century has Serbia had the social conditions for real political pluralism. A predominantly monolithic, structurally non-stratified society is a basis for the creation of a monolithic political system, regulated completely by the rule of one party, permeating all levels of state and society. A weakly differentiated society has weakly differentiated interests, and political parties cannot institute their representatives or influence the state in their name. An egalitarian society with small differences and needs does not achieve balance and leadership by political activity, limiting and controlling society and state, but its interests lie in a strong state and government as a guarantee of social stability and security. Political action is not a natural and spontaneous expression of social action, nor are political parties representatives of individual parts of society or their interests before the state. Thus the political pluralization of the post-Communist world presents an interesting historical experiment, because it does not spring from the pluralization of society, as happened in the West, but has the opposite conception: it appears as a possible *condition* for society's development and differentiation. Democratic theory still does not have a solution to the question of whether such an inversion is possible, for there is insufficient similar experience (G. Hermet 1993).

Until the appearance and dominance of political organizations claiming to be equal to the whole population, it follows that an undeveloped society does not have expressive 'individual-citizens, nor *demos*, nor profiled subjects of the democratic process' (J. Trkulja 1993: 148). In such sub-urban societies it is not possible to constitute an individual-citizen, as a political subject assuming political pluralism and parliamentarianism. The citizen is absorbed into the collective; no difference is seen between his interests and those of the collective; and by right, great missionary, collective ideas that will change the known world are the most accessible to him. For this reason poor societies often elect the political form of populism, giving the simplest answers to the most complicated questions (G. Hermet 1993: 174; N. Popov 1993).

The social conditions in Serbia had the effect that 'the fundamental homeland constitution of the "democratic" political territory was above the individual, a collective-national interest' (J. Trkulja 1993: 38). Parties did not come into being spontaneously or gradually, growing out of the various internal, opposing needs of a social group, but rather grew from the political ideas of their leaders. This method of creating a party, from the head downwards, favours a leading, charismatic type of party, recognizable by its leadership and not by its programme (V. Milić 1994). The party leader becomes a symbol, incomparably more important than the policy promoted by the party, and the promotion of personal attributes becomes a sign of recognition and suggestion to voters (for example Vuk Drašković, the romantic rebel; successful and talented Zoran Djindić; strong and uncompromising Vojislav Šešelj).

The most outstanding example of this kind of portrayal is the Serbian Renewal Party (SPO) and its charismatic leader Vuk Drašković. This party was the first formed on the principle of a pyramid construction. This kind of party has an unimpeachable leader at the head, whose rights are completely unlimited.[6] Then comes a narrow circle of party leadership (most frequently composed of the party leader's friends). In the case of the Serbian Democratic Party (DSS) there was also the independent institution of adviser to the party Presidency, who did not need to be a member of the party (for example Leon Kojen). Next comes the wider party body, membership, voters, and finally people who attend meetings.

The question of party formation is no less important than the contents of the party programme. Indeed, analysis of programmes shows that these two aspects are deeply connected and that the organizational changes in the DS (Democratic Party) and DSS came as consequences of policy changes and their movement from being parties of the civil centre to those with a right-wing, national orientation. The political approach to populism produced the effect that the modern structure of party institutions on which they had insisted at first was abandoned (the Democratic Party's loyalty to institutional decision making regarding the party organs, where the general and executive boards, at that time separated, were called together for every important question of policy, was particularly brought to public attention). Abandoning the previous democratic form, procedure and institutional system, the DS and DSS became parties of leadership, fitting into the ruling, authoritarian cultural model that confirmed their current activity. The Democratic Party's election result best confirms this: at the time of their loyalty to procedures and politics of the centre they obtained 7 per cent of votes in the first elections, whereas in the 'Djindjić phase' they achieved 16.4 per cent of votes in the 1993 elections (Statlab 1993).

Kosovo and Yugoslav trauma in national programmes

The political and social conditions in Serbia, the way in which parties were formed, and their type of organization, decisively influenced their ideology and political activity. Election analysis points to a conclusion that the policy of the Serbian opposition should be considered on two levels: the level of their agenda; and the level of their political activity.

Analysis of party agendas, manifestos and pre-election speeches of party leaders, and of elections where the basic party assignments were mentioned, reveal that clashing parties offered the same national agendas. The ruling SPS also offered the same national programme, showing that the main plurality in Serbia was caught in a dilemma between Communist and anti-Communist nationalism (Goati 1991: 20). Their agendas joined to a regime, the parties wasted time outdoing each other and the government in 'patriotism', and in this game, the party in power had incomparably stronger arguments (e.g. the army). Parties tried to oppose the government's arguments, heading out into extreme nationalism, thus losing their democratic identity and failing to pose essential questions about the neglected Serbian state, or to show an alternative way of thinking or acting.

Research into texts published in church periodicals and in *Knjižecne novine* show that the year in which the opposition opened the national question can be taken as 1986. The question of Kosovo (see the contribution of Olga Zirojevic, this volume) was raised just as Slobodan Milošević formulated it in his attack on the constitutional system of Yugoslavia: as the right of Serbia to statehood, and the right of Serbian people to equality (Lj. Tadić 1986). This demagogic formula carried in it the essential programme which led to the breakup of Yugoslavia.

In the notorious 1980s, part of the Serbian intellectual elite, who were later to form opposition parties, formulated the Kosovo trauma in mythical style, offering an intellectual framework for Milošević's policy. In May 1987, at the 'On Kosovo—for Kosovo' meeting of the Association of Writers, Ljubomir Simović (later to become a member of the non-party section of DEPOS [Democratic Movement of Serbia]) pronounced the words with which Slobodan Milošević would come to power four months later: 'At once, immediately,' said Simović 'are the first words of a new speech by which a betrayed and humiliated people are announced ... These people have stood up, and to those whom they have penitently listened to up until now, they have begun to give orders and settle terms'. (*KN* 1 June 1987). Later that phenomenon would be used in an identical way and formally expressed as 'a happening of the people' by the government.

'The voice of the people' was the most important introductory political argument of the nationally oriented intelligentsia in the mid-1980s, and of their representatives who would later form political parties. They would oppose the still sacred 'working class' with 'people' as their political toy, creating the illusion that the issue was of a new political concept. The illusion of change was founded on the proffered image of 'people' materialized into the shape of a body (I. Čolović 1993: 149), whose soul and being groaned under the burden of history, their 'reality' already pressed down to a spent, abstract 'working people'. By the transplantation of one collective force into another, any essential political change was frustrated, but the transformation of 'workers' into 'Serbian people' (Čolović 1993: 149) enabled the completely imperceptible move from totalitarianism in the name of a class, to totalitarianism in the name of a nation.

However, the future opposition leadership did not just formulate new ideas, but also a good proportion of concrete political projects, later to be accepted by Slobodan Milošević. Thus, for example, in April 1988, in discussions between Serbian intellectuals and Albanian representatives held in *Dom Omladine*, Milan Komnenić (vice-president of the SPO) said: 'Hand on heart, I have nothing to discuss with you. You have already said clearly enough and done what you intended. For that I offer you bitter thanks ... Sir, we are at war. As we already know this, why do we hide it. A segment of the Albanian people—I don't know how many—has brought war against the Serbian people, without notice. If they haven't declared war with weapons, they have done so with their consciences' (*KN* 1 May 1988).

A few months later, in the summer of 1988, Serbia was shaken by 'solidarity rallies' at which the Albanians were notified of the authority of Slobodan Milošević, and the whole of Yugoslavia informed that the Serbs could 'no longer retreat' and that they had essentially changed the rules of the game. That summer Yugoslav television screens displayed the crazed and distorted faces of hundreds of thousands of participants at the meetings, whose 'self sanctified' trance became the argument and material force of ruling populism. The whole 'cultural revolution' movement would not have been possible without the ideas formed and previously offered by the Serbian intelligentsia. These ideas were as important to Milošević as they had been to them.

This was confirmed by the following example. The megalomanic celebration of the six-hundredth anniversary of the Battle of Kosovo signified the peak of the meetings movement and served as a stage from which war was pronounced for the first time. Before this ultimately political use, the Kosovo trauma had appropriately been solemnly fermented in the ranks of the Serbian intellectual elite. Thus one of their most important representatives, Matija Bećković (later a central figure in DEPOS) announced, three months before the celebration: 'Should we not announce at the six hundredth Kosovo anniversary that "Kosovo is Serbia"? That fact does not depend on Albanian birth rates, nor Serbian mortality. There is so much Serbian blood and so many Serbian shrines there that it will be Serbian even when not one Serb remains' (*P*. 5 March 1989). Using a gnomic formulation, Bećković announced a new Serbian political trend, the basis of which would not depend on realpolitik but that would be inclined towards the stronger, the older, or whatever first comes to mind. The adventure into which Serbian politics would move in these years could not be packed into a modern language or form, since in essence it was anachronistic. The political project intended to create the idea of 'each to his own' in the Serbian people (even where 'there is not one Serb'), just as each and every project that places the rights of one group above the rights of another group has to be tied to a higher, heavenly or metaphysical reason. Anti-modern aspirations can only be justified with anti-modern motives and expressed in anachronistic forms. Such a form was given to Milošević's policy by Serbian nationalism, later the opposition intelligentsia. They formulated and pronounced this 'meta'-side very concretely at a time when even Milošević had shunned it. The essence of the war for 'the other side' (the other side of the Drina, the Sava and the Danube), a war against the living in the name of the dead, was best formulated by Bećković in an address which he gave to North American Serbs in 1988: 'The grave is the greatest shrine and the oldest church of the Serbian people. The grave is our longest and most enduring faith. We still swear by bones and graves, we have no firmer support or better medicine, nor firmer conviction ... States have gone to war because of bones, states are held with bones, with bones they are founded and built' (*GC* March 1988).

The poetic framework of Milošević's policy pointed to a deep, symbiotic relationship of the nationally orientated, later oppositional elites with the new leaders, frequently expressed as open support for Milošević. Once again the most explicit, concrete support was from Matija Bećković. Twenty days before passing the amendments to the Serbian constitution, by which lawful aggression was executed against the constitutional system of Yugoslavia, at an extraordinary session of the Association of Writers of Serbia (AWS), the essence of the new amendments were again expressed 'poetically': 'Serbia, the Republic which is not, cannot have a more important assignment than to be' (*P.* 5 March 1989).

Vuk Drašković sought fast action, as Milošević had needed: 'We (the Serbian intelligentsia) are late in Kosovo. We will pay for our delay and indifference to our destiny fatally and probably with no chance of historical justification, if we do not, as soon as possible, immediately, demand the programme and conditions that we want or don't want' (*KN* 15 March 1989).

Gojko Djogo, one of thirteen initiators of the Democratic Party, spoke in the same tone at the party's founding assembly: 'From Kosovo until today, Serbs have not had a greater shrine than

Kosovo. They have handed themselves over to that shrine, and over six centuries have returned to her the most expensive sacrifices, blood sacrifices ... I don't know how or how far we will go, but I know that we must. For a Serbian state without Kosovo would be like a Serb stabbed in the heart ... Kosovo is a Serbian problem and we must resolve it once and for all' (*De.* 9 March 1990).

Quotations show that the majority of leading people in the subsequent opposition parties publicly showed the Kosovo problem in a very similar way, nearer to an epic tale than a real confrontation with an actual situation and having a possible political remedy. Forming a corpus of political ideas on which Milošević would later base his clash with the previous Serbian leadership and come to power, a section of the Serbian intelligentsia drew out the national question as the one, pressing political problem. All other problems of Serbian society (living through a deep crisis) looked tiny in comparison with the shrines and testament ideas, and insistence on them was non-essential. Thus the social blows and traumas heralded by the collapse of the system were averted by exchanging them with a trauma six hundred years older. All state, social and economic problems in Yugoslavia were substituted by national problems and reduced to national problems. Transition was delayed for an unspecified period, to be acted on when national problems were resolved, and the old system remained unmoved. Since a large proportion of the Serbian elite, and even the section that would later form opposition parties, prepared and supported the enthronement of people as a political force, and treated the national question as a priority, it can be said that there was no readiness for transition in Serbia.

Raising the Serbian national question in Kosovo had one further significance. As in the case of Slobodan Milošević's policy, the Serbian opposition also used Kosovo to raise the even more complex issue of interethnic relations in Yugoslavia. Matija Bećković formulated the connection between the Kosovo issue and the Serbian national problem most precisely when he said: 'Long ago Kosovo arrived at Jadovno (a burial place), and it's a real miracle that the whole Serbian territory didn't get the name Kosovo' (*KN.* 15 June 1998). The problem of the Serbs and Albanians thus grew into a problem of the Serbs' relations with all other ethnic groups, through raising the question of what this meant, and how far Serbian territory stretched. In essence, leaders of all the opposition parties would agree on the answer to that question, regardless of differing terminology.

The first concept about which they would all agree was the idea that Yugoslavia ought to be a 'democratic federation'. Thus, in their 'recommended national programme' the Democratic Party would support Yugoslavia 'as a democratic federation with full equal rights of federal units and citizens'.[7] In the name of this principle (which in practice meant introducing a two-house parliament and 'one person, one vote'), the party supported the introduction of a new constitution, establishing a new state organization in place of the existing one, 'in which confederate elements that do not suit the collective Yugoslavian state would overrule–since internal borders between individual federal units would tend towards differing and mutually opposing principles–the principle of ethnic homogeneity and that of cultural-historical identity'.[8] The DS explained its objection to a confederate organization in that the issue was about 'historical survival and undemocratic state forms that neglected civilian freedom and subordinated this to national sovereignty', and with a warning that entry into a confederate organization might lead to a civil war.[9]

In its first programme, the Serbian Renewal Movement (SPO) allowed the possibility of the existence of Yugoslavia as a federal state alongside the demand for unity of Serbian lands, provided that Yugoslavia tolerated serious constitutional changes.[10] Only by such changes (of which more will be said later) could historical injustice, described in the programme as the Serbian peoples' trauma, be corrected: 'The graves of Serbs killed in this century's wars have not yet been counted, and many have not been dug or marked. Nevertheless, they all bear the mark of Yugoslavia. From 1912 to 1918 one generation was mowed down in order to create Yugoslavia. From 1941 to 1945 another generation fell to recreate Yugoslavia. For the survival of a united Yugoslavia we denied ourselves faith, history and tradition, in the hope that in this way we would subdue the hatred of those who did not include state, culture, shrines, dynasties, epochs, flags, or laws in Yugoslavia, for these they simply did not have ... In a stroke, Yugoslavia turned the Serbian victories of the twentieth century into their defeat.'[11]

These programme departures, with an open lack of esteem and intolerance towards other Yugoslav peoples, meant that the Serbs' assent to Yugoslavia supposed bringing international relations down to an imaginary 'historical final account' by which 'payment' would be justly made. The people would enter into this creation, supposing this imaginary 'payment'. In essence, this was about the concept of a Serbian Yugoslavia, politically dominated by the Serbian people for ever, a final offer to the other Yugoslav peoples.[12] However, they were not ready to accept such a project.

The programme of the Serbian Radical Party was the only one that rejected any possibility of preserving Yugoslavia. The national objective was formulated as follows: 'the return of a free, independent and democratic Serbian state, to include all that is Serbian and all Serb territories, so that within her own borders she would have, alongside the current Serbian federal unit, Montenegro, Serbian Bosnia, Hercegovina, Dubrovnik, Dalmatia, Lika, Kordun, Banija, Slavonija, West Srem, Baranja and Macedonia'.[13]

The Serbian Democratic Party and the Civil Alliance of Serbia were formed at a time when the breakup of Yugoslavia had already come about, so that in their programme there was no concrete recommendation to preserve Yugoslavia.

The acceptance of a Yugoslav federation by the SPO and the DS was subject to important constitutional changes. The DS programme predicted that 'it would be worthwhile securing a constitutional possibility if, in the framework of individual federal units, territorial autonomy is honoured, in so far as the population on territories with specific ethnic composition or cultural-historical identity decide this by referendum. The final decision to honour autonomous regions would be made by the parliaments of the federal units'.[14]

By the same principle, the SPO sought the formation of an autonomous region of Serbian Krajina, Istria and Dubrovnik in Croatia, and four autonomous, national areas in Bosnia-Hercegovina, specifying the districts in its programme of May 1990. A few months later the events in Croatia started to move along that road.

Alongside these projects there also appeared the concept of organizing the Yugoslav area, in the event that the breakup of Yugoslavia had already occurred. The future opposition leaders were the first to raise the issue of creating new ethnic borders in the event of dissolution, much earlier than the issue was raised in the programme of the ruling party. At the beginning of 1989, at an extraordinary session of the AWS, Vuk Drašković raised the question of the restriction of Yugoslav peoples: 'where are the western borders of Serbia, and how far do they extend? We must establish this. Those borders were surely specified by Ante Pavelić [leader of the Croatian Ustasha during the Second World War]. They are where Serbian graves and pits lie! It is essential that these borders are marked in the Serbian national programme ... Croats must know ahead of time that in the event of the dissolution of Yugoslavia, the AVNOJ and Brioni [Communist leadership congresses at which the federal borders of Yugoslavia were determined] borders would cease, and a true vote would be made by both Jasenovac and Jadovno [Croatian concentration camps during the Second World War], and by all our burial places, and by all Serbs who were driven or relocated from Croatia, Slavonia, Bosnia, Dalmatia, Hercegovina, Kordun, Lika and Banija' (*KN*, 18 March 1989).

A year later, at the founding of his first National Serbian Renewal Party on 7 January 1990, Drašković did not mention the possibility of preserving Yugoslavia, but pronounced the following as the goal of his party: 'the creation of a democratic, multiparty Serbian state within her historical and ethnic borders' (*P*, 8 January 1990).

As shown above, the SPO programme predicted the possibility of preserving a democratic, federal Yugoslavia, but in the event of a confederation foresaw the following: 'territory cannot be removed from current Yugoslavia, or made confederate to the disadvantage of the Serbian people, if it formed part of the Kingdom of Serbia on 1 December 1918, the day on which Yugoslavia was created, or if it comprises regions in which Serbs formed the majority before the Ustasha genocide. Such territory is the unchallengeable, historical and ethnic property of the Serbian people' (*SR*, 1 June 1990). According to this stance, Serbian territorial demands depended on two different principles: historical (in which case Macedonia should have entered into the future Serbian state, since it was in the Kingdom of Serbia in 1918); and ethnic (by which, on the basis of natural law, regions with a Serb majority should belong to the Serbian state).

In 1991, at the outbreak of the wars which we could call the Yugoslav Wars, Drašković crucially changed the direction of his political activity and offered a strategy to resolve the crisis in a peaceful way. That plan was contained in a 1994 party programme. It repeated that the boundary limitation with Croatia, on the basis of the ethnic map of 6 April 1941 (the day on which Germany attacked the Kingdom of Yugoslavia) was unavoidable. A reconstruction of Yugoslav areas should be along the following principles: 'part of Baranja, Western Srem, and the Serbian part of Eastern Slavonia ought to enter into the composition of Serbia, and the remaining part of current Serbian Krajina should enter into the composition of Bosnia-Hercegovina. In return, Croatia should receive West Hercegovina, to the right of Neretva'.[15] The programme envisaged the cantonization of Bosnia-Hercegovina, and the creation of a combined state of Bosnia-Hercegovina, Serbia, Montenegro and Vardar Macedonia, which would be identical to an earlier formula for Serbian historical and ethnic borders.

Essentially, the SPO programme remained unchanged. Today it is simply offered in a more modern form, and written in modern, political and not epic language. The party left a programme faithful to the principle of newly composed areas of former Yugoslavia, which, regardless of whether the Serbian borders were original or determined 'by Serbian skulls', or in a second phase based on current economic, trade or political justification, remained the same: the creation of a state in which all Serbs should live.

The committee of the Democratic Party which formulated the 'Recommended National Programme of the Democratic Party', saw the national interests of Serbia in the same light—as lying in the creation of a Serbian national state: 'the Democratic Party considers legitimate the desire of any people to gather as many as possible of their own compatriots under one state roof ... The national policy of a Serbian state, as in other national states, must aim at bringing all territories predominantly populated by Serbs into the composition of one state'.[16] In the event of secession of any peoples from Yugoslavia, they envisaged the following: 'they should be informed that in the event of departure from Yugoslavia and the creation of independent states, they cannot claim the right to territory which is predominantly populated by other Yugoslav peoples'.[17] The last sentence of the programme stated: 'In the final analysis, this policy of a Serbian state should be managed with good understanding of the national interest: that the Serbian people as a whole, or as a majority, live in one state'. Thus the DS, which in its political activity had a different discourse from the SPO, and in its policy behaved as a party of the civil centre, in essence bent towards the greatest acceptance of a national programme, confirming that between the government and the most influential political parties, there was no difference at that moment and on that key political question. In fear of being isolated and judged as anti-national, the party went out with a national programme at variance with its democratic principles and right at the start opened the way for its gradual move to the right. Even if this were the result of a necessary compromise within the framework of its ideologically differing leadership, this shows that the compromise was not sufficient to keep the thirteen original party founders together. The first to depart from their ranks was Slobodan Inić, largely due to his disagreement with the party move towards nationalism. However, that move was insufficient on the part of the DS leadership who, led by Kosta Čavoski and Nikola Milošević, would form the more right-wing and expressly nationally oriented Serbian Liberal Party. In the same way, a section would leave because of that, and other, reasons in 1992 and, led by Vojislav Kostutnica, form the Serbian Democratic Party. Finally, the battle over national policy would be one of the reasons for replacing the party president, Dragoljub Mišunović (1994), and the start of a strengthened national wave which would bring to the fore the new party leader, Zoran Djindjić. These battles and the split in the DS show the essence of opposition programme swings and show how, under the prevailing circumstances, the DS wandered further from its democratic and civil principles, accepting national criteria as the only policy measure and thus moving gradually from its position at the moderate centre. From its inception, the Serbian Radical Party represented the idea of united Serbian lands, with no possibility for the survival of Yugoslavia. It differed from other parties in that, even before the outbreak of the Yugoslav Wars, its leader Vojislav Šešelj had already effectively expressed its programme commitment in the famous 'Karlobag-Karlovac-Virovitica' formula. In the 1991 and 1994 programme texts,[18] the national aspiration was set out in the first point: 'the restoration of a free, independent and democratic Serbian state, encompassing the whole of Serbdom, all Serbian lands, which means that within its borders it will have the current Republic of Serbia, Montenegro, the Serbian Republic and the Serbian Republic of Krajina'. This latest programme differed from the first party programme only in that the unrecognized Serbian states were named as regions, and in that it did not mention 'Serbian Dubrovnik and Serbian Dalmatia' (J. Turkulja 1993: 182).

Only in DEPOS in 1992 was there a different tone from the above.[19] This coalition favoured a new Serbia which would, in the words of Vuk Drašković, 'rest on rich, free citizenship, on a cult of peace and not war, life and not death, reconciliation and not extermination'.[20] Opposing the war lobby, Ljubomir Simović says, in the same place, '"Away with you"! should be said to everyone who today, at the end of the twentieth century, offers a militarized Serbdom, a state of bayonets and army helmets instead of heads, who, in fanatical ecstasy offers a "heavenly" Serbia with no substance ... We should abandon the "kingdom of heaven" as a political project because it is the fastest route to pure suffering, only another name for thoughts and ideas by which nebulous creators, official propagandists and necrology writers are raised up'. Vuk Drašković also spoke in a similar, reconciliatory spirit before the 1992 elections: 'We will offer both hands in reconciliation to Muslims and Croats. In this war we are all both executioners and victims' (*SR*, 16 December 1992).

However, DEPOS did not use its authority and massive support to offer a recognizably different national programme. It is correct to say that the political discourse had been vitally changed; that for the first time the opposition raised some existential social questions; and that for the first time it was clearly emphasized that Serbia could not be subordinated to 'peripheral parts of Serbdom'. But this was not sufficient to create an authentic opposition identity founded on a programme qualitatively different from that of the government. DEPOS's success and that of Milan Panić (in the 1992 elections DEPOS won 17.3% of the votes) showed that at that moment, up to the time of the outbreak of war in Bosnia and the imposition of sanctions against Serbia, there was perhaps space in Serbia to offer a programme founded on a completely different concept, but no one took the risk of 'national betrayal'. Amongst other things, programmes of the associated opposition parties who formed the coalition did not allow an essential withdrawal from the idea of uniting all Serbs.

An analysis of the programmes shows that at the time of the breakup of Yugoslavia, the most influential opposition parties in parliament did not publicly propose an alternative national programme which would in any way differ from the words of Slobodan Milošević, 'all Serbs in one state'. There are many reasons for this, from the above-mentioned parties' lack of a social base, to the fact that the parties were formed when the fate of Yugoslavia had perhaps already been determined. They had no time to form clearly different political platforms, but rather at the last moment jumped on a train that had already started moving. However, perhaps the absence of an alternative national programme disseminated in Serbian political circles the idea that the question of redistributing Yugoslav territory had been opened, and that Serbia faced an historical opportunity to wipe out the consequences of the twentieth-century wars and follow a 'Serbian state' programme which, in the history of Serbian political ideas, had endured for more than a century beside the Yugoslav programmes. It seemed to everyone that the breakup of Yugoslavia opened a possibility 'finally to resolve the Serbian problem', but no one wanted to take responsibility for wasting the opportunity. Desiring that Milošević should let them share the historical limelight, the opposition parties were brought into a situation of having to share with him the responsibility for the deconstruction of Yugoslavia—and with it, for the war. Thus Serbia entered the war with no alternative solution to the Yugoslav question to offer, with no way to reduce the risk of entering war, and no way to provide a social and political remedy.

The political operations of Serbian opposition parties

The period from 1986 to 1994 can be divided into two parts with respect to the activities of political parties. The first period closed at the outbreak of the war. It was characterized by ideological initiatives of the opposition in relation to the government. The second period started with the first armed confrontations in spring 1991. The government seized the initiative, and the main thrust of the opposition was its increased determination to oppose Milošević's actions.

In the first period of the opposition's ideological initiatives, a corpus of ideas had been prepared which was later accepted and led the parties into power. This relates particularly to the period before Milošević came to power, when, from 1986, members of the opposition formulated all the ideas (from Kosovo, to the constitutional reorganization of Serbia and Yugoslavia) which were later to become the basis for Milošević's programme and success.

After the Eighth Session in 1987 (a meeting of Serbian Communists at which Milošević took control of the SKS) the still unsure government opened a period of association with opposition-oriented intellectuals. They then began to write in the previously inaccessible *Politika* or *NIN*. They openly supported Milošević's moves. Dobrica Ćosić returned to the public eye for the first time in twenty years. Matija Bećković received the 7th July prize. Mića Popović (an artist) was additionally given a prize that had not been presented in 1972 for political reasons. This period of association lasted from the end of 1987 to the middle or end of 1989.

Besides this co-operation, there existed between the two sides a certain rivalry, in which each tried to make political use of the other. The Serbian national opposition remained partially distrustful towards the Communist Milošević, intending to use him for unpleasant activity, especially that in Kosovo, and then later to reduce support and benefit from the rivalry. However, it happened that Milošević's appraisal was more precise, and he played the game better. He used the opposition members' strong intellectual authority which had first prepared the ground for him, and then, having the ideological initiative, they continued to open new important and complicated questions which he would later take over as required.

The middle of 1989 marked the end of this co-operation, when individuals in the opposition became dissatisfied with what Mi-

lošević had done and when the destruction of Communism in
Eastern Europe gave them the idea that, pursuing their programme
alone, they could seize power. Then Milan Komnenić announced:
'Instead of a government which vacillates in Belgrade, we will lead
Serbia into death or into glory.'

However, the authority of Slobodan Milošević was strong and
stable and he no longer needed the co-operation of Serbian opposition intelligentsia. Occupying the national seat, Milošević pushed
them out to an extreme political position, by which the potential
number of their voters was reduced at the start.

The most noticeable opposition party—the SPO—would continue
to attack the government from extreme national positions, seeking
a firmer attitude and a quick, efficient solution to the Serbian question, right up to the first elections and the shocking opposition
defeat. In this way, the SPO played the part of a pace-setter in a
race. The fact that from July to December 1990, one-third of the
pre-election messages of the SPO were connected to the national
question testifies to this; only 6 per cent of DS and SPS messages
concerned this issue (Goati 1992: 168). To a large degree it is
down to the SPO that the national question dominated the whole
of Serbia and formed the basis for all political divisions. It was also
thanks to the SPO that, in relation to them, the nationalism of the
Serbian government was moderate, leaving an impression with
voters of a wise, moderate policy which would attempt anything to
save Yugoslavia. Although the Democratic Party had the same national programme as the SPO, their political activities left a different impression. In the foreground was a devotion to democracy,
with which 19 per cent of DS political speeches were concerned
(while in the case of the SPO, the proportion was only 10%). Talking about parliamentarianism, an independent judiciary, an economy independent of politics, civil equality and private property,
this party gave the impression of a party of the centre. From such a
platform the party won 7.4 per cent of votes in the first elections
(Goati 1992: 168).

The shock of the election defeat at the beginning of 1991 began
to change the relations between the opposition parties and their
political expression. The SPO would begin gradually to move towards the centre. In May 1991, immediately before the outbreak of
the war, Vuk Drašković was interviewed by *NIN* about which had
priority, democracy or nation. He stated: 'It is clear which direction
is essential: first democracy, after that democracy, and in third
place, democracy. Everything else will follow by itself.' His anti-war
messages announced before the outbreak of war show that he had

rejected national extremism and that he would offer Serbia different rhetoric in the stormy times ahead.

After their election failure, the Democratic Party began to accentuate a national policy. In May 1991 Mirko Petrović asked the Serbian Parliament to determine the 'western borders of Serbdom', and Zoran Djindić, speaking about the Serbs in Croatia, announced, to the applause of the Socialists, 'We also plead for a peaceful solution, but peace under these conditions is not peace–rather capitulation. Peace can be achieved now at the cost of retreating from autonomy, at the cost of holding a meeting of Serb loyalty to the Croatian government in Jelacic square ... Such peace is only illusory and we cannot agree to it, because our lives are at issue'" (*De*, 24 May 1991).

Disarray on the opposition scene had already prepared a situation in which Milošević would take full initiative at the outbreak of war. He would direct the war, negotiate and sign peace agreements. The opposition would remain stuck in the programme for which the war was being fought, waver in their political expression, and in time lose their identity. An analysis of their bearing leads to the conclusion that the nationalist opposition parties abandoned every policy, principle, programme and idea, and that the main focus of their political activity became Slobodan Milošević. In time they would speak less about Serbdom, war, borders, Serbs, democracy, economic trade or any other question of principle, and more about Milošević and his activity. Their principle attitude became 'be against, even when this requires a change in party policy, a split in the party, or compromise with the extreme war positions directed from Pale'.

Above all, this related to the Democratic Party which would first play its card against Milošević at the time of the Vanse plan in January 1992. The rejection of the UN peace plan by the Democratic Party, support for the Knin leader, Milan Babić, and the meeting of Dragoljub Mićunović with Babić and Karadžić, were flatly against maintaining the already fragile truce in Croatia. There then began the policy of a party which accused Milošević of leaving the war without getting done anything that he had planned on entering it. This would be repeated and confirmed in all subsequent situations: on the occasion of the Vanse-Owen plan for Bosnia; on the occasion of the Owen-Stoltenburg plan; and finally with the Contact Group's plan when, in August 1994, in the conflict between Milošević and Karadžić, Zoran Djindjić would stand completely on the side of the Bosnian leadership and become a frequent visitor to Pale.

The DSS began as a party concentrated on the problems of Serbia itself, as opposed to those of Serbs living in other republics. It featured a plum (a symbol of Serbia) on its posters. In its manifesto it stated that 'a state of Serbia and Montenegro is the best solution to the state question', and also foresaw the possibility of 'transforming Serbia into an independent and sovereign state'.[21] However, at the time of the political split over the Vanse-Owen plan the party changed its policy, placing itself on the side of the Bosnian leadership. By this turn they abandoned all the axioms on which the party had been formed and because of which they had left the Democratic Party (the party abandoned the DEPOS coalition for which they had split from the DS and concentrated their policy on the problems of Serbia). The party's manifesto, adopted in 1994, was crucially changed from its first programme. Now, 'moving from the right to self-determination' the DSS 'supports the just battle of the Serbian people outside our state and gives its backing to all efforts leading to the creation of Serbian unity'. They arrived at this position since 'only in a Serbian state can the Serbian people realize their full creative potential and so, having in mind the experience of the first and second Yugoslavia, the Democratic Party decisively opposes any recreation of Yugoslavia or association at state level with neighbouring peoples'.[22]

From its inception, the Serbian Radical Party occupied an extreme, national position. In the name of creating its programme, the SRP formed paramilitary units comprising volunteers from the Chetnik movement and from the party itself. These units participated in the first armed conflicts in Croatia and their brutality produced a real war psychosis. Vojislav Šešelj said of these first successes: 'Led by Oliver Denis Baret they have won the first great Serbian victory in Borov Selo.'[23] In addition to these first victories, Šešelj set out the precise achievement of his party in the following words: 'alongside what it has informed its volunteers of, the Serbian Radical Party has participated in gathering fighters from defeated armed units, in improving mobilization and in preventing chaos wherever we have been able to, and where we have known how to do so'. In connection with the Bosnian battlefields he said, 'Serbian Radical Party volunteers have fought on all fronts of the territory of former Bosnia-Hercegovina.'

By his extreme national policy, Šešelj took over the role of 'pacesetter' from Vuk Drašković in the middle of 1991. With his extreme chauvinistic views expressed on the most popular state television (from the claim that Croats should be killed with rusty spoons to a public announcement of the need to expel Croats from Serbia), he served as a kind of test of public endurance in the uncertain time of war. Although he never formed a coalition with the SPS he performed all that was needed for Milošević's unpleasant work, both on republican and federal levels (e.g. replacing federal premier Milan Panić and Dobrica Ćosić, SRJ president). For these services, Milošević called him his 'favourite opposition'.

At the end of April 1993, Milošević and Šešelj came into conflict when the Serbian president accepted the Vanse-Owen plan for Bosnia. In that political turn Šešelj became ballast to Milošević, and at that time a struggle for power with the radicals began. Šcšclj said of his own separation from Milošević: 'We wouldn't have publicly attacked him again if our people hadn't been arrested. We knew that, in a completely irrational way, he has a lot of sympathy in Serbia ... from the aspect of our party's interests it would be better not to touch him. But we had to "hit him on the head" so that our people are no longer arrested.'[24]

After that Šešelj became Milošević's most outspoken opponent and was even in prison for four months in 1994 because of his trenchant words. In addition to his personal attacks on Milošević, Šešelj opposed the ruling policy, using every opportunity to support the leadership of the Bosnian Serbs when they rejected the peace plans of the world community, with the persistent aim: 'Serbia from Negotin to Knin'.

This short overview shows that three of the five opposition parties in parliament sought their identity in extreme national positions in the war years, attacking Milošević for national betrayal and insisting on 'unification of all Serbian lands'. This policy was in accord with their programmes which, as shown above, envisaged the creation of a Serbian state in the event of the dissolution of Yugoslavia. However, the DS and the DSS presented themselves on policy level as parties of the civil centre and their entry onto national terrain brought changes in their identity and the re-composition of the Serbian political scene. Creating a strong right-wing block, they created a vacuum into which Milošević would enter in August 1994 as the bearer of a peace-making policy. Milošević's turn to peace was made possible because the centre parties had not contemplated the purpose and aims of the war and Milošević's responsibility, but rather, seeking their own identities and the support of the electorate, they presented themselves as parties which would lead the war better. Leaving the 'peace terrain' to Milošević, they closed the circle of Serbian political confusion, closing also the possibility for any catharsis.

From its formation in November 1992, the Civil Alliance of Serbia (GSS) consistently defended the civil option and an anti-war position, these becoming postulates in the policy of the UJDI, the Association of Reform Forces of Serbia, and the Republican Club.[25] The basic task of the party was concern for the citizen-individual who is not 'simply a city inhabitant or a passive citizen, but an individual who does public work'.[26] Simply by separating the citizen as a political subject, this party differed from the other parties/conglomerates on the political scene. From there flowed its political uniqueness, for, acting for the cause of the individual, it had as its goal the struggle against national collectivism which binds citizens, and was against 'the ideology of national exclusiveness which leads to territorial war, "ethnic cleansing", and the subordination of the whole of private life to a militant national policy' (*The role of the citizen...*). In the cause of harmony between a civilly organized state and national feelings which people nurture towards the community to which they belong, it condemned 'illtempered, primitive and aggressive nationalism, which stirs up fear, hatred and violence, provokes wars, provides a foundation for dictatorship' (ibid.). It therefore saw its responsibility in affirming realism in the resolution of state and national questions. In the party's manifesto this realistic national policy was reduced to the following priorities: '1) The affirmation of truthful peace-loving politics with the goal of normalizing the SRY's international position by strengthening its diplomatic relations at the highest level and by accession to international organizations; 2) The affirmation of freedom and protection of all Serbian people instead of a reduction in this protection, from the whole national question to the territorial question. This reduction of the national question draws all of Serbia and the Serbs into endless battles with their neighbours, extensively damaging their long-term developmental interests.'

By these programme assignments the GSS bowed to the thin but long tradition of liberal thinking in Serbia, which from its inception in the time of Jevrem Gruljić (in the mid-nineteenth century) gave political priority to harmony between internal and external freedom, or between national freedom and democracy. This political direction had never dominated in Serbia, but its long continuity (through the United Youth of Serbia, Svetozar Marković, Vladimir Jovanović, Dragiša Stanojević, Svetozar Marković, Slobodan Jovanović and Jovan Skerlić) shows that the concept had lasted as an alternative through a century and a half of Serbian state development (N. Popov 1991). This continuity was confirmed in GSS policy, but also in that, not having a base in a dominant cultural model, such an essentially liberal direction could not yet have any mass support in Serbia. Nevertheless, during the war years the GSS had an important role in anti-war organization and peace-making activity in Belgrade, showing that even in a war environment, with deafening war propaganda, it could oppose the dominating majority mood.

The paradigmatic case of political confusion and inability to come out with an alternative programme or offer a real way out of a situation was given by the Serbian Renewal Party. In most of his public appearances, Vuk Drašković repeated and confirmed the contradictory policy and position of his party, by which he contributed to the falling away of nationally oriented members and voters from the SPO, and the fact that the civilly and liberally oriented did not join him. Thus Drašković became more and more just a symbol of a Serbian opposition leader, a symbol with less and less political weight. As a groundless liberal, an anti-war activist with a nationalistic programme, a reconciler of alienated people, with his party paramilitary guard, a European and Westerner with an epic appearance and village background, Drašković filled the stage of a politically unstable Serbian opposition.

The political contradictions in Vuk Drašković's viewpoint can be seen, for example, in the lecture that he gave in the Centre for Political Studies in London, in June 1991, three days before the Yugoslav Wars broke out. Speaking in favour of Yugoslavia as the only reasonable solution, he explained that ethnic partition of the country was not possible: 'The ethnic map of the largest part of Yugoslavia resembles a leopard skin ... there is no magician who can draw clean ethnic borders over that leopard skin or between a thousand husbands, wives and their children' (*SR*, 8 August 1991). However, despite this real conclusion, in the same lecture he said: 'In that event [Croatia and Slovenia breaking away], 40 per cent of Serbs would find themselves outside the current borders of Serbia. Besides this, the Croats would make state use of the genocide begun against the Serbs. We consider that in the case of the breakup of Yugoslavia, all territory with which the Kingdom of Serbia entered Yugoslavia must belong to her now, along with all provinces and Bosnia-Hercegovina, in which Serbs were in the majority before the Ustasha genocide.'

The contradictions are obvious. Basically, Drašković realized the impossibility of confining the Yugoslav peoples, but he forgot that realization, offering a solution to a concrete problem which would involve the breakup of Yugoslavia. Although at that time he had already declared himself against the war, and warned of terrible crimes, the unavoidable consequences of a war for clean ethnic borders between mixed peoples, he nevertheless drew those borders. Deeply contradictory in his policies, Drašković remained in a crevice between two mutually repelling political poles which he represented in parallel. Standing somewhere between them, he lost that support on which he could have started political change in Serbia.

Drašković was the only leader of the 'national opposition' who protested against the bombing of Dubrovnik, and of the 'Vukovar victory' he wrote: 'I cannot applaud the Vukovar victory, which is so euphorically celebrated in the war propaganda of intoxicated Serbia. I cannot, for I won't violate the victims, thousands of dead, nor the pain and misfortune of all Vukovar survivors ... [Vukovar] is the Hiroshima of both Croatian and Serbian madness ... Everyone in this state, Serbs but especially Croats, have experienced days of the greatest shame and fall' (*SR,* 9 December 1991). In January 1992, two months before the start of the war in Bosnia-Hercegovina, at the government and opposition round table in Sarajevo, he warned: 'Surely it's clear to us that we don't want a Vukovar, surely it's clear to us that such a violent settlement of our future, using force in the heart of what was Yugoslavia, in Bosnia-Hercegovina, would mean half this people leaving for refuge and the country looking like Vukovar, signifying a flame of total war brought to the Balkans and beyond' (*SR,* 20 January 1992).

In the edition of *Srpska Reč* for the week ending 6 April, the day war broke out in Bosnia, Drašković announced 'An appeal to the citizens of Bosnia-Hercegovina': 'In these judgement hours when Bosnia and Hercegovina are gambling between war and peace, between life and death, I join all people in protest against chauvinistic-fascist madness ... This is the last moment for citizens of Bosnia and Hercegovina to push their religious, national or party feelings into the background, and for everyone, above all, to talk and embrace each other like people ... for the protection of national interests, the principle is legalized that they can create their own right and happiness from the injustice and unhappiness of a neighbour. Blood flows from that kind of policy. That policy will transform the whole of our Bosnia and Hercegovina into a grave if their citizens do not take their fate into their own hands' (*SR,* 13 April 1992).

In keeping with his anti-war appearances, Drašković accepted all the peace offers of the world community: the Hague Declaration, the Vanse Plan to end the war in Croatia, the Vanse-Owen Plan for Bosnia, the Owen-Stoltenburg Plan, and finally he gave full support to Milošević on the occasion of his turn to peace and his conflict with Karadžić in August 1994.

Parallel with these appearances, Drašković kept one foot in the war programme as soon as the dichotomy of his policy was confirmed. In his programme he stayed faithful to the idea of a 'Serbian commonwealth' and the final separation from Croatia, which was the idea that led to war, despite his devotion to the anti-war cause. During the war in Croatia he attacked the JNA for conducting the war so badly and favoured the creation of a Serbian army which could achieve better results: 'We want to perish for those borders in a Serbian army, under Serbian national flags, led by Serbian commanders. We must' (*SR*, 14 October 1991). These words, pronounced at the time of the siege of Vukovar, implied that the JNA was not capable of conducting a war because of the absence of a national symbol and the still 'unclean' commanding elements. For those reasons Drašković formed his own party paramilitary unit, the 'Serbian Guard', whose war successes are recorded time after time in *Srpska reč*. Drašković said of his own army, at the funeral of his commander, Djordje Božović–Giška: 'This is an army with the soul of a girl, the behaviour of a priest, and the heart of Obilić. This is an army which protects its own, and does not seize what belongs to a stranger. This is an army whose commanders always command: "Follow me, heroes!"… this is an army whose flags will never be captured.'[27]

Publicly voicing its criticism of the war, the SPO had an opportunity to occupy the place of a real alternative and pledge its pre-war authority to a policy which would offer a different solution for Serbia from that offered by the government. However, essentially abandoning its programme, the SPO did not have the strength to take the risk of 'national betrayal' and the responsibility for suggesting a new programme which would offer Serbia and the whole Yugoslav region a way out of the war. Perhaps the SPO could not do that. Existing as they did as a populist, nationalist and anti-Communist front and movement, it was difficult for them to set out for something completely opposite. Basically, the SPO did not have the force to become a modern European civic party offering Serbia a modern rational programme, an end to the war and a position among modern states. Internal shocks and the party's abandonment of both the complete leadership and its recognized representatives showed that the issue was more about the personal maturity of Vuk Drašković than the maturity and different formulation of the party itself. A captive of his personal image and former policy, the SPO flew into a nationalistic political trap set against the

whole opposition by Slobodan Milošević, and became a double
hostage. As a hostage to personal nationalism it had a narrowed
space to manoeuvre with the electorate and could not fully abandon the 'Serbian track'. Determined by this internal party interest
and reason, the SPO created an amalgam of mutually opposing
political stances, sending an old message to old voters, but convert-
ing the Serbia who felt the consequences of a war which was not
hers with its new, anti-war policy. With this internal dichotomy the
SPO entered into another external circle of dependency, fixed by
Milošević. Proclaimed as traitor in the government's war propaganda, Drašković was forced by this external reason to maintain
part of his pre-war national image and to protect himself from accusations which threatened to disqualify him, by great activity and
many statements. Thus he could not take the essential step towards
raising the issue of the essential causes of the war in former Yugoslavia, nor could he single-mindedly explain in public that the programme 'all Serbs in one country' could not have been completed
without war. Thus the anti-war position of the SPO remained, but
without serious foundation. As the opportunity had not been taken
to explain and to attack the national programme that had led to
war, room was left for Milošević's transition to a peace-making
policy without recanting on his war objectives and programmes.
Since the SPO, as the most influential Serbian opposition party, had
not openly pointed out in advance the causes of the war, the ruling
party could present itself in a new suit and fly into the media space
with a propaganda formula about the continuity of its peace-
making mission. The subsequent delays in that formula did not
take effect, so that the creators of the war now baled Serbia out of
that war. Thus the opportunity was lost for Serbia publicly to face
the problems of war maturely and rationally and to thus emerge
from it.

Carrying out research into the Serbian opposition is like examining a traumatic vicious circle. Formed from the nationally oriented
intellectual elite, the opposition began its political activity by
opening up the Serbian national question in the mid–1980s. When
the ideas of these opposing and nationally oriented intellectuals
became the ruling ideas with the accession of Milošević to power,
great numbers of them supported his policy, thus strengthening the
impression of political unity, monolithic, and finally 'differentiated'
Serbia. A 'national consensus' was created concerning key issues of
national relations in the Yugoslav state, a consensus which in essence was not brought into question even when individuals from
the opposition separated from Milošević to form their own parties.

Thus, paradoxically, a multiparty system strengthened a programme which would lead Serbia into war, for parties which had been in different political positions offered the basis of the project by which Serbs had to separate from the other ethnic groups and form a nationally clean state. The consensus reached over this project speaks of an idea with deep, compounded historical roots, which cannot simply be interpreted as adventurous irresponsibility on the part of Communist leaders who would do anything to stay in power. The idea of 'all Serbs in one country' united the Serbian left, the right and the centre (as far as this can be said, in general, about such developed political division) showing its foundational strength. But it also showed the deep crisis in Serbian society and the Serbian elite, who in times fatal for all Yugoslav peoples, were not able to formulate a programme founded on modern principles of integration. Unity between the national programmes of both the Serbian opposition and the government indicates that the Yugoslav Wars were not a post-Communist phenomenon, but that their causes were deep and their essence lay in the struggle for domination in these regions.

Notes

1 As a criterion one can take, e.g., state-directed economy and a party state. See V. Goati 1991: 9.

2 E.g. authentic revolution, a 'personal' road to socialism, the independent position of Serbia in international relations, workers' self-management, the decentralization of the political system, open borders, economic links with the world. (See V. Goati 1991.)

3 See the contribution of Aleksandar Nenadović, this volume.

4 Stenographic minutes of the National Parliament, Extraordinary Session 1906: 113.

5 Cultural models suppose the widest understanding of principles which determine complete relations in a society, from value systems to political relations. Historically they start from a range of factors which are conditional on the political, economic, social and cultural development of a specific group. In time, this web of circumstances influences the formation of the dominant cultural model which, like a half-moving phenomenon with slow rhythm influences events, political life, or peoples' actions, or influences the 'historical time with faster rhythm'. In this joining of long-lasting processes and events whose historical time is short, history is connected to current phenomena (Braudel 1991). On cultural models as the basis for political relations see Guy Hermet 1986: 67–77.

6 In its by-laws the president of the SPO has discretionary authority: he announces penalties, appoints the general secretary, decides on the vice-presidents, and has a casting vote if the Presidency is divided. See *Statute* 1994.

7 Recommendation for the Democratic Party's National Programme, 1990.

8 See the Programme of the Democratic Party in Pečujlić and Milić 1990: 287.

9 Proposal for the Democratic Party's National Programme.

10 From the SPO's draft programme, 1990.

11 Ibid.

12 The programme states as follows: 'The Serbian people obviously have nothing more to sacrifice to the ideal of Yugoslav unity, neither are they willing to continue with disastrous self-mutilation.'

13 Serbian Radical Party programme, 1991.

14 Democratic Party Programme, 1990; Pečujlić and Milić 1990: 288

15 SPO programme, 1994.

16 Proposal for the Democratic Party National Programme, 1990.

17 Ibid.

18 Serbian Radical Party Programme, 1994.

19 Since DEPOS as a wider coalition did not have its own programme, analysis will be reduced to that of its leaders' statements.

20 First DEPOS Assembly, 1992.

21 DSS Programme, 1992.

22 DSS Programme.

23 Third Homeland Congress, SRS, 1994.

24 Ibid.: 6.

25 For the policy of the UJDI, the Association of Reform Forces and the Republican Club see the contribution of Bojana Šušak, this volume.

26 *The role of the citizen*, Civil Alliance Programme, 1994.

27 'Dear Giška, brother, Obilić, commander', pronounced September 1991; 'all my betrayals', *Srpska reč*, special edition November 1992.

An Alternative to War

BOJANA ŠUŠAK

This article[1] will survey the political parties, citizens' groups and associations which, from the very beginning of the war (and in some cases even before the war), through their explicit anti-war stance, demonstrated that there existed 'another Serbia'. This 'other Serbia' admittedly exerted only 'a limited influence on the events, but its existence nevertheless gives us hope in the knowledge that there is at least someone who resolutely delineates the limits of violence not according to maps, but according to contemporary criteria of humanity and civilized existence' (Popov 1994: 115).

If we consider their fundamental goals and the direction of their actions as the criterion for inclusion, we can count among these alternative actors certain movements and political parties, autonomous women's groups, peace or anti-war organizations, and organizations for the protection of human rights and freedoms.

Movements and political parties

At the end of the 1980s, when the fall of the Berlin Wall symbolized the end of socialist regimes throughout Eastern Europe, Yugoslavia, and especially Serbia, were shaken by new movements of a different order. In each of the republics nationalist parties entered the political scene and began competing for power with the ruling League of Communists , which had shortly before fragmented into eight antagonistic parties due to long-term disagreements among its republican and provincial leaderships.

At that time, when 'the political, cultural and economic conditions in Yugoslavia forecast a decline in the gains made during the previous years, when a considerable number of its citizens found themselves living in increasingly difficult living conditions, when national and social divisions prevented a common life in the country, and when the absence of a democratic political order dispelled any hope that things may improve',[2] the Association for a Yugoslav Democratic Initiative (UJDI, *Udruženje za jugoslovensku demokratsku inicijativu*) entered the political scene as the first autonomous political organization.

The UJDI was founded in Zagreb on 3 February 1989 at the initiative of a group of intellectuals who rallied around the idea of the democratic restructuring of Yugoslav society. According to the UJDI programme, the fundamental reason for the founding of the organization was the fact that 'in Yugoslavia [today] there does not exist a political option which is both Yugoslav and democratic'. The authorities in both Zagreb and Belgrade rejected their request for legal status, and it was only on 29 December 1989 that the organization was finally registered in Titograd (Montenegro), which entitled it to act on the entire territory of Yugoslavia.

With the enactment of the Act on Citizens' Associations, Social Organizations, and Political Parties Established for the Territory of the Socialist Federal Republic of Yugoslavia (SFRY), and with the enactment of analogous legislation in Serbia, the UJDI was entered in the register of political organizations in Serbia, with its main office in Belgrade, as a 'subtenant' at the Duško 'Radović' theatre. Its founders wished to promote awareness of democratic ideas, and thus organized debating clubs in Belgrade and Zagreb, as well as a Round Table for the Co-ordination of Democratic Initiatives. The UJDI also issued public statements in response to critical political events, and its members individually made frequent public appearances. The organization's political strategy consisted of attempts to pressure the regime immediately to enact laws ensuring civil liberties, and to open a parliamentary procedure for drafting a new constitution. Individual UJDI members frequently made personal initiatives to promote union rights, the depoliticization of the police and the military, remedies for social problems, and other issues. By initiating a dialogue about Kosovo at round tables in Mostar, Priština, and Belgrade, the UJDI also contributed to the development of democratic procedures for resolving complex problems and to the development of a democratic public opinion. The conclusions reached during the UJDI-sponsored discussions differed markedly from the 'official' perspectives on Kosovo in many aspects, particularly in their uncompromising insistence on the non-violent resolution of disputes and conflicts, especially with regard to the questions of Serbian emigration, rapes, and other criminal acts (*Kosovski Čvor*, 1990).

The UJDI proposed to the Federal Assembly that it pass an amendment to elect a Constitutional Convention which would determine the fate of Yugoslavia. In this struggle to promote a democratic constitution, the UJDI could be characterized both as a party and as a movement. It could be seen as one aspect of a movement that would effect changes, and also as a political party which would then co-operate with other parties in establishing democratic rule, although not in executing power, as its final goal rested with the passage of a democratic constitution. UJDI members envisioned a new, democratic Yugoslavia reconstituted as a 'union of citizens and federal units'. The organization held conventions in Sarajevo and Belgrade, and organized round tables in Belgrade, Sarajevo, Titograd, Mostar and Priština, demonstrating a respect for the unity of Yugoslav cultural and political space.

In the summer of 1990, another all-Yugoslav party was established–the Alliance of Reformist Forces of Yugoslavia (SRSJ, *Savez reformskih snaga Jugoslavije*). Its founding was announced by the then president of the Federal Executive Committee [Federal Prime Minister] Ante Marković 'at a meeting on the mountain named Kozara, speaking before some 100,000 people' (Kovačević and Dajić 1994: 27). This party, as a 'nucleus of a growing pan-Yugoslav movement for reform', called together 'all citizens, parties and associations who believe that their joint efforts can achieve peace, a better quality of life, economic advancement, mutual respect and freedom' (*Programmatic Declaration of the Alliance of Reformist Forces of Yugoslavia*). The Reformists proceeded from the thesis that 'a good Yugoslavia is one in which all citizens, nations and nationalities wish to live together. The Alliance is for an arrangement within Yugoslavia which would enable each and every citizen, nation and republic complete political, economic and social self-determination. It is for a new democratic contract between all citizens and their states based on economic and political reform' (ibid.). The Reformists were proposing a programme of economic and political reforms that included democracy[3], economic recovery and the overhaul of the banking system, a market economy, and unfettered competition based on knowledge and ability. They wished to abandon the practices of classical political parties and to strengthen individual initiative. In response to the charge that their sole purpose was to promote Ante Marković, the Serbian Reformists declared that the reason for their existence was 'not to defend every move of the regime, but to struggle for a democratic mode of existence for Serbia and Yugoslavia. It [was] not an expression of "sentimental Yugoslavism" but an association based on mutual interest with the principal task of defeating the nationalist hatred which [was] engulfing society.'[4]

At the beginning of 1991, the SRSJ and the UJDI advanced their co-operation by jointly developing an outline for a new programme of economic and political reforms which was published in *Republika* (No. 16, 16 March 1991) and thus submitted for public consideration. This document specified their principal argument: through political action based on socio-economic changes, the equality of national groups and respect for individual liberties, a solid and enduring foundation for a Yugoslav state could be built. A careful reading of the elements presented in the joint outline reveals an alternative but reliable path to a new democratic state.

After the opposition's demonstrations in March 1991, the UJDI and the SRSJ participated in the establishment of the United Opposition of Serbia, along with the Serbian Renewal Movement (SPO, *Srpski pokret obnove*), the Democratic Party (DS, *Demokratska stranka*), and the National Party of Serbia (NSS, *Narodna stranka Srbije*). Their joint statements and participation in meetings of the opposition on 13 and 27 March indicate an attempt to build a coalition of opposition parties.

UJDI members perceived the above-mentioned demonstrations as a possibility to move the debate beyond the confines of nationalism. It later became clear, however, that their statements were too hopeful and optimistic, and that they harboured too many illusions. The March demonstrations not only failed to upset the ruling party, but it became clear that this party could resist democratic changes. It also became evident that members of the opposition were unwilling to co-operate and unable to effect democratization. There was a conflict between the two most influential opposition parties, the SPO and the DS, with regard to some essential questions. Moreover, they had both entered into competition with the ruling party in the expression of 'patriotism'.

In a survey of political actors having a predominantly civic orientation, one must certainly elaborate on the European Movement in Yugoslavia (EPJ, *Evropski pokret u Jugoslaviji*) Founded on 25 March 1991 as a recognized member of the European Movement, the EPJ proclaimed that 'it would promote a European spirit and unity with the goal that Yugoslavia accede in all European processes and integration, and thus become a part of a unitary European space' (*Programmatic Declaration the EPJ*). In their programme declaration, the EPJ clearly identified national exclusiveness as an essential problem which jeopardized not only Yugoslavia but potentially the whole of Europe. 'The EPJ cannot, and will not, attempt to assume the role of arbiter with regard to the internal political questions in Yugoslavia. It will, however, decisively and continuously strive to promote a political, economic and social life in Yugoslavia that is compatible with the framework of standards and goals of the European Movement' (ibid.). One of the tasks of the EPJ was to acquaint world institutions and the European public with the existing Yugoslav reality. But this organization/movement likewise failed to resonate among the public and to grow into a real movement. It, too, became eclipsed by the processes of national homogenization along republican lines that were gaining momentum in the months before the war.

In April 1991, several months before the *official* beginning of war in Yugoslavia, within the framework of the debating club that had been convening for three years in the Duško Radović theatre, the UJDI organized a public forum on the subject 'How to End a Civil War'. Participants in the debate represented opposing views on the issues. Some claimed that the civil war which had started in 1941 had not been concluded; others maintained that a new civil war had already begun; and others still insisted that there was only a threat of war. Nevertheless, the majority of the participants endorsed peace initiatives. On 3 May 1991, after the first armed conflicts in Croatia, the UJDI dispatched letters to the Federal Assembly, the Serbian Parliament and the Croatian *Sabor*, in which it expressed 'deep grief for the victims and concern for the onslaught of violence and national hatred'. The letter further suggested that a joint parliamentary commission be formed to 'determine responsibly and inform the public of the causes and consequences of state terror and anti-state terrorism in the crisis spots of Croatia' (*R*, No.20, 16 May 1991: 8–9).

The UJDI reconsidered its role in the United Opposition of Serbia after a meeting on 9 May 1991, as it became apparent that members of the opposition were increasingly espousing pro-war positions. This coalition never fully materialized despite attempts to act together through joint statements and meetings. After this key meeting, the UJDI, the Reformists and the NSS abandoned the coalition. Neither the government nor the opposition offered an alternative to the growing wave of chaos and violence. Along with the above-mentioned proposals to the parliament to adopt a constitutional amendment that would enable elections to a Constitutional Convention, the UJDI also advocated forming anti-war alliances and coalitions for the totality of Yugoslav space. They insisted that holding federal elections, followed by new republican

elections, represented the only way to introduce a civil state that
would guarantee a peaceful life for all its citizens.[5]

On 24 June 1991, immediately preceding the outbreak of armed
conflict in Slovenia, the Second Session of the Preliminary Parliament of Yugoslavia took place in Sarajevo. Created a year earlier at
the initiative of the UJDI, the Preliminary Parliament represented a
unique attempt at co-operation, or rather, at coalition building,
engaging some thirty civic-oriented parties, movements and associations. The joint goal was to find a peaceful solution to Yugoslav
conflicts. They attempted to respond to questions such as 'Is it
possible to prevent catastrophe?' and 'What are the chances for a
civil society?' The Second Session of the Preliminary Parliament
was held at the time when the regular rotation of the president of
the Federal Presidency had been sabotaged and the constitutional
crisis was reaching its peak, while among the people there was
widespread fear of hatred, violence and war over disputed republic borders. The Preliminary Parliament recommended to the highest republican and federal organs that two decisions be taken: one
on passing a constitutional act that would define responsibilities
for Yugoslavia as a common state, and the second on scheduling
free multiparty elections to the Federal Chamber (*Savezno Veće*)[6]
and adopting an appropriate election law which would provide for
equal representation of citizens, nations, republics and provinces.
The result of such elections would have permitted the creation of a
democratically legitimate civil government that would decide the
future of Yugoslavia. The Third Session of the Preliminary Parliament conveyed a request to the appropriate government bodies to
stop the intensification of armed conflicts and to respect the decisions reached by the civil authorities and the agreements made
with representatives of the European Community (EC) and the
Conference on Security and Co-operation in Europe (*CSCE*). They
also reiterated a previous request to form a government–
opposition Round Table comprising representatives of the Federal
Assembly (*Skupština*), the federal government, republic and provincial parliaments and governments, along with representatives of
the Preliminary Parliament. Sadly, despite all the initiatives, protests and efforts of the civic opposition, armed conflicts continued
to escalate and real war commenced.

In response to the irrefutable onset of an absurd war, members
of the SRSJ for Serbia, the UJDI and the EPJ held a joint press conference claiming their citizens' right to refuse participation in a
civil war, and publicly criticizing the leaderships' 'cynical diplomacy'.[7]

A truly unique institution was founded in Sarajevo at the initiative of the Preliminary Parliament of Yugoslavia, with the aim of ending armed conflict in Croatia and preventing its expansion into Bosnia-Hercegovina–that is, a Round Table of government repre sentatives and members of the opposition. Its first session was held on 28 July 1991, at the same time and in the same city where YUTEL[8] sponsored a concert for peace. At the time, the media devoted more attention to the concert than to the session of the Paraparliament and the Round Table. The Round Table met for a total of six sessions between 28 July 1991 and 18 January 1992. At the final session, the participants concluded that only systematic co-operation among domestic political actors, and foreign initiatives, could have any meaningful impact on ending the war and on re-establishing political dialogue. The end result was a proposal to draft a peace agreement which would be approved by all the republics, which would regulate the retreat from the use of force in resolving conflicts, and which would establish a new Interparliamentary Council,[9] the founding of which would conclude the work of the Round Table. Participants of the Round Table demonstrated great endurance and optimism in their efforts to end a war that was gaining momentum, and to prevent the onset of war in Bosnia-Hercegovina, a development which would have constituted 'total war'.[10]

While similar Round Tables contributed to achieving political stabilization in states like Poland and Hungary, those held in Yugoslavia not only failed to resolve key problems, but their very substance can be called into doubt: the government made no attempt to reach a compromise with the opposition; as an idea, they failed to resonate with the public; and even the 'anti-war' media provided them with little visibility. What is more, many of the most significant political actors on the Yugoslav scene declined invitations to participate in them.

Towards the end of 1991, due to increasing difficulties in communication, UJDI regional activities began to decline and the organization devolved into a loose association of group projects. Within the UJDI there emerged three separate definitions of its mission: some wanted it to remain an association with a cultural/political character which would limit its activities with respect to the public promotion of its principles and initiatives; others believed that it should become a political party that would participate in the long-term competition for power; others still thought it could act as a framework for the co-ordination of like-minded political initiatives, parties and movements.

Concluding that in Serbia there existed a pressing need to form new political organizations, one segment of the UJDI membership launched a new party. By the beginning of the following year, they had published in the pages of *Republika* the Announcement of the Republican Club and the Proposal of Programmatic Principles. Like the UJDI and the Reformists, this party's goals included promoting democratic changes through the reform of the state, the economy, social politics and culture. One section of the Proposal for Programmatic Principles reads as follows: 'Let us be realistic, let us turn towards the future. Only in the future can we form new values and new forms of life. The past has already brought us to this unbearable condition. Let us begin with democracy anew, and without delay, because later it will be far more difficult.' The Republicans wished to promote the broadest possible co-operation with all democratic parties, independent trade unions and peace groups, along with citizens' associations and groups that advocated establishing a lasting peace; they wished to resolve the Yugoslav crisis through dialogue; they wanted to promote a sovereign and democratic Serbia, the development of a market economy, the welfare of all citizens, a secular state, and openness towards the world. The Republicans believed that private property and entrepreneurial initiative stood at the foundation of the free-market system, and that the independence of citizens from the government represented a necessary precondition. At a time when nationalist parties were emerging as the political heirs of the future, the Republican Club openly promoted a state in which the sovereign citizens represented the core of political power, where the fundamental problems of society and the state would be a *public matter* (*res publica*), and in which a future Constitutional Convention would decide on the actual form of the state order: republic or monarchy. They also supported the formation of a democratic public sphere. 'Founded on the values and the ideas of the European Enlightenment, individualism and humanism, and their reverberations in our culture' the primary goal of the Republican Club was to 'extend the boundaries of personal liberties in all realms of public life' (*Action Programme RK*, Spring 1992). They presented themselves as a party of the civic Left that would transform Serbia into a democratic republic, promote the entry of young people into public life, and uphold the unification of the democratic and peace processes. They also continued the UJDI's tradition of organizing public dialogue and debating clubs that addressed current societal problems.[11]

While it seemed to many that the war in Croatia was finally nearing its end, a far more savage conflict was about to erupt in Bosnia-

Hercegovina. After the bloody anti-war demonstrations of 5 April 1992 in Sarajevo, a Proclamation Against the War was signed by the Belgrade Circle, the Republican Club, the Centre for Anti-War Action, and the UJDI. They addressed the citizens of Bosnia-Hercegovina directly. 'It would be too modest to say that we believe your tears and that we commiserate in your losses and suffering. Without a doubt, this is the last opportunity for citizens to organize into parties, unions, associations, and, if need be, into a liberation movement, to confront organized murderers and thieves, and finally to stop the inferno of war ... If we do not stop them, they will continue to destroy us ... In order to stop them, it is also imperative that we increase the pressure on the authorities in Serbia, so that we can determine the responsibility of all those who incited and participated in the war. We expect others to follow. Only in this manner can we thwart all those who have enmeshed us in this war' (*R*, No. 41–42, 1 April 1992: 32).

The Republican Club warned the public that 'Serbia may have to face the consequences of a lost war: international condemnation of aggression, retaliation by war adversaries, and growing internal chaos. We are threatened by Serbian fascism as the ultimate means of maintaining an anti-democratic regime in Serbia and in increasingly numerous "Serbian states", and as a means of settling accounts with all internal opposition' (*R*, No. 43, 1 May 1992: 32). There was a growing fear of advancing fascism in Serbia because of a coalition[12] between the ruling party—the Socialist Party of Serbia (SPS, *Socijalisticka partija Srbije*)—and the Serbian Radical Party (SRS, *Srpska radikalna stranka*).

In the summer of 1992, the Civic Alliance (GS, *Gradjanski savez*) was formed. It was a pre-campaign coalition of four parties—the Republican Club, the Reformists, the NSS and the League of Social Democrats of Vojvodina (LSV, *Liga socijaldemokrata Vojvodine*). In the December 1992 elections, the Civic Alliance won only a small number of votes at republican and local levels. After the elections, while many of the parties disintegrated, the Reformist Party and the Republican Club united to form a new party called the Civic Alliance of Serbia (GSS, *Gradjanski savez Srbije*). The other two parties, LSV and NSS, continued their independent political activities.

The GSS continued its political activity as a party with clear and well-defined objectives: ending economic sanctions and the international isolation of Serbia; uniting all the actors capable of effecting the transformation of Serbia into a parliamentary, civic, rule-of-law state around a programme of anti-war and democratic principles; promoting respect for human rights and freedoms, and for the rights of national minorities; preventing the resurgence of state-sponsored nationalism and the continuation of war; and articulating a political programme for Serbia based on international norms defined in the Preamble of the United Nations Charter and the political principles of the *CSCE*, so that Serbia could become an equal and respected member of the international community (*Platform GSS*, 1994). The GSS pledged to 'act faithfully on behalf of freedom and peace, democracy and equality, human dignity and social justice, the reform of the economy and an rise in the standard of living of the citizens' (*Program GSS*, 1994).

Just as the UJDI, the Reformists and the Republican Club had done before them, the GSS likewise endeavoured to effect democratic changes by way of reforms, believing that 'social reform demands the emancipation of all spheres of social life from the patronage of the state', while 'without economic reform there can be no economic development nor social progress, nor a better life for all citizens' (ibid.). The GSS's similarity to the parties mentioned above is especially evident with regard to its position on private property: 'Without a free market and private property there can be neither economic efficiency nor prosperity' (ibid.). With such emphasis on economic reforms, these parties clearly contradicted the existing political regime, or rather, the ruling party. The ruling party, by contrast, emphasized the 'solution' to the national question before all else, so that all attempts at the economic transformation of society remained marginalized or 'postponed'. The same delay applied to the question of democratization more generally—it was deferred pending a 'military solution to the *Serbian question*'.

There were indeed few parties which both before and during the war sought political rather than military solutions to the intranational conflicts and disputes. The parties mentioned in this text belong to a small group identifiable by their consistent anti-war positions. They made joint efforts to promote non-violent resolutions to national conflicts, and a politics of peace, dialogue and compromise. At the onset of the great nationalist campaign during 1991 and 1992, both the ruling party and the majority of the opposition denounced the UJDI and the Reformists as 'national traitors' and 'fifth columnists' because they espoused an pan-Yugoslav political position. A possible explanation for this attack may have been the regime's fear of real political alternatives, with these accusations and attempts at marginalization representing an attempt to silence them. The GSS met a similar fate somewhat later—it was accused of 'anationalism' by the leaders of the Serbian Radical Party, the coalition partner of the SPS at the time.

Later on, however, the new 'peace-making' profile of the ruling party somewhat eclipsed the GSS' politics of peace. Paradoxically, the very same players who had forged the war became the peace-makers in the public eye, while the true and uncompromised opposition to war remained marginalized, even disparaged as 'NATO pacifists', 'traitors', and the like.

Autonomous women's organizations

These organizations had already come into being in the late 1970s, which means that they were the very first alternative groups in the country. As a part of a new social movement–the feminist movement–they represented a new form of interest-based associations in Yugoslav society. They sought to supersede the institutionalized 'surrogate movements' such as the Conference for Social Activities for Women (*Konferencija za društvenu aktivnost žena*), which, in the feminists' opinion, 'did nothing to advance the position of women'. The ultimate aim of this movement was to achieve 'true equality for women' in society.

The feminist group Women and Society (*Žene i društvo*) was founded in 1973, 'during the era of a one-party political system in Yugoslavia when feminism was regarded as "an evil from the West and a hostile element which needs to be extirpated"'.[13] To this day there exists a type of informal co-ordination among the various women's groups, most of which have been formed at the initiative of activists from this original group. One of their more successful initiatives has been an SOS telephone hotline, a volunteer telephone service devoted to deal with all forms of violence which women and children routinely face.

The Belgrade Women's Lobby (*Beogradski ženski lobi*) was founded with the aim of organizing political pressure directed at the regime, the institutions of the system and the political parties, 'so that women's experiences and women's demands would no longer remain below the threshold of social visibility and sensibilities' (ibid.: 24). From the time of its formation in May 1990, this group acted in opposition to the regime. It worked on exposing sexism and gender-based discrimination against women in public and cultural life, and it voiced numerous protests against discrimi-

natory statements made by party leaders and parliamentary representatives. It also made public statements against war and violence.
It was one of the few organizations which protested against the
official reception in the National Assembly of an Italian Fascist
Party delegation. It circulated various petitions, such as those
against the Proposal for a Resolution on the Renewal of the Citizenry of Serbia, the Outline for a Law on Family Planning, and
other laws that were being adopted by the 'illegitimate male parliament'. It also issued public appeals and protests in reaction to
key political events, but primarily against the war.[14]

Dissatisfied with the small proportion of women elected to the
National Parliament of Serbia, women from the above-mentioned
groups began an initiative to form the Women's Parliament
(*Ženski parlament*) which would endeavour to eliminate all forms
of discrimination against women. One of the main goals of the
Women's Parliament was to oppose all attempts to violate and re-
peal the women's rights that had already been secured. Their slogan was 'Let us make visible the violence against women'.

The Belgrade SOS telephone hotline later founded a separate initiative for assisting women who had been raped during the war.
This new group evolved into the Autonomous Women's Centre
Against Sexual Violence (*Autonomni Ženski centar protiv seksu-
alnog nasilja*).

Women in Black (*Žene u crnom*) came into being at the beginning of October 1991, at the time of armed hostilities against Dubrovnik. Since the group's founding, these women gathered every
Wednesday to express their protest against the war and militarism,
appearing peacefully and silently in public places, dressed in black.
Armed with slogans and banners, they appealed to fellow citizens
to disobey the warmongering and militaristic regime. Their slogan
was 'Let us banish war from history and from our lives'. On the
anniversary of their existence, they issued a public statement proclaiming that 'wars which are conducted on the territory of the
former Yugoslavia benefit only the elites in power, bullies, murderers, war profiteers and paramilitary formations. The Serbian
regime has provoked the introduction of sanctions because it profits from these sanctions, for they encourage various mafia and
black-market enterprises. This regime protects the *status quo*
while continually shifting the blame to others, expecting that it
will escape unpunished for its bellicose politics and crimes which
it has either ordered or itself committed. Women in Black support
the initiatives of international organizations for human rights that
call for the immediate establishment of an international court for

war crimes. Collective guilt can be mitigated only through investigations of individual acts, and to be free of this collective guilt, the citizens of Serbia must end their silence' (*R*, No. 54, 16 October 1992: 6).

Autonomous women's groups did not enter the competition for power; their strategy for political action consisted of oppositional activities that would pressure the regime, and the staging of public disturbances. To date, the majority of these women's groups in Belgrade remain assembled at the same address, at the Autonomous Women's Centre.

Peace or anti-war organizations

In Serbia, the Centre for Anti-War Action (CAA, *Centar za anti-ratnu akciju*) stands among the first organizations that appeared in response to the citizens' need to resist the war and its expansion. As early as 15 July 1991, immediately after the outbreak of hostilities in Slovenia, and in an attempt to 'block the path of war madness', members of several alternative organizations—including the EPJ, the UJDI, the Women's Parliament, the Women's Party, the Helsinki Committee of Yugoslavia, the Helsinki Citizens' Parliament, and the Forum for Ethnic Relations—formed the CAA to represent 'all those individuals whose war this is not'. They began from the premise that everyone has the right to life and the right to civil disobedience. Their goals included preventing the war, disseminating anti-war ideas and attitudes, mitigating the consequences of war in the areas where fighting had already broken out, and promoting the demilitarization of the Yugoslav space. It was envisioned that the Centre's activities would encompass providing legal aid for all those who refused conscription or mobilization; defending conscientious objectors; organizing anti-war demonstrations, peace concerts and other methods of lobbying for peace; observing and registering individuals who incited conflicts with the goal of summoning them to assume responsibility for these actions; investigating and initiating proceedings against those who disobeyed humanitarian norms and international conventions; collecting documentation on those media that misinformed the citizenry, criminally disseminated religious and national hatred, or otherwise incited war (*The Proclamation of the CAA*, *R*, No. 25–26, 1 August 1992: 11).

The founding of the Centre ushered in a new era in the struggle for peace. The Centre initiated several peace activities and demonstrations such as the 'Walks for Peace', the first of which took place around the Federal Assembly on 25 July 1991. At this event, CAA activists gathered signatures for a petition that called for an end to armed conflict and for the augmentation of the corps of negotiators willing to compromise; an end to hate propaganda; and an end to the killing, destruction, burning, looting and expulsion of people from their homes and homelands. Under the slogan 'PEACE NOW', they issued an appeal for peace signed by 127 intellectuals, calling for a return to reason, the laying down of weapons, and the commencement of concrete negotiations to cease all military operations. With hindsight, some of the public statements made at the time appear almost prophetic. In a CAA declaration made on 15 September 1991, they urged: 'Let us stop pretending that we do not know ... Don't we realize that only the Serbian leadership supports the dark intentions of this army, which will inevitably lead to the demise of the Serbian people. We are on the verge of complete catastrophe. Let us save ourselves from death, shame before the entire world, isolation and poverty. Let us do away with political adventurers and false patriots, this is our last chance!' (*R*, No. 29, 1 October 1991: 5).

Shortly after this, at a peace conference organized in response to the attack on Dubrovnik, Belgrade historians Ljubinka Trgovčević, Sima Ćirković, Andrej Mitrović and Ivan Djurić circulated a petition which they called 'Save Dubrovnik'. A new group was formed—the Committee for the Protection of Dubrovnik (*Odbor za zaštitu Dubrovnika*)—primarily composed of people originally from Dubrovnik, but long-time residents of Belgrade. They formulated a list of special demands for the protection of Dubrovnik and its residents from all wartime threats which they submitted to the then Federal Secretariat for National Defence (SSNO, *Savezni sekreterijat za narodnu odbranu*). At that moment, the CAA also undertook some explicitly political activities—letters to President Milošević with demands for civil overseeing of the Yugoslav People's Army (JNA, *Jugoslovenska narodna armija*), that is, the transfer of command of the JNA to parliament. The CAA also regularly monitored the activities surrounding the preparation for the Sarajevo Round Table meetings between the members of the opposition and the ruling parties.

The initiative to form a similar peace organization—the Citizens' Action for Peace (GAMA, *Gradjanske akcije za mir*)—took place at approximately the same time as the initiative to form the CAA—that is, the middle of July 1991. Their goals were almost identical: 'preventing war and promoting civic consciousness, the consciousness of peace and non-violence' (Petrović and Paunović 1994: 59). With the onset of war, the GAMA organized an 'Open Anti-War Forum' which operated for six months at the Belgrade Youth Centre (*Dom omladine*).

To a certain extent, this activity functioned in tandem with the Belgrade Anti-War Marathon, a parallel initiative which attracted a significant number of participants to open forums at the Duško Radović theatre and to anti-war demonstrations that were held between October 1991 and February 1992. The Marathon consisted of weekly meetings on the subject 'How do you envision the end of the war?', at which numerous scientists and public servants spoke about the consequences of war, and each event bore the 'stamp' of the profession featured at the session.[15] A Marathon bulletin was published in co-operation with Radio B–92.

The forums at the Youth Centre and at the Duško Radović theatre (which ended with forcible eviction from the theatre) were followed by additional forums organized by the newly founded Belgrade Circle of Independent Intellectuals at the Student Cultural Centre.

During the Belgrade Anti-War Marathon, and later, in the park located between the buildings of the federal and Serbian parliaments and in front of the office of the president of Serbia, people gathered each evening to light candles as a symbol of protest against the war.[16] Some one hundred people gathered there expressing solidarity with all the war victims. They read lists of victims, and started a book of mourning for Miroslav Milenković,[17] the soldier who committed suicide rather than participate in the war.

Despite both the considerable number, and the frequency, of anti-war activities, only a narrow segment of the public knew about these events. The weeklies *Borba* and *Vreme*, and the television stations NTV and Studio B, occasionally covered these activities. The only media that followed the anti-war events fully and regularly were the weekly *Republika* and the independent radio station B–92. At the same time, the state-controlled media circulated only stories about genocide and crimes committed against the Serbian people by the 'other side'.[18]

In response to the propaganda campaign launched by the regime media, the CAA forwarded a letter with the following message to the editors-in-chief of all radio and television stations and all daily and weekly publications, and to the ministers of information: 'We demand that you stop this monstrous manipulation of human dramas and unimaginable tragedies which this war exacts every day. We demand that you immediately cease using dead children, women and men to incite even greater evil and hatred. We demand that you stop being a tool in the hands of the people who are carrying out this endlessly dirty and bestial war. We demand that you publish the identity of every victim, along with the time and the place of their burial' (November 1991).

Another anti-war group which emerged on the scene at the time was the organization of mothers whose sons were conscripted to fight in the war. At the beginning of July 1991, this group succeeded in disrupting a session of the National Parliament, after which other women's groups and anti-war organizations supported their demand for the return of soldiers who had completed their military service and soldiers who were stationed in the territories where war was being waged. Unfortunately, these parents' organizations disbanded as soon as their demands had been met: with the return of children—soldiers to their homes, all of their anti-war initiatives ceased. The parents acted strictly through self-interest, and their activity was only temporary, prompted by a passing social disruption. As a result, one cannot properly categorize their organizations as a part of the anti-war movement as defined here.

By 1992, certain anti-war demonstrations attracted tens of thousands of people, according to some estimates. Among them was the peace concert 'Don't Count on Us', organized by the CAA and Radio B–92 on 22 April, which provided an opportunity for young people to express their anti-war feelings through music. After the bombing of Sarajevo on 31 May, several anti-war groups organized the citizens of Belgrade in a procession which carried a 1,300-metre-long black ribbon. The column stretched from the Albanija building in the central Terazije Square to Slavija Square, and it symbolized protest, solidarity and mourning for the thousands of victims of the war in Bosnia-Hercegovina. In describing the event on 1 June 1992, the newspaper *Politika* noted that 'it was difficult to estimate how many people were actually present because the line of people was constantly moving'. According to the estimates of Radio 202, Studio B and *Borba*, there were several tens of thousands of people. Associated Press reported some 50,000 participants.

The next cycle of massive demonstrations against the regime and its warmongering politics was organized jointly by the GSS, the Civic Resistance Movement, the CAA, the United Trade Unions called 'Independence' (*Nezavisnost*), the Belgrade Circle, and Women In Black. They also received 'appropriate coverage' in *Politika*, the foremost state-controlled daily newspaper. Between the texts '*Litija*[19] for the Salvation of Serbian People' which described a mass held in the Sabor Church, and 'First *Litija* from the Church Opened after 50 Years' Separation of People and Church', there was a brief story under the title 'Peacemakers Among the Believers' which stated that 'The first free [ritual processions] held yesterday took place in peace and dignity. On the way from the Ružica Church to the Sabor Church, however, the line of believers was interrupted by a vehicle resembling an army truck, equipped with a loud-speaker system and a bell, and occupied by members of the CAA who called on the believers to join them. Some of the believers saluted this anti-war gesture, while others declared that this kind of anti-war protest is incompatible with religious rituals.' Another story in the same issue of *Politika*, 'The Last Bell Tolling for Peace', described the event as follows: 'Some three thousand residents of Belgrade assembled in front of the Federal Assembly yesterday carrying bells, alarm clocks, key rings, even kitchen utensils and pots and pans, to signal to their fellow citizens of Serbia that this is the final "wake up call"'. The treatment of these events in *Politika* clearly demonstrates the degree of significance afforded to anti-war and anti-regime gatherings.

Another demonstration jointly organized by the CAA (which marked its first anniversary with this demonstration), the Civic Resistance Movement, the GSS and the Belgrade Circle was held on 15 July. *Politika* covered the event for the public in the following manner: '"I am an Orthodox, Catholic, Muslim, Jew, Buddhist and Atheist" was one of the most prominent banners seen at the demonstration held yesterday evening before the Federal Assembly under the title "Yellow Ribbon", which was supposed to symbolize the unjust treatment of other faiths and national groups in Belgrade.' The article further stated that it was a gathering of several hundred persons, and its primary message was interpreted as follows: 'By rising up in defence of Hungarians, Croats, Slovenes, Muslims, Albanians and others, Serbs are defending the honour and nobility of the Serbian nation, and the lives of Serbs in Zagreb, Sarajevo and Mostar.' (*P*, 16 July 1992).

This was the last of the anti-war demonstrations jointly organized by several alternative groups.

The group known as *Most* (Bridge) was founded as an independent organization and was a collective member of the CAA with the mission of educating the public in the culture of peace and non-violent conflict resolution by means of mediation, negotiation and reconciliation. Their project—'Eliminating the Glorification of War, Nationalism, Ethnocentrism and Sexism from School Textbooks'—was a study of how children in schools were socialized, and the goal was to offer alternative programmes and to affirm the values of peace-loving and democratic societies.[20] The study was published in Serbian and in English in *War, Patriotism and Patriarchy*. It identified the basic models for the 'official' socialization of children from the perspectives of valuing war, the concept of patriotism, and gender roles. A follow-up to the project, 'Comparative Studies of School Textbooks in Balkan States' was also planned at the time.

This group attempted to 'introduce new models of non-violent conflict resolution as a substitute for the existing inflexible, ineffective, aggressive, violence-based model' by organizing seminars and training workshops, and by developing a network of like-minded groups throughout Serbia (ibid.: 6). By the end of 1993, they had started the project *Pakrac* in co-operation with the Zagreb Anti-War Campaign. The goal was to 'initiate and support activities which would normalize life in certain communities, starting with the rebuilding of objects necessary for the normal life of residents' (ibid.: 8). This, and other successful projects, demonstrated that non-violent conflict resolution is not only an abstract category, but a practical, living technique.

Early in 1994, activists from various alternative organizations came together in support of a group project Living in Sarajevo. The primary goal was to collect and send aid to Sarajevo, and to initiate various activities which would contribute to the peace process and an end to the war. One of their most prominent actions was the collection of aid for a unitary Sarajevo. At the beginning of 1995 they observed the one-thousandth day of the siege of Sarajevo, travelled to Sarajevo twice, and hosted a group from Sarajevo once. At the end of May of that year, they also organized an exhibition about life in wartime Sarajevo at the Centre for Cultural Decontamination. They endeavoured to establish immediate alternative communication with residents of Sarajevo—first in Belgrade and in Sarajevo, then in Tuzla in October 1995—demonstrating a commitment to promoting co-operation between various alternative groups and to establishing communication among political parties, associations and the media in Serbia and Bosnia-Hercegovina.

The protection of human rights and freedoms

With the end of the 1970s and the beginning of the 1980s, a genuine movement to promote fundamental human rights and civil liberties began to form. The stirrings of such a movement can be found in the writing of petitions and in the appearance of committees for the protection of freedom of thought and the defence of human rights. The nationalist euphoria emerging before the war halted its development. Yet the war itself also spurred a renewal of these initiatives, for it threatened the most fundamental human right—*the right to life*.

One of the organizations which emerged during this period was the Helsinki Citizens' Parliament which was created with the goal of aiding the development of civil society, confirming the autonomy and freedoms of citizens, and promoting co-operation among civic initiatives, movements, groups and individuals. From the start, its members participated in all the anti-war protests and gatherings. They themselves likewise initiated many of these events. Between 25 and 30 September 1991, they organized the Peace Caravan of Citizens of Europe which travelled to Rijeka, Ljubljana, Zagreb, Subotica, Novi Sad, Belgrade, Užice, Sarajevo and Skopje. The very same month, they also started *Yugofax*, a publication of the Helsinki Citizens' Parliament focusing on updates of war developments, as well as the *War Report*. On 7 July 1992 they organized a meeting under the title 'The Disintegration of Yugoslavia–European Integration', at which they introduced the Project for Balkan Peace and Integration. They also organized several conferences and meetings analysing the status of national minorities, and a Round Table on 'Prospects for a Democratic Alternative in Serbia'.

The initiative to launch the Civic Resistance Movement (*Civilni pokret otpora*) began at the very onset of the war. It is difficult to classify its activities with precision as it concerned itself with anti-war activities as well as with the protection of human rights. The organization promoted 'the rights of persons from ethnically mixed marriages, those who identified themselves in terms of region, and those who considered themselves of Yugoslav nationality. They also represented national minorities in the Yugoslav states, members of major Yugoslav nations who lived outside their "mother states", and individuals who chose not to identify themselves as belonging to specific national groups due to citizenship preferences. They insisted that no matter what fate ultimately befell the Yugoslav state, and no matter how many states ultimately emerged on the territory of the former Yugoslavia, these individuals would have to be recognized as persons having irrevocable simultaneous citizenship of all the new states, and as persons who are not subject to military service in any conflict among those states, except in cases where these states are attacked by a third state' (*R*, No. 39, 15 March 1992: 14). Their demands were published in a pamphlet which they called *A Freedom Charter* which outlined recommendations to states for regulating the right of citizens to hold multiple citizenship. They also participated in anti-war demonstrations and began various other anti-war initiatives.

Towards the end of 1992, the Fund For Humanitarian Law (*Fond za humanitarno pravo*) was founded as a humanitarian, non-governmental, non-profit organization. The Fund primarily collected data on crimes and violations of fundamental human rights and freedoms occurring in the war on the territory of the former Yugoslavia, violations of human rights and freedoms in the Federal Republic of Yugoslavia, and violations of minority rights. The idea was to use this reliable data to promote respect for human rights among governmental bodies (in the state and in the world), public figures, as well as among the democratic public. By collecting and analysing press reports and other means of public information, by compiling immediate eyewitness accounts and documents, by carrying out fieldwork and verifying data among several independent sources, and by exchanging information with other similar organizations in the country and abroad, the Fund for Humanitarian Law established a documentation centre which collected and classified information about various crimes and human and minority rights abuses on the territory of the former Yugoslavia and the Federal Republic of Yugoslavia. They also issued reports on human rights violations and the *abuse of international humanitarian rights* ('Anti-War Activities', *R,* special issue, February 1993).

At the beginning of 1993, the CAA founded a Council on Human Rights (*Veće za ljudska prava*) which engaged several well-known experts in the field. The organization also generated a lively interest among young people. They were involved in many of the same issues as the Fund for Humanitarian Law: the systematic registration of human rights abuses; continuous pressure on the Serbian government to take the necessary measures to protect human rights; and dissemination of ideas about human rights in public life by popularizing the Universal Declaration of Human Rights and lobbying for its inclusion in school curricula. Its long-term projects included: a comparative legal analysis of the individual articles of the International Covenant on Civil and Political Rights with the corresponding sections of the Yugoslav Constitution and other laws which relate to those rights; human rights education; examination of the relationship of the principle of conscientious objection with military service obligations in Yugoslavia; the tracking of expressions of hate in the Yugoslav media; and the establishment of an SOS telephone hotline for victims of discrimination.[21]

At the end of 1994 the Helsinki Committee for Human Rights was also founded in Belgrade, and its activities were almost identical to the activities of the Fund for Humanitarian Law and the Council for Human Rights. The organization distinguished itself later, however, by offering legal aid to refugees from Croatia who wished to return to their homes.

On 25 January 1992 the Association of Independent Intellectuals Belgrade Circle (*Beogradski krug*) was founded. As with other civic- and peace-minded groups formed at the time, it emerged as a 'reaction to political circumstances in which hatred and war have brought into question the fundamental questions of life within society' (Petrović and Paunović 1994: 271). Considering the fact that few intellectuals resisted the politics of hatred and war and the ideas arising from this kind of politics, and remembering that the voice of those who do resist is seldom heard and even more seldom listened to, the Belgrade Circle worked on 'promoting ideas, actions and activities which affirm the values of a democratic, civic and pluralistic society' ('Founding Act', *Another Serbia*, 1992, Preface). All their meetings were open to the public, and by organizing symposia, debates, round tables and lectures, they consistently worked to affirm culture and creativity. The Belgrade Circle organized two important lecture series—'Another Serbia' (held from the beginning of April until the end of June 1992 at the Student Cultural Centre) and 'Intellectuals and War' (held from the beginning of October 1992 to May 1993 at the Belgrade Youth Centre)—the proceedings of which were subsequently published.

Besides the lecture series, the Belgrade Circle also organized a series of public forums addressing current topics such as ethnic cleansing, Sandžak and Bosnia-Hercegovina, as well as the 'Student Protest of '92'. Many respected intellectuals from various European countries appeared as guests at these events, and members of the Belgrade Circle accordingly attended numerous peace meetings in Europe and in the United States. Moreover, in addition to encouraging international co-operation, the Belgrade Circle planned to promote co-operation among the successor states of Yugoslavia, so that its efforts would resonate beyond Belgrade.

The independent weekly *Naša Borba* reported regularly on the Belgrade Circle's Saturday public forums, devoting a section of its Monday editions to detailed reports on the events.

From its very inception, the Belgrade Circle attempted to hasten the end of the war by warning of its consequences. In co-operation with the parties mentioned above, and with anti-war organizations, the Belgrade Circle made its contribution to the quest for an alternative to war through the activities described, and through the writing of numerous protests letters and petitions. In addition to holding forums addressing the problems and consequences of war, it also contributed to the 'anti-war education' of the public by publishing several books with explicitly anti-war themes. And with the founding of the Centre for Cultural Decontamination, it furthermore launched an institution for promoting alternative culture.

Student demonstrations in 1991 and the 'Student Protest of '92'

After the initial protest on 9 March, a series of student demonstrations took place in Terazije Square from 10 to 14 March. They gave rise to the Terazije Parliament Forum (FTP, *Forum terazijskog parlamenta*), the primary aim of which was to eliminate all manipulations and falsehoods associated with these student demonstrations. The Forum was founded spontaneously by students who gathered around the Terazije fountain. They also formed a student demonstrations committee which met with numerous public figures. The FTP endeavoured to gather all relevant documents associated with the demonstrations, 'so that the domestic and international public would obtain a complete picture of the awakening of democracy in Serbia'. The Forum was conceived to act as a 'restraint, both on the regime and the opposition, poised to summon the "extra-party" student parliament to defend the fundamental principles of freedom and democracy'.[22] Although it was conceived with serious goals in mind, the Terazije Parliament Forum failed to develop a clear political position (i.e. the FTP never explained how it intended to act as a 'restraint, both on the regime and the opposition'), and its activities soon subsided. It ceased to exist, with the explanation that it had been disrupted by break-ins into its offices and by increasingly frequent provocation.

One year later, despite the absence of university students, there was a large gathering of middle-school students who 'conquered Terazije Square with their colourfulness, optimism, slogans and messages' (Radovanović 1992: 14).

'The month of March, last year and this year, represent the mid-way point of the most tragic period of the post-war history of Serbia. It seems that man gets used to anything and forgets quickly. When we make the effort clearly to remember last year, it is difficult to grasp all that has changed in that year: Yugoslavia fell apart, a bloody war erupted and ended, and Serbia has found itself in isolation and on the verge of economic ruin, full of refugees and the wounded' (Popadić 1992: 18–19).

The conspicuous absence of university students might be explained by the seemingly unrealistic demands[23], or perhaps by the conspicuous presence of the political opposition in the organization of these assemblies. Another reason may lie in the previous year's failure to influence the direction and work of the students' own organization—they did not manage to oust the president of the Student Alliance who, at the time, was not a student and did not have a valid mandate. Whatever the reason, the students did not appear in Terazije Square on the anniversary of 10 March to voice the demand for the resignation of the president of Serbia.

The massive student protest of June/July 1992 was announced by the huge gathering of university students in front of the Belgrade Electrotechnical and Law Faculties in early June (see Kuzmanović et al. 1993). Students gathered in front of the buildings of the technical faculties to announce to 'all concerned' their first clearly formulated demand that a 'government of national salvation' [a type of grand coalition] be formed. They drafted the rest of their demands by 15 June when the student demonstrations 'marathon', actually began.

The June demonstrations differed from those held in the previous March in at least one important respect: instead of avoiding the political opposition, this time the students made no attempt to appear apolitical. Many opposition party leaders were granted a hearing at the public forums organized at Belgrade faculties during that period. Students' demands were likewise anything but apolitical: the dissolution of the National Parliament and the Serbian government, the resignation of President Milošević, the formation of a Government of National Salvation, and the organization of elections for a Constitutional Convention (*Student Proclamation*, 8 June 1992).

Judging by its concrete results, the student protest could be considered a failure. But if the judgement were founded on other criteria (its thirty-day duration, the students' activities, their decision to 'actively participate in changing the present and in creating a decent future ... [which has] convinced us that we can reach our objective—the democratic transformation of our society—only by following the activist school of democracy'), one may reach a different conclusion (Golubović 1992: 17). A research project on the relationship of the students to the protest, and on the students themselves (both the participants in the protests and the collaborators on the project), concluded that it was difficult to define precisely, or to compare this protest with the previous public manifestations, because the most recent protest contained political, cultural and social elements. Students were both the organizers and the audience, so that all aspects of the event were executed according to students' desires (Kuzmanović et al. 1993: 85). The research also concluded that students were realistic about their demands and about the likelihood of their fulfilment. They seemed to have been conscious of the fact that 'the student protest would probably remain only a small step forward in the continuing democratization of society, and that the chances that their demands would be met were small indeed (particularly their most radical demand—Milošević's resignation)' (ibid.: 85). The students' attitudes with regard to the current political questions differed markedly. They only shared an 'extremely negative attitude toward the regime, and particularly toward the president of the Republic' (ibid.: 110). The same monograph contained a section on the students' party affiliations, which demonstrated a distribution of positions reflecting the distribution of political parties, primarily according to the position of those parties on the sanctions and the war (a position which would have been formulated before the implementation of sanctions).

The common position regarding Milošević, however, did not imply any homogeneity of political attitudes and party affiliations. The survey did not even approach 'questions about the causes of war, about the responsibility of other parties for the current events, nor about the (non-)existence of alternatives for the resolution of the Yugoslav crisis among the parties. These were something of "taboo-topics" in the protest' (ibid.: 129). B. Kuzmanović perhaps best described the protest in his assessment that 'the protest was more a reaction to the current social situation—an expression of accumulated and pending frustrations—than an indication of clear, firm and relatively enduring political convictions and values, or recognized spiritual needs which could be articulated into some type of social programme ... There was a small chance that the protest could have turned into a movement if its leaders had redirected it towards a struggle for the autonomy of the university.'

The student protest has been included in this survey despite the fact that the students did not articulate a clear anti-war position. In a way, it demonstrated that an alternative mass gathering could provoke the attention of the media (which followed it for the whole of its thirty day duration), and that it could thereby gain a measure of *power*. Unfortunately, to effect real changes in a state, a great deal more is needed.

An attempt at a comparative analysis of the anti-war scene

It is difficult to define precisely the activities of the groups discussed in the survey, as their political activities overlap. There was a series of joint actions that seemed to indicate co-operation, but this co-operation lasted only during the summer of 1992, during the period of massive anti-war demonstrations. Even then, they made no joint public appearances, nor did they manage to capture and hold public attention. Additional problems were also identified in carrying out this analysis.

In the majority of cases, a certain number of people reappear as the initiators of new organizations. This is particularly evident with women's organizations, and with anti-war and human rights groups. This *duplication of initiatives and groups* contributed to the fragmentation of existing organizations. Many similar organizations were founded: some of them survived, others did not. Yet the leaders of these failed initiatives seldom elected to join the organizations that survived, but instead attempted to start new groups. The most obvious example of this kind of duplication is the simultaneous initiative to form two practically identical organizations—the Centre for Anti-War Action and the Civic Actions for Peace (GAMA). There was so little collaboration between these two organizations, that they occasionally inadvertently organized public forums during the Anti-War Marathon during the same time slot.

The poor communication among these groups is also remarkable, and it presents additional evidence of activists' inadequate
knowledge of projects being carried out by other groups. Even
more serious is the lack of communication with the victims of the
war, in whose name they often spoke before the political leadership or the public. Many organizations also undermined one another's work through excessive competitiveness, which resulted in
the further marginalization both of themselves and of the issues
they were trying to promote.

Another problem rests with the lack of concrete alternatives offered by anti-war organizations. They often addressed *moral condemnations* in the form of petitions and proclamations to the political elite and to the public, but seldom did they offer proposals
for an alternative resolution of the conflicts.

Finally, there was no joint independent publication following all
the activities of the alternative initiatives. *Republika* attempted to
follow systematically[24] all the events on the alternative scene, but
it did not succeed entirely. The other media were largely uninter-
ested, and when they did report on the alternative scene, the result
was most often simply ideologically motivated criticism.

The above problems, along with the organizations' small membership, all hindered the formation of a proper anti-war or peace
movement. A. Turen claimed that 'social movements represent
organized collective action in a specific concretely historical period, through which class actors struggle for the social governance
of historicity' (A. Turen 1983: 79). Although many of these organizations called themselves 'movements', they themselves, or in concert with other organizations on the opposition scene, failed to
generate a movement that would effect changes. These organizations' powerlessness to influence public opinion was also significant, because power, as Turen defined it, belongs to those who are
capable of taking initiatives, who have access to newspapers, who
can occasionally lift themselves above the law–in one word, elites.
Power is nothing more than the ability to introduce, direct and
exploit changes (ibid.: 93).

In the end, one question must be asked: 'Was there an alternative
to the war?' The parties who believed that there was an alternative
expressed this in programmes of economic and political reforms,
which they thought could be realized through the democratic transformation of the whole of Yugoslavia. Their struggle for power and
for the implementation of economic programmes represented an
attempt to avoid war. Unfortunately, they were overwhelmed by the
bellicose cries of the ruling party and a segment of the opposition.

An important characteristic of the groups discussed is their truly civic orientation: they were all initiatives begun by ordinary individuals, there was no formal leader who spoke in the name of them all, and after the 'happenings of the people' when the words 'Serbian nation', 'enemies', and 'genocide' gained currency, these groups distinguished themselves from the ruling and opposition parties even in their vocabulary. In public statements they did not speak to the nation or in the name of the nation, but they addressed citizens. Their terminology did not catch the attention of the majority because they rejected nationalism as the leading ideology, and their rhetoric of peace was too unfamiliar in Serbian society.

Regardless of the failure to create a broader movement, the existence of these organizations represents a possible path towards civil society, if we define civil society as the 'totality of social communications and social networks, social institutions and social values, in which the primary actor is the citizen with his civil rights, civic (non-political and non-governmental) organizations, associations, social movements and civic institutions, and all that constitutes the public sphere in a modern society'.[25]

The anti-war scene was pushed to the margins of society to such an extent that it remained largely invisible to the public. When one writes about alternative actors, one generally speaks of their 'powerlessness' *vis-à-vis* the ruling party as the sole holder of power. From 1987, the ruling party demonstrated its power through the media, making it known that it was the sole entity entitled to decide about war and peace in the name of all. Much blood has been spilled between the official position of 'Serbia will not bow' and the slogan 'Peace has no alternative'. During that time the alternative groups acted following the dictates of their conscience, never coming to terms with the official positions of the government and a sizeable section of the opposition.

The actions of the anti-war activists on the Serbian political scene demonstrated that there existed alternative solutions which, if they could not save Serbia, could have certainly directed its citizens out of the war madness in which they were enmeshed.

Notes

1 In addition to the weekly *Republika*, one of the principal sources for this text is a book by Branka Petrović and Žarko Paunović (1994). These

authors continue to monitor and report on the alternative scene in *Republika* and *Odgovor* (a publication for refugees).

2 From the 'UJDI Manifesto' published in *Republika*, No. 4, Zagreb, October 1989.

3 'Ownership of goods should not be confined to a small number of individuals. Let us keep the positive aspects of self-management and let us expand the economic opportunities and security of workers by making them stock holders in the firms in which they are working, to the success of which they have already contributed. Let us also extend this opportunity to all the citizens of Yugoslavia, so that property and the wealth of society derived in the future phase of development will have their base in the labour, capital and wisdom of millions of people, rather than state or anonymous social property without owners and without responsibility for their proper use. That is how we will build a proprietary democracy' (*Programmatic Declaration SRSJ*).

4 Vojin Dimitrijević, at one of the founding assemblies (*R*, No.15, 1 March 1991).

5 Confronting a situation in which armed skirmishes were already claiming lives, and in which bellicose ideological positions advocated national exclusiveness and hatred, proposing violent final solutions for social and national disputes and conflicts, according to the UJDI the only chance for peace was to hold free elections to the Federal Assembly of Yugoslavia, in which sovereign citizens could articulate their interests, beliefs and political will for a peaceful and democratic change to the current political, economic and spiritual situation (*R*, No. 21, 1 June 1991: 16).

6 Translator's note: the Federal Chamber is the main chamber of the Federal Assembly.

7 The SSNO was the first institution to respond to this statement: 'Such pseudo-democratic equating of the JNA and the so-called armed forces of Slovenia during the course of recent events in Slovenia is both unacceptable and unprincipled ... such equating of the lawful actions of the JNA with the unilateral and unconstitutional actions of bodies in Slovenia can be considered neither a thoughtful nor a well-intentioned effort to find a peaceful solution to the crisis in Yugoslavia, nor a patriotic act of those who believe this' (*P*, 6 July 1991). A few days later, the same journalist who reported on the press conference wrote for *Politika*: 'A clumsy statement calling for desertion from the JNA which could be heard at last week's joint press conference of the SRSJ, UJDI and EPJ, not only alarmed the public, but it divided the members and the sympathizers of the Reformists. The truth about the views of the SRSJ in Serbia regarding the army is altogether different, however.' The statement of the president of the Belgrade committee of the SRSJ in Serbia, Žarko Korać ('We are against all paramilitary and party formations. The only armed force that should exist in the state is the JNA, of course transformed and depoliticized'), was used for the title of the text 'Only the JNA Can Prevent National Conflict' (*P*, 11 July 1991).

8 Translator's note: YUTEL was the only non-republican, i.e. all-Yugoslav television station, founded by Prime Minister Ante Marković.

9 'The goal of the Interparliamentary Council would be to strengthen the peace process in the former Yugoslav space, to help reverse the consequences of armed conflict, to rebuild co-operation among Yugoslav peoples, to promote the respect of individual and collective human rights, the establishment of the rule of law, and the extension of demilitarized zones, and to help enter the processes of European integration' (from the *'Proposal for the Founding of an Interparliamentary Council*).

10 A special edition of *Republika*, No. 29, 1 October 1991, 'How to prevent total war', was published in book form in the English language.

11 One public forum organized by the local Republican Club took place at the end of the summer of 1992 in Zrenjanin. Discussions on the theme 'War and Tolerance' lasted seven days.

12 One of the consequences of this *alliance* was a 'cleansing' in Pančevo, when the SPS-SRS-dominated Parliament unlawfully revoked the right to operate of Radio Pančevo and the journal *Pančevac*. These two media were remarkable for their many years of markedly anti-war editorial politics, ever since the populist gatherings orchestrated by Slobodan Milošević. Radio Pančevo was the only station to broadcast the July 1988 meeting in Novi Sad (the infamous *yogurt revolution*) when the arrival of national socialism on the political scene in Serbia was announced.

13 'For us, this feminist group is a resource for various women's initiatives and personal change, and a support for changing reality' (Women For Women [Žene za žene], 1993: 23).

14 On 12 May 1991, at a meeting of this group, the first anti-war slogans were formulated, including 'Let us talk/negotiate, even if it is pointless', 'Leaders, shake hands', 'We love Slovenes, Croats, Muslims, Serbs, Montenegrins, Albanians and Roma', and 'Leaders, bury the hatchets' (ibid.: 43).

15 Historians discussed the destruction of cultural-historical monuments (regardless of their national or religious heritage); psychologists addressed the serious consequences of war on all direct participants—the difficulties with respect to their reintegration in society, and especially the scars that war inflicts on the psyche of children.

16 This gesture should not be interpreted as a religious act because members of many different faiths, and large numbers of atheists, participated equally. There are traces of melted candles on that place to this day—neither wind nor snow have washed them away. They will serve as a reminder that not everyone supported the war.

17 Many of these epitaphs were collected for a book given the title *A Tomb for Miroslav Milenković*, published by several peace organizations.

18 See contributions by Aleksandar Nenadović, Snježana Milivojević, and Rade Veljanovski, this volume, and *Hate Speech*, 1995.

19 Translator's note: *Litija* is an aspect of orthodox ceremony consisting of a public procession.

20 Cited in the *Report on Activities in 1994 and Plans for 1995*, CAA, Belgrade, February 1995.
21 A more detailed account of these and other activities of the Council on Human Rights and the CAA can be found in their bulletin *Gals (Voice)*.
22 From the Proclamation of the Terazije Parliament Forum which was signed by over 100,000 people.
23 The demands were the following: the resignation of President Milošević; elections for a Constitutional Convention and the formation of a transitional government; an amnesty for all individuals who evaded conscription; an accurate list of all Serbs killed in a war in which Serbia [officially] did not participate; the dismissal of the existing Student Alliance and the formation of a Student Parliament as the only legitimate representative of the students.
24 Texts by Vesna Pešić and Miljenka Dereta (*R*, No. 125–126, 1 October 1995), in reaction to an earlier text by Žarko Paunović (*R*, No. 123, 1 September 1995), opened a dialogue about the alternative regarding questions that have yet to be formulated.
25 The definition of civil society used here is 'the theoretical category for the analysis and explication of those dimensions of social life which can be defined as such, and which exist in reality', from V. Pavlović, ed., 1995: 248.

The Army's Use of Trauma

MIROSLAV HADŽIĆ

The Yugoslav war confirmed the high motivational power of the ideology of 'blood and soil'. At the same time it was a reminder that motivation for war is unlimited. The motivation for war among the participants arose from a range of sources of different rank and origin. Contemporary and historical, national and religious, political and ideological, economic and social, individual and group, internal and external, (pro-)war motives overlapped, each providing stimulus for the other.

With the deepening of the Yugoslav crisis, the use, as well as the efficacy, of national traumas from the historical memory was growing fast; such traumas became the key mechanisms in the collective and individual rationalization of the war: by invoking them, the collective and individual actors were ensuring for themselves, in advance or post factum, 'indulgences' for various kinds of destruction, including war crimes.

The mass interiorization of traumas revealed the indoctrinating nature of the political socialization that had gone before. The widely accepted theory of 'special war' showed its frightening efficacy only when used against collective 'internal enemies'—formerly fraternal peoples. Systematic depersonalization, based on the systematic weakening of individuals, coupled with ignorance and ideological thinking, led to a high degree of readiness, and even the need, to submit to political manipulation. The 'blank spots' of history, preserved by the lack of catharsis, in a very short time turned into a new historical ignorance and 'knowledge'.

The basic lack of integration of the state and the social community, strengthened by a non-democratic constitution, made the Yugoslav peoples rivals instead of co-operators, due to their different aspirations. Lack of integration meant that a state of permanent conflict was maintained, which took on differing forms, accents and intensity. The collective national dissatisfaction with the common state and with the other peoples within it, initiated and articulated by politics, produced a permanent feeling of historical and concrete deprivation.

In these circumstances, collective frustration directed the accumulated aggression towards the other members of the same community. Small nations, which had appeared late on the historical scene, through their narcissism strengthened by ideology, found the main reasons for their own troubles among the 'others', those nearest to them.

The absence of any catharsis after 1945 inevitably stimulated the 'black-market production' of historical traumas. Situated in the 'black-market zone' of thinking, these traumas gained both in strength and persuasiveness, thus increasing their motivational power. The absence of catharsis repressed, but also 'modernized' traumas, laying them open to daily political interpretation. Above all, the lack of any systemic instruments for checking and censuring barbarism, encouraged the politically desired move towards 'lower levels of consciousness'.

In focusing attention on the army, several considerations should be borne in mind. The use of the seemingly self-explanatory name 'The Yugoslav People's Army' (JNA) implies that the army was seen as a monolithic, impersonal organization. Since the name does not reveal any information about the internal distribution of power, the persons making the actual decisions on the use of the army remained hidden behind that name. The hierarchical structure of the JNA therefore points to the corps of generals as the holders of central political military power. The course of its (pre-)war involvement was clearly determined by three of the most influential generals—Veljko Kadijević, Stane Brovet and Blagoje Adžić—of whom Kadijević had the first and last word (see Đ. Stanić 1992: 7). Nevertheless, there was enough room left for his subordinates to make a 'creative contribution' to the new war trauma of their own people and of other peoples.

Focusing on the army is justified for a number of reasons. Firstly, although the JNA and its military leadership was the ideological, political and security mainstay of the regime of the second Yugoslavia, it contributed objectively to the country's self-destruction. Secondly, in the period from the death of Josip Broz to the eve of the war, the corps of generals acted as a relatively independent political subject with considerable power. In the final stage of the Yugoslav crisis, the generals, through their ideological interventions, contributed to its intensification in the direction of war.

Above all, the focus on the military leadership is dictated by the fact that this leadership, through its biased and destructive involvement in the armed conflicts among the various peoples, directly (co-)operated, among other things, in the revival of the old traumas and in the creation of new ones.

The physical consequences of the traumatic use of army power are clearly visible require no particular proofs. The context of the crisis and the existing situation may partially explain concrete actions taken by the army, but they do not reveal the reasons for the destructive activity of the quondam army of all thepeople. The question arises whether within the army—in its structure and its way of functioning—there already existed the potential for traumatization of the Yugoslav peoples. If the answer is affirmative, how and why was this potential realized?

A more complete answer to these questions would first require an analysis of the military–social nature of the army. This would have to be followed by a study of the mode of involvement of the JNA in the war, and an analysis of its role in the war. However, such analyses are not possible without uncovering the interaction between the military establishment and the national–republican actors.[1] This opens up a new area of investigative and cognitive problems, which are beyond the scope of this paper.

We shall therefore limit ourselves to a concise and selective review of the speed and the contents of the ideological–political preparations of the JNA for involvement in the Yugoslav war. By establishing as points of reference the attitude of the generals towards the Yugoslav crisis, we shall try to contribute to the understanding of the transformation of the army from the defender of the constitution into the destroyer of its own state and people.

The scope of this review is limited by the inaccessibility of the relevant documents which could explain more reliably the cause and the significance of the army's (pre-)war activity, that is, its inactivity. The secondary, publicly accessible sources on the role of the JNA in the destruction of Yugoslavia therefore acquire temporarily the status of primary sources.

The army and catharsis

In 1945 catharsis did not present the Communists with any problem, nor did they have any need of catharsis. Triumph in the war and the winning of power had cleansed their 'souls' and liberated them from any anxiety. The traumatic division within and among individual peoples not only did not bother them, it became an additional source for the renewal of 'revolutionary' energies. The permanent revolution was reduced to an incessant (fifty-year-long) 'struggle' against the same enemy.[2] Thence the impression that the latest Yugoslav war was only a continuation of the previous one.

The need for catharsis was removed by pushing traumas into the background. By combining various procedures, the traumas were first modified and made relative. The closing of this problem prevented the recently ended (fratricidal) war from becoming a matter of public consideration. By redefining the situational and historical circumstances, the autochthonous causes of mutual traumatization of the Yugoslav peoples were smothered. By making them void of any concrete content—by the depersonalization of both the executioners and the victims—the traumas were generalized. They were reduced to being a regular phenomenon of the anti-fascist war. By a proportional distribution of the liberation and the criminal actions by means of the formula according to which 'everybody is (a little bit) guilty'[3], the intra-national gap was falsely bridged and the trail towards ideological brotherhood and unity was blazed. Instead of de-Nazification, in the name of 'love' among the Yugoslav peoples, the past was forgiven, but not forgotten.

Catharsis was definitely removed from the agenda by the party's redirecting of social energy towards the 'construction' of socialism. The traumas were relegated to the past, under the onslaught of the 'bright' present and future. Since that time, they have been used to remind the forgetful of what would have happened had it not been for the revolution, the party, the army and Tito.

The inevitability of this 'construction' was justified later on by the deep roots of (the idea of) socialism, and by the will among the Yugoslav peoples to live under such a system. It was followed by the ideological reinterpretation of the party and the social past, the recent past as well as the more distant. A relation of inverse proportion was established: as the distance in time lengthened, the reliability of the knowledge of previous events diminished, which inevitably led to the new (party) version of history.[4]

This point marks the beginning and the end of the story of the army's role in the prevention of post-war catharsis. In the first place, catharsis, as a process of social self-interrogation and cleansing, did not occur at all. Secondly, the army, as a mouthpiece of the party, was active in the 'mass production' of the socialist consciousness. In co-operation with other sub-systems (education, schools, information, culture, etc.) it was active in the elimination of remnants of the old consciousness and the 'introduction' of the new one. Only in that sense was the JNA just one of the participants in the prevention of catharsis and the suppression of traumas.

The army's strengths and weaknesses

Nominally, the position and the sphere of activity of the JNA in the second Yugoslavia were, without any ideological content[5], determined by the constitution.[6] However, the real (political) power of the army surpassed the systemic framework and was calibrated according to the needs of the party and the Leader. The army functioned as a complex, isolated and protected (non-)systemic essence of the one-party state.

The special position of the JNA in all areas, first established according to the needs of its special links with the Leader, was constantly being extended to new areas of exclusivity. Its revolutionary pedigree was enhanced by its role as the guardian of the purity of the ideas of socialism, and by its achievements as well. Its monopoly over the defence of the country against outside aggression was extended in time, but also redirected towards the internal defence of party (ideological) values and the aims of the regime.

The peculiarity of the political role of the army was supported by the special social status of the JNA and its members. The legal possibilities for systemic control of the army were narrowed by transferring the constitutional and legal authority to ministerial decrees. Thus, the possibilities for hierarchical arbitrariness in relations within the army were increased. The professional separateness of army personnel was enhanced by new attributes. The system of vertically increasing benefits gave privileges to army employees according to status.[7] At the same time, the social separateness of the army was preserved. In order to enter the military profession it was necessary to have not only certain mental and physical abilities, but also an appropriate social (class) origin, as well as party and security clearances (which required the vetting of relatives, too).

The total separateness of the JNA suggested the outlines of a military corporation under the patronage of the party.[8] It was expressed through, among other things, the autarchic tendencies of the army's leadership, the composition of which was constantly changing. Naturally, all this was justified in terms of the higher needs of defence. The creation of the military–industrial complex[9] was meant to secure technological and economic independence in the production of arms and equipment. The development of the system of military farms contributed to an increase in the logistic independence of the army.

The final consequence of these processes was the intra-army re-production of a corporate spirit *sui generis*–awareness of its exceptional character produced an awareness of the separateness of the army's (material and political) interests, and, even more importantly, an awareness of the justifiability of affirming its group interests and its right (and duty) to defend them.

The party domination over the army resulted in the ideological organization of the JNA, and, accordingly, of the whole defence system.

The General People's Defence and Social Self-Protection (ONO-DSZ) system, which comprised the JNA and the Territorial Defence (TO), and the concept behind this system, were founded on a double ideological turn of events. Firstly, the party's project of socialism was proclaimed a reality, and subsequently, the ideological reality became the source and demigod of the General People's Defence.

It was for this reason that the party was installed at the centre of the system–through the committees for ONO-DSZ it controlled all defence forces outside the army,[10] and through the organization of the League of Communists of Yugoslavia (SKJ) within the JNA it controlled all the army's defence forces.[11] The party allotted to itself the leading and directing role.[12] The party parameters determined the combat morale,[13] training and education, as well as the management and command.[14] Ideological criteria were used to appraise the 'moral and political conditions' (MPC)–the crucial element of combat readiness of (all) armed forces.[15]

The combat morale of the troops was derived from the 'revolutionary and popular character of the JNA' (*Instructions for MPC in the JNA*, Article 2). Within the army, the status was appraised on the basis of the relation of its members 'to constitutional order, socialist self-management, brotherhood, unity and the equality of peoples and nationalities in the SFRY, to the leading role of the League of Communists of Yugoslavia, to the independent and non-aligned foreign policy of the SFRY, to General People's Defence and Social Self- Protection' (*Instructions for MPC in the TO*, Article 3). Political activities in the army units served as an indicator of individual and collective loyalty to the state and the party.[16] The whole approach to the MPC was built on the conviction that self-managing socialism produced a corpus of unchangeable motivational aims and defence values, about which there existed a high degree of unity among citizens and members of the Armed Forces (OS).

A whole system of instruments was developed for the evaluation and endorsement of the party loyalty of members of the JNA/OS. As a preventative measure the whole army was pervaded by a network of party organizations[17]—the military structure had its own party analogue. The professional and party roles of officers and NCOs were merged,[18] and in the functioning of the army ideological considerations were above professional ones.[19]

The overlapping of the line of command and of the forging of the party's monolithic unity increased the arsenal of disciplinary measures along the hierarchical vertical. The final aim was to secure, if need be by force, the ideological unanimity of all members of the army.[20] For that purpose, a comprehensive system of ideological and political education (IPE) was created for officers, NCOs and soldiers.

The character of the IPE for officers is best described by its declared aims: 'By acquiring a knowledge of the basic characteristics of the social and political situation in the country and in the world, from the standpoint of strengthening ideological and political unity among the members of the armed forces in accordance with the programme and policy of the SKJ, and by forging brotherhood and unity within the OS and by educating them in the spirit of Yugoslav socialist patriotism, the officers and NCOs were prepared "for direct political activity in the units and institutions of our armed forces."'[21] Conspicuous in the formulation of these aims is the absence of any mention of the duties of the JNA/OS, that is, of its officers and NCOs, towards the state. It was on this basis that the redefinition of the character of patriotism was carried out. By adding the prefix 'socialist', the central duty of the army was transferred from the defence of the state to the defence of the regime and its ideology.

The ideological loyalty of officers and NCOs was also endorsed by official grading, on which their status in the service depended. Political suitability and the possibility of promotion were dependent on 'Marxist and social political knowledge, political activity in the military units/institutions, political activity in local communities, interpersonal relationships, criticism and self-criticism, general and political vigilance' (*Rules on the grading of military personnel:* 30).

In addition to all this, the army leadership did not renounce its ambition to influence conscripts ideologically. The 'political education and training of soldiers' was supposed to secure 'the strengthening of their morale and their ideological and political consciousness on the basis of scientific knowledge, grounded in Marxism, about the society and the individual, about the working class as the main protagonist of revolutionary changes, about the National Liberation War and the socialist revolution' etc. (*The Plan and Programme of the Political Education and Training of Soldiers/Marines in the JNA:* 9).

Apart from the fact that the tasks assigned were too great even for an average faculty of political sciences, this political activity was meant to create, in the fifteen months of obligatory military service, 'ideologically and politically conscious, morally unshakeable, loyal and resolute fighters for the development and defence of the freedom, independence and constitutional order of the SFRY'. One should note that, judging by the aims, the soldiers were being prepared—although on ideological grounds—for the defence of the state and the constitutional order, and their commanding officers and NCOs for activities on the basis of the programme of the SKJ!

In order not to leave anything to chance, the ideological shaping of the members of the JNA was rounded off in the party organizations. Everything that was 'taught' in the compulsory programme of the IPE was repeated in the party organizations.

The ideological strongpoint of the indoctrination was the cult of J.B. Tito. During his life, but also after his death, Broz was used in the JNA/OS as a model, a theoretical and methodological matrix,[22] the source of revolutionary (self-)legitimation, and also as a totem[23].

The connecting warp and woof of the ideological indoctrination of the members of the JNA/OS was the struggle against 'special warfare'.[24] In the tradition of the best Communist sectarianism and exclusiveness, individuals, ideas, movements, nations and states were classified as friends or enemies.[25] Yugoslavia, its regime and the army were surrounded by a conspiratorial world, which permanently used 'their own weaknesses' in order to destroy them.[26]

Under the guise of sharpening their sense of political vigilance and security, the officers and NCOs were constantly warned against a departure from party policy and falling under foreign (enemy) ideological influence.[27] The whole system and every individual within it were under close scrutiny by the army security organs, while their activity remained secret to the majority of members of the JNA.[28]

The real reach of the (self-)shaping of the army by the party and the police became apparent only within the proper and broader social and systemic environment. Permanent ideological and security pressures resulted in the army's ignorance of reality. The ease with which complex socio-political processes were classified and (dis)qualified according to black-and-white schema speaks volumes of the dominance of a Manichaean perception.

The rigidity of official and interpersonal relations within the army fitted perfectly into the authoritarian texture of society. The factual separateness of the army from the system made it possible, after the Leader's death, for political and military elites to come close together behind the stage. At the same time, it left the generals complete freedom in decision making within the army.

The existential dependence and social 'corruptness' of permanent personnel, caused by the principles of 'the one-commander system' and ideological monolithism, turned the officers' corps into an amorphous mass susceptible to all kinds of manipulation. The crowning proof for this is the lack of any—let alone any organized—professional or political resistance on the part of the officers and NCOs to the (pro)war policy of the generals in command.

The key after-effect of the ideological self-determination of the army was its professional incapacitation. The absence of public and systemic control permitted those in command of the army to be arbitrary in estimating the degree of combat readiness of the JNA/OS. Self-estimating, in which ideological criteria were implemented, created both in society and in the army a false impression[29] of its factual capacities and abilities.

The army's rejection of reality

The political end to the Yugoslav crisis[30] brought to the public stage the army leadership as well. The radical change in the political topography, and the controversial reactions of the party-state organs were creating a kind of political *galimatias*. The least that could have been expected was that the army leadership would find its way in the confusion. The blockade of federal centres stimulated the process of its political independence and increased its aspirations.

The collapse of one-party socialism which occurred in a context in which Revolution, the party and Tito were no longer taboo subjects, endangered the very foundation of the army's existence. The constitutional and systemic bases of the functioning of the JNA were also undermined. The first breaches appeared in the army's previously untouchable preserve-the organizing of society along military lines (cf. B. Mamula 1987: 12). There were suggestions that the social and the political position of the army should be looked into again and that its power should be curtailed.

The changes in the army environment had a destructive influence, although with a delayed effect. The revitalization of nationalistic ideas and movements was rapidly undermining the status, the reputation and the political influence of the army. The multinational harmony within the army was also damaged. A long-lasting process of nationalistic differentiation in the commanding corps was initiated, although it was not visible at first.[31]

During 1989 and 1990, the army leadership became directly involved in the political dispute. As the crisis was heightening, the frequency of the public appearances of the army leadership, which were ideologically and politically uncompromising, was increasing, while their ability effectively to prevent the disintegration of Yugoslavia by war was diminishing. The army intervention in the Yugoslav crisis was characterized by two constants: the generals, by their political actions, were continuously overreaching their authority, and by their non-action (or wrong actions) within the sphere of their authority they accelerated the destruction, through war, of their native country.

General defence of heritage

The army leadership placed the first line of defence around socialism. The generals' desire for socialism was stronger than reasons of state and state interests, which had already been partly amputated. The first great switching of theses occurred: the state interest—the preservation of the territorial integrity and intactness of Yugoslavia—was reduced to the preservation of socialism within it, at all costs.

The army leadership were pursuing the policy of the party instead of the policy of the state. They therefore invested all their authority and energy into the preservation of the SKJ.[32] After the congress preceding the disintegration of the party, the generals took over the initiative for the salvation and renewal of the (remaining) SKJ.[33]

At the same time, they wanted to prevent party pluralism at all costs. In the beginning the generals gave a legalistic form to their resistance,[34] and later they looked for salvation in non-party pluralism, claiming that 'at the present stage of social development any form of institutionalization of political pluralism in the form of multiparty organizing is unacceptable' (*The Ninth Conference of the OSKJ in the JNA*, 1990: 25).

The introduction of the multiparty system would inevitably lead to the depoliticization of the JNA and to the dissolution of the military branch of the party. Even putting this issue on the agenda was unacceptable to the army leadership.[35] They rejected any hope that ideology would be taken out of the army, and they emphasized primarily 'preserving and strengthening the morale and political unity of the army based both on the programme of safeguarding and further developing the achievements of the socialist revolution, and on the revolutionary thinking of Josip Broz Tito' (V. Kadijević 1989: 16).

Since they were not able to prevent the disintegration of the SKJ, the army leadership decided to preserve, as long as possible, the army branch of the SKJ. Its dissolution was postponed in every conceivable way,[36] and then, by a roundabout manoeuvre, the Communists in the army were collectively enrolled in the League of Communists–Movement for Yugoslavia (SK–PJ) (*The Decision of the Tenth Conference of the OLC in the JNA*, 1991: 19).

The last call to the members of the army to defend socialist Yugoslavia was formulated in the document *Information of the Political Department* of the Federal Secretariat for National Defence (SSNO). In early 1991, the generals came to the conclusion that, in spite of the international anti-Communist conspiracy, 'real prospects for the preservation of the country as a federal and socialist community still existed'. They maintained that the Western script-writers 'failed to destroy Communism in any country where the revolution was autochthonous', and they 'understood that the idea of Yugoslavia and the option for socialism had much deeper roots than they had estimated'. Later on, a party and military mission followed—to make the SK–PJ, 'in the next five to six months, the main political force on the Yugoslav scene', as 'at this moment that is the only pan-Yugoslav political force', and, accordingly, 'the chance for the survival of federal Yugoslavia and of the army itself' (*B*, 31 January 1991: 4).

The central army ramparts were built around the 'modern federation'. This was quite understandable, since requests for the recomposition of the federal state and the final redistribution of power in favour of the republics directly jeopardized the essential interests of the army and the generals. The relation of the generals towards constitutional changes can be qualified as federalism which was 'combative and in the form of an ultimatum'. The army leadership first launched the slogan that 'Yugoslavia can exist only as a true federation, or, in our [their M. H.] opinion, it will cease to exist' (V. Kadijević 1988: 53). A decisive message to the public and to their opponents was delivered by the announcement of the battle for Yugoslavia: 'If somebody has already declared the battle for Yugoslavia, it will not be waged without the JNA and millions of working people on its side' (P. Šimić 1989: 15).

The army's indispensability was based on two premises: 1) that the 'Decisions of the Second Session of the Anti-Fascist Council for the National Liberation of Yugoslavia (AVNOJ) have the character of a permanent historical and social covenant, and they cannot be haggled about on a daily basis' (*The Ninth Conference of the OSKJ in the JNA*, 61); and 2) that 'The Constitution of the SFRY should be the highest political and legal act. The constitutions of the republics should be in harmony with the Constitution of the SFRY' (V. Kadijević 1989: 11).

The debates on the (re)arrangement of the federal state inevitably had a nationalistic character. By stressing their Yugoslav orientation, the army leadership was constantly giving evidence of the army's equidistance from the so-called separatist and unitarist nationalisms, but they were constantly facing the danger of annihilating their request for the strengthening of the central state by their criticism of unitarism. The problem was being solved by resorting to the Authority, since 'in harmony with Tito's ideas of Yugoslavia and Yugoslav socialist patriotism the members of the army are resolutely against any nationalism—whether separatist or nationalist—... and at the same time are against those tendencies which claim that social movements in the direction of the strengthening of the country's unity are unitarism' (B. Mamula 1987 :11).[37]

The gist of the army's political announcements was directed at the preservation of the constitutional, systemic and factual position of the JNA. The first breach in the untouchability of the army was achieved by alternative movements. The political and professional autonomy of the JNA was opened to question, and changes in its role and systemic position were requested. The issue of the rationality of the system and the concept of the ONO was also opened to discussion. Changes in the conscription system, the right to do national service as a civilian, and recognition of the right of individuals to be conscientious objectors were also requested.[38]

By reacting sharply to the requests of the alternative movements, the army leadership began a political offensive against the so-called anti-army forces, which did not slacken until the onset of the war. The key counter-argument was condensed into the statement that 'Any change in the social role of the army would lead to the destruction of the SFRY as a state and as a social community' (S. Mirković 1988: 30). The generals explicitly refused any debate on the position of the army in its statement that 'there can be no discussion about the tasks of the armed forces in the defence of the country, determined by the Constitution of the SFRY and by federal law' (V. Kadijević 1989: 8).

An insoluble problem for the army leadership was the organization, in the course of 1990, of the national (para-)armies in Slovenia and Croatia. The disintegration of the federal state and the ideological self-blockade, enhanced by the illusion of the strength of the army's power,[39] reduced the generals to the role of threatening observers. The military triumvirate regularly recorded and informed the public of all constitutional and legal violations, claiming that 'the SSNO will not allow the formation of any kind of armed forces in any part of the Yugoslav territory outside those established by the Constitution of the SFRY' (*B*, 1 October 1990: 3). The army leadership was compensating for its inability to act by convincing the public (citizens) of the readiness of the army to fulfil its constitutional role.

The army's offensive defence could not remain without response, just as that defence itself was a response to current political processes. The groupings and re-groupings of political forces, which started along the lines of Communism vs. anti-Communism, were quickly transformed into national (nationalistic) differentiation along the confederal–federal axis.

On that basis the army leadership, during 1990, in its internal communications with its constitutional superiors—the Presidency of the SFRY and the Federal Executive Council (SIV)—used a differentiated approach. By using federal and socialist criteria, it classified them as suitable or not suitable, loyalists or traitors.[40] Its support for the economic reforms orchestrated by the SIV was only declarative. It recognized in the reform a return to capitalism and the abolition of the privileged position of the army.

The complete identity of their interests brought the army leadership closer to the federalist group.[41] This closeness of interests was accompanied by an ideological closeness. Behind the scenes there existed strategic and tactical co-ordination.[42] This partly explains the double political standards of the army leadership. Thus, among other things, the adoption of a separate[43] Constitution of Serbia did not provoke any reactions from the army.

On the other hand, the conflict of the army leadership with the leaders of Slovenia and Croatia was evident even during the existence of the SKJ. After the election victories of DEMOS and HDZ, a direct confrontation occurred between the irreconcilable ideologics and exclusive (pro-)state interests. The army leadership irrevocably weakened its position by sticking to its Yugoslav ideology and exclusive federalism; the ideological bias and the bias of interests disqualified them from playing a mediating or pacifying role in the denouement of the crisis, a role that was feasible, at least in principle. Daily political and propagandistic appearances by the leading generals became directly counterproductive—they delivered plenty of material to the secessionist republics for the defamation of the JNA on the grounds of being Communist and Serbophile.

The classic army propaganda did not abandon the framework of the revolution–counter-revolution antithesis and its derivatives. With the introduction of party pluralism the arsenal was widened, but special attention was paid to the nationality of the participants in the propaganda action.[44] However, after the victory of the opposition in Slovenia and Croatia priority was given to the matrix '41'. It is interesting to note that (anti-)fascist qualifiers were never used for the events taking place in Slovenia, even after its secession. After the victory of the HDZ in Croatia, and Serbian reactions to it, the army moved first the political and then the military focus of its activities to Croatia.

The illusion of self-transformation

In the last phase of the Yugoslav crisis laden with conflicts, the army leadership were forced to devote special attention to the situation within the army itself. In order to diminish the outside influences on the JNA, a number of self-defensive measures were undertaken. The ideological, political and informational activities directed towards the permanent structure of the army were intensified by the participation of the leading generals. A special emphasis was put on the obligations of the JNA in the preservation of socialism and of Yugoslavia. The process of making the army monolithic was facilitated by the radicalism of the officers based on the illusion of (pre)cognition of the essence of the crisis and of the ways to a solution.

As a safeguard, the top generals increased their pressure on their subordinates. For instance, members of the JNA in Slovenia and Croatia were instructed, by an internal cable, to vote for the Left. The climax of the pressure was reached on the occasion of the founding of SK–PJ; the signing of application forms was raised to the status of a patriotic duty and those who did not sign were dismissed from the ranks.[45]

The army leadership started to re-examine, internally and gradually, the ONO system and the concept behind it of the. This was followed by a series of normative adaptations and by changes to the names of the institutions. The Political Department was renamed the Morale Department; the Law on the ONO and the Rules of Service were cleansed of ideological content. Partial changes were made in the IPE of officers and NCOs, and a programme of moral education for soldiers was introduced. Ideological points of reference were removed from moral and political education and the focus was moved to the defence of the SFRY and patriotism. The official norms regarding the treatment of religious believers were changed—believers were permitted to visit places of worship in their free time, etc.

A debate was launched on the very concept of ONO.[46] Generally speaking, the debates opened important questions on the functioning of the defence, but in the final remarks of the chief of General Staff it was concluded that the concept of the ONO had proved to be valid and adequate (*VD*, special edition: 24). The improvements were reduced to the establishment of unity between the concept, doctrine and system of the ONO, that is, the unity of the OS. The goal was to prevent the take-over of the Territorial Defence by the republics.

It was not possible to evade a series of problems related to current political processes. A warning on the counter-productivity of the daily political activity of the army was rejected—it was concluded that a neutral status for the JNA was unacceptable.[47] The need for the political activity of the army was specially underlined.[48]

However, nothing was done to identify the critical point of the concept and system of defence. The situation demanded that the sturdiness of all elements of the system be rigorously examined. By listing the necessary and momentarily feasible changes, it could have been possible, at least partially, to repair this dysfunction. The problem can be best seen in the example of the TO. Only when it was realized that the republican staffs and units of the TO could become (as they indeed did) the nuclei of the national armies did the generals discover that this component of defence was over-sized[49] and inefficient. As the peace-time location of army corps was identical to the republican borders, changes were made in the organization and formation of large army units.[50]

The tardiness of the generals in all phases of the crisis reached its peak, six months later, in the statement made by the federal secretary for Defence, Veljko Kadijević, that 'the Territorial Defence, as created in the late sixties and early seventies, was objectively a great deceit'.[51]

The generals directed the major part of their activities towards preparing the army for the oncoming (war) events. We cannot judge the military plans for extraordinary circumstances[52] as they are highly secret, but, according to the results the JNA achieved, it can be stated that either the top army leadership had no plans for extraordinary circumstances; or if they had plans, they were poor; or if they had good plans in principle, then they no longer had the power to realize them, which is, in practice, the same thing—the plans were poor, since they did not take into account the power (i.e. the powerlessness) of the JNA.

It seems that the top military leadership misjudged its future enemies and allies in the war. One of the reasons for this was the fact that during 1990 the army leadership still doubted, according to its confidential estimates, that the Yugoslav crisis would end in war. They counted on a great majority of the population standing by the army in order to prevent mutual war. They completely overlooked the fact that in the newly created situation, and in accordance with the nature of the internal war among the nations, the intervention of the JNA could be met by general resistance, primarily among the peoples of the north-western republics.

The army leadership did not want to face the fact that the crisis and national homogenization directly made worthless the foundations of the concept and system of the ONO and its military functionality. This refers primarily to the principle of 'reliance on one's own forces', which meant the use of internal material resources and mass voluntary involvement of the populations in the internal defence of socialism and of Yugoslavia. To put it briefly, in the estimate of the JNA's prospects for fulfilling its constitutional duty, the generals did not proceed from the most unfavourable variant for themselves, but from the most favourable.

The army abandons Yugoslavia

Generally speaking, the JNA could not have escaped the fate of Yugoslavia—the disappearance of the state led to the disappearance of its army. However, the course, tempo and forms of disintegration of the former state were directly dependent on the way in which the JNA was used.

The army's abstaining from the use of force increased, in principle, the possibility for a peaceful separation. However, this did not depend only on the JNA. In another variant, the army leadership could have prevented (or tried to prevent), by the independent use of force, the dissolution of the state in civil war. The circumstances and all the political actors were working against the independent use of the army. In addition to all this, the generals did not succeed, as their results prove, in elaborating and/or implementing any adequate variant of the protection of their state and the people within it.

The political dissolution of Yugoslavia was followed, but also facilitated, by an invisible entropy of the military system. The army leadership faced several questions, to which they had to give—or should have given—their own responses: 1) should Yugoslavia be defended at all costs and by all means, including the use of armed force? 2) was it possible to defend it by force, and if the answer was affirmative, how it was to be done? 3) what was the probability of success and what was the price of the defence by force of a state which had been rejected and abandoned by all? 4) would the JNA have reliable internal allies in this endeavour, and who were they? 5) what would be the reaction of international factors to the use of force? and 6) what should the army do with the state if it succeeded in defending it?

To make the irony even greater, nobody asked the army leadership for instructions concerning the defence of the state. However, all the participants in the process of destroying/saving the country assigned a different role to it, according to their own needs (B. Jović: 161–163).

To use an operational idiom, the army leadership did not have a single element precisely defined for independent action by the army. It was not even able to decide against whom to use it. It still cherished the hope that the link between the nationalistic elites and the seduced masses was not strong and that the impending war danger would sober up the people and reduce military intervention to the removal of the holders of power.[53]

In early 1991 the time arrived for the army leadership to make concrete decisions. By a series of military–political initiatives, an impression was created among the public that they were determined to fulfil their (constitutional) role well and fully.[54]

The generals directed a major part of their activities toward the Presidency of the SFRY, the government and the Federal Parliament–they bombarded them with their estimates of the military–political and security situation, suggesting a number of steps and activities aimed at removing the danger.

If their estimates, based on the theory of 'special war', were fairly accurate, the generals did not draw accurate conclusions from them. First of all, they did not undertake the necessary military measures[55] concordant with their estimate that internal war was approaching. The degree of confusion within the army leadership can best be seen in the inefficient, incomplete and inconsistent realization of loudly announced actions. Half-measures became the hallmark of their activity. None of the (self-)prescribed and (self-)chosen tasks were formulated or realized efficiently or fully. This is demonstrated by the failure of the order of the Presidency of SFRY on the disarmament of paramilitary units.[56] This order introduced a series of orders and acts by the army leadership and the Presidency that were never to be realized. This is best shown by the fate of the television documentary[57] on the illegal import of weapons, and by the trial of Martin Špegelj, Croatian minister of defence (*VPI*, No. 4/91: 16–25).

However, the true image of the army generals emerged at the March 1991 session of the Presidency of the SFRY, when they proposed the introduction of a state of emergency (*B*, 14 March 1991: 16–17). By doing this they drew a line under their previous activity and made the only move left open to them—responsibility for the army's (in)action was dropped into the lap of the Supreme Command (the Presidency of the SFRY).[58] After the failure of the 'constitutional coup', the army leadership, in a letter to the Presidency, dissociated itself from the future course of the Yugoslav crisis and the multiplying of paramilitary units (see the *Communication of the Supreme Command of 19 March*, 1991: 7). This moment marks the beginning of the visible political disengagement of the army.

The fiasco surrounding the proposal to introduce a state of emergency was the last occasion for the Serbian top army leadership to re-examine their attitude towards Yugoslavia. In this interval, the decisive move for Yugoslavia and for the JNA was made—the generals desisted from defending the state at all costs and submitted themselves to the Serbian leadership (B. Jović: 349).

At the beginning of the war, the consequences of this decision became apparent: the feigned war in Slovenia was not the end of the anti-constitutional withdrawal of the JNA; the system of mobilization was abandoned, the troops were re-grouped in the territories populated by the Serbs in Croatia and Bosnia-Hercegovina, and so forth. The war in Croatia fully revealed the teaming up of the Serbian and the army leaderships, and turned the JNA into an instrument of the Serbian regime's policy.

The balance of trauma

The end of June 1991 marked the beginning of the final, armed, settling of various accounts in Yugoslavia—from the historical to the individual—according to the intentions of the actors. The Yugoslav war therefore had a very differentiated structure. The republics and nations, belonging to the same federal state, were warring among themselves. At the same time, the federal army, roaming destructively across the battlefields, was searching for a valid goal and justification. It waged war against some people on the account of others who did not officially enter the war, formally undeclared. All this was done on behalf of saving Yugoslavia and safeguarding peace until the achieving of a 'democratic solution' to its fate.

All those who believed[59] in the patriotic liberation mission of the leaders of the nations entered into mutual bloody conflicts. Nor did those who had nowhere to go and nothing to take along with them stay out of the war. The guns were used to convince them of the inevitability of the war (among nations) and to instil in them the desired fighting spirit–surviving demanded killing. As a logical consequence, former neighbours and relatives became mortal enemies. This was a war waged within the family, in courtyards, precincts and foyers. Thus it turned into a general war among the nations, as there are no relations which cannot be severed by bombs. As the contribution of the different actors in the preparation of the war was not equal, neither were the accounts. Common to all of them was the fact that in the war they all started to reap the harvest of their previous (in)action. They were caught up, literally and metaphorically, in the destructive consequences of their previous actions. The first preliminary estimates are known, but the final balance cannot even be guessed, let alone calculated and settled.

The price of the war will be paid by the people, while the leaders will go into history. The generals of the former JNA are also candidates for the history textbooks.[60] The following list of the traumatic effects of their arbitrary use of the JNA can also be added to the material for their biographies:

1) by guaranteeing the citizens a peaceful solution to the Yugoslav crisis and the prevention of internal war, they facilitated and favoured individual and group flirting with nationalism and war;

2) by their ideological, and finally egotistical, treatment of the Yugoslav crisis, they facilitated the instalment of authoritarian regimes and helped them to acquire national legitimacy;

3) by accepting the war alternative, they left the citizens of Yugoslavia without a homeland and herded them into one-nation states;

4) by using the army for the goals of the Serbian regime, they traumatized, physically and mentally, all the non-Serbian peoples of the second Yugoslavia;

5) by transforming the Yugoslav People's Army into a Serbian army, they abused the subordinate rank and file; and

6) by pretending to defend the Serbian people, the generals contributed to bringing it into the war and facilitated the abuse of traumas from its historical memory–through the war they provided a pseudo-catharsis for the Serbian people (the settling of historical accounts), only traumatizing it once again.

Notes

1 V. Kadijević (1993) and B. Jović (1995) partly shed light on the behind-the-scenes intrigues in Yugoslavia, but it is important to look at what 'the authors wanted to say' (and why).

2 Cf. *The Programme of the League of Communists of Yugoslavia*, the section 'The decisive struggle of Communists against anti-socialist manifestations and tendencies', in *The Seventh Congress of the SKJ*, 413.

3 The idea of all-round symmetry of the Yugoslav peoples was fully elaborated in the speech by J. Broz, delivered at the Fifth Congress of the Communist Party of Yugoslavia (cf. *The Fifth Congress of the KPJ*, 9–118).

4 In this way the inception of the concept and system of the General People's Defence and the Social Self-Protection was removed into the

remote party past: 'The social and historical embryos of the creation of the General People's Defence in Yugoslavia are linked with the period of ideological and organizational stabilization of the KPJ from the mid-1930s, namely, from the time when Josip Broz Tito came to its head' (B. Sikimić 1985: 81).

5 Cf. *The Constitutional Development of Yugoslavia, 1988; The Constitution of the Federal People's Republic of Yugoslavia (1946)*, Arts. 134 and 135; *The Constitution of the Socialist Federal Republic of Yugoslavia* (1963), Arts. 252–257; *The Constitutional Amendments XX–XLII* (1971), Amendment XLI, Arts. 2 and 3, and *The Constitution of the SFRY* (1974), The Basic Principles, Part VI, 466 and Arts. 237–243.

6 'The armed forces of the SFRY protect the independence, sovereignty, territorial integrity and social order established by this Constitution' (*The Constitution of the SFRY,* Art. 240, para.1)

7 The army had its own housing fund, a closed system of vacation facilities, a chain of army stores with subsidized prices was in the making, etc.

8 On the essential reasons for the subordination of the army to the party in socialism see K. Rajs, 1991: 172–191, particularly 180–183.

9 The arms and equipment industry comprised, in 1990, a total of 53 enterprises with 80,000 employees and 1,000 outside suppliers (*B*, 5 March 1990: 8)

10 'The committees of the ONO and DSZ represent, in the system of leadership, the bodies for co-ordination and operational tactics ... For their work of implementing the attitudes and the policy of the SKJ in the ONO and DSZ, these committees are responsible to the organs which appoint them and to the SKJ' (*The Strategy of the Armed Struggle*, 1983: 59).

11 'The leading ideological and political role [of the organization of the SKJ] in the armed forces is based on the role of the SKJ in our society and its special responsibility for the defence and protection of the socialist self-managing Yugoslavia, established by the Constitution of the SFRY' (ibid.: 140)

12 'The League of Communists carries out its leading role in the ONO and DSZ by acting within the political system of socialist self-management ... The League of Communists has a special role and responsibility for the organization and work of the committees for General People's Defence and Social Self-Protection' (ibid.: 49).

13 'The combat morale is primarily based on the socialist self-managing consciousness, on freedom-loving and revolutionary traditions, on the belief of our working people and citizens in the justice of the aims for which they struggle' (ibid.: 67).

14 'The basis of the unity of the management and commandment is the unity of the military and political goals, the ideological and political unity of the commanders, staffs, military units and commanding officers' (ibid.: 126).

15 'The moral and political conditions are inter-related with other elements of combat readiness, in which they have a primary role' (*Instructions for the MPC in the TO*, 1985: 8).

16 Thus, for instance, the members of the Territorial Defence were appraised according to 'the level of socialist self-managing consciousness',
'acceptance and adoption... of the aims and paths of developments', as
well as 'the level of belief in the success and in the perspective of our
socialist self-managing society' *(Instructions for MPC in the TO,* 7-8).

17 In 1988, within the JNA, the SKJ had 2,543 basic organizations with
75,924 members, 54% of whom were persons on active military duty,
and 33% civilians employed by the JNA *(Documents for the Ninth Conference of the OSKJ in the JNA,* 125-126).

18 'Persons in the service of the armed forces are obliged to work actively
on the implementation of the policy of the League of Communists of
Yugoslavia in their military units or institutions, in social-political and
other organizations, as well as in the community in which they live'
(The Rules of Service in the Armed Force, Art. 13)

19 A good example of this are the chapter titles in the *Report of the Ninth
Conference*: 'Ideological problems in the modernization of the JNA',
'Current ideological problems in training and education', 'The forging
of moral strength and political unity in the army', 'Ideological questions
in personnel policy', 'Security and self-protection', etc. (ibid.: 8-24).

20 The military party 'must continue to be a decisive factor in the
strengthening of the consciousness and the moral-political unity of the
JNA, of guarding and intensifying the revolutionary, the class, and the
character of the JNA as the army of all the peoples and as the Yugoslav
army' *(The programme for the ideological-political tasks of the OSKJ in
the JNA,* 69).

21 *The Programme of the IPE of Officers and NCOs and of Civilians in the
Service of the OS of the SFRY,* 2; the aim of the Programme was not
changed for the following year (1989).

22 'His [Tito's] strategic thought and practice are beyond the narrow and
traditional framework of military activity and include all areas of social
activities, each of them having its own strategy and tactics. Above all of
them is a general revolutionary strategy, namely the strategy of the
General Peoples' Defence' (N. Ljubičić 1977: 39).

23 For instance, the panels bearing photographs of J. Broz's burial remained in all military facilities for ten years, and every anniversary was
marked by a collective oath of the members of the JNA not to depart
'from his path'.

24 '(1) The political system of socialist self-management; (2) independent
and non-aligned foreign policy; and (3) the importance of the geo-
strategic position of Yugoslavia' are 'the reasons why the SFRY is a frequent and a prime object of attack by the superpowers and their allies
using the method of "special warfare"' *(Special Warfare against the
SFRY,* 1981: 44).

25 'Engaged in special warfare are ... the remnants of the class enemy,
nationalistic, irredentist, unitarist, bureaucratic-statist, liberal, clerical
and other counter-revolutionary and reactionary forces *(The Strategy of
the Armed Combat,* 31).

26 'Yugoslavia is threatened by the activities of the forces of special war-fare. Aggressive and other reactionary forces from abroad, connected with the internal enemy, are trying to disturb the internal stability of the socialist self-managing system, to compromise its international re-nown and its non-aligned foreign policy and to weaken the defensive-protective readiness of Yugoslavia' (ibid.: 30).

27 The whole system of ideological and political education and teaching in the OS was also directed at the development of the resistance of members of the OS to noxious ideological influence and psychological propaganda actions (*The Special War against the SFRY,* 117).

28 The entire regulation of the status and rights of the military security service organs by laws and rules was a military secret for a great major-ity of officers and NCOs.

29 'The state of crisis in the society did not affect in any considerable way the defensive potentials of the country ... The system of General Peo-ples' Defence and Social Self-Protection , and particularly the armed force, control defence mechanisms which protect them from the ef-fects of the crisis' (S. Mirković 1988: 59).

30 We place it in the period between the First Conference of the SKJ (29–30 May 1988) and the Order of the Presidency of the SFRY on the Dis-armament of Paramilitary Formations (9 January 1991); due to the lack of space the context of the crisis will be taken as understood and the key positions of the national–republican leaders will not be de-scribed.

31 A high correlation between national/republican origin and the political views of military and civilian personnel in the JNA was established by the 'Survey of the opinions of members of the SKJ on social reform and the transformation of the SKJ' (P. Šipka and M. Hadžić 1989: 72).

32 'The Communists in the army do not accept the splitting of the SKJ into several parties, namely, the transformation of the SKJ into a social-democratic party and the changing of its name' (P. Simic, *B.* 15 February 1990: 1 and 5).

33 For this purpose, the military party drew up and published 'The Basic Ideas for the Continuation of the Fourteenth Extraordinary Congress of the SKJ', 11–13.

34 'All democratic institutions of society must be based on law. In the present circumstances in Yugoslavia, and with the Yugoslav historical experience, returning to party pluralism would be a long step back-wards' (V. Kadijević 1989: 15).

35 'Therefore, in considering this deep permeation of society and its de-fence, I cannot visualize the way our OS would look and perform their social function, should they be, as some want it, depoliticized, meaning cut off from society's basic problems' (B. Adžić *VPI,* No. 1/90, 10)

36 By the order of the federal secretary for defence, issued on 8 October 1990, every form of political organization in the army was forbidden.

37 See the introductory speech of Admiral Šimić at the Conference of the OSKJ in the JNA, *VPI,* No.8/88: 7–14.

38 See the list of the basic requests and of the army's counter-arguments in M. Daljević, 1987: 20–26)

39 'We are witnessing the revival and the extremely aggressive onslaught of anti-Yugoslav and anti-socialist forces. These are the same forces which once before caused the collapse of Yugoslavia. In the National Liberation War (NOB) they collaborated with the occupying powers and were politically and militarily defeated. They are in for another defeat' (V. Kadijević 1990: 7).

40 For instance, General Kadijević was internally treating the president of the SIV, Ante Marković, as an American spy and a concealed Croatian separatist (cf. B. Jović: 176)

41 I trace the rise of the Serbian–army alliance in 1995: 281–301.

42 The excerpts of the diary of B. Jović are full of proofs of this co-ordination (B. Jović 1995).

43 'If acts of the agencies of the Federation or acts of the agencies of another republic, in contravention of the rights and duties it has under the Constitution of the Socialist Federal Republic of Yugoslavia, violate the equality of the Republic of Serbia or in any other way threaten its interests, without providing compensation, the republic agencies shall issue acts to protect the interests of the Republic of Serbia.' (*The Constitution of the Republic of Serbia*, Art. 135, para. 2).

44 The army newspaper *Narodna Armija* (The People's Army) was a very important channel for the presentation of the standpoint of the army leadership. It was permanently engaged in the disqualification of leaders of new parties and movements; on the eve of the elections in Croatia it stated that 'Tudjman, his gang and those like them ... should be immediately and resolutely stopped in their destructive and fascistic onslaught, in the very name of real democracy and of the future of this country' (*B*, 1 March 1990: 7); Vuk Drašković (*NA*, 15 March 1990: 5), Jože Pučnik and DEMOS (*B*, 29 March 1990: 9), as well as Vojislav Šešelj (*NA*, 27 September 1990: 6) were treated in a similar way.

45 Admiral Stane Brovet spoke along these lines to those attending the Centre of High Military Schools in January 1991.

46 A gathering of scientific experts was held in May 1990 in Belgrade; part of the proceedings were published in the army magazine *Vojno delo*, No.3-4/90, and the complete text was published in a special edition (for restricted circulation).

47 'Our army cannot be separated from the achievements of the revolution, it cannot depart from socialism. It must fight for a new, more humane type of socialism, but it must remain in line with socialism. Some other army after us could fight against socialism, but this one cannot do that... This army cannot exist without being a Yugoslav army. But how can one be above this and remain neutral when there are new governments in parts of Yugoslavia which are against Yugoslavia and which have national armies?' (Retired General D. Dozet, *VD*, special edition: 317).

48 'Without the presence of the army and its objective political power and clearly defined political standpoint on all basic questions of the future

of Yugoslavia, the pro-Yugoslav forces would remain without one of their powerful supports' (S. Brovet, *VD*: 322).

49 The TO grew to one and a half million members and the defence plans were elaborated by 125,000 social organizations and institutions (*VD*: 25 and 361).

50 Instead of five army districts (the First and Second in Serbia, the Third in Macedonia, the Fifth in Croatia, the Seventh in Bosnia-Herzegovina, the Ninth in Slovenia and an independent corps in Montenegro), three military districts were formed (the first one encompassed the majority of Serbia and parts of Bosnia-Herzegovina and Croatia, the third one encompassed southern Serbia, Montenegro and Macedonia, and the fifth one Slovenia and the majority of Croatia).

51 V. Kadijević, 1989: 9; these viewpoints were later supported by the then official theoretician of the concept of the ONO, General (now retired) Radovan Radinović, who only recently revealed that 'it was clear to everyone that the Territorial Defence was developing fully as a parallel military system to the Yugoslav People's Army and that it was only a matter of days before it would be transformed into its rival and adversary' (1994: 287). Neither of the two generals inform us of the real reasons for the lateness of their fundamental discoveries.

52 'It is the duty of all participants of the ONO and DSZ to make plans for extraordinary circumstances, in addition to regular defence plans... In elaborating plans for extraordinary circumstances special importance and weight has to be given to the appraisal of the political and security situation, an appraisal which must be complex and objective, in order to give as realistic an idea as possible of the real situation and possible developments in the case of escalation of the activities of the enemy forces' (The *Strategy of the ONO and DSZ*: 152).

53 Admiral Brovet stated in the Federal Parliament that 'the JNA, if the situation and the development of events got out of hand, would not enter into conflict with the people, but with those who prepare, organize and provoke conflicts and lead the peoples of Yugoslavia into bloodshed and war' (*NA*, 16 May 1991: 13).

54 An interesting analysis of the then controversies between the army position and its proclaimed goals was carried out by Z. Đinđić (1991: 2)

55 The result was that the army remained in the barracks which were easily blockaded at the onset of the war.

56 Regardless of this, the army leadership continued to claim that 'The Order ... is in force and we will execute it; it is our duty to do so, since no one has yet withdrawn it ' (S. Brovet, *NA*, 21 February 1991: 5).

57 The documentary was shown on 25 January 1991, only on parts of the Yugoslav national TV network; for a wider context and data regarding the SSNO on the import of arms, see 'A Supplement to the Information on Illegal Organization of Armed Military Units in the SFRY' (*VPI* , No. 3/91: 19–24).

58 An analysis of the performance and of the proposed measures is beyond the scope of this paper, but one should note that the army leader-

ship withdrew its demands on failing to obtain the approval of the Presidency, which was something to be expected in advance.

59 'It is the people on whom history is performed, although its creators prefer to say that the people is the cause of the performance' (B. Pekić 1992: 110).

60 Veljko Kadijević filled in his application form with 'my own viewpoints on the collapse', when he stated that the aim of the JNA (and also his own) was the creation of three Serbian armies (1993: 128 and 163).

MEDIA WAR

Politika in the Storm of Nationalism

ALEKSANDAR NENADOVIĆ

In this article we shall deal primarily with the daily newspaper *Politika*, while other publications of this publishing house will be touched upon only in passing. Needless to say, it is not because these other publications do not merit this kind of investigation. Far from it. Some of them are almost impossible to pass over, particularly the weekly *NIN* and the daily *Politika Ekspres*. However, the role of *Politika* as the flagship newspaper of this publishing house and as a political daily was, and still is, predominant. Launched at the dawn of the twentieth century, this newspaper remains to the present day, and in its own genre, the paper with the strongest influence on public opinion, exerting, at the same time, a strong influence on Serbian political evolution in this century.

Until the unstoppable mass breakthrough of electronic media, which, in the conditions prevailing in Serbia, meant that Radio-Television Serbia (*RTS*) grew to be the most powerful, practically monopolistic information network controlled by the governing party and ideology, *Politika* also served as a vital public forum for all those who, in a manner of speaking, cared for social legitimacy. Anyone who did not appear in *Politika*, that is, on the pages of the political daily which was believed, with good reason, to be read by the most intelligent and the most influential readership, could hardly count on serious support, particularly political support, among the pubic. It was for this reason that the most powerful political and state authorities, including the autocratic ('socialistic' or nationalistic) authorities to which, by definition, democratic procedures are alien, needed this forum to test and confirm their supremacy and to keep abreast of the times.

Here one has to keep in mind that the importance of *Politika* was due not only to its steadily high circulation on the local press market, nor to its convincingly high level of professionalism compared with the existing Belgrade and Serbian journals. Its most important feature was its very high level of credibility; it was a medium through which an important influence was exerted, if not on the nation as a whole, then certainly on its more educated political and cultural elite. It is for this reason that the battles for influence over the daily *Politika*, for the use and abuse of its media penetration, were always important, sometimes even crucial, in the recent political history of Serbia, and partly in all three Yugoslavias.

The first journalistic staff of *Politika* differed in many respects from their counterparts at its Belgrade rivals, which were numerous, but professionally poor and economically weak. The difference was especially visible in the composition of *Politika's* first homogeneous editorial and journalistic team. The members of this team were, for a time, its founder Vladislav Ribnikar, an intellectual educated in Europe and an established writer (Ribnikar was Slovenian, and had a Czech father); Stanoje Stanojević, a Serb; and Tješimir Starčević, of Croatian origin. With such a cosmopolitan (Yugoslav) staff, *Politika* entered Serbia in the early twentieth century with the ambition to offer to the Serbian (in the beginning mostly to the Belgrade) readership something more than the usual fare it had been offered until then. The aim of the new daily, as expressed in one of the first statements by its small but ambitious editorial staff, was 'to widen the horizon of general views'. Soon after its launch, a commendable tradition was initiated in the new daily—to engage as permanent or part-time contributors leading literary and scientific authors.

That was the way it was in the first days of *Politika*. The very fact that it survived for such a long time in this, to put it mildly, fragile part of the European south-east, makes it easier to understand its heritage, which has, to a great extent, something of the nature of a cult. Its presses were stopped only three times, either by the force of circumstances or at the decision of its owners and editors: twice because of the foreign occupation of Belgrade and Serbia during World Wars I and II, and once because of a strike by its journalists and workers, organized by its management, on 31 July and 1 August 1992.

The changes which followed World War II altered essentially the politically liberal character of the pre-war *Politika*—although formally it continued to act as a private share company until nationalization on 29 April 1949. In the party state, *Politika's* founding declaration to be a non-party and impartial newspaper became 'a traditionalistic formality'. As the marginal attempts of the opposition were stifled, all media, including *Politika*, came under the regime's direction. It should to be pointed out, however, that this monolithic environment was not accepted willingly, even in the face of the most severe threats and pressures exerted over more than four decades of one-party autocracy.

As a matter of fact, one could say that right up to the mid-1980s, or, to be more precise, up to the introduction of the practically unlimited predominance of aggressive nationalism, there was no shortage of editors and journalists who were inclined to 'disobedience'. By making use of every loosening of ideological and bureaucratic restraint after the break with Moscow in 1948, as well as of liberal tendencies in the ranks of the groups in power, the more audacious editors and the more skilful reporters contrived, in every feasible way, to give more space to truthful information from within the country and from abroad, even if it meant 'writing between the lines'.

Pressure and resistance

In the 1980s, at the beginning of the end of the Yugoslav community, the journalistic staff of the most powerful daily in the capital found itself between a rock and a hard place. On the one hand, it was bound by its pledge to defend the, in theory, indisputable principle of objective information, a principle much lauded by the political and editorial elite as well, who on solemn occasions liked to recall the glorious tradition of the newspaper, although in practice they had less and less use for it. On the other hand, *Politika's* professionalism was, at the same time, strongly challenged not only by the officially discarded, but still tenacious, Stalinist dogmatism, but also by aggressive national-chauvinism, not only in Serbia, which was gaining more room for manoeuvre.

Attempts to save *Politika's* professional identity clashed, chronologically and politically, with the crucial turn in the political fate of Serbia and Yugoslavia. At the Eighth Session of the Central Committee of the League of Communists of Serbia (23–25 September 1987), which was politically decisive for the future of the whole of former Yugoslavia, this turn was endorsed irrevocably: by a formal political (a party forum) legitimization of Greater Serbian nationalism as the dominant ideological option, on the one hand, and of Slobodan Milošević, as an almost untouchable, charismatic and cult figure at the pinnacle of the governing political oligarchy on the other.

This course of events inevitably led to a reduction in the already narrow space for the professional autonomy of journalists. The struggle for power in the political arena, which in Serbia reached its most intense stage in the mid-1980s, favoured the awakening of the 'national consciousness' among journalists as well. This was the case, more or less, in every strata of society. It seemed that it was happening more rapidly and to a more considerable degree among the editors of *Politika*. In the most influential Belgrade daily, the polarization was also deepened by scandals, such as the one which would be remembered as the 'Vojko and Savle' affair—so named after a pseudo-satire by the same title—and which, in effect, was a joint federal, republican, political and police onslaught on the personality of the free-thinking and indomitable member of the Serbian Academy of Arts and Science, Gojko Nikoliš, in order to intimidate the ever louder critics of a decaying but overbearing one-party system.

In the unpleasant confrontations, which lasted for several months in 1987, the obvious involvement in the scandal of the editorial core, particularly of the editor-in-chief of the newspaper was at the centre of attention.[1]

The newspaper, in which the torch of professional dignity that had been defended for decades still flickered, found itself in the midst of a dispute into which it had been drawn by the party-state ruling oligarchy who were ready to resort to any means available. However, as time passed, while participants and accomplices were becoming more and more enmeshed in the controversy, it was obvious that the majority of innocent journalists were looking for an answer to one crucial question: who was actually deciding what could or could not be published in *Politika*?

The fact that nobody, not even the editor-in-chief, could offer a convincing answer to the question of who had commissioned and written the pamphlet 'Vojko and Savle' or how it had found its way into *Politika*, led the editorial staff to the logical and inevitable conclusion: powerful outside forces were beginning to edit *Politika* directly, with no heed for the elementary norms of the profession.[2]

Trying to gain an edge over the unprecedentedly alienated editor-in-chief and his top associates, the most resistant professionals could, for a while, count on the support—the passive support, at least—of the majority, even in the organization of the League of Communists within *Politika*. However, the commission formed by this organization on 4 June 1987, concluded that, following an investigation which lasted twenty days, it was not possible to ascertain precisely who had written the text 'Vojko and Savle' and how, or on whose orders, it had reached *Politika*. It was, nevertheless, given approval for its crowning political conclusion that neither the editor-in-chief nor his close associates had 'respected elementary editorial obligations', which, 'in the case of the editor-in-chief meant that he allowed his newspaper to be edited from outside'. ('Report on the case of Vojko and Savle', *NIN*, 29 September 1987).

A disastrous 'editorial feat'

Departure from objective information as a primary obligation, that is, the trampling on *Politika*'s professional autonomy on behalf of the dictate of the 'people's' will, accelerated with the introduction of the column 'Echoes and Reactions'. At first, this editorial 'construction' may have looked relatively harmless to the uninitiated, something like the immoderate and distasteful national overflowing of the editorial team's latest concerns into the space reserved for readers' letters. It soon became obvious that this antijournalistic diversion had grown into a particular political revival of Stalinist methods, which left a permanent stain on the face of *Politika*, and on that of Serbia as well.

The pseudo-patriotic and chauvinistic pamphleteering offensive, not only against political opponents and those within Serbia with different opinions, but also against whole nations outside Serbia, lasted almost three full years (from July 1988 to March 1991). *Politika*'s innocent, traditionally strictly neutral column 'Medju nama' ('Among Us') was gradually mutilated and pushed into a corner. With the new column 'Echoes and Reactions', which was given a much larger space, the name of *Politika* and its reputation would be overtaken more and more aggressively by the sowers of a spontaneous and commissioned wrath on behalf of the defence of Serbia and the Serbs, warriors for the inviolable project of Yugoslav and Serbian development mapped out at the 'historical' Eighth Session.

The non-nationalistic opposition, tragically fettered and practically marginalized as it was, and the dwindling number of resistant but helpless journalistic professionals, received this 'catastrophically successful' innovation on the pages of *Politika* as a humiliation. At the same time, the authorities did not conceal their delight. On the occasion of the eighty-fifth anniversary of the launch of *Politika*, Radmila Anđelković, speaking on behalf of the highest political leadership of Serbia, praised the column 'Echoes and Reactions' as 'the editorial feat' of the director and editor-in-chief Živorad Minović.

Without removing the inherited logo, in their nationalistic fervour the editorial team of *Politika*, led by Živorad Minović, announced its 'editorial feat' by adding the word *reactions* under the logo, in larger letters. It was under this header that the letter by Vjera Baletić was published, with the banner headline 'A jet of clean water washes away untruth' printed across the whole page. It was a pointed personal and political attack on Koča Popović, prompted by the review of his book *Notes from the War* written by Sveta Lukić. The other text on the same page was not of a political character.

On the following day, 9 July, the same formula and the same format appeared, but there were three contributions. The place of honour was given to a militant defence of Slobodan Milošević's political views, that is, of his criticism of the autonomy of Kosovo and Vojvodina in the form of the famous answers to forty-nine questions put to him by the weekly *NIN*.

After a two-day pause, the next appearance of the extended column 'Among Us', as a precursor to the massive 'Echoes and Reactions' (12 July), raised the temperature by publishing only one, distinctly militant political letter across the whole page of the newspaper. The author was Blažo Perović, Ph.D., and the title ('Separatism will not pass') was suited to the attempt to dramatize an increasingly aggressive attack by Serbia's leadership on the autonomy of Kosovo and Vojvodina.

In the 13 July issue, the dramatization of the issue continued, in the form of seven fiery reactions to, as stated moderately under the additional heading ('reactions'), 'the stay of Serbs and Montenegrins from Kosovo in Vojvodina'.[3] The first contribution was a letter written by professor Gordana Dovijanić, who, hurling severe accusations at Vojvodina's leader Boško Krunić, among other things stated with delight: 'On Saturday, it could be seen in the streets, on the squares, in windows, in front of the Parliament, that the people understand the people, but that you do not understand them. The people of Novi Sad said what you wanted to leave unsaid; they spoke the truth together with the people from Kosovo, and demanded one Serbia, one Constitution, one Court.'

The title used by the editors—'The people understood the people'—was completely in harmony with the intimation of an inevitable future. The message of the editors left no room for ambiguity: a new force was being born to which *Politika* submitted itself without reserve, shutting off its professional senses even in the face of the tautological absurdity of the bombastic title.

A programmed dramatization

Two days later, the space reserved for letters to the editor under the old heading 'Among Us', was reduced to three columns, and the contents of the only political contribution appeared as a mysterious brake on the debate. The letter was sent from Slovenia, its author was a Slovenian (Matjaž Anžujev), and its political pro-Yugoslavia attitude was conciliatory and rational. By virtue of his 'peasant common sense', he expressed, among other things, the Slovenian disposition towards the Serbs in the following way: 'Five per cent are the enemies of Serbia, five per cent are true friends of Serbia and the rest are a crowd which can be easily manipulated ... In Slovenia the bourgeois right does exist, but no more than in Belgrade. And what is the fate of the Yugoslav worker today, to which nobody pays any heed? He is poorly paid , he lives in misery, and in exchange he is offered an enemy which for a Slovenian is a Serbian worker and vice versa' (*P*, 15 July 1988).

The pause was short and deceptive. Only two days later, after the meeting of the Central Committee of the League of Communists of Serbia, the old column 'Among Us' was returned with the new heading 'Reactions', like a torch flame hovering over everything. For the first time, a contribution covered more than one whole page. It came from the pen of writer Radoslav Zlatanović, who, pointing to Boško Krunić as a protector of Vojvodina's autonomists, warned threateningly: 'If no radical constitutional changes occur ... expect us Serbs and Montenegrins in Novi Sad again, where we shall seek a place for our homes and land, or at least some temporary shelter, as has happened to the Serbs many times before when they have had to flee their enemies ...' (*P*, 17 July 1988).

This not particularly subtle message from Kosovo, made plain the crucial role of *Politika* in the campaign of public branding, which began to spread like an epidemic. On the following day (18 July), the newspaper set aside five pages for 'reactions after the delayed publication of the discussion held at the closed session of the Provincial Committee of the League of Communists of Vojvodina', with the reports from all parts of Serbia and titles in the style of party agitation and propaganda ('Every honest citizen is embittered', 'Ascertain the responsibility of Stojišić, Matić and Krunić', 'The leaders of Vojvodina divide the working class').

In tune with this obviously carefully prepared programmed dramatization of the 'people's will', the column intended for letters to the editor took wings, as it were: with two very long and two somewhat shorter protest contributions, it spread over two whole pages of the newspaper. The tone of the contributions in the 'Reactions' column was suited to the development of tumultuous events, that is, to the political and propaganda needs of the Belgrade Serbian leadership. For example, the already politically defeated leaders of Vojvodina were apparently sent a directive via a letter to the editor written by Miladin Grabovac: 'A leadership without the support of the people should resign' (*P*, 21 July 1988).

The organizers of the 'socialist tidal wave' (as the mass requests for constitutional changes were defined by professor Dragomir Drašković, later one of the leaders of the League of Communists-Movement for Yugoslavia), unselfishly obliged the thus incited people. They were led by Slobodan Milošević, chairman of the Central Committee, who, in a headline across three columns on the front page of *Politika*, sent a message which read loud and clear: 'All citizens of Serbia can rest assured that we shall not desist from changes'. However, even this promise, as the act of a leader, was not free of the mimicry in which passion gets the upper hand over reason. Counting on the influence of *Politika*, the Serbian leader seemed to try, by an icy expression of indomitable self-confidence, to create the mythical impression that it was the people itself who spoke through him and that faced with this historical turning point for Serbia, no leadership, either in the provinces or in Yugoslavia, was of any importance.

Through *Politika*, which put itself unreservedly at his disposal, Slobodan Milošević expressed this mythological pretension of Serbian populism: 'Some say that one or other popular meeting is supported by certain leaders. The people does not need support, nor is the leadership authorized to give support to the people. Only the people, the citizens, the public, can give or withhold support for the leadership' (*P*, 23 July 1988).

Joining the executioners

This direction was adhered to loyally by all political-informative publications produced by the publishers *Politika*, particularly by the editors of 'Reactions' who surpassed even the official propaganda machinery; their selection of texts was becoming more and more zealous and was given absolute priority in the daily. *Politika's* professionalism was pushed to the sidelines, or even written off as anti-Serbian behaviour.[4]

An important date for the column by means of which 'the people' edited *Politika* and put Serbia in order was 5 August 1988. It was on that day that it was given its full name for the first time. Inconspicuous letters in the traditional 'Among Us' column were moved under a barely visible heading, below which a new, higher level of national revival was announced in bold letters: *'Echoes and Reactions'* (given the name 'screams and howls' by the decimated ranks of the intellectual opposition). On the following day (6

August 1988), the editors strengthened the editorial power of the intangible 'people' by introducing another column of the same genre, also across the whole page, under the heading 'On the Trail of the Letters to *Politika*'. Conceived as some sort of occasional help to the 'Echoes and Reactions' column on special occasions, the new column on that day was devoted fully to the 'liberation' of Vojvodina. The method used put the whole force of *Politika*'s influence behind the request, in the form of an ultimatum to the Municipal Committee of the League of Communists of Serbia in Sombor, to withhold support from 'a section of the provincial leadership'. Another two examples from Vojvodina are also characteristic of the direct involvement of *Politika* in the execution of the affairs of the state-party machinery. The first one is found in the 24 August 1988 issue, when a venomous condemnation of a certain Vojvodina leader who dared ask the question 'Who pays for the solidarity meetings', was published, with the headline set across four columns. The other example is even more striking, since it reveals the contribution of technology to the production of massive support for the 'solidarity meetings'. On 8 August 1988, the editors of 'Echoes and Reactions' published at the top of the page, framed and in bold type, a letter from one hundred and fifty disabled veterans from Novi Sad, who wholeheartedly supported trade union members in the 'Jugoalat' company in their intention to attend the solidarity meeting in Titov Vrbas. A really touching helping hand!

It was, in fact, becoming clearer every day that the 'national revival' as preached by *Politika* recognized no limits or arguments where the creation of 'a united and strong Serbia' was at stake. It was important to show that it encompassed all strata, even the disabled veterans. As for the newspaper itself, its endeavours included the campaign which had to permeate all informative columns of the newspaper—from the home affairs column to the foreign affairs and cultural columns, not leaving out even the sports reports.[5]

Editorial interventions (titles, subtitles, headings, etc.) in contributions to the 'Echoes and Reactions' column, through which the 'people' expressed their feelings in the most direct way, speak for themselves. They include the following examples:

'The indifference of Josip Vrhovac'; 'The masks were taken off and the real face emerged'; 'The people know best what is good for them' (8 August 1988);

'He who is afraid of his own people has no right to represent them' (from the letter by Jovan Striković, M.D., Ph.D., set across five columns of *Politika*);

'Serbia must become a state now, without delay or compromise'; 'Why Kolj Široka did not say who the traitors were' (14 August 1988);

'The Plenum of the Central Committee of the League of Communists unmasked those leaders who are deaf to the demands of the people' and who 'do not hear the cries of mothers whose children were raped in Kosovo' (15 August 1988);

'It is high time for those who prevent the settlement of the situation in Kosovo, the constitutional reform and the statehood of Serbia, to leave' (22 August 1988);

'It is a great mistake that the security forces in Kosovo have been decimated' (30 August 1988);

'The people warn strongly'; 'It is not autonomy that is lost, but the positions of power'; 'The Constitution should correspond to the wishes of the people'; 'Serbia lies on both banks of the Danube' (4 September 1988, on the occasion of the 'solidarity meetings' in Šumadija and Vojvodina);

'Constitutional changes only on the basis of the people's wishes'; 'Immediately—we accept no other deadline'; 'The leadership of Serbia has become one with the people'; 'We demand from the Central Committee of the League of Communists of Yugoslavia that it differentiate among its ranks at its Seventeenth Session (5 September 1988, in the titles of reports on the meeting in Crvenka);

'Constitutional power in Serbia was taken spontaneously by the people itself' (a contribution by Professor Ratko Marković, Ph.D., to the discussion on constitutional reforms); 'The pressure of the people cannot be undemocratic' (9 August 1988);

'To fellow journalists who are on the wrong side' (the title of an article by Miloš Ćorović, across the whole page of 'Echoes and Reactions', wholly devoted to a sharp condemnation of disobedient journalists (16 July 1988);

'They have used their right to speak, now it is time for them to answer' (title of an article by Zoran Čičak, later an official of the League of Communists-Movement for Yugoslavia, against those with different opinions, published in 'Echoes and Reactions', 17 July 1988);

'The aspirin is of no help any more; what Serbia needs is a surgical operation. It is vital to have a political, moral and ethical revolution' (Radoš Smiljković, Ph.D., at the meeting in Bački Ratkovac); 'There is no bargaining over the fact that there is a counter-revolution in Kosovo' (18 July 1988);

'The Seventeenth Session of the Central Committee of the League of Communists of Yugoslavia must dissociate itself from leaders criticized by the majority of the people' (27 September 1988);

'The people said what they had to say; the next move is up to the Central Committee of the League of Communists of Yugoslavia' (29 September 1988);

'A word from the children' (the title of the telegram sent from Smederevska Palanka, printed in bold type and framed, the contents of which go beyond the most blatant propaganda imaginable, in attributing to innocent children this 'opinion' on the undesirable consequences of the crisis in Kosovo: 'Peoples of Yugoslavia, your children send you this message: everyone who belittles or fails to understand the magnitude of this problem is not only the enemy of Yugoslavia, but an overt enemy of its children and their future' 10 October 1988);

'The new constitution will be written by the people'; 'To be indifferent means to be an accomplice' (30 October 1988).

Immersed in this obsessive propaganda, the newspaper, in its basic, informative function, resembled its former self less and less. Only here and there, although more and more rarely, a flicker of professional spirit would occasionally appear—as was the case with a cartoon created by Ivo Kušanić: a political gathering is opened by its chairman with the following words: 'Allow me to open the discussion on constitutional changes in the Province. To start with, let me first read the conclusions...!' For a while, the occasional mild commentary would pass through, directed at undesired allies in 'the happening of the people', such as the Chetniks and former party members arrested during the Cominform clash in 1948. But the wave of 'people's wrath', launched and precisely directed from the top, to which *Politika* was also subordinate as a key 'transmitter', left no room for any kind of serious corrections on behalf of professional autonomy. During that time, the 'Echoes and Reactions' column was growing and asserting itself in the role of internal censor of the whole editorial staff; it imposed itself by destroying, with no consequences, all norms in *Politika* and in the journalistic profession, as a privileged instigator of nationalistic exclusiveness.

In that nationalistic fire, which it had been stoking day in day out on behalf of the people, *Politika*, like the power it served unflinchingly, eventually began to forge a 'people' suited to its mission, that is, readers who learnt from it how to think and how to speak in order to become model Serbian patriots. In this vein, a letter published on 17 July 1988, in the 'Echoes and Reactions' column was particularly eye-catching. With the angry message 'I am not going to read this any more' included in the heading by the editor, a certain Boško Jović from Kuršumlija gave vent to his Serbian ire in these words: Serbia was enslaved for five hundred years, we could have endured slavery for as many years, but we cannot be servants for a single day. As a veteran reader of *Politika*, I ask the editors to stop publishing articles from Slovenian and Croatian newspapers. I am not going to read this any more. We in Serbia have more urgent and important business to attend to.

The fact that Slovenians and Croats were still citizens of the common homeland at the time such views on persons and peoples living outside Serbia were being promoted, seemed not to have bothered the editors of *Politika*. The important thing was to have 'the voice of the people' heard as far as possible. They therefore started to write the noun 'people' with a capital 'P'. The reader Vitomir Pušonjić, in a letter that was given the heading

'I have a candidate' (on the occasion of the election of the new president of the Federal Executive Council), self-confidently offered a political recipe (which *Politika* printed smugly)in which a myth seemed to turn into the only reality:

> If a candidate is judged by what he does from the moment of his election, then my candidate for all functions, not only those in the Federal Executive Council, would be the PEOPLE, as it has demonstrated, in a very short time, to be the most mature, the most honest, the most courageous, the most dignified, the most incorruptible... By representing itself, the People has proved that government business could be carried out in the People's idiom which is known to all, and that there is no need to make vast studies on subjective weaknesses and objective difficulties, when there are simple and precise words, such as 'thief', 'liar', and 'shirker', while the word *'foteljaš'* [from *fotelja* (armchair), used of a person who comfortably sits in the armchair of power and does not want to leave it] significantly abbreviates our political vocabulary ... (*P*, 18 July 1989)

In this signal to the intrepid fighters in the 'anti-bureaucratic revolution' there is something authentically plebeian, but also undoubtedly violent, impelling, totalitarian. Pseudo-libertarianism which annihilates the right to differences and different opinion can be even worse than cruel bureaucratic force. This is also the way in which 'liberated' journalism, in the service of the populist autocracy, can be reduced to the destruction of the profession without whose freedom there is no democratic political culture.

Thus spoke the leader of Politika

The discontent which was also, undoubtedly, authentic, was accompanied by unrestricted manipulation, including manipulation by means which were obviously unscrupulous, chauvinistic and warmongering. However, in spite of being blatantly at odds with ethical and other professional obligations, the 'Echoes and Reactions' column was aggressively promoted as a model of *Politika*'s 'liberated' Serbian journalism.

Seen from that angle, the course of development of the leader of the most powerful newspaper publishing house deserves the attention of everyone who is interested in understanding the role and responsibility of the editorial team of the daily *Politika* during the difficult trials of Serbian society in the second half of the 1980s and in the early 1990s, even more so as Živorad Minović acted, more than any other editor-in-chief, as a holder of political titles and authorities, first locally (in Belgrade), and later, as the iron propagandist fist of the republic's top leadership. For the purposes of this article, we shall single out several indicative, seemingly contradictory traces of this unusual, to put it mildly, advance.

The first incident is from early 1985. At that time, Minović was still behaving as a fearless defender of socialism, of brotherhood and unity, of self-management, of the party and of Tito. As the chairman of the Information Commission of the Belgrade Committee of the League of Communists of Serbia, he demanded keen 'differentiation' among the Belgrade journalists, saying, inter alia: 'No one can deny remarkable progress in the editorial policy. However, it is becoming obvious that further differentiation, not only in the area of ideology but also in the area of work, is necessary in order to achieve a clearer socialistic orientation of the media... We cannot ignore the fact that some media have still not eliminated either the filth of liberalism, dogmatism, and even nationalistic intonations, or the old editorial mythologies, imitation and various types of bourgeois inferiority ...'

In autumn the following year (28 September 1986), Minović still seemed to waver. At the common session of two ideological commissions of the Central Committee of the League of Communists of Serbia, he singled out nationalism as the greatest threat: 'What we have here is the reviving of nationalism, with some media showing great zeal for it. The Serbian nationalists vary their old slogan that the Serbs lost in peace what they had won in war. They inflame hatred and want to estrange the Serbian people from all other nations and nationalities. They strive to create not only anti-Albanian, but also anti-Croatian, and anti-Slovenian sentiment ...' This was the way in which the political leader of *Politika* spoke in 1985 and 1986, prior to the Eighth Session, while the torrent of 'national revival' was only appearing through the thick clouds of the inherited ideological doctrinairism; while the defence of Tito's work, revolution and socialism was still in vogue, and along with it, a doctrinaire bureaucratic anti-nationalistic rhetoric. However, two years later (in January 1988, on the occasion of the eighty-fifth anniversary of the launch of *Politika*), the same editor-in-chief of the same newspaper, now a member of the Central Committee and many other forums, was an ardent promoter of a radically opposite editorial policy. He said, literally, that the newspaper *Politika* that had been entrusted to him 'has no right to think differently from the people'.

Since then everything was in the spirit of the 'anti-bureaucratic revolution', and serving that cause was offered as a freedom unknown not only in Serbian and Yugoslav journalism, but in international journalism as well. 'The people' (not a person, a citizen, a reader) turned into a force which all had to serve submissively, a mantra and justification for everything; everything was permitted in its name; nobody dared utter a sound against this illusory abstraction. Those whose opinion differed had either to shift lanes quickly or be cast off, as an obstacle not tolerated by the angry people.[6]

'The People among peoples'

Naturally, it was already known that *Politika* was irrevocably included in the 'anti-bureaucratic revolution', at the expense of even the very delusion of objective information. However, this time things were different. Formerly, the Party established rules for everyone, including journalists. Now, 'the people' controlled everything, including even the party and journalism. Minović prepared the last warning for the doubting Thomases: 'The citizens, whose self-consciousness has lately grown to an undreamed of extent, are not ready to accept excuses any longer or to tolerate insults at the expense of the Serbian people. As the Serbian people, to paraphrase the poet, is not only a people among the plum trees, but also *a people among peoples*; it is, above all, as history has shown, an uprising among the peoples, an uprising against injustice ...' (author's emphasis).

A year later (on 13 February 1989), Minović stated triumphantly: 'In all these happenings, both *Politika* and its publications have changed, as has public opinion. I am sure that this is primarily due to the fact that public opinion has influenced our publications, but that our publications have also influenced public opinion ... This represents a great cross-roads in Yugoslav journalism.'

That is, indeed, what it was: a great cross-roads. But where did this cross-roads lead *Politika*? The noisily overacted infatuation with the people was used to impose obedience in journalism as well; it was reduced to absolute submission to the autocratic power which, in the name of the defence of the honour and dignity of all Serbdom, separated Serbia from the civilized world, and its oldest and most influential newspaper from the realm of free, independent journalism.

However, in autumn 1989 the perspectives of the 'anti-bureaucratic revolution' were undisturbed; its promoters and propagandists were marching forward as an unstoppable force; awards to the most deserving were being handed out all round. Nor was the head of the *Politika* publishing house left out. In early 1990 he was elected director and editor-in-chief, and was praised loudly, although far more by outsiders than by the editorial staff. The chairwoman of the Republic Conference of the Socialist Alliance of the Working People of Serbia, Radmila Anđelković, portrayed him as a shining star on the political sky of Serbia for his contribution to the Eighth Session. 'At the crucial moments', she commented, Minović 'made an important contribution to the unmasking of all those forces which prior to, during and after the Eighth Session tried to stop the inevitable progressive aspirations of the League of Communists of Serbia.'

This political recognition given to the editor-in-chief of the main daily in Serbia could have been seen as the ritual suicide of the profession: it seemed as if the main activity of *Politika* was no longer providing truthful information about events within and outside the country, but the merciless 'unmasking' of the opponents of the Eighth Session.[7]

However, power is similar to Diogenes's fire: he who comes too close to it can burn himself. Was the most ambitious politician among the Serbian journalists aware of this danger?

Two years after the moments of glory he experienced on the occasion of his re-election as director and editor-in-chief, Minović, in the summer of 1992, provoked (doubters would say 'staged') a political duel unforeseen by anyone: he attacked the authorities, to which hardly anyone was as close as he was himself.[8]

Seen from outside, it was a fierce clash with the then Serbian prime minister, Radoman Božović, that is, 'with the government and the governing party'. According to Minović, the reason for it was the declared intention of the authorities to prevent 'the transformation of ownership' of the *Politika* publishing house by putting it, with the blessing of Parliament, under the control of the government.

The deeper motives for this duel, which, at least formally, ended without a winner, remained incomprehensible to the public. But Minović's public dramatization of the conflict, slowly and skilfully performed, was, in fact, quite effective. This was due, in the first place, to his publicly announced and seemingly irrevocable intention to liberate, in the name of independent and objective information, the most powerful newspaper publisher in Serbia from the guardianship of nationalistic autocracy.

Quite a number of people had hopes at that time (too early, as it turned out) that at the top of the nationalistically oriented governing pyramid, serious, maybe irreparable, cracks were opening, through which *Politika*, if strong enough, could pull through and once more stand on its own feet. Its head, who answered Božović's threats by organizing, with lightning speed, a general strike and a stoppage of *Politika*'s presses, did not mention Milošević in person. However, he cunningly threatened to do that as well, if he had to. 'Nobody can silence our house, he threatened unexpectedly, 'not even those who were assisted by *Politika* in their climb to power.'[9]

The confession of one of the most prominent associates and minions of the 'governing circles' had the effect of a true sensation. Maybe it was even the intimation of a catharsis for *Politika* after the great traumas—in the creation of which it had also had a hand. At the same time, it was a great riddle, since, to put it mildly, many things remained unclear, including the real intentions of *Politika*'s head, a man who was shooting poisoned arrows at the regime which the daily he headed served so obediently. Had he suddenly begun to defend journalism against the guardianship of autocratic power, or, suspecting that someone was out to attack him, was he trying to remain both in *Politika* and in the governing 'structure' by blackmail, threatening disobedience within the strongest newspaper publishing house? Or perhaps there was a third reason, a more modest and seemingly a more natural one: that one of the most responsible participants in the defence of the Greater Serbia project, which had reduced Serbia to poverty, was trying to protect himself from harmful consequences while there was still time and to secure an alibi by disassociating himself from Milošević's power?

The section of Minović's statement in which he described *Politika* and himself as almost innocent victims, pointed to this third possibility: 'It is a known fact that the house of *Politika* was taking part in the national revival until a few years ago. But from the moment Serbia took a different road, our house started to follow its own historical logic of independence.'

This ambiguity, which was meant to provide an alibi, could perhaps have been convincing had subsequent events confirmed it. However, if that was his intention, he failed—nor did he even attempt to step out of this ambiguity. On the contrary, he seemed to repent as time went by.[10]

Politika's Kosovo

Politika's painful oscillation between the traumas which undermined its professional foundation and the increasingly ambiguous catharsis, entered a new phase. Let us go back once more, however, to the beginning of its professional shipwreck, on the eve of, and during, the political disintegration of Yugoslavia and the armed conflicts. The journalists of *Politika* had the opportunity to see for themselves that the future was not smiling upon the independence of the journalistic profession, even before the ominous 'Vojko and Savle' affair (1987) had announced the hopeless restrictions to be imposed on professional autonomy. They had seen enough from the two sentences uttered by Slobodan Milošević at a session of the Belgrade Party Committee, on 18 February 1987.

By announcing a radical political and personal 'differentiation' in Serbian journalism, the speaker made it clear that the independence of the media was becoming pure illusion: 'The editor-in-chief of *Duga* has been replaced, but the situation in *Duga* will not change before we execute broader changes in the editorial staff of *Duga*. We are talking about a new editor-in-chief of the weekly *NIN*. Regardless of the solution we reach, we shall not solve the problem in *NIN* unless a serious reconstruction is carried out.' The settling of accounts among Serbia's top leaders was approaching, while the tidal wave of 'national revival' was becoming stronger and stronger. Under its onslaught, the professionalism of *Politika* became more and more shaky. This was to be confirmed, on the eve of the Eighth Session, by reports on the cruel tragedy in the Paraćin barracks. On 3 September 1987, a soldier on night duty, an Albanian by the name of Azis Kelmendi, killed four soldiers and wounded five others while they were asleep.

The top editors of *Politika* gave this event maximum coverage–which is understandable–accompanied by a mild criticism of national revanchism and anti-Albanian incidents in certain towns in Serbia. However, as the coverage of the burial of the victims, and of other events, became more extensive, the political (nationalistic) dimension of texts related to this event and published by *Politika* became more and more noticeable. For example, the report by *Politika*'s Priština correspondent at the time from Dušanovo, the birthplace of the perpetrator of the crime, Azis Kelmendi, reflected not only a departure from the reasonable assumption that this was an insane act by an individual, but also a less than subtle suggestion that it was the result of a perfidious anti-Serbian conspiracy. In a style characteristic of departure from objectivity in favour of a loose generalization typical of the agitation and propaganda department, *Politika*'s reporter wrote, inter alia, that 'The unprecedented assassination of the soldiers has shocked all Yugoslavia. In Kosovo, it provoked astonishment and confusion among a majority of honest people, and prompted the question: has it come to this? ... Immediately after the burial of the murderer Kelmendi, in the village of Dušanovo which has a population of around 7,000 inhabitants, only 208 of whom are Serbs, the decision of the local community on the boycotting of the Kelmendi family became effective. In *respectable households* (author's emphasis) the meetings of local precincts were held and the decision on the boycott was unanimously accepted ...'

The contents and the manner of presentation of this allegedly objective information are striking for the way in which *Politika*'s eyewitness reporter, or rather his managing editor at the newspaper, turned a blind eye to the glaring ambiguities inherent in this politically and psychologically inflammable text. For example, who made the decision to boycott a whole Albanian household because of a crime committed by one of its members, when not one of those who were in charge made the slightest mention of there being accomplices to the crime; on what grounds was that decision made, and how? How was it possible legitimately to adopt such a brutal anti-Albanian decision in a local community with 7,000 inhabitants, only 208 of whom were Serbs? Did the description of these painful events imply that the Albanians in that particular community all voted, to the last man, for the cruel boycott of their compatriots, or were *Politika*'s reporter and his editor keen to stir up anti-Albanian feelings at the expense of the unfortunate soldier/murderer's family? It seemed that the border between professional integrity and obsequiousness had already crumbled.[11]

Two years later it was the turn of Kosovo Field, a grandiose 'happening of the people'. It was the final message to all that Serbia, with its new leadership endorsed by the Eighth Session, had decided, in the name of historical justice and equality with others, to become, once and for all, 'united and strong'. The gathering in Kosovo Field was planned as a magnificent proof of the unwavering resoluteness of the people and their leaders to complete, sparing no expense, the 'anti-bureaucratic revolution' in Serbia and elsewhere.

On the eve of the great celebration, on 27 June 1989, *Politika* came out with headlines which were printed in letters larger than any used by the leading world newspapers to announce the beginning of the Second World War. A separate page, with special contributions, resembled a militant political leaflet calling for pan-Serbian national revival through a common return to the past. The heading, headline and subtitles spoke for themselves: 'Six centuries after the battle of Kosovo', 'The time of Kosovo', and, finally, a political message for those who thought differently, in the manner of a final warning: 'The Serbian people has glorified and still glorifies its heroes and recognizes its traitors'.

It is interesting to look at some of the other characteristic headlines on the rest of the pages dedicated to the Kosovo events. A common feature was the unlimited triumphalism, which would have been out of place even in newspapers with much less professional experience and tradition. Several of the most conspicuous ones are quoted here:

'Kosovo is a dream dreamt by generations' (This particular title requires some deciphering: the editor, it seems, has failed to follow the rules of elementary logic, since if Kosovo is a historical symbol and a national dream for Serbia, then it means that the defeat is a Serbian national ideal).

'For six centuries Kosovo has been waiting for its sons to come back and say: it is ours and shall remain ours'. (The use of the thoughts of ordinary people as headlines in the leading political daily has nothing to do with the kind of journalism that strives to maintain high standards. However, it must be admitted that this is a very expressive example of the nationalistic promotion of the national legend, its ideological profanation for the sake of the requirements of a momentary and aggressive national strategy.)

'Millions wished for this celebration to take place'. (By replacing journalistic and editorial professionalism with celebratory, populist banality, the editor, obviously caught up in the mood himself, puts the report from the Kosovo meeting into the service of theatrically mobilizing emotions, in accordance with the needs of the new political order born out of the movement known as 'the happening of the people'.)

No less characteristic of the increasingly obvious submerging of professional journalistic ethics, in this case *Politika's*, in the ever murkier waters of politically volatile national euphoria, was the poetic report that was given special treatment in the issue dedicated to the celebration in Kosovo. The report, which reads like a mixture of revolutionary rhetoric borrowed from the French and the October revolutions, Serbian style, begins with the following lines by *Politika's* ambitious author:

> Today is 28 June 1989, one of the days on which our thoughts turn to the past, six centuries ago, and alight in Kosovo Field, amid the rattling of swords, in the midst of the clash between the Serbian and the Turkish armies on 28 June 1389. The Battle of Kosovo. The Serbian army, on the ramparts of civilization, defending Serbian glory and the European cross. We did not save Serbia, but we did save Europe ...[12]

In order to get a more complete insight into *Politika's* role and responsibility, as well as into the political circumstances and traumas to which, in the late 1980s and early 1990s, it was making a very active and important contribution, we should take into consideration some interesting thoughts of Eric Hobsbawm, a political scientist from New York. He says that myths and fantasies are of essential importance in creating the identities by which people today define themselves—ethnically and religiously, in relation to former or present state frontiers—while trying to find some certainty in this uncertain world under the slogan 'We are different and better than the others'. History, Hobsbawm says, is the raw material for nationalistic, ethnic and fundamentalist ideologies, just as poppy seeds are the raw material for making opium. He points out that the past is an essential, maybe the most essential, element of these ideologies.

However, to return to Kosovo Field and *Politika* and its reporting on the celebration of the six-hundredth anniversary of St. Vitus's Day, an interesting omission in its reports from the spot is revealed. It is striking that the editors of the daily did not deem it necessary to display prominently, by means of the graphic presentation in these unforgettable editions, the one detail that was most dramatic for the outside world. I refer to what was politically probably the most lethal, and by its consequences certainly the most far-reaching, message delivered by Slobodan Milošević in his speech in front of a nearly one-million-strong audience at Gazimestan: 'Six centuries later were are again in battle and facing new battles. They have not been armed battles so far, but even such battles cannot be ruled out.' These words were certainly not chosen at random, they were prophetic and unforgettable, a kind of announcement of the Yugoslav and Serbian tragedy.

'The People is coming...'

Probably convinced that this message was sufficiently militant not to require further dramatization, *Politika* gave the highest priority, and most of its space, to its duties as a fervent agitator, abiding by the well-known pseudo-professional concept that the 'voice of the people' is paramount, particularly when that voice is in harmony with precisely programmed expectations. The following are additional illustrations taken from reports of the Kosovo meetings.

Quoting a certain Dragan Jelisijević, an economist from Zagreb who joined the stream of participants in the celebration in Kosovo with a camera in his hands, *Politika*'s reporter recorded the his vow that 'I will make a big album and dedicate it to my children. Let them see how their people, summoned by their tradition and future, came to pay their respects before its largest wound– Kosovo.'

This is followed by the reporter's comment on this unprecedented event: 'Thousands and thousands of people are descending the roads leading from the gentle slopes to the Great Field ... The people are coming and nothing can stop them any longer.'

Another touching note follows, this time on the ecstatic mood which gave wings to visions of Serbia and the Serbs as an exceptional phenomenon of planetary dimensions. Milan Tribrenčić, born in Jasenovac, who was taken prisoner of war in 1941 and who came to the six-hundredth anniversary of the Battle of Kosovo from Pennsylvania, told *Politika*'s reporter that he felt absolutely reborn at this pan-Serbian meeting: 'All the pains and sufferings which have followed me throughout my life have been healed today ...'

Miodrag Jović from Niš, who, according to *Politika*, reached Gazimestan at the crack of dawn with the intention of getting a place in the front row at the meeting, showed a euphoria which took little heed of human limitations: 'I would wait twenty-four hours if necessary; this is a big day for Serbia. After six centuries, the Serbs have realized that they can enter the new age only if united, and this unity has been achieved thanks to Slobodan Mi-lošević. The most important thing now is the loan for the economic revival of Serbia which must surpass expectations, just as the number of participants at this magnificent manifestation has done today. We are grateful for this to the present Serbian leadership, in the first place to Slobodan Milošević, whom the people trust without reserve.'

Leaving aside the authentic or inferred depth of feelings shown by this so-called ordinary man, in this case a Serb, this kind of journalistic prose will be remembered as a clear example of the abandonment of professionalism. The reporting from Kosovo is only one illustration of this sad fact: the oldest political daily in Serbia and Yugoslavia had shamed itself, as never before, with reports and comments worthy of an agitprop department, first from various meetings and conferences, and later from the battlefields of nationalist armed conflicts in Croatia and Bosnia-Hercegovina.

Contrary to all previous 'isms', and to one-party or other monopolies, the new order, announced and inaugurated by the 'solidarity meetings', and promoted by shouting from all rooftops 'as a spontaneous happening of the people' by a politically precisely directed organization, demanded from *Politika* more than an unconditional, absolute support. It demanded, and unfortunately received, the professional and moral capitulation of its editorial team in the name of the revival of Serbian statehood and unity. As for the consequences, it was the most painful fall for *Politika* and its readers, and for journalistic and political culture in Serbia.

It is self-evident that this brief appraisal from a professional journalistic angle neither implies nor suggests the division of the whole history of *Politika* into only two epochs—the first eighty years and the last ten or so years of its development. As all other political newspapers in this area, and in the rest of the world as well, *Politika* was always too heterogeneous and too dependent on various influences, circumstances and troubles for any of its successes and trials to be treated as independent and separate phenomena.

However, if the core of modern journalism is indisputable—that is, that 'information is the fuel of democracy' (Ronald Berkman and Laura Kich 1986), there can be no dispute about the lesson deriving from it, either: every ideological-political, state and party control over information is the strongest arm of all examples of undemocratic societies. To quote once again the political scientists from Brooklyn, New York, information is 'of crucial importance in a society whose citizens are to participate in political decision making'.

In the period under observation (approximately and conditionally from the Eighth Session in the autumn of 1987 to the strike and 'liberation' made public in the summer of 1992), *Politika*, as if in a trance, started to go the other way: by accepting primarily the role of agitation and propaganda, it prepared the citizens, its readers, not for independent reasoning about everything that was happening, but for an uncritical servility 'to higher national interests'. To put it more precisely: by neglecting and deserting the battle for objective and independent information, *Politika* accepted its own, professional surrender.

To make things worse, the heads of *Politika*, overcome by the illusory warmth of national euphoria, rushed to give to the aggressive ideology which had taken them under its wing even more than it expected from them: they became not only model followers, but also the agitprop activists, particularly in the promotion and strengthening of the collective myth surrounding the injustice and dangers which had been putting Serbia and the Serbs in peril from time immemorial and from every direction. Thus, they opened the doors wide, in the name of the right to self-determination and self-defence, to every kind of violence, including armed violence.

Turning their backs on their profession and vocation, and by demagogically vowing to 'serve the people', the editors rubbed their hands in satisfaction at the increase in circulation, paying no heed to the price they paid for this 'success'. They opened almost all their political and informative pages to the unrestricted flow not only of kitsch and vulgar pseudo-patriotism, chauvinism and unrestrained political gossip, but also to true eruptions of blind hatred aimed at Albanians, Croats, Moslems, Slovenians, Macedonians... as well as at Serbian 'traitors'. In this way, *Politika* experienced a unique, and not only a journalistic, *salto mortale*.

The reputation and the influence which *Politika* had been acquiring for decades enabled it to make true legends even out of the modestly known people around it. It also became a legend in its own right for many of those who wished to see their reflection in its glow. For them, it was more than a newspaper, even the most influential of its kind; it was accepted, praised and glorified, used and abused, as a prime national institution as well.

Citizens who asked for 'the newspaper' at news stands with *Politika* in mind, did not have to be invented by marketing specialists in the sales department; they only made use of the legend of *Politika* as the only true newspaper. Then came the cruel twist of fate: the most influential political daily of Serbia, which, as a bulwark of independent and objective information, reached a pinnacle of power, hit rock bottom. In Serbia, and to an even greater extent outside it, the paper was condemned and pointed to as a chauvinistic rabble-rouser encouraging hatred and war, mostly, and with the greatest anger and pain, by those who sincerely respected it because of its former professional qualities and achievements which had done credit to the Serbian culture.

In the turmoil of the Yugoslav and Serbian nationalistic debacle, *Politika*, ironically, became a drastic example of the disastrous anti-professionalism about which the far-sighted Walter Lippman warned as early as 1920. At that time he said that people without relevant information about the environment in which they live unavoidably turn into victims of agitation and propaganda. Babblers, charlatans, chauvinists and terrorists can multiply, he maintained, only in those milieux where public are deprived of independent information.

Lippmann's diagnosis of the serious trials of modern journalism could be taken, at first glance, as proof that here, in the crisis which severely tested journalists both within *Politika* and around it, nothing happened that had not happened before in the history of international journalism. To support this, we can also add another fact: it was not only *Politika* which surrendered, but almost everyone else. Not only in journalism, but more or less everywhere. With some honourable exceptions, *Politika* broke down because it did not have any immunity in itself or any defence in its surroundings. The nationalistic avalanche, intensified by the tragic disintegration of almost the whole territory of the former Yugoslavia, was destroying the already shallow material and social foundations of enlightenment and democratic political awareness. *Politika* was not able to raise itself above the reality of contemporary Serbia and former Yugoslavia.

Politika shared the sorrowful fate of the whole of Serbian society, but as it was 'the newspaper', a concept wider than its name, and an institution the influence of which was not measured only by the number of its readers, its responsibility for the epidemic of demagogic populism and aggressive nationalism was, and still is, unique and great.

It is true that the 'differentiation' lasting several years and the 'national revival' were gaining all the more destructive acceleration from the force of the avenging, national-chauvinistic storm, which, hitting the civilizationally fragile foundations of a greater part of former Yugoslavia, also brought to their knees institutions which were stronger than *Politika*. But it is also true that resistance in the name of the defence of professionalism was becoming an increasingly hopeless task, due, among other reason, to the disastrous, apolitical and careerist readiness of the leaders of the editorial staff to join, without any reserve, the front lines of the 'anti-bureaucratic revolution' and the national madness and xenophobia ignited by it.

It is also important to keep in mind the totality of all relevant, domestic and outside circumstances in which *Politika*, promoted to its role as the champion of professional independence, turned out to be both a silent prisoner and a vocal proponent of collective innocence, that is, of national autism. We should not forget that the plunge of *Politika*'s famous professionalism took place at the time of the collapse of Eastern European 'Communism', the tearing down of the Berlin wall, the end of the Cold War and other past evils. The beginning of a democratic renaissance, of human rights and civil liberties was being celebrated, prepared for or promised nearly everywhere. Why was it that *Politika*, as 'the newspaper' without rival in history in this part of the world, as an institution of special importance, chose just that moment to fall into the arms of the power and ideology which recoils from those who think differently and cannot stand independent media? How great was the role of outside pressure, supported by autocratic absolutism; and how great was the internal journalistic weakness? Finally, was not the defensive potential of *Politika*'s professionalism irreparably weakened by the purges carried out in *Politika* in previous periods?

More precise and detailed answers to the questions surrounding *Politika*'s professional cataclysm in the period of nationalistic autocracy in Serbia and outside it, will undoubtedly require further research.

Notes

1 The controversial so-called humoresque was published in the Sunday edition of *Politika* on 18 January 1987. It provoked protest from a considerable part of the political and cultural public, particularly in Belgrade, and for almost a year held the whole house of *Politika* in a kind of convulsion. The reason lay partly in the fact that behind the not very skilfully written scandalous pamphlet one could discern very clearly the methodology of an autocratic model of political governance and of the settling of accounts, as dangerous as it was trite.

2 Actually, this shameful situation, without precedent in the history of *Politika*, could not pass without consequences. On 20 January, 67 of *Politika*'s journalists sent a letter of protest addressed to the editor-in-chief, requesting that the disgraced newspaper send a public apology to the innocent Nikoliš family. A few days later (on 26 January), proof appeared that the public was also deeply upset: 126 citizens, some of the most prominent intellectuals among them, signed an 'Open Letter' in which they summarized in the following way the disgrace of Serbia and *Politika*: 'That article does not bring shame on those you intended to shame, but on our people, whose written and public words have been equated with *Politika* for almost a century.'

3 The new 'Reactions' column, through which the torrent of 'organized' pan-Serbian dissatisfaction with autonomism, separatism and other dark forces flowed, had a peculiar profile of contributors. Among the authors of the seven contributions published that day (*P*, 13 July 1988), three signed themselves as 'professor', two used the letters Ph.D. after their names, while no occupation was given for the last two.

4 The proof of this is the involvement of *Politika* in campaigns against journalists from nationally 'unsuitable' media, in Belgrade, Novi Sad and other places. At the session of the Commission for Ideological Activity of the Central Committee of the League of Communists of Serbia (chaired by its chief, Živorad Minović), Dušan Mitević expressed the political avant-gardism of the top editors of *Politika*: 'At this moment, while we are discussing matters, and while many are shedding false tears over the oppressed Serbs and Montenegrins in Kosovo, *Rilindija*, for example, has published a text stating that the people are migrating from the Province for economic reasons. Will the Communists on the spot take care of this text, *or will Politika have to do it?*' (author's emphasis).

5 Serials are another matter. This section of *Politika*'s space would remain, even after the closing down of the 'Echoes and Reactions' column, an irreplaceable platform for the ideological troubadours of the 'anti-bureaucratic revolution' and the Eighth Session. It was used particularly for the frequent chauvinistically toned 'exposing' of Croatian, Moslem, Slovenian, Albanian, Vatican, German, American and other 'anti-Serbian conspiracies', through texts with scholarly pretensions the argumentation of which, to put it mildly, remained unverified.

6 *Politika*'s editor-in-chief eliminated any dilemmas and acted as if the people as a whole were prompting him as to what to say. 'We have begun to print words that change life itself. Words in the service of the truth ... This provokes opposition, as we do not want drawing-room and bureaucratic journalism. Some ironically call our attitude "buckling before populism". We are a witness, but we do not hide that we are also a fighter for the truth... At the great cross-roads of Yugoslav journalism, *Politika*, celebrating its anniversary, can repeat that it has no other editorial programme but to be with the people.'

7 Several months earlier, on 20 September 1989, the jury of the Association of Journalists of Serbia awarded Minović, by a majority vote, 'the

highest recognition for editorial journalistic work', the Dimitrije Davi-dović Prize. In the explanation of the decision, along with other pane-gyrics, it was said that the winner, as the head of *Politika* 'boldly ac-cepted the challenges of the awakened consciousness of the people which have become the mainstay of its editorial policy'.

8 According to the findings of S. Đukić, Minović, as early as the time of the severe anti-regime demonstrations of 9 March 1991, came to the conclusion that the power of Milošević was heading toward disaster and began to retreat and look for support among the leaders of the op-position parties (S. Đukić 1994).

9 The *pièce de résistance* of this dramatization, which motivated even the anti-nationalistic, democratic, and especially intellectual circles in Ser-bia to accept the call for defence, i.e. the liberation of the oldest news-paper house, was Minović's provocative declaration in front of the cameras of his (*Politika*'s) television station, on 30 July 1992. In a melodramatic text, in which the long inaccessible director of the news-paper publishing house *Politika* seemed to inform the public that he was in physical danger as well, the following accusations were cited against the government and the political regime of Serbia: 'Is this the humanity of the respected gentlemen from the government which sends us threatening messages, like in a thriller? If it is already obvious that the freedom of the press is threatened, why do they have to threaten our families as well ... The violence of the leadership has been lasting for years. Perhaps we were cowards not to have raised our voices earlier. But, believe me, it is difficult to work under stress and pressure, in the atmosphere of hypocrisy, ignorance and nepotism that exists in the governing circles ...'

10 In the summer of 1994, two years after the shocking rebellious state-ment given to *Politika*'s television station, the unpredictable Minović, as the company's president, questioned the modest results of profes-sional rehabilitation announced by the strike of 1992. By a speedy deci-sion of the Board of Directors, which he controlled, disobedient jour-nalists and undesirable information, including whole programmes, quickly disappeared from *RTV Politika*, while the position of director was given to Slobodan Ignjatović, former federal information minister, a former journalist with *Politika Ekspres*, and better known as a tireless fighter against foreign and domestic 'conspiracies'. All this was, natu-rally, done in a 'strictly legal way', according to Minović, and, certainly, in agreement with the authorities he had angrily bared his teeth at two years earlier. At that time he had vowed to be faithful to the glorious traditions of *Politika*'s journalistic school; by taking over its electronic media, he seemingly returned to what he was not able to, or did not want to, resist.

11 To make things worse, the ostentatiously suggestive (mis)information offered by *Politika*'s reporter from Dušanovo on the explosion of popu-lar (Serbian) anger caused by the horrific murders in the barracks was spiced with a strikingly anti-professional surfeit of emotion. Instead of

doing his duty conscientiously and objectively, he seemed to be stirring up passion for revenge, and, in a verdict without appeal, he concluded as follows: 'The Kelmendi family remains isolated. The doors to this house have not been opened by any local residents for several days ...' (*P*, 8 July 1989).

12 In the special issue dedicated to the six-hundredth anniversary of the St.Vitus's Day battle which would be used for a monumental, primarily political, reconstruction of the Serbian collective myth, *Politika,* as its contribution to this reconstruction, published a number of articles written by outside contributors, well-known public figures. Among them was an article by Radomir Lukić, a member of the Serbian Academy of Arts and Science, written to suit the occasion. The editors condensed the ideas it contained into the double subtitle 'The choice of the heavenly kingdom, although a religious one, as heaven and earth are bound together, is nevertheless not glorification of suicide, but the revelation of the road to salvation–The heavenly kingdom is the soul of the people'.

Turning the Electronic Media Around

RADE VELJANOVSKI

An analysis of the role of Radio Television Belgrade (RTB) and Radio Television Serbia (RTS, founded 1991) in events in former Yugoslavia is a daunting task. Unlike the printed media which leaves a trail through which the researcher can retrace his or her steps, the transience of electronic media makes study over any length of time difficult. In this particular case, ten years or so is a long period and what remains in the memory cannot always be verified by reliable sources or research material. Most radio and television broadcasts are simply not preserved and, in the political situation prevailing when this research was carried out, radio and TV archival material was not available to the objective or critical analyst.

However, this does not mean that it is not possible to search for cause and effect in the behaviour of the most influential media, or that such research bound to be superficial. Under the circumstances, one has, to a certain extent, resort to the reconstruction of the events and messages broadcast on radio and television. For this we have to use other relevant sources such as professional publications and papers, the daily and weekly press, radio and TV reviews, documents from RTB/RTS round tables and programme meetings, the writings and notes of people involved in certain events, journalists, editors and others employed in the media. It should be said that the further back we go in time, the fewer available data there are, but contemporary events also bear witness to what preceded them.

The phenomenon we are dealing with has its own genesis. The work of RTB/RTS in the 1980s and up to 1992 and later can be divided into three stages. The first begins with the events of 1981 in Kosovo and continues up to 1987 and the Eighth Session of the Central Committee of the Serbian Socialist Party; the second runs from the Eighth Session to 31 July 1991 and the passing of a new radio-television law; the third follows the passing of this law, which joined three radio and television centres, Belgrade, Novi Sad and Priština, into Radio-TV Serbia. After this, major structural and programming changes took place. These periods in the work of RTB/RTS do not exactly coincide with the work of other media, especially the daily and weekly press. Part of the press, led by Politika publishing house, first broke the taboo against fostering nationalism and mythomania in Serbia. Within RTB/RTS, not all departments and programmes had a unified approach to the problem. From time to time there were also significant differences between the programmes of Radio Belgrade and Television Belgrade.

Controlling the turnaround

Up to 1987 there was a gradual increase in freedom in Yugoslav journalism in dealing with subjects that had not been ordered 'from above'. This did not mean that a desirable level of editorial and media autonomy had been attained. However, there were increasing demands and efforts, mostly by individual journalists or departments, to penetrate the tightly controlled monolith of editorial policy. On the other hand, the government was not yet prepared to yield. This stand-off between liberal journalists on the one hand, and bureaucratic authority on the other, is best illustrated by a true anecdote: when journalists asked for the embargo on news from Kosovo to be lifted since Reuters was already broadcasting it, a certain Yugoslav politician gave the order to 'Stop Reuters!'.

The mounting tension between the need for a free press and the determination of the power structures that no such freedom was going to endanger their own position, boiled over at one point, only to head at once in the wrong direction.

The government did not succeed in relieving the tension but it did manage to divert it: the national leadership in the republics and autonomous provinces permitted the freest and most radical criticism of events, as long as they were happening in other republics. Thus, it was the Serbian press that revealed the Agrokomerc affair and wrote openly about the villas at Neum, while the media in Slovenia, Croatia and other parts of Yugoslavia reported in the harshest terms on protests by Serbs and Montenegrins from Kosovo, calling them nationalists even when they were not, or not merely so.

During this period, RTB programmes carried on pretty much as before, upholding the idea of 'brotherhood and unity' at all costs. However, the events in Kosovo in 1981 were to change all that.

Following the Kosovo demonstrations, a series of party meetings laid down guidelines for editorial policy in Radio Belgrade and Television Belgrade. According to these, a 'counter-revolution' was threatening the southern province, and this was followed by increasing—and erroneous—references to 'irredentism'. Later, the term 'separatism' crept in. In his book *The Time of Radio*, Radio Belgrade journalist and chronicler Živomir Simović notes that on 27 July 1981, a meeting of the RTB Programme Council was held, chaired by Radovan Pantović. The meeting concluded that significant results had been achieved in keeping the public politically informed. 'It was thought that the journalists had fulfilled their allotted task when reporting on the counter-revolution in Kosovo and the action taken by society, especially the Socialist Party', writes Simović (1984: 338)

However, besides this global tenet that enemy forces in Kosovo, by exerting constant pressure on Serbs and Montenegrins, were bent on ethnically cleansing the province, thus accomplishing the dream of an Albanian Republic which would in time secede, programmes in the early 1980s were not yet attempting to rouse Serb national myths or nationalism. Editors strove for objective reporting from Kosovo, on–the-spot reports being most in demand. This usually took the form of news or features. Reports frequently included a comment reflecting official policy, but not as yet evoking the past or involving the abuse of history. Journalists who helped unmask hostile conspiracies were praised.

Increasingly frequent discussion of, and efforts to solve, the Kosovo problem naturally meant an increase in the number of programmes dealing with the subject on radio and television. At that time, journalists and editors were still making an effort not to exaggerate but to provide objective reports for the public. Criticism of enemy action in Kosovo was, in accordance with the politics of the time, permitted only by 'self–management' and socialist circles. The many dissidents known to be champions of the Serbian cause, or those against whom there were ideological reservations, were not allowed into these circles. At that time it was the events themselves, not editorial purpose or dictates, that helped increase the number of programmes on Kosovo, which in turn helped raise the tension surrounding the issue.

Editorial policy in RTB at the time still kept its distance from any public manifestation of Serb nationalism. It was particularly critical of the activity of The Writers' Association of Serbia, known as 'Francuska 7' after its Belgrade address, and of certain groups within the Serbian Academy of Arts and Sciences (SANU). As irrefutable evidence, we could cite writings on the SANU Memorandum and reports and comments on the Extraordinary Assembly of the Academy devoted to this never-finished document. Not a single broadcast by Belgrade radio or television gave the slightest hint of any support for the Memorandum. On the contrary, a commentary on Radio Belgrade's First Channel pointed to the misuse of history and the gravity of the moment at which this document had emerged.

There were reasons why radio and television in the republican and provincial capitals were far more restrained in their support for 'national agendas' and reluctant to give air space to nationalists, who were increasingly present elsewhere. Radio and TV stations had co-operated for years within a Yugoslav Radio-Television, an association that was practically a substitute for a proper Yugoslav radio and TV channel. It was assumed that all stations were pro-Yugoslav in policy and only then republican or national. Even when sniping between the republics and provinces in the daily and weekly papers had become commonplace, Yugoslav radio and television stations were still producing joint programmes and projects. A number of illustrations are cited below.

In late 1985 and early 1986, the news and political departments of all eight radio stations produced two special programmes on Kosovo. The preparation and production were a joint effort and all the stations, regardless of language differences, broadcast these programmes. There was a regular daily exchange of material for all types of programmes, especially in news and current affairs: The 'Morning News', 'News of the Day' and 'Dnevnik', the main news broadcast at prime time in the evening. There were late-night programmes for Yugoslav workers abroad, such as 'Together Tonight', aimed at all, regardless of republic or nationality, while Radio Yugoslavia broadcast contributions from all republic and provincial stations in turn.

Co-operation among TV stations, despite the increasingly unfavourable political situation, also continued in news and current affairs. Informing foreign audiences was the joint concern of the TV stations, which broadcast via a TV Zagreb transmitter. In 1983 there were fifty-one joint programmes made up of joint contributions, twenty-six 'Hello Yugoslavia' broadcasts to German Television, and 'Mosaic', for Yugoslavs living in France (T. Jošanović 1984: 71–84). The same sources show that a report on Kosovo for foreign broadcast was made by Television Pristina on behalf of Yugoslav Radio-Television. This goes to show that while republic and provincial stations worked individually, there was a mutual trust which lasted for some time.

Evidence of co-operation among the state electronic media can be found in the anniversary of sound broadcasting in Yugoslavia. The date taken as the starting point was 15 May 1926, the day on which Radio Zagreb began regular broadcasts. This was chosen as the official Yugoslav Radio Day. Radio Belgrade joined in the celebrations and a programme called 'The Ever Present Voice', created by Sonja Malovrazić, won an award at the 'Week of Radio 1986' in Ohrid, Macedonia. The programme described the beginnings of radio in Yugoslavia, citing Radio Zagreb as the first, followed by Radio Ljubljana and thirdly Radio Belgrade (RTV TP, 44/1986: 29–37). This is of particular interest because in 1993, after the collapse of Yugoslavia, RTS announced that the first radio programme in Yugoslavia had been broadcast by Radio Belgrade in October 1924. It was not that radio historians were unaware of this, but it was thought that it could not be taken as the beginning of sound broadcasting in Yugoslavia because an initial experimental period had been followed by a lengthy break. As national euphoria took hold, and solely for political reasons, 1 October was declared as RTS Day. To the government of the time it was highly convenient to have another proof that Serbia had always been first in everything.

As we have mentioned, 1987 was a turning point for the media. A round table held at the Ohrid radio festival stated that 'It has been noted with increasing frequency that a routine visit by "one's own" politician is enough to eclipse the events of the day in another republic, or even the Federation.' The idea of 'my republic' or 'someone else's republic or region' began to creep into radio and television. Co-operation, although it still existed, was not as idyllic as before. All programmes, including RTB's, began to be permeated by the political views of the mother republic, if not yet by the propagation of nationalism and hatred, especially not that of journalists or other people involved in programme making.

The media happening

The media war, already being waged for some time in print, began to take over the electronic media. In the departments of Belgrade Radio and Television, resistance to the incitement of nationalism and retaliation could still be heard. It was impossible, however, to refuse to devote attention or space to one particular kind of occurrence, which directly involved the public and helped to form the collective idea of a threat to the Serb nation and of an 'unprincipled coalition' working against it.

The visit of Slobodan Milošević to Kosovo Polje on 24 April 1987, the Eighth Session of the Central Committee of the Serbian Socialist Party (CKSKS), the so-called truth rallies held throughout Serbia, the overthrow of the provincial leadership in Vojvodina and then in Kosovo, and the Seventeenth Session of the Central Committee of the Yugoslav Socialist Party on Kosovo, were all given wide media coverage. Sessions of political forums were either covered live or presented in voluminous reports and special broadcasts so that everything that was said reached the public. At that time, speakers were already thundering about the danger threatening the Serbian people, about Serbia as a winner in war and a loser in peace, about Yugoslavia in which all the nations had gained and only the Serbs had lost.

From 1987 on, certain differences could be seen in the behaviour of Radio Belgrade and Belgrade Television. The Eighth Session of the CKSKS had attracted varied comment. No news reporter on television was willing to write the kind of commentary which, according to contemporary practice, was expected to support the winner, so a volunteer from the cultural department was found who distinguished himself by his apologetic delivery. On the radio, a commentary in the 'Sunday at Ten' programme made the point that this was in fact a struggle for supremacy between two factions in the party.

The year 1988 will be remembered for the 'happenings of the people' and the 'meetings of truth', upheld and encouraged by the Serbian political leadership. Combined with the need to report on events, this turned RTB into a vehicle by which militant, pro-war, nationalistic messages reached the greatest number of people. The fact that no official policy representative opposed any of this and that all was heard and seen on state radio and television had an impact of its own. In addition, television, in a unique way, brought into viewers' homes the entire iconography of these meetings: threatening slogans, images of saints and of Slobodan Milošević, bearded faces, and the cockades, costumes, uniforms and flags of the past.

Myths of a 'heavenly Serbia' and the eternally wronged Serbian people were nourished by the electronic media, especially television, in full view of the nation. Television and radio broadcasts such as prime-time and regular news programmes, current affairs programmes and so on were full of this sort of thing.

A sort of parallel life emerged in RTB programmes, especially the radio. Aware of the awful reality, but also aware of how their own media were contributing to stoking emotions, many journalists rose to the challenge. One such success was the programme 'Oh What a Lovely Day' by Dušanka Gikić, Predrag Tomić and Branislava Stefanović, broadcast by Radio Belgrade's Second Channel. This reconstructed in a persuasive, ironic way, with the use of radiophonics, many of the events concerning Kosovo, treating them as if they had happened in a single day. The attitude towards the 'meetings of truth', presented in a slightly allegoric manner, was a very clear criticism of the manipulation of the masses. This was appreciated by the jury at the Ohrid Radio Festival who, despite changed criteria and the body blows already delivered to Yugoslav unity, awarded this programme first prize. The votes were cast by representatives of all radio stations from Ljubljana to Skopje.

At this time, television and radio began a serious broaching of issues hitherto unthinkable in the media. In a reference to Belgrade television programmes, journalist and radio-television critic Branka Otašević calls this process the democratization of the media: 'In the general democratization, television also opened up to issues which had recently been taboo, showing a critical interest in the personalities who were creating history; it moved into the centre of events and explored their background ...' (RTV, TP, 54/1989: 95). The author does not say which taboo issues she meant, but as this was 1989, we may recall that these were usually themes from the recent past, such as the post-war prison camp on the island of Goli Otok, or the personality of Josip Broz Tito. Many lengthy reports were made about Goli Otok on both Belgrade television and radio, while talk of Tito became increasingly critical and negative in tone. This came not only from those who had always been his opponents, but also from his former fellow-revolutionaries and allies. With the demystification of recent history, the dilemma most often heard was whether or not Yugoslavia had been the right choice for the various nations, or whether it was an artificial structure imposed on the Serbian people. Gradually, the relationship between Chetniks and Partisans, and the roles of both in World War II, were dragged into the open, with passing mention of national reconciliation.

The state electronic media reflected increasing differences between the republic and provincial leaderships. Joint news programmes created daily friction, as TV stations would insert into programmes intended for all, items which upheld the viewpoints of its own leadership but were critically slanted towards those of other republics. This was especially true of Belgrade Television. Serbia's introduction of emergency measures in Kosovo caused enormous controversy in news and current affairs departments. Reporting on the miners' strike in the Stari Trg mine at Trepča in

Kosovo differed fundamentally from one TV station to another: while for Belgrade the strike was an example of the enemy's manipulation of the miners, for the rest, especially Slovenia and Croatia, the miners were protesting against the tyranny of the Serbian government and merely defending their rights.

One of the events of 1989 which contributed most to the 'national awakening' in Serbia and gave rein to nationalist passion, was the six-hundredth anniversary of the battle of Kosovo. What was said at and about the commemoration is not the issue here. The fact is that it was given exceptionally wide media coverage, that it was reported live by RTB, and that many programmes devoted special emphasis to rebroadcasting Slobodan Milošević's speech, either in its entirety or or in part.

At that time, Belgrade Television made an official decision to use the Cyrillic alphabet in subtitles for foreign films and programmes intended for Yugoslav audiences. Notwithstanding the irritation this caused to other TV stations, Belgrade Television stuck to its decision.

Despite the ever growing tension, co-operation between stations continued. In 1989, a fortnightly current affairs TV programme called 'Parliamentary Chronicle', and a weekly radio programme 'The Course of Reform', were launched on the initiative of the federal government. This was one of the last efforts of Prime Minister Ante Marković to provide at least elementary information on debate and decision making among the federal leadership. These programmes were prepared jointly by the parliamentary reporters, but reluctantly and without much support from the radio and television stations. They did not last long.

As proof that the radio made more of an effort to uphold co-operation among the republics throughout 1989, a monthly series called 'Radio Bridge' was started. It was initiated by Radio Sarajevo, with planning input from Radio Belgrade's First Channel news department. This programme provided tangible evidence that with good will, even under difficult circumstances, it was still possible to speak objectively and openly on burning issues. The hosts were the republic and provincial stations in turn, with the participation of all the others. It was broadcast live, with phone-in facilities allowing listeners from all over Yugoslavia to put questions to the guests in the studio. It was an extraordinary media experiment. The topics were 'Yugoslavia and the Kosovo question', 'Federation or Confederation', 'How to achieve political pluralism', 'The majority-minority relationship inside the Communist Party', 'Market economy—examples and experiences'. The selection shows that thorny subjects were not avoided. This series was one attempt by media professionals to stave off looming disintegration.

In 1989 there was a palpable difference in editorial policy between Belgrade Radio and Television. Journalists felt a growing need to break free of government dictates and one-way-only, monolithic editorial policies. Guest personalities, hitherto proscribed by the authorities, began to appear on Radio Belgrade, as well as politicians from other republics who were not popular among politicians in Serbia. A young journalist, Dragan Štavljanin, held interviews with Slovenian leaders such as Milan Kučan, Sonja Lokar and Ciril Ribičič. These interviews attracted attention because of their objective approach which, without avoiding tricky questions, paid due respect to the interviewee. The Slovenian press wrote favourably about them. On the radio, there were talks with people who were critical of the political system and its prime movers. Similar efforts on Belgrade Television, especially in the field of culture and news, resulted in the banning of some of the best-known and popular programmes such as 'Kino Oko' ('Cinema Eye'). Teams working on 'Dnevnik' and 'Zip Magazine' were changed. This happened for two reasons: television as the more powerful media was more important to the government, and the most important places in it were occupied by people ready to act on every whim of those in power. At Radio Belgrade, in contrast, a session of the Programme Council in April 1990 officially adopted a multinational editorial policy. Even though the director of Radio Belgrade and the editor-in-chief of Channel One had previously been warned by the Serbian CKSK leadership that they would be replaced if they allowed critics of the party or system on air, a pluralist concept was nevertheless taking hold. On radio, this meant the airing of different opinions, confronting the manipulation and abuse of the media for day-to-day political purposes.

The year 1990 was interesting from several aspects: it saw the first multiparty elections since World War II in all republics, with Serbia and Montenegro bringing up the rear.

The Serbian political leadership, aware that it would not be able to avoid multiparty elections, tried to keep a tight grip on the most influential media. The then director-general of RTB, Dušan Mitević, stated openly at meetings of top programme and management working groups (*Kolegijum*), that 'We have to do everything to make sure the Socialists win'. At the same time, a negative attitude was fostered towards the rest of Yugoslavia. A meeting of the *Kolegijum* was told, in the form of confidential information from the Serbian political leadership, that 'Nothing will come of Yugoslavia' and 'Serbia doesn't need Yugoslavia'. These statements, made at meetings of RTB top management, were meant as guidelines for action. Since Radio Belgrade put up unflagging resistance to this, many top-level meetings began with Mitević saying 'All right then, how long do you at the radio intend to carry on like this? I can't go to the Main SPS Committee any more without being asked "What do those people of yours think they're doing?"'.

Threats that the radio management would be 'cleansed' arrived every day from different quarters, although officially and publicly the question was never raised.

Differences in editorial policy between radio and television were most obvious in attitudes towards the new political parties now mushrooming daily, but also towards other questions which are the topic of this research. Thus, for example, the RTB *Kolegijum* at one time was explicitly instructed not to release news of an incident involving the Chetniks of Vojislav Šešelj at the Prohor Pčinjski monastery, when they broke the memorial tablet commemorating the ASOM Session. Radio Belgrade, however, reported it, and in the evening it was shown on television. In other words, approval was issued subsequently to the television, without informing the radio. As it turned out, the people at the radio had done well to take matters into their own hands.

The famous opposition demonstration of 13 June 1990, at which demands were made for multiparty elections as soon as possible, was another opportunity for government manipulation of the media. Professionals at Radio Belgrade could not reconcile themselves to not using authentic recordings and promptly protested. The mistake was rectified over the next few days when Channels One and Two broadcast numerous on-the-spot recordings, together with exclusive testimony from Ljubiša Mitić whose collarbone had been broken in a street clash with the police. In 'Sunday at Ten' Mitić was able to deny claims by the Serbian interior minister, Radmilo Bogdanović, who said in an official statement that Mitić had been injured by one of the mob. Mitić clearly said that he had been hurt by the police.

One of the most flagrant instances of media abuse in the interests of a single party, with tolerance towards an outburst of Serb nationalism, was the way in which the public was informed of a rally to launch the Reform Forces as part of the run-up to the multinational elections of 1990. At this meeting, Federal Premier Ante Marković [a Croat], together with Serbian presidential candidate Ivan Djurić and their associates, were greeted in the packed Socialist Youth Centre by Šešelj and a group of his cronies with cries of

'Ustasha, Ustasha', followed by a roar of 'Yugoslavia, Yugoslavia'. After an incident involving the hurling of a camera, which injured the novelist Mirko Kovač, and an appearance by Vojislav Šešelj on the platform, the Chetniks left the hall, having put an end to the launch by the Reformists. The following day, at the RTB Programme *Kolegijum,* Dušan Mitević ordered the radio and television to issue the following comment: 'No more than two hundred people turned up to the Reformist launch, which was totally broken up by Šešelj's Chetniks. Ante Marković and his associates did not manage to answer a single question put from the floor.' The commentary was read out in the course of the prime-time evening news, 'Dnevnik', by Milorad Komrakov. By way of contrast, no one at the radio would write the item. On the contrary, Channel One's 'News of the Day' broadcast a comment by Dragan Mihović condemning the uncivilized behaviour of Šešelj's supporters. There could be no doubt that Belgrade TV's failure to condemn hostile behaviour and nationalist insults towards the federal government and its premier was all part of the anti-Yugoslav campaign which was then in full swing in Serbia.

The difference in approach to many key political issues between Belgrade Radio and Television was demonstrated just before the elections on 9 December 1991 when there was drastic misuse of RTB's Third Channel. The editor-in-chief, Ivan Krivec, spoke to journalist Mila Štula for a full three hours after the period of pre-election silence had been declared. Formerly a Zagreb journalist who 'knew the situation in Croatia', Štula talked all the time about how the best outcome for Serbia and the Serbian people was for Slobodan Milošević to win the elections. One of the presidential candidates, Vuk Drašković, was shown in the worst possible light. All this took place with the full participation of the host and chief editor, Krivec. The three-hour programme was not only out of line from the point of view of election regulations, but also a glaring misuse of the ravaged relations between the Yugoslav nations for the politics of the moment.

The extent to which state television, the most influential media, was misused, is illustrated by a film, shot in secret, of arms imports into Croatia by Croatian defence minister Martin Špegelj, who is seen plotting with his associates. As nothing was done to stop the import of arms even though it was known to be taking place (the film was made by the JNA) it may be no exaggeration to conclude that even this served the Serbian political leadership as propaganda. The public had to be shown obvious proof of how the Serbian people were in danger from the Croatian people.

The reaction of the democratic public and of opposition parties to the television partisanship at, prior to, and during, the election period is shown most dramatically in the events of 9 March 1991. The demonstrations provided a frame for the ruling party to attempt to use radio and television to abuse patriotism for party goals. Having accepted the idea of his own resignation, Dušan Mitević ordered at a meeting of the Programme *Kolegijum* on 11 March that the SPS rally at Ušće should be broadcast live by all radio and television stations, including Novi Sad and Priština (which were not yet part of RTS) and the association of radio stations of Serbia. He then stressed that they should 'make programme adjustments in the patriotic sense as contained in the RTS Declaration'.

When, at the end of March, the Serbian National Parliament passed judgement on the work of RTB over the past year, both the opposition and the party in power, under pressure from the public, concluded that Radio Belgrade had done its job professionally and honestly whilst the Belgrade Television was biased in favour of the Socialist Party. The director-general of RTB, Dušan Mitević, was sacked, together with the entire television management, while at the radio all those in positions of responsibility remained. This 'victory' of democratic forces was of short duration. The party in power was not at all prepared to come to terms with a loss of influence in the strongest media and was intent on getting it back by all means. RTB's acting director-general, Ratomir Vico, who had held this position two years previously, in his very first meetings with the press showed that he intended to continue where Mitević had left off. At a meeting with TV news journalists on 18 March 1991, he complained of 'obstruction' and 'fraud' by journalists on the home desk and insisted that things would be done the way he said. The journalists asked for more professionalism and proposed the promotion of trusted and reputed colleagues such as Milorad Petrović, Branka Mihajlović and Milica Lučić Čavić to key editorial positions. The meeting was adjourned but was never reconvened (*I*, 396, March 1991: 3)

In April 1990, when the RTB *Kolegijum* was considering programming for 1991, Ratomir Vico demanded that the document should 'emphasise links with Serbs living outside Serbia (in Knin and Bosnia) and include some of their programmes in RTB'.

The existing personnel structure, somewhat improved after 9 March, and journalists who wanted to do their work objectively and professionally, prevented the government from being able to count fully on complete use of the most influential media. A law designed to change this was therefore prepared in secret. Some of those in positions of responsibility at Radio Belgrade initiated a demand to inform the public and in-house staff of this intention. At RTB, a working group was formed to introduce the law, but all this fell through. The Radio and Television Act passed on 31 July 1991 was a definitive defeat for democratic forces within RTB. The entire radio and television management was dismissed. A giant system of three stations, or 'centres' was formed: Belgrade, Novi Sad and Priština. This collective of about eight thousand employees was solely to serve the interests of a single party. Its entire real estate was nationalized, while all authority over RTS was transferred to the government, which then, and subsequently, apart from some minor exceptions, consisted of one party.

Revealing real intentions

The new law enabled those in power to do away with all personnel who opposed their calamitous editorial policies–policies which promoted war and hatred among the nations and the break-up of the state. At the outset, the government did not volunteer a single word of explanation as to its position on staffing policy within RTS; ten months later, however, the deputy Speaker of the Serbian Parliament and chairman of the RTS Board of Management, Vukašin Jokanović, stated in 'Epoch':

> RTS, as the national and state television, is of exceptional importance. It cannot, at this time of pressure and genocide against the Serbian people and the denial of their basic national and human rights, be a-national or refuse to protect the vital national interest ... In the various news departments, there are people who arrived at various periods, none of whom have left. Belgrade Radio and Television, for instance, was more Yugoslav than representative of Belgrade and Serbia. This is also the case with a number of papers and magazines. In these media there are people who actually work against Serbia. These are the Serbs of Ante [Marković], who do harm, create bad relations and fight among themselves, all of which weakens these media houses and prevents them from organizing themselves properly. (I, 407, March 1992: 4)

This statement, coming from a key figure in the government-RTS relationship, vindicated not only several waves of sackings of unreliable editors and journalists, but also the drastic about-face in editorial policy. Previous insistence on national agendas or the inordinate broaching of taboos and myth which had slipped through disguised as everyday reporting on events or speeches by politicians, now became editorial strategy. The masks were off. It is a paradox that this took place just as the SPS and Slobodan Milošević were doing their utmost to convince the public at home and abroad that they supported the preservation of Yugoslavia. Their actions, which had quite a lot to do with the media, proved otherwise.

The outbreak of war just before the passing of the new law on radio and television obviously helped the Serbian authorities to introduce censorship into RTS. Programmes, especially news and current affairs, were prepared in accordance with the rules of war propaganda. Radio and television journalists in the war zones reported on the endangered Serbian people, Serb refugees, torn-down Serb houses, atrocities inflicted on the Serb nation. No one mentioned the killing of Croats and Muslims, their refugees and orphans, the atrocities committed against them or their property. These details were mentioned only when there was friction between Croats and Muslims, when it suited those who pulled the strings of war to appear for a moment to be giving support to one side or the other.

The 'FEDOR 1991' Festival, referred to above, bears witness to the use of radio writers for political ends. A well-known reporter on Radio Belgrade's First Channel, Radovan Brankov, in his travelogue 'The Dead are There', as Raško V. Jovanović notes, used 'many sound effects recorded on the ground, and numerous interviews revealing the appalling ferocity of the fighting and reprisals against the innocent population. The absurdity of the war in the areas around Dalj and Knin comes through in countless testimonies by victims but at the same time strengthens the fighters' conviction that the rabid spectre of fascism has to be stopped' (R. V. Jovanović 1992: 55). The author, of course, speaks only of the sufferings of the Serb people and the hopes of the Serb fighters. Jovanović, a radio critic, notes in the same article that this travelogue referred to the Croat intention of 'bleeding the Serbs to death', showing a vast number of waiting bottles by way of evidence!

Jovanović also describes a Belgrade Radio Channel Two report, 'Monument', by Milica Ostojić Pušara. The report describes 'clean-up operations' in a Serb village in Hercegovina during World War II in which a priest, Radojica Perišić, first led the uprising against the occupying forces. 'When Broz got news of this', Jovanović relates, 'he sent Petar Drapšin and his soldiers, who divided the rebels into Partisans and Chetniks and sparked off a fratricidal war, to the delight of the Muslims' (ibid.: 56). 'Echoes from the Pit' by Bojan Lazović and Nada Zamfirović of Radio Novi Sad, shown at the FEDOR Festival, 'draws a parallel between the victims of World

War II and current events ... Remembrance of the horrors of the 1941–1945 war is blended with events of this year as the sufferings of not only one family but of a village and several others' (ibid.: 56). A documentary by Nenad Purić called 'The docile head shall not be cut off by the sabre' from the same radio festival (ibid.: 58), also grafts the past on to the present, accompanied by the inevitable revival of memories of the slaughter of innocent Serbs by the Ustasha.

The national interest, as seen by current policy in Serbia, or rather how to make use of it for one's own interests, affected all departments in RTS. Music by non-Serb composers or performers from other republics (whether folk, light or classical) was very quickly banned. Religion became increasingly present; no Orthodox feast day was allowed to pass without a mention, accompanied by an extensive report on how it was celebrated. For the major holidays of Christmas and Easter, entire church ceremonies were broadcast live. Representatives of the Serbian Orthodox Church began to invade not only RTS programmes but also the departments.

RTS used the period following the new Radio Television Law and the outbreak of war quite openly to bring about the dream of a Greater Serbia. This is evident from programmes especially made to propagate this idea, while criticizing any who were opposed to it or who were seen as insufficiently supportive. On 9 June 1992, an RTS First Channel programme invited Dr. Manojlo Bročić, Academy (SANU) member Mihailo Marković, Brana Crnčević, Dr. Vojislav Šešelj and Gavro Perazic. Criticizing a number of his academic colleagues (obviously Matija Becković and others) who were at that moment critical of the Serbian government, Marković said:

> The SANU Memorandum laid the groundwork for all that is happening now, foreseeing as it did the coming together of all Serbs from Croatia, Bosnia-Hercegovina and the ethnic borders, thus enabling a clash with the creators of the new world order ... That's why these academics who are now members of DEPOS have no moral right to oppose the politics they themselves have created, and which Milosevic is carrying out by general consensus... Haven't some opposition parties who declare borders everywhere they find Serbian bones, now asked that the president who implemented this policy should resign on moral grounds?

The Language of Hatred, a book published in late 1994 by the Anti-War Action Centre, contains a study carried out in 1992 and 1993. This notes many examples of stereotype projection in which

Serbs are inevitably the victims, while Croats and Muslims are villains who often kill 'for religious reasons'. The following examples are taken from the book.

On 31 July 1992, Belgrade Television 'broadcast a report from Bratunac on the slaughter of 114 Serbs, said by the reporter to have been carried out "in the name of Allah"... In a weekly main news programme from the Priština studio on 2 August, a reporter from Hercegovina announced that "Croatian and Muslim forces want to exterminate all that is Serb in these parts"' (B. Mihajlović 1994: 22). The author of this section tof the 'Language of Hatred', Branka Mihajlović, says that RTS did not report truthfully on the Bosnian Serb blockade and shelling of Sarajevo; on the other hand, the rhetoric of war propaganda was enriched with terms such as 'the knights of the Jihad', for example, or 'Tudman's and Alia's warriors', or 'The green berets, the HOS-ites and those from the Sandzak withdrew to Goražde where they are committing evil against the Serbs' (ibid.). The script also recalls a clip shown on Belgrade TV at the time, which called on Hercegovina refugees to join their brothers in battle. The clip used the national anthem of the Kingdom of Yugoslavia, '*Bože Pravde*' ('Oh God of Justice') over a picture of Serb fighters in action. Branka Mihajlović also notes that RTS was silent on the expulsion of ethnic Croats from the Vojvodina village of Hrtkovci, and when on 20 August a report was broadcast of this case, none of the minority affected were approached for their opinion, an interview with those suspected of ethnic cleansing being shown instead.

Also in *Language of Hate*, Lola Stamenković notes examples of propaganda on Radio Belgrade which include the following.

'The Patriotic Union of Zavidovići calls on all Serbs to "defend" this town because it "has always been and will remain Serb"' (prime-time news, 19 February 1993) (L. Stamenković, 1994: 35); 'Maslenica must fall even if it means going through Zagreb' (statement by 'Captain Dragan' to a correspondent from Knin, 23 March 1993) (ibid.); 'The Serb people are a galactic nation who will, like Nikola Tesla, gather all just people together' (interview with the painter Milić Stanković on Radio Belgrade, 10 April 1993) (ibid.); 'The Serbs are victims of political vindictiveness of the German-Catholic alliance. Serbs are not only being killed by enemies in Bosnia, but by the sledgehammers wielded by the great powers' (prime-time news, 22 March 1993, interview with Dr. Radovan Karadžić) (ibid.).

In a meticulous analysis of two television stations, RTS and the independent Studio B, during the election campaign of 1992,

Snježana Milivojević and Jovanka Matić point to details of that are of interest in the present research. Their study *Screening the Elections* reveals the technique of manipulatively placing information and an arbitrary and deliberate emphasis on certain events, combined with the over-use of certain ideas. The authors confirm the fact that in the period under review, 72.4 per cent of the prime-time TV news programme 'Dnevnik' was actually voice-overs by newsreaders, reporters or anchorpersons. 'The structure of evening news broadcasts shows the importance of the interpretative over the factual in the RTS main news programme, 'Dnevnik' ... RTS-speak is based much less on reporting facts than on transmitting interpretations' (S. Milivojević and J. Matić 1993: 29).

Propaganda techniques of this kind produced programmes in which the struggle of the Bosnian Serbs was 'markedly designated as just'. They were 'fighting for freedom', 'defending' and 'protecting' their 'homes, wives and children', and preserving their 'native heath' (ibid.: 36). Serbs, the authors conclude, are represented solely in the role of victim, Croats and Muslims as aggressors and evildoers. In addition, RTS main news insisted on the religious character of the Muslim struggle. The authors quote a sentence from one programme: 'The Jihad and Muslims are inseparable, they are twins.' An entire arsenal of media-fomented hatred was noted in RTS news broadcasts. Croat and Muslim forces were 'malefactors', 'cut–throats', 'Ustasha', 'Islamic Ustasha', 'Mujahidin', warriors of the Jihad', 'terrorist diversionary groups', and 'Muslim extremists'. Serb soldiers were 'Serb fighters' and 'Serb defenders' (ibid.: 37).

Quotes from RTS television broadcasts point to manipulation at various levels. This chiefly meant emphasizing that Serbs were never guilty of anything, whatever the situation, while all the rest were—for no apparent reason—disposed to be hostile to them and to commit atrocities. There was very notable insistence on the innately democratic character of the Serb nation. All this added up to a manipulative twisting by the TV programme makers and representatives of the ruling party working in close co-operation with them.

At this time, Radio Belgrade, the editorial polices of which once differed from those of the Television, did not lag behind. First Channel news broadcasts yield examples of combined propaganda. In a commentary by Živojin Jerotijević in the main news of 1 December 1992, the presidential candidate standing against Milošević, Milan Panić, was described as 'a drunken sailor who roams the seas looking for foreign support for his policy'. Claiming that

on his travels Panić had belittled his political opponents in a no-
holds-barred fashion, the commentator added that 'he delighted to
the point of euphoria those circles at home and abroad whose
dream was to see Serbia confined to the *Pashaluk* of Belgrade ...'
Discrediting a presidential candidate, and thereby violating the
ground rules of behaviour by the state media during an electoral
campaign, was in this way embellished by insinuating that Panić
saw eye to eye with all enemies who would like to see Serbia reduced to a Turkish administrative district. A traumatic memory
from the past was projected onto the present for obvious political
reasons, while providing indirect support to the existing president.

In 'War Chronicle', also on Radio Belgrade's Channel One main
news, expressions already mentioned occurred, such as 'Muslim
armed forces and their mercenaries, Muslim knights of the Jihad'
'an Ustasha-Muslim breakthrough' (Milivoje Savić), and 'armed
provocation by Croat-Muslim warriors' (a newsreader). An interesting detail here confirms that reporters were frequently unable to
check the real state of affairs for themselves but accepted information served up to them. Vlado Trišić, reporting from Mt. Majevica,
in a short sound-bite quoted 'competent military bodies' three
times as his source.

The choice of sound material recorded on location for use in
broadcasts was always accompanied by support for the ruling
party and Slobodan Milosevic. This was taken care of both by reporters and editors. Visits by Slobodan Milošević to places in Serbia
during the election campaign, formally unconnected to promotion
of either the party or himself, were charged with nationalism. In a
main radio news broadcast on 15 December 1992, there are inserts
in which Milošević strongly asserts the state and national interests
'on account of which we cannot agree to abandon the defence of
freedom and democracy in our country or to abandon defence of
the interests of all the people of Serbia and the entire Serb nation ...
Today, various capitals of who-knows-where throughout the world
would like to tell us how we should behave in our own country.
We shall behave as we wish in our own country, as free people,
and not in accordance with the dictates of politicians from who-
knows-where.' The same report contains a sound-bite from Milošević's speech following the laying of a wreath at a monument to
the heroes of Kosovo at Kruševac: 'I would like to tell you here, at
this monument to the heroes of Kosovo, that Serbia will not yield.
Serbia throughout its history has placed all of Europe in its debt by
its struggle against the conqueror, since in fighting for its own
freedom, it protected those countries who now dispute these same

rights of our Republic and our nation ... You can rest assured and be convinced that we have all the prerequisites for successful, free, democratic, economic and cultural development and that we will see this development through, all of us together.' Thus, 'capitals of who-knows-where' and 'politicians from who-knows-where' were not invented by journalists, but by the president of the Republic in person. The idea that all of Europe was indebted to Serbia and now returned this by injustice, and particularly the idea of Serbia's ability to make progress–despite the blockade–in democratic, economic and cultural development, as stated by its highest leader and carefully chosen and placed by those in the media, had no other source on which to call.

The political circumstances in Serbia, their influence on events and on RTS editorial policy, are indissolubly linked. Parallel to the entrenchment of the authority of the SPS and Slobodan Milošević, there was growing repression of RTS journalists who did not want to be the instruments of war propaganda, while those who concurred were increasingly called upon to make a contribution. The abuse of history and tradition, and of religious and national feeling also grew.

On 11 January 1993, some eleven thousand RTS employees were sent home on enforced leave. Among them were all programme staff, engineers, technicians and trade union activists who had resisted repression and warmongering. Dozens of the most distinguished and creative personalities, international award winners, were removed from radio and television. The most popular programmes were turned into a means of propaganda. This was particularly true of the prime-time news and TV programmes such as 'ZIP', radio programmes such as 'Another Argument' or 'Sunday at Ten' on the First Channel, 'Page One', 'No one like Me' and 'Green Megahertz' on the Second Channel.

The newly promoted editors and programme hosts promptly showed their loyalty to an editorial policy tailored to 'the national interest'. Host and editor Dobrica Miličević, in an introduction to 'Sunday at Ten', said: 'Our nation tends to make mistakes and finds it hard to rid itself of them. It would be hard to find another people who have experienced a bloodier historical confirmation of the hostility of certain nations towards our own, and here we are again, caught unawares and off our guard by their latest reprisals.' Setting aside the author's poor attempt at style–an unimportant consideration at the time–the intention is clearly to point out that the struggle of the Serbs in Croatia and Bosnia was not only justified, but that the Serbs were not as well prepared for it as they should have been in view of their historical experience. The speaker calls Croats fighting Serbs in the Knin krajina 'Ustasha'. An on-the-spot report by Spomenka Deretić, a long-time journalist from the cultural department, might serve as an insert in an encyclopaedia of this kind of quasi-journalism: 'They were ten to one and this, unfortunately, is no epic metaphor. The Ustasha set on fire, and for the first two days overran, Ravna Kotara. What I saw and heard from the poor Serb refugees will haunt me like the whistle of a shell, like the smell of burning Serb villages, or the weeping of children and keening of women. Milja from Islam Grčki told me that she is sorrier about the burning of the Janković Stojan tower and the destroyed church of St. George than for her own house. Her three-year-old Rade sobs: "Daddy, don't let the Ustasha get me". In Smoković, the Ustasha hanged Serb children from the olive trees—from olive trees!' The horrors of war, which undoubtedly occurred, are again seen only from the point of view of the Serb nation, reported without any reliable data, inflated by personal impression, epic pathos and heightened emotion into an interpretative report.

As part of the defence of 'patriotic' journalism and current policy, RTS programmes regularly denounced and attacked opponents of such policy and the independent media. The newsreader on Belgrade TV of 27 May read: 'In Belgrade, for the first time since the war began, so-called peace-lovers are carrying black mourning streamers through the streets. The international media competes in anti-Serb hysteria. At home, they are joined by Belgrade papers such as *Borba* and *Vreme*.' The headlines preceding the news projected 'the truth' which it was hoped would be accepted without a murmur. Unfortunately, it is a fact that the majority of average viewers did indeed accept these messages from the lips of state TV announcers.

Even news that had nothing to do with the war situation was overshadowed by the trauma of national division. An air disaster that killed over a hundred citizens of Serbia and Yugoslavia was reported ten minutes into TV Belgrade news on 21 November 1993. The reason for this treatment was clear: the dead were Kosovo Albanians.

Not only news and current affairs were used at this time to abuse tradition. The new wave of 'spirituality' and the stoking of national feeling in those in whom it appeared to be lacking, occurred in programmes which at first sight appeared to be quite benign. 'A Glass of Water from the Spring', a series in which Serbian folk music was presented in a knowledgeable and careful manner, began to appear in a somewhat ambivalent atmosphere. One programme on 21 February 1994, showed amateurs and professional folk singers competing in what looked like a typical village celebration. Children with Serbian caps skipped about and chattered, women spun, the men engaged in manly conversation. The scene was hung with icons, images of the saints, sugar hearts. In the centre of the action was a group of men, some of whom were in battle fatigues, singing hunting songs.

The crowning glory of aggressive propaganda on RTS TV was a series called 'Horoscope', introduced by a former actress, turned seer and 'astrologer', Milja Vujanović, on the Third Channel. Once a week for several months at peak viewing time, in programmes which lasted for forty-five minutes to an hour, Ms Vujanović harnessed her powers as a seer in the struggle of Serbs against the whole world. Calling on various horoscopes, the Bible and historical events, the prophetess produced 'indisputable evidence' of the corruption of Europe and the world and their inevitable doom. 'What lies ahead for a Europe gone mad and for its Pharisees, writers and journalists?' she wondered during the 8 March 1994 programme. Journalists were particularly targeted for transgressing the Ninth Commandment; they should think about where they would live when one day 'it all comes out in the open'. On 14 June the same year, Milja Vujanović spoke of 'the Serbs who often defended the Slovene, Croatian and Macedonian borders, so they might defend their own', adding that 'war is inevitable, it is a normal occurrence. By war is territory possessed and borders defined ...' Like other forms of war propaganda, this was removed from the TV screens when it had outrun its usefulness, that is, in late 1994, when the Serbian political leadership decided to initiate a policy of peace.

A large broadcasting system such as RTS, like RTB before it, because of its range and influence, has been of tremendous importance in social upheaval in Yugoslavia and Serbia for the past decade and a half. The obverse is also true. All that happened in society was reflected in the relationships existing inside this huge organization and, even more importantly, through its public function. Therefore, a more detailed study of the internal processes within the various departments and the external influences reaching them would be needed to understand why certain programmes were put before the public at certain times.

From the early 1980s to just before the second half of the 1990s, the status, organization and staffing of state radio and television, particularly in terms of programming, underwent changes which, in the prevailing environment, enabled the free discussion of the taboos and traumas of the past. These issues would have been broached even if Yugoslavia had not collapsed. A much more difficult question to answer is what came first, and whether the opening up of these taboos contributed, directly or indirectly, to the disintegration of the country.

There is sufficient evidence argument to claim that it was the press rather than the electronic media which was responsible for the monstrous fashion in which this was done. However, in the initial period, particularly from 1987 on, radio and television as the transmitters rather than sources of nationalist politics brought the paranoia of threat, danger and revenge together with the need for a novel historical argumentation into every household. As soon as the war began, however, the state radio and television, RTS, surpassed the printed media both in covering up the truth about events in the zones of escalation and in encouraging the militant mood.

When state coercion and repression finally broke down the resistance of reason, which had certainly existed in RTS, the latter began to function as a one-track, orchestrated broadcasting station, in which the traumas of the past had no incidental role. On the contrary, their use and abuse served to build a propaganda strategy. The last chance was lost for democratic processes already initiated to be reflected in their programmes, or for creative and talented professionals to approach issues now covered by the mould of time. The intentions of professional journalists to take on this work in a serious and constructive way were shattered by the intent of political power centres to use the past in accordance with their own views of the present and future. The effects were devastating and socially damaging insofar as the media produced fresh trauma, from which an entire generation will find it difficult to recover.

The Nation: Victim and Vengeance

ZORAN M. MARKOVIĆ

This chapter reviews the attitude of some of the less serious Serbian magazines on the topic 'Serbia as victim', from September 1987 to September 1991. Although magazines do not essentially differ from the rest of the printed media they have some distinguishing characteristics. Apart from differences of style, the breadth of content makes them different from the news and political press. Their aim is to inform and entertain, to popularize, shock and incite to action, something they achieve through writing on a wide range of issues in a style acceptable to a wide circle of readers.

In this discussion three magazines have been taken as representative: *Duga, Ilustrovana Politika* and *TV Novosti*[1]. These are published by three different publishers: BIGZ, Politika and Borba. They are read by a wide range of social classes: *Duga* mostly by the upper and middle classes, *Ilustrovana Politika* by the middle class and *TV Novosti* by the middle and lower classes. The style of journalism also differs, *Duga* going in for 'historical journalism', *Ilustrovana Politika* tending towards a more literary style, while *TV Novosti* aims to entertain the masses.

In striving to please their consumers, magazines produce their own concept of reality and their own value system; they also tend to ideologize their subject matter. These tendencies are immanent but not completely autonomous. They are, to a major extent, the reflection of prevailing values, which is why any analysis of the press is also an analysis of society.

The period from 1987 to 1991 was of enormous importance for Yugoslav society. It was a time when nationalism came to dominate all spheres of life. Within this process, a key indicator is the body of writing on Serbs as victims. Insistence on looming danger, exploitation and the suffering and hardship of the nation is always aimed at mobilizing it and making it homogeneous, the overall goal being that the political elite 'riding the wave' should take over. It is of no importance whether or not facts speak differently, as examples are provided to show that only one side is in the right. There is no understanding for the rejection of one's own position, while the opposite position is aggressively negated. The insulted tone that goes with this lack of understanding is almost expected and in fact forms part of the ritual. When the means of mass communication become enmeshed in this game, they break the rule that facts are sacred. It is unavoidable that in this mode of journalism, the truth is first to be sacrificed. If in a society in conflict, and a multinational one at that, there is understanding only for one side while the other is seen as the guilty party or enemy, then this kind of journalism is no different from what the politicians are doing and becomes, in fact, an active element in the conflict.

Perhaps the most significant characteristic bred by the Balkan region is the eternal play of minority and majority, victims and executioners. This tragic game, in which the roles of minority and majority are endlessly interchangeable, appearing and reappearing in various combinations and coalitions the logic of which is hard to fathom, creates an atmosphere of insecurity in which all can be victims. A negative experience by a minority warns of the fatality of history repeating itself following the principle: the fact that we are paranoid does not mean we are not being persecuted.

Tito's post-war attempt at solving the national question by forgiving and forgetting while forbidding the settling of historical accounts was, apart from the occasional dissonant note, fairly successful. It was nonetheless incapable of preventing the eruption of reawakened national dissatisfaction from the moment when the supreme authority ceased to exist and the political elite of the various republics began to take power. It may be that part of the blame for the scale of the Balkan tragedy in the 1990s lies in the choking off of these valves of discontent.

The main reason for the non-release of tension lies in the dominant model of communications in Yugoslav society from World War II onwards.[2] This model, which served a so-called non-conflict society (a society of 'harmony') could not adequately respond to new challenges.

Early troubles (1987–1988)

Although the first awakenings of nationalism go back to 1986, it was articulated in clearly political terms only at the Eighth Session of the Central Committee of the Serbian Socialist Party (23 and 24

September 1987). The pivotal disagreement at this meeting was between the faction led by Slobodan Milošević (who had already experienced the intoxicating scent of populism during his appearance at Kosovo polje in April that year) and the line followed by Ivan Stambolić, who sought the use of 'legal methods' and pointed to the danger of making use of Serb nationalism. The faction which wanted a 'fast solution' to the Kosovo problem won.

The magazines faithfully monitored political events in Serbia, if not always with total consistency. *Duga*, for example, was unusually ambivalent. On the one hand, it had contributors such as Brana Crnčević, who ran a feature called 'Serb Business', and Dragoš Kalajić, whose openly racist theories were frequently defended by the editors; while on the other hand it printed Croatian writers such as Igor Mandić and Miljenko Smoje.

The *Ilustrovana Politika* of the time dealt with subjects through the prism of socialist self-management, with the idea of covering the south-east of the country (Bosnia-Hercegovina and especially Macedonia in addition to Serbia and Montenegro).

TV Novosti tried to retain its Yugoslav character, thus 'brotherhood and unity' was the paper's ideology, which did not, however, apply to Kosovo Albanians.

Typical articles of this period described the Serbs as victims, whether between the lines, in parable form or in coy semi-concealment. Perhaps the following extract from Rajko Djurdjević's 'What became of the Nemanjić's Treasure?' on the danger to Serb monasteries and archaeological sites such as Sopoćani, Djurdjevi stupovi, Petrova crkva, Pazarište and Gradina as a result of the construction of a fish-farm and a rubbish dump may help to illustrate this. The article concludes:

> There is no pressure ... No one is bothered even by the first day of Ramadan... No one considers it a rebuke when here and there people say aloud at the workplace that 'this series on Vuk [Karadžić] is silly, who needs it after all this time', no one complains that there are no pork scratchings to be found in factory canteens or pork in the town's butcher shops ... No one criticizes aloud the fact that the entire Old Quarter of Novi Pazar has only one retail outlet under a Serb name ... No, no one here criticizes the fact that there is not a single letter of Cyrillic to be seen in the town except in the sign 'Museum' engraved over the door. (*Duga*, No. 362, 9–22 January 1988)

Brana Crnčević explained the Serb position in his feature 'Serb Business': 'In the struggle for the most secure position in civilization in Yugoslavia, my dear Petronije, the backward south hardly dares to raise its voice (always timid and entreating, sometimes a touch hysterical and temperamental as becomes the backward southerners) against the developed north' (*Duga*, No. 359, 28 November–11 December 1987).

The style of *Ilustrovana Politika* differed in several respects from *Duga*'s dashing open-and-closed style. Its prevailing subject was Kosovo, usually seen through some individual tragedy. Jevrem Damnjanović wrote movingly of a mother whose son had been killed by Albanians before her eyes.

> 'Ah, my own darling,' a deep, painful sigh was wrenched from her. 'Two of them held you while a third hit you on the head with a stick. I ran up and they came at me with their stick, cursing my Serbian mother. My neighbour Vida Živanović ran up pleading: "Please, for God's sake, don't! Let him go." Then Ferat, may he be cursed for all time, knelt on you and pulled out his gun. I threw myself forward to cover you and protect you but the gun went off. They got you in the heart. If that criminal had aimed next to your heart, maybe you would have lived. Maybe, my Daša, you would have said something to your mother ...' (*IP*, No. 1543, 31 May 1988)

Another subject in *Ilustrovana Politika* which warily touched on the danger threatening the Serbs, was the use of the Cyrillic alphabet.

An article by Ljiljana Biničanin contains a statement by Professor Djordje Trifunović: 'I do not want to go into how other nations here would feel if their alphabet were to be suppressed, but I think this tolerance of ours is a reflection of our national broadmindedness. And this is no small matter, because this is the Serb nation which has suffered most on account of this very alphabet' (*IP*, No. 1512, 27 October 1987).

Almost every issue of *TV Novosti* at the time contained an article on Kosovo. Given the editors' concentration on the world of entertainment, it seemed something of an anachronism, a sort of obligation. In the well-known case of Fadil Hodza, formerly a high ranking Kosovo official, regarding a statement made by him in 1986 (that 'Albanian women do not let themselves be raped, but Serbian and other women are sympathetic to it') and not made public, alas, until 1987, Predrag Živančević writes of a gathering of Kosovo women:

> The archaic response of 'Freedom to the people!' which made the rafters ring in the Hall of Culture in Kosovo Polje contained the entire depth-charge of deep bitterness aroused in the Serb and Monte-

negrin women of Kosovo–Metohija by two indirect causes: the recently published statement by Fadil Hodza ... as the basic motive and an attempt by a group of Albanian boys to rape H. F., a Serb minor, in the Vuk Karadžić School in Pristina (together with statements by the authorities on the case); these two incidents represented the final drop in their cup of bitterness. (*TVN*, No. 1191, 23 October 1987)

Articles which 'liberated' Serbian music were particularly popular in this paper. Predrag Živančević in 'Politically Unsuitable Songs' writes:

The night between 13 and 14 January [Serbian Orthodox New Year] was long the cause of particular excitement; it gave rise to special 'directives' and produced a special kind of behaviour. We well remember the authorized comrades in their long leather coats [secret police], energetically and intently monitoring the behaviour of the few guests of the few city cafés, while the café orchestras carried on, under orders not to play a single Serbian dance number that night. (*TVN*, No. 1209, 26 February 1988)

In another article, Dragan Damjanović points to a kind of symmetry which is to the detriment of Serbs:

Last weekend in Peć, three young Serb girls were attacked. The young criminal took out a knife and threatened and abused them, saying he would, if need be, cut their throats. Somewhat later, the attacker was apprehended and brought before a magistrate who sentenced him to fifteen days. At the other end of Kosovo that same afternoon, a magistrate in Uroševac was called from home to preside at the case of Nedeljko Jelić (21), a worker ... who had been singing a song about Vojvoda Sindjelić. The Uroševac magistrate, in contrast to his colleague in Peć, was harsher: despite the fact that some witnesses claimed that he had not sung the song at all, Jelić was sentenced to forty days, to begin immediately. (*TVN*, No. 1214, 1 April 1988)

The end of this period in Serb magazines was characterized by Brana Crnčević at a round table with the Ljubljana *Teleks* and Belgrade *Duga*:

As neither you nor we have a free press as yet and restricted as we are by current laws against causing public unrest, we in the papers write by touch, trying to correspond with one another between the lines. Writing between the lines is recommendable in one language, but difficult in two. What we write between the lines to the Slovenes and they to us, only a small number of people understand. Our comrades from Croatia are not here to make up the threesome, but we can simply tell one another what we think and see if some of those ideas might be worth something. For I do not believe that Yugoslavia, in the state it is in now, is capable of taking from its citizens the right to speak and of telling them to be quiet. They have been quiet for too long; they have been talking rubbish for too long. So if we want the truth, let's run this conversation differently. (*Duga*, No. 365, 20 February–4 March 1988)

The conversation did indeed start to run on different lines. A media war broke out.

Media war–Revealing 'the truth' (1988–1990)

The time for revealing 'the truth' began in the first half of 1988. The salient characteristic of this period was the increasingly open way in which various 'cases' became political. The public was faced day after day with shocking 'truths'. Before this, scandalous affairs (known as 'cases') had not been over-used to make political hay, and where 'excesses' of the kind had occurred, editors would restrict these tendencies. This, of course, was not autonomous. A good example was the 'Keljmendi case'[an incident in which a recruit of Albanian nationality killed six recruits of Serbian nationality]. When the massacre at the Paracin barracks began to be used to manipulate national feelings and incite retaliation, the reaction which followed helped to cool passions. Ilija Rapaić, editor-in-chief of *Duga,* for instance, stood up in an editorial against the Serbian desire for vengeance, the neighbourhood boycott of the Kelmendi family, demands from the Prizren Veterans' Association that they should be ejected from their home and Kelmendi's sister expelled from the Socialist Youth and from school, pointing out that the casualties were not only Serbs but 'the youth of Yugoslavia' (*Duga*, No. 354, 19 September–2 October 1987).

However, by the middle of 1988, as the battle of the Serbian political leadership to change Serbia's Constitution and place it on a more equal footing in the Federation was in full swing—something which had taken place partly thanks to the 'meetings of truth'—politicization was total. A no-holds-barred media war broke out. Certain journalists were given the task of monitoring the position of Serbs outside Serbia. A very organized, if sometimes hysterical, wail went up over the general danger threatening Serbs.

Kosovo continued to be the predominant issue, but there was also the story of the exploitation of Serbia by Slovenia and Croatia, and the laying of charges at the Ustasha's door of genocide against Serbs in World War II.

One journalist who dealt mainly with Kosovo was Milisav Milić, RTV Belgrade's chief correspondent in Priština. In addition to his regular work, he managed to publish occasional articles in magazines, while offering his services to other reporters who came to Kosovo. His style was very recognizable, his articles full of information on the family and other ties of Albanian offenders. Here is a sample from *Duga*:

> Stanojlo Mihajlović was wounded in Novo Selo (municipality of Kosovska Vitina). He was shot by Hisen Aljiu from the village of Trpeza, grandson of Hise Trpeza, the notorious enemy of the people, leader of the emigrant Albanian extremists in Chicago ... Svetozar Stojankić died of a broken heart when he saw fifty-six trees cut down and his wheat trampled on. This act of vandalism was perpetrated by the Behluli brothers. They are related to the Hodža Hacif Behluli, who bought up all the Serb houses in one street in Gušnica ... (*Duga*, No. 370, 30 April–13 May 1988).

The Milić mind-set resembles the militant nationalist mind-set among the Serbs. Asked in an interview with *TV Novosti* how he had arrived at the idea of arming himself, Milisav Milić replied:

> Here's how: I'm fifty years old and I've never borne arms. I was warned by the police, however, not to go into chaotic situations such as demonstrations and other street unrest. I respected the suggestion and my entire life began to be reduced to apartment–car–studio. One day I simply got bored living like that. It was a fine day and I went out into the street. A man with a child and a woman were coming towards me. He was the sort of man of whom you would say at first glance that he didn't possess a radio, never mind a television set. He seemed—if you'll excuse the expression—to belong to the lower classes, a man you would never imagine as seeing me as the object of his hatred. However, I heard him say to his wife as he passed by: 'Cure ceni, kopli skau' (See that dog, that Serb bastard). That very moment I went back to the studio and asked the authorities for a weapon. I thought: if I'm a dog and a Serb bastard to a man like that, what must those who look better than he does think of me? I was devastated by this discovery. (*TVN*, No. 1313, 23 February 1990)

Reaching for a weapon in frustrating situations was later to become the rule.

Kosovo is in any case fertile ground for all sorts of manipulation and abuse in the interests of propaganda. An article by Rajko Djurdjević, called 'They burn, rape, heat, stone, destroy, break, desecrate', written following the attempted rape of the Abbess of Gračanica Monastery, Tatjana Todorović, by a policeman, Ahmet Latifi, was accompanied by a photograph of a nun holding a rifle. Underneath was written: 'Musutište: Abbess Ilirija guards the holy places, carabine in hand' (*Duga*, No. 380,17-30 September 1988). The manipulation of religious persons is obvious.

The Kosovo question was the cause of conflict among the elite in the republics. Milošević's taking power with the help of 'meetings of truth' worried the other members of the federation. The altercation with the Slovenes (and Croats) was merciless. In an interview with *TV Novosti*, actor Bata Živojinović said: 'A Slovenian representative went to Kosovo and says he saw what the situation was. Where did you see it from? Through a window? From a car? From a plane? Where did you see it?'(*TVN*, No. 1240, 30 September, 1998). Later in the same interview his rhetorical scepticism suddenly collapsed when he talked of the meetings in Serbia:

> We are not such a primitive people that we have to resort to guns and knives. Why, there wasn't as much as a glass broken at any of these gatherings. Look at these young politicians, all scientists, all doctors, these are well-versed people, people who don't pull knives, people who don't shoot in parliament. Let the people gather, why shouldn't they when they don't have anything else?
> 'You went to the meetings?'
> No, but it's just as if I did... (Ibid.)

This shows intolerance of other peoples' opinions and how standards suddenly change when speaking of one's own environment. On a broader scale, this model demonstrates how in this community, only *I* may concern myself with internal affairs: any other opinion is an insult.

The economic exploitation outlined in the Memorandum of the SANU, that is, the inequality and backwardness of Serbia within the SFRJ, was now plainly given form in magazines. While earlier these accusations tended to be blurred they were now out in the open. Zoran Nikodijević and Rade Grujić wrote:

> This high GNP, high efficiency of investments, high rate of employment, high hard currency exports, high personal incomes, high standards, people's high cultural and political level ... Are the Slovenes really doing that well? And why are they doing so well? The answer

to this question for many outside Slovenia looks perfectly simple: The Slovenes are doing well because the others are not! That is, Slovenia is making intelligent use of all the illogicality in economic life—to put it simply. (*Duga*, No. 367, 19 March–1 April 1988)

Milorad Vučelić resorted to statistics:

In the past year, let's say, Serbia was the only republic to record an increase in the volume of production; even so, at the end of the financial year it was found to have made the greatest losses. At least half of these were due to cheap electrical energy (about 560 billion dinars) which served as the basis of production in other republics. Serbia, like the others, although underdeveloped itself, earmarked around 72 per cent of its own earnings for the underdeveloped regions ... The prices of industrial products were 0.5 per cent lower in Serbia than the Yugoslav average, while in Slovenia they were higher by 19.4 per cent ... If we add to all this various abnormalities to do with exports, problems with food production and the way Serbia is treated within the Federation, it is completely obvious that over the past decades there has been a systematic and systemic exploitation of Serbia. (*Duga*, No. 397, 13–19 May 1989)

Having 'revealed' economic exploitation by Slovenia, it was now the turn of Slovenian chauvinism. The victims were southerners. In an introduction to a description of the trial of Janez Janša (and the overall situation in Slovenia) Jovan Antonijević said: 'In public places there are more and more incomprehensible graffiti. One urging that "Serbs [should be hung from] the willows" was discovered in a firm in Kranj (*IP*, No. 1547, 28 June 1988).

The favourite story at this time was the 'discovery' of Serb victims of genocide. For Brana Crnčević it became a *leitmotiv*: 'The people of Srem, Banat and Bačka were heroes a hundred times over. They were in the NDH (they knew the way to Jasenovac and other concentration camps) ... The victims from across the Danube had no reason and no place to hide. Those who live north of the Danube know better than others how much the Serb nation has been persecuted just for being Serb' (*Duga*, No. 376, 23 July–5 August 1988). 'The number of dead Serbs (in theory) is reduced in order to prove to anyone interested: you are not really killed, tortured and victimized as much as all that. The number of executioners who took part in the genocide is linked to the number of victims; if there are fewer victims, the number of executioners is automatically reduced' (*Duga*, No. 396, 29 April–12 May 1989). Counting the dead became a national pastime. The monk Atanasije

Jevtić, writer of the book *From Kosovo to Doomsday,* in an interview with *Duga* said: 'What hurt most was the disowning of our innocent victims, who number a million. When our guts were spilled in Kosovo and Metohija they sneered at the suffering of our nation, clinching political deals and bargains over it; these people had to have it thrust under their noses, as the saying goes. Or, as Slobodan Milošević said: "They humiliated a proud nation". Thanks should go to Milošević for being among the first to realize this' (*Duga,* No. 403, 5–18 August 1989).

Day after day, more Serb killing-fields and the lack of a proper attitude towards them were busily 'revealed'. Snežana Milošević, in an article citing the Croat source 'We shall remove and exterminate the Serb people', wrote:

> At Donja Gradina in Bosnia-Hercegovina, part of the commemoration area where from Janurary 1942 to April 1945 over 360,000 victims were killed, nothing whatsoever is marked. At Stara Gradiška, where tens of thousands of camp inmates were liquidated, there is a playing field of the local reformatory and a development of holiday homes! Seeing all this three years ago, a delegation of the Serbian Academy of Arts and Sciences stated with bitterness that whereas in the rest of Europe all the large concentration camps had been preserved and reconstructed, the worst of them all—Jasenovac—had been turned into a tourist venue on the Sava. So everything has been done to wipe out the memory of hundreds of thousands of innocent people, so villainously killed. (*IP,* No. 1570, 6 December 1988)

The idea of genocide entered the public mind only with the appearance of a book called *The Vatican and Jasenovac* (1987) (Ljubomir Kljakić, *TVN,* No. 1322, 27 April 1990). Laying all the evils of this world at the door of the Catholic Church is commonplace among Serb nationalists. In an interview with *Ilustrovana Politika,* Milan Bulajić clarifies the connection: 'There is no doubt that the Ustasha were too few in number to carry out all this if they had not been backed by a powerful organization such as the Catholic Church, who instigated the ideology of a "religiously pure area" in the battle for domination over the Orthodox "schismatics". The Catholic Church today, too, identifies with the Croat nation, representing itself as the "Catholic Church of the Croats"' (*IP,* No. 1578, 31 January 1989).

Yugoslav magazines very rarely showed any consideration for victims of other nationalities. Predrag Živancević wrote of the victims among the Albanian demonstrators of March 1989 in Dečani: 'No one wanted to grasp the fact that the casualties—whether demonstrators or innocent bystanders—were nonetheless in the line of fire between the demonstrators who were attacking and the police who were defending themselves, or the fact that the general condemnation was aimed only at the consequences of these tragic events, not at what caused them. The victims are therefore incidental, the culprits—unknown!' (*TVN*, No. 1268, 14 April 1989).

The sabre rattling began in 1988. First it was local vigilantes. In the Kosovo village of Prekale, groups of this kind were organized in August 1988. But a year was to go by before the war cry went up following Milošević's speech on St. Vitus's Day at Gazimestan, when he said: 'Today, six centuries later, we are once more engaged in battles and facing battles. These are not armed conflicts, although this has still not been ruled out' (*P*, 29 June 1989).

The fomenting of 'brotherhood and unity' [as it was ironically called], began by quarrels over the constitutional status of Serbia in the Federation, and spread to include the unequal position, or even danger, in which all Serbs in Yugoslavia found themselves. There was increasing focus on the status of Serbs in Croatia. Brana Crnčević wrote: 'The Serbs in Croatia need nothing. They share a language with the Croats, and as far as the written word is concerned, they tossed and lost. That is why there are no Cyrillic newspapers or magazines' (*Duga*, No. 377, 6–20 August 1988).

The Knin krajina was 'revealed' in early 1989: 'According to some estimates, 87 per cent of Serbs live in the Knin krajina, but it is not difficult to sense that they still feel threatened as a nation'(*IP*, No. 1585, 21 March 1989).

The hot summer of 1989 was heralded by reactions to Slavica Bajan, who proposed an amendment to an amendment in the Croatian Parliament: 'The Socialist Republic of Croatia is the national state of the Croatian people and the state of other nations and nationalities who live in it.' The Croatian Constitution of the time declared Croatia to be: 'The national state of the Croatian people, the state of the Serb people in Croatia and the state of other nations and nationalities who live in it.' Even though the amendment was rejected, this was clearly a warning signal to Serbs in Croatia (and elsewhere).

Duga dedicated an issue to the Serbs in Croatia. Veljko Djurić wrote about the village of Vrana, near Biograd on the coast:

> Last summer a newly planted vineyard was destroyed. This summer the watermelons were destroyed to the last one ... Two or three months ago, unidentified persons destroyed and stole around ten irrigation generators ... Breaking down fences, blocking roads, throw-

ing rocks on house roofs and poisoning wells have became daily occurrences in this village, close to an attractive lake. All this vandalism
of private property, unrecorded up to now, at least in the civilized
western hemisphere of our country, has only one common denominator: The owners of the damaged property are all Serbs. (*Duga*, No.
404, 19 August–2 September 1989)

Dobrica Ćosić's speech concerning the arrest of Jovan Opačić,
delivered at a protest evening at 'Francuska 7', summed up all the
preoccupations of magazines in this period:

> For decades, Serbs in Socialist Croatia have not had the national
> rights they enjoyed under the Austrian Empire. They bear this as a
> misfortune sent by heaven, and we their compatriots are silent out of
> fear, indifference, self-interest ... In fact, the creation of the second
> Yugoslavia and the way in which it was constituted, ensured that nei-
> ther the genocide suffered by Serbs in Croatia, nor the anti-fascist war
> of liberation in which their blood was copiously shed, nor the declared
> programme of the Communist Party, nor the various constitutions of
> the Socialist Federative Republic of Yugoslavia, nor the last constitu-
> tional amendments, nor the latest projects for political reform of the
> existing order, nor the political programmes of the opposition parties
> now being formed only in name in Croatia, have given the Croatian
> Serbs equality of citizenship with the Croats, or even with national mi-
> norities living in Croatia—the Italians, Hungarians or Czechs.

From Starčević and Franko to Šuvar and Vrhovec, the Serbs in
Croatia have failed to acquire the rights of a politically recognized
nation. Until we clarify to ourselves why this is so, until we definitely understand what this is about, we can ask these questions:

> 'Is the destiny of Serbs in Croatia genocide in times of war, and
> discrimination and assimilation in times of socialist peace?'
> 'Is the Cyrillic alphabet and Serb tongue the same for Croats who
> consider themselves Communists and democrats as for the Ustasha?'
> 'Is it possible that the founding of the first and only Serbian cul-
> tural society in Croatia is a greater political crime in the eyes of the
> Presidency of the Socialist Republic of Croatia and the Central Com-
> mittee of the Croatian Communist Party than chauvinist orgies at the
> sports stadiums of Zagreb and Split, chauvinist violence against Serb
> children and workers at Dalmatian coastal resorts and the beating up
> of people from Belgrade on the Adriatic highway?'
> 'Is the Serbs' demand to reopen the forbidden Partisan *Prosvjeta* a
> more dangerous nationalism than the deliberate forgery by "scholars"
> and cardinals of the number of victims of Ustasha genocide, the truth
> about Jasenovac, Nova Gradiška, Hercegovina and the pits of Lika?'

Asking these questions of myself and of you, I can also point to the answer: all this is so because the predominant Croatian national ideology and politics have been historically consistent in their aims: Croatia is the homeland of the Croats; the Croat nation must be united spiritually, economically, territorially; the Croatian state must be ethnically pure, regardless of its links with, and the historical past of, its fellow tribes; it cannot have any Serb '*corpus separatum*', any politically or culturally autonomous areas. On these national-ideological postulates Croatian Communist policy is based, and under it the assimilation of Serbs has been carried out for decades. (*Duga*, No. 406, 16–29 September 1989)

Articles pointing out that the Yugoslav National Army (JNA), Serbs and the 'southerners' in general were not wanted in Slovenia became more frequent. *Ilustrovana Politika* wrote: 'An officer and his wife were attacked in Novo Mesto. He was hit on the chin by a group of young people and asked: "What are you officers doing here? You should be barred from Slovenia". In Celje, an officer was slapped and slightly injured for warning a group of youngsters not to make a racket near the building in which he lived. He was also told: "Southerners go home. We feed you. Learn Slovenian." In Ptuj, three soldiers were beaten with chains ... Threatening letters, threats over the telephone, insults because of nationality ...' (*IP*, No. 1593, 16 May 1989).

To strained relations with Croatia and Slovenia, the Serbs added Bosnia and Hercegovina. Reports from sensitive areas increased. Slobodan Reljić of *Ilustrovana politika* had the mechanics of Bosnian repression of the Serbs explained to him by an anonymous interviewee from Bratunac:

When I finished [university] and left Sarajevo it seemed that all would go well. A job was advertised and I applied. And what happens? They take a guy who graduated after me and hadn't done his military service—a Muslim. He hadn't even been working three months when he went into the army and I was employed to replace him until he came back ... However, you know, you won't find any open pressure here: harassment, rape, attacks on houses. Here everything is done quietly, through the institutions ... The people in power always work that way so that people feel they are being separated out, different. Like, Bosnia will be a Muslim country and the Serbs should go to Serbia. (*IP*, No. 1618, 7 November 1989)

TV Novosti published an article based on information from the Serbian State Security (SDB) on population movement out of Bosnia-Hercegovina: 'In the general atmosphere of Muslim nationalism, certain villages have been badly hit, such as Bosanska Crkvica, a village bordering on Bajina Bašta and entirely inhabited by Serbs who were left out of urban planning, road construction and the supply of a phone service. At the same time, Muslim villages on hilly and inaccessible terrain have been connected by road, telephone etc.' (*TVN*, No. 1298, 10 November 1989).

Vesna Mališić reported to *Duga* from East Bosnia: 'National sensitivity grows into hyper-sensitivity. Serbs are increasingly irritated by the absence of pork in the butchers' shops and of music during Ramadan at the town restaurant, the favourite gathering place of young people [Srebrenica] ... Neither is Bratunac municipality spared of nationalist quarrels and fist-fights. People still talk of the rape of a female minor and of the rapist, Hajro, who was considered normal when he applied for a job, but went to hospital instead of prison following the rape' (*Duga*, No. 410, 11–24 November 1989).

The past and present—joined in war (1990–1991)

The time of discovering 'the truth' accomplished its mission and the Serbs were now informed of their position. Even those who had thought the SFRY a rather nice place to live began to have their doubts. Media pressure would have turned even cooler heads. People adjusted to a life of semi-war. Serbs had finally realized they were the victims. All that was left was for the leader to strike his fist on the table and say: 'This can't go on!' Or as composer Enriko Josif poetically put it, illustrating the interdependence of victim and leader:

> After forty-four years of parliamentary, holy silence and the devoted exertion of his entire self in order to extract the finest possible sense out of a utopian community of fraternal nations, two voices spoke out. The first, that of the non-survivors of the bloodiest, most horrendous, most appalling, most perverted and cruel crimes of killing, slaughtering, burning, tearing limb from limb and raping, only because they were Serbs, for no other reason; in the voice of those unblemished victims, buried without ceremony. And the second voice: the speaking voice of the Serbian people and its true son, through whom with wondrous simplicity, clarity, courage and uprightness was spoken all that had lain virtuously in the heart, soul and spirit of the Serbian people. It is no accident that freedom's name is freedom or that a day is called day. (*Duga*, No. 414, 5–18 January 1990)

The most important characteristic of magazine writing between 1990 and 1991 was the connecting of the past (where the Serbs are the victims) with the present (when they awaken and rebel) and the future (which they face as avengers, heroes and conquerors).[3]

The end of 1989 and early 1990 initiated the swift fall of the Yugoslav Federation, the disintegration of the Yugoslav Communist Party, the start of multiparty politics, the new economic programme of federal premier Ante Marković, and a wave of demonstrations in Kosovo as the province exploded again. Jovan Antonijević wrote: 'Terrorism is reality in today's Kosovo—the pictures of madness and destruction so often seen in Beirut have became part of life in Kosovo. Especially at night ... militant groups of twenty-year-olds stop the rare and frightened travellers on Kosovo roads, checking their papers, harrassing and beating them, overturning and burning cars' (*IP*, No. 1631, 6 March 1990).

Kosovo at this period was used as proof that the danger threatening Serbs could be solved by armed force. Leading *TV Novosti* writer on Kosovo, Predrag Živancević, wrote: 'During the last three days which separated the chaos in Kosovo from the effective entry of mechanized units of the JNA, the Serb and Montenegrin population was forced day and night to take arms to defend itself from terrorist attacks by aggressive gangs of a Greater Albania' (*TVN*, No. 1311, 9 February 1990).

Brana Crnčević also warned of the threat to human rights in Kosovo: 'Who is against human rights? The minute the Shiptars acknowledge the human rights of Serbs in Kosovo, Serbia will be whole and democratic! It is nice and democratic to acknowledge the human rights of those who do not return the compliment. Nice and dangerous. The Serb state cannot and dare not, simply in order to please the world, enter into an adventure that would ruin the Serbs and Serbia' (*Duga*, No. 417, 17 February–2 March 1990).

As the Kosovo question was now 'solved', attention turned towards Croatia. *Ilustrovana Politika,* in a report from Benkovac, quotes the words of an anonymous 'young man with a beard':

I think that hard times are yet to come. In Kašić, everyone was up all night. It seams there was news from the village of Poličnik that they could expect a visit. We know what that means. Yesterday in Stankovac two men entered a bus: 'So, Serbs, where are you then?' they started to provoke us ... The three of us reported this to the police. They asked us for names. How could I tell them? I have a wife and two children. I travel to Šibenik every day where I work. These days no one talks to anybody. Not while working, nor during the coffee break. Everything is clear. But this time they won't surprise us that easily. Today is worse than 1971. (*IP*, No. 1638, 27 March 1990)

Duga found some Serbs who had moved from Croatia to the Belgrade suburb of Kaludjerica. Their stories tell of the impossibility of living with the Croats and they see moving to Serbia as the only alternative (*Duga*, No. 414, 5–18 January 1990).

The situation in Croatia deteriorated with the appearance on the scene of Franjo Tudjman. The first major incident took place in May 1990, described as follows by *TV Novosti*:

The news of the stabbing of Miroslav Mlinar on Saturday , May 19, at number 8 Milanko Djelanović Street, after 10 p.m., has caused consternation, anger and fear in Benkovac, Krajina and other parts of Yugoslavia. 'You see, the "Tudjman" psychosis has begun,' we were told by Zdravko Zečević, a member of the Executive Board of the Serbian Democratic Party and vice-chairman of the 'Zora' society. They're getting bold; Tudjman has put the knives into their hands. (*TVN*, No. 1326, 25 May 1990)

To *Duga*'s editor-in-chief, Ilija Rapaić, the appearance of Franjo Tudjman looked like a perfectly good alibi:

Unfortunately, Mr. Tudjman has unambiguously confirmed what this paper has continually written, for which it has been accused of nationalism and malice by the Zagreb press and home-bred ideologists such as Cicak and Co. We wrote that the politics and dark designs that ended in the NDH genocide of people whose only guilt was to be Serb, Jewish or Gypsy must be brought to light ... We did so in order to awaken the consciences of Croatia's ruling Communists and Yugoslav patriots, by pointing out the fatal consequences of policies of forgetting the Ustasha atrocities, which gloss over them or make political symmetry. (*Duga*, No. 418, 3–16 March 1990)

The attitude of Serb opposition leaders towards the enemies of the Serbs was no different; Vuk Drašković was heard to say:

The Serbs are a people who take an awfully long time to work out who their enemy is and to get him in their sights, but when they do, he's done for ... The Serb people never declared anyone to be their enemy by accident and have never made a mistake in doing so. This is why they take a long time to pinpoint him, weigh him up, draw back, forgive; but when nothing else helps and their back is to the wall, then they say: 'Ah, so it was you!' and it's all up with him. The Serb people are close to finding out something which is true, that the main indicator of all conspiracies against the Serb people and in the Balkans is the Zagreb Kapitol [the residence of the Catholic Archbishop]. (*Duga*, No. 422, 28 April–11 May 1990)

The past and the present gave each other mutual recognition in order that Serbs might mobilize Here is Steva Jakšić writing in *Duga*'s regular column 'Genocide': 'The Ustasha priest Dionizije Juričević addresses his congregation thus: "Today it is not a sin to kill even a small child who stands in the way of the Ustasha movement. Don't think that just because I am a priest I cannot take a machine-gun into my own hands and mow them all down, to the bay in the cradle". From platforms today in Split, Osijek, Zagreb ... similar proposals are flying, only wrapped in a packet labelled democracy and political pluralism' (*Duga*, No. 422, 28 April–11 May 1990).

TV Novosti, in a report from the referendum in Knin under the headline 'Peace, but a relative peace', wrote: '"The time has come that at eighty-five years of age I am keeping guard again like I used to in 1941. Then they used to take away the guns, and then slaughter people", a wiry old man recalls. "Now they want to take away our Cyrillic and then move us out. They say that we already have our own state, so there's nothing for it but to take up our guns--or it's feet first into the pit"' (*TVN*, No. 1339, 24 August 1990).

The 'solution-by-war' was ever clearer on the horizon. Zoran Sekulić hinted at this in his regular column: 'Threats and the deliberate frightening of the Serb people in Croatia that have not ceased since Tudjman's party came to power have now turned into an open use of force. Everything is irresistibly reminiscent of 1941. But the Serb people in Croatia have learned this appalling history lesson well. Never again will they wait in the death ranks of Jasenovac, Jadovno, Gradiška ... They will, if necessary, respond to force by force' (*Duga*, No. 434, 12–26 October 1990).

Duga promoted an uncompromising, belligerent type of journalism, often chauvinistic. The subtitle of a report from the Bosnian elections ran: 'We shall live together–how threatening that sounds' (*Duga*, No. 437, 23 November–7 December 1990). Another example from Zoran Sekulić reads: 'When the "finest and most courageous Croats" are joined with the "noblest Albanians" what do we get? Sulphuric acid. And even primary pupils know how that stinks!' (*Duga*, No. 442, 2–16 February 1991).

In early 1991 the war games began to speed up and the drawers of maps, the first harbingers of war, took up their positions. Budimir Košutić in *Ilustrovana politika* said:

If the secessionist trend really leads to seriously posing the question of retailoring Yugoslavia's internal borders and forming small national states, we will perforce have to consider the real historical facts and not amateurish calculations based on irrational wishes. We shall also have to respect international law and the demographic maps made in 1936 according to the census of 1931. In other words, it would be immoral to take the present situation in Bosnia-Hercegovina and Croatia as a starting point because that would mean profiting from genocide, and not recognizing the fact that the Croats didn't even have their own state before the forming of Yugoslavia. (*IP*, No. 1684, 12 February 1991)

The same author also wrote in *Duga*:

After the terrible genocide of Serbs in the Independent State of Croatia (in which some of the Catholic clergy took part) during World War II, and the revival of the idea of a Croatian political nation in present-day Croatia and their inclusion in the Croatian Constitution, the Serb nation must be extremely cautious. Every citizen, therefore, should be as fully informed as possible of the consequences of using the right of every Yugoslav nation to self-determination, up to and including secession, to work out a satisfactory division of assets from 1918 to today, and above all to acquaint themselves with the impossibility of turning the present administrative boundary lines into the borders of the state. (*Duga*, No. 441, 19 January–2 February 1991)

Serbian magazines in early 1991 openly point to an identical situation in 1941 in Croatia. The TV broadcast of a secretly shot film of Martin Špegelj, Croatian defence minister, importing weapons from Hungary, shocked the Yugoslav public, while the reaction proved how one type of chauvinism feeds another.

The shots at Pakrac (a Croatian town with a substantial Serbian population, 6 March 1991) are an illustration of the over-heated atmosphere and a proof that 'patriotic' journalism creates a war psychosis. Some reports were that several had been killed, which was later shown to be untrue. No one, of course, was held responsible for this error.

A report from Borovo Selo, three weeks before the much-reported fighting with the Croat police which marked the beginning of the war, foreshadowed the inevitability of future events.

The Serbs of Borovo Selo trust no one anymore. They have reason enough for their consolidated attitude. These past few days, they say, they have been taken in by promises, stories, lies. There will be no more compromise or concessions. They are fed up with beatings, night attacks, bursts of gunfire, false representations, accusations, ugly names ... This state of affairs is intolerable, there is no end to the harassment, so the inhabitants, nine thousand of them and mostly Serbs, have closed off approach roads to the village. Up to 1 April, the police were parading through the village and beating up anyone they chose according to some criteria of their own. When the villagers heard that Goran Hadžić and Borivoj Savić had been arrested and beaten bloody, then accused, without grounds, of acts which could mean sentences of ten or more years, they realized the fat was in the fire. They shut themselves up in their village, oiled their ancient weapons and decided to sell their skins as dearly as possible. (*IP*, No. 1693, 16 April 1991)[4]

The mini-war provoked by Slovenia's declaration of independence on 25 June 1991 meant new victims for the Serbs. The press, of course, wrote in suitable fashion of these events. *Ilustrovana Politika*, in an article under the title 'The Dirty Slovene War' and headlined 'Treacherously, Without a Soldier's Honour', recited the details of this military defeat: 'They left a young private, Dejan Bjelogrlić, to bleed to death, shot Captain Blagoje Stanojević in the back and then refused to operate on him at Maribor Hospital, killed Dragan Rodić with dum-dum bullets and then shot him again when he was dead' (*IP*, No. 1705, 9 July 1991). Olga Dzoljić of Belgrade told *TV Novosti*: 'Hitler's army gave first-aid to our soldiers, but the Slovenes would not allow them to come near the wounded and shot them in the back! And at least some of these "heroes" ate Serb bread during the [Second World] War' (*TVN*, No. 1385, 12 July 1991). Predrag Zivancević skilfully summed up events:

Just after the armed uprising in Slovenia and the virtual capitulation of the Yugoslav National Army and its military-political leadership, in a situation when—very significantly—the spectre of civil war had flared along Croatia's administrative borders with Serbia, the rule was proved whereby ignoring history condemns one to repeat it as tragedy. Concealed by the so-called 'Brioni Declaration', which in fact simply froze the Yugoslav Army disaster in Slovenia while obliging the army in Croatia to withdraw to barracks, leaving the Serb-inhabited areas at the mercy of the new pro-Ustasha government— whose genocidal intentions could not be doubted—it is hardly necessary to draw the parallel with the Yugoslav catastrophe of April 1941. (*TVN*, No. 1386, 12 July 1991)

The commander of the war headquarters at Dvor na Uni, Bogdan Vajagić, drew an easy analogy: 'The duty of the defence of Dvor na Uni is to prevent fresh forces, ammunition or weapons reaching

Ustasha formations which would terrorize Serb villages and put down the resistance at Glina, Vrgin Most, Vojnić ... With great effort we are managing to do this. Our motive is not to allow a repeat of 1941 when the Ustasha, the ancestors of today's HDZ, massacred the people here' (*IP*, No. 1708, 30 July 1991).

The sequence of events was similar in Bosnia-Hercegovina. The enemy's name was easily changed, so that instead of the Catholic Church there were Islamic fundamentalists, and instead of the Ustasha, Muslim warriors, and so on. The point was that Serbs were in danger here also. Radovan Karadžić complained: 'This nation has been politically headless for too long. Just remember what happened to the intelligentsia whenever they showed the slightest sign of disobedience or hardihood. Such people would disappear from public life overnight without trace and be replaced by incompetents. The more incompetent they were, the faster they advanced. And anyway, when did this nation ever live in its own country? It doesn't feel at home even now. Until recently, it could not celebrate its family feast days or attend its own church' (*Duga*, No. 430,18–31 August 1990). Serbs were ill-treated in Bosnia too. The story of Todor, in a report from Foca, is a case in point: 'We set off for the market ... when we met Dzevad Himzo and his wife Bera ... next-door neighbours. And he says to me: "Where you off to? To sing songs to Milošević, to stick up for the Chetnik side, you motherfucker?" He had a stone in his hand and he cracked me on the head, and I saw him hit my wife the same way, and she fainted' (*Duga*, No. 432, 14–28 September 1990).

Constantly encumbered by the weight of the past, every ethnic group in the Balkans is torn apart by uncertainty for the future, fear of suffering the fate of a minority, or revenge. This state of affairs endlessly prolongs the reopening of wounds, while any action that might have the opposite effect is met with hostility and incomprehension.

Magazines in Serbia between 1987 and 1991 faithfully followed the impetus provided by the political and ideological subsystem, bounded by the Eighth Session and Slobodan Milošević's St. Vitus's Day message, shaping the facts according to the requirements of the moment. In contrast to an analytical and critical attitude which assumes that facts will be checked, this kind of journalism does not consider it important. The overriding aim is to arouse emotions and attitudes.

Magazines also, by their very nature, tended to focus on the extremes of social and political life, making the picture of reality in Yugoslavia even more lurid. Their immanent sensationalism was not intended to make them commercially viable (a secondary consideration at the time) but to mobilize the masses.

This type of journalism, which serves politics and rejects autonomy, contributed to creating and spreading an authoritarian society which left no opening for a democratic solution to the conflicts. The Serbs were victims. All were victims.

Notes

1 The first issue of *Duga* (The Rainbow) appeared on 22 July 1945. After a long break, a new series began again on 1 January 1974. It comes out twice a month and is printed in Roman type. Between 1987 and 1991, the editor-in-chief was Ilija Rapaic. Circulation figures were never published. The weekly *Ilustrovana Politika* (Politika Illustrated) first came out on 11 November 1985 and is printed in Cyrillic. Chief editors in the period under review were Mirko Bojic, followed by Rade Soskic. Circulation was over 200,000 per issue (average circulation for September 1987 was 260,000 and 210,000 in September 1988). The weekly *TV Novosti* first appeared as a special edition of *Vecernje Novosti* and is printed in Cyrillic. The editor-in-chief is Zika Sreckovic. It claimed to have the largest weekly circulation in the former Yugoslavia.

2 A comprehensive study by Stjepan Gredelj on changes in communication models in Yugoslav society, based on an analysis of the dailies *Borba* and *Politika* between 1945 and 1975, confirms the premise that 'communication systems in socialist societies are given a very restricted role, which stems from their subjugation to the ideological, political subsystem' (S. Gredelj 1986: 15).

3 This, like the other characteristics of magazines, was *ideel-typisch* (in Weber's sense).

4 A report in *Duga* on the strike at Borovo on 20 August 1987 showed that people then had other problems. One statement by a striker read: 'Go past the baker's on the 10th and the 25th and you'll see when people buy most bread... We have to turn off our own electricity and water, it's better than having them coming into our houses to turn them off. We can't pay the bills any more. What will we do for fuel this winter?'

The Nationalization of Everyday Life

SNJEŽANA MILIVOJEVIĆ

The war which brought about the collapse of SFR Yugoslavia revealed the non-existence of social institutions for mediation, as
well as the lack of appropriate communication strategies for conflict resolution. Without guaranteed autonomy, the mass media
were easily instrumentalized and transformed into a tool of the
ruling ideology. This tool functioned smoothly, enabling the adjustment of the media, and subsequently of the whole of public
discourse as well, in accordance with the political aims of the ruling regime. Domination of the media scene was facilitated by the
structural characteristics of Yugoslav society: the one-party system,
state ownership, crude political control of the media, the absence
of media autonomy, a lack of professional standards among journalists, an insufficient domestic supply of printing paper and the
centrally controlled import there of, the undeveloped market,
modest market profits, low purchasing power, and the level of
(il)literacy of the population.

The government's attack on the media sphere was very strong. It
preceded the final phase of the crisis and contributed to its tragic
end. This forcefulness was, certainly, a result of the importance of
the mass media in the process of socialization: such media help
everyday life, and secure the adoption of the knowledge necessary
for orientation in everyday life.[1] They also act as translators of expert knowledge into the lay formulas indispensable for the cognitive mastering of everyday life. Media products strengthen the
mythological basis of a community through the production of
metaphors for popular use. A colonization of the media space is
the best shortcut to everyday life for a totalitarian government. It
is, at the same time, a great challenge, since the media can be instrumentalized much more directly than in pluralist societies.

The government's interventions were obvious through a combination of direct and indirect actions directed against media auton-

omy, and professional journalists enabled the success of the whole operation through a change in media standards, in accord with the new social circumstances.

Media autonomy was violated by direct changes of editorial boards, by appointing and pressurizing editors, and by firing or favouring employees according to extra-professional, primarily political criteria. Equally efficient in terms of this strategy were the granting of radio frequencies, the granting of permits, and government fiscal interventions (granting freedom from, or introducing additional, taxes, funding, subsidies for equipment and printing material, etc.). The extent of these interventions depended partly on the quality of the editorial board, the media tradition, the needs of the media, and the readiness of the media personnel to co-operate, although at the time the regime was coming into power, the government directly controlled all the influential media.

Another important process was the internal professional degeneration during the time of crisis. By 'interiorizing' tasks that were in the vast undertaking of state reorganization allocated to the media, the chief creators of professional standards became advocates of the ideas required to practice 'patriotic journalism'.

The contribution made by the mass media to the preparations for war is important precisely because of the way in which they defined the crisis and identified its main aspects and actors. By controlling the media, the government upheld the rule of the interpretative formula that had been valid for the last half century, and defended the illusion of continuity. The old vocabulary and the old iconography convinced the public that the crisis had not gone beyond the capacities of socialism, and that it could be solved through measures taken from the existing repertoire. Events were defined totally outside the context of global changes in Communist countries.

Empirical evidence was gathered through analysing articles in the magazine *Duga* from 1985 to 1991. *Duga* was the first illustrated magazine launched in Yugoslavia after World War II. During the whole period, it was one of the magazines with the highest circulation—in concept it was the closest to a 'family' magazine. As a fortnightly publication, it had the opportunity to develop a more sophisticated approach and to promote a more modern style of journalistic expression. Throughout the decade preceding this research, it had a reputation as a provocative, free-thinking, or even 'opposition' magazine (in terms of the opposition allowed at the time). Its history is directly connected to the general events in Serbia, which makes it an almost paradigmatic media example of the late 1980s.

In autumn 1985, a new series of the magazine was launched, and *Duga* was conceptually, and visually, modernized. At the first anniversary of this new series, the liberal and critical position of the magazine was already criticized for 'content and messages in contrast to the policies of the League of Communists of Yugoslavia (SKJ)', for articles which were not 'a social critique, but an oppositional political attitude, which does not contribute to the solving of social conflicts and the stabilization of situations, but contributes to tension' (Savo Kržavac, *Duga* No. 335). This opened a major debate between the editorial board and the relevant political authorities. The discussions ended with the dismissal of the editor in spring 1987. In the first issues published after this change, a new editorial policy was highly correlated with a new political course. The editorial change at *Duga* temporally coincided with the establishment of the new regime in Serbia and the changes it initiated. This was a symbolic announcement of the new government's intention to intervene directly in the field of popular culture, and to control the instruments that formed popular tastes. The developing political project was systematically popularized in the magazine, the status of which was based on its mix of opposition (it published articles which more or less openly flirted with nationalism and anti-Communism, and it also published articles by people who could not get published in the official media) and entertainment.

This was the first dismissal of an editor of a large-circulation publication. It was carried out according to the pattern of the then prevailing ideological disciplining of the press (that is, following a clash between the editorial board and a party committee in charge of 'information'), but it also marked the development of direct conflicts between various media houses (*Politika* actively participated in the dismissal, as a mediator and interpreter of the government's efforts to discipline 'certain' media). This 'family feud' followed the logic of hierarchization characteristic of the whole period of the disintegration of the Yugoslav community: provocation in defining reality, characteristic in the early phase of the crisis for magazines and reviews, was taken over (at the same time changing the symbolic instruments) by the 'serious' informative-political press, while in the final phase of the crisis the symbolic sphere was dominated completely by the only existing television–state television.

Changes in crisis talk

A general term which could be used to define the participation of *Duga* in public communication in the whole period under analysis would be the systematic 'nationalization' of speech. By nationalization is meant the formulating of the crisis in Yugoslav reality in the terms and repertoire of the nationalist idiom. Several sources served as a semantic reservoir for this operation: populism (the 'happenings of the people', the glorification of the leader, the devaluation of social institutions); anti-Communism (de-Brozovization,[2] de-Bolshevization); and nationalism (the mythologizing of the national past, national exclusiveness, and xenophobia). As a component of the collective memory, national history was adjusted for immediate political use through a series of romanticized stories. The redefinition of the past left new tasks for the present (the unification of all Serb lands, all Serbs in a single state, the creation of the national state). *Duga* built a particular discourse on these presuppositions. Thus, the object of this essay is the media product, not the events that caused it: these events are only external points of reference from which *Duga* selected.

This analysis requires that the multiplicity of meanings contained in the articles published be ignored, and that a 'preferred meaning' be determined.[3] The aim is to show how a prevailing meaning is developed through symbolic means, and how the possibility of different readings is narrowed according to media requirements. No matter how crude, this semantic control which has as its effect an obvious schematizing of reality, can never exclude the possibility of different interpretations. However, differences in individual readings (alternative, even oppositional interpretations) is not the object of this analysis. What is of interest here is the sense being favoured through the media. It is for this reason that the research is based on identifying frames shaping the patterns of the *Duga* narrative, and not on quantitative content analysis or on determining the characteristics of content as a whole. By presenting all the complexity and scope of the contents , it is possible to separate three phases in the realization of this 'nationalization' of speech.

The first phase (1985–1987) was characterized by a defence of the past. After a distinctive initial (1985–1986) critical attitude, this phase involved the suppressing of demands for changes and the defence of continuity, the blocking of the liberalization achieved so far, criticism of anti-socialist and anti-Communist tendencies, opposition to the legalization of political pluralism, advocating the maintenance of Yugoslavia on the 'original' principles, a lack of agreement on the project of reform, and the gradual transfer of the crisis from economic to political language, with the Kosovo problem defined as central to the Yugoslav crisis.

The second phase (1987–1989) was characterized by a distinctive re-examination of the past, a gradual recuperation of nationalist projections, the romanticization and mythologization of the national past, the reworking of the anti-Communist idiom and its translation into the acceptable form of 'de-Brozovization', fierce criticism of the creators of the Communist system (Tito and Kardelj) as representatives of the anti-Serb, Vatican-Comintern conspiracy, the mobilization of support for the project of change to the Serbian constitution, the channelling of popular dissatisfaction into the national sphere, the domination of Kosovo as the main cause of the Yugoslav crisis, the launching of the populist identification formula, the politicization of the crisis, conflict with the reform attempts in other republics (the 'anti-Serb coalition'), and insistence on national unity as a dam against pluralism.

The third phase (1989–1991) was characterized by the mending of the past, a significant redefinition of national history, the affirmation of the new constitution and the reorganization of relations within Serbia, the demand for a solution to the Serb national question in Yugoslavia, the Kosovization of Croatia, a definitive denouncement of togetherness and the non-acceptance of reforms, the denouncing of the opposition and the caricaturing of political pluralism, aggressive advocacy of the unity of Yugoslavia and non-acceptance of the borders as defined at the Anti-Fascist Council for the National Liberation of Yugoslavia (AVNOJ), the settling of all conflicts within Serbia and the projection of the same model for Yugoslavia, the affirmation of national consensus and the reaffirmation of the strategy exposed in the Memorandum of the SANU, confirmation of the indisputable role of the leader, and affirmation of the populist achievements of the 'happening of the people'.

In each of these phases, concepts were forced into the existing frames by means of the 'naturalization' of new, and often contradictory stories.[4] This naturalization explains how the public reconciled mostly irreconcilable positions into a coherent whole, and simultaneously accepted both the defence of Yugoslavia as an aim and the conviction that a common state was the worst solution for Serbia; that there was a change of government in Serbia, while at the same time continuity was maintained; that Serbia was at the same time both the initiator of changes and the guardian of tradition; that the West was both anti-Communist and anti-Serb, although Serbia was the greatest adversary of Communism; that Communism and Bolshevism had been forced on Serbia, while at the same time Serbia had most difficulties getting rid of them; that

Serbia consistently advocated democratic and equal relations in the federation, while there was a growing anxiety in the federation because of political processes in Serbia. The coexistence of these contradictions in the collective consciousness shows that the equalizing of the totalizing interpretative frames was the first task of the media, and that the government tried to determine that process.

What is stopping us?

The narrative of crisis appeared in the Yugoslav press only in the second half of the 1980s. Until then, crisis was mentioned in a symbolic domain, and only conditionally and fragmentarily. Only individual and limited aspects of reality were defined in terms of crisis (debt crisis, economic crisis, education crisis), never the system as a whole. Also, certain individual scandals had a purifying function, although they came relatively late in the everyday repertoire of the Yugoslav press in its role as a media instrument ('Agrokomerc' was the first real scandal).[5] Even complex Kosovo themes were treated as a series of individual cases, and only in the mid–1980s were numerous cases thematized in a unique 'crisis focus'. For the media that, until then, had functioned as an instrument for the fabrication of reality without conflicts, this meant a visible change. Circulation began to rise, and some papers, especially reviews and the student press, liberalized to the maximum extent the journalistic standards that existed at the time. It was in these circumstances that the new series of *Duga* started (autumn 1985), one that was extremely open and critical of the existing situation. Its character as a review enabled the kind of criticism that was impossible for the informative-political press. The unusual provocative nature of its articles placed *Duga* in that section of the press that contributed to the ending of taboos with respect to both contemporary and important historical events. Interventions by party and state institutions increased, and were manifested in different ways: from changes in the editorial board, to the discrediting of liberal public personalities.[6]

The general situation was most often defined as a 'crisis of the system's efficiency'. Inefficiency was primarily due to economic reasons, and the whole crisis narrative began with the problematization of economic factors. The inadequate speed of development was discussed. 'Nobody wants to understand that in those "happy years" the problems of today were piling up. Those years, before 1980, were something abnormal for us, we did not spend our own money, but someone else's and that was suicidal. Many people do not want to understand that we are, along with Albania and Portugal, the least developed country in Europe' (Popov, *Duga* No. 301).

The gradual definition of the crisis as political in nature first took place through interviews in the series 'What is Stopping Us?'. The series started as an open invitation to public, scientific and political workers to add their input to the debate on the political system and the preparations for the forthcoming congresses, and to try to find answers to the questions 'What is it that undermines Yugoslavia? What is keeping us from the ideals written in those days of revolutionary enthusiasm and later enshrined in the most important documents? What is stopping us from being a society with greater socialism, self-management, equality, social justice and solidarity?' (*Duga*, No. 312).

Claims that apart from the economic crisis there was also a serious political crisis, were becoming more frequent. Before long, they were being openly formulated: 'For almost ten years there was ideological outwitting and name-changing with respect to the status of the Yugoslav state community. At first, when the first signs of a serious crisis became apparent, it was only admitted that we had encountered "certain economic difficulties", and that their causes were to be found outside the Yugoslav borders, in the world energy crisis ... This attitude was crowned by a statement from a high-ranking party functionary from Serbia: "The political situation in the country is excellent, but the economic one is—bad"' (Todorović, *Duga* No. 322).

The main obstacle to development came from the privileged social classes: within Serbia, those who enjoyed the privileges of the regime (bureaucracy); and within Yugoslavia, the economically more developed republics. This attitude became generally accepted, and almost all those involved in discussions sided with it, claiming that social inequalities and inflation benefited the rich, and that the rich were afraid of changes. However, despite identifying classes and groups which were hindering development, nothing changed significantly; sharp polemic and harsh criticism produced no social improvement. This quasi-politicization was to continue in later phases of the crisis: despite huge energy and continuous communication, there were no results. Even then it was obvious that potential for change was blocked within the system: the most radical critics of the system were its creators, thus establishing their power over doubt. The government controlled criticism by producing it itself, thus satisfying public demand for radical criticism (Letica, *Duga* No. 315).

Faced with growing dissatisfaction, various attempts at stabilization were offered as solutions for the crisis (long-term programs, economic and party commissions), with maintenance of the ideological foundations and the basic political solutions. All the instruments for defining the crisis were taken from the value system and were declared in the idiom of the 'old regime'. Crisis management was based on the assumption that the socialist order was indisputable, that the system was good, but that it did not function, and that this functional deficit could be corrected through partial reforms. Political rhetoric respected the code of the 'leading role of workers': 'Workers visiting the Central Committee (CK)'; 'The eyes of the workers are directed towards the Party'; 'The Party also shows signs of increasing orientation to workers'; 'One cannot exist without the other'; 'A body without a head is the same as a head without a body' (Mijović, *Duga*, No. 335). Just prior to the League of Communists of Yugoslavia (SKJ) Congress (beginning with issue No. 322), a series of interviews with national figures was started ('The Congress Interviews'), focusing on their suggestions for getting out of the crisis. An extremely critical attitude towards the present was disproportional with the defence of the past. The past was still guarded, primarily through the defence of the main symbol of the order, the reputation of Josip Broz. In the article 'What does Jovanka Broz want?', reprinted from *Nedjeljna Dalmacija*, members of Tito's family were criticized for starting proceedings to divide the property of the late president. 'If you want to hear what the public think, the most frequent question they ask is: "Why do Broz's heirs disgrace Comrade Tito? Why does this happen?"'

When the new series was started, *Duga* published quite openly comments on the new democratic tendencies in Slovenia. The interview with Dimitrij Rupel (*Duga*, No. 322), who expressed the positions of intellectuals gathered around *Nova revija*, provoked a storm of protests, and maybe one of the biggest polemics in the Yugoslav press after World War II. Most protests were caused by a 'Slovenian' view of the Kosovo problem: 'I am not annoyed by boys who shout Kosovo Republic. Why should I care if some boy shouts slogans like that? So what if someone sings in a tavern? What does it have to with the state? And here, the sensibility is very high, and it only inflames the situation and creates a crisis. I think that Serbs should make a deal with Albanians on how they will live in this country and a common republic.'

Duga was criticized for the interview, but at the time it was also widely read in Slovenia. The relationship to Slovenia continued to have a prominent place, but the initial understanding and tolerance retreated before the increasingly loud denouncement. One of the last voices of reason was published in early 1987, with the message that one 'should have more patience for the new movements in Slovenia'. 'Fear of the unknown is a great fear. A Slovenian experiment–let us call it that although we think that it includes many authentic expressions of the Yugoslav political system–merits attention, to say the least. Especially at a time when we are burdened with a difficult crisis, and when people mourn their own destiny, more than they create fresh ideas' (Đukić, *Duga*, No. 338). Before long, the relationship to this member of the federation changed to the view that 'Slovenia provokes the rest of Yugoslavia'.

In the already highly politicized crisis, the Kosovo conflict became more important in the light of debates on the constitutional and legal organization of the state. Public pressure to solve the problems in Kosovo was represented in all areas. The arrival in Belgrade of dissatisfied Serbs and Montenegrins from Kosovo to to stage a protest, was described as a 'document on socialism with a blanket over the window': that 'ethnic purity' is threatening Kosovo is not the most horrific thing, there are much more important things at stake–the foundations of the Yugoslav community and the basic achievements of civilization (Spasović, *Duga*, No. 317). In the same issue, in the article 'From the diary of a retired activist', the event was described as an announcement of the awakening of national self-consciousness in Kosovo and of the lack of understanding in Belgrade: 'Serbs and Montenegrins complain to the Sava Centre. Four thousand citizens of Belgrade came to listen to Pogorelic, and merely a hundred to hear Serbs and Montenegrins ... The people have learnt to speak. The people do not stutter. The people demand justice' (Crnčević, *Duga*, No. 317). The lack of understanding for the Kosovo problem is not only characteristic for the citizens of Belgrade. State and party institutions did not follow adequate policies. In the series 'Across the full line', the question was asked: 'Is the Kosovo lobby so strong, that Serbia cannot confront the counter-revolution with the system of legal protection?', 'The UN Charter says that when there are flags of another country in one country's territory, that territory is debatable. And then, as everyone knows, the army enters the scene' (Golubović, *Duga*, No. 336).

The problematizing of Kosovo themes culminated at the time of the Central Committee of the League of Communists of Serbia

(CKSKS) in its plenary session on Kosovo. 'We sincerely hope that 26 June this year marks a turn-around and a new political practice. We believe that the session put an end to political phraseology according to which the situation in Kosovo has been stabilizing for the last six years (which should mean that it is improving), while the exodus of Serbs and Montenegrins continues' (Rapajić, *Duga*, No. 349). Slobodan Milošević's platform at the session was presented in detail. It was based on the formula 'equality, freedom, unity'.

This issue was completely dominated by Kosovo themes. There was discussion on a number of aspects of the Kosovo reality—the historical (What did Tito say about Hoxha and Albania during a visit to Kosovo? Tito was lied to by the members of the Gjakove line...), demographic ('The birth rate in Kosovo—A directive from Heaven'), and cultural ('Monuments change faith—The process of transforming Serb monuments into "mosques"'), and there were series about the past ('The deep roots of irredentism') (*Duga*, No. 350).

The definitive transformation of the frame 'the politicization of the Yugoslav crisis', with Kosovo at its centre, was completed in June 1987. This frame was based on the demand for changes (the unacceptable situation in Kosovo), on preserving continuity (the denouncement of Albanian irredentism as an attempt to bring about the disintegration of the country), on the decontextualization of the events in Yugoslavia (not showing the global character of changes in socialism), and on an increasingly obvious nationalization of the crisis. By autumn 1987 and with the change in the Serb leadership, all publications were similar. In the lengthy report on '36 hours of insomnia', a 'democratic ritual of political sacrifice' was described: the clash between bravery and reluctance. 'The political courage of the last session of the CKSKS actually lies in the acknowledgement of the facts of life, returning politics to the primordial collective images of the world, from which it can draw its power ... The leadership that made such a decision, decided to take full responsibility before the people. And it has decided that awareness of public opinion (admittedly imperfect, but the best we have) should become a true factor in the political struggle. For now, politics has acknowledged that the people are right ... Could things revert to the way they used to be, now that it has finally been admitted after great reluctance and political struggles that the people are right...?' The hint of a more efficient phase in Serb politics was soon tied to a preparation of the constitutional changes in the already announced code of the 'happening of the people'. Thus, the Kosovo problem became the first on the list of problems to be solved, and the frame in which the solution would be sought was given. The first phase of the nationalization of the language of *Duga* took place in the formulation of the Kosovo crisis.

Is there a way out of nowhere?

A radicalization of the crisis narrative and its increasingly obvious politicization started in 1987 and continued during 1988. The dominance of Kosovo themes resulted in the first special issue of *Duga* that was completely devoted to Kosovo ('The Truth about Kosovo') in June 1988, and culminated in the June 1989 special issue dedicated to the Memorandum of the SANU. The final phase of the defining of the Yugoslav crisis and its complete symbolic nationalization took place in this period. A frame which favoured a dramatic resolution to the crisis, involving war, was definitively set up. Possibilities of alternative solutions remained beyond the scope offered by this frame. It was mainly for this reason that it was important to consider both the frames and the symbolic actions they constituted.

The special issue was 'a particular reply to Branko Horvat's book *Kosovsko pitanje* [The Kosovo Issue], and was characterized by the author's particular political exclusivism based on the "falsifying of history, the abuse of science, the forging of the history of a nation (Serbs), and the ideologizing of the past of another nation (Albanians)", which was used in order to provide the politically indefensible theses and conclusions with the alleged scientific dignity." With such a book, no serious profession could establish a fruitful dialogue, so the articles in this issue dealt more with 'issues of the destiny of a history of several hundred years of our nations and nationalities, seeing them in the light of scientific facts, without forced manipulation and symmetry, without granting amnesty to any people for historical responsibility for the past and the present situation in Kosovo' (Vučelić and Dautović, *Duga*, June 1988).

Between these two special issues, politicians gave their interpretation of the Kosovo situation: 'After the fall of the Vojvodina autonomists, I would say that the anti-Serb and anti-Yugoslav coalition lost its trump, so it had to use another one, Kosovo. This, I would say, is a very dangerous one for Yugoslavia, since Albanian national bureaucracy is connected directly to Albanian nationalism' (Trajković, *Duga*, No. 391). Respected Church officials said that 'Kosovo is the memory of the Serbian people, and Albanians have suffered a spiritual loss ... those who led their own people betrayed its national interests, Shqiptars lost all their roots in Albania, and here they never had any ... so what then is a nation which has grown and has no roots?' (Radović, *Duga*, No. 388).

People wrote about Kosovo on the occasion of important events, such as the drawing up of the Serbian Constitution, an event that marked 'the end of a reign of fear' (Košutić, *Duga*, No. 394). There were particularly lengthy commentaries on the occasion of the celebration of the six-hundredth anniversary of the Battle of Kosovo. Almost all the best-known journalists were in the team of reporters. Using six pages and through eleven contributions, they described the celebration ('Six centuries after the victory, six years after the defeat'), 'in which it was simple to be a Serb. But nothing was simple any more in the press. They measured each of our words, counted every bus, looked under the seats; they envied us, and did not dare to admit it, they scolded us, even while their teeth chattered in fear, ugly creatures of Rugova, boys and guys.[7] And now again we have to swear that we won't do anything to them' (Bogavac, *Duga*, No. 401). The celebration was also marked by a spirit of reconciliation: 'The time has come again for our people to applaud sincerely its leaders. And it was only yesterday when it threatened to send them back where they came from ... All too easily this people renounced its national pride and treasure in the name of some higher and brighter goals, only to become totally impoverished and disgraced, stumbling in darkness, realizing a brutal and irreconcilable class struggle both in Heaven and on earth' (Jovanić, *Duga*, No. 401).

This was the situation when, in June 1989, a special issue of *Duga* was published, completely dedicated to the Memorandum of the SANU. The explanation was that, with the exception of the journal *Naše teme* (January 1989), this was the first publication of the entire text for the public. The introductory text stresses a demand to 'de-ideologize all the open issues', and to look at the Memorandum as a collective contribution of the members of the Academy to the social efforts to come out of the crisis. 'The Kosovo issue today represents a kind of ontological energy of the Serbian people, and a national historical consciousness based on the Kosovo legend, the basis of the consciousness of Serb ethnic particularity ... This only proves that for this people something serious was endangered, their national identity ... Of course, the Memorandum is like an incentive, like a constitutive element of democracy itself, the fundamental energy of people who are on the move, and for whom its historical and actual advantages then come to the fore.' Regarding the accusations that the Memorandum influenced events in Serbia, Milorad Vučelić stated that it should be known that the Serb people was not some 'paper nation, moved by words written on paper, no matter how correctly, smartly, and relevantly. Its movement is much more influenced by the totality of its basic interests and as a response to the call of the times, as well as the heritage of alienated history and tradition ...' In the same issue, Antonije Isaković saw the movement of the Serbian people as 'the search for one's own face. I think that this nation of ours is at this time going through some sort of a moral purification, a catharsis, a rejection of abandonment. The Serb people have, as far as I see it, and I think I see it correctly, found themselves again.'

Besides the integral text of the Memorandum, the whole history of the 'case' provoked by the 'thieves in police uniforms' was published. Although it was claimed that the Memorandum was not a Serb national programme, the context of its publication implied a full nationalization of the Yugoslav situation. The nationalization of the crisis meant defining that crisis in terms of the national problems of the Serbian question, its solution within the framework of the national optics and the wealth of the Serb nation. This wealth was soon consolidated, enumerated and formulated for popular use in the nationalized crisis narrative. Public representations on Serbia's capacities to resolve the crisis of the community had been translated from the ideologically political, to the national level. The initial anti-Communist and anti-socialist potential was placed within a nationalist idiom and the favouring of national homogenization, as opposed to ideological pluralization. In this action, national homogenization, the leader, national interests and communality were favoured above any kind of pluralism. This was only confirmed by the publication of the Memorandum of the SANU, almost four years after it had been published for the first time.

The dominance of the Kosovo themes was followed by an anti-Communist strategy (pronounced de-Brozovization and de-bolshevization) through the demand for a re-evaluation of the national past, a re-examination of history, and a re-examination of the founding principles of the federation. That re-examination contained a strategy for solving the crisis through a specific combination of preserving continuity and allowing changes, or accepting changes which would defend and maintain the political *status quo*. This recuperation of energy and demands for change in the maintenance of the already existing situation occurred through the offer of constitutional changes (the reorganization of Serbia, hints at the possibility of changes in the federation), in exchange for the political continuity of the existing government. A wide consensus of political and cultural elites on the national issue and on possibilities for its solution was established in Serbia. The necessity for changes in the constitution was explained both by experts and by the *Duga's* authors.

Through its full support for the winning current in the leadership and for the 'happening of the people', *Duga* followed a programme of 'settling' the situation in Yugoslavia. Slovenia was first on the timetable. The choice of a multiparty system was interpreted as provocation directed at the rest of Yugoslavia–through a series of translations, ideological and programmatic differences between the two leaderships were transformed to the level of national confrontations between two nations.

The Slovenian model for resolving the crisis was later formulated as anti-socialist and anti-Yugoslav, which led to a complete lack of understanding of the processes in Slovenia. Not only were the political programmes in Slovenia unacceptable, but *Duga* entered into a direct polemic with the media and a personality from Slovenia, regarded as a representative of the 'Serbian' side. The final touches to the negative depiction of Slovenia were added in the form of an article on Dimitrij Rupel (Duška Jovanić, 'Rupel Wants to Crawl into Europe', *Duga*, No. 321). With respect to his statements of two years earlier, *Duga* had already been drawn into the polemic and criticized as an 'anti-socialist' magazine. This time a similar polemic was caused by an interview with Josip Vidmar, although Vidmar immediately distanced himself from the content the interview (*Duga*, No. 393).

Many ideas emerging from Slovenia were understood as a direct attack on socialism. At a time when the possibility of legalizing the multiparty system was not even mentioned in Serbia, a poll in Slovenia showed that two-thirds of the voters were in favour of introducing a multiparty system, and that only 9.6 per cent of voters intended to vote for the Communists at the eventual elections (*Duga*, No. 388). A meeting at the *Cankarjev dom* in Ljubljana was interpreted as the greatest provocation, and writers in Belgrade reacted immediately andat an extraordinary assembly, the Association of Writers of Serbia (UKS) said that they refused 'to betray their own people'.

Relations with other members of the federation were affected by the 'happening of the people'. After Vojvodina, a wave of political changes hit Montenegro, in what was reported as the 'Montenegrin uprising', and as a rebellion of the people against the coalition. In a special report covering seven pages of the magazine,

'The Mountain Wreath Live' was described (*Duga*, No. 389). Political changes were interpreted as the authentic expression of the popular will, and in one of these formulations, Nenad Bućin stated that 'In Vojvodina and Montenegro there was a "happening of the people", but not in the form of a "mob" as some like to say, but as people, as something self-sufficient, as the basis of an overall legitimacy ... What "happened" was the people who had been silent for a long time and who had suffered within themselves what had been done to them, in their name' (*Duga*, No. 392).

The new leadership received support and were given space for representing their ideas. In the interview 'Five Armchairs do not Constitute the System', the newly elected Milo Đukanović said that 'By a forceful entry of the people into politics, what until recently was reserved for the privileged is falling down, like a house of cards ... I do not believe that our option in the political system is the one that should be followed ... I even have tremendous reservations about the potential to help of that which is being offered to us ever more aggressively. The more politically experienced I become, the more convinced I am that pluralism can be articulated much more successfully and much more fruitfully in a non-party system (as ours should be), than in a multi-party system. Through its democratic and avant-garde activity, the League of Communists (SK) would have to stimulate itself its own "socialist opposition" to make a constructive difference' (*Duga*, No. 391).

National homogenization also presupposed the indisputable role of the leader who enabled it. Slobodan Milošević, the president of the Socialist Party of Serbia (SPS) and president of Serbia, was declared man of the year, with the explanation that 'changes were made according to his project ... and the apathy of Serbian people was transformed into Serb victory'. In other republics, the rise of this man was regarded as a scandal. With regard to that statement, *Duga* explained what it was that was actually scandalous about it: 'A guilt complex is being imposed on the Serbs ... They are being pushed into anti-Communism. So far, Milošević has declared the only real programme in the market of political ideas ... This nation has opened its eyes' (*Duga*, No. 388). The same issue reprints affirmative articles on Slobodan Milošević from the world press, and in the next issue his role as 'the man of changes' was analysed.

Duga confirmed the indisputable popularity of President Milošević even when this had to be done through polemic with media from other regions. On the occasion of claims in the Zagreb press that Dobrica Ćosić did not support the policies of Slobodan

Milošević, Milorad Vučelić wrote that 'Ćosić said that he undoubtedly supports Milošević in his democratic orientation, for the equality of the Serbian people and the constituting of Serbia as a republic equal with others... The Serbian intelligentsia thinks the same way ... The movement in Serbia is deeply democratic, anti-bolshevik and anti-conservative; it is a movement of the people who have been burnt down to their nails ...; it stands for free elections, the abolishment of the delegate system and for other aims, like others in Yugoslavia ... The whole of this planned treachery is aimed at suggesting a division and a polarization between the leading Serbian politician and one of the central literary cultural figures in Serbia' (*Duga*, No. 394).

In an interview given the night before he left the country for a long period of time, Emir Kusturica said to a *Duga* journalist: 'If there needs to be a general clean-up in this country, it refers to the irrational fear of Slobodan Milošević and depends on whether he will become a new leader. He is a Serb, with an Orthodox sub-text that could endanger some Catholic Slovenian ... Before I would criticize too easily a man who has recently come into politics, and who, thanks to an emotional event in Kosovo, acquired the sympathies of the people ... [let me say that] for the first time in my life, I saw a Yugoslav politician who had a pale face, and whose voice was trembling, which proves that this man really spends himself emotionally while performing his actions and earning his salary' (*Duga*, No. 391).

National homogenization in Serbia was regarded with displeasure by other parts of the federation. That dissatisfaction was interpreted as anti-Serb hostility, but Serbia also lacked international support for its project of changes. The international context at the time of the Yugoslav crisis was interpreted in Dragoš Kalajić's articles 'A View of the World' which discussed 'the third way of Serbia':

> The witches of supra-national capitalism are angered by the importance given in Serbia to the values of human personality, contrary to centuries of convincing that man is not worth anything, or that he is just a servant—of structures, of production forces ... The usurers are particularly worried, since instead of asking them for credits or being enslaved by them, Serbia looks for funds for its economic recuperation from her own ideal sources, across the world, Serb Diaspora and solidarity ... Brezezinsky is afraid of supra-party homogenization, of the primacy of mutuality and solidarity which are a powerful barrier protecting independence and sovereignty against the chaos of the multiparty crumbling of the community, according to the formula of 'divide and rule'. Homogenization is followed by the awaken-

ing of the ethno-cultural conscience of the people ... Serbia is a negligible part, but the masters of the capital's pseudo-empire are afraid
that it could become a contagious example for the others that could
ruin their plans ... In the unjust struggle, Serbia will certainly win if it
retains the homogenization acquired, if it realizes the great importance of the spontaneous tendencies of its movement for changes,
and if it persists in the direction of the reification of the initial hints
at the "third way" alternative. Spiritual socialism according to the
formula 'one step to the right (towards the economy of common
sense), three steps up (through the vertical of spiritual, ethical, ethnic and cultural renewal)', which becomes the central basis... The
third way is a vertical overcoming of the artificial ideological dualism
of the modern world. (*Duga*, No. 402)

At the celebration on the occasion of the four-hundredth issue,
Dragan Barjaktarević, editorial reporter and assistant editor, evaluated the quality of writing in the magazine, expressing his pleasure
at the fact that 'there are fewer naked women in *Duga* than naked
truths'. Under the pressure of the everyday crisis, important decisions had had to be made, and most of them had been correct: out
of around thirty interviews, only the one with Josip Vidmar was
deemed to have been a failure. The greatest editorial mistake was
the negative evaluation of the author's work by Emir Kusturica.
The greatest praise was for the series 'Serb Business' by Brana
Crnčević, about which 'we do not dare speak, since with these
texts *Duga* directly enters into the history of modern satire' (*Duga*,
No. 401).

The smartening up of de-smartened Serbia

Up until the beginning of war, already defined elements of the
frame of everyday communication were kept through a further
radicalization, since, following 1989, in relations with other federal
units, a recipe already used within Serbia was propagated, as 'the
smartening up of de-smartened Serbia' (Đuretić, *Duga*, No. 416).
Any alternative was still rejected, the importance of emerging political opposition dismissed, unity favoured, the past mythologized,
and the *status quo* defended. This defence of the existing
('preservation of Yugoslavia') did not mean that the character of
the community which it was intended to maintain would not be
changed. The change was visible in the denouncement of the principles on which the federation was based, and in the continuous

disintegration of the elements of community. The style of writing in *Duga* in that period hinged on the presentation of two characteristic processes: the Kosovization of Croatia, and the marginalization of the political opposition within Serbia. It was in the form of the Kosovization of Croatia that the nationalization of speech was continued, and in the form of the marginalization of the opposition that support for the ruling political project was continued.

That political project was increasingly formulated as a tendency to resolve the Serb national question within a single–Serb–state. Brana Crnčević wrote 'Your job, lad, is to create a Serbia which can do it alone; this country should enable Serbs to express their national feelings' (*Duga*, No. 417); 'Others around the world were allowed to be Slovenes, Croats, Macedonians, and, by the way, Yugoslavs; it was only the Serbs, wherever they lived, who had to be Yugoslavs, and, by the way, Serbs' (*Duga*, No. 421). Thus 'whoever wants Yugoslavia without us, will not build it with us' (*Duga*, No. 422), since 'Serbia is the only Yugoslav state that can [survive] both with Yugoslavia and without it. In case of the dissolution of this ever more impotent community, only Serbia would acclimatize itself, and not be lost within Europe' (*Duga*, No. 423).

Immediately after the new constitution, Kosovo ceased to be a topic of interest for Duga. At the same time more was written about the situation. Non-participation of official Croatia in disputes between Slovenia and Serbia, 'Croatian silence', was broken after more numerous interethnic conflicts in the Knin Krajina. After unrest at the celebration of the anniversary of the Battle of Kosovo in the Knin Krajina ('Dalmatian Kosovo') and the arrest of one of the Serb leaders, Jovan Opačić, the Croatian reply was clear 'They complain about us... finally, the Croats have spoken. God, how excited they were about Knin! ... That would do forty days for them! Do they think it is harmless? Do they hope that Serb patience is measured in centuries and not in days?' (Crnčević, *Duga*, No. 402). 'Croatian quasi-democrats are organizing real Stalinist trials where people are being accused because they shook hands, because they applauded, or because they carried someone's portrait. One writer made the lucid observation, "We cannot hide our conviction that through the Serbs in Croatia, they want to settle accounts with Serbia and its leadership. If they are sentenced to jail for carrying photographs, how big a sentence would they give the one on the photograph?" From those for whom the survival of Yugoslavia is conditioned by the inequality of the Serbian people, since they are the most numerous, which automatically means the danger of hegemony for the smaller peoples, that is, for those well accustomed to factual inequality, the Serb leadership asks too much' (Ilija Rapa-jić, *Duga*, No. 406).

Numerous texts on Serbs leaving Croatia ('Where did "Little Serbia" go', 'Serbs Don't Live Here Any More', 'The March across the River Drina', together with metaphors recognizable from the Kosovo surroundings—'house for sale') display what is, in political evaluations, formulated as the 'defeat of the winner': 'The Serbs in Croatia are deprived of all the elementary national rights' (*Duga*, No. 420), and their personal security is not guaranteed. One article read: 'My grandchild asks me: "Granny, will they slit our throats?" And cries. But I am not afraid of anything on this which I have earned. Whatever happens' (*Duga*, No. 420). The reasons for the Serb-Croatian conflict are put into a historical perspective, and history is actualized through a recognition of the past (Ustasha crimes, the World War II genocide) in the present (aggressive nationalist rhetoric and iconography of the political parties, the revival of pro-Ustasha ideas and symbolism). At the time of, and immediately following, the Croatian Democratic Union (HDZ) victory in the Croatian elections, much was written, and frequently, about the new Croatian president, Franjo Tuđman (including a series on the election manifesto of the HDZ 'Who is Tuđman'; and a series on Tuđman's trial 'Tuđman in the World Press: Democracy Does Not Live Here Any More').

One important theme was, in the tradition of *Duga*, summarized in a special issue, 'Serbs in Croatia' (July 1990). Brana Crnčević wrote about the Serbs in Croatia: 'If the news says that Serbs will soon assault Serbs, don't believe the news. If they tell you that Serbia, no matter where you live, would abandon you, don't believe what they hope for. If they say you are few, just let them count us. If they are united by our discord, their unification will not allow our discord to last. The Serbs will not allow themselves or others to serve them up, carved up and cooked, at a suddenly democratic dining table. Hopefully, the world will not again miss the holy truth that the Serb-eaters are, after all, only man-eaters. Hopefully, we have not created the Serb state out of nothing only to be returned to nothing by our discord' (*Duga*, No. 446).

After the demonstrations of 9 March 1991 in Belgrade, at the time of major polarizations in Serbia, *Duga* did everything to prevent a potential political conflict and to interpret all political differences as dangerous 'Serb-Serb' divisions. The idiom of 'Serb disunity' was used in order to present any polarization as dangerous for the integrity of the community at a difficult historical time.

Neutralization of political differences was eased through trivializing of the opposition that had taken place earlier, and its almost complete marginalization. This treatment of the opposition had begun at the time of the appearance of the first parties, and especially following the first multiparty elections. Election results were commented on in the editorial 'Responsibility for the Defcat': 'Socialists in Serbia and Communists in Montenegro gained the huge trust of the people and new moral and political credit. The Serb opposition criticized the socialists and its people for not rejoicing at the victory! And it was wrong again. There is no time for celebration and triumphalism ... Generally speaking, Serb people deserve much better and more mature opposition. The opposition of today tried in its impotence, accusing socialists of being "Bolshevists" and criticizing its own people, especially in the Zagreb press, using the Jesuit-Bolshevik principle that "the end justifies the means", uniting political options which cannot be united in the second round of the elections in order to get into power at least once, or to return to the power again. But the trick did not work ...' (*Duga*, No. 440).

The political elections were interpreted in the article 'Freedom for One Use Only': 'People whose opinion nobody here has cared about for a long time, for half a century were not able to choose, so it is understandable that on 9 December they voted for the one who gave them the possibility for the first time ... The Serb people knew very well what they were choosing. Why let someone get away, almost run away, and peacefully and with dignity leave after the elections, instead of staying and stewing in the pot he himself had prepared, and for which he had to be responsible... The Serb people have shown in everything else that they are not naďve at all. Smartly and intelligently, they have tricked those they wanted to. The people simply did not have the heart to push into government the diligent, the honest, and the honourable, since not only could those people not govern, but they would not be able to do anything in a country which cannot be saved' (Duška Jovanić, *Duga*, No. 440).

When, several months later, in *Duga's* terminology 'Serbia happened to Serbia', the great protest against the government and the demands for changes were neutralized by peaceful texts on the danger of intra-Serb conflict. Political differences were not overcome in the area of normal social consensus on the basic principles of the community, but were suppressed through the renewed dominance (after a short consolidation period) of the political arrangement on which the regime existed. Political confrontation was negated through the argument of authority ('however, it is impossible just to accept the often suspicious and even counterproductive thesis of the leftists that history is created by angry or enlightened masses. We really need some authority and order in the place of chaos ...' Jovanić, *Duga*, No. 445), as well as through moral principles ('That is why honest people avoided the stench of politics and politicians. But, that is also why the ablest minds of Serbia, at the inertia of social repulsion, stayed well aside from the newly composed parties made up mostly of former "Communists", or human refuse from the decades-long race of the politically correct for high social positions and privileges. They do not feel moral repulsion towards politics. Quite the contrary' Kalajić, *Duga*, No. 446).

In the reconciled Serbia of *Duga*, soon all the more important regime institutions were interpretatively put back in their appropriate places. It began with an analysis of the media portrait of President Milošević, based on the 'Kennedy syndrome'–'the expression of the magic of extremism in specific, generally acceptable media packaging. The essence of that extremism lies in the disruption of the so-called natural flow (the revolution that flows), in the changes, but without significant disturbance of the tradition and causality of the historical continuity.' Contrary to those who tended to give a Mussolinian meaning to Milosevic's gesture of raising his chin, the explanation of Dragoš Kalajić was quoted, according to which 'the gesture of raising the chin should be read in the context of the Slav idiom of the body, where it signifies the movement of rising from humiliation, defiance at enemies and troubles, determination and self-defence ... People did not carry Milošević's pictures to glorify him personally, but in order symbolically to destroy the old, remembered in other photographs. The rallies are like the "Muppet Show"' (Tirnanić, *Duga*, No. 447).

The nationalization of everyday life in *Duga* terminated in mid–1991. Started during the crisis in Yugoslavia through a re-working of the past, it ended in a homogeneous and isolated Serbia, through the blocking of the future.

Notes

1 On the relation between everyday knowledge and everyday life, see Silverstone 1988: 20–47.

2 Translator's note: This is a reference to Josip Broz Tito (1892–1980).

3 I use 'preferred meaning' in the sense defined by Stuart Hall, based on Parkin's distinction among the systems of meaning. I speak here about the way in which a preferred meaning is 'read into' the text, in accordance with the author's intent (see Hall 1980).

4 In cultural studies, naturalization is defined as the process of representing the cultural and historical as natural, and it is an important characteristic of ideological discourse (O'Sullivan 1994).

5 The 'Agrokomerc affair' was a big economic and political affair, which broke in the agro-industrial company in Bosnia in autumn 1987.

6 The editorial board of the weekly *Student* was dismissed after controversy over its title page, which, allegedly, associated to the 'exorcism' of Josip Broz (as a 'vampire') with the hawthorn post.

7 Translator's note: In the original, *fantje i dečki.* refers to Slovenes and Croats respectively.

CONFLICT AND COMPROMISE

The International Community and the Yugoslav Crisis

VOJIN DIMITRIJEVIĆ

Inevitably, the crisis in the Socialist Federal Republic of Yugoslavia (SFRY) has had its international component. The interest shown by the rest of the world, by foreign states, by the international community[1]—or whatever one wishes to call the environment in which Yugoslavia existed, acted, and lived its difficult last days—needs no special explanation. Suffice it to say that the SFRY enjoyed a specific status in Europe as a country which internally belonged to 'existing socialism' but retained a large measure of autonomy in foreign policy, relying on its formal membership and former leading role in the predominantly non-European non-aligned movement. In this sense, and in geopolitical terms, the Yugoslav space constituted a 'grey zone' between the two military-political blocks, and also contained some important strategic routes, such as Russia's access to the Mediterranean, the valley of the rivers Morava and Vardar, the Ljubljana 'gate', etc.

As the only relatively lasting and effective multinational construction in the Balkans, Yugoslavia was taken to represent the possibility of forming a nucleus of Balkan co-operation and lessening the risk of 'Balkanization', which did not lie solely in the creation of a series of small states, but also in the fact that all Balkan nationalisms had been tinged with the 'great nation' idea (i.e., the creation of individual 'great' states), leading to the 'national interest' of every people being, as a rule, defined to the detriment of neighbouring peoples.

The final, and now forgotten, circumstance is that in the first half of the 1980s the idea of self-management appeared attractive abroad, much more than in Yugoslavia itself, and in leftist intellectual circles seemed a possible model for humanizing and softening the Eastern bloc, the imminent demise of which most foreign observers and distinguished 'Kremlinologists' did not foresee.

Yugoslavia and the world

The situation in Yugoslavia started worsening in the second half of the 1980s, almost simultaneously with the first hints that the situation in the USSR and the socialist bloc was changing fundamentally. Sober analyses demonstrated that the political and economic system in the USSR could not be changed and saved through reforms–Gorbachov's or anybody else's–and that the weakening of the socialist super-power would show that socialist rule in the remaining countries of the Eastern bloc was based practically exclusively on the power of the USSR and fear of its intervention. Strife in the USSR threatened its surroundings and the whole world with far worse consequences than strife in Yugoslavia, if for no other reason than because of the existence of Soviet nuclear weaponry on two continents. For a long time, Yugoslavia was not the centre of attention in Western diplomacy or international diplomacy in general, and this has to be taken into account when judging the first reactions to events in this country. In other words, what started seeming dramatic and dangerous to inhabitants of the SFRY from 1987, did not seem this way to foreigners.

It is still hard to ascertain what the attitude of local, Yugoslav decision makers was towards foreign countries. More precisely, it is clear that forces which dreamt of separation from Yugoslavia, or of obtaining autonomous or confederal status within it, were interested in support from abroad, knowing that the new states, unable to rely on previous record of independence, could not survive without international support and recognition. As such groups were also anti-Communist, or at least opposed to the Yugoslav variant of 'existing socialism', it is quite natural that they turned to the West and, sincerely or not, adapted to its standards of civic democracy and its notions of human rights.

On the other hand, this was not the way of thinking of the people who slowly took over control of the SFRY, finally turning it into the Federal Republic of Yugoslavia (FRY), and in whom we are mainly interested here. Serbian leaders, who during the crisis gradually assumed formal decision making in the Yugoslav federation, seem to have relied, just like the Serbian national intelligentsia, on the Serbian people's proven 'state-creating' attribute[2], on the fact that Serbia as a state has had uninterrupted international continuity from the nineteenth century, and that it was on the winning side in both world wars. This gave rise to the belief that the Serbs and Serbia were beloved in the whole world, and that they had friends in all states except in those which were their traditional enemies, whom they had defeated in World War II (Germany, Austria). At first, this socialist-national current hoped that the world would accept that the preservation of Yugoslavia meant a 'modern federation' which would ensure a favourable position for the Serbian leadership (as representatives of all the Serbs in the country) and—what seemed more important—also the preservation of an intact one-party system, social ownership and other attributes of socialist self-management. It is characteristic that their primary demands for changes to the 1974 Constitution referred to those short parts dealing with the relationships of the republics and provinces and centralized political decision making, and not to the enormous number of ideological provisions dealing with self-management in 'organizations of associated labour', with 'local communities' and the 'delegate system' arising from it, and with other forms of cancellation of democracy through its mediation. Likewise, nobody from Serbia asked for the abolishing of the Law on Associated Labour which paralysed the economy more than the supposed mutual exploitation of the republics, insisted on by Yugoslav economists, each, naturally, with his own republic in the role of victim[3].

The group which wanted to oppose both these tendencies consisted of those parts of the administrative class gathered around the programme of the Federal Executive Council (SIV)[4] of Ante Marković. Like the party which Marković later formed, they basically relied on the managerial caste, on Communists inclined to adaptation and reform, and on those parts of the population which could not find identity primarily on a national basis. Although they were not close to Marković's Alliance of Reformist Forces, nor to Marković himself, the then federal secretary for foreign affairs, Budimir Lončar, and the leading professional officials of his Secretariat, showed a strong inclination to preserve Yugoslavia, relying on those foreign countries which they believed had an interest in this, primarily the USA, Great Britain, France and the non-aligned countries. With this aim, a series of diplomatic initiatives led by them was undertaken in order to achieve closer links with European organizations such as the Council of Europe and the European Community (as it was then known)[5]. In time, the Federal Executive Council increasingly lost influence because of resistance by three republics—Serbia, Croatia and Slovenia. This also applies to those forces which supported Marković's foreign and domestic policies, especially to the Federal Secretariat for Foreign Affairs[6]. Their definition of the international situation and the foreign-policy aims based on it were irrelevant at least from early 1991, so they shall be discussed no more in this article[7].

The most important and innermost circles of the Serbian and federal leaderships were not in the least civically oriented, and their aim was to save the cause of socialism in Yugoslavia, indeed outside it as well, even at the cost of a risky alliance with Serbian nationalism. This ideological orientation was strengthened by the interests of this class, which saw in the market economy ('restoration of capitalism'), political pluralism and democracy, huge dangers for its social position. This especially applies to the highest command of the Yugoslav People's Army (JNA). This current had inherited earlier views on the foreign, and especially the non-socialist, environment as inimical. According to these views, the capitalist world was constantly trying to destroy existing socialism by any means, including violent ones, which in peacetime were combined into 'special war', but in times of crisis could take the form of indirect or direct aggression. This basic attitude was accompanied by intense xenophobia and ignorance or dismissal of Western democratic mechanisms, which were seen only as a mask for decisions taken in international centres, some sort of 'central committees' or 'politburos' of international capitalism[8].

This part of the 'leadership' saw potential allies and supporters only in powerful socialist countries, represented for them by the USSR and China. In the former case, faith was not invested in Gorbachov, whom some considered to be a foreign agent sent to destroy socialism, but rather in those who opposed *perestroika* and *glasnost*, and who would try to depose him in August 1991[9]. Therefore, in critical moments, help was asked only from the Soviet military leadership, and not from the Soviet government or Communist Party. Intending to carry out a military take-over after the events in Belgrade on 9 March 1991, in spite of the resistance of the Presidency, the federal secretary for national defence, with the approval of the Presidency member from Serbia who was then head of this body, asked (unsuccessfully) the Soviet military leaders for assurances that they would defend the regime from Western intervention[10]. The president of the Presidency himself journeyed to China that year in order to gain its support in opposing the petrol embargo being considered by the UN[11].

In this perspective, traditional friendships between peoples was not what mattered, but ideological affinity, thus not the help of *any* Soviet Union or *any* Russia was expected, but only of 'progressive forces' in these countries. That is why the federal and Serbian leaderships were never neutral towards internal political events in the USSR and Russia, but invested great hopes in those who wished to overthrow first Gorbachov, and later Yeltsin[12]. On the other hand, election outcomes and the possibility of changes of government in the West were not interesting, in keeping with the belief that nothing good could come from the capitalist West for socialism and, later, for the Serbian people, which was amalgamated with socialism as its only defender.

There is also the impression that the 'foreign factor'—as foreign countries, primarily meaning Western ones, were referred to in internal discussion, under the influence of JNA vocabulary—was both over- and underestimated. It was overestimated regarding its influence on internal events in Yugoslavia, and underestimated where its intervention could be expected, in diplomacy, economy and the use of armed force. It was expected that the 'foreign factor' would resort only to 'special', not to real war. In keeping with the dominant doctrine that citizens of the SFRY and their groups could not have autonomous political attitudes, and that every criticism of the socialist system had to be ordered or induced from abroad, it was thought best to prevent it by police methods, either through use of classical secret or public police, or through the use of the army as police (*coup d'état*). The 1989 estimates of the federal army and police ministers are in keeping with this.

The federal secretary for national defence 'estimates that this is part of the special war against socialism and communism in general ...' He and his police colleagues considered it 'evident that there is a wish to prevent the League of Communists of Yugoslavia from carrying out reforms and remaining on the stage, they wish to break it up, push it off stage, and introduce the system of Western democracy ... it is clear that the foreign factor will not allow a consensus to be reached on socialist orientation, because their aim is the fall of socialism and, at least, the introduction of Western-type social-democracy'. They went so far as to say that the West (for only the West was considered to be the 'foreign factor') was weighing two variants: introducing bourgeois democracy immediately into Slovenia and Croatia and 'liquidating socialism only in the western part of Yugoslavia', or, in the long run, preserving the unity of the country and 'facilitating the penetration of anti-socialist ideology into the territory of the whole Yugoslavia through its western parts' [13].

Such an attitude towards foreign countries reveals a lot about the relationship towards its own population, the 'people', who would not be asked about any of these combinations, or whether they wanted democracy or whether they could think at all, as it ideas were being implanted into them from abroad, like *murti-bing* pills (after *The Captive Mind* by Czeslaw Milosz). In such thoughts from 1989, one can see the beginnings of the later joining of real socialism and (great) 'Serbdom': the vanishing of socialism only in the western parts of the country was a lesser evil than its fall in the whole Yugoslavia, presumably because the Serbian people (probably following the Eighth Session of the Central Committee of the League of Communists of Serbia), when Milošević came to power, were more socialist, or at least more immune to capitalism and 'bourgeois' democracy than others[14].

It was therefore considered that the best protection against foreign countries lay in the activities of the secret police. On the basis of such estimates, the already largely independent Serbian administrative leadership of the SFRY which was closely connected to the military and the police, opted in November 1989 for a large-scale operation to expose links with foreign services in order to save Yugoslavia. This was done without informing the Presidency of the SFRY[15]. This was the period before the multiparty elections: all members of the Presidency were still trusted Communists, or at least members of the League of Communists of Yugoslavia. Having in mind the above-mentioned fear of social-democracy, it is evident that not even Communists were inclined towards reforms.

As already hinted, the 'foreign factor' was underestimated just where it normally acted and was most efficient: in foreign policy and economy. There is no sign that the emerging Serbian military centre paid especial attention to avoiding isolation and finding allies, or at least gaining the benevolent neutrality of countries which were not ideologically close, and there were few that were. There was no attempt to win over either governments or public opinion. Representatives of the Western states, governmental and parliamentary, were received carelessly and consciously humiliated (e.g., the members of the famous EEC troika, and especially Hans van den Broek, Senator Robert Dole, etc.)[16]. State, regime and national propaganda was turned exclusively inwards, mostly towards the Serb population[17]. The international propaganda of Serbia, and, under its influence, of the last authorities of the SFRY and the first ones of the FRY, had the same content, as it was directed towards the Serbian diaspora[18]. It was completely unadapted to the environments to which it was being broadcast, asking them only to adopt the 'truth' about Serbs, the regime in Serbia and, later, the new Serb state constructs, already adopted with enthusiasm by the local Serbian public[19]. Foreign journalists were unwillingly received, accused of bias and espionage, even expelled[20].

When the war in Croatia was starting, the federal Serb side, unlike the enormous efforts of Croatian propaganda, did nothing to win over foreign correspondents: JNA commanders, such as General Andrija Biorčević, told Western journalists to go home, and that the JNA in Slavonia was defending the southern borders of Russia. The 'propaganda war' was not lost–it was not even waged in an organized fashion because of indifference to the 'foreign factor'. Spontaneous and badly organized attempts by some patriotic Serbian groups and organizations could not make up for this lack of will– their representatives, too, addressed persons of Serbian origin instead of influential segments of the foreign public, increasingly using unsuitable official arguments in which there was little democratic reasoning, and much historical, legalistic and strategic thinking[21].

Bearing all this in mind, it is clear that the aims of those who had taken over the Presidency of the SFRY and command of the JNA would have to change. From preserving Yugoslavia and socialism within it, they turned to acquiring as much territory as possible for the new Yugoslavia, which would include all territories inhabited by Serbs, and which would be, regardless of its name, a Serb state[22]. This change was a result of the abandonment of the unsuitable strategy of preserving socialist Yugoslavia with the aid of Serbian nationalism. In accord with this was the writing off of ethnically homogeneous Slovenia, after the initial anger and trade sanctions imposed following its ban of the Serbian 'Meetings of Truth' in Ljubljana on 29 November 1989[23]. The change was finalized during the war in Croatia: the JNA finally abandoned the strategy of struggle for a socialist Yugoslavia, which included the removal of non-socialist regimes in Croatia and other republics, and 'put itself in the vanguard' of the new state, in which 'Serbs and those who wanted to live with them' would remain[24]. Ideology made way for an ethnically defined 'national interest'[25].

From that point forward, the aims of Yugoslav foreign policy could be approximately defined as follows: foreign countries were to be persuaded to accept the proposition that Serbs as a people had the right to take over all territories which they themselves, or their leaderships, considered to be Serbian (historically, or according to actual population percentages); that the Serbs' right to self-determination included the right to alter earlier · republican boundaries; that the Serbs had the right and the historical mission to be dominant on the territory of their lessened (but not new) state, with minimal rights for minorities; that this state had the right to aid all Serb independence movements outside its borders;

that the two republics of Serbia and Montenegro were sufficient to extend the Yugoslav federation in full continuity, including the status of sole successor of the SFRY as regarded property, membership in international organizations and the recognition that the departing republics had violated national and international law through their 'violent secession', thus bearing all the moral and historical responsibility for the tragedy in Yugoslavia (but not for its disintegration, as it supposedly did not happen, the FRY officially being what was left over of Yugoslavia after secession)[26]. We can spare no more space for all the possible interpretations of these aims, except to mention that the tendency to conquer territory in some circles in Serbia, and also in the new Serb outposts outside Serbia, took on the irrational form of conquering territory and at the same time vacating it of non-Serbs, which practice, regardless of altruistic statements about humane population exchange, the impossibility of joint life, etc.[27], must be termed ethnic cleansing.

The world and Yugoslavia

The institutions of the international community reacted to events in Yugoslavia, which worsened suddenly from 1989, through several mediators who principally represented the Western countries, as the Soviet Union was, until its dissolution, preoccupied with its own problems and the states created from it could not react to international events quickly enough, except for Russia, which became involved in Yugoslav events after the disappearance of the SFRY. International organizations which tried to take on the role of mediator were the Conference on (later Organization for) European Security and Co-operation (CSCE/OSCE), the European Community (later Union), the United Nations and the North Atlantic Treaty Organization (NATO). The non-aligned movement and the Islamic Conference had only a tangential role, mainly in connection with events in Bosnia-Hercegovina.

Several phases can be discerned in the attitude towards Yugoslavia. The first reaction was to plead for the preservation of Yugoslavia as an unchanged state, based on the belief that like other East and Central European countries, it would show a tendency to rid itself of existing socialism, become democratic and change the economic system. This approach continued well into 1991, and was personified by the Council of Europe, which expected that Yugoslavia would be the first country of 'existing socialism' to become a member; the European Community which, through its first ministerial troika (Jacques Poos, Gianni de Michelis, Hans van den Broek), said, in as late as April 1991, that its aim was the preservation of Yugoslavia and the solving of conflicts within it in a peaceful fashion, and which adopted an identical declaration on Yugoslavia at foreign minister level in May; and the CSCE at its Berlin ministerial meeting (19 June 1991). Support for the preservation of Yugoslavia was also shown by the USA (there was a visit by Secretary of State James Baker to Yugoslavia in June 1991). The insistence of the ministerial troika during their second visit that Stipe Mesić be elected president of the Presidency (1 July 1991) demonstrates that at that time it was still thought that the SFRY could function on the basis of the 1974 Constitution, even though the fact that the US State Department had, in November 1990, published instructions for the holding of free election in the republics which had still not had them, testifies that this referred only to the functioning of the federal structure and not to an extension of the existing system in the republics[28].

Support for the existing federal Yugoslavia was gradually replaced by attempts to preserve the country as a loose federation or confederation of republics. This was apparent in the EC Declaration on Yugoslavia of 3 September 1991, and in the manner in which the Hague Conference on Yugoslavia was conducted. The text finally put forward by the chairman of the Conference, Lord Carrington, gave the Yugoslav republics, which became sovereign, the possibility of deciding on forms of their mutual co-operation, from the firmest to those which could be seen as relations between separate states. The Treaty Provisions for the Convention attempted to compensate for the non-coincidence of ethnic and republican borders with broad guarantees of minority rights. The plan did not succeed because the delegation of the Republic of Serbia refused to accept it[29], although it left its mark on the conditions which the new states on the territory of the former Yugoslavia had to fulfil in order to be recognized, especially regarding the guarantees of rights for minority communities[30].

The transition from support for the federation towards a solution which would be based on a system of relationships among sovereign republics paralleled awareness of the situation in the country. There is an unavoidable impression that at first the foreign participants were unprepared, and that they did not know the political situation and the tendencies of the main actors. Later they became acquainted with these superficially, but self-confidently. Support for the preservation of the SFRY was therefore declarative, and it was unclear what exactly was meant by this. In any case, the SFRY was subjected to the general expectations of countries finally leaving existing socialism, where matters of democratization, human rights improvements and economy were paramount.

It was for this reason that pressure to hold free multiparty elections was the strongest, especially from the USA. Because of opposition from Slovenia and Serbia, they could be held only at republican level, and brought to power those parties which put into the foreground the question of an individual state, and only within such a state saw possibilities of democratization, transition and human rights—if they had them in mind at all[31]. Thus, the mediators in the Yugoslav crisis simplified its extent and causes, reducing them only to ethnic conflicts. The opportunity was missed while Yugoslavia still existed to resolve other important matters, also at the roots of the crisis, such as that of conditions for political pluralism, economic transformation and human rights. All the inhabitants of Yugoslavia, by will of their national leaders, but now also with the help of the international community, were forced into collectivity, without the opportunity of understanding and expressing themselves differently. Democratic forces, which could have had a favourable influence on events in the SFRY by co-operating and helping each other across republican borders, were divided, forced to adopt patriotic rhetoric for the sake of political survival, and reduced to acting in a confined space. The most affected by this everywhere was the social-democratic left, which by its nature crosses ethnic barriers in multinational communities most easily[32].

Recognizing the national leaders as legitimate negotiating partners without satisfactory democratic proof, the EC gave them the legitimacy of statesmen and of embodiments of national aspirations, which referred primarily to the creation and strengthening of archaic nineteenth-century states with unlimited sovereignty over their own territory and population and all its attributes, especially the military ones[33]. It is no wonder, therefore, that later on national leaders of extremely doubtful democratic legitimacy, either self-proclaimed or imposed from outside, especially in Bosnia-Hercegovina, easily gained the position of respected partners in international negotiations. Contrary to the initial democratic inspiration, Western mediators and crisis solvers actually adopted local nationalist attitudes: it became important to them to solve problems among nations and states in order to prevent wider conflicts and graver consequences for the surrounding region, completely forgetting in the process about the people who were supposed to live with the new arrangements.

The failure of the Hague Conference, and German pressure, forced the EU to seek simpler and more radical solutions, in the form of the adoption of the Slovenian-Croat version of the disappearance of the SFRY through disintegration, and not through secession of a large number of federal units. The extraordinary ministerial session of this organization, held on 16 December 1991, adopted a Declaration on Yugoslavia putting forward the agreed views on recognition of all Yugoslav republics which should ask for it. Those states could be recognized which, among other things, fulfilled the conditions set forth in the declaration on guidelines for recognizing new states in Eastern Europe and the Soviet Union, adopted by the same gathering on the same day[34]. On the basis of this last document, all these states had to respect the provisions of the UN Charter and the obligations accepted in the Helsinki Agreement and Paris Charter, especially as regarded the rule of law, democracy, and human rights, and to guarantee the rights of all ethnic and national groups and minorities in keeping with obligations undertaken at the CSCE. Additionally, the Yugoslav republics had to declare that they accepted the provisions of the draft convention[35]—especially those in Chapter I, dealing with human rights and national or ethnic group rights.

A circumstance which must be kept in mind here is that the Yugoslav question was the first serious test of the common European foreign policy, that is, of the EU foreign policy made possible by the Maastricht Treaty, and that the destructive potential of the Yugoslav crisis, which was not foreseen abroad, paled beside the danger of joint decision making and co-ordination in the new foreign-policy area of the Union proving to be impossible, thus preventing the Union from dealing with the whole post-Communist complex in the East and setting up as an equal partner for the USA. That is why German pressure to recognize Slovenia and Croatia as soon as possible had even greater weight. The Yugoslav republics were thus presented with an opportunity which, historically, has rarely been offered to secessionist and independence movements. Croatia and Slovenia took it up with alacrity, and Macedonia and Bosnia-Hercegovina out of necessity, because otherwise they would have had to remain within Yugoslavia under conditions controlled by the Serb military institutions in Belgrade, which would be formally strengthened by the decrease in number of members of the Presidency of the SFRY[36]. The decision on recognition was to be taken jointly on the basis of the findings of the Badinter arbitration commission. However, Germany threatened unilateral recognition, and forced the Union to act swiftly and, in early 1992, recognize all the republics which had asked for recognition, save for Macedonia. These moves were dogged by inconsistency from the beginning: Croatia was recognized even without the recommendation of the arbitration commission, but Macedonia was not, in spite of the commission's recommendation, because Greece was opposed on grounds not covered by the Declaration. It subsequently turned out that conditions referring to human rights were quickly forgotten: none of the states recognized was ever warned, in spite of sufficient reasons for doing so, that on the basis of unilateral acceptance of all the conditions set forth by the Declaration it was obliged to guarantee the highest standards of human and minority rights.

The haste in giving international recognition to Croatia and Slovenia, and later to Bosnia-Hercegovina, is considered a mistake on the part of the EU, not only because, apart from Slovenia, they did not fulfil the traditional demands for the existence of a state (authority, territory and population), but also because Croatia did not fulfil the new, democratic conditions set forth in the EU Declaration. However, a more important objection, voiced particularly by Lord Carrington, was of a political nature, and referred to Slovenia. After international recognition of their basic tendency to create independent states, the western Yugoslav republics would have achieved their most important and primary aim, and would lose interest in further participation in solving the remaining questions of the SFRY, and the international community would have deprived itself of the means to extract concessions from them by imposing further conditions for their recognition[37].

Another consequence was a sudden loss of interest by the recognized republics in improving the living conditions of the people in the rest of Yugoslavia. Official Slovenia was the first to hasten to behave as if it had never belonged to Yugoslavia, and had never had any connection with it. Among other things, the Slovenians' earlier marked interest in the fate of the Albanians and other members of national minorities in Serbia vanished. Looking back, this presents the Slovenian interest in human rights as a means to achieving their own basic end, Slovenian independence. Relations were raised to state level, and only matters of state were on the agenda.

The behaviour of Germany deserves special analysis. The many hysterical assertions put forward in Serbia, according to which Germany was the main inspirer of the disintegration of Yugoslavia so that it could achieve its strategic aims ('access to warm seas', domination in the Balkans, *Drang nach Osten*, nuclear waste storage etc.), avenge its defeat in the Second World War, or realize its pathological hatred towards the Serbs, must not prevent us from seeing that it was in Germany and Austria that the bias which marked Europe's attitude towards the participants in the Yugoslav events during the following period was initiated. Understanding ethnic nationalism is part of the German tradition, which, in contrast to the state patriotism typical of the tradition of the French Revolution, is often termed the Germanic version of nationalism[38]. In Germany, therefore, nationalism itself was not considered outmoded or dangerous, and this paved the way for the acceptance of 'good' nationalisms. This was the road taken whole-heartedly by some Slovenian and Croatian intellectuals, who thought that nationalism was a positive characteristic, while bad nationalism had to be called by more pejorative names, such as 'fascism, xenophobia, chauvinism, racism, political ethnocentrism' etc.[39]. That Serbian nationalism should become the paradigm of bad nationalism in Germany was abetted by at least two factors. One was the perception of Serbs as brutal intruders, enemies and terrorists[40]. The other was that the Federal Republic of Germany was a haven for Croatian nationalist and rightist emigrants, who interpreted post-1945 events in Yugoslavia exclusively in terms of Serbian Communist domination. These interpretations were not restricted to the easily recognizable publications of the émigré groups, but, through entry of the new emigrants into scholarly institutions, for which they were qualified by knowledge of the language and circumstances of south-eastern Europe, also became points of view with scholarly, or at least expert, legitimacy. Various circumstances, among them the personal experience of editor-in-chief Reismüller, contributed to one of Germany's previously most respected dailies (certainly the most influential in the northern part of Germany), the *Frankfurter allgemeine Zeitung*, completely adopting the view of Serbs as non-European and backward negative heroes of the Yugoslav drama[41].

However, it must be said that the atmosphere in favour of the recognition of the 'secessionist republics' was strongly fuelled by the behaviour of the JNA and the Serbian paramilitary units under its cover and command during the war in Croatia. Not only did the foreign media show the needless destruction of towns, but the propaganda machinery in Yugoslavia, with the herostratic pleasure of the victor, provided them with abundant visual and written material for this[42]. The negative consequences of the strategy of destruction of towns which the JNA had chosen were both military and psychological: the targets chosen (such as Dubrovnik, and later

Sarajevo, cities known to wide circles of Western media consumers) were symbolically important abroad, and gave occasion to the estimate that this was a campaign being waged by cruel and uncultured people.

What acted unfavourably for the Serbs in all Western environments was a consequence of the great misunderstanding in Serbia and Montenegro between the regime born at the Eighth Session of the League of Communists of Serbia on the one hand, and the national intelligentsia and the majority of nationally oriented voters on the other. The latter, as many of them later realized with regret, made their choice in the belief that the transformation at that historical meeting and the ascension of Slobodan Milošević as head of party and state had made the whole decision-making class into strong and sincere fighters for the Serb people and its interests. The continuance of 'Communist' symbols, rituals and rhetoric seemed like an unimportant and necessary evil for the sake of higher efficacy in combating the 'Communists' from other republics. The new image of the Communist Party was supported by leading dissidents at home and abroad, who, on account of their problems with the pre-Milošević or Titoist authorities, cannot be accused of pro-Communist tendencies.

When election time came around, the majority in Serbia and Montenegro voted for *Communists as nationalists*. The Communist Party in Serbia disguised itself as socialist belatedly and thinly, and in Montenegro it kept the unchanged name of League of Communists for the elections. And while in the other republics the Communists and their evidently non-nationalist inheritors had been defeated, in Serbia they won 46 per cent of the vote, and in Montenegro a total of 64 per cent[43]. With a little malice and ignorance, and with the already described help of official Serbian propaganda, it was easy to come to the conclusion that the Serbs had voted for Communism, and everybody else for liberal democracy; even when the nationalist inspiration of the Serb electoral body was found out, it could be concluded that Serbian nationalism was Communist and retrograde, while the other Yugoslav nationalisms, especially those in the western republics, were democratic, capitalist and liberal, even when they were known to be rightist. Subsequently, it could be concluded that the Serb people in Serbia and outside it shared a system of values and a world-view similar to those of the Staff of the High Command and the members of the SFRY Presidency close to it.

All this created the basis for behaviour in subsequent phases, characterized by the preconception that the Serbs did not wish to fit into Europe and the world of democracy, market and human rights, but that they exclusively tended to dominate others and impose on them obsolete forms of social and political organization. Naturally, the already described behaviour of Serb emissaries and generals, regardless of whether they spoke as representatives of the SFRY, the FRY, Serbia or the Serb 'entities', for a long time reinforced such a conception. In a way, the prophecy of the military ideologues was fulfilled, the West tried to 'take away' from Communism as large a part of Yugoslavia as possible by denying it to Communist Serbia[44]. This may explain the many wrangles in interpretation of the rules of international law and morality, even some of the controversial decisions of the Badinter commission[45]. It should be kept in mind that attitudes towards the nations in Yugoslavia and their leaders were being formed in 1990 and 1991, when it still seemed that the USSR could endure as a Communist superpower and use its enormous military potential, especially if leadership was reassumed by the 'healthy forces' of *perestroika* opponents[46].

In the next phase, aversion towards the Serbian regime and Serbs in general went hand in hand with the belief that Yugoslavia had broken up into new states, and that norms of international law governing relationships between states, including those dealing with aggression, should be applied to the relations among them. It was thus easy to come to the conclusion that Serbia, now in the guise of the FR of Yugoslavia, was helping the Serb side in the fighting in Bosnia-Hercegovina sufficiently to warrant qualification as a threat to international peace and the application of measures from Chapter VI of the UN Charter, popularly and incorrectly known as 'sanctions'[47].

Mistrust of Serb subjects, which in turn caused among them a growing defiance and a stubborn search for partners outside the UN and other organizations, lasted for a very long time, and could not be removed by fine-tuning at the top of the FRY leadership. It was equally on display towards the government of Milan Panić, which was not taken seriously, nor was his relative success in the presidential elections in Serbia[48]. It seems that all opposition in Serbia was ignored long before it became nationalistically warlike. The Vidovdan (St. Vitus's Day) Assembly and massive student demonstrations in Belgrade in 1992 went unnoticed, or were interpreted only as outbursts of nationalism.

As could be expected on the basis of earlier experience with the application of economic embargoes against states in a similar situation, the Security Council measures produced their effect: in the short term they deformed and radicalized political life and strengthened the regime, and only in the long term did they perhaps force the authorities in Serbia and the FRY to make some concessions[49]. As early as 1993, two years before the Dayton Accords, they showed signs of desisting from maximalist plans in Bosnia-Hercegovina, and the burden of the 'sanctions' was not the only reason. The gaining of about half of the Bosnian-Hercegovinian territory for the Serb side (with the clear possibility of its joining the FRY) seemed quite realistic, and further support of the one-party leadership in the Republika Srpska unattractive, because Radovan Karadžić's Serbian Democratic Party (SDS) and its rightist allies could become dangerous rivals to the Socialist Party of Serbia and the President of Serbia, not only in the Republika Srpska, but also in Serbia itself and in the future unified state. *The political centre in Belgrade was during the whole crisis primarily motivated by preservation of its own power*[50].

There are two further reasons for claiming that sanctions against the FRY and (indirectly) against the Republika Srpska did not work in their mainly economic thrust. The result, as measured by its definition and the initial intentions of the Security Council, was achieved only halfway: instead of the FRY completely pulling out of Bosnia-Hercegovina, it retained influence on 49 per cent of its territory; instead of the JNA withdrawing, its men were disguised as the Army of the Republika Srpska, enjoying strategic, personnel and logistic support from the Army of Yugoslavia all the time. Besides, the decisive turnabout was not achieved through sanctions, but through the use, in summer 1995, of armed force by NATO against the Bosnian Serbs and, indirectly, the Army of Yugoslavia, which had important reconnaissance, information and command elements destroyed. In that way, the advantage of the Serb-Yugoslav side in armaments and equipment was decreased, and the long hesitation of the Western countries to commit ground forces without US participation was overcome as Croat and Bosnian units, which had interest and motivation, took their place.

The United Nations joined the solving of the Yugoslav crisis after European institutions. It is presumed that the federal Serbian leadership wanted this in order to avoid the excessive influence of Germany in Europe. The first move by the SFRY diplomacy was shrewd: with its approval, the Security Council adopted, on 25 September 1991, Resolution 713 (1991) banning, on the basis of Chapter VI of the UN Charter, all delivery of weapons and military equipment to Yugoslavia. This made more difficult the provision of weaponry for the secessionist republics, and ensured a long-lasting supremacy for the JNA, which became especially apparent during the fighting in Bosnia-Hercegovina. The second move by the Security Council also followed at the initiative of the ruling group in Belgrade. They demanded that UN forces be sent to Croatia to safeguard the advantages which the local Serbs had achieved without further involvement of the JNA, which, according to Borisav Jović, would have required increasingly large-scale call-ups in Serbia, and 'this was completely counter-productive for our policies'[51]. In Resolution 721 (1991) of 27 November 1991, the Security Council supported this initiative, which developed into the Vance plan. Accepting Vance's concept of 'inkblot' disposition of forces, the Security Council did not fully live up to Belgrade's expectations that 'now the Serb people in these territories have power, we should ask the United Nations that they (sic) protect them with their peace forces'[52]. Up to the adoption of the measures ('sanctions') against the FRY, the Security Council tried to keep to a 'statist' but neutral approach to the actors in the events in Yugoslav territory, but the General Assembly, influenced by the non-aligned majority, increasingly opted for a critical attitude towards the Serb side. Various factors influenced this majority: from racist and white-supremacist tones in Serbian propaganda which portrayed non-alignment as Tito's expensive 'nigger' adventure, through strong attempts by Belgrade and Serb nationalist associations to establish connections with Israel and the Jewish lobby, to–perhaps most importantly–the Bosnian Serb treatment of Muslims and the increasingly frequent official attempts by official Serbian science and quasi-science to qualify all Bosnian Muslims as fundamentalists, and even to treat the Kosovo Albanians in the same way[53]. When, in mid-1992, the awful crimes and ethnic cleansing in Bosnia-Hercegovina became known, the Serbs definitely acquired the reputation of the negative hero of the Yugoslav tragedy, and the only one, at that, until evidence surfaced that the policies of Croatian nationalism and the new Croatian state were based on the idea of territorial conquest of ethnically vacant territories, and that they supported all crimes supposedly necessary to achieve this aim.

Principles and pragmatism

Revulsion at atrocities, concentration camps, rape, forced resettlement and similar acts engulfed the world public and international non-governmental organizations, but was not easily transferred to governments. This was completely in keeping with the shift of focus, at the end of 1991, from the (internal) problems of people and their organizations in Yugoslavia to the international relations of the monolithic post-Yugoslav nations and their states. Consequently, collective subjects could be accused of aggression against other subjects, but not of attempting to fight for their own privileged position or of striving to protect national interests. Their collective responsibility was seen as the responsibility for aggressive acts only, which brought about the 'sanctions' against the FRY (and later against the Republika Srpska, with the FRY's bizarre mediation). However, their attitude towards their own populations ceased to be of interest, except in the case of bad treatment of collective entities, among which, due to the preoccupation with national concerns, national (but not other) minorities were most prominent.

From the tension between the state and humanitarian approaches, and because of frustration caused by the failure of the measures against the FRY to stop the war in Bosnia, the gradual knowledge that the war was part of the Serb-Croat plan for partition of Bosnia-Hercegovina, the development of the Muslim-Croat conflict and announcements of criminal acts by Croatian army and paramilitary units against Muslims and Serbs and the ethnic cleansing of Krajina, there arose the need to separate the 'moral' approach to the Yugoslav actors from the 'pragmatic' one. As there was no basis to consider only one side as the moral offender, and as the division into good and bad is very difficult in any conflict with more than two participants, the solution was found in individual criminal responsibility. With this in mind, the International Criminal Tribunal for the Former Yugoslavia (Hague Tribunal) was founded in May 1993[54]. Those accused and indicted appear before it as individuals, so it was thought that collective judgement of the nations to which they belonged would be avoided[55].

Collective judgement became superfluous, as non-Serb nationalisms lost the reputation of being 'better'[56]. The only nationalism on Yugoslav territory which still encounters understanding in the West as 'good' is Albanian nationalism.

Diplomats and strategists, who as a rule see moral and legal judgements as outbursts of unrealistic and emaciate sentimentality, could thus turn back to negotiating with those who promised them success in ending the war and its consequences for the wider environs and for international relations in general. These were primarily those men who had power and control of the army, regardless of their democratic origin and legitimacy and their choice of means in carrying out their domestic and foreign policies. The co-chairmen of the International Conference on the Former Yugo-slavia, Thorvald Stoltenberg, representing the UN, and Lord Owen, representing the EU, became personifications of this approach[57]. The 'peace process' could, therefore, be conducted like any other mediation between states: the premise was that every leader was legitimate and equally good or bad, and the measure of his qualifi-cations lay only in his ability to control the means of power. For greater security, the Statute of the Hague Tribunal did not include crimes against peace (such as, for example, initiating a war of ag-gression), with which the principal participants in the peace proc-ess could possibly be charged.

The use of force against the Bosnian Serbs was not the expres-sion of a moral, but of a pragmatic principle: it was intended to achieve military balance and to force the militarily stronger side to adhere to agreements. It was aimed at the political leadership of the SDS and the now independent Bosnian-Hercegovinian branch of the JNA, who had demonstrated that they took moral judge-ments very easily, but turns of fortune and battlefield defeat very hard. This strengthened the only Serbian actor who, albeit very belatedly, had begun behaving rationally (relative to himself) and paying attention to the previously underestimated 'foreign factor'. The president of the Republic of Serbia was given the mandate of completing the 'peace process' in the way which he found suitable, but still keeping to international demands. These no longer in-cluded punishment for what was originally considered aggression, so long as that aggression, that is, the annexation of Bosnia-Hercegovina, did not bear all its intended fruits, and form was ob-served in the survival of Bosnia-Hercegovina as a unified subject of international law.

And the moral approach? It was partly preserved in the transfer to the plane of individual responsibility. Regardless of the future fate of the Hague Tribunal, with which all post-Yugoslav states and 'entities' have to cooperage according to the Dayton Accords, its prosecutor had the right of veto for high political appointments in Bosnia-Hercegovina. For somebody's candidacy to be invalid, it was not necessary that he or she be convicted by the Tribunal, but only that one of its judges approve an indictment against that person.

The reasons why the intervention of the institutions of the in-ternational community in Yugoslavia is considered unsuccessful are known. Some have already been pointed out, but all can be recapitulated by pointing to the lack of readiness, disunity and inability of European institutions to become acquainted with the crisis and realize its real causes; to the view of the conflict as pri marily a collective struggle among nations, or at least a struggle among national states; to gradual acceptance of nationalist arguments, to support of sides who verbally represented themselves as 'pro-Western'; to the inability to take a position in complex conflicts with more than two participants; to facile acceptance of theses on centuries-old animosities among semi-wild Balkan peoples; to overestimation of the role of religion; to underestimation of the economic factor, etc. All this was abetted by confusion and uncertainty in the USSR and the Eastern bloc, rivalry between Europe and the USA, which led to the temporary disengagement of the only remaining superpower, and by the fear that south-eastern Europe would return to its pre-1914 state, where the European powers would again exhaust themselves in the struggle for spheres of interest, possibly entering into a new world war.

On the basis of the preceding analysis, some further remarks need to be added. Even if we consider that at the end of 1995 a somewhat more durable solution was found, it cannot be deemed successful, as it left in its wake and in the largest part of the territory of ex-Yugoslavia economic devastation, hundreds of thousands of displaced persons, ravaged and criminalized societies and states and semi-states which have little chance of becoming, in the near future, democratic societies under the rule of law.

Vacillation between two opposed approaches, the amoral-diplomatic on the one hand, and the moral on the other, made the whole undertaking more difficult, confusing the majority of the inhabitants of the Yugoslav space and, in some of its parts, giving rise to mistrust of international institutions and international law, and the unwilling acceptance of the feeling of having been eternally banished to the periphery of the world.

Lack of interest in the human content of the solutions proposed and accepted, and the preference given to those who were undisputedly in power, strengthened authoritarian tendencies in all post-Yugoslav states, especially in those most involved in the armed conflict. Communication from abroad with democratic and anti-war forces was left to non-governmental organizations and individuals, while officially it was superficial, lacking in interest and inventiveness. The democratic opposition was everywhere in a politically even more unfavourable position: even though it was supposedly traitorous because of its alleged links to foreign countries, it was precisely in this area that it was helpless and ineffective, because foreign countries did not respect it, either.

The conflict in Yugoslavia was marked by a double dosage of irrationality. First, at the end of the twentieth century, most of the aims which the nationalist elites set themselves were irrational. This does not apply only to the evident obscurantism and attempts to return to the ancient past and isolation from the world, but primarily to the tendency towards acquisition of territory which was not grounded in any sort of economic justification. Second, most of the participants were led by irrational men, even if we apply a limited definition of rationality as the tendency to choose suitable, available and permissible means to an end, even if the end in itself is immoral, or even irrational. They all showed a strong tendency to violence, both in domestic and in foreign policy.

Abroad, the irrationality of the leaders and decision makers was gradually recognized, for which there is increasingly clear testimony from those who, in keeping with the pragmatic approach, had to negotiate with them, even pretending to find them rational. However, many foreign representatives, even experts on Yugoslavia, did not recognize the irrationality of the aims, especially of the territorial aims. They either became used to accepting them, gradually endorsing the explanation that the conflict on Yugoslav territory was eternal, dating back to the division of the Roman Empire, or they applied norms dear to the 'realists' and strategic thinkers and geopoliticians (who have great influence on professional diplomats), according to which what was rational in the sixteenth or nineteenth century was still rational–possession of territory and (military) control of space. There is no need to stress how much this differs from the real state of affairs, where the well-being of people mostly depends on economic development, good organization and the ability of democratic institutions and decision making to fulfil human needs. It is paradoxical that this was happening at a time of European integration, and under the aegis of the European Union, which was set up in order to eliminate motives for territorial conquest and the conflicts connected with it in Europe.

Notes

1 'The international community' is a term which marks the sum of all subjects of international relations. The word 'community' only suggests that the existence of common values is somewhat greater than in sums termed 'societies'. Nowadays, usually the institutions of the international community are meant, wherein states and other subjects do not act anarchically and independently, but through forums for joint consultation and decision making, generally meaning international organizations. In Yugoslavia, however, the habit set in of differentiating be-

tween the international community and one's own state or people, or even of taking up an antagonistic position towards it. Testimony to this were the vociferous proposals that Serbia and the FR of Yugoslavia leave all organized forms of the international community, such as, e.g., the United Nations. Further testimony is to be found in terms such as 'the so-called international community' and prophecies of the end of the United Nations.

2 The preamble to the Constitution of the Republic of Serbia cites the 'state-creating traditions' of the Serbian people. As far as the author of this text knows, this is the only constitution which uses this word.

3 See Ljubomir Madjar, 'Ko koga eksploatiše', *Republika*, Beograd, 1995, No. 123.

4 *Savezno izvršno veće*: corresponded to the federal government in other countries.

5 In 1991 Yugoslavia was visited, at the initiative of the Federal Secretariat for Foreign Affairs, by delegations of the Council of Europe (secretary general and Speaker of the European Parliament) and the European Community. Such visits had been even more frequent previously, and it was believed that Yugoslavia was on the threshold of membership in the Council of Europe. See Slobodanka Kovačević and Putnik Dajić, *Hronologija jugoslovenske krize 1942–1993*, Beograd, Institut za evropske studije, 1994.

6 One example is sufficient: the Federal Secretariat for Foreign Affairs insisted on obtaining from the president of France an invitation for the president of the Presidency of the SFRY to attend the official celebration of the two-hundredth anniversary of the French Revolution in June 1989. The Serbian leadership concluded that the 'imposition' of Drnovšek was 'beneath the dignity' of the state, and the member of the Presidency from Serbia all but demanded the resignations of the president of the Presidency and of the federal secretary of foreign affairs. A diary entry by this member from Serbia, Borisav Jović, is worth quoting: 'Slobodan Milošević was right when he said in Novi Sad that we want to go to Europe, but with dignity, and not as lackeys. He certainly knew whom to address' (B. Jović, *Poslednji dani SFRJ*, Politika, Beograd 1995: 36). Professional diplomats know, of course, that the diplomatic services of small countries have to make great efforts to have their heads of state invited to such significant ceremonial occasions.

7 The success of the Federal Executive Council depended to a large extent on foreign support. It did not materialize, probably because the Western public paid more attention to the outcome of the first multiparty elections in the republics, where the Reformists did not do well. Marković's popularity, which peaked in 1990 (79% support in Yugoslavia, 93% in Bosnia-Herzegovina, 89% in Vojvodina and Macedonia, 83% in Croatia, 81% in Serbia, 59% in Slovenia and 42% in Kosovo-Metohija) was not sufficiently convincing when compared to the outcomes of the elections and the unambiguous attitudes of the old and new leaderships of Serbia, Croatia and Slovenia against preserving Yugoslavia through

the changes called for in Marković's programme. See Susan Woodward, *Balkan Tragedy*, Washington, D.C., The Brookings Institute, 1995: 128ff. Together with Gorbachov, Marković was branded a traitor, even an executor of Ustasha plans in Yugoslavia (Ilija Petrović and Budimir Košutić in a special broadcast on Serbian Television). See Lazar Lalić, *Tri TV godine u Srbiji*, Nezavisni sindikat medija, Beograd, 1995: 68.

8 Lately, the leading candidate for this role was the Trilateral Commission. As representative of many similar works, see Vojislav Mićović, *Specijalni rat i Jugoslavija*, Beograd, Rad, 1986; Dušan Miljanić, Radovan Radinović et al., *Opštenarodna odbrana i društvena samozaštita SFRJ*, Beograd, Zavod za udžbnike i nastavna sredstva, no date.: 120ff; and the contributions to *Novi svetski poredak i politika odbrane Savezne Republike Jugoslavije*, Beograd, Savezno ministarstvo odbrane, Uprava za strategijske studije i politiku odbrane, 1993. In the latter, a very respectable and expensive official publication, one of the authors (Lieutenant-Colonel Svetozar Radišić, MA) even discusses an international conspiracy against Serbian history (141)!

9 See: Veljko Kadijević, *Moje viđenje raspada. Vojska bez države*, Politika, Beograd, 1993.

10 The president of the SIV found out about this secret visit by a member of his government, Veljko Kadijević, to his Soviet colleague, General Yazov, only six months later, and then demanded his resignation without success (18 September 1991). Kovačević and Dajić, op. cit. As far back as November 1989, the Serbian leadership had been considering Kadijević as the best candidate for the post of president of the SIV (B. Jović, op. cit.: 265, 269).

11 Ibid.: 411.

12 The mistaken perception of contemporary Russian intellectuals and politicians as generally highly conservative, traditionalist, mystical and archaic Orthodox Slavophiles should be the matter of a separate discussion. The impression is that this was helped not only by frequent visits of such personages to Yugoslavia, but also by the reporting of all media. For a start, see the critical articles published in *Republika*, e.g., 'Rusija u magli', No. 125–26, October 1995: 2.

13 V. Kadijević, op. cit.: 63, 67, 67–68. In an interview published on 3 December 1990, after the Communists had been defeated in elections held in all republics except Serbia, Kadijević still pleaded for a 'united and socialist' Yugoslavia. Kovačević-Dajić, op. cit.

14 The version offered by the subsequent rightist allies of this group of fighters against the 'new world order' is amazingly similar: the Serbian people, according to them, is 'authentic', and thus not susceptible to the false charms of democracy, the market and 'financial capital'. That is why it was faced with an alliance of the USA, who control the UN and the OSCE, the European Union, dominated by Germany, Turkey, as a vassal of America and leader of the Islamic world, and revanchist neighbours such as Austria, Albania and Hungary. Dragoš Kalajić, 'Na braniku Evrope, protiv novog svetskog poretka', paper at a conference

organized by the Directorate for Strategic Studies and Defence Policy of the Federal Ministry of Defence of the FRY in February 1993. *Novi svetski poredak i politika odbrane Savezne Republike Jugoslavije*, 106ff.

15 The decision was taken by the federal secretary for national defence, Veljko Kadijević, the federal secretary for internal affairs, Petar Gračanin, and the Presidency member from Serbia, and its head, Borisav Jović. According to Jović, 'Veljko has the habit of presenting such analyses to me, and for understandable reasons does not want to present them to the whole Presidency'. B. Jović, op. cit.: 68. The same attitude towards the suitability or lack thereof of functionaries of the Federation is evinced by General Kadijević, op. cit.: 6, 109.

16 More examples can be found in Henry Weynaends, *L'engrenage. Chroniques Yougoslaves juillet 1991-âout 1992*, Paris, Denoel, 1993.

17 It could be said that intensive nationalist propaganda was necessary in Serbia, because nationalism was not developed in the population, unlike in the intellectual elite. Its greater success among emigrants can be ascribed to already existing nationalism in the diaspora. For this note I am indebted to Vesna Petrović.

18 The introduction of satellite broadcasts *in Serbian* by Serbian Radio-Television is clear testimony. Experts considered this an ill-advised and expensive move, thinking that its aim was to influence foreign public opinion. However, it turned out that 'the dish', with the help of newly formed Serbian associations financed from Yugoslavia, such as 'All Serbs of the World', etc., was a very powerful lever in mobilizing Serbs in the diaspora to support the aims of the Serbian leadership. Having in mind the rightist, even Chetnik and Ljotić origin of most of the Serbian political emigration, and the fact that the Serb-Yugoslav leadership did not much alter its Communist style, this was a veritable propaganda miracle.

19 See, e.g., Prvoslav Ralić and Mile Nedeljković, eds., *Rečnik zabluda: sto neistina o srpskom narodu, i odgovori na njih* (A Dictionary of Misconceptions: a hundred falsities about Serbia and Serbs and answers to them), Beograd, Ministarstvo za informacije Srbije, 1994.

20 Except for chosen ones, like, for example, an Italian correspondent and the Belgrade correspondent of Reuters (a Yugoslav citizen) who supposedly saw the corpses of forty-one Serb children with their throats cut in Borovo Naselje. The news was later denied both by the JNA and the British agency, so finally Serbian television, which had devoted great attention to these journalists, had to do so, too. Lalić, op. cit.: 95, 99.

21 As representative of many such works, see *The Violent Dissolution of Yugoslavia. Truth and Deceit 1991–1994. One Hundred Irrefutable Facts*, San Francisco, North American News Analysis Group, s.a. This opens with a reproduction map of Greater Serbia, supposedly drawn up in a secret London agreement with Italy in 1915, whereby the powers of the Entente promised that Italy would gain Austro-Hungarian territories in Dalmatia in return for entering the war on their side. These Ser-

bian borders include, among other places, Split. Regardless of the accuracy of this claim, the lack of its appeal to the American public, which remembered that at the end of World War I President Wilson was strictly opposed to secret diplomacy and its results, is remarkable.

22 Regarding the preservation of socialism, differences remained, surfacing later in the internal politics of the FRY and the Republika Srpska.

23 See B. Jović, op. cit.: 77ff. The Serbian national intelligentsia used its influence on Slobodan Milošević and circles close to him even earlier, in order to suggest that they abandon the idea of Yugoslavia and declare, in the interest of the Serbs, that it simply no longer existed. Ibid.: 28, 130.

24 V. Kadijević, op. cit.; B. Jović, op. cit.: 388. Jović says that Kadijević described opposition to this attitude as 'a typical example of special war'.

25 In the scholarly terminology of international relations, 'national interest' does not refer to the (ethnic) nation but to the state. See Andrija Miletić, *Nacionalni interes u američkoj teoriji medunarodnih odnosa,* Beograd, Savremena administracija, 1978. Vojin Dimitrijević and Radoslav Stojanović, *Medunarodni odnosi,* Beograd, Centar za publikacije Pravnog fakulteta, 1988: 300ff.

26 Thence the instruction to the state administration and media to use only the expression '*former* Yugoslavia'.

27 See Vojin Dimitrijević, *The Fate of Non-Members of Dominant Nations in Post-Communist European Countries,* Firenze, European University Institute, 1995: 21.

28 Facts from Kovačević and Dajić, op. cit., under the corresponding dates.

29 The president of Montenegro accepted it, and this led to a crisis in the relations of the Serbian and Montenegrin leaderships.

30 There are suggestions that it was precisely these provisions which caused Serbia's rejection of Carrington's plan, because they also referred to Serbia, and could be interpreted in favour of the Kosovo Albanians. See Laura Silber and Alan Little, *The Death of Yugoslavia,* London, Penguin-BBC, 1995: 213. There is no support for this in Borisav Jović's memoirs: according to him, the reasons for rejecting the plan were that it 'breaks up Yugoslavia, divides the Serb people into several states, leaves the Serbs in Croatia, etc.', B. Jović, op. cit.: 400. As far as can be discerned, the Serbian expert team at the conference on Yugoslavia in The Hague and Brussels, headed by academician Kosta Mihailović, reasoned similarly: they were principally bothered by the language used, which in their view implied that the republics had already become subjects of international law, and by the fact that only one option was proposed, that of sovereign independent republics. See 'Sudbina haško-briselske konferencije o Jugoslaviji', *Ekonomska misao,* XXV, off print, 3.

31 Practically without exception, human rights were envisaged as the *collective* rights of one's own nation, primarily the right to self-determination, serving to set up a state first, which would then guarantee individual rights, broader for members of the majority, and somewhat reduced for minority nations.

32 See Eric Hobsbawm, *Nations and Nationalism* Since 1780, 2nd edition, Cambridge University Press, 1990.

33 See Woodward, op. cit.: 198.

34 Both declarations were published in document UN S/23292, 17 December 1991.

35 Carrington's plan.

36 According to the 1974 Constitution, Serbia had one seat in the federal Presidency, its two autonomous provinces two, and the remaining five republics one each. In 1991 the Serbian regime controlled four of the eight Presidency members: those of Serbia, Montenegro, Vojvodina and Kosovo-Metohija. These four (the so-called semi-Presidency) claimed that they could take decisions by themselves, but would have had a clear majority as soon as the number of federation members fell to five because of the departure of Slovenia.

37 'The only incentive we had to get anyone to agree to anything was the ultimate recognition of their independence. Otherwise there was no carrot. You just threw it away, just like that.' Lord Carrington in Silber and Little, op. cit.: 221.

38 See Egbert Jahn, 'Demokracija i nacionalizam—jedinstvo ili protuvslovlje?', *Politička misao*, 1992/4: 48.

39 Tomaz Mastnak, 'Is the nation-state really obsolete?', *The Times Literary Supplement*, 7 August 1992: 11. See also Franjo Zenko, 'Demokracija i nacionalna država', *Politička misao*, 1992/4: 70.

40 Thomas Mann's *Doktor Faustus* describes a Munich soirée in 1915 which is pervaded by fear at the rumour that Serb terrorists are in town.

41 The power of the Frankfurt daily can be compared to the position of *Politika* in Serbia, which the leaders of the 'anti-bureaucratic revolution' knew how to use so well. Like *Politika* in Serbia, in Germany outside Bavaria the *Frankfurter allgemeine Zeitung* is referred to as 'the newspaper'.

42 See Lalić, op. cit.: 74ff.

43 Owing to the electoral system, this majority in Serbia was translated into 77.6% of seats in parliament, and into only 66% in Montenegro. See Vladimir Goati, 'Korak u demokratiju', *Oslobodjenje*, 7,8,9 April 1991.

44 For the same reasons, non-nationalist leaders in Macedonia and Bosnia-Hercegovina, aware of economic and strategic difficulties, shied away from Serbia, to be joined later by similar forces in Montenegro.

45 For example, the legal argumentation in Commission Opinion No. 1, according to which the SFRY was 'in the process of disintegration'; No 2, according to which the Serb population in Bosnia-Hercegovina did not have the right to self-determination; and No. 3 , on equating internal with international boundaries. 'Process of disintegration' is not a legal term: in law, something either is, or is not, it either exists, or does not exist. It is impossible to determine a process on the basis of legal norms. A man is either alive or dead: whether he is dying is determined by doctors, not lawyers. In these, as in other opinions, the legal argumentation could have been different if the basic inclinations had been different.

The opinions have been published in Branislav Milinković (ed.), *Rezolucije saveta bezbednosti UN o krizi u bivšoj Jugoslaviji (i drugi dokumenti), Beograd, Medunarodna politika* - Pravni fakultet - Fakultet političkih nauka, 1995: 103ff.

46 The open support of Serbia and the Socialist Party of Serbia for the putsch against Gorbachov in August 1991 could in no way work in the Serbs' favour.

47 A sanction is a punishment, while the Charter envisages measures which should persuade the addressee to stop behaving in an impermissible manner, i.e., the FRY and the JNA to stop operations in Bosnia-Hercegovina. In Resolution 752 (1992) of 15 May 1992, the Security Council asked that 'JNA units and elements of the Croatian army' retreat from Bosnia-Hercegovina, or be placed under the control of the Bosnian government. Finding that the JNA had not fulfilled this condition, the Security Council adopted, on 30 May, Resolution 757 (1992) on measures against Serbia and Montenegro (FRY). That the Security Council did not find it necessary to implement measures against Croatia even though 'elements' of its army were yet to withdraw, is testimony to the already described general attitude towards the Serb side and the role of the FRY.

48 See A. M. Rosenthal, 'American Allies in Serbia', *New York Times*, January 1993.

49 See Vojin Dimitrijević and Jelena Pejić, 'UN Sanctions Against Yugoslavia: Two Years Later', Dimitris Bourantonis and Jarrod Wiener, *The United Nations in the New World Order. The World Organisation at Fifty,* London, Macmillan, 1995: 124ff.

50 See B. Jović, op. cit.: e.g. 310. Unexpected confirmation is found in deliberation over the matter of succession and continuity in the report of the aforementioned expert group of the Republic of Serbia at the Conference on Yugoslavia. According to their opinion of July 1992, non-recognition of the SFRY-FRY continuity contained many dangers, among them 'producing constitutional and political changes in the FR of Yugoslavia, primarily in Serbia', new elections 'with the aim of changing ruling parties'. 'Sudbina haško-briselske konferencije ...' (n. 25): 8. The interpretation that in case of succession only, without continuity, new elections are demanded has no grounding. However, the experts were alluding to the conditions for recognition from the EU Declaration which demands that a state be democratic and have free elections. The onstitutions of Serbia and the FRY proclaimed free elections, and these experts were representing a government which had come to office after the first multiparty elections in Serbia, in 1990, which had been celebrated as democratic, and had given the ruling party a large majority. The danger, therefore, had no legal grounding, but was quite in keeping with the cold-war fear of the 'foreign factor' and its internal representatives in the opposition.

51 B. Jović, op. cit.: 407. A way was found to convey this proposal to the Security Council without the participation of the SFRY's permanent en-

voy to the UN, Darko Šilović, because, being a Croat, he was mistrusted. Ibid.: 408.

52 Ibid.: 407.

53 See, e.g., Miroljub Jeftić, 'Međunarodne pretpostavke islamske trans-formacije u BiH', 'Novi svetski poredak i međunarodni islamski faktor', *Novi svetski poredak...* (n. 7): 190ff., 500ff.

54 The full name is 'International tribunal for the prosecution of persons responsible for serious violations of international humanitarian law committed in the territory of the former Yugoslavia since 1991'. The Tribunal was established by UN Security Council Resolution 827 (1993) of 25 May 1993.

55 Judging by the vehement reactions in Serbia and Croatia to every indictment drawn up against a Serb or a Croat, this impression is still absent in those countries.

56 As is natural, turnabout and disappointment are most drastic where exaggerated inclination had existed first. For example, criticism of the Croatian regime was most frequent in Austria. See the Vienna dailies *Die Presse* and *Der Standard* in October and November 1995.

57 Characteristic of this approach was a statement by Lord Owen. Asked what he thought of Milošević after the 1992 elections and the dismissal of Milan Panić, he said that former UN representative Cyrus Vance and he always talked to Milošević, even when he was 'electorally unpopular', as they saw in the Serbian president a potentially powerful figure who should be convinced to force the Bosnian Serbs to accept the peace plan. It was unrealistic to expect that he would assist the peace process in December 1992, as this would only favour Milan Panić's government, Owen added. 'The Future of the Balkans. An Interview with David Owen', *Foreign Affairs*, Vol. 72, No. 3, 1993: 9.

Bibliography

Aćin, Jovica. *Gatanje po pepelu. O izgnanstvima i logorima* (Roaming through the ashes. On exiles and camps). Belgrade: Vreme knjige, 1993.

Adorno, Theodor W., Ernst Bloch, Hannah Arendt, Walter Benjamin et al. *Zivilisationsbruch. Denken nach Auschwitz.* Frankfurt am Main: Fischer Verlag, 1968.

Agani, Fehmi. "Kritički osvrt na politički diskurs o Kosovu i Albancima" (A critical review of the political discourse on Kosovo and Albanians). In *Kosovo–Srbija–Jugoslavija* (Kosovo–Serbia–Yugoslavia). Ljubljana: KRT ZSMS,1989.

Anderson, Benedict. *Imagined Communities. Reflections on the Origin and Spread of Nationalism.* London: Verso, 1983.

Anderson, Kenneth. "Illiberal tolerance: an essay on the fall of Yugoslavia and the rise of multiculturalism in the United States." *Virginia Journal of International Law* 33 (1992).

"Antiratne akcije" (Anti-war actions). Special issue of *Republika*. Belgrade, February 1993.

Antonijević, Dragoslav. "Kult kneza Lazara u folklornoj tradiciji" (The cult of Knez Lazar in the folklore tradition). In *Kosovska bitka 1389. godine i njene posledice* (The 1389 Kosovo battle and its consequences). Belgrade, 1991.

Antonijević, Dragoslav. "Les Tzintzares dans la diaspora." In *La culture urbaine des Balkans.* Belgrade and Paris: Institute des études balkaniques, 1991.

"Apel" (An Appeal). *Pravoslavlje* no. 366 (15 June 1982).

Apih, Milan. *Enajsta šola Andreja Klasa* (The eleventh school of Andrej Klas). Ljubljana: Založba Borec, 1984.

Apih, Milan. *Nadaljnje življenje Andreja Klasa* (The further life of Andrej Klas). Ljubljana: Cankarjeva založba, 1987.

Arendt, Hannah. "Organisierte Schuld." In Hermann Glaser (ed.). *Bundesrepublikanisches Lesebuch. Drei Jahrzehnte geistiger Auseinandersetzung.* Munich and Vienna, 1978: 227-235.

Auerbach, Philip. "Das Einigende Suchen." In Knud C. Knudsen (ed.). *Welt ohne Hass. Führende Wissenschaftler aller Fakultäten nehmen Stellung zu brennenden Problemen. Aufsätze und Ansprachen zum 1. Kongreß über bessere menschliche Beziehungen.* München, Berlin, Hamburg and Stuttgart, 1950: 105-109.

Avramov, D. "Kosovo—poslednja oaza visokog fertiliteta u Evropi" (Kosovo—the last oasis of high fertility in Europe). In *Prilozi demografskim i ekonomskim naukama* (Contributions to demographic and economic sciences). Belgrade: Serbian Academy of Sciences and Arts, 1994.

Babović, Milosav. "Kosovski mit u Njegoševom 'Gorskom vijencu'" (The Kosovan myth in Njegoš's "The Mountain Wreath"). In *Kosovski boj u istoriji, tradiciji i stvaralaštvu Crne Gore* (The Kosovo battle in the history, tradition and art of Montenegro). Titograd, 1990.

Bajić, Nevenka. "Junski ustanak u gornjoj Hercegovini" (The june uprising in upper Herzegovina). In *Godišnjak istorijskog društva Bosne i Hercegovine* (The Historical Society of Bosnia-Herzegovina yearly). Sarajevo, 1965.

Bakhunin, Mikhail. *Države i slobode* (States and liberties). Zagreb: Globus, 1979.

Bandić, Dušan. *Carstvo zemaljsko i carstvo nebesko, ogledi o narodnoj religiji* (Earthly kingdom and heavenly kingdom, essays on the people's religion). Belgrade, 1990.

Bandić, Dušan. *Narodna religija u Srba, u 100 pojmova* (The people's religion of Serbs in 100 concepts). Belgrade, 1991.

Bartoszewski, Wladyslaw. *Es lohnt sich, anständig zu sein*. Freiburg: Verlag Herder, 1995.

Basta-Posavec, Lidija. "Constitutional requirements of democracy and non-democratic (constitution of) society. Serbia under the Constitution of 1990." *Bulletin of the Australian Society of Legal Philosophy* 17 (1992).

Bataković, Dušan T. "Značaj kosovskog predanja u održanju srpskog naroda na Kosovu i Metohiji u XIX veku" (The importance of the Kosovan legend for the preservation of the Serbian people in Kosovo and Metohija in the XIX century). In *Kosovska bitka 1389. godine i njene posledice* (The 1389 Kosovo battle and its consequences). Belgrade, 1991.

Bazler-Madžar, Marta. "Regionalni razvoj u Jugoslaviji—dugoročne tendencije" (Regional development in Yugoslavia—long-term tendencies). *Ekonomska analiza* 25, no. 2 (1991): 137-154.

Beckett, J. C. *A Short History of Ireland*. 6th edition. London: Hutchinson, 1979.

Bećković, Matija. "Srbija nema prečih zadataka nego da je ima" (Serbia has no goal more important than its existence). *Književne novine* no. 772 (1989).

Bećković, Matija. "Kosovo—najskuplja srpska reč" (Kosovo—the dearest Serbian word). *Književne novine* no. 779-780 (1989).

Bećković, Matija. "Ostatak zaklanog naroda" (The remains of the slaughtered people). *Književne novine* no. 782 (1989).

Bećković, Matija. "Nema poslednje utopije" (There is no last utopia). *Književne novine* no. 807 (1990).

Beldiceanu, N. "L'influence ottomane sur la vie urbaine des Balkans et des principoutés roumains." In *La culture urbaine des Balkans*. Belgrade and Paris: Institute des études balkaniques, 1991.

Benc, Ernest. "Veličina i slabost pravoslavlja" (The strength and weakness of Orthodoxy). In Dragoljub Đorđević (ed.). *Pravoslavlje izmedu neba i zemlje* (Orthodoxy between heaven and earth). Niš: Gradina, 1991.

Benevolo, L. *Histoire de l'architecture moderne.* Volume I. Paris: Dunod, 1979.

Bergmann, Werner. "Sind die Deutschen antisemitisch? Meinungsumfragen von 1946–1987 in der Bundesrepublik Deutschland." In Werner Bergmann and Rainer Werner (eds.). *Antisemitismus in der politischen Kultur seit 1945.* Opladen, 1990: 108–130.

Berlin, Isaiah. *Against the Current. Essays in the History of Ideas.* Viking Press: New York 1980.

Bilandžić, Dušan. "Skriveni nacionalni programi u SKJ" (Hidden national programs in the League of Communists of Yugoslavia). *Filozofija i društvo* IV (1993).

Biro, Mikloš. *Psihologija postkomunizma* (Psychology of post-Communism). Belgrade: Beogradski krug, 1994.

"Biti Urukalo" (To be Urukalo). *Vojska Krajine* (October-November 1993).

Blagojević, Marina. "Slam i geto" (Slum and ghetto). *Kultura* no. 70 (1985).

Blagojević, Marina. "Srpske seobe sa Kosova od kraja 60-ih godina, društveni činioci" (Serbian migrations from Kosovo since the late 1960s, social factors). In *Srbi i Albanci u XX veku* (Serbs and Albanians in the XX century). Belgrade: Serbian Academy of Sciences and Arts, 1991.

Blagojević, Miloš. "Jugoslovenski kontekst: sekularizacija i desekularizacija" (The Yugoslav context: secularization and desecularization). *Gradina* no. 10–12 (1993).

Blagojević, Miloš. "Vezanost ljudi za religiju i crkvu na pravoslavno homogenim prostorima" (People's attachment to religion and the church in the Orthodox homogeneous regions). In *Religija–rat–mir*, (Religion-war-peace). Niš, 1994.

Bloom, William. *Personal Identity, National Identity and International Relations.* Cambridge: Cambridge University Press, 1990.

Bodemann, Michael. "Staat und Ethnizität: Der Aufbau der jüdischen Gemeinden im Kalten Krieg." In Misha Brumlik et al. (eds.). *Jüdisches Leben in Deutschland seit 1945.* Frankfurt am Main, 1988: 49–69.

Bogdanović, Bogdan. *Grad i smrt* (City and death). Belgrade: Beogradski krug, 1994.

Bogetić, Boško. "Nametnuti stavovi" (Imposed positions). *Književne novine* no. 751 (1988).

Bogoev, Ksente. "Regionalno prelivanje dohotka fiskalnim mehanizmom centralnih vlasti" (Regional surplus of income by the fiscal mechanism of the central government). In Ksente Bogoev (ed.). *Problemi reforme privrednog sistema SFR Jugoslavije* (Problems of reform of the economic system of the Socialist Federal Republic of Yugoslavia). Zagreb: Globus, 1989: 259–272.

Bogosavljević, Aleksa. *O Arnautima* (On Arnauts). Niš, 1897.

Bogosavljević, Srđan. "Bosna i Hercegovina u ogledalu statistike" (Bosnia-Herzegovina in the mirror of statistics). In Srđan Bogosavljević et al.

Bosna i Hercegovina između rata i mira (Bosnia-Herzegovina between war and peace). Belgrade: Institut ekonomskih nauka, 1992.

Bogosavljević, Srđan. "Statistička slika srpsko-albanskih odnosa" (Statistical picture of Serbian-Albanian relations). In Dušan Janjić and Skelzen Maliqi (eds.). *Sukob ili dijalog* (Conflict or dialogue). Subotica: Otvoreni univerzitet and EGCRK, 1994.

Boj na Kosovu, starija i novija saznanja (The battle of Kosovo, older and more recent discoveries). Belgrade, 1992.

Bojić, Vera. "Transformacija kosovskog mita u poeziji Milutina Bojića" (The transformation of the Kosovan myth in the poetry of Milutin Bojić). In *Kosovski boj u književnom i kulturnom nasledu* (The Kosovo battle in literary and cultural heritage). Belgrade, 1991.

Bojović, Boško "Geneza kosovske izdaje u prvim postkosovskim hagiografsko-istoriografskim spisima" (The genesis of Kosovo betrayal in post-Kosovan hagiographical and historiographical writings). In *Kosovska bitka 1389. godine i njene posledice* (The 1389 Kosovo battle and its consequences). Belgrade, 1991.

Bojović, Jovan R. "O Vidovdanu u Crnoj Gori" (On St. Vitus Day in Montenegro). In *Sveti knez Lazar, Spomenica o šestoj stogodišnjici kosovskog boja 1389–1989* (St. knez Lazar, in commemoration of the six-hundredth anniversary of the Kosovo battle, 1389–1989). Belgrade, 1989.

Bovan, Vladimir. "Usmena tradicija o kosovskoj bici na Kosovu" (The oral tradition about the Kosovo battle in Kosovo). In *Kosovski boj u književnom i kulturnom nasledu* (The Kosovo battle in literary and cultural heritage). Belgrade, 1991.

Bower, Tom. *Blind Eye to Murder. Britain, America and the Purging of Nazi Germany. A Pledge Betrayed.* London, 1981.

Boyd, Robin. *Ireland: Christianity Discredited or Pilgrim's Progress?* Geneva: ORK, 1988.

Božić, Ivan. "Postanak i razvoj Univerziteta u Srbiji" (The establishment and development of the university in Serbia). In *Univerzitet u Beogradu* (University in Belgrade). Belgrade, 1988.

Braudel, Fernand. *Civilisation matérielle et capitalisme XVe–XVIIIe siècle.* 1967, 1979.

Braduel, Fernand. *Écrits sur l'histoire.* Flammarion: Paris, 1991.

Braun, Maximilian. *Kosovo. Die Schlacht auf dem Amsevelde in geschichtlicher und epischer Ueberlieferung.* Leipzig, 1937.

Bromberger, Christian, Alain Hayot Jean-Marc Mariottini. "Allez L'OM! Forza Juve! La passion pour le football à Marseille et Turin" (Allez L'OM! Forza Juve! Passion for soccer in Marseille and Turin). *Terrain* (8 April 1987).

Brown, Michael. *Ethnic Conflict and International Security.* Princeton: Princeton University Press, 1993.

Brubaker, Rogers. "Nationhood and the National Question in the Soviet Union and Post Soviet Eurasia: An Institutionalist Account." *Theory and Society* 23 (February 1994), no. 1.

Brubaker, Rogers. "Nationalism Reframed: The New National Question in Eastern Europe." Paper presented at the conference organized by the Institute on Global Conflict and Cooperation of the University of California, September 1994.

Brumlik, Misha et al. (eds.). *Jüdisches Leben in Deutschland seit 1945*. Frankfurt am Main, 1988.

Bulić, Vanja. "Pričalice sa beogradskog asfalta" (Stories from the Belgrade asphalt). *Duga* no. 509, 1993.

Caruso, Igor A. *Soziale Aspekte der Psychanalyse*. Stuttgart: Klett, 1962.

Cohen, J. Leonard. *Broken Bonds – The Disintegration of Yugoslavia*. Boulder and San Francisco: Westview Press, 1993.

Connor, Walker. *The National Question in Marxist-Leninist Theory and Strategy*. Princeton: Princeton University Press, 1984.

Connor, Walker. *Ethnonationalism—Quest for Understanding*. Princeton: Princeton University Press, 1994.

Crnčević, Brana. "Ne postoji demokratija protiv nekog" (There is no democracy against someone). *Književne novine* no. 772 (1989).

Crnjanski, Miloš. "Vidovdanske pesme" (St. Vitus Day poems). In Vojislav Đurić. *Kosovski boj u srpskoj književnosti* (The Kosovo battle in Serbian literature). Belgrade, 1990.

La culture urbaine des Balkans (The urban culture of the Balkans). Belgrade and Paris: Institute des études balkaniques, 1991.

Cvijlć, Jovan. *Balkansko poluostrvo i južnoslovenske zemlje* (The Balkan peninsula and the south Slav lands). Collected works (see 1965 and 1966 editions). Belgrade: Zavod za izdavanje udžbenika i nastavna sredstva, 1987.

Čajkanović, Veselin. *Mit i religija u Srba* (Myth and religion in Serbs). Belgrade: SKZ, 1973.

Čajkanović, Veselin. *O vrhovnom bogu u staroj srpskoj religiji* (On supreme god in the old Serbian religion). Belgrade: SKZ, 1994.

Čavoški, Kosta. *Iz istorije stvaranja nove Jugoslavije* (From the history of creation of new Yugoslavia). London: Naša reč, 1987.

Čolović, Ivan. *Bordel ratnika* (The warriors' brothel). Belgrade: Bibl. XX vek, 1993.

Čolović, Ivan. *Pucanje od zdravlja* (Healthy like hell). Belgrade: Beogradski krug, 1994.

Čolović, Ivan. "Skerlić i srpski politički mitovi" (Skerlić and the Serbian political myths). In *Srbija u modernizacijskim procesima XX veka* (Serbia in the modernization processes of the XX century). Belgrade: Institut za noviju istoriju, 1994.

Čolović, Ivan. "I majka i ljubavnica" (Both a mother and a lover). *NIN* (11 November 1994).

Čuljak, Milan. "Kako je Adamič upoznao širu američku javnost o Kosovu" (How Adamič introduced Kosovo to the American public). In *Kosovski boj u književnom i kulturnom nasledu* (The Kosovo battle in literary and cultural heritage). Belgrade, 1991.

Čupić, Drago. "Leksika i sintagmatika u 'Gorskom vijencu'" (Lexics and Syntagmathics in "The mountain wreath"). In *Kosovski boj u istoriji, tradiciji i stvaralaštvu Crne Gore* (The Kosovo battle in the history, tradition and art of Montenegro). Titograd, 1990.

Čupić, Drago. "Kosovski mit i Crna Gora" (The Kosovan myth and Montenegro). In *Kosovska bitka 1389. godine i njene posledice* (The 1389 Kosovo battle and its consequences). Belgrade, 1991.

Ćirković, Sima. "O Kosovskom boju 1389" (On the Kosovo battle of 1389). In *Zadužbine Kosova, Spomenici i znamenja srpskog naroda* (Foundations of Kosovo, monuments and memorials of the Serbian people). Prizren, Belgrade and Ljubljana, 1987.

Ćirković, Sima M. "Kosovska bitka kao istorijski problem" (The Kosovo battle as a historical problem). In *Okrugli sto: Kosovska bitka u istoriografiji* (Round table: The Kosovo battle in historiography). Belgrade, 1992.

Ćirković, Sima M. "'O Knezu Lazaru', Studija Ilariona Ruvarca" ("On knez Lazar," the study of Ilarion Ruvarac). In *Boj na Kosovu, starija i novija saznanja* (The battle of Kosovo, older and more recent discoveries). Belgrade, 1992.

Ćirković, Sima. "Urbanizacija kao tema srpske istorije" (Urbanization as a theme in Serbian history). In *Socijalna struktura srpskih gradskih naselja* (Social structure of the Serbian urban settlements). Smederevo and Belgrade, 1992.

Ćosić, Dobrica. *Grešnik* (The Sinner). Belgrade: BIGZ, 1985.

Ćosić, Dobrica. "Koliko smo sami krivi" (To what extent is it our own fault). *Književne novine* no. 733 (1987).

Ćosić, Dobrica. "Srpsko pitanje—demokratsko pitanje" (Serbian question—a democratic question). *Književne novine* no. 743 (1987).

Ćosić, Dobrica. "Istina iz patnje?" (Truth from suffering?). *Književne novine* no. 782 (1989).

Ćosić, Dobrica. "Velika obmana srpskog naroda" (A great cheating of the Serbian people). *Politika* (10 January 1991).

Ćosić, Dobrica. *Promene* (Changes). Novi Sad: Dnevnik, 1992.

Ćosić, Dobrica. *Srpsko pitanje—demokratsko pitanje* (Serbian question—a democratic question). Belgrade, 1992.

Ćosja, Redžep. "Patnje Albanaca" (The suffering of the Albanians). *Književne novine* no. 753 (1988).

Daljević, Milan. "Izlaganje na SSRNJ" (Expose at a SSRNJ meeting). *Vojno-politički informator* no. 2 (1987).

Daly, Gabriel. "Forgiveness and Community." In Alan D. Falconer (ed.). *Reconciling Memories*. Dublin: Columbia Press, 1988.

D'Arcy May, John. "Political Ecumenism: Church Structures and the Political Process." *Studies* 79 (1990).

Davičo, Oskar. "Kao i 'Nova revija'" (Like "Nova revija"). *Književne novine* no. 751 (1988).

Dedijer, Vladimir. *Sarajevo 1914*. Second edition. Volumes I-II. Belgrade: Prosveta, 1978.

De Jasay, Anthony. *The State*. Oxford: Basil Blackwell Ltd, 1985.

Delić, Jovan. *Tradicija i Vuk Stefanović Karadžić* (Tradition and Vuk Stefanović Karadžić). Belgrade: BIGZ, 1990.

Denitch, Bette. "Dismembering of Yugoslavia. Nationalist Ideology and the Symbolic Revival of Genocide." *American Ethnologist* 21 (1994), no. 2.

Denitch, Bogdan. *The End of a Cold War*. Minneapolis: University of Minnesota Press, 1990.

Dereta, Miljenko. "Pogrešno usmereni jed" (Anger in a wrong direction). *Republika* no. 125-126.

"Deseti kongres Saveza komunista Srbije" (The tenth congress of the League of Communists of Serbia). *Komunist*, 1986.

Deutschkron, Inge. *Israel und die Deutschen*. Köln, 1983.

Deutschland und seine östlichen Nachbarn. Beiträge zu einer evangelischen Denkschrift. Stuttgart: Kreuz Verlag, 1966.

"Deveta konferencija OSKJ u JNA, dokumenti" (The ninth conference of OSKJ in JNA, documents). *Vojnopolitički informator* no. 1 (1990).

Dimitrieva, Elka and Lila Stošić. "Prelivanje sredstava Fonda federacije i razvoja nedovoljno razvijenih područja u Jugoslaviji" (Outflow from the Federation fund and the development of the insufficiently developed regions in Yugoslavia). In Ksente Bogoev (ed.). *Problemi reforme privrednog sistema SFR Jugoslavije* (Problems of reform of the economic system of the Socialist Federal Republic of Yugoslavia). Zagreb: Globus, 1989: 421-437.

Dimitrijević, Vojin. "Međunarodno zaštićena ljudska prava i Jugoslavija" (Internationally protected human rights and Yugoslavia). *Anali Pravnog fakulteta u Beogradu*, 1987.

Dimitrijević, Vojin. "Freedom of opinion and expression." In A. Rosas and J. Helgesen (eds.). *Human Rights in a Changing East–West Perspective*. London and New York: Pinter, 1990.

Dimitrijević, Vojin. *The Fate of non Members of Dominant Nations in Post-Communist European Countries*. Florence: European University Institute, 1995.

Dimitrijević, Vojin and Jelena Pejić. "UN Sanctions Against Yugoslavia: Two Years Later." In Dimitris Bourantonis and Jarrod Wiener. *The United Nations in the New World Order. The World Organization at Fifty*. London: Macmillan, 1995.

Dimitrijević, Vojin and Radoslav Stojanović. *Medunarodni odnosi* (International relations). Belgrade: Centar za publikacije Pravnog fakulteta, 1988.

Dinić-Knežević, Dušanka. "Doprinos Đorđa Sp. Radojčića proučavanju Kosovske bitke" (The contribution of Đorđe Sp. Radojčić to the study of the Kosovo battle). In *Okrugli sto: Kosovska bitka u istoriografiji* (Round table: The Kosovo battle in historiography). Belgrade, 1990.

Dinkić, Mlađan. *Ekonomija destrukcije. Velika pljačka naroda* (The economy of destruction. The big rip-off of the people). Belgrade: VIN, 1995.

Dmitrów, Edmund. "Obraz Niemców w Polsce w latach 1945-1948" (Image of the Germans in Poland in the years 1945-1948). *Historia LXXIX* (1991).

Dokumenta za 9. konferenciju OSKJ u JNA (Documents for the ninth conference of OSKJ in JNA). Belgrade, 1989.

"Dokumenti (jun–lipanj 1968)" (Documents (June 1968)). *Praxis* (1971).

Dotterweich, Volker. "Die 'Entnazifizierung.'" In Josef Becker et al. (eds.). *Vorgeschichte der Bundesrepublik Deutschland. Zwischen Kapitulation und Grundgesetz*. München, 1979: 123–161.

Drašković, Čedomir. "Religija kao djelatnost ljudskog duha" (Religion as an activity of the human spirit). In *Religija i nacija* (Religion and nation). Zagreb, 1984.

Drašković, Vuk. "Nespremni za istoriju" (Not ready for history). *Književne novine* no. 772 (1989).

Druga Srbija (The other Serbia). Belgrade, 1992.

Dučić, Jovan. "Himna pobednika" (The anthem of the victors). Originally published in 1918). In Vojislav Đurić. *Kosovski boj u srpskoj književnosti* (The Kosovo battle in Serbian literature). Belgrade, 1990.

Duer, Hans Peter. *Traumzeit. Über die Grenze zwischen Wildnis und Zivilisation*. Frankfurt am Main: Suhrkamp, 1985.

Durković Jakšić, Ljubomir. "Udeo Cetinjske mitropolije u borbi za uspostavljanje redovnog stanja u SPC" (The role of the Cetinje archbishopric in the struggle for the establishment of order in the Serbian Orthodox Church). In *Srpska pravoslavna crkva 1219–1969*. Belgrade.

Durković Jakšić, Ljubomir. "Ustanovljenje u vaskrsloj Srbiji Vidovdana za državni praznik" (Establishment of St. Vitus Day as a holiday in ressurected Serbia). In *Sveti knez Lazar, Spomenica o šestoj stogodišnjici kosovskog boja 1389–1989* (St. knez Lazar, in commemoration of the six-hundredth anniversary of the Kosovo battle, 1389–1989). Belgrade, 1989.

Durković Jakšić, Ljubomir. *Mitropolija cetinjska nikada nije bila autokefalna* (The Cetinje archbishopric was never autocephalous). Cetinje, 1991.

Dušanić, Svetozar. "Osvrt na jedan govor" (A review of a speech). *Pravoslavlje* no. 493, (1 October 1987).

Džadžić, Petar. *Homo balcanicus, homo heroicus*. Belgrade: BIGZ, 1987.

Đekić, Mirko. *Upotreba Srbije: optužbe i priznanja Draže Markovića* (The use of Serbia: accusations and admissions of Draža Marković). Belgrade: Besede, 1990.

Đilas, Aleksa. "Osporavana zemlja" (The contested country). *Književne novine*, 1990.

Đinđić, Zoran. *Jugoslavija kao nedovršena država* (Yugoslavia as an unfinished state). Novi Sad: Književna zajednica Novog Sada, 1988.

Đorđević, Dragoljub B. "Opšta socioreligijska i konfesionalna panorama stanovništva u SFRJ" (General socio-religious and confessional panorama of the population in the Socialist Federal Republic of Yugoslavia). In *Religija i društvo* (Religion and society). Belgrade, 1988.

Đorđević, Dragoljub B. *Sile mraka i bezumlja. Niški studentski protest '92* (Forces of darkness and unreason. The Niš student protest 1992). Niš: Naučni podmladak and SKC, 1992.

Đorđević, Dragoljub B (ed.). *Povratak svetog* (The return of the sacred). (1993). *Gradina* nos. 10–12 (1993).

Đorđević, Dragoljub B. (ed.). *Pravoslavlje izmedu neba i zemlje* (Orthodoxy between heaven and earth). Niš: Gradina, 1991.

Đorđević, Dragoljub B. and Bogdan Đurović. "Sekularizacija i pravoslavlje: slučaj Srba" (Secularization and Orthodoxy: the Serbian Case). *Gradina* no. 10-12 (1993).

Đorđević, Dimitrije. *Ogledi iz novije balkanske istorije* (Essays in recent Balkan history). Belgrade: SKZ, 1989.

Đorđević, Dimitrije. "The Yugoslav phenomenon." In Joseph Held (ed.). *The Columbia History of Europe in the Twentieth Century*. New York: Columbia University Press, 1992.

Đorđević, Dragoljub B. and Zoran Milošević. "Pravoslavlje, rat i stradanje" (Orthodoxy, war and suffering). In *Religija–rat–mir* (Religion–war–peace). Niš, 1994.

Đorđević, Jovan. "La Constitution de 1974." In *Questions actuelles du Socialisme*, Belgrade, 1984.

Đorđević, Mirko. "Rusija u magli" (Russia in fog). *Republika* no. 125-126 (1995).

Đorđević, Vladan. *Moja odbrana pred sudom* (My defense before the court). Belgrade: Narodna štamparija, 1906.

Đorđević, Života. "Franjevci u Montekarlu" (Franciscans in Monte Carlo). *NIN* no. 1127 and 1128 (1972).

Đorđević, Života. "Preseljenje industrije Srbije od 1944. do 1953. godine" (The moving of the Serbian industry, 1944 to 1953). *Industrija* XIX (1992), no. 4: 61-67.

Đukić, Slavoljub. *Čovek u svom vremenu* (A man in his time). Belgrade, 1989.

Đukić, Slavoljub. *Slom srpskih liberala. Tehnologija političkih obračuna Josipa Broza* (The fall of the Serbian liberals. The technology of political showdowns of Josip Broz). Belgrade: Filip Višnjić, 1990.

Đukić, Slavoljub. *Kako se dogodio voda* (How the leader happened). Belgrade: Filip Višnjić, 1992.

Đukić, Slavoljub. *Između slave i anateme—Politička biografija Slobodana Miloševića* (Between fame and anathema—political biography of Slobodan Milošević). Belgrade: Filip Višnjić, 1994.

Đurđević, Rajko. "Naoružana droga" (Armed drugs). *NIN* no. 2040.

Đurđević-Lukić, Svetlana. "Jesen studentskog nezadovoljstva" (The fall of the student discontent). *NIN* no. 2180 (1992).

Đurić, Vojislav. *Kosovski boj u srpskoj književnosti* (The Kosovo battle in Serbian literature). Belgrade, 1990.

Egbert, Jahn. "Demokracija i nacionalizam—jedinstvo ili protuslovlje?" (Democracy and nationalism—unity or contradiction?). *Politička misao* no. 4 (1992).

Ehrenberg, Alain. "La rage de paraître". *L'amour foot, Autrement*, no. 80 (1986).

Ekmečić, Milorad. *Ratni ciljevi Srbije 1914* (War goals of Serbia in 1914). Belgrade: SKZ, 1990.

Elaborat o politici ekonomskih odnosa SR Jugoslavije sa Slovenijom, Hrvatskom, Makedonijom i Bosnom i Hercegovinom (Report on the policies of economic relations of the Federal Republic of Yugoslavia with Slovenia, Croatia, Macedonia and Bosnia-Herzegovina). Belgrade: Ekonomski institut, 1993

Eliade, Mircea, "Mit i istorija" (Myth and history). In *Mit, tradicija savremenosti* (Myth, the tradition of contemporaneity). Belgrade: Delo and Argumenti.

Emerson, R. "Nacionalizam i demokratija: nekad i sad" (Nationalism and democracy: before and today). *Ekonomika* no. 1–3 (1994).

Emmaunel, Arghiri. *Unequal Exchange—a Study of the Imperialism of Trade*. New York: Monthly Reviews Press, 1972.

Enzensberger, Hans Magnus. *Civil wars*. New York: New Press, 1994.

Erdeljan, Olivera. "Jevreji ponovo raspinju Hrista" (Jews are crucifying Christ again). *Pravoslavlje* no. 597 (1992).

Eschenburg, Theodor. *Jahre der Besatzung 1945–1949*. Stuttgart and Wiesbaden, 1983.

Evropski diskurs rata (The European war discourse). Savić, Obrad (ed.). Belgrade: Beogradski krug, 1995.

Faith and Politics Groups. "Burying Our Dead: Political Funerals in Northern Ireland." In *Breaking Down the Enmity*, 1993.

Felkl, Ekehard. "Obračuni u Hrvatskoj" (Showdowns in Croatia). *Naša Borba*, 5 May 1995.

Fira, Aleksandar. "Federalism under the new Constitution of the SFR Yugoslavia." *Review of International Affairs* no. 574 (1974).

Fitzgerald, Garet. "The ghosts of past Europe's." *The Irish Times* (4. 01. 1992).

Flajner, Tomas. "Federalističke i demokratske institucije i metodi za rešavanje etničkih konflikata" (Federalist and democratic istitutions and methods for ethnic conflict resolution). In Tomas Flajner and Slobodan Samardžić (eds.). *Federalizam i problem manjina u višenacionalnim zajednicama* (Federalism and problems of minorities in multiethnic communities). Belgrade: Institut za evropske studije, 1995.

Flanz, Gisbert H. "Yugoslavia." In Albert P. Blaustain and Gisbert H. Flanz (eds.). *Constitutions of the Countries of the World*. New York, Dobbs Ferry and Oceana, 1986.

Fotiev, C. *The Living God*. London: Overseas Publications Interchange, 1989.

Frajnd, Marta. "Transformacija tumačenja kosovske legende u srpskoj istoriografskoj drami" (The transformation of interpretations of the Kosovan legend in Serbian historiographical drama). In *Kosovski boj u književnom i kulturnom nasledu* (The Kosovo battle in literary and cultural heritage). Belgrade, 1991.

Fricke, Otto. "Wir Christen und die Juden." In Hans Kallenbach (ed.). *Die Juden und wir Christen*. Frankfurt am Main, 1950: 41–49.

Friedrich, Jörg. *Die Kalte Amnestie. NS—Täter in der Bundesrepublik*. Frankfurt am Main, 1984.

Gagnon, V. P. Jr. "Serbia's Road to War." *Journal of Democracy* 5 (April 1994), no. 2.

Gallagher, Eric and Stanley Worrall. *Christians in Ulster 1968–1980*. Oxford: Oxford University Press, 1982.

Gelanson, Gregory. *Federalism and Nationalism—The Struggle for Republican Rights in USSR*. San Francisco: Westview Press, 1990.

Gellner, Ernest. "Nationalism in the Vacuum." In Alexander Motyl (ed.). *Thinking Theoreticaly about Soviet Nationalities*. New York: Columbia University Press, 1992.

Gesammelte slavistische und balkanologische Abhandlungen (in serbokroatischer Sprache). Volume IV. Munich, 1970.

Gezeman, Gerhard. *Čojstvo i junaštvo starih Crnogoraca* (Nobility and courage of old Montenegrins). Cetinje, 1968.

Gezeman, Gerhard. "O karakterologiji životnog stila" (On the "characterology" of lifestyles). In Bojan Jovanović (ed.). *Karakterologija Srba*. Belgrade: Naučna knjiga, 1992.

Giljferding, Aleksandar F. *Putovanje po Hercegovini, Bosni i staroj Srbiji* (Travels in Herzegovina, Bosnia and Old Serbia). Sarajevo, 1972.

Giordano, Ralph. *Die zweite Schuld oder von der Last Deutscher zu Sein*. Hamburg and Zürich, 1987.

Glenny, Misha. *The Fall of Yugoslavia—The Third Balkan War*. New York: Penguin, 1992.

Gligorov, Vladimir. *Why do Countries Break Up?* Uppsala: Acta Universitatis Upsaliensis, 1994.

Goati, Vladimir. *Jugoslavija na prekretnici. Od monizma do građanskog rata* (Yugoslavia at the crossroads. From monism to civil war). Belgrade, 1991.

Goati, Vladimir. "Korak u demokratiju" (Step into democracy). *Oslobođenje* (7–9 March 1991).

Goati, Vladimir. "Višepartijski mozaik Srbije" (Multiparty mosaic in Serbia). In *Rađanje javnog mnenja i političkih stranaka* (The birth of public opinion and political parties). Belgrade: IDN, 1992.

Goati, Vladimir. "Socijalna osnova političkih partija u Srbiji" (The social basis of political parties in Serbia). In Vukašin Pavlović (ed.). *Potisnuto civilno društvo* (Civil society supressed). Belgrade: Ekocentar, 1995.

Godišnjak SANU (The Serbian Academy of Sciences and Arts Yearly) XCI (1984). Belgrade, 1985.

Godišnjak SANU (The Serbian Academy of Sciences and Arts Yearly) XCII (1985). Belgrade, 1986.

Golubović, Zagorka. *Kriza identiteta savremenog jugoslovenskog društva* (The identity crisis of contemporary Yugoslav society). Belgrade: Filip Višnjić, 1988.

Golubović, Zagorka. "Šta smo naučili iz studentskog protesta '92?" (What did we learn from the student protest of 1992?). *Republika* no. 49–50 (1992).

Golubović, Zagorka. "Nasilje nad univerzitetom" (Violence over the university). *Republika* no. 61 (1993).

Golubović, Zagorka. "Da li je Univerzitet već izgubio bitku za svoju autonomiju?" (Did the university lose the battle for its autonomy?). *Republika* no. 62 (1993).

Golubović, Zagorka, Bora Kuzmanović and Mirjana Vasović. *Društveni karakter i društvene promene u svetlu nacionalnih sukoba* (Social character and social changes in the light of ethnic conflicts). Belgrade: Institut za filozofiju i društvenu teoriju and Filip Višnjić, 1995.

Goodwin, Robert E. "Exploiting a Situation and Exploiting a Person." In Andrew Reeve (ed.). *Modern Theories of Exploitation*. London: Sage Publications, 1987: 166–200.

Gottlieb, Gidon. "Nations without States." *Foreign Affairs* (May/June 1994).

Gow, James. *Legitimacy and the Military*. New York: St Martin's Press, 1992.

Graf, Friedrich Wilhelm. "In großer Ferne zur Demokratie. Evangelische Kirche in der Nachkriegszeit." In *Frankfurter Allgemeine Zeitung* (14 September 1989). Besprechung von Clemens Vollnhals, Evangelische Kirche und Entnazifizierung 1945–1959. Die Last der nationalsozialistischen Vergangenheit, München.

Gredelj, Stjepan. *S onu stranu ogledala* (From the other side of the mirror). Belgrade: IICSSO Srbije, 1986.

Gredelj, Stjepan. "Dominantne vrijednosne orijentacije" (The dominant values of orientation). In Mladen Lazić et al. *Razaranje društva* (The destruction of society). Belgrade: Filip Višnjić, 1994.

Greeley, Andrew M. "Are the Irish Really Losing the Faith?" *Doctrine and Life* no. 44 (1994).

Greenfeld, Liah. *Nationalism—Five Roads to Modernity*. Cambridge: Harvard University Press, 1992.

Greenfeld, Liah and Danile Chirot. "Nationalism and Agression." *Theory and Society* 23 (February 1994), no. 1.

Grković, Milica. *Rečnik ličnih imena kod Srba* (Dictionary of Serbian personal names). Belgrade, 1977.

Grosser, Alfred. "Odgovornost za razumevanje prošlosti" (Responsibility for understanding the past). *Republika* no. 128 (1995).

Grubačić, Bratislav and Momir Tomić. *Srpske slave* (Serbian *slava* celebrations). Belgrade, 1988.

Habermas, Jürgen. *Javno mnenje* (Public opinion). Belgrade: Kultura, 1969.

Hadžić, Miroslav. "Srpski kraj jugoslovenske vojske" (The Serbian end of the Yugoslav army). In Dušan Janjić (ed.). *Srbija između prošlosti i budućnosti* (Serbia between past and future). Belgrade: NIP Radnička štampa, Institut društvenih nauka and Forum za etničke odnose, 1995.

Hall, S. *Culture, Media, Language*. London: Hutchinson, 1980.

Hassner, Pierre. "Beyond Nationalism and Internationalism." In Michael E. Brown (ed.). *Ethnic Conflict and International Security*. Princeton: Princeton University Press, 1993.

Hayek, Friedrich A. *The Road to Serfdom*. Originally published in 1944. London: Routledge and Kegan Paul, 1979.

Henke, Klaus-Dietmar. *Politische Säuberung unter französischer Besatzung*. Stuttgart, 1981.

Hermet, Guy. *Sociologie de la construction democratique*. Paris, 1986.

Hermet, Guy. *Culture et democratie*. Paris, 1993.

Heuberger, Rachel and Helga Krohn. *Hinaus aus dem Ghetto. Juden in Frankfurt am Main 1800–1950*. Frankfurt am Main, 1988.

Hirsch, Kurt. *Die Blutlinie. Ein Beitrag zur Geschichte des Antikommunismus in Deutschland.* Frankfurt am Main, 1960.

Historia LXXIX (Wokól stereotypów Polaków i Niemców). Wroclaw, 1991.

Historia CXIV. Wroclaw, 1993.

Hobsbawm, Eric. *Nations and Nationalism since 1780.* 2nd edition. Cambridge: Cambridge University Press, 1990.

Horvat, Branko. *Kosovsko pitanje* (The question of Kosovo). Zagreb: Globus, 1989.

Hudelist, Darko. *Martin Špegelj (intervju)* (Martin Špegelj, an interview). *Erazmus* no. 9 (1994).

Hurem, Rasim. *Kriza NOP-a u Bosni i Hercegovini krajem 1941. i početkom 1942 godine* (The crisis of the national liberation movement in Bosnia-Herzegovina in late 1941 and early 1942). Sarajevo: Svjetlost, 1970.

Hurley, S. J. *Reconciliation in Religion and Society.* Dublin.

Igrić, Gordana. "Tajna arkanskih depoa..." (The secret of clandestine depots...). *NIN* no. 2302 (10 February 1995).

Ilić, Mile. *Zapisano—ostvareno, Socijalistička partija Srbije u Nišu (april 1990—jun 1993)* (Written down—achieved. The Socialist party of Serbia in Niš, April 1990—June 1993). Niš, 1993.

Inter-Church Group on Faith and Politics. "Remembering our Past." In *Breaking Down the Enmity: Faith and Politics in the Northern Ireland Conflict.* Belfast, 1993.

Inter-Church Group on Faith and Politics. *The Things that Make for Peace.* Belfast, 1995.

Islami, H. "Demografska stvarnost Kosova" (The demographic reality of Kosovo). In Dušan Janjić and Skelzen Maliqi (eds.). *Sukob ili dijalog* (Conflict or dialogue). Subotica: Otvoreni univerzitet and EGCRK, 1994.

Istorija Crne Gore (A history of Montenegro). Volumes I–III. Titograd, 1975.

Istorija srpskog naroda (A history of the Serbian people). Volume V2. Belgrade: SKZ, 1981.

Istorija srpskog naroda (A history of the Serbian people). Volume VI1. Belgrade: SKZ, 1983.

Istorija srpskog naroda (A history of the Serbian people). Belgrade: SKZ, 1993.

Istorijski arhiv KPJ (The historical archive of the Communist party of Yugoslavia). Belgrad, 1949.

Ivanković-Vojta, Zvonko. *Hebrang.* Zagreb: Scientia Yugoslavia, 1988.

Ivić, Ivan and Olga Perazić. "Obrazovni nivo stanovništva i razvoj" (The educational level of the population and development). *Republika* no. 91 (1994).

Ivić, Pavle. "Natalitet i politika" (Birth rate and politics). *Književne novine* no. 753 (1988).

Jacobmeyer, Wolfgang. "Die Lager der jüdischen Displaced Persons in den deutschen Westzonen 1946/47, als Ort jüdischer Selbstvergewisserung."

In Brumlik, Misha et al. (eds.). *Jüdisches Leben in Deutschland seit 1945.* Frankfurt am Main, 1988: 31-48.

Jacobmeyer, Wolfgang. *Vom Zwangsarbeiter zum heimatlosen Ausländer. Die Displaced Persons in Westdeutschland 1945-1951.* Göttingen, 1985.

Jakšić, Božidar. *Svest socijalnog protesta* (The consciousness of social protest). Belgrade: IICS, 1986.

Jasper, Gotthard. "Wiedergutmachung und Westintegration. Die halbherzige justitielle Aufarbeitung der NS Vergangenheit in den frühen Bundesrepublik." In Ludolf Herbst (ed.). *Westdeutschland 1945-1955.* München, 1986: 183-202.

Jeftić, Miroljub. "Međunarodne pretpostavke islamske transformacije u BiH" (International preconditions of the Islamic transformation in Bosnia-Herzegovina). In Yugoslav Federal Ministry of Defense. *Novi svetski poredak i politika odbrane Savezne Republike Jugoslavije* (New world order and the politicies of defense of the Federal Republic of Yugoslavia) Belgrade, 1993.

Jerotić, Vladeta. *Darovi naših rodaka* (Gifts of our relatives). Volumes I–II. Belgrade: Prosveta, 1993.

Jerotić, Vladeta. "Praštati, zaboravljati ili se svetiti?" (Forgive, forget or revenge?). *Istočnik* (1994).

Jerotić, Vladeta. *Vera i nacija* (Faith and nation). Belgrade: Tersit, 1995.

Jevtić, Atanasije. "Kosovsko opredeljenje za carstvo nebesko u istorijskoj sudbini srpskog naroda" (The Kosovan choice of heavenly kingdom in the historical fate of the Serbian people). In *Sveti knez Lazar, Spomenica o šestoj stogodišnjici kosovskog boja 1389-1989* (St. knez Lazar, in commemoration of the six-hundredth anniversary of the Kosovo battle, 1389-1989). Belgrade, 1989.

Jochmann, Werner. "Evangelische Kirche und Politik in der Phase des Neubeginns 1945-1950." In Viktor Cunzemius et al. (eds.). *Die Zeit nach 1945 als Thema kirchlicher Zeitgeschichte.* Göttingen, 1988: 194-212.

Josić Višnjić, Miroslav (ed.) *Saopštenja, zapisnici i pisma Odbora za zaštitu umetničke slobode pri beogradskoj sekciji pisaca u Udruženju književnika Srbije* (Addresses, minutes and letters of the Committee for the protection of artistic freedom at the Belgrade section of the Writers' union of Serbia). Belgrade, 1984.

Jovadžić, Radivoje. *Dijalektika odbrane.* Belgrade: VIZ, 1983.

Jovanić, Duška. "Udba ili Praksis" (Udba [secret police] or Praxis). *Duga* no. 418 (1994).

Jovanić, Duška. "Prvi pali borci antisrpske zavere" (The first fallen soldiers of the anti-Serbian conspiracy). *Duga* no. 523 (1994).

Jovanić, Duška. "Srpski Lun kralj ponoći" (Serbian Lun, king of midnight). *Duga* no. 529 (1994).

Jovanov, Neca. *Štrajkovi u SFRJ* (Strikes in the Socialist Federal Republic of Yugoslavia). Belgrade: Zapis, 1979.

Jovanović, Bojan. "Neobuzdana i viša pravda" (Unbound higher justice). *Istočnik* (1994).

Jovanović, Dragoslav. *Muzej živih ljudi* (The museum of the living people). Volumes I–II. Belgrade: Rad, 1990.

Jovanović, Slobodan. *Primeri političke sociologije* (Examples of political sociology). Belgrade, 1940.

Jovanović, Slobodan. *Moji savremenici* (My contemporaries). Windsor, 1968.

Jovanović, Slobodan. *Vlada Aleksandra Obrenovića* (The government of Aleksandar Obrenović). Belgrade: SKZ, 1990.

Jovanović, Slobodan. *Iz istorije i književnosti* (From history and literature). Collected works, volumes I-II, books 11–12. Belgrade, 1991.

Jovanović, Vladimir. "The sources of self-management law." *Yugoslav Law* (1981).

Jović, Borisav. *Poslednji dani SFRJ. Izvodi iz dnevnika* (The last days of the Socialist Federal Republic of Yugoslavia. Excerpts from a diary). Belgrade: Kompanija Politika, 1995.

Jugoslavija 1918–1988. Belgrade: SZS, 1989.

Jurančić, Janko. *Slovensko-srbskohrvatski slovar* (Slovene-Serbo-Croatian dictionary). Ljubljana: Državna založba Slovenije, 1981.

Kadijević, Veljko. "Reč u diskusiji na 17. sednici CKSKJ" (Speech at the discussion at the 17th session of the Central Committee of the League of Communists of Yugoslavia). *Vojnopolitički informator* no. 11 (1988).

Kadijević, Veljko. Articles and interviews in *Vojnopolitički informator* nos. 1 and 11 (1989).

Kadijević, Veljko. Interview to *Narodna armija* (6. December 1990).

Kadijević, Veljko. *Moje viđenje raspada—Vojska bez države* (My view of the breakup—army without a state). Belgrade: Politika—izdavačka delatnost, 1993.

"Kako sprečiti totalni rat?" (How to prevent a total war?). Inlay of *Republika* no. 29.

Kalajić, Dragoš. "Na braniku Evrope, protiv novog svetskog poretka" (On the front line of defense of Europe, against the New world order). In Yugoslav Federal Ministry of Defense. *Novi svetski poredak i politika odbrane Savezne Republike Jugoslavije* (New world order and the politicies of defense of the Federal Republic of Yugoslavia) Belgrade, 1993.

Kalajić, Dragoš. "Život bez budilnika" (Life without an alarm-clock). *Duga* no. 521 (1994).

Kalezić, Dimitrije M. "Religiozno-filozofske dimenzije kosovske tradicije" (Religious-philosophical dimensions of the Kosovan tradition). In *Sveti knez Lazar, Spomenica o šestoj stogodišnjici kosovskog boja 1389–1989* (St. knez Lazar, in commemoration of the six-hundredth anniversary of the Kosovo battle, 1389–1989). Belgrade, 1989.

Kallenbach, Hans (ed.). *Die Juden und wir Christen.* Frankfurt am Main, 1950.

Kambovski, Vlado. "Od ideala do stvarnosti" (From ideal to reality). Special edition of *Borba* (November 1991).

Kanic, Feliks. *Srbija, zemlja i stanovništvo od rimskog doba do kraja XIX veka* (Serbia, land and population from the Roman times to the end of the XIX century). Volumes I-II Belgrade: SKZ, 1985.

Kapetanović-Jovanović, Fahrija. *Vjera i strah* (Faith and fear). Belgrade: Filip Višnjić, 1986.

Karadžić, Vuk. "Srbi svi i svuda" (Serbs, all and everywhere). *Kovčežić*, Vienna (1849).

Karadžić, Vuk. *Kritike i polemike* (Critiques and polemics). Volume II of *Srpska književnost u sto knjiga* (Serbian literature in one hundred books), book 16. Novi Sad and Belgrade: Matica srpska and SKZ, 1960.

Kardelj, Edvard. *Pravci razvoja političkog sistema socijalističkog samoupravljanja* (Directions of development of the political system of socialist self-management). Belgrade: Izdavački centar Komunist, 1977.

Kecmanović, Dušan. *Masovna psihologija nacionalizma* (Mass psychology of nationalism). Belgrade: Vreme knjige, 1995.

Kempfer, Frank. "Početak kulta kneza Lazara" (The beginning of the cult of knez Lazar). In *O knezu Lazaru, naučni skup u Kruševcu 1971* (On knez Lazar: a symposium in Kruševac in 1971). Belgrade, 1975.

Kilibarda, Novak. "Kosovski mit u Crnoj Gori" (The Kosovan myth in Montenegro). In *Kosovo u usmenoj i srednjovekovnoj književnosti* (Kosovo in oral and medieval literature), 1989.

Kirtis, Žan Luj. *Questions ŕ la litterature*. Paris: Stock (1973).

Kiš, Danilo. *Čas anatomije* (The anatomy lesson). Belgrade: Nolit, 1978.

Klajn, Hugo. *Ratna neuroza Jugoslovena* (The war neurosis of the Yugoslavs). Belgrade: Tersit, 1995.

Kleßmann, Christoph. *Die doppelte Staatsgründung. Deutsche Geschichte 1945–1955*. Göttingen, 1986.

Knežević, Aleksandar and Vojislav Tufegdžić. *Kriminal koji je izmenio Srbiju* (Crime that changed Serbia). Belgrade: B92, 1995.

Knudsen, Knud C. (ed.). *Welt ohne Hass. Führende Wissenschaftler aller Fakultäten nehmen Stellung zu brennenden Problemen. Aufsätze und Ansprachen zum 1. Kongreß über bessere menschliche Bezienhungen.* München, Berlin, Hamburg and Stuttgart, 1950.

Kočović, Bogoljub. *Žrtve II svetskog rata u Jugoslaviji* (Victims of World War II in Yugoslavia). London: Naše delo, 1985.

Kogon, Eugen. *Der SS-Staat. Das System der deutschen Konzentrationslager.* Frankfurt am Main, 1946.

Kolarić, J. *Pravoslavni* (The Orthodox). Zagreb, 1985.

Komanin, Žarko. "Vladavina mržnje" (The reign of hatred). *Književne novine* no. 783 (1989).

Komlenović, Uroš. "Sahrana autonomije" (Burial of the autonomy). *Vreme* no. 135 (1993).

Komnenić, Milan. "Ćutanje i zločin" (Silence and crime). *Književne novine* no. 753 (1988).

Komnenić, Milan. "Glas praštaoca" (The voice of the forgiver). *Književne novine* no. 783 (1989).

Komnenić, Milan. *Obraćanja* (Addresses). Valjevo, 1989.

Komunistička internacionala, Stenogrami i dokumenti kongresa (The Communist international. Minutes and documents of the congress). Volume VII. Gornji Milanovac: Dečje novine, 1982.

Konstantinović, Radomir. *Filozofija palanke* (Philosophy of small town). Belgrade: Nolit, 1981.

Kosanović, Dejan. "Kosovski boj i filmska snimanja" (The Kosovo battle and film production). In *Kosovo u pamćenju i stvaralaštvu* (Kosovo in memory and art). Belgrade: Raskovnik, 1989.

Kosovo i Metohija u srpskoj istoriji (Kosovo and Metohija in Serbian history). Belgrade, 1989.

Kosovo u pamćenju i stvaralaštvu (Kosovo in memory and art). Belgrade: Raskovnik, 1989.

Kosovska bitka 1389. godine i njene posledice (The 1389 Kosovo battle and its consequences). Belgrade, 1991.

Kosovska bitka u istoriografiji. Okrugli sto (The Kosovo battle in historiography. A Round Table). Belgrade, 1990.

Kosovski boj u istoriji, tradiciji i stvaralaštvu Crne Gore (The Kosovo battle in the history, tradition and art of Montenegro). Titograd, 1990.

Kosovski boj u likovnim umetnostima, Kosovska spomenica 1389-1989 (The Kosovo battle in visual arts, the Kosovo memorial 1389-1989). Belgrade, 1990.

Kosovski boj u književnom i kulturnom nasleđu (The Kosovo battle in literary and cultural heritage). Belgrade, 1991.

Kosovski čvor—drešiti ili seći (The Kosovo knot—untie it or cut it). Belgrade: Chronos, 1990.

Kosovski čvor sve zamršeniji (The Kosovo knot ever more complicated). Special issue of *Republika* (1994).

Kostić, Laza. *Knjiga o Zmaju* (The book about Zmaj). Originally published in Sombor in 1902. See also the 1989 edition by Matica srpska, Novi Sad. Belgrade: Prosveta, 1984.

Kovačević, Ivan. "Fudbalski ritual" (The soccer ritual). *Gledišta* no. 5-6 (1987).

Kovačević, M. "Srbi kao žrtve rata u II svetskom ratu" (Serbs as war casualties in World War II). *Stanovništvo* (1992).

Kovačević, Mlađen. *Faktori konkurentnosti jugoslovenskog izvoza* (The factors of competitiveness of Yugoslav exports). Belgrade: Privredno-finansijski vodič, 1973.

Kovačević, Slobodanka and Dajić, Putnik. *Hronologija jugoslovenske krize 1942-1993* (Chronology of the Yugoslav crisis, 1942-1993). Belgrade: Institut za evropske studije, 1994.

Kovačević-Kojić, D. "Les villes médiévales de Serbie et de Bosnie avant et apres l'instauration du pouvoir ottoman." In *La culture urbaine des Balkans*. Belgrade and Paris: Institute des études balkaniques, 1991.

Kraljačić, Toma. "Petstogodišnjica Kosovske bitke u Bosni i Hercegovini" (The five-hundredth anniversary of the Kosovo battle in Bosnia-Herzegovina). In *Kosovska bitka 1389. godine i njene posledice* (The 1389 Kosovo battle and its consequences). Belgrade, 1991.

Krivokapić, Boro. *Dahauski procesi* (The Dachau trials). Belgrade: Partizanska knjiga, 1986.

Krivokapić, Boro. *Miodrag Bulatović, Preobraženska krv* (Miodrag Bulatović's "Preobraženska krv"). Belgrade: Politika, 1994.

Krleža, Miroslav. "Dijalektički antibarbarus" (Dialectical antibarbarus). *Pečat* no. 8–9 (1939).

Krstić Branimir. *Kosovo između istorijskog i etničkog prava* (Kosovo between historical and ethnic right). Belgrade: Kuća Vid, 1994.

Krstić, Branislav. "Postanak i razvoj narodnih pesama o kosovskom boju" (The genesis and development of folk poems about the Kosovo battle). In *Treći kongres folklorista Jugoslavije* (The third congress of the folklorists of Yugoslavia). Cetinje, 1958.

Kržišnik-Bukić, Vera. *Cazinska buna 1950* (The Cazin uprising of 1950). Sarajevo: Svjetlost, 1991.

Kuk, Albert. *Mit i jezik* (Myth and language). Belgrade, 1986.

Kulišić, Špiro. *Stara slovenska religija u svjetlu novijih istraživanja, posebno balkanoloških* (The old Slavic religion in the light of recent research, especially the balkanological ones). Sarajevo, 1979.

Kuzmanović, Bora et al. *Studentski protest '92* (The student protest of 1992). Belgrade: Institut za psihologiju Filozofskog fakulteta, 1993.

Kymlicka, Will. *Multicultural Citizenship: A Liberal Theory of Minority Rights*. Manuscript.

Lah, Ivo. "Metod izračunavanja budućeg stanovništva" (The method of calculation of future population) *Statistička revija* 1951.

Lalić, Dražen. "Nasilništvo nogometnih navijača. Geneza fenomena u Jugoslaviji" (Violence of soccer fans. A genesis of the phenomenon in Yugoslavia). *Kultura* no. 88–90 (1990).

Lalić, Lazar. *Tri TV godine u Srbiji* (Three TV years in Serbia). Belgrade: Nezavisni sindikat medija, 1995.

Laplanche, J. *Vocabulaire de la Psychanalyse*. Paris: PU, 1990. Zagreb: August Cesarec, 1992.

Lauer, Reinhardt. "Od ubica postaju junaci—o herojskoj poeziji Srba" (Murderers become heroes—on poetry of heroics of the Serbs). *Zbilja* 31 May 1994.

Lazić, Mladen. "Društveni činioci raspada Jugoslavije" (Social factors of the breakup of Yugoslavia). *Sociološki pregled* no. 2 (1994).

Lazić, Mladen et al. *Razaranje društva* (Destruction of society). Belgrade: Filip Višnjić, 1994.

Lee, J. J. *Politics and Society*. Cambridge: Cambridge University Press, 1989.

Lennon, Brian. *After the Ceasefires: Catholics and the Future of Northern Ireland*. Dublin: Columbia Press, 1995.

Leski, Albin *Grčka tragedija* (Greek tragedy). Novi Sad: Svetovi, 1995.

Liebich, Andre. "Minorities in Eastern Europe: obstacles to a reliable count." In *RFE/RL Research Report*. Volume I, 1992.

Liechty, Joe. "Roots of Sectarianism in Ireland." In *The Report of the Working Party on Sectarianism: A Discussion Document for Presentation to the Irish Inter Church Meeting*, Belfast, 1993.

Limbergen, Kris van. "Fudbalski vandalizam" (Soccer vandalism). *Kultura* no. 88–90 (1990).

Lions, F. S. L. *Ireland Since the Famine*. London: Colins Fontana, 1973.

Lipgens, Walter. "Christen und Juden heute." *Freiburger Rundbrief* 49 (1960): 26–28.

Loughlin, Sean. "The Role of the Churches in the Northern Ireland Conflict." *Studies* 78 (1989).

Lovrić, Ivica. *Delegatski sistem—uloga, značaj i pretpostavke za njegovo funkcionisanje* (The delegate system—role, importance and preconditions for its functioning). Sarajevo: Oslobođenje, 1974.

Lukić, Radomir. "Značaj boja na Kosovu, kosovska epika i kosovski mit—simbol očuvanja srpske nacionalne svesti" (The importance of the battle of Kosovo Kosovan epics and the Kosovan myth—the symbol of preservation of the Serbian national consciousness). *Politika* 28 june 1989.

Lukić, Vojin. *Sećanja i saznanja. Aleksandar Ranković i brionski plenum* (Memories and new moments: Aleksandar Ranković and the Congress of Brioni). Titograd, 1989.

Ljubičić, Nikola. *Opštenarodna odbrana strategije mira* (The national defense of the strategy of peace). Belgrade: VIZ, 1977.

Ljubinković, Nenad. "Kosovska legenda u ruskom rukopisnom svodu iz vremena cara Ivana IV Groznog" (The Kosovan legend in Russian manuscripts in the time of Ivan IV Grozny). In *Studije i grada za istoriju književnosti*. Volume I. Belgrade: Institut za književnost i umetnost, 1980.

Ljubinković, Nenad. "Kosovska bitka u svome vremenu i u viđenju potomaka ili logika razvoja epskih legendi o kosovskom boju" (The Kosovo battle in its time and in the view of heirs, or the logic of development of epic legends about the Kosovo battle). In *Kosovo u pamćenju i stvaralaštvu* (Kosovo in memory and art). Belgrade: Raskovnik, 1989.

Ljubinković, Nenad. "Od kosovske bitke do kosovske legende" (From the Kosovo battle to the Kosovan legend). In *Kosovski boj u književnom i kulturnom nasledu* (The Kosovo battle in literary and cultural heritage). Belgrade, 1991.

Ljudske i materijalne žrtve Jugoslavije. Izveštaj Vlade (Human and material Yugoslav casualties. Government report). Belgrade, 1945.

Macura, V. *Čaršija i gradski centar* (Urban community and the city center). Niš and Kragujevac: Gradina and Svetlost, 1984.

Madžar, Ljubomir. "Privredni sistem i mobilnost faktora proizvodnje" (Economic system and the mobility of factors of production). *Ekonomist* XVIII (1965), no. 1–2: 28–48.

Madžar, Ljubomir. "Revalorizacija zaliha, fiktivna akumulacija i iluzija rasta" (Revaluing of stocks, fictitious accumulation, and the illusion of growth). *Ekonomist* XXXVIII (1985), no. 3–4: 327–347.

Madžar, Ljubomir. *Suton socijalističkih privreda* (Twilight of socialist economies). Belgrade: Ekonomika and Institut ekonomskih nauka, 1990.

Madžar, Ljubomir. "Anatomija jugoslovenskog privrednog čuda" (Anatomy of the Yugoslav economic miracle). *Ekonomski anali* XXXVI (1992), no. 113: 45–76.

Maffesoli, Michel. "Hooligans." *Globe* no. 49 (1990).

Malinvaud, Edmond. *Theorie macroeconomique.* Volume II. Paris: Dunod, 1982.

Maliqi, S. "Kosovo kao katalizator jugoslovenske krize" (Kosovo as a catalyst of the Yugoslav crisis). In *Kosovo–Srbija–Jugoslavija* (Kosovo–Serbia–Yugoslavia). Ljubljana: KRT ZSMS,1989.

Malja, Agim. "Na Kosovu nema genocida" (There is no genocide in Kosovo). *Književne novine* no. 753 (1988).

Mamula, Branko. "Ekspoze u Skupštini SFRJ" (Expose in the Federal Assembly). *Vojnopolitički informator* no. 2 (1988)

Manević, Z. "Transformations des villes en Serbie au cours du XIXe siècle." In *La culture urbaine des Balkans.* Belgrade and Paris: Institute des études balkaniques, 1991.

"Manifest UJDI-ja" (The manifesto of the Association for the Yugoslav Democratic Initiative). *Republika* no. 4 (October 1989).

Marić, Milomir. "Svetac u službi davola" (A saint working for the Devil). *Duga* (1986).

Marić, Milomir. *Deca komunizma* (The children of Communism). Belgrade: Mladost, 1987.

Marić, Milomir. "Arkan kao mislilac" (Arkan as a thinker). *Borba* (1993).

Markov, Mladen. *Isterivanje boga* (Exorcising God). Volumes I–II. Belgrade: Prosveta, 1984.

Marković, Dragoslav-Draža. *Život i politika 1967–1978* (Life and politics, 1967–1978). Volume I. Belgrade: Rad, 1987.

Marković, Mihailo. "O jeziku ideologije" (On the language of ideology). *Theoria* no. 1 (1981).

Marković, Mira. *Odgovor* (The answer). Belgrade: BIGZ, 1993.

Marković, Mira. *Noć i dan* (Night and day). Belgrade: BIGZ, 1994.

Marković, P. *Beograd i Evropa: 1918–1941* (Belgrade and Europe: 1918–1941). Belgrade: Savremena administracija, 1992.

Marković, Peđa. "Teorija modernizacije i njena primena na međuratnu Jugoslaviju i Beograd" (The theory of modernization and its application to inter-war Yugoslavia and Belgrade). In *Srbija u modernizacijskim procesima XX veka* (Serbia in the modernization processes of the XX century). Belgrade: Institut za noviju istoriju, 1994.

Marković, Slobodan Ž. "Kosovska tradicija" (The tradition of Kosovo). In *Zabavnik,* inlay of *Srpske novine.* Quoted in *Kosovski boj u književnom i kulturnom nasledu* (The Kosovo battle in literary and cultural heritage). Belgrade, 1991.

Marković, Vera. "Zašto su samo navijači u napadu?" (Why are only the fans on the offense?). *Kultura* no. 88–90 (1990).

Mason, Dijan. "Pour une nouvelle Serbie." *Diagonales* no. 39 (1996).

Marsenić, Dragutin. "Kolika je i kakva (pre svega ekonomski) Savezna Republika Jugoslavija" (How big and how sound (primarily in economic terms) is the Federal Republic of Yugoslavia). *Ekonomski anali* XXXVI (1992), no. 113: 5–44.

Mastnak, Tomaž. "Is the Nation State really Obsolete?" *The Times Literary Supplement* (7 August 1992).

Maticki, Miodrag. "Slovar kosovske bitke (Kosovo polje)" (Dictionary of the Kosovo battle (Kosovo field)). In *Kosovski boj u književnom i kulturnom nasleđu* (The Kosovo battle in literary and cultural heritage). Belgrade, 1991.

Maticki, Miodrag. "Karađorđe u usmenoj narodnoj istoriji" (Karađorđe in the oral folk tradition). *Danica*, Serbian illustrated calendar for 1995, 1994.

Matić, Vojin. *Psihoanaliza mitske prošlosti* (Psychoanalysis of the mythical past). Volume I. Belgrade: Prosveta, 1976.

Matr, Harry. *Über den Wiederaufbau der jüdischen Gemeiden Deutschlands seit 1945*. Mainz, 1960.

Mayer, Alfred. "Die Situation der Juden im heutigen Deutschland." In Knudsen, Knud C. (ed.). *Welt ohne Hass. Führende Wissenschaftler aller Fakultäten nehmen Stellung zu brennenden Problemen. Aufsätze und Ansprachen zum 1. Kongreß über bessere menschliche Bezienhungen*. München, Berlin, Hamburg and Stuttgart, 1950: 157–164.

McDonagh, Enda. "Europe, the Faith and Ireland." *Studies* 78 (1989).

McDonagh, Enda. *The Gracing of Society*. Dublin: Gill and Macmillan, 1989.

McGarry, John and Brendan O'Leary (eds.). *The Politics of Ethnic Conflict*. London: Routledge, 1993.

McGarry, John and O'Leary, Brendan. "Introduction. The macro-political regulations of ethnic conflict." In McGarry, John and Brendan O'Leary (eds.). *The Politics of Ethnic Conflict*. London: Routledge, 1993.

Meinecke, Friedrich. *Die deutsche Katastrophe. Betrachungen und Erinnerungen*. Wiesbaden, 1946.

Memorandum Srpske akademije nauka i umetnosti (The Memorandum of the Serbian academy of sciences and arts). Originally published in 1986. Special edition of *Duga* (June 1989). See also *Novosti 8* (12 February 1991).

Mensing, Hans Peter (ed.). *Adenauer. Briefe 1945–1947*. Berlin, 1983.

Merrit, Anna J. and Richard L. (eds.) *Public Opinion in Occupied Germany. The OMGUS Surveys, 1945–1949*. Urbana, Chicago and London, 1970.

Merton, Robert. *Social Theory and Social Structure*. New York: The Free Press, 1968.

Mićović, Vojislav. *Specijalni rat i Jugoslavija* (Special war and Yugoslavia). Belgrade: Rad, 1986.

Mihailović, Dragoslav. *Goli otok* (The Naked island). Belgrade: NIP Politika, 1990.

Mihailović, Dragoslav. *Goli otok* (The Naked island). Volume III. Belgrade: SKZ–BIGZ, 1995.

Mihailović, Dušan. "'I voljaše carstvu nebeskome', 'Kosovska tetralogija' Nikole T. Đurića" ('And they leaned towards the heavenly kingdom.' 'The Kosovo tetralogy' of Nikola T. Đurić). In *Kosovski boj u književnom i kulturnom nasleđu* (The Kosovo battle in literary and cultural heritage). Belgrade, 1991.

Mihailović, Kosta and Vasilijc Krestić. *Memorandum SANU. Odgovori na kritike* (The Memorandum of the Serbian Academy of Sciences and Arts. Replies to criticisms). Belgrade: SANU, 1995.

682   *Bibliography*

Mihaljčić, Rade. *Boj na Kosovu, kraj Srpskog carstva* (The Kosovo battle. The end of the Serbian kingdom). Belgrade: BIGZ, 1989.

Mihaljčić, Rade. *Junaci kosovske legende* (The heroes of the Kosovan legend). Belgrade: BIGZ, 1989.

Mihaljčić, Rade. *Lazar Hrebeljanović, istorija, kult, predanje* (Lazar Hrebeljanović. History, cult, legend). Belgrade, BIGZ, 1989.

Mihaljčić, Rade (1990), "Motiv izdaje u istoriografiji" (The motive of betrayal in historiography). In *Okrugli sto: Kosovska bitka u istoriografiji* (Round table: The Kosovo battle in historiography). Belgrade, 1992.

Mijač, Božidar. "Eshatologija" (Eschatology). *Teološki pogledi* nos. 1–2 (1988).

Mijatović, Boško *Efekti poreske politike SFRJ–Pristup opšte ravnoteže* (The effects of the policy of taxation of the Socialist Federal Republic of Yugoslavia–the approach of the general equilibrium). Belgrade: Ekonomski fakultet, 1989.

Mikitenko, Oksana. "Kosovska tradicija u narodnoj tužbalici" (The tradition of Kosovo in the folk cry-songs). In *Kosovski boj u književnom i kulturnom nasleđu* (The Kosovo battle in literary and cultural heritage). Belgrade, 1991.

Milanović, Branko. *Protiv nacizma* (Against Nazism). Belgrade: Radio B–92,1994.

Milaš, Nikodim. *Pravoslavno crkveno pravo* (The Orthodox church law). Belgrade, 1926.

Miletić, Andrej. *Nacionalni interes u američkoj teoriji međunarodnih odnosa* (The national interest in the American theory of international relations). Belgrade: Savremena administracija, 1976.

Milin, Lazar. "Vidovdan" (St. Vitus Day). *Pravoslavni misionar* no. 3 (1982).

Milin, Lazar. "Razgovori o veri" (Conversations about faith). In *Apologetska čitanka* (The Apologetic reader). Belgrade: Bogoslovski fakultet, 1985.

Milinković, Branko. *Rezolucije Saveta bezbednosti UN o krizi u bivšoj Jugoslaviji (i drugi dokumenti)* (The resolutions of the United Nations Security Council about the crisis in the former Yugoslavia and other documents). Belgrade: Međunarodna politika, Pravni fakultet and Fakultet političkih nauka, 1995.

Milivojević, Zdenka. "Mediji u Srbiji od 1985. do 1994" (The media in Serbia from 1985 until 1994). In Dušan Janjić (ed.). *Srbija između prošlosti i budućnosti* (Serbia between past and future). Belgrade: NIP Radnička štampa, Institut društvenih nauka and Forum za etničke odnose, 1995.

Miller, David. "Exploitation in the Market." In Andrew Reeve (ed.). *Modern Theories of Exploitation*. London: Sage Publications, 1987: 149–165.

Miljanić, Dušan, Radovan Radinović et al. *Opštenarodna odbrana i društvena samozaštita SFRJ* (National defense and the social self-protection of the Socialist Federal Republic of Yugoslavia). Belgrade: Zavod za udžbenike i nastavna sredstva.

Miljovski, Kiril. "Ekonomski regioni u jugoslovenskoj teoriji i praksi" (Ecoonomic regions in Yugoslav theory and practice). In Kiril Miljovski (ed.). *Neravnomerni regionalni razvoj u ekonomskoj teoriji i praksi* (Uneven regional development in economic theory and practice). Skopje: MANU, 1980: 19–49.

Milosavljević, A. *Kultura vlasti* (The culture of the governing). Belgrade: Radio B-92.

Milošević, Milan. "Odbrana ognjišta" (The defense of hearths). *Vreme* no. 90 (1992).

Milošević, Zoran. "SPS, SPC i religija" (The Socialist Party of Serbia, the Serbian Orthodox Church and religion). In Dragoljub Đorđević (ed.). *Pravoslavlje između neba i zemlje* (Orthodoxy between heaven and earth). Niš: Gradina, 1991.

Milošević-Đorđević, Nada. "Lik kneza Lazara i kulturno-istorijska predanja" (The character of knez Lazar and cultural-historical legends). In *Sveti knez Lazar, Spomenica o šestoj stogodišnjici kosovskog boja 1389–1989* (St. knez Lazar, in commemoration of the six-hundredth anniversary of the Kosovo battle, 1389–1989). Belgrade, 1989.

Milutinović Krstić, Nebojša. *Politika i obraz za vaskrs raspetog srbstva* (Politics and ethics for the ressurection of the crusified Serbdom). Beograd, 1993.

Milza, Pierre. "Le football italien." After Ignacio Ramonet. "Le football, c'est la guerre." *Quel Corps?* (July 1990).

Mirković, Stevan. Article in *Vojnopolitički informator* no. 7 (1988).

Mirković, Stevan. "Reč u diskusiji na 17. sednici CKSKJ" (Speech at the discussion at the 17th session of the Central Committee of the League of Communists of Yugoslavia). *Vojnopolitički informator* no. 11 (1988).

„Mišljenje SANU o promenama Ustava SR Srbije" (The opinion of the Serbian Academy of Sciences and Arts about the changes in the Constitution of the Socialist Republic of Serbia). *Politika* (19 November 1988).

Momčilović, Branko. "Proslava Vidovdana u Velikoj Britaniji 1916. godine" (The celebration of St. Vitus day in Great Britain in 1916). In *Kosovski boj u književnom i kulturnom nasledu* (The Kosovo battle in literary and cultural heritage). Belgrade, 1991.

Mommsen, Hans. "Was haben die Deutschen vom Völkermord an den Juden gewusst?" In Walter H. Pehle (ed.) Walter H. *Der Judenpogrom 1938. Von der "Reichskristallnacht" zum Völkermord*. Frankfurt am Main, 1988: 176–200.

Morrow, Duncan et al. *The Churches and Inter–Community Relationships*. Oleraine: University of Ulster, 1991.

Mostov, Julie. "Endangered Citizenship." In Michael Kraus and Ronald Liebovitz (eds.). *Russian and East Europe Transition*. Westview Press, 1995.

Motyl, Alexander J. "Nach der Sintflut: Totalitarismus und Nationalismus im ehemaligen Sowjetreich." *Österreichische Osthefte* (1993).

Mumford, L. *Grad u historiji*. Zagreb: Naprijed, 1968.

Murray, Charles. "The Pursuit of Happiness under Socialism and Capitalism." *The Cato Journal* XI (Fall 1991), no. 2, 239–258.

"Nacrt programa SPO" (Draft of the program of the Serbian renewal movement). *Srpska reč* (1 June 1990).

Navres, Reneé de. "Democratization and Ethnic Conflict." In Michael Brown (ed.). *Ethnic Conflict and International Security*. Princeton: Princeton University Press, 1993.

Nedeljković, Mile. "Kosovo i Metohija u svesti i na usnama naroda" (Kosovo and Metohija in the consciousness and on the lips of the people). In *Kosovo u pamćenju i stvaralaštvu* (Kosovo in memory and art). Belgrade: Raskovnik, 1989.

Nedeljković, Mile. *Godišnji običaji u Srba* (Annual rites of the Serbs). Belgrade, 1990.

"Nekoliko osnovnih činjenica o položaju srpskog naroda u Hrvatskoj" (A few basic facts about the condition of the Serbian people in Croatia). Report of the Serbian Academy of Sciences and Arts. *Politika* (16. October 1991).

Niethammer, Lutz. *Die Mitläuferfabrik. Die Entnazifizierung am Beispiel Bayerns*. Berlin and Bonn, 1982.

Nikezić, Zvonimir (project leader). *Prestrukturiranje jugoslovenske privrede—analiza i ocena stanja* (Restructuring of the Yugoslav economy—analysis and the report on the current condition). Belgrade: Institut za ekonomiku industrije, 1987.

Nikolajević, Dušan S. "Naš demokratizam" (Our democratic inclinations). *Nedeljni pregled* (1910).

Nikolić, Pavle. "Basic characteristics of the system of delegates." *Review of International Affairs* no. 576 (1974).

Nikprelević, Đ. "Uzeto kao darovano" (Taken like received as a present). In *Koliko nas košta Kosovo?* (How much does Kosovo cost us?). Special issue of *Privredni pregled* (1989).

Nipperday, Th. "Romantischer Nationalismus." In *Nachdenken über deutsche Geschichte*. München, 1986.

Nodilo, Nadko. "Religija Srba i Hrvata, na glavnoj osnovi pjesama, priča i govora narodnog" (Religion of Serbs and Croats, on the main basis of songs, stories, and folk speech). *Rad* LXXVII. Originally published in Zagreb in 1885.

Noormann, Harry. *Protestantismus und politisches Mandat 1945–1949*. 2 Volumes. Gütersloh, 1985.

Novi srpski forum (New Serbian forum). *Republika* mo. 77 (1993).

Novi svetski poredak i politika odbrane Savezne Republike Jugoslavije (New world order and the politicies of defense of the Federal Republic of Yugoslavia) Yugoslav Federal Ministry of Defense. Belgrade, 1993.

Novi ustavi na tlu bivše Jugoslavije (New constitutions on the soil of the former Yugoslavia). Belgrade. Međunarodna politika, Pravni fakultet and Fakultet političkih nauka, 1995.

Novija srpska književnost i kritika ideologije (Recent Serbian literature and the critique of ideology). Belgrade: SANU, 1989.

Numić, Selim. *Dobra zemljo, lažu. Do istine o brionskoj aferi prisluškivanja* (They are lying, good country. Towards truth about the Brioni affair of surveillance). Belgrade: Filip Višnjić, 1989.

Njegoš, Petar Petrović. *Gorski vijenac* (The mountain wreath). Belgrade.

O knezu Lazaru, naučni skup u Kruševcu 1971 (On knez Lazar: a symposium in Kruševac in 1971). Belgrade, 1975.

O'Brien, Conor Cruise. *Ancestral Voices: Religion and Nationalism in Ireland*. Dublin: Poolbeg Press, 1994.

Ocić, Č. (ed.). *Privredni razvoj Kosova* (The economic development of Kosovo). Belgrade: MC CKSKS, 1990.

Odajnik, V. V. *Jung i politika. Političke i sociološke ideje K. G. Junga* (Jung and politics. Political and sociological ideas of Karl Gustav Jung). Belgrade: Esoterija, 1994.

"Odluka 10. konferencije OSKJ u JNA" (The decision of the 10th conference of OSKJ in JNA). *Vojnopolitički informator* no. 2 (1990).

Oduprite se Zapadu (Resist the West). Message of the Russian Slavophiles to their Serbian brothers. *Republika* no. 4 (1992).

Offe, Claus. "Ethnic Politics in Eastern European Transitions." Paper presented at the conference *Nationalisms in Europe Revisited*. Tulane university, New Orleans, 1994.

Okrugli sto: Kosovska bitka u istoriografiji (Round table: The Kosovo battle in historiography). Belgrade, 1992.

Orbin(i), Mavro. *Il regno degli Slavi*. Pesaro, 1601.

Orhanović, S. M. "Jedan eshatološki motiv u staroj kosovskoj poeziji" (An eschatological motive in old Kosovan poetry). In *Prilozi proučavanju narodne poezije* (Contributions to the study of folk poetry), 1934.

Ornstein, Hans. "Christlich-jüdische Zusammenarbeit: ihr Wesen und ihre Ziele." *Judaica* 3 (1947): 210–235.

Osnove programa Socijalističke partije Srbije (Fundaments of the program of the Socialist party of Serbia). Belgrade, 1993.

"Osnovna zamisao za nastavak 14. vanrednog kongresa SKJ" (The basic thought about the continuation of the 14th extraordinary congress of the League of Communists of Yugoslavia). *Vojnopolitički informator* no. 6 (1990).

Owen, David. "The Future of the Balkans. An Interview with David Owen." *Foreign Affairs* 72 (1993), no. 3.

Pages, Didier. "Football: Ceux qui vont mourir te saluent ou a qui profite le crime?" *Quel Corps?* (July 1990).

Paić, Gordana (1991). "SPC i kriza" (The Serbian Orthodox Church and the crisis). In Đorđević, Dragoljub B. (ed.). *Pravoslavlje između neba i zemlje* (Orthodoxy between heaven and earth). Niš: Gradina, 1991.

Palavestra, Predrag. "Kritička književnost kao oblik očišćenja" (Critical literature as a means of purification). *Književne novine* (8 April 1982).

Pantić, Dragomir. "Nacionalna distanca građana Jugoslavije" (The national distance between the citizens of Yugoslavia). In *Jugoslavija na kriznoj prekretnici* (Yugoslavia at the crossroads of the crisis). Belgrade: IDN, 1991.

Pantić, Miroslav. "Narodno (usmeno) pesništvo" (Oral folk poetry). In *Istorija srpskog naroda* (A history of the Serbian people). Volume IV, "Srbi u XVIII veku" (Serbs in the XVIII century). Belgrade, 1986.

Park, R. L. "Grad: predlozi za istraživanje ljudskog ponašanja u gradskoj sredini" (The city: propositions for research of human behavior in the urban area). In Sreten Vujović (ed.). *Sociologtju grada* (Sociology of the city). Belgrade: Zavod za izdavanje udžbenika, 1988.

"Partizanski zločini u Srbiji 1944–45: 150.000 neznanih grobova" (Partisan crimes in Serbia, 1944–1945: 150,000 of unknown graves). Special edition of *Pogledi* (June 1991).

Paunović, Žarko. "Simuliranje aktivnosti" (Simulating activity). *Republika* no. 123.

Pavlović, Dragiša. *Olako obećana brzina* (Easily promised speed). Zagreb: Globus, 1988.

Pavlović, Leontije. *Kultovi lica kod Srba i Makedonaca* (The cults of face in Serbs and Macedonians). Smederevo, 1965.

Pavlović, Miodrag. "Epsko pevanje o kosovskom boju" (Epic poetry about the Kosovo battle).

Pavlović, Vukašin (ed.). *Potisnuto civilno društvo* (Civil society supressed). Belgrade: Ekocentar, 1995.

Pejin, Jovan. "Obeležavanje petstogodišnjice Kosovskog boja u Ugarskoj i širenje kosovske legende" (Commemorating the five-hundredth anniversary of the Kosovo battle in Hungary and the spreading of the Kosovo legend). In *Kosovska bitka 1389. godine i njene posledice* (The 1389 Kosovo battle and its consequences). Belgrade, 1991.

Pekić, Borislav. *Godine koje su pojeli skakavci* (The years eaten away by the grasshoppers). Volumes I–II. Belgrade: BIGZ, 1989 (1987).

Pekić, Borislav. *Sentimentalna povest Britanskog carstva* (Sentimental history of the British empire). Belgrade: BIGZ, 1992.

Pelikán, Jan. "Tri studie o modernim srbském nacionalismu." *Slovanský prehled* no. 4 (1995).

Perasović, Benjamin. "Sportsko huliganstvo kao subkulturna pojava" (Sport hooliganism as a subcultural phenomenon). *Pitanja* nos. 5–6 (1988).

Perišić, Miodrag. "Kraj utopije, početak mržnje" (The end of utopia, a beginning of hatred). *Književne novine* no. 807 (1990).

Perović, Latinka. Srpski socijalisti XIX veka (Serbian socialists of the XIX century). Belgrade, 1985.

Perović, Latinka. "Yugoslavia was defeated from inside." In Sonja Biserko (ed.). *Yugoslavia: Collapse, War Crimes.* Belgrade: Center for Antiwar Action and Belgrade Circle, 1993.

Perović, Latinka. *Srpsko-ruske revolucionarne veze. Prilozi za istoriju narodnjaštva u Srbiji* (Serbian-Russian revolutionary ties. Contributions to the history of populism in Serbia). Belgrade, 1993.

Perrot, M. "La vielle et ses faubourgs au XIXe siècle" In *Citoyenneté et urbanité.* Paris: Esprit, 1991.

Pešić, Radmila and Nada Milošević-Đorđević. *Narodna književnost* (National literature). Belgrade, 1984.

Pešić, Vesna. *Kratki kurs o jednakosti* (A shourt course on equality). Belgrade: Sociološko društvo Srbije, 1988.

Pešić, Vesna. "Nationalism, war and disintegration of Communist federations: the Yugoslav case." In Sonja Biserko (ed.). *Yugoslavia: Collapse,*

War Crimes. Belgrade: Center for Antiwar Action and Belgrade Circle, 1993.

Pešić, Vesna. "Neraspakovano pravo na samoopredeljenje: zdravorazumsko i naučno prikrivanje stvarnih ratnih ciljeva" (Unpacked right to self-determination. Commonsensical and scientific representation of real war goals). *Republika* no. 123 (1995).

Pešić, Vesna. "Treniranje strogoće" (Practising rigidity). *Republika* nos. 125–126 (1995).

Peti kongres KPJ, Stenografske beleške (The fifth congress of the Communist party of Yugoslavia. Minutes). Belgrade: Kultura, 1949.

Petranović, Branko. "O levim skretanjima KPJ krajem 1941. i u prvoj polovini 1942. godine" (On leftist radicalism of the Communist party of Yugoslavia in late 1941 and the first half of 1942). *Zbornik za istoriju* no. 4 (1971). Novi Sad: Matica srpska.

Petranović, Branko and Momčilo Zečević. *Agonija dve Jugoslavije* (The agony of two Yugoslavias). Belgrade and Šabac: Edicija svedočanstva, Zaslon, 1991.

Petrov, Aleksandar. "Šta pisci da čine" (What should writers do). *Književne novine* no. 753 (1988).

Petrović, Branka and Žarko Paunović. *Nevladine organizacije u SR Jugoslaviji* (Non-governmental organizations in the Federal Republic of Yugoslavia). Subotica: Otvoreni univerzitet and Evropski građanski centar za rešavanje konflikata, 1994.

Petrović, Krešimir. "Nasilje i sport" (Violence and sport). *Kultura* nos. 88–90 (1990).

Petrović, Lidija. "Oktobarski štrajk studenata 1905" (The October student strike of 1905). In *Univerzitet u Beogradu* (University in Belgrade). Belgrade, 1988.

Petrović, Nikola. "Istorijsko mesto, uloga i značaj Ujedinjene omladine srpske" (Historical place, role and importance of the United Serbian youth). In *Ujedinjena omladina srpska* (The United Serbian youth). Novi Sad: Matica srpska, 1968.

Petrović, Pavle and Cvjetićanin, Danijel (eds.). *Tranzicija privrede Srbije* (The transition of the Serbian economy). Belgrade: Ekonomski institut, 1991.

Petrović, Ruža. *Etnički aspekt i migracije* (The ethnic aspect of migration). Belgrade: IIC SSO, 1987.

Petrović, Ruža. "Demografske osobenosti razvoja Kosova i etničke prilike" (Demographic pecularities of the development of Kosovo and the ethnic relations). In *Srbi i Albanci u XX veku* (Serbs and Albanians in the XX century). Belgrade: Serbian Academy of Sciences and Arts, 1991.

Petrović, Ruža and Marina Blagojević. "The Educational Structure of Ethnic Groups in Yugoslavia (Results of the 1981 Census)." In *Razprave in gradivo* no. 18 (1986).

Petrović, Ruža and Marina Blagojević. *Seobe Srba i Crnogoraca sa Kosova i iz Metohije* (Migrations of Serbs and Montenegrins from Kosovo and Metohija). Belgrade: SANU, 1989.

Pilon, Roger. "Individual Rights, Democracy and Constitutional Order: On the Foundations of Legitimacy." *The Cato Journal* XI (Winter 1992) no. 3: 373-390.

Piroćanac, Milan. *Dnevnik*. Arhiv SANU (Archive of the Serbian Academy of Sciences and Arts), no. 9989.

"Pismo HAZU upućeno SANU početkom oktobra 1991" (The letter of the Croatian academy of sciences and arts to the Serbian Academy of Sciences and Arts from the beginning of October 1991). In *Godišnjak SANU za 1992*. Belgrade, 1993.

Plan i program političkog obrazovanja i vaspitanja vojnika/mornara u JNA (Plan and program of political education of soldiers and sailors in the Yugoslav People's Army). Belgrade: SSNO and PU, 1988.

Podunavac, Milan. "Princip građanstva i priroda političkog režima u post-komunizmu: slučaj Srbija" (The principle of citizenship and the nature of the political regimes in post-Communism: the case of Serbia). In Vukašin Pavlović (ed.). *Potisnuto civilno društvo* (Civil society supressed). Belgrade: Ekocentar, 1995.

Polovina, Vesna. "Lingvističko-pragmatički aspekti nekih iskaza u tekstovima o proslavi Kosovskog boja 1389. i 1989. godine" (Linguistical-pragmatist aspects of some statements in the text about celebration of the Kosovo battle in 1389 and 1989). In *Kosovski boj u književnom i kulturnom nasleđu* (The Kosovo battle in literary and cultural heritage). Belgrade, 1991.

Polovina, Gojko. *Svedočenja. Prva godina ustanka u Lici* (Testimonies. The first year of the uprising in Lika). Belgrade: Rad, 1988.

Popadić, Dragan. "Prvi i drugi deseti mart" (The first and the second 10th of March). *Republika* nos. 41-42 (1992).

Popadić, Dragan. "Studentski protest '92" (The student protest of 1992). *Republika* nos. 49-50 (1992).

Popov, Nebojša. *Društveni sukobi—izazov sociologiji* (Social conflicts—a challenge to sociology). Belgrade: CFDT, 1983.

Popov, Nebojša. "Živeti slobodno" (To live freely). *Književne novine* nos. 723-4 (1987).

Popov, Nebojša. *Contra fatum. Slučaj grupe profesora Filozofskog fakulteta (1968-1988)* (Contra fatum. A case of a group of professors from the Faculty of philosophy, 1968-1988). Belgrade: Mladost, 1988.

Popov, Nebojša. *Kriza međuratnog jugoslovenskog društva* (The crisis of the inter-war Yugoslav society). Belgrade: CFDT, 1989.

Popov, Nebojša. *Jugoslavija pod naponom promena* (Yugoslavia under the tension of changes) Belgrade, 1990.

Popov, Nebojša. "Unutrašnja i spoljna sloboda" (Internal and external freedom). In *Potrebe društvenog razvoja* (The needs for social development). Volume 1. Belgrade, SANU, 1991.

Popov, Nebojša. *Srpski populizam. Od marginalne do dominantne pojave* (Serbian populism. From a marginal to the dominant phenomenon). Special edition of *Vreme* br. 135 (1993).

Popov, Nebojša. *Republikanac* (Republican). Zrenjanin: Građanska čitaonica Banat, 1994.

Popov, Nebojša. "Teškoće s dijalogom" (Difficulties with dialogue). *Republika*, thematic issue no. 9 (1994).

Popović, Danko. *Knjiga o Milutinu* (Book about Milutin). Belgrade: NIRO Književne novine, 1986.

Popović, Justin. *Dogmatika pravoslavne crkve* (The dogmatics of the Orthodox church). Volumes I–III. Belgrade, 1978.

Popović, Justin. *Na bogočovečanskom putu* (On the godly-manly road). Belgrade, 1980.

Popović, Justin. "Svetosavlje–pravoslavno hrišćanstvo srpskog stila i iskustva" (The cult of St. Sava–Orthodox Christianity of Serbian style and experience). *Pravoslavni misionar* no. 4 (1985).

Popović, Justin. "Svetosavska filozofija kulture" (The cult of St. Sava and its philosophy of culture). *Glas crkve* no. 3 (1985).

Popović, Justin. "Svetosavska filozofija prosvete" (The cult of St. Sava and its philosophy of education). *Glas crkve* no. 3 (1996).

Popović, Justin. *Crkva i država* (Church and state).

Popović, Miodrag. *Vidovdan i časni krst, Ogled iz književne arheologije* (St. Vitus day and the Holy cross. An essay in literary archaeology). Belgrade, 1976.

Popović, Miroslav. *Udri bandu* (Hit the bandits). Belgrade: Filip Višnjić, 1988.

Popović, Radovan. *Pisci u službi naroda* (Writers in the service of the people). Belgrade, 1991.

Popović, Srđa. "Kriza modernosti" (The crisis of modernity). *Republika*, thematic issue no. 8, "Sloveni i Zapad" (Slavs and the West). Belgrade, 1994.

Popović, T. "La 'čarši' balkanique aux XVIe et XVIIe siècles." In *La culture urbaine des Balkans*. Belgrade and Paris: Institute des études balkaniques, 1991.

Popović-Obradović, Olga. "Političke stranke i izbori u Kraljevini Srbiji 1903–1914. Prilog istoriji stranačkog pluralizma" (Political parties and elections in the Kingdom of Serbia, 1903–1914. A contribution to the history of party pluralism). In *Srbija u modernizacijskim procesima XX veka* (Serbia in the modernization processes of the XX century). Belgrade: Institut za noviju istoriju, 1994.

Popović-Obradović, Olga. "Zablude o 'zlatnom dobu'" (Misconceptions about the 'golden age'). *Republika* no. 115 (1995).

Posen, Barry R. "The Security Dilemma and Ethnic Conflict." In Michael Brown (ed.). *Ethnic Conflict and International Security*. Princeton: Princeton University Press, 1993.

Potrebe društvenog razvoja (The needs for social development). Volume 1. Belgrade, SANU, 1991.

Povratak bogova (The return of gods). Special edition of *Duga* (April 1986).

Pravilnik o ocenjivanju vojnih lica (Regulations determining the grading of military persons). Belgrade: SSNO, Personalna uprava, 1980.

Pravilo službe Oružanih snaga (Regulations of service in the armed forces). Belgrade: SSNO, 1985.

"Predlog nacionalnog programa Demokratske stranke" (A proposed national program of the Democratic party). *Demokratija* (18 September 1990).

"Prilozi za slovenački nacionalni program" (Contributions to the Slovene national program). *Nova Revija* no. 57 (1987).

Prodanović, Mileta. *Pas prebijene kičme* (A dog with a broken spine). Belgrade: Plato, 1993.

"Program Demokratske stranke" (The program of the Democratic party). In Miroslav Pečujlićand Vladimir Milić. *Političke stranke u Jugoslaviji* (Political parties in Yugoslavia). Belgrade, 1990.

Program Demokratske stranke Srbije (Program of the Democratic party of Serbia). Belgrade, 1994 (1992).

Program Građanskog saveza Srbije (Program of the Civil Alliance of Serbia). Belgrade, 1994.

"Program idejno-političkih zadataka OSKJ u JNA" (Program of the ideo-political goals of OSKJ in JNA). In *Dokumenta za 9. konferenciju OSKJ u JNA* (Documents for the ninth conference of OSKJ in JNA). Belgrade, 1989.

Program SKJ. VII kongres SKJ (Program of the League of Communists of Yugoslavia. VII congress of the League of Communists of Yugoslavia). Belgrade: Kultura, 1958.

Program SPO (Program of the Serbian Renewal Movement). Belgrade, 1994.

Program Srpske radikalne stranke (Program of the Serbian Radical Party). Belgrade, 1991.

"Program Srpske radikalne stranke" (Program of the Serbian Radical Party). *Velika Srbija* (March 1994).

Programske osnove i Statut Socijalističke partije Srbije (Programatic foundations and the Statute of the Socialist Party of Serbia). Belgrade, 1990.

Programske osnove i Statut Socijalističke partije Srbije (Programatic foundations and the Statute of the Socialist Party of Serbia). Belgrade, 1993.

Prstojević, M. *Sarajevo—ranjeni grad* (Sarajevo—a wounded city). Sarajevo: DAF Grafika and PP Ideja, 1994.

"Prva skupština DEPOS-a" (The first congress of the Democratic Movement of Serbia). *Srpska reč* (26 October 1992).

Pučnik, Jože. *Članki in spomini (1957–1985)* (Articles and memories). Maribor: Znamenja, 1986.

Puhovski, Žarko. "Moguće je padati još dublje. Intervju sa M. Vučelićem „ (It is possible to sink even further. An interview with Milorad Vučelić). *Književne novine* no. 727 (1987).

Pula G. and E. Beqiri. "Kosova: Colonial Oppression of Albanians in Yugoslavia." In *Kosova Watch*. Volume I, no. 1. Pristina: Kosova Helsinki Committee, 1992.

Pusić, Eugen. "Identitet-diverzitet-kapacitet" (Identity–diversity–capacity). *Erasmus* no. 11 (1995).

Puslojić, Adam. "Srbija bez anateme" (Serbia without the anathema). *Književne novine* no. 772 (1989).

Radinović, Radovan. "Moć i nemoć vojske u raspadu Jugoslavije" (Power and powerlessness of the army in the breakup of Yugoslavia). *Sociološki pregled* no. 2 (1994).

Radović, Amfilohije. "Pravoslavno shvatanje nacije" (Understanding of the nation in Orthodoxy). In *Religija i nacija* (Religion and nation). Zagreb, 1984.

Radović, Borislav. "Ne prihvatam Nacrt u celini" (I do not accept the draft in its entirety). *Književne novine* no. 751 (1988).

Radović, Nastasja. "Platite nas barem kao tramvajdžije" (Pay us at least as much as you pay tram-drivers). *Republika* no. 22 (1991).

Radovanović, Rade. "Deca marta na vetrometini" (The children of March in the wind). *Republika* nos. 41–42 (1992).

Radovanović, Vojislav S. *Sveti Miloš Obilić, Južnosrbijanski kult narodnog heroja* (Saint Miloš Obilić. A southern-Serbian cult of a national hero). Belgrade: Život i rad, 1929.

Rajić, Ljubiša. "Navikavanje na opoziciju" (Getting used to the opposition). *Republika* no. 16 (1991).

Rajs, Kondoliza. "Vojska u demokratskom poretku" (The military in a democratic order). *Treći program* nos. 90–91 (1991).

Rakić, Laza. *Nadalj*. Novi Sad, 1988.

Rakočević, Novica. "Kosovski kult u Crnoj Gori tokom XIX i na početku XX vijeka" (The cult of Kosovo in Montenegro during the XIX and at the beginning of the XX century). In *Sveti knez Lazar, Spomenica o šestoj stogodišnjici kosovskog boja 1389–1989* (St. knez Lazar, in commemoration of the six-hundredth anniversary of the Kosovo battle, 1389–1989). Belgrade, 1989.

Ralić, Prvoslav and Mile Nedeljković (eds.). *Rečnik zabluda: sto neistina o srpskom narodu i odgovori na njih. A Dictionary of Misconceptions: A Hundred Falsities about Serbia and Answers to them*. Belgrade: Ministarstvo za informacije Srbije, 1994.

Ramet, Sabrina Petra. *Nationalism and Federalism in Yugoslavia 1962–1992*. 2nd edition. Bloomington and Indianapolis: Indiana University Press, 1992.

Ramet, Sabrina Petra. "War in the Balkans." *Foreign Affairs* 71 (1992).

Rapi, Đerd. *Savremene albanske zadružne porodice na Kosovu* (Contemporary Albanian extended families in Kosovo). Belgrade: ISI FF, 1995.

Rašević, Mirjana. *Ka razumevanju abortusa u Srbiji* (Towards understanding of abortion in Serbia). Belgrade: CDJ IDN, 1994.

Rašković, Jovan. *Luda zemlja* (The crazy country). Belgrade: Akvarijus, 1990.

Rea, Desmond. *Political Co-Operation in Divided Societies*. Dublin: Gill and Macmillan, 1982.

Redžep, Jelka. "Kosovska legenda i Priča o boju kosovskom" (The Kosovan legend and the narrative of the Kosovo battle). In *Kosovska bitka 1389. godine i njene posledice* (The 1389 Kosovo battle and its consequences). Belgrade, 1991.

Redžep, Jelka. "Razvitak kosovske legende" (The development of the Kosovan legend). In *Boj na Kosovu, starija i novija saznanja* (The battle of Kosovo, older and more recent discoveries). Belgrade, 1992.

Reeve, Andrew (ed.). *Modern Theories of Exploitation*. London: Sage Publications, 1987.

Reich, Wilhelm. *Masovna psihologija fašizma* (The mass psychology of Fascism). Belgrade: Ideje, 1990.

Reichel, Peter. "Vergangenheitsbewältigung als Problem unserer politischen Kultur. Einstellungen zum Dritten Reich und seinen Folgen." In Peter Steinbach and Jürgen Weber (eds.). *Vergangenheitsbewältigung durch Strafverfahren? NS-Prozesse in der Bundesrepublik Deutschland*. München, 1984: 145–163.

Religija i društvo (Religion and society). Belgrade, 1988.

Religija i nacija (Religion and nation). Zagreb, 1984.

Religija–rat–mir (Religion–war–peace). Niš, 1994.

Rendtorff, Ralf and Hans Hermann Henrix (eds.). *Die Kirchen und das Judentum. Dokumente von 1945 bis 1985*. Paderborn and München, 1988.

Rezultati Popisa 1948 i 1953 (Results from the censuses of 1948 and 1953). Belgrade: SZS, 1989.

Richards, L. A. *Načela književne kritike* (The principles of literary criticism). Sarajevo: Veselin Masleša, 1964.

Richtman-Augustin, Dunja. "Junaci i klijenti. Skica za istraživanje mortaliteta" (Heroes and clients. A sketch for the study of mortality rates). *Erasmus* no. 16 (1996).

Ristić, Žarko and Dušan Jovanović. *Komparativni fiskalni sistemi* (Comparative fiscal systems). Belgrade: Službeni list SFRJ, 1992.

Roksandić, Drago. "Ljudska i građanska prava i otvorena pitanja personalne i kulturne autonomije Srba u Hrvatskoj" (Human and civil rights and the open questions of the personal and cultural autonomy of the Serbs in Croatia). *Scientia Yugoslavica* 16, nos. 3–4 (1990).

Rosandić, R. and V. Pešić (eds.). *Ratništvo, patriotizam, patrijarhalnost* (Warriorship, patriotism, patriarchality). Belgrade: Centar za antiratnu akciju, 1994.

Rosenthal, A. M. "American Allies in Serbia." *The New York Times* (January 1993).

Rožič, Marjan. "The delegation system and the Socialist Alliance." *Review of International Affairs* no. 589 (1974).

Ršumović, Lj., R. Stanojević and M. Tomić. *Crvena zvezda. Monografija* (Red star. A monograph). Belgrade, 1986.

Rugova, Ibrahim. "Albanci su Iliri" (Albanians are Illyrians). *Književne novine* no. 753 (1988).

(Rushdie) Ruždi, Salman. "Bosna u mojim mislima" (Bosnia in my thoughts). *Beogradski krug* no. 1 (1994).

Rusinow, Dennison. *The Yugoslav Experiment 1948–1974*. London: C. Hurt and Company, 1977.

Ruvarac, Ilija. "Prilog ispitivanju srpskih narodnih pesama" (A contribution to the study of the Serbian folk poetry). In *Dve studentske rasprave*. Novi Sad, 1984.

Sachs, Jeffrey D. and Felipe B. Laraine. *Macroeconomics in the Global Economy.* New York and London: Harvester and Wheatsheaf, 1993.

Samardžić, Radovan. "Pravoslavlje u savremenim političkim prilikama" (Orthodoxy in the contemporary political setting). In *Religija i društvo* (Religion and society). Belgrade, 1988.

Samardžić, Radovan. "Istorija prvih progona" (The history of the first persecutions). *Književne novine* no. 753 (1988).

Samardžić, Radovan. *Kosovsko opredeljenje. Istorijski ogledi* (The Kosovan decision. Essays in history). Belgrade, 1990.

Samardžić, Radovan. "Za carstvo nebesko" (For the heavenly kingdom). In *Kosovska bitka 1389. godine i njene posledice* (The 1389 Kosovo battle and its consequences). Belgrade, 1991.

Samardžić, Slobodan. "Jugoreformska dilema—izmedu nacionalnog i demokratskog" (Yugo-reform dilemma—between the national and the democratic). In *Kosovo-Srbija-Jugoslavija* (Kosovo-Serbia-Yugoslavia). Ljubljana: KRT ZSMS,1989.

(Ninčić, Roksanda, Miloš Vasić, Aleksandar Ćirić and Dragoljub Žarković.) "Samo bi rat bio gori" (Only war would be worse). *Vreme* no. 20 (1991).

"Saopštenje IO Predsedništva SANU, od 15. 10. 1991" (Announcement of the Executive committee of the Presidency of the Serbian Academy of Sciences and Arts from 15 October 1991). *Politika* (23 November 1991).

"Saopštenje Štaba Vrhovne komande od 19. 03. 1991" (Announcement of the Headquarters of the High Command from 19 March 1991). *Vojnopolitički informator* no. 4 (1991).

Schmaus, Alois. "Miloš Obilić u narodnom pesništvu i kod Njegoša" (Miloš Obilić in folk poetry and in Njegoš). In *Gesammelte slavistische und balkanologische Abhandlungen (in serbokroatischer Sprache).* Volume IV. Munich, 1970.

Schmaus, Michael. *Begegnung zwischen katholischen Christentum und nationalsozialistischer Weltanschauung.* München, 1933.

Schoeps, Hans-Joachim. "Probleme der Christlich-jüdischen Verständigung." In Knud C. Knudsen (ed.). *Welt ohne Hass. Führende Wissenschaftler aller Fakultäten nehmen Stellung zu brennenden Problemen. Aufsätze und Ansprachen zum 1. Kongreß über bessere menschliche Bezienhungen.* München, Berlin, Hamburg and Stuttgart, 1950: 70–80.

Schöpflin, George. "Croatian Nationalism." *Survey, Journal of East and West Studies* 19 (Winter 1973), no. 1.

Schöpflin, George. "The rise and fall of Yugoslavia." In John McGarry and Brendan O'Leary (eds.). *The Politics of Ethnic Conflict.* London: Routledge, 1993.

Schöpflin, George. "Civilno društvo i nacionalitet" (Civil society and nationality). In Vukašin Pavlović (ed.). *Potisnuto civilno društvo* (Civil society supressed). Belgrade: Ekocentar, 1995.

Sebastijan, Nikola and Rok Šamfor. *Maksime i misli* (Maxims and thoughts). Gornji Milanovac: Milprom, 1994.

Sekelj, Vojislav. *Beograd se dogodio u Beogradu* (Belgrade happened in Belgrade). Subotica: ŽIG, 1995.

Shinnar, Felix E. *Bericht eines Beauftragten. Die deutsch-israelischen Beziehungen 1951–1966.* Tübingen, 1967.

Shoup, Paul. *Communism and the National Question.* New York: Columbia University Press, 1968.

Shoup, Paul. "Crisis and reform in Yugoslavia." *Telos* 79 (1989).

Sikimić, Borislav. *Odbrana u ustavnom sistemu SFRJ* (Defense in the constitutional system of the Socialist Federal Republic of Yugoslavia). Belgrade: VIZ, 1985.

Silber, Laura and Allan Little. *The Death of Yugoslavia.* London: BBC and Penguin Books, 1995.

Sliverstone, R. "Television, Myth and Culture." In J. W. Carey. *Media, Myths and Narratives.* London: Sage Publications, 1988: 20–47.

Simeon, Rikard. *Enciklopedijski rječnik* (Encyclopedic dictionary). Zagreb: Matica hrvatska, 1969.

Simić, Nenad M. "Kult Vidovdana u našoj crkvenoj umetnosti XVIII i XIX veka" (The cult of the St. Vitus day in the church art of the XVIII and XIX centuries). *Glasnik Srpske pravoslavne crkve* 129 (1957).

Simović, Ljubomir. "Kosovski jezici" (The languages of Kosovo). *Književne novine* no. 733 (1987).

Skerlić, Jovan. *Omladina i njena književnost (1848–1871). Izučavanja o nacionalnom i književnom romantizmu kod Srba* (The youth and its literature, 1848–1871. Studies of national and litarary romanticism of the Serbs). Volume I. Belgrade: Srpska kraljevska akademija, 1906.

Skerlić, Jovan. *Feljtoni, skice i govori* (Feuilltons, sketches, speeches). Belgrade: Prosveta, 1964.

Slijepčević, Đoko. *Istorija srpske pravoslavne crkve* (A history of the Serbian Orthodox Church). Volume I. Duesseldorf, 1978.

Slijepčević, Pero. "O našoj patrijarhalnoj kulturi" (On our patriarchal culture). *Književne novine* (1 February 1989).

Sloterdijk, Peter. *Kritika ciničnog uma* (A critique of the cynical reason). Zagreb: Globus, 1992.

"Slovenci i Srbi danas." (Slovenes and Serbs today). *Književne novine* no. 743.

"Sloveni i Zapad." (The Slavs and the West). *Republika*, no. 85 (1994).

Smolka, Leonard. "Symbolika polsko-niemieckiego obrazu wroga doby powstan i plebiscytu górnoslaskiego." *Historia* CXIV (1993).

Solzhenitsyn, A. I. *The Gulag Archipelago.* London: Collins: Havrill Press, 1974.

Specijalni rat protiv SFRJ (The special warfare against the Socialist Federal Republic of Yugoslavia). Belgrade: GŠ JNA, 1981.

Spremić, Momčilo. "Kosovska bitka—problem izdaje" (The Kosovo battle—a problem of betrayal). In *Kosovska bitka 1389. godine i njene posledice* (The 1389 Kosovo battle and its consequences). Belgrade, 1991.

Srbija i Albanci u XIX i početkom XX veka (Serbs and Albanians in XIX and the beginning of the XX century). Belgrade: SANU, Odeljenje istorijskih nauka, 1990.

Srbija između prošlosti i budućnosti (Serbia between past and future). Janjić, Dušan (ed.). Belgrade: NIP Radnička štampa, Institut društvenih nauka and Forum za etničke odnose, 1995.

Srbija krajem osamdesetih (Serbia at the end of the 1980s). Belgrade: ISIFF, 1991.

Srbija u modernizacijskim procesima XX veka (Serbia in the modernization processes of the XX century). Belgrade: Institut za noviju istoriju, 1994.

Srpski mitološki rečnik (Serbian mythological dictionary). Belgrade, 1970.

Stanić, Đorđe. "Istine i zablude o ulozi Armije u jugoslovenskom građanskom ratu" (Truths and misconceptions about the role of the military in the Yugoslav civil war). *Vojno delo* no. 6 (1992).

Staniszewski, Andzej. "Stereotyp Niemca i Polaka w prasie zaboru pruskiego." *Historia* LXXIX (1991).

Stanković, Đorđe Đ. "Beogradski univerzitet—političke i istorijske kontroverze" (Belgrade University—political and historical controversies). *Marksistička misao* no. 5 (1983).

Stanovništvo, Popis '91 (The population. The census of 1991). Volume 2. Belgrade, 1993.

Statističke publikacije o stanovništvu i izveštaji popisa (1948-1994) (The statistical publications about the population and the reports on censuses, 1948-1994). Belgrade, SZS.

Statistički godišnjak Jugoslavije 1988 (The statistical yearly of Yugoslavia, 1988). Belgrade: Savezni zavod za statistiku, 1988.

Statut Srpskog pokreta obnove (The Statute of the Serbian Renewal Movement). Belgrade, 1994.

Stefanović, Nenad Lj. "Duh moderne Srbije" (The spirit of modern Serbia). *Vreme* no. 88 (1992).

Steiner, Hillel. "Exploitation: A Liberal Theory Amended, Defended and Extended." In Andrew Reeve (ed.). *Modern Theories of Exploitation.* London: Sage Publications, 1987: 132-148.

Stenografske beleške Narodne skupštine, vanredni saziv 1906 (Minutes of the extraordinary 1906 session of the National Assembly).

Stenografske beleške Narodne skupštine Srbije za 1980. i 1981 (Minutes of the sessions of the National Assembly of Serbia in 1980 and 1981). Belgrade, 1981.

Stewart, A. T. Q. *A Deeper Silence: The Hidden Origins of the United Irishmen.* London: Faber and Faber, 1993.

Stojanović, Ljuba. "Stari srpski zapisi i natpisi" (Old Serbian writings and titles). *III* no. 5284 (1994).

Stojanović, Milinko B. *Goli otok—anatomija zločina, Svjedočanstva golootočkih zločina, Na golootočkom poprištu* (The Naked island—an anatomy of crime; Testimonies of crimes on the Naked island; On the Naked island's battleground). Three volumes. Belgrade: Stručna knjiga, 1993-94.

Stojanović, Radoslav. "Antisrpski kontinuitet" (The anti-Serbian continuity). *Književne novine* no. 753 (1988).

Stojčić, Đoko. "Budimo realni" (Let us be realistic). *Književne novine* no. 751 (1988).

Stokes, Gale. *The Walls Came Tumbling Down. The Collapse of Communism in Eastern Europe.* New York and Oxford, 1993.

Stokes, Gale. "Nationalism, Responsibility and the People-as-one." *Studies in Eastern European Thought* 46 (1994).

Stoyanne, D. "Mali rječnik jugoslovenskog građanskog rata" (A small dictionary of the Yugoslav civil war). *Luča* IX (1992), no. 2.

Strategija oružane borbe (The strategy of armed combat). Belgrade: SSNO, 1983.

"Studentski protest 1991–1992" (The student protest, 1991–1992). Parts 1 and 2. Thematic issue of *Republika* (1993).

Sudetic, Chuck. "As Croatia Goes, Will All Yugoslavia?" *The New York Times* (5 May 1990).

Sutherland, Peter, John Bradley and Eithna Murphy. Contributions to "Europe: What Kind of Solidarity?" Thematic issue of *Studies* no. 78 (1989).

Sukob ili dijalog (Conflict or dialogue). Dušan Janjić and Skelzen Maliqi (eds.). Subotica: Otvoreni univerzitet and EGCRK, 1994.

Sullivan, O. *Key Concepts in Communication and Cultural Studies.* London: Routledge, 1994.

Supek, Rudi. *Živjeti nakon historije. Prilog dijalektici oslobođenja* (Living after history. A contribution to the dialectics of liberation). Belgrade: Biblioteka Slobodana Mašića, 1986.

Supek, Rudi. *Grad po mjeri čovjeka* (City in accordance with man). Zagreb: Globus, 1987.

"Sve moje izdaje" (All my betrayals). Special edition of *Srpska reč* (November 1992).

Sveti knez Lazar, Spomenica o šestoj stogodišnjici kosovskog boja 1389–1989 (St. knez Lazar, in commemoration of the six-hundredth anniversary of the Kosovo battle, 1389–1989). Belgrade, 1989.

Szarota, Tomasz. "Polak w karykaturze niemieckiej 1914–1944" (The Pole in the German cartoons, 1914–1944). *Historia* LXXIX (1991).

Šakota, Slobodan. "Priprema i prve ustaničke borbe u Hercegovini" (Preparations and the first insurrection fights in Herzegovina). *Vojnoistorijski glasnik* no. 1 (1954).

Šimić, Petar. "Uvodno izlaganje na Konferenciji OSKJ u JNA" (The introductory exposition at the Conference of OSKJ in the Yugoslav People's Army). *Vojnopolitički informator* no. 8 (1988).

Šimić, Petar. "Reč u diskusiji na 20. sednici CKSKJ" (Speech at the discussion at the twentieth session of the Central Committee of the League of Communists of Yugoslavia). *Vojnopolitički informator* no. 3 (1989).

Šipka, Pero and Miroslav Hadžić. *Komitet SKJ u JNA* (The committee of the League of Communists of Yugoslavia in the Yugoslav People's Army). Belgrade, 1989.

Štraus, Leo. "Jerusalim i Atina" (Jerusalem and Athens). Translation of a manuscript. *Treći program RTS* (1994).

Tadić, Ljubomir. "Intervju" (An interview), *Književne novine* (1 May 1986).

Tasić, Dragoljub. *Popis stanovništva 1948* (The census of the population in 1948). Foreword in Volume I. Belgrade: SZS, 1949.

Tašić, Predrag. *Kako je ubijena druga Jugoslavija* (How the second Yugoslavia was killed). Skopje: Štamparija Katje, 1994.

The stars and stripes. The European edition. 7 March 1948.

The Violent Dissolution of Yugoslavia. Truth and Deceit 1991–1994. One Hundred Irrefutable Facts. San Francisco: North American New Analysis Group, no year of publication.

"Thesen christlicher Lehrverkündigung. Schwalbacher Fassung der Seelisberger Thesen." In Hans Kallenbach (ed.). *Die Juden und wir Christen*. Frankfurt am Main, 1950: 61–65.

Thompson, John. "The Churches in Northern Ireland—Problem of Solution? A Presbyterian Perspective." *Irish Theological Quartely* 58 (1992).

Tilly, Charles. "Prisoners of the State." *Historical Sociology* 44 (August 1992), no. 3.

Tilly, Charles. "States and Nationalism in Europe, 1492–1992." *Theory and Society* 23 (February 1994), no. 1.

Todorov, Cvetan. *Mi i drugi. Francuska misao o ljudskoj raznolikosti* (Us and others. The French thought about human diversity). Belgrade: Biblioteka XX vek, samostalno autorsko izdanje Ivana Čolovića i Ivana Mesnera, 1994.

Todorović, Mijalko. "Yugoslavia's new Constitution." *Review of Iternational Affairs* no. 574 (1974).

Tokin, B. *Terazije*. Belgrade, 1932.

Tomašcvić, Katarina. "'Pasija Svetog kneza Lazara' Rajka Maksimovića" ('The *pasija* of St. knez Lazar' by Rajko Maksimović). In *Kosovski boj u književnom i kulturnom nasledu* (The Kosovo battle in literary and cultural heritage). Belgrade, 1991.

Tomaševski, B. V. *Teorija književnosti* (The theory of literature). Belgrade: SKZ, 1972.

Tompson Mark. *Proizvodnja rata* (The production of war). Belgrade: Media centar and Radio B–92, 1995.

Torkar, Igor. *Umiranje na rate* (Dying piecemeal). Zagreb: Globus, 1984.

Treći otadžbinski kongres SRS (The third Fatherland Congree of the Serbian Radical Party). *Velika Srbija* (March 1994).

Trifunović, Đorđe. "Kosovsko stradanje i nebesko carstvo" (The suffering of Kosovo and the heavenly kingdom). In *O knezu Lazaru, naučni skup u Kruševcu 1971* (On knez Lazar: a symposium in Kruševac in 1971). Belgrade, 1975.

Trkulja, Jovica. *Osvajanje demokratije, Ogled o postkomunizmu* (Conquering democracy. An essay on post-Communism). Belgrade, 1993.

Tucović, Dimitrije. *Srbija i Arbanija* (Serbia and Albania). Belgrade: Nova štamparija Save Radenkovića i brata, 1914. Reprinted by Radnička štampa, 1974.

Uloga građanina, Program Građanskog saveza Srbije (The role of the citizen. Program of the Civic alliance of Serbia). Belgrade, 1994.

Uoči stogodišnjice (On the eve of the hundredth anniversary). Belgrade: SANU, 1985.

Uputstvo za praćenje i procenjivanje MPS u JNA (Guidelines for monitoring and estimating MPS in the Yugoslav People's Army). Belgrade: SSNO, 1979.

Uputstvo za praćenje i procenjivanje MPS u TO (Guidelines for monitoring and estimating MPS in the Territorial Defense). Belgrade: SSNO, 1985.

Ustav Republike Srbije (The Constitution of the Republic of Serbia). Belgrade: Službeni list SFRJ, 1990.

Ustav SFRJ (The Constitution of the Socialist Federal Republic of Yugoslavia). Split: Vojna štamparija, 1974.

Van Dam, Hendrik G. "Die Juden in Deutschland nach 1945." In Franz Böhm and Walter Dirks (eds.). *Judentum. Schicksal, Wesen und Gegenwart.* 2 Volumes. Wiesbaden, 1965. Volume II: 888–915.

Vasić, Dragiša. *Devetsto treća* (Nineteen-hundred and three). Belgrade: Prosveta, 1990.

Vasilijević, Vladan. "Ostvarivanje i zaštita prava čoveka" (Establishing and protecting the rights of man). In Dušan Janjić and Skelzen Maliqi (eds.). *Sukob ili dijalog* (Conflict or dialogue). Subotica: Otvoreni univerzitet and EGCRK, 1994.

"Vaskrsenje šćućurene duše. Razgovor sa gospodinom Radovanom Karadžićem" (The resurrection of the timid soul. A conversation with Mr. Radovan Karadžić). *Svetigora* nos. 35–36 (1995).

Velimirović, Nikolaj. *Rat i Biblija* (War and the Bible). Kragujevac, 1931.

Velimirović, Nikolaj. *Nacionalizam Svetog Save* (The nationalism of St. Sava). Belgrade: Mala narodna biblioteka, 1938.

[Velimirović] Nikolaj, bishop. *Govori srpskom narodu kroz tamnički prozor* (Speeches to the Serbian people through the prison window). Himelstir, 1985.

Velimirović, Nikolaj. *Kosovo i Vidovdan* (Kosovo and St. Vitus day). 3rd edition. Šabac, 1988.

Velmar-Janković, Vladimir. *Pogled s Kalemegdana* (A view from the Kalemegdan fortress). Belgrade: Biblioteka grada Beograda, 1991.

Vernant, Jean Pierre. *Les origines de la pensée grecque.* Paris: PUF, 1990.

Vernant, Jean Pierre and Pierre Vidal Nake. *Mit i tragedija u antičkoj Grčkoj* (Myth and tragedy in ancient Greece). Translated by Živojin Živojnović and Jovan Popov. Sremski Karlovci and Novi Sad: Izdavačka knjižarnica Zorana Stojanovića, 1995 (1993).

Die Verträge der Bundesrepublik Deutschland mit der Union der Sozialistichen Sowjetrepubliken und mit der Volksrepublik Polen. Bonn: Presse und Informationsamt der Bundesregierung, 1971.

Vidović, Žarko. "Zavet—izvorno načelo evropske istorije" (The covenant—the original principle of European history). In *Kosovska bitku 1389. godine i njene posledice* (The 1389 Kosovo battle and its consequences). Belgrade, 1991.

Vitalne statistike predratne i poratne Jugoslavije (The vital statistics of pre- and post-war Yugoslavia). Belgrade: SZS, 1989.

Vlahović, Veljko. "Referat na Osmom kongresu SKJ" (The report at the eighth congress of the League of Communists of Yugoslavia). In *Osmi kongres SKJ* (The eighth congress of the League of Communists of Yugoslavia). Belgrade: Komunist, 1964.

Vogelnik, Dolfe. "Demografski gubici Jugoslavije u II svetskom ratu" (The demographic losses of Yugoslavia in World War II). *Statistička revija* (1952).

Vojvodić, Mihailo. "Demonstracije velikoškolaca 1902. godine" (Student demonstrations of 1902). In *Univerzitet u Beogradu* (University in Belgrade). Belgrade, 1988.

Vojvodić, Mihailo. "Srpsko-turski odnosi i proslava petstogodišnjice Kosovske bitke" (Serbian-Turkish relations and the celebration of the five-hundredth anniversary of the Kosovo battle). In *Boj na Kosovu, starija i novija saznanju* (The battle of Kosovo, older and more recent discoveries). Belgrade, 1992.

Vučković, Vojislav. "Prikaz knjige B. Kočovića" (Review of a book by,B. Kočović). Paris: *Naša reč*, 1989.

Vučurević, Božidar. *Pjesme borbe, mira i slobode* (Poems of struggle, peace and liberty). Trebinje, 1988.

Vujačić, Veljko. *Communism and Nationalism in Russia and Serbia*. PhD dissertation. University of California, Berkeley, 1994.

Vujasinović, Dada. "Pedagoška poema. Tajni dosije Arkan: rani radovi, stara revolucija i parlamentarna rehabilitacija" (A pedagogical poem. Secret dossier Arkan: early works, the old revolution and the parliamentary rehabilitation). *Duga* no. 494 (1993).

Vukadinović, Alek. "Srpska tuga" (Serbian sorrow). *Književne novine* no. 783 (1989).

Vukanović, Tatomir. *Srbi na Kosovu* (Serbs in Kosovo). Volumes I-II. Vranje, 1986.

Vukanović, Tatomir. "Prilozi proučavanju narodnih umotvorina o kosovskom boju na području Kosova i Metohije" (Contributions to the study of folk wisdom about the Kosovo battle in the region of Kosovo and Metohija). In *Kosovo u pamćenju i stvaralaštvu* (Kosovo in memory and art). Belgrade: Raskovnik, 1989.

Vukmanović, Svetozar-Tempo. *Memoari (1966-1969)* (Memoirs, 1966-1969). Belgrade and Zagreb: Narodna knjiga and Naprijed, 1985.

Vuković, Zdravko. *Od deformacija SDB do maspoka i liberalizma. Moji stenografski zapisi 1966-1972* (From the deformations of the Agency of State Security to the mass movement and liberalism. My minutes, 1966-1972). Belgrade: Narodna knjiga, 1989.

Wasmund, Klaus. *Politische Plakate aus dem Nachkriegsdeutschland. Zwischen Kapitulation und Staatsgründung*. Frankfurt am Main, 1986.

Wellek, R. and A. Warren. *Theory of Literature*. New York: Harcourt Brace, 1956.

Wetzel, Juliane. "'Mir szeinen doh'. München und Umgebung als Zuflucht Überlebenden des Holocaust 1945-1948." In Martin Broszat et al. (eds.). *Von Stalingrad zur Währungsreform. Zur Sozialgeschichte des Umbruchs in Deutschland*. München, 1989: 327-364.

Whyte, John. *Church and State in Modern Ireland, 1923-1979*. Dublin: Gill and Macmillan, 1980.

Whyte, John. *Interpreting Northern Ireland*. Oxford: Clarendon Press, 1990.

Woodward, Susan L. *Balkan Tragedy–Chaos and Dissolution after the Cold War.* Washington D. C.: The Brookings Institution, 1995.

World Bank. *Yugoslavia: Small Scale Industry and Industrial Policy.* Document of the World Bank. 28 August 1981.

Wright, Frank. *Northern Ireland: A Comparative Analysis.* Dublin: Gill and Macmillan, 1987.

Wright, Frank. "Reconciling the Histories of Protestant and Catholic in Northern Ireland." In Alan D. Falconer (ed.). *Reconciling Memories.* Dublin: Columbia Press, 1988.

Wright, Frank. "Northern Ireland and the British-Irish Relationship." *Studies 78* (1989). Thematic edition: *Memory and Reconciliation.*

Wynaends, Henry. *L'engrenage. Chroniques Yougoslaves juillet 1991 – août 1992.* Paris: Denoel, 1993.

Zadužbine Kosova, Spomenici i znamenja srpskog naroda (Foundations of Kosovo, monuments and memorials of the Serbian people). Prizren, Belgrade and Ljubljana, 1987.

"Zakon o političkim organizacijama" (The law on political organizations). *Službeni glasnik SRS* no. 37 (19 July 1990).

Zapisi Jevrema Grujića (1922. i 1923) (Writings of Jevrem Grujić, 1922–1923). Volumes I-III. Belgrade: Srpska kraljevska akademija.

Zaslavsky, Victor. "Nationalism and Democratic Transition in Postcommunist Societies." *Daedalus* 121 (Spring 1992), no. 2.

Zbornik okruglog stola o naučnom istraživanju Kosova (Proceedings of the round table on the scientific study of Kosovo). Belgrade: SANU, 1988.

Zečević, Miodrag. *Ustav Socijalističke Federativne Republike Jugoslavije* (The Constitution of the Socialist Federal Republic of Yugoslavia). Belgrade: Privredni pregled, 1978.

Žanić, Ivo. *Smrt crvenog fiće* (The death of the red fića). Zagreb: Studio grafičkih ideja, 1933.

Žene za žene (Women for women). Extraordinary issue of SOS bulletin. No. 5 (November 1993).

Žerjavić, Vladimir. *Gubici stanovništva Jugoslavije u II svjetskom ratu* (The losses of the population of Yugoslavia in World War II). Zagreb: JVD, 1989.

Žižek, Slavoj. *Metastaze uživanja* (Metasthases of enjoyment). Belgrade: Biblioteka XX vek, 1996.

Žrtve rata 1941–1945; rezultati popisa (Casualties of war, 1941–1945; results of the censuses), Belgrade: SZS, 1966.

Žrtve rata 1941–1945; rezultati popisa iz 1964 (Casualties of war, 1941–1945; results of the 1964 census). Reprinted edition. Belgrade: SZS, 1992.

Županov, Josip. "Dominantne vrijednosti hrvatskog društva" (Dominant values in the Croatian society). *Erasmus* no. 2 (1993).

List of Contributors

Marina Blagojević
Associate professor at the Faculty of Philosophy, University of Belgrade, and lecturer at the Center for Women's Studies in Belgrade.

Srđan Bogosavljević
Associate professor at the Faculty of Organizational Sciences, University of Belgrade

Ivan Čolović
Senior research fellow at the Ethnographic Institute of the Serbian Academy of Sciences and Arts.

Vojin Dimitrijević
Full professor at the Faculty of Law, University of Belgrade.

Mirko Đorđević
Former professor at the Pedagogical Academy, Belgrade.

Drinka Gojković
Editor-in-chief of the magazine for foreign literature *Mostovi*.

Miroslav Hadžić
Former colonel in the Yugoslav People's Army, research fellow at the Institute of Social Sciences, University of Belgrade.

Ljubomir Madžar
Full professor at the Faculty of Economics, University of Belgrade.

Zoran Marković
Former journalist of weekly magazine *NIN*.

Snježana Milivojević
Assistant professor at the Faculty of Political Sciences, University of Belgrade.

Olivera Milosavljević
Assistant professor at the Faculty of Philosophy, University of Belgrade.

Aleksandar Nenadović
Former correspondent from London and New York, former editor-in-chief at the Belgrade daily *Politika*.

Marija Obradović
Research fellow at the Institute for Modern Serbian History, Belgrade.

Latinka Perović
Research fellow at the Institute for Modern Serbian History, Belgrade.

Vesna Pešić
Research fellow at the Institute for Philosophy and Social Theory, University of Belgrade.

Nebojša Popov
Research fellow at the Institute for Philosophy and Social Theory, University of Belgrade.

Radmila Radić
Research fellow at the Institute for Modern Serbian History, Belgrade.

Dubravka Stojanović
Assistant professor at the Faculty of Philosophy, University of Belgrade.

Bojana Šušak
Faculty of Philosophy, University of Belgrade.

Rade Veljanovski
Former editor-in-chief of Belgrade Radio's First Program. Currently a free lance journalist and media researcher.

Sreten Vujović
Full professor at the Faculty of Philosophy, University of Belgrade.

Olga Zirojević
Research fellow at the Institute of History, Serbian Academy of Sciences and Arts.

Name Index

Adorno, Theodor 3
Adžić, Blagoje 510, 531
Aghiri, Emmanuel 163, 178
Aksakov, K. 372
Albahari, David 350
Aleksić, Snežana 316
Allport, Gordon 124
Anđelković, Radmila 541, 551
Anderson, Benedict 48
Anderson, Kenneth 661
Antić, Radomir 379
Antonijević, Jovan 595, 601
Anžujev, Matjaž 543
Artemije, episkop SPC 259, 265
Avramov, Dragana 215, 220, 221

Babić, Milan 16, 469
Babović, Milosav 197, 198
Bajan, Slavica 597
Bajić, Nevenka 89
Baker, James 42, 641
Bakhunin, Mikhail 325
Bakočević, Aleksandar 318
Bandić, Dušan 195
Barjaktarević, Dragan 624
Bataković, Dušan 201, 203
Bećković, Matija 290, 337, 339, 340, 341, 363, 381, 458, 459, 460, 467
Begović, Vlajko 92
Behluli, Hacif 593
Berkman, Ronald 558
Berlin, Isaiah 1, 9, 41, 87, 93, 97, 137, 143, 304, 311, 425, 479, 561, 641
Bigović, Radovan 257, 260
Bijedić, Džemal 413

Biorčević, Andrija 639
Biro, Mikloš 98, 105, 211, 444
Bjelica, Isidora 137
Bjelogrlić, Dejan 605
Blagojević, Marina 46
Blaustein, Albert P. 422
Bloom, William 37
Bogavac, Zoran 619
Bogdanović, Bogdan 88, 133, 139, 145, 574
Bogetić, Boško 343
Bogoev, Ksente 167, 169
Bogosavljević, Srđan 146
Bojić, Milutin 206
Bokan, Dragoslav 137
Bovan, Milovan 191
Božić, Ivan 303, 306
Božović, Radoman 552
Brankov, Radovan 578
Branković, Vuk 189, 192, 193, 197, 205, 207, 208, 209, 210
Braudel, Fernand 143
Braun, Maximilian 664
Breuilly, John 47
Brezhnev, Leonid Ilyich 401
Breznik, Dušan 154
Broćić, Manojlo 579
Broek, Hans van der 638, 641
Bromberger, Christian 396
Brovet, Stane 510, 532, 533
Broz, Jovanka 615
Brubaker, Rogers 16, 41, 42
Bruk, Hans van den 638, 641
Bučar, France 56, 58, 59, 63, 79
Bućin, Nenad 622

Buha, Aleksa 137
Bulić, Vanja 93
Bulović, Irinej 248, 259, 269
Büchner, Georg 327

Carrington, Lord 261, 266, 291, 641, 644, 657, 658
Caruso Igor A. 3, 100
Chirot, Danile 36
Cohen, L. J. 32
Connor, Walker 42, 45
Crnčević, Brana 137, 138, 340, 381, 579, 589, 591, 595, 597, 601, 616, 624, 625, 626
Crnjanski, Miloš 137, 206
Cvetković, Vladimir 380
Cvijić, Jovan 120, 127, 128, 129, 134, 206, 211

Čajkanović, Veselin 199
Čarnojević, Arsenije 209
Čavoški, Kosta 464
Čičak, Zoran 546
Čobeljić, Nikola 300
Čolović, Ivan 83, 118, 132, 202, 208, 373, 395, 396, 457
Čupić, Drago 197
Ćirić, Aleksandar 326
Ćirković, Sima 132, 189, 205, 283, 293, 492
Ćopić, Branko 310
Ćorović, Miloš 546
Ćosić, Dobrica 20, 44, 45, 50, 80, 117, 119, 258, 274, 275, 276, 287, 290, 294, 295, 302, 332, 333, 334, 337, 338, 340, 341, 342, 356, 357, 362, 368, 372, 422, 432, 467, 471, 598, 622
Ćosja, Redžep 335

Dahrendorf, Ralf 116
Dajić, Putnik 74, 348, 349, 350, 481, 654, 655, 657
Daljević, Milan 532
Damjanović, Dragan 591
Damnjanović, Jevrem 590
Danojlić, Milovan 350

Darwin, Charles 251
Dautović, Savo 618
Davičo, Oskar 343
David, Filip 133
Davidov, Dinko 132
Davidović, Dimitrije 563
de Gaulle, Charles 313
Dedijer, Vladimir 308
Demaqi, Adem 328
Dereta, Miljenko 508
Deretić, Jovan 584
Dimitrijević, Vojin 44, 399, 409, 418, 506, 633, 657, 659
Dinkić, Mlađan 93, 447
Dizdarević, Raif 318
Dmitrović, Ratko 133
Dolanc, Stane 70, 401
Dole, Richard 638
Dovijanić, Gordana 542
Dozet, Dušan 532
Dožić, Gavrilo 195
Drašković, Aleksandar 138
Drašković, Dragomir 544
Drašković, Vuk 255, 258, 356, 376, 385, 395, 452, 455, 459, 462, 465, 468, 470, 473, 475, 532, 575, 602
Drnovšek, Janez 338, 349, 654
Dučić, Jovan 129, 206
Dušanić, Svetozar 253
Džadžić, Petar 381

Đekić, Mirko 31
Đilas, Milovan 23
Đinđić, Zoran 26, 30, 533
Đogo, Gojko 80
Đukanović, Milo 622
Đukić, Milan 16
Đuretić, Veselin 624

Egbert, Jahn 658
Egerić, Miroslav 114
Ehrenberg, Alain 393
Ekmečić, Milorad 50, 51, 287, 290, 294, 301
Eliade, Mircea 194
Ellis, Norbert 394
Enzensberger, Hans Magnus 139

Name Index 705

Felkl, Ekehard 105
Filipović, Dragoljub 206
Fira, Aleksandar 407
Flajner, Tomas 42
Flanz, Gisbert H. 403, 422
Franz, Ferdinand 202

Gaćinović, Vladimir 308
Gagnon, V. P. 17
Gams, Andrija 23
Gavrilović, Žarko 249
Gellner, Ernest 47
German, patriarch 113, 255, 257, 259
Gezeman, Gerhard 129, 198
Gikić, Dušanka 571
Goati, Vladimir 447, 448, 451, 456, 468, 477, 658
Gojković, Drinka 46, 327
Goljevšček, Alenka 61, 79
Golubić, Mustafa 92
Golubović, Zagorka 23, 324, 325
Gorbachov, Mikhail 39, 634, 636, 637, 655, 659
Gow, James 45
Gračanin, Petar 656
Grafenauer, Niko 79
Gredelj, Stjepan 143, 607
Grković, Milica 210
Grujić, Jevrem 304, 305
Grujić, Rade 594
Grujović, Božidar 304

Habermas, Jürgen 142
Hadžić, Goran 605
Hadžić, Miroslav 509
Hafner, Vinko 70
Hall, S. 590, 628
Hasani, Sinan 412
Hassner, Pierre 28
Hayek, Friedrich A. 160, 672
Hebrang, Andrija 94
Hermet, Guy 455, 478
Hitler, Adolf 133, 258, 429, 605
Hobsbawm, Eric 556, 658
Horvat, Branko 329, 618
Hrebeljanović, Lazar, prince 189

Hribar, Spomenka 57, 61, 63, 78
Hribar, Tine 57, 61, 62, 63, 78
Hurd, Douglas 266
Hurem, Rasim 89

Ignjatović, Slobodan 563
Igrić, Gordana 123
Ilić, Mihailo 306
Imširović, Pavle 95, 312
Inić, Slobodan 464
Isaković, Antonije 112, 284, 287, 290, 300, 302, 620
Islami, Hivzi 216, 217, 218, 220, 221, 222, 232, 237, 238
Ivanković, Zvonko Vojta 94
Ivić, Pavle 291, 300, 335
Izetbegović, Alija 262, 264, 291

Jakšić, Božidar 312
Jambrek, Peter 79
Jančar, Drago 58, 79
Janković, Milovan 304, 305
Janša, Janez 73, 595
Jeftić, Miroljub 660
Jelić, Nedeljko 591
Jelisijević, Dragan 557
Jerotić, Vladeta 83, 102, 105, 265
Jerotijević, Živojin 581
Jerovšek, Janez 79
Jevtić, Atanasije 195, 248, 250, 253, 255, 257, 258, 260
Jokanović, Vukašin 577
Josić Višnjić, Miroslav 347
Josif, Enriko 600
Jovan, Pavle 95, 258, 259, 260, 261, 262, 264, 265, 266, 269, 273, 283, 291, 300, 335, 365
Jovanić, Duška 93, 619, 621, 627, 628
Jovanović, Raško V. 578
Jovanović, Slobodan 119, 128, 203, 206, 472
Jovanović, Vladimir 305, 472
Jović, Borisav 260, 430, 437, 441, 649, 654, 656, 657
Jović, Boško 548
Jović, Miodrag 557

Jovičić, Miodrag 112
Jurančić, Janko 79
Jusufspahić, Hadži Hamdija 262

Kadijević, Veljko 40, 48, 49, 415, 424, 430, 438, 439, 441, 510, 519, 520, 521, 524, 528, 531, 532, 533, 534, 655, 656, 657
Kalajić, Dragoš 87, 136, 589, 623, 628, 655
Kalezić, Dimitrije M. 190
Kambovski, Vlado 417
Kanazir, Dušan 112, 276, 284, 285, 286, 288, 295, 299, 300, 301
Kandić, Nataša 347
Kapor, Momo 136, 138
Karađorđe 83
Karadžić, Radovan 103, 134, 136, 145, 268, 290, 291, 580, 606, 648
Karadžić, Sonja 136
Karadžić, Vuk 127, 199, 202, 208, 210, 253, 591
Kardelj, Edvard 24, 53, 58, 280, 281, 301, 405, 422, 423, 424, 612
Kelmendi, Asis 592
Kertes, Mihalj 70, 131
Kich, Laura 558
Kilibarda, Novak 195
Kiš, Danilo 357, 371
Kljajić, Jelka 95, 312
Kljakić, Ljubomir 596
Kočović, Bogoljub 147, 149, 150, 151, 157, 158
Kojen, Leon 456
Kolarić, J. 247
Komanin, Žarko 338, 341
Komlenović, Uroš 323
Komnenić, Milan 258, 336, 339, 341, 363, 458, 468
Komrakov, Milorad 575
Konstantinović, Radomir 125, 130
Korać, Žarko 506
Kosančić, Ivan 192
Kostić, Branko 262
Kostić, Laza 353, 354, 355, 357, 368, 371, 372
Košutić, Budimir 655

Kovač, Mirko 133, 575
Kovačević, Ivan 396
Kovačević, Ljubomir 205
Kovačević, Slobodanka 654
Krajišnik, Momčilo 135
Krestić, Vasilije 300, 301
Krivokapić, Boro 90
Krunić, Boško 70, 542, 543
Kržavac, Savo 313, 610
Kučan, Milan 42, 439, 573
Kuharić, Franjo 257, 261, 266
Kulišić, Špiro 199
Kušanić, Ivo 547
Kustić, Živko 255
Kusturica, Emir 623, 624
Kuzmanović, Bora 124, 501, 502
Kymlicka, Will 11

Lah, Ivo 147, 150
Lalić, Dražen 395
Lalić, Lazar 655
Lauer, Reinhard 210, 678
Lazić, Mladen 99, 124
Lazović, Bojan 578
Lenin, Vladimir Ilyich 88, 359
Leskovac, Rade 184, 396
Letica, Slaven 615
Liebich, Andre 423
Lippmann, Walter 560
Little, Allan 626, 657, 658
Latifi, Ahmet 594
Ljotić, Vladimir 305
Ljubinković, Nenad 190, 191
Lokar, Sonja 573
Lončar, Budimir 635
Lovrić, Ivica 403
Lukić, Radomir 564
Lukić, Sveta 542
Lukić, Vladan 389
Lukijan, bishop 260, 273

Macura, Miloš 287, 300
Madžar, Ljubomir 160, 165, 171, 172, 179, 184
Maffesoli, Michel 393
Maksimović, Ivan 294, 300

Maliqi, Skelzen 223, 224, 228, 233, 243
Mališić, Vesna 600
Mala, Agim 336
Maljković, Božidar 378
Maljković, Nebojša 316
Malovrazić, Sonja 569
Mamula, Branko 518, 520
Mandić, Igor 589
Manević, Z. 126
Marjanović, Jovan 44
Marković, Ante 75, 287, 413, 438, 440, 441, 481, 506, 532, 572, 574, 601, 635
Marković, Dragan 313
Marković, Mihailo 113, 287, 300, 324, 579
Marković, Mira 316
Marković, Mirko 92
Marković, Svetozar 305, 450, 472
Marković, Vera 396
Marsenić, Dragutin 161
Martić, Milan 16
Marx, Karl 88, 175, 251, 310
Masaryk, Tomáš 368
Mastnak, Tomaž 658
Matić, Jovanka 581
Maticki, Miodrag 193
McGarry, John 420
Medaković, Dejan 112, 294, 300, 301
Merton, Robert 19, 43
Mesić, Stipe 349, 350, 641
Mežnarić, Silva 329
Michelis, Gianni de 641
Mićović, Vojislav 313, 655
Mićunović, Dragoljub 469
Midić, Ignatije 264
Mihailović, Dragoslav 105
Mihailović, Kosta 657
Mihajlov, Mihajlo 23
Mihajlović, Branka 576, 580
Mihajlović, Siniša 389
Mihajlović, Stanojlo 593
Mihaljčić, Rade 190, 191, 205
Mihović, Dragan 575
Mijač, Božidar 264
Mijanović, Vladimir 95, 312, 328, 347

Mijatović, Boško 204
Mijović, Vlastimir 615
Mikitenko, Oksana 210
Mikulić, Branko 413
Milaš, Nikodim 248
Milenković, Miroslav 493, 507
Milin, Lazar 251
Milinković, Branko 659
Milivojević, Snježana 507, 581, 608
Miljanić, Dušan 655
Mill, John Stewart 143, 305
Milosavljević, Olivera 50
Milošević, Nikola 464
Milošević, Slobodan 29, 39, 45, 48, 49, 52, 65, 70, 71, 97, 115, 117, 207, 208, 260, 262, 263, 284, 286, 296, 317, 319, 331, 347, 363, 376, 385, 414, 425, 426, 428, 429, 430, 437, 439, 441, 442, 450, 452, 457, 458, 460, 466, 468, 469, 476, 507, 539, 542, 544, 553, 557, 558, 570, 572, 575, 578, 582, 583, 589, 596, 606, 617, 622, 623, 646, 654, 657
Minović, Živorad 285, 541, 549, 550, 551, 552, 553, 562, 563
Mirković, Stevan 521, 531
Mišić, Zoran 195
Mišković, Ivan 325
Mišković, Jovan 204
Mitević, Dušan 562, 573, 575, 576
Mitić, Ljubiša 574
Mitrović, Andrej 132, 492
Mladić, Ratko 138, 267
Mlinar, Miroslav 602
Muhić, Fuad 313
Mussolini, Benito 258

Navres, Reneé de 44
Nedeljković, Mile 211, 656
Nedić, Milan 78
Nemanjić, Sava 83, 198, 203, 253, 589
Nenadović, Aleksandar 102, 477, 507, 537
Nenadović, Ljuba 210
Nietzsche, Friedrich 47, 251

Nikezić, Marko 24, 400
Nikodijević, Zoran 594
Nikolaj, bishop 196, 251, 252, 253, 254, 269
Nikolajević, Dušan S. 120
Nikolić, Milan 95, 312, 347
Nikoliš, Gojko 540, 562
Nikprelević, Đ. 217
Ninčić, Roksanda 326
Nixon, Richard 401
Nodilo, Nadko 199
Novak, Boris 79
Novaković, Stojan 121
Numić, Selim 94
Nušić, Branislav 206

O'Leary, Brendan 420
Obilić, Miloš 70, 189, 191, 192, 193, 196, 197, 198, 203, 208, 209, 210, 475, 478
Obradović, Dositej 303, 325
Obradović, Marija 425
Obrenović, Aleksandar 83
Obrenović, Mihailo 303, 304
Obrenović, Miloš 126, 303
Opačić, Jovan Jovo 16, 337, 338, 339, 341, 342, 349, 598, 625
Orwell, George, 136
Ostojić, Pušara Milica 578
Owen, David 469, 470, 471, 474, 651, 660

Pajkić, Nebojša 137
Pandurović, Sima 206
Panić, Milan 466, 471, 581, 647, 660
Pantić, Miroslav 300
Pantić, Nikola 300
Pašić, Nikola 196, 379
Paunović, Žarko 493, 499, 505, 508
Pavelić, Ante 98, 462
Pavičić, Marko 422
Pavle, bishop 258, 259, 260, 261, 262, 264, 265, 266, 269, 273
Pavlović, Dragiša 316, 326
Pavlović, Leontije 209
Pavlović, Miodrag 350

Pečujlić, Miroslav 447, 478
Pejanović, Obrad 318
Pejin, Jovan 205
Pekić, Borislav 92, 311, 452, 534
Perasović, Benjamin 395, 396
Perišić, Radojica 578
Perović, Blažo 542
Perović, Latinka 2, 24
Pešić, Vesna 508
Petković, Vladislav Dis 206
Petranović, Branko 90
Petrov, Aleksandar 335, 338
Petrović, Branka 505
Petrović, Ilija 655
Petrović, Ljupko 378
Petrović, Milorad 576
Petrović, Mirko 469
Petrović, Nikola 198
Petrović, Rastislav 138
Petrović, Rastko 206
Petrović, Veljko 206
Petrović, Vesna 656
Piroćanac, Milan 120, 122
Planinc, Milka 46, 413
Plavšić, Biljana 145
Poos, Jacques 641
Popadić, Dragan 323, 391, 501
Popov, Nebojša 81, 301, 325, 329, 355
Popović, Danko 256, 352
Popović, Jovan Sterija 304
Popović, Justin 251, 259
Popović, Koča 542
Popović, Mića 158, 467
Popović, Miodrag 194
Popović, Radovan 327
Princip, Gavrilo 202
Prstojević, Miroslav 134
Pučnik, Jože 58, 61, 62, 63, 79, 105, 532
Puhovski, Žarko 329, 330
Pula, G. 214, 222, 223
Pupovac, Milorad 16
Purić, Jagoš 316
Purić, Nenad 579
Puslojić, Adam 342
Pušonjić, Boško 548

Račan, Ivica 439
Rački, Franjo 205
Radić, Radmila 46
Radinović, Radovan 533, 655
Radišić, Svetozar 655
Radosavljević, Đorđe 254
Radović, Amfilohije 259, 268, 290
Radović, Borislav 343
Rajs, Kondoliza 529
Rakić, Ljubiša 300
Rakić, Milan 206
Rakitić, Slobodan 258
Rakočević, Novica 210
Ralić, Prvoslav 656
Ramet, Sabrina Petra 21, 26, 42, 45, 46
Ranković, Aleksandar 22, 23, 43, 46, 94, 232, 233, 312, 325, 400, 422
Rapajić, Ilija 617, 626
Rapi, Đerd , 221
Rašković, Jovan 16, 104, 290
Ražnatović, Željko Arkan 138, 273, 386, 387, 388, 396
Redžep, Jelka 190, 191, 193, 209, 210, 335
Reljić, Slobodan 599
Ribnikar, Vladislav 538
Richards, L. A. 369
Ringelblum, Emanuel 3
Rosandić, Ružica 105
Rosenthal, A. M. 659
Rožanc, Marjan 79
Ršumović, Ljubivoje 391
Rugova, Ibrahim 335, 376, 619
Rupel, Dimitrije 58, 78, 376, 615, 621
Rus, Veljko 79
Rushdie, Salman 144
Rusinow, Dennison 20, 21, 24, 26, 43, 44
Ruvarac, Ilarion 205

Sachs, Jeffrey D. 164
Samardžić, Radovan 114, 133, 284, 300, 335
Sarić, Petar 340
Sava, bishop 129, 265, 267
Savić, Borivoj 605

Savić, Milivoje 582
Savić, Pavle 283
Schöpflin, George 13, 18, 24, 41, 43, 44, 420, 422, 423
Sekulić, Isidora 355
Sekulić, Zoran 603
Selenić, Slobodan 355
Selimoski, Hadži Jakub 264, 266
Shakespeare, William 210
Shoup, Paul 19
Sikimić, Borislav 529
Silber, Laura 657, 658
Silverstone, R. 628
Simeon, bishop 258
Simić, Miroslav 287
Simović, Ljubomir 206, 338, 457, 465
Simović, Živomir 567
Skerlić, Jovan 83, 202, 304, 305, 325, 449, 472
Slapšak, Svetlana 254, 347
Sloterdijk, Peter 4
Smiljković, Radoš 316, 546
Smoje, Miljenko 589
Solzhenitsyn, A. I. 91, 694
Sombart, Werner 141
Spasović, Grujica, 616
Spencer, Herbert 394
Stalin, Iosif Vissarionovich 88, 91, 307, 309, 399
Stambolić, Ivan 32, 283, 317, 326, 589
Stambolić, Petar 45
Stamenković, Lola 580
Stanić, Đorđe 510
Stanković, Milić (od Mačve) 580
Stanojević, Blagoje 605
Stanojević, Dragiša 305, 472
Stanojević, Stanoje 538
Starčević, Tješimir 538
Stefanović, Branislava 571
Stipčević, Nikša 114
Stojanović, Lazar 95, 312, 347
Stojanović, Miodrag 312
Stojanović, Radoslav 258, 335, 657
Stojčić, Đoko 343
Stokes, Gale 426

Stoltenberg, Torvald 651
Stošić, Lila 170
Stoyanne, D. 136
Striković, Jovan 545
Sullivan, D. 629
Supek, Rudi 4

Šainović, Nikola 446
Šakota, Slobodan 89
Šantić, Aleksa 206
Šeks, Vladimir 80, 328
Šešelj, Vojislav 328, 455, 465, 470, 471, 532, 574, 579
Šilović, Darko 660
Šimić, Petar 520, 531
Šipka, Pero 531
Široka, Kolj 546
Špegelj, Martin 526, 575, 604
Štavljanin, Dragan 573
Štula, Mila 575
Šušak, Bojana 301, 478
Šuvar, Stipe 313, 598

Tasić, Dragoljub 147
Terzić, Dragan 256, 264
Tesla, Nikola 580
Tilly 47
Timotijević, Milutin 258
Tirnanić, Bogdan 628
Tocqueville, Alexis de 109
Todorović, Bata 93
Todorović, Mijalko 405
Todorović, Tatjana 594
Toholj, Miroslav 137
Tokin, Boško 130
Tomc, Gregor 62, 79
Tomić, Dragan 318
Tomić, Milan 378
Tomić, Predrag 571
Torkar, Igor , 90
Tošić, Desimir 158
Trajković, Momčilo 618
Trgovčević, Ljubinka 132, 492
Tribrenčić, Milan 557
Trifunović, Bogdan 318
Trišić, Vlado 582
Trkulja, Jovica 455

Trotsky, Lev Davidovich 359, 367
Tucović, Dimitrije 84
Tudman, Franjo 98, 580, 626
Tufegdžić, Vojislav 93
Turen, Alen 504

Ubiparipović, Dragomir 255, 267
Udovički, Danilo 95, 312, 347
Unković, Slobodan 317

Vajagić, Bogdan 605
Vance, Syrus 649, 660
Vasić, Dragiša 325
Vasić, Miloš 326
Vasilije, bishop 269
Vasilijević, Vladan 222
Velimirović, Nikolaj 251, 252, 269
Veljak, Lino 312
Veljanovski, Rade 48, 105, 507, 565
Vico, Ratomir 576
Vidaković, Miloš 206
Vidmar, Josip 621, 624
Vinogradov, J. 354
Vlahović, Veljko 43
Vlasi, Azem 318, 385, 396
Vogelnik, Dolfe 147, 150
Vojvodić, Momir 138
Vračar, Rajko 319, 324
Vračar, Stevan 23
Vrhovec, Josip 70, 598
Vučelić, Milorad 595, 618, 620, 623
Vučković, Slobodan 258
Vujanović, Milja 585
Vujasinović, Dada 93
Vujović, Sreten 123
Vukadinović, Alek 341
Vukanović, Tatomir 200
Vukčević, Vojislav 149, 150
Vukmanović, Svetozar Tempo 325
Vukobratović, Miomir 300
Vuković, Zdravko 189, 209, 325
Warren, A. 351, 360, 370
Weber, Max 48, 141, 607
Wilson, Woodraw 657
Woodward, Susan 46, 655, 658

Yeats, William Butler 123

Zaler, Vinko 312
Zamfirović, Nada 578
Zečević, Zdravko 602
Zenko, Franjo 658
Zirojević, Olga 46, 189, 213, 249
Zlatanović, Radoslav 331, 543
Zloković, Simeon 258

Žanić, Ivo 104
Žarković, Dragoljub 326
Žerjavić, Vladimir 147, 149, 150, 151, 157
Živančević, Predrag 590, 591
Živojinović, Bata 594
Žižek, Slavoj 5
Žujović, Zoran 391
Županov, Josip 4, 447